The Coase Theorem
Volume II

## Economic Approaches to Law

*Series Editors*: Richard A. Posner
*Judge, United States Court of Appeals for the Seventh Circuit and Senior Lecturer, University of Chicago Law School, USA*
Francesco Parisi
*Oppenheimer Wolff and Donnelly Professor of Law, University of Minnesota Law School, USA and Professor of Economics, University of Bologna, Italy*

Wherever possible, the articles in these volumes have been reproduced as originally published using facsimile reproduction, inclusive of footnotes and pagination to facilitate ease of reference.

For a full list of published and future titles in this series and a list of all Edward Elgar published titles visit our website at www.e-elgar.com

# The Coase Theorem Volume II

## Criticisms and Applications

*Edited by*

Richard A. Posner

*Judge, United States Court of Appeals for the Seventh Circuit and Senior Lecturer, University of Chicago Law School, USA*

*and*

Francesco Parisi

*Oppenheimer Wolff and Donnelly Professor of Law*
*University of Minnesota Law School, USA*
*and Professor of Economics*
*University of Bologna, Italy*

ECONOMIC APPROACHES TO LAW

**An Elgar Research Collection**
Cheltenham, UK • Northampton, MA, USA

Published by
Edward Elgar Publishing Limited
The Lypiatts
15 Lansdown Road
Cheltenham
Glos GL50 2JA
UK

Edward Elgar Publishing, Inc.
William Pratt House
9 Dewey Court
Northampton
Massachusetts 01060
USA

A catalogue record for this book is available from the British Library

Library of Congress Control Number: 2012951755

MIX
Paper from responsible sources
FSC www.fsc.org FSC® C018575

ISBN 978 0 85793 791 9 (2 volume set)

Printed and bound by MPG Books Group, UK

# Contents

# Acknowledgements

The editors and publishers wish to thank the authors and the following publishers who have kindly given permission for the use of copyright material.

American Economic Association for article: William Schulze and Ralph C. D'Arge (1974), 'The Coase Proposition, Information Constraints and Long-Run Equilibrium', *American Economic Review*, **64** (4), September, 763–72.

Blackwell Publishing Ltd for articles: Stanislaw Wellisz (1964), 'On External Diseconomies and the Government-Assisted Invisible Hand', *Economica New Series*, **31** (124), November, 345–62; Varouj A. Aivazian, Jeffrey L. Callen and Irwin Lipnowski (1987), 'The Coase Theorem and Coalitional Stability', *Economica*, **54** (216), November, 517–20; Glenn W. Harrison, Elizabeth Hoffman, E.E. Rutström and Matthew L. Spitzer (1987), 'Coasian Solutions to the Externality Problem in Experimental Markets', *Economic Journal*, **97** (386), June, 388–402; Luca Anderlini and Leonardo Felli (2006), 'Transaction Costs and the Robustness of the Coase Theorem', *Economic Journal*, **116** (508), January, 223–45.

*Duke Law Journal* for article: J. Gregory Sidak (1991), 'The Inverse Coase Theorem and Declarations of War', *Duke Law Journal*, **41** (2), November, 325–8.

Elsevier Ltd for articles: Ken-Ichi Inada and Kiyoshi Kuga (1973), 'Limitations of the "Coase Theorem" on Liability Rules', *Journal of Economic Theory*, **6** (6), December, 606–13; Paul Samuelson (1995), 'Some Uneasiness with the Coase Theorem', *Japan and the World Economy*, **7** (1), May, 1–7; Peter Bernholz (1997), 'Property Rights, Contracts, Cyclical Social Preferences and the Coase Theorem: A Synthesis', *European Journal of Political Economy*, **13** (3), September, 419–42; Peter Bernholz (1999) 'The Generalized Coase Theorem and Separable Individual Preferences: An Extension', *European Journal of Political Economy*, **15** (2), June, 331–35; Avinash Dixit and Mancur Olson (2000), 'Does Voluntary Participation Undermine the Coase Theorem?', *Journal of Public Economics*, **76** (3), June, 309–35.

Kluwer Law International for excerpt: A. Mitchell Polinsky (2011), 'The Coase Theorem', 'First Application-Nuisance Law', 'Second Application-Breach of Contract' and 'Third Application-Automobile Accidents' in *An Introduction to Law and Economics*, Chapter 3, Chapter 4, Chapter 5 and Chapter 6, 13–16, 17–27, 29–41 and 43–56.

*Natural Resources Journal* and James M. Buchanan for article: James M. Buchanan (1973), 'The Coase Theorem and the Theory of the State', *Natural Resources Journal*, **13**, 579–94.

Palgrave Macmillan for excerpts: Robert D. Cooter (1987), 'Coase Theorem', in John Eatwell, Murray Milgate and Peter Newman (eds) *The New Palgrave: A Dictionary of Economics, Volume I*, 457–60; Francesco Parisi (2008), 'Coase Theorem', in Lawrence E. Blume and Steven N. Durlauf (eds) *The New Palgrave: A Dictionary of Economics, Volume I*, 2nd Edition, 855–61.

Springer Science and Business Media B.V. for article: Francesco Parisi (2003), 'Political Coase Theorem', *Public Choice*, **115** (1/2), April, 1–36.

*Stanford Law Review* via the Copyright Clearance Center for article: Robert C. Ellickson (1986), 'Of Coase and Cattle: Dispute Resolution Among Neighbors in Shasta County', *Stanford Law Review*, **38** (3), February, 623–87.

Southern Economic Association for article: Timothy R. Hylan, Maureen J. Lage and Michael Treglia (1996), 'The Coase Theorem, Free Agency, and Major League Baseball: A Panel Study of Pitcher Mobility from 1961 to 1992', *Southern Economic Journal*, **62** (4), April, 1029–42.

Taylor and Francis Group, LLC (http://www.taylorandfrancis.com) for article: James Halteman (2005), 'Externalities and the Coase Theorem: A Diagrammatic Presentation', *Journal of Economic Education*, **36** (4), Fall, 385–90.

University of Chicago Press for articles: Guido Calabresi (1968), 'Transaction Costs, Resource Allocation and Liability Rules – A Comment', *Journal of Law and Economics*, **11** (1), April, 67–73; G. Warren Nutter (1968), 'The Coase Theorem on Social Cost: A Footnote', *Journal of Law and Economics*, **11** (2), October, 503–7; Harold Demsetz (1972), 'When Does the Rule of Liability Matter?', *Journal of Legal Studies*, **1** (1), January, 13–28; Donald H. Regan (1972), 'The Problem of Social Cost Revisited', *Journal of Law and Economics*, **15** (2), October, 427–37; Varouj A. Aivazian and Jeffrey L. Callen (1981), 'The Coase Theorem and the Empty Core', *Journal of Law and Economics*, **24** (1), April, 175–81; Robert Cooter (1982), 'The Cost of Coase', *Journal of Legal Studies*, **11** (1), January, 1–33; Elizabeth Hoffman and Matthew L. Spitzer (1982), 'The Coase Theorem: Some Experimental Tests', *Journal of Law and Economics*, **25** (1), April, 73–98; Glenn W. Harrison and Michael McKee (1985), 'Experimental Evaluation of the Coase Theorem', *Journal of Law and Economics*, **28** (3), October, 653–70; Elizabeth Hoffman and Matthew L. Spitzer (1986), 'Experimental Tests of the Coase Theorem with Large Bargaining Groups', *Journal of Legal Studies*, **15** (1), January, 149–71; Kenneth R. Vogel (1987), 'The Coase Theorem and California Animal Trespass Law', *Journal of Legal Studies*, **16** (1), January, 149–87; Daniel Kahneman, Jack L. Knetsch and Richard H. Thaler (1990), 'Experimental Tests of the Endowment Effect and the Coase Theorem', *Journal of Political Economy*, **98** (6), December, 1325–48; A.W. Brian Simpson (1996), '"Coase v. Pigou" Reexamined', *Journal of Legal Studies*, **25** (1), January, 53–97; Varouj A. Aivazian, Jeffrey L. Callen and Susan McCracken (2009), 'Experimental Tests of Core Theory and the Coase Theorem: Inefficiency and Cycling', *Journal of Law and Economics*, **52** (4), November, 745–59.

Every effort has been made to trace all the copyright holders but if any have been inadvertently overlooked the publishers will be pleased to make the necessary arrangement at the first opportunity.

In addition the publishers wish to thank the Library of Indiana University at Bloomington, USA for their assistance in obtaining these articles.

# Part I
# Surveys and Applications

# [1]

## THE COASE THEOREM

One of the central ideas in the economic analysis of law was developed in an article by Ronald H. Coase in 1960.[7] This idea, which has since been named the *Coase Theorem,* is most easily described by an example. Consider a factory whose smoke causes damage to the laundry hung outdoors by five nearby residents. In the absence of any corrective action each resident would suffer $75 in damages, a total of $375. The smoke damage can be eliminated in either of two ways: a smokescreen can be installed on the factory's chimney, at a cost of $150, or each resident can be provided an electric dryer, at a cost of $50 per resident. The efficient solution is clearly to install the smokescreen because it eliminates total damages of $375 for an outlay of only $150, and it is cheaper than purchasing five dryers for $250.

### Zero Transaction Costs

The question asked by Coase was whether the efficient outcome would result if the right to clean air is assigned to the residents or if the right to pollute is given to the factory. If there is a right to clean air, then the factory has three choices: pollute and pay $375 in damages, install a smokescreen for $150, or purchase five dryers for the residents at a total cost of $250. Clearly, the factory would install the smokescreen,

7. Ronald H. Coase, The Problem of Social Cost, 3 J.L. & Econ. 1 (1960).

the efficient solution. If there is a right to pollute, then the residents face three choices: suffer their collective damages of $375, purchase five dryers for $250, or buy a smokescreen for the factory for $150. The residents also would purchase the smokescreen. In other words, the efficient outcome will be achieved regardless of the assignment of the legal right.

It was implicitly assumed in the preceding paragraph that the residents could costlessly get together and negotiate with the factory. In Coase's language, this is referred to as the assumption of *zero transaction costs*. In general, transaction costs include the costs of identifying the parties with whom one has to bargain, the costs of getting together with them, the costs of the bargaining process itself, and the costs of enforcing any bargain reached. With this general definition of transaction costs in mind, we can now state the simple version of the Coase Theorem: If there are zero transaction costs, the efficient outcome will occur regardless of the choice of legal rule.

Note that, although the choice of the legal rule does not affect the attainment of the efficient solution when there are zero transaction costs, it does affect the distribution of income. If the residents have the right to clean air, the factory pays $150 for the smokescreen, whereas if the factory has the right to pollute, the residents pay for the smokescreen. Thus, the choice of the legal rule redistributes income by the amount of the least-cost solution to the conflict. Because it is assumed for now that income can be costlessly redistributed, this distributional effect is of no consequence—if it is not desired, it can be easily corrected.

## Positive Transaction Costs

The assumption of zero transaction costs obviously is unrealistic in many conflict situations. At the very least, the disputing parties usually would have to spend time and/or money to get together to discuss the dispute. To see the consequences of positive transaction costs, suppose in the example that it costs each resident $60 to get together with the others (due, say, to transportation costs and the value of each resident's time). If the residents have a right to clean air, the factory again faces the choice of paying damages, buying a smokescreen, or buying five dryers. The factory again would purchase the smokescreen, the efficient solution. If the factory has a right to pollute, each resident now has to decide whether to bear the loss of $75, buy a dryer for $50, or get together with the other residents for $60 to collectively buy a smokescreen for $150. Clearly, each resident will choose to purchase a dryer, an inefficient outcome. Thus, given the transaction costs described, the right to clean air is efficient, but the right to pollute is not.

Note that in the example the preferred legal rule minimized the effects of transaction costs in the following sense. Under the right to clean air, the factory had to decide whether to pay damages, install a smokescreen, or buy five dryers. Because it was not necessary for the factory to get together with the residents to decide what to do, the transaction costs—the costs of the residents to get together—did not have any effect. Under the right to pollute, the residents had to decide what to do. Because the residents were induced to choose an inefficient solution in order to avoid the cost of getting together, the transaction costs did have an effect. Thus, even though no transaction costs were actually incurred under the right to pollute because the residents did not get together, the effects of transaction costs were greater under that rule.

We can now state the more complicated version of the Coase Theorem: If there are positive transaction costs, the efficient outcome may not occur under every legal rule. In these circumstances, the preferred legal rule is the rule that minimizes the effects of transaction costs. These effects include actually incurring transaction costs as well as the inefficient choices induced by a desire to avoid transaction costs.

The distributional consequences of legal rules are somewhat more complicated when there are transaction costs. It is no longer true, as it was when there were zero transaction costs, that the choice of the rule redistributes income by the amount of the least-cost solution. In the example, if the residents have the right to clean air, the factory pays $150 for the smokescreen, whereas if the factory has the right to pollute, the residents pay $250 for five dryers.

Although the simple version of the Coase Theorem makes an unrealistic assumption about transaction costs, it provides a useful way to begin thinking about legal problems because it suggests the kinds of transactions that would have to occur under each legal rule in order for that rule to be efficient. Once these required transactions are identified, it may be apparent that, given more realistic assumptions about transaction costs, one rule clearly is preferable to another on efficiency grounds. The more complicated version of the Coase Theorem provides a guide to choosing legal rules in this situation. All of the applications investigated in this book—including nuisance law, breach of contract, automobile accidents, pollution control, products liability, and litigation—can be approached in this way, although some fit more naturally into the Coasian framework than others.

# FIRST APPLICATION — NUISANCE LAW

One area of law that can be readily examined in terms of the Coase Theorem is nuisance law. Nuisance cases result from incompatible land uses and typically involve a small number of individuals bargaining with each other, as when emissions from a factory fall upon neighboring property, bright lights or noise disturb someone's sleep, or an unsightly building spoils an attractive residential neighborhood.

Adopting a framework first suggested by Guido Calabresi and A. Douglas Melamed,[8] the resolution of a nuisance dispute may be viewed as involving two steps. First, an *entitlement* must be chosen — that is, a determination must be made regarding who is entitled to prevail. The injurer can be granted the right to engage in the activity that causes harm, or the victim can be granted the right to be free from harm. Then, a decision must be made about how to protect the entitlement. One possibility is to grant the holder of the entitlement an *injunction*. If the victim holds the entitlement, protecting it by an injunction means that she can prohibit the injurer from causing harm. Thus, the injurer can cause damage only if he "buys off" the victim. Similarly, if the injurer holds the entitlement, protecting it by an injunction means that the victim must buy off the injurer if she wants damages reduced.

8. Guido Calabresi & A. Douglas Melamed, Property Rules, Liability Rules and Inalienability: One View of the Cathedral, 85 Harv. L. Rev. 1089 (1972).

An alternative method of protecting entitlements is to give the holder of the entitlement an amount of money—*damages*—that some governmental body, such as a court, determines. If the victim has the entitlement, she has the right to be compensated, but she cannot prohibit the injurer from causing harm, as she could under an injunctive remedy.[9] Analogously, if the injurer holds the entitlement, protecting him by a damage remedy would mean that the victim could restrict the injurer's activity but would have to compensate the injurer for the injurer's "damages" (for example, forgone profits). This last combination—entitling the injurer to damages—is unconventional, but it has been used.[10] Thus, there are four possible solutions, corresponding to who is given the entitlement and how it is protected.

In this chapter, we will examine whether the efficiency criterion can determine which entitlement to choose and which remedy to use to protect it. The analysis will be based on an example of a polluting factory located next to a single resident. The example is described in Table 1. The factory can produce zero, one, two, or three units of output. Increasing

**TABLE 1**

**Nuisance Law Example**

| *Output of Factory* | *Additional Profits of Factory* | *Total Profits of Factory* | *Additional Damages of Resident* | *Total Damages of Resident* | *Total Profits Less Total Damages* |
|---|---|---|---|---|---|
| 0 | — | $0 | — | $0 | $0 |
| 1 | $10,000 | $10,000 | $1,000 | $1,000 | $9,000 |
| 2 | $4,000 | $14,000 | $15,000 | $16,000 | –$2,000 |
| 3 | $2,000 | $16,000 | $20,000 | $36,000 | –$20,000 |

9. A leading American nuisance case illustrating this version of the damage remedy is Boomer v. Atlantic Cement Co., 26 N.Y.2d 219, 257 N.E.2d 870, 309 N.Y.S.2d 312 (1970).

10. See Spur Industries, Inc. v. Del E. Webb Development Co., 108 Ariz. 178, 494 P.2d 700 (1972).

output results in additional profits for the factory and additional damages to the resident. If the factory produces one unit, the factory obtains $10,000 in profits and the resident suffers $1,000 in damages. Total profits less total damages are $9,000. If the factory produces a second unit, the factory's additional profits are $4,000—so the factory's total profits are $14,000—and the resident's additional damages are $15,000—so the resident's total damages are $16,000. Then total profits less total damages are −$2,000. If the factory produces a third unit, the results are described similarly.

Maximizing the size of the pie in the nuisance law example is equivalent to maximizing the factory's profits net of the resident's damages. Given the data in Table 1, this occurs when the factory produces one unit of output (see the last column). In other words, one unit of output is the efficient solution.

## Zero Transaction Costs

We know from the discussion in the previous chapter that if there are zero transaction costs, then the factory will end up producing the efficient output regardless of the choice of remedy or entitlement. It will be useful to see how this comes about in the example before considering more realistic assumptions about transaction costs.

Under the injunctive remedy, suppose, for example, that an entitlement to clean air is given to the resident. This corresponds to giving the resident the right to force the factory to produce zero output. The factory, however, would gain $10,000 in profits from producing one unit, and the resident would suffer only $1,000 in damages. Thus, it is in each party's interest to reach an agreement in which the factory would pay the resident some amount between $1,000 and $10,000 for permission to produce one unit. Assuming zero transaction costs, which is interpreted to imply cooperative behavior, such an agreement will be reached. It will not be mutually beneficial for the factory to produce a second unit because the factory would gain only an additional $4,000 in profits, whereas the resident would suffer an additional $15,000 in damages. Similarly, it would not be mutually beneficial for the factory to produce three units. Thus, the parties would remain at one unit, the efficient solution.

Under the damage remedy, suppose that an entitlement to clean air is given to the resident, as before, and that the court makes the factory liable for the resident's actual damages. Because the factory would gain $10,000 from producing one unit and would be liable for only $1,000, the factory clearly will choose to produce at least one unit. It will not be in the factory's interest to produce the second unit, however, because the increase in the factory's profits is $4,000 and its additional liability is $15,000. Similarly, the factory would be worse off if it produced three units. Thus, the factory would choose to produce the efficient output.

### Strategic Behavior

The assumption of zero transaction costs obviously is unrealistic in many respects. We will first consider the possibility that the parties will behave strategically;[11] for instance, to establish a reputation as a tough bargainer, a party may "hold out" for a disproportionate share of the gains from any agreement. If both parties are stubborn in this sense, they may not be able to reach an agreement even when both could be made better off. Such behavior is not uncommon; for example, parties often go to court rather than settle out of court more cheaply.[12] We will now reconsider the nuisance remedies assuming that the parties behave strategically.

11. Although strategic behavior does not necessarily generate any out-of-pocket costs or costs associated with lost time, it will be treated as a type of transaction cost. It is like other transaction costs in that it may prevent the parties from reaching an efficient agreement.

12. There may be reasons other than strategic behavior why parties litigate rather than settle. For example, the parties may disagree about the plaintiff's chance of winning at trial and therefore may not perceive a mutually beneficial settlement. See Chapter 16 below.

Under the injunctive remedy with an entitlement to clean air, we saw that it would be in each party's interest to reach an agreement in which the factory paid the resident some amount between $1,000 and $10,000. However, because of strategic behavior, the resident may, for example, hold out for $8,000, while the factory may refuse to pay anything over $5,000. As a result, the resident might enforce the injunction and shut down the factory (at least for some period), an inefficient outcome.

The problem of strategic behavior under the injunctive remedy can be overcome by the appropriate choice of the entitlement. Instead of an entitlement corresponding to zero output of the factory — an *absolute* entitlement to clean air — suppose that the court were to choose an entitlement corresponding to one unit of output — an *intermediate* entitlement. Under the injunctive remedy, this would mean that the factory could produce one unit, but no more, without having to obtain the permission of the resident. Starting at one unit of output, it would not be mutually beneficial to produce a second or third unit because the factory's gains are less than the resident's losses. Likewise, it would not be mutually beneficial to reduce output to zero because the resident's gain (in the form of reduced damages) is less than the factory's loss (in the form of reduced profits). Thus, starting at an intermediate entitlement of one unit, the parties will remain there. Strategic behavior cannot upset this outcome because no beneficial changes can be made that would require negotiation.

This discussion illustrates a general principle: Under the injunctive remedy, to overcome strategic behavior it is necessary to choose an entitlement corresponding to the efficient outcome. This is because, starting from any other entitlement, the parties must reach an agreement to get to the efficient outcome; and strategic behavior may prevent this agreement from being reached.

Under the damage remedy with an entitlement to clean air and liability equal to actual damages, we saw that the factory would choose to produce the efficient output of one unit. The presence of strategic behavior does not affect this result because there are no bargains that the parties have to reach. Also, there are no threats that the factory can make because, given that the factory is liable for actual damages, the resident is indifferent among all levels of the factory's output.

It is essential to the conclusion of the previous paragraph that liability equals actual damages. To see why, suppose that the factory's liability is $7,000 for the first unit—exceeding the resident's damages of $1,000—and, as before, is equal to the resident's damages for the second and third units. If the factory produces one unit of output it will gain $3,000 ($10,000 – $7,000). The resident also will gain $6,000, the amount by which the liability payment exceeds actual damages ($7,000 – $1,000). But the factory can deny this gain to the resident by not producing the first unit of output. Therefore, if the factory believes that it can bargain more effectively than the resident, it might threaten to not produce unless the resident pays some specified amount up to her full gain of $6,000. However, if the resident believes that she is the better bargainer, she might not give in to the factory's demand. As a result, the factory might carry out its threat, if only to make future threats credible, and produce at an inefficient output.

The kind of "extortion" threat just described cannot occur if liability is equal to actual damages. Because the resident then is not overcompensated, and so gains nothing from an increase in the factory's output, the factory's threat to not produce the first unit of output has no effect. With full compensation, the resident is indifferent to whether the first unit is produced and is likewise indifferent with respect to the second and third units. Thus, the factory will maximize its after-liability profits by increasing production to the efficient output of one unit.

This discussion illustrates another general principle: Under the damage remedy, to overcome strategic behavior it is necessary to set liability equal to actual damages. If liability exceeds actual damages, then the party who is liable has an incentive to threaten to deny the other party's overcompensation by choosing an inefficient outcome.[13]

13. More generally, strategic behavior can be overcome under the damage remedy if liability is less than or equal to actual damages up to the efficient output and greater than or equal to actual damages beyond

## Imperfect Information

The analysis of strategic behavior under the injunctive and damage remedies suggests another way in which the assumption of zero transaction costs is likely to be unrealistic. For both remedies, it was seen that the court must have certain information about the nuisance dispute in order to achieve the efficient solution. Under the injunctive remedy, the court needs to know the efficient outcome to choose an entitlement corresponding to it. And under the damage remedy, the court needs to know the resident's damages to set liability equal to actual damages. It was implicitly assumed that the court had whatever information was required. We will now reconsider the remedies when this information is imperfect. The assumption of strategic behavior will be maintained in this discussion.

Suppose that the court has limited information of the following sort: It knows the resident's schedule of damages but does not know the factory's schedule of profits. For example, the court might easily be able to obtain information about the damage to property from pollution but not about the cost to the polluter of changing production methods to abate pollution.[14]

Under the injunctive remedy, the court no longer can achieve the efficient outcome. To reach that outcome, strategic behavior must be avoided, which requires under the injunctive remedy that the entitlement coincide with the efficient output. But to determine the efficient output, the court must know when the factory's profits net of the resident's damages are maximized. Knowing the damage schedule alone obviously is insufficient to determine this level of output. Although the court could attempt to estimate the efficient output, if it makes a

the efficient output. It is beyond the scope of this chapter to explain this more general proposition. Note, however, that the statements and examples in the text are consistent with it.

14. The alternative case in which the court knows the factory's profit schedule but not the resident's damage schedule will not be analyzed because it is analogous to the case discussed in the text.

mistake, as it generally will, strategic behavior might prevent the parties from bargaining to the efficient output.

The damage remedy can reach the efficient outcome despite the court's imperfect information. This result can be guaranteed, however, only if the court gives an absolute entitlement to clean air to the resident and sets liability equal to actual damages. Any other entitlement might lead to the efficient outcome, but it need not. For example, suppose that the court assigns an intermediate entitlement to pollute to the factory corresponding to two units of output and makes the factory liable thereafter for the resident's damages. Initially, the factory would choose to produce two units because there is no liability up to and including the second unit, and liability for the third unit—equal to the resident's damages of $20,000—exceeds the factory's additional profits—equal to $2,000. The resident then would have an incentive to "bribe" the factory to reduce output from two units to the efficient output of one unit, but because of strategic behavior the parties might not reach that output.

On the other hand, if the court chooses an entitlement corresponding to zero or one unit of output and sets liability thereafter equal to actual damages, the damage remedy will lead the factory to produce at the efficient output. In other words, with liability equal to actual damages, the damage remedy leads to the efficient outcome if, and only if, the entitlement is at or below the efficient output. However, because the court cannot determine the efficient output with its limited information, the only way it can guarantee the efficient result is to choose the entitlement corresponding to the lowest possible output—an absolute entitlement to the resident.

The discussion thus far has shown that if the court knows the victim's schedule of damages but not the injurer's schedule of profits, it generally cannot implement an efficient injunctive remedy but it can implement an efficient damage remedy. However, in many nuisance situations the court might not be able to easily determine the victim's damages. For example, although a court might be able to accurately estimate the market price of someone's home, this price generally is less than the damages that would be suffered by the resident if she were forced to move, because it does not reflect the special attachment she might have for that location and house. Damages often include a subjective or idiosyncratic element of this sort that is difficult or impossible to measure.[15] We will therefore briefly reconsider the remedies when the court is assumed to underestimate the resident's damages (and, as before, to not know anything about the factory's profits). For concreteness, suppose in the example that the court's estimate of damages is $500 per unit of output.

Because the court obviously still cannot implement an efficient injunctive remedy, the discussion will focus on the damage remedy. Suppose an absolute entitlement is awarded to the resident. If damages were measured accurately, then, as we saw above, the damage remedy would lead to the efficient outcome. Now, however, with damages underestimated, the factory generally will overshoot the efficient output. In the example, with liability equal to $500 per unit of output, the factory will choose to produce three units because its additional profit from producing each unit exceeds $500 (see Table 1).

Starting at an output of three units, the resident would be better off by $19,500 if output were reduced by one unit — she would lose a $500 liability payment, but her damages would decline by $20,000 (see Table 1). The factory would lose only $1,500 as a result of this change — its profits would fall by $2,000, but it would avoid a $500 liability payment. Thus, if the parties could reach an agreement in which the resident paid the factory some amount between $1,500 and $19,500 to reduce output by one unit, both parties would be better off. However, because of strategic behavior, such a deal will not necessarily occur. And even if an agreement were reached with respect to this change from three units to two units, the parties might fail to reach an agreement when they negotiate over reducing output from two units to the efficient output of one unit.

15. In practice, this element of damages generally is excluded from a damage award.

The general point of this discussion can be simply stated. If courts underestimate the victim's damages, then the damage remedy initially will lead to an excessive output and this inefficiency might not be corrected because of strategic behavior. There is then no general reason to believe that a damage remedy would be preferable to an injunctive remedy. For example, suppose that, starting with an absolute entitlement to the resident, the damage remedy would lead to an output of three units for the reasons described in the previous paragraph, and the injunctive remedy would lead to an output of zero units because of strategic behavior. The injunctive outcome then is more efficient than the damage outcome because total profits less total damages are $0 rather than –$20,000 (see Table 1). In general, however, either remedy could be the more efficient one.

We can now summarize the results in this chapter regarding the efficiency analysis of nuisance remedies. If the parties can be expected to bargain cooperatively (and there are no other transaction costs), then any choice of entitlement and remedy will be efficient. If the parties are likely to act strategically, then the efficient outcome still can be achieved under both remedies if the court has adequate information. Strategic behavior can be overcome under the injunctive remedy by choosing the entitlement that corresponds to the efficient outcome, which can be determined if the court knows the injurer's benefits from engaging in the harmful activity and the victim's damages. And strategic behavior can be overcome under the damage remedy by giving an absolute entitlement to the victim and setting liability equal to actual damages, which obviously requires knowledge of the victim's damages. If the court only knows the victim's damages, the injunctive remedy generally will fail because the court cannot accurately set the entitlement equal to the efficient outcome, but the damage remedy still can guarantee the efficient outcome. However, if the court underestimates the victim's damages, then the damage remedy generally will lead to excessive output and may be less desirable than the injunctive remedy.

Although in theory either remedy could therefore be more efficient, it may be apparent in particular circumstances that one remedy is likely to be better than the other. For example, suppose that a court is confident that its estimate of the victim's damages is close to the truth, but believes that its estimate of the injurer's benefits is inaccurate. Then an entitlement to the victim protected by a damage remedy generally would be preferred because this would be likely to lead to an outcome close to the efficient solution. Alternatively, suppose that a court has poor information both about the victim's damages and the injurer's benefits, but is confident that the efficiency loss from too little activity by the injurer is small relative to the efficiency loss from excessive activity. Then an entitlement to the victim protected by an injunctive remedy would be desirable because this would guarantee that the final outcome will not be too bad. Thus, the efficiency analysis of nuisance law may be helpful even when there is some uncertainty about which entitlement and remedy to choose.

# SECOND APPLICATION—BREACH OF CONTRACT

Another area of law that can be discussed within the Coasian framework of bargaining among a small number of individuals is contract law. Unlike the normal nuisance law situation, however, the parties to a contract negotiate with each other before any dispute arises. Since the parties can decide in advance how to resolve potential disputes, it might be asked whether it is necessary or desirable to have general legal rules that govern contract disputes. The reason contract rules are desirable is, of course, that it would be prohibitively costly (if even possible) to negotiate and draft a contract that provides for every conceivable contingency. For contingencies that are thought to be unlikely or that do not affect the parties' costs and benefits very much, it is not worth going to the trouble to specify in advance what to do if the contingency should occur.

Contract law can be viewed as filling in these "gaps" in the contract—attempting to reproduce what the parties would have agreed to if they could have costlessly planned for the event initially. Since the parties would have included contract terms that maximize their joint benefits net of their joint costs—both parties can thereby be made better off—this approach is equivalent to designing contract law according to the efficiency criterion.[16]

16. The statement that the parties would have maximized their joint benefits net of their joint costs obviously presumes that they would have bargained cooperatively. Also, the conclusion that the maximization of the parties' joint benefits net of their joint costs is the goal of efficiency presumes that no one else is affected by the contract.

In this chapter, we will examine three remedies for breach of contract from this perspective. One, *expectation damages*, awards the breached-against party an amount of money that puts her in the same position she would have been in had the contract been completed. Another, *reliance damages*, awards an amount of money that places the breached-against party in the position she would have been in had she never entered into the contract initially. The last, *restitution damages*, awards the breached-against party an amount of money corresponding to any benefits that she has conferred upon the breaching party.[17]

The analysis will be undertaken using an example in which a seller, *S*, can produce a good called a "widget" for $150. Widgets are not generally available. For this reason, a buyer, *B1*, who values the widget at $200, enters into a contract with *S* for the future delivery of a widget. The contract price is paid in advance. In order to use the widget, *B1* must make an expenditure of $10 prior to delivery (for example, she might have to modify her warehouse to store the widget). This will be referred to as her *reliance expenditure* or *reliance investment*. If the contract is not completed, this expenditure is assumed to have no value.[18]

Before delivery occurs, there is a chance that some other buyer, *B2*, may also want the widget. The value *B2* attaches to the widget is not known at the time *S* and *B1* enter into their contract. For simplicity, it is assumed that *B2*'s value will be either $0, $180, or $250, and that he will offer this amount for it. Thus, after *S* and *B1* have entered into their contract, there is a chance that *B2* will offer more for the widget than *B1* did. Both *S* and *B1* are assumed to be aware of this possibility. The facts of this example are summarized in Table 2 (ignore for now the note at the bottom of the table).

17. Another remedy, liquidated damages, will be discussed in Chapter 8 below.

18. The assumptions that the contract price is paid in advance and that the reliance investment has no value in the event of breach are not essential and do not affect any of the general conclusions in this chapter.

**TABLE 2**

**Breach of Contract Example**

*S* is the seller:

*S*'s cost to produce the widget is $150.

*B1* is the initial buyer:

*B1* values the widget at $200.

*B1*'s reliance expenditure is $10.[a]

*B1* pays *S* the contract price in advance.

*B2* is the second buyer:

*B2* values the widget at $0 or $180 or $250.

a. The possibility that *B1* can spend an additional $24 on reliance and thereby increase the value of the widget to her by $30 also is considered.

It also will be assumed in this chapter that the parties are *risk neutral.* This means that they only care about the *expected value* of a risky situation—that is, the magnitude of a potential loss or gain multiplied by the probability of the loss or gain occurring. For example, the expected gain in a situation involving a 50 percent chance of winning $10,000 is $5,000. A risk-neutral person would, by definition, be indifferent between this situation and any other one with the same expected gain—such as a situation involving a 25 percent chance of winning $20,000, or one involving a certainty of winning $5,000.

## A Fully Specified Contract

Before considering how breach of contract remedies fill in the gaps in incompletely specified contracts, it will be useful to examine the contract between *S* and *B1* when everything is specified in advance. Suppose the contract has the following provisions. First, the contract price, payable in advance, is $175. Second, if the value *B2* attaches to the widget is $0 or

$180, then *S* is to deliver the widget to *B1*. In this case, *S*'s profit is $25—the contract price of $175 less *S*'s production cost of $150—and *B1*'s profit is $15—the $200 value of the widget to *B1* less her $10 reliance expenditure and less the contract price of $175. Third, the contract states that in the event that *B2* values the widget at $250, *S* is to sell it to *B2* rather than *B1*, but then must pay *B1* $225. In this case *S*'s profit is $50—the contract price of $175 less *S*'s production cost of $150, plus *B2*'s payment to *S* of $250 less *S*'s payment to *B1* of $225. *B1*'s profit is then $40—the $225 payment from *S* less the reliance expenditure of $10 and less the contract price paid in advance of $175.

It is clear that this fully specified contract between *S* and *B1* is efficient. The only choice the parties have to make that affects their *joint* profits is whether *S* is to sell to *B2* if *B2* wants the widget. If *S* does not sell to *B2*, then the joint profits of *S* and *B1* are $40—*S*'s profit of $25 plus *B1*'s profit of $15. If *S* does sell to *B2* when *B2* values the widget at $250, then the joint profits of *S* and *B1* rise to $90—*S*'s profit of $50 plus *B1*'s profit of $40. However, if *S* were to sell to *B2* when *B2* values the widget at $180, the joint profits of *S* and *B1* would fall to $20 because, together, they would have revenue of $180 and costs of $160 (*S*'s production cost of $150 plus *B1*'s reliance expenditure of $10). Thus, the provisions in the contract that call for *S* to sell the widget to *B2* if *B2* values it at $250, but not if he values it at $0 or $180, are efficient.[19]

It is important to note that there is a close relationship between the contract price and the amount of money *S* has to pay to *B1* if *S* sells the widget to *B2*. In general, the higher the amount paid to *B1*, the higher the contract price. For example, suppose *S* has to pay *B1* $240 rather than $225 in the event that the widget is sold to *B2*. *B1* clearly would prefer to receive the higher payment in the event of a breach, and *S* clearly would prefer to pay the lower amount. Presumably,

19. Since *B2* is assumed to offer an amount equal to the value he attaches to the widget, his profits are not affected by how valuable the widget is to him. This is why *B2*'s profits do not need to be taken into account in determining the efficient contract provisions.

therefore, *S* will demand, and *B1* will be willing to offer, a higher contract price in advance—say $180 instead of $175.

### Efficient Breach

Thus far, the example illustrates a simple but fundamental principle in the economic analysis of contract law: A fully specified contract is efficient. In practice, however, the cost of contracting will lead the parties to ignore relatively unimportant contingencies. Therefore, now suppose that because *S* and *B1* believe that an offer from *B2* is unlikely, they do not bother to include a provision in the contract that deals with the possibility that *B2* will offer more for the widget. The contract simply states that *S* is to deliver a widget to *B1* at some price payable in advance. We will now examine whether the expectation, reliance, and restitution remedies for breach of contract are efficient alternatives to an explicit contract provision regarding when the widget should be sold to *B2* rather than to *B1*. An important assumption in the following analysis is that if *S* wants to breach the contract, *B1* will not find it worthwhile (because of bargaining costs) to attempt to stop *S* from breaching or to repurchase the widget from *B2* after the breach. (If it were costless for *B1* to negotiate with *S* or *B2*, then the Coasian analysis in Chapter 3 implies that every remedy would be efficient.)

First consider a breach of the contract when the expectation remedy is applicable. If the contract had been completed, *B1* would have made a profit equal to the $200 value she places on the widget less her reliance expenditure and less the contract price she paid in advance. Thus, to put *B1* in the same position she would have been in had the contract been completed, it is necessary to compensate *B1* $200 (because *B1* has already incurred the reliance expense and has paid *S* the contract price). Given a damage payment of $200, *S* will decide to breach if *B2* offers $250 for the widget, but not if he offers $180 (or, of course, $0). Thus, the expectation remedy leads to the efficient outcome. Put differently, the expectation remedy is an efficient substitute for explicit contract provisions governing when *S* is to sell the widget to *B1* or *B2*. It thereby saves the parties the cost and inconvenience of dealing with unlikely contingencies every time they enter into a contract. Instead, they can simply rely on a breach of contract remedy in the few instances when the contingency arises.

Note that the conclusion that the expectation remedy induces efficient breach decisions does not depend on what the contract price is. *S* will have to pay *B1* $200 in the event of a breach regardless of the contract price because, given that *B1* paid the contract price (and incurred the reliance expense) in advance, $200 is the amount of money necessary to put *B1* in the same position she would have been in had the contract been completed. Thus, regardless of the contract price, *S* will breach in order to sell to *B2* only if *B2* offers more than $200 for the widget.

Next consider the reliance remedy. If *B1* had not entered into the contract with *S*, it is assumed that she would have earned zero profit.[20] Thus, to put *B1* in the same position she would have been in had she never entered into the contract, it is necessary to compensate *B1* for her $10 reliance investment and to return to her the contract price that she paid in advance. In other words, the reliance measure of damages equals the reliance expenditure plus the contract price.

To determine the effects of the reliance remedy on *S*'s decision to breach, it is therefore necessary to examine the setting of the contract price. Since *S*'s production cost is $150, he will not be willing to accept less than this amount. *B1* will be willing to pay up to $190 for the widget because she values it at $200 but has to make the $10 reliance investment. Thus, the contract price will be somewhere between $150 and $190, the exact price depending on the relative bargaining strengths of the parties. Suppose, for concreteness, that it is $160.

Given a reliance expenditure of $10 and a contract price of $160, the reliance remedy would award *B1* $170 in the event of a breach by *S*. Therefore, *S* will breach the contract if *B2* offers

20. This assumption is not essential and does not affect any of the general conclusions about the reliance remedy.

either \$180 or \$250 for the widget because *S* has to pay only \$170 in damages. If *B2*'s value is \$180, the breach will be inefficient because the value *B2* attaches to the widget is less than the \$200 value *B1* attaches to it. In other words, the reliance remedy might lead to an inefficient breach.

Finally, consider the restitution remedy. The only benefit *B1* has conferred on *S* is the contract price that she paid in advance. Thus, to award *B1* an amount of money corresponding to the benefit she has conferred, it is necessary to force *S* to return the contract price to *B1*. In other words, restitution damages equal the contract price. For the same reasons discussed with respect to the reliance remedy, the contract price will be between \$150 and \$190. If it is below \$180, then the restitution remedy also will lead to an inefficient breach when *B2* values the widget at \$180.

In general, the restitution remedy is more likely to lead to inefficient breaches than the reliance remedy for the following reasons. First note that the contract price under the restitution remedy tends to be less than the contract price under the reliance remedy. Intuitively, this is because the seller (*S* in the example) does not have to compensate the buyer (*B1* in the example) for her reliance expenditure under the restitution remedy, but he does have to under the reliance remedy. Consequently, the buyer presumably would not be willing to pay as much for the contract under the restitution remedy, and the seller presumably would be willing to accept less. Given a lower contract price under the restitution remedy, the damage payment also would be lower under that remedy because restitution damages equal the contract price, whereas reliance damages equal the contract price plus the reliance expenditure. One would expect inefficient breaches to be more likely under the restitution remedy because of the lower damage payment.

The discussion thus far illustrates several general conclusions about the economic effects of contract law. The key result is that the expectation remedy is the only remedy that creates efficient incentives with respect to breaches of contracts. This is because the expectation remedy forces the breaching party to pay damages equal to the value of the good to the breached-against party. If another buyer values the good more than this, then it is efficient for that buyer to have the good. Given the expectation measure of damages, the seller will have an incentive to breach in order to obtain the higher offer. If another buyer values the good less than the original buyer, a breach is not efficient and the expectation remedy will appropriately discourage breaches. Any other measure of damages for breach of contract generally will be inefficient. If damages exceed expectation damages, then a breach might not occur even though it would be efficient. For example, if damages were $260 in the example, then *S* would not breach when *B2* offers $250. And if damages are less than expectation damages, an inefficient breach might occur. This is the problem with the reliance remedy, because it leads to a level of damages below the expectation level. The restitution remedy is worse because it results in even lower damages than those under the reliance measure.

## Efficient Reliance

Inducing optimal breaches of contracts is not the only problem with which contract law has to deal. Another issue of concern relates to reliance expenditures. In the example, it was assumed that *B1*'s reliance investment was fixed at $10. In general, this expenditure can vary, and the more spent on reliance, the more valuable the contract will be to the buyer if it is completed. For example, the buyer might be able to purchase various customized pieces of equipment, each of which is capable of transforming the widget into a more valuable final product. (Because widgets are perishable, this equipment must be obtained before delivery.) In the remainder of this chapter we will analyze how remedies for breach of contract affect the amount invested in reliance.

In order to examine the reliance decision, the example used earlier needs to be made slightly more complicated. We will continue to assume that the original buyer *B1* must spend at least $10 on reliance and that the widget will be worth $200 to her if this is all that she spends. But now she will have the option of spending an *additional* \$24 on reliance and thereby raising the value of the widget to her by \$30. As before, if the contract is not completed, the reliance expenditure will have no value. It also will be assumed that the three values the second buyer *B2* might attach to the widget—\$0, \$180, or \$250—are all equally likely. The relevance of this assumption will become apparent shortly.

Although it might seem that the efficiency criterion would dictate having *B1* make the additional reliance investment—because this investment seems to increase the value of the widget by \$30 at a cost of only \$24—this conclusion is incorrect. The increase in value occurs only if the contract is completed and *B1* obtains the widget. But, as we have seen, it is efficient for *S* to breach the contract with *B1* in order to sell to *B2* if the value of the widget to *B2* turns out to be \$250. Given the assumption at the end of the previous paragraph, there is a one-in-three chance that *B2* will value the widget this much. In other words, if the breach decision is efficient, there is only a two-thirds chance that *B1* will obtain the widget. Thus, while the \$24 cost of reliance is certain, the \$30 benefit from reliance is uncertain. The *expected* benefit—the benefit multiplied by the probability of its realization—is only \$20. It is inefficient to incur a \$24 cost to obtain a \$20 expected benefit.

If *S* and *B1* had been able to costlessly negotiate and draft their contract initially, they would have included a provision that specified that *B1* is not to make the additional \$24 reliance investment. However, negotiating over *B1*'s reliance decision is not a simple matter. For example, if it is difficult for *S* to verify how much additional benefit *B1* would obtain from the additional reliance expenditure, *B1* might be able to take advantage of *S*'s imperfect information. Thus, analogously to the breach of contract decision, it is reasonable to suppose that a provision regarding the reliance decision was not included in the contract. We will therefore examine whether some breach of contract remedy can serve as a substitute for this missing provision.

Under the expectation remedy, *B1* either will receive the widget (if the contract is performed) or be given an amount of money equivalent to the value of the widget (if the contract is breached). If *B1* spends just $10 on reliance, the widget will be worth $200 to her, so expectation damages would equal $200. If she spends an additional $24 on reliance, the widget will be worth an additional $30 to her, so expectation damages would equal $230. Thus, by spending an extra $24, she will obtain a $30 benefit either because the widget will be delivered or higher expectation damages will be paid. Clearly, *B1* will invest the additional $24 in reliance, an inefficient outcome for the reasons discussed above. In other words, because the expectation remedy *in effect* guarantees performance, it does not force *B1* to take into account the fact that the reliance expenditure will be worthless if the contract is breached. It therefore encourages excessive reliance investments.

Under the reliance remedy, *B1* either will receive the widget or be given an amount of money equal to her reliance expenditure plus the contract price. Thus, if the contract is performed, the extra $24 investment in reliance will have been worthwhile because it will have raised the value of the widget by $30. If the contract is breached, the extra $24 will be returned because reliance damages will be that much higher. *B1* therefore will have an incentive to spend the extra $24 on reliance because this expenditure is, in effect, an investment that has no "downside" risk but that does have "upside" potential. In other words, the reliance remedy also encourages excessive reliance expenditures.

Under the restitution remedy, *B1* either will receive the widget or be given an amount of money equal to the contract price. Unlike under the expectation remedy, she is not effectively guaranteed performance, and, unlike under the reliance remedy, she does not get her reliance investment back in the event of breach. *B1*'s reliance expenditure is now, in effect, a risky investment with a positive payoff in the event of performance and no payoff in the event of breach. Therefore, in order for *B1* to determine whether it is worthwhile to spend the extra $24 on reliance, she needs to know the probabilities of performance and breach. Suppose *S* breaches only when it is efficient for a breach to occur—that is, only when *B2* values the widget at $250.[21] Given the assumption that the three values *B2* might attach to the widget—$0, $180, and $250—are all equally likely, there is a two-thirds chance of performance and a one-third chance of breach. Thus, the *expected* benefit to *B1* of the reliance expenditure is $20—the $30 increase in value of the widget multiplied by the probability of obtaining this value. *B1* will not spend an extra $24 in reliance to obtain this expected benefit. In other words, the restitution remedy leads to the efficient reliance investment.

This discussion of the effects of breach of contract remedies on the reliance decision illustrates several general results. The principal one is that, among the remedies considered, only the restitution remedy induces efficient reliance investments. It does this because it forces the party investing in reliance to take into account the fact that the reliance expenditure is worthless if the contract is breached.[22] The expectation remedy generally leads to too much reliance because it gives the relying party the value that would have been created by the reliance investment if the contract had been performed. The reliance remedy also generally induces excessive reliance because it reimburses the relying party for the cost of reliance in the event of breach.

Another consideration in the economic analysis of breach of contract remedies is the cost of obtaining the information needed to implement each remedy. The expectation remedy requires a court to estimate what the value of the contract would have been to the breached-against party if the contract had been completed. In many contract situations, this value

21. The supposition that *S* breaches only when it is efficient for a breach to occur is clearly counterfactual in general under the restitution remedy. This supposition is used nonetheless because it allows the effect of the restitution remedy on the extent of the reliance investment to be illustrated most easily.

22. The "remedy" of no damages at all also would lead to the efficient reliance investment for the same reason.

may be difficult to determine. For example, suppose the buyer is purchasing specialized memory chips for the production of a newly designed laptop computer. The court would have to predict how profitable the new computer would have been. The restitution and reliance remedies both require knowledge of the contract price, which should be readily available. The reliance remedy also requires information about the breached-against party's reliance expenditures. Since these expenditures will have been made prior to the parties' coming to the court, it should be easier for the court to obtain this information than the information required by the expectation remedy. Thus, in general, the expectation remedy probably would be the most costly to implement, the restitution remedy would be the cheapest, and the reliance remedy would be somewhere in-between.

Note also that if the court incorrectly estimates the value of performance to the breached-against party, then the conclusions regarding the effects of the expectation remedy on the breach decision and on the reliance decision would have to be modified. Similarly, if the breached-against party's reliance expenditures are likely to be incorrectly determined, the conclusions regarding the effects of the reliance remedy also would be different.

The discussion in this chapter has shown that, in general, there does not exist a breach of contract remedy that is efficient with respect to both the breach decision and the reliance decision. With respect to breach, the expectation remedy is ideal, whereas with respect to reliance, the restitution remedy is ideal. Thus, which remedy is best overall depends on whether the breach decision or the reliance decision is more important in terms of efficiency. For instance, in the example used in this chapter an inefficient breach occurred when *S* sold the widget to *B2* when *B2*'s value was \$180. Because *B1* valued the widget at \$200, there was an efficiency loss of \$20 from the inefficient breach; assuming this occurs with a one-third chance (the chance that *B2* values the widget at \$180), the expected value of the efficiency loss is \$6.67 (1/3 × \$20).

Inefficient reliance occurred when *B1* spent the additional $24 in reliance. Because the expected benefit of reliance only was $20, there was an efficiency loss of $4 from inefficient reliance. Thus, in this example, because the efficiency loss from inefficient breach exceeds the efficiency loss from inefficient reliance, the expectation remedy would be preferred.

A key assumption in the discussion in this chapter was that the parties were neutral with regard to risk. In Chapter 8 we will reconsider breach of contract remedies when the parties are assumed to be averse to risk and see that, in general, none of the remedies discussed here are ideal with respect to risk allocation.

# THIRD APPLICATION — AUTOMOBILE ACCIDENTS

In both of the applications discussed thus far — nuisance law and breach of contract — it was appropriate to consider the possibility that bargaining among the parties could lead to the efficient solution. Thus, the framework of the Coase Theorem was directly applicable to these kinds of disputes. In the next application that we will examine — automobile accidents involving pedestrians — bargaining obviously cannot lead to the efficient outcome because neither drivers nor pedestrians know in advance with whom to bargain. The Coase Theorem may be helpful nonetheless. Efficient legal rules for dealing with driver-pedestrian accidents still can be derived by imagining what rules a driver and a pedestrian would have chosen if they could have costlessly gotten together before the accident. As in the other applications, the parties would have agreed to remedies that lead them to behave so as to maximize their joint benefits net of their joint costs.

A simple example will be used to investigate the efficiency of different legal remedies in driver-pedestrian accidents. In this example, it is assumed that drivers and pedestrians are risk neutral; the discussion therefore will be in terms of the *expected* accident cost to a pedestrian — the magnitude of the harm if an accident occurs multiplied by its probability of occurrence. It also is assumed initially that only the speed of drivers affects the pedestrians' expected harm. (The example will be extended later in this chapter to include the possibilities that the number of miles driven or the care exercised by pedestrians also affect the expected harm.) The driver has

TABLE 3

Automobile Accident Example—Driver's Care Affects Expected Accident Cost

| *Behavior of Driver* | *Benefit to Driver* | *Expected Accident Cost to Pedestrian* | *Benefit Minus Cost* |
|---|---|---|---|
| Drive rapidly | $120 | $100 | $20 |
| Drive moderately | $80 | $40 | $40 |
| Drive slowly | $50 | $20 | $30 |

three choices: drive rapidly, drive moderately, or drive slowly. Each choice results in some benefit to the driver and some expected accident cost to the pedestrian. The driver's benefit from driving faster might be the dollar value he places on saving time. The pedestrian's harm also is assumed to have a monetary value.[23]

The data for the example are described in Table 3. For each choice of the driver, the table lists the benefit to the driver and the expected accident cost to the pedestrian. The efficient outcome requires that the driver act so as to maximize benefit less cost. Given the data in Table 3, it is efficient for the driver to drive moderately. Relative to this outcome, driving rapidly is inefficient because it increases the pedestrian's expected losses by $60 while increasing the driver's benefits only by $40. And driving slowly is inefficient because it lowers the driver's benefits by $30 while lowering the pedestrian's expected losses only by $20.

### The Driver's Care

We will now consider the effects on the driver's behavior of two alternative rules of liability in accident law—*strict*

23. As suggested in note 6 above and in the accompanying text, economic analysis still can be used when the harm is not equivalent to the loss of money (as is the case with pain and suffering). However, the discussion would be more complicated.

*liability* and *negligence.* Under each, the driver will choose the action that maximizes his benefits net of his expected liability payments. Under the rule of *strict liability,* the driver will be made liable for the pedestrian's accident losses regardless of the driver's care. Thus, for each action, the driver's benefit net of his expected liability payments is the same as the last column in Table 3. The driver therefore will choose to drive moderately — the efficient outcome. In essence, the rule of strict liability results in efficient behavior because it forces the injurer — in this example, the driver — to take into account all of the adverse effects of his behavior on the victim — the pedestrian.

For the rule of strict liability to be efficient, the court generally must be able to obtain correct information about the victim's damages. To see why, suppose in the example that the court estimates damages to be one-half of the victim's actual damages. Then, referring to Table 3, the driver's benefits net of his expected liability payments would be $70 if he drives rapidly ($120 – $50), $60 if he drives moderately ($80 – $20), and $40 if he drives slowly ($50 – $10). He therefore would choose to drive rapidly — faster than is efficient.[24] Conversely, suppose the court estimates damages to be twice what they actually are. Then the driver's benefits net of his expected liability payments would be, respectively, –$80 ($120 – $200), $0 ($80 – $80), and $10 ($50 – $40). Thus, the driver would choose to drive slowly — too slow relative to desired driving behavior. In order to focus on other considerations, it will be assumed hereafter that the court has accurate information about the victim's damages.

Under the rule of *negligence,* the driver will be made liable for the pedestrian's accident losses only if the driver does not meet some standard of care. Suppose this standard is determined by the care that would be taken if the driver acted efficiently. In the example, this corresponds to driving at

24. For analogous reasons, the driver also generally would drive faster than is efficient if, given his income or wealth, he does not expect to be able to pay the full amount of the victim's damages.

moderate speed. Thus, the driver would be liable for the pedestrian's accident losses only if the driver chooses to drive rapidly. Therefore, if he drives rapidly his benefit net of his expected liability payments is $20 (a $120 benefit less a $100 expected liability payment). If he drives moderately, it is $80 (just the benefit because there is no liability), and if he drives slowly it is $50 (again, just the benefit). Consequently, under the rule of negligence with this standard of care, the driver will choose the efficient outcome of driving moderately. In essence, the rule of negligence leads to the efficient outcome because the injurer prefers to comply with the standard of care—to avoid having liability increase from zero to the victim's damages if the standard is violated—and the standard is selected to correspond to the desired behavior.

For the rule of negligence to be efficient, it is necessary for the court to have enough information to determine the efficient outcome so that the standard of care can be chosen to correspond to it. To see why, suppose in the example that the court mistakenly believes that it is efficient for the driver to drive slowly and therefore makes this behavior the standard of care. In other words, the driver is liable for the pedestrian's losses if he drives rapidly or moderately, but not if he drives slowly. Then, referring to Table 3, the driver's benefit net of his expected liability payments is $20 if he drives rapidly ($120 – $100), $40 if he drives moderately ($80 – $40), and $50 if he drives slowly ($50 – $0). Thus, the driver would choose to drive slowly, an inefficient outcome. Similarly, if the court were to make the standard of care too lenient rather than too strict, the driver would choose to drive faster than would be efficient. It will be assumed hereafter that the court has enough information to select the standard of care that corresponds to the efficient outcome.

The discussion thus far illustrates a general principle in the economic analysis of accident law: In accident situations in which the only issue is how to induce the injurer to take appropriate care, both strict liability and negligence are efficient, provided that liability equals actual damages if strict liability is used and that the standard of care corresponds to the efficient outcome if negligence is used.

## The Pedestrian's Care

In many accident situations, however, the problem is not just to control the injurer's behavior. In general, both the injurer and the victim can affect the probability and the magnitude of the harm. For example, a pedestrian can walk rather than run while crossing a street, or a cyclist can wear a protective helmet. When both the injurer and the victim can affect the expected harm, the issue is how to induce both parties to take appropriate care. We will now reexamine the rules of strict liability and negligence with respect to this additional consideration.

To allow for the expected harm to be determined by the behavior of both the driver and the pedestrian, it is necessary to extend the example used above. It will now be assumed that the pedestrian has one choice — whether to walk or to run. If she walks, then her expected accident loss is $100 if the driver drives rapidly, $40 if the driver drives moderately, and $20 if the driver drives slowly. These are the same values used in Table 3. If the pedestrian runs, her corresponding expected accident losses are $110, $50, and $30. In other words, running is assumed to raise the expected harm by $10 regardless of the driver's behavior.[25] The data for the extended example are summarized in Table 4, where it also is assumed that the driver's benefits from driving are the same as in Table 3.

The efficient solution to the accident problem now involves a specific action both by the driver and by the pedestrian. If the pedestrian walks, the problem is the same as before, and the efficient outcome with respect to the driver's behavior is for him to drive moderately. If the pedestrian runs, Table 4 shows that benefits minus costs also are maximized when the driver drives

25. In general, the effect of the pedestrian's care on expected accident losses would depend on the driver's behavior. For example, suppose the pedestrian's decision whether to walk or to run determines the probability of an accident, while the driver's speed determines the magnitude of the harm if an accident occurs. Then the faster the driver drives, the more the expected harm will be raised by the pedestrian's decision to run. The assumption made in the text — that running raises the expected harm by an amount that does not depend on the driver's behavior — simplifies the subsequent analysis without affecting the general conclusions.

TABLE 4

**Automobile Accident Example—Driver's Care and Pedestrian's Care Affect Expected Accident Cost**

| *Behavior of Driver* | *Benefit to Driver* | *Expected Accident Cost to Pedestrian (Depending on Pedestrian's Behavior)* | *Benefit Minus Cost (Depending on Pedestrian's Behavior)* |
|---|---|---|---|
| Drive rapidly | $120 | $100 (walks) | $20 (walks) |
| | | $110 (runs) | $10 (runs) |
| Drive moderately | $80 | $40 (walks) | $40 (walks) |
| | | $50 (runs) | $30 (runs) |
| Drive slowly | $50 | $20 (walks) | $30 (walks) |
| | | $30 (runs) | $20 (runs) |

moderately. Thus, regardless of the pedestrian's behavior, the efficient solution involves driving moderately. Whether it is efficient for the pedestrian to walk or to run depends on the relevant costs and benefits. Running rather than walking increases the pedestrian's expected harm by $10 (regardless of the driver's behavior). It will be assumed that running provides additional benefits to the pedestrian valued at $5—for example, due to the saving of time. Thus, given these costs and benefits, the efficient solution involves the pedestrian walking.[26]

Now reconsider the rule of strict liability. The driver's benefit net of his expected liability payments corresponds to the last column in Table 4. If the pedestrian walks, the relevant values are $20, $40, and $30, depending on whether the driver drives rapidly, moderately, or slowly. The driver therefore

26. For simplicity, the benefit to the pedestrian from running or walking is not included in Table 4. Thus, Table 4 focuses on the benefits and costs associated with the driver's behavior (which depend in part on the pedestrian's behavior).

would choose to drive moderately. If the pedestrian runs, the corresponding values are $10, $30, and $20, and the driver also would choose to drive moderately. Thus, regardless of the pedestrian's behavior, the rule of strict liability will lead the driver to behave efficiently in this example. However, the rule of strict liability will not be efficient with respect to the pedestrian's behavior. Because the pedestrian will be fully compensated for her losses, she will ignore these losses when deciding whether to walk or to run. She only will consider the $5 extra benefit from running. The pedestrian therefore will choose to run even though running increases expected accident costs by $10.

The problem of controlling the victim's behavior under the rule of strict liability can be solved by adding a defense of *contributory negligence.* Then, the injurer is strictly liable unless the victim is contributorily negligent. This rule will result in the desired behavior of both parties.

To see this in the example, let the standard of care applicable to the pedestrian correspond to the efficient behavior of the pedestrian — walking. Thus, if the pedestrian walks, she is not contributorily negligent, so the driver would be strictly liable. If she runs, she is contributorily negligent, so the driver would be free of liability. The pedestrian then has to bear her own losses. Thus, while running rather than walking provides benefits valued at $5, it increases the expected accident cost borne by the pedestrian from zero to $110, $50, or $30, depending on whether the driver drives rapidly, moderately, or slowly (see Table 4). Clearly, the pedestrian will choose to walk in order to avoid having to bear her own losses. Given this choice by the pedestrian, the driver will be strictly liable. We already have seen that this will lead the driver to choose to drive moderately. Thus, the rule of strict liability with a defense of contributory negligence will cause both parties to take an efficient amount of care.

Next, reconsider the rule of negligence in terms of the incentives it creates for both parties to take appropriate care. Assume, as before, that the driver is negligent only if he drives rapidly. If the pedestrian walks, the driver's benefits net of his expected liability payments are the same as discussed earlier under the negligence rule, so the driver will choose to drive moderately. If the pedestrian runs, the driver's benefits net of his expected liability payments are \$10 if he drives rapidly (\$120 – \$110), \$80 if he drives moderately (\$80 – \$0), and \$50 if he drives slowly (\$50 – \$0). Thus, the driver will choose to drive moderately regardless of what the pedestrian does. Because the driver therefore will not be negligent, the pedestrian will bear her own losses. She will then compare the \$5 extra benefit from running to the \$10 increase in expected accident costs and will choose to walk. Thus, the rule of negligence will lead both parties to take an efficient amount of care.

Note that under the negligence rule it is not necessary to add a defense of contributory negligence to induce the victim to take proper precautions. If a contributory negligence defense were added, it would not affect the conclusion that both parties will take an efficient amount of care. The victim would meet the standard of care applied to her to avoid being contributorily negligent and having to bear her own losses. Given that the victim is not contributorily negligent, the injurer will meet the standard of care applied to him to avoid being negligent and having to compensate the victim for her losses.

The preceding discussion of the accident problem when both parties can affect the expected harm illustrates another general result in the economic analysis of liability rules: In accident situations in which the problem is to induce both the injurer and the victim to take appropriate care, a rule of strict liability with a defense of contributory negligence *or* a rule of negligence—with or without a defense of contributory negligence—is efficient.

### The Activity-Level Issue

In many accident situations, expected accident losses depend not only on the care exercised by each party, but also on the extent to which each party participates in the activity that is the source of the dispute. For example, the number of driver-pedestrian accidents depends in part on how much drivers drive and on how frequently pedestrians travel by foot (rather than, say, by bus). The efficient level of participation in the dispute-creating activity is determined by comparing the benefits a party obtains from greater participation — for example, from the more extensive use of one's car — to the resulting increase in expected accident costs. In general, then, the problem to be solved by liability rules is how to induce both parties to take appropriate care *and* to engage in the activity to an appropriate extent.

To examine whether the rules of strict liability and negligence lead to the efficient level of participation in the activity, the simple version of the driver-pedestrian example — in which only the driver's speed affects the pedestrian's expected accident costs — will be extended to include the number of miles driven. (The more general case in which expected losses also are affected by the pedestrian's care and level of participation in the activity will be discussed below.) Now suppose that expected accident costs depend not only on whether the driver drives slowly, moderately, or rapidly, but also on whether he drives "a little" or "a lot." If he drives a little, then the relevant data are assumed to be the same as in the simple version of the example — that is, the same as in Table 3. If he drives a lot, then his benefits are assumed to increase by \$20 and the pedestrian's expected accident costs are assumed to rise by \$30, regardless of the speed at which he drives.[27] The data for the extended example are summarized in Table 5.

Because the additional benefits from driving a lot are less than the increase in expected accident costs, the efficient solution involves driving a little. If the driver drives only a little, the problem is the same as that discussed in the simple version of the driver-pedestrian example, where it was efficient for the driver to drive at moderate speed. Put differently, driving moderately and only a little maximizes benefits less costs. This can be seen directly in the last column of Table 5.

Under strict liability, the driver's benefit net of his expected liability payments corresponds to the last column

27. A point analogous to the one made in note 25 above applies here.

TABLE 5

**Automobile Accident Example—Driver's Care and Activity Level Affect Expected Accident Cost**

| *Behavior of Driver* | *Benefit to Driver (Depending on How Much Driver Drives)* | *Expected Accident Cost to Pedestrian (Depending on How Much Driver Drives)* | *Benefit Minus Cost (Depending on How Much Driver Drives)* |
|---|---|---|---|
| Drive rapidly | $120 (a little) | $100 (a little) | $20 (a little) |
| | $140 (a lot) | $130 (a lot) | $10 (a lot) |
| Drive moderately | $80 (a little) | $40 (a little) | $40 (a little) |
| | $100 (a lot) | $70 (a lot) | $30 (a lot) |
| Drive slowly | $50 (a little) | $20 (a little) | $30 (a little) |
| | $70 (a lot) | $50 (a lot) | $20 (a lot) |

in Table 5. Thus, the driver will choose to drive moderately and only a little. As in the earlier versions of the driver-pedestrian example, strict liability leads the injurer to behave efficiently because it forces him to take into account the adverse effects of his behavior on the victim. The only difference now is that one relevant aspect of his behavior is the extent of his participation in the activity.

Under negligence, suppose, as in the earlier versions of the example, that the driver is negligent only if he drives rapidly. Then, if his participation in the activity corresponds to driving a little, his benefit net of his expected liability payment is $20 ($120 – $100) if he drives rapidly, $80 ($80 – $0) if he drives moderately, and $50 ($50 – $0) if he drives slowly. If he drives a lot, the comparable values are $10 ($140 – $130) if he drives rapidly, $100 ($100 – $0) if he drives moderately, and $70 ($70 – $0) if he drives slowly. The driver therefore will choose to drive a lot and to drive at moderate speed. In other words, the negligence rule with this standard of care is efficient with respect to the injurer's care but not with respect to his level of participation in the activity.

Recall from the discussion of the negligence rule in the simple version of the driver-pedestrian example that this rule is efficient only if the standard of care corresponds to the efficient behavior of the injurer.[28] The negligence rule is not efficient in the present version of the example precisely because the standard of care does not take into account one relevant aspect of the injurer's behavior — the extent of his participation in the activity. If the standard of care were to correspond to the efficient outcome of driving moderately and only a little — so that the driver *would* be negligent if he drives a lot even if he drives moderately — then the negligence rule also would lead to the efficient outcome.

In practice, however, it often is not feasible to include the level of participation in the activity as an aspect of the standard of care. For example, it would be virtually impossible for a court to determine how many miles a particular person drives each year since that person might drive a car that is shared with other family members or he might drive different cars owned by the household. If the injurer's level of participation in the activity is omitted from the standard of care, then a negligence rule generally will lead him to participate in the activity to an excessive degree. The reason for this is straightforward. If the care he exercises meets the standard of care, he will not be liable for any damages. Therefore, in deciding how much to participate in the activity, he will consider the additional benefits from greater participation but not the increase in expected accident costs. This problem with the negligence rule was illustrated by the driver-pedestrian example. Given a standard of care based only on the driver's speed, the driver chose to meet the standard by driving moderately. But he also chose to drive a lot, exceeding the efficient level of participation in the activity.

The discussion thus far of the activity-level issue can be summarized as follows: In accident situations in which the problem is to induce the injurer both to take appropriate care and to participate in the activity at an appropriate level, strict

28. See pp. 45-46 above.

liability is efficient. Negligence also is efficient if the standard of care encompasses both the injurer's care and his level of participation in the activity. However, if the standard does not include the injurer's activity level, then the negligence rule will lead to excessive participation in the activity. In practice, the negligence rule is likely to be inefficient for this reason.

In some accident situations, the expected accident losses may depend not only on the injurer's care and activity level, but also on the victim's care and activity level. In this more general setting, results analogous to those just discussed would occur. Strict liability with a defense of contributory negligence would be efficient if the standard of care applicable to the victim encompasses both the victim's care and her activity level. However, if it includes only her care, then the victim will engage in the activity to an excessive degree. Similarly, negligence would be efficient if the standard of care applicable to the injurer includes both aspects of his behavior. If it includes only his care, then he will participate in the activity too much. Thus, if it is not feasible to include either party's activity level in the standard of care, the preferred liability rule depends on whether it is more important to control the injurer's or the victim's activity level. If the injurer's activity level is of greater concern, then strict liability with a defense of contributory negligence should be used. If the victim's activity level is more important, then negligence is preferable.

The final consideration in the economic analysis of liability rules that will be discussed in this chapter is the effect of each rule on the administrative costs of resolving accident disputes. These costs depend both on the number of cases litigated and on the cost of resolving each case.[29] The negligence rule would be expected to generate less litigation than the strict liability rule for the following reason. Consider the

29. Although the following discussion is concerned with disputes that are litigated, similar points could be made with respect to disputes that are settled after costly negotiation.

negligence rule in an accident situation in which the injurer's care was very likely to have satisfied the standard of care. Given the cost to the victim of litigating, she might not find it worthwhile to bring an action against the injurer because of the low probability of success. Yet, under the strict liability rule, she might be willing to bring an action in this accident situation because the injurer's care is not a bar to a successful suit.

Although there may be fewer cases under the negligence rule, the administrative cost of resolving each one is likely to be higher than under the strict liability rule. The justification for this conclusion is easiest to see when the only problem is to induce the injurer to take appropriate care. To apply a strict liability rule, the court needs to know the victim's damages. But to apply a negligence rule, the court not only needs to know the victim's damages and the injurer's benefits at different levels of the injurer's care—in order to choose a standard of care that corresponds to the efficient outcome—but also how the injurer behaved—in order to determine whether he met the standard. (When the problem is to induce both the injurer and the victim to take appropriate care, this argument does not apply because the strict liability rule then requires a defense of contributory negligence to be efficient.)

On balance, therefore, administrative cost considerations do not clearly favor either rule. While the negligence rule is likely to lead to fewer cases being litigated than the strict liability rule, it may well generate higher administrative costs in each case.

This chapter has shown that in accident situations in which the only problem is to create incentives for the parties to take appropriate care, both strict liability with a defense of contributory negligence and negligence are efficient. If the problem also is to induce the parties to engage in the dispute-creating activity to an appropriate extent, then both rules still are efficient provided that the relevant standards of care—the victim's under the contributory negligence defense and the injurer's under the negligence rule—incorporate the activity-level decision of the party to whom the standard applies. In practice, however, this is not likely to be feasible. If the standard of care refers only to the relevant party's level of care, then strict liability with a defense of contributory negligence will lead to excessive participation in the activity by the victim, and negligence will lead to excessive participation by the injurer. In many accident situations it may be apparent that one party's activity level matters more than the other's, in which case the superiority of one of the rules will be clear.

An important assumption in the discussion in this chapter was that both drivers and pedestrians were risk neutral. When accident law is reconsidered in Chapter 9 under the assumption of risk aversion, it will be seen that strict liability and negligence may no longer be efficient even in accident situations in which only the injurer's care determines the victim's expected losses.

# [2]

# Externalities and the Coase Theorem: A Diagrammatic Presentation

James Halteman

*Abstract:* In intermediate microeconomic textbooks the reciprocal nature of externalities is presented using numerical examples of costs and benefits. This treatment of the Coase theorem obscures the fact that externality costs and benefits are best understood as being on a continuum where costs vary with the degree of intensity of the externality. When these cost-and-benefit functions are portrayed as continuous, it is possible to analyze optimal levels of the externality. Total costs and benefits can be observed so that efficiency can be evaluated under conditions of zero transactions costs, positive transactions costs, and auction bidding for property rights. This approach also reinforces several other general principles of microeconomic theory.

Key words: Coase theorem, externalities
JEL codes: A22, H23

The significance of Coase's (1960) insights into the reciprocal nature of externalities is widely recognized in the economics profession. Those insights suggest, "When the parties affected by externalities can negotiate costlessly with one another, an efficient outcome results no matter how the law assigns responsibility for damages" (Frank 2003, 623). Unfortunately, undergraduates often miss the importance of this claim for two reasons. First, the subject is usually situated near the end of intermediate microeconomics textbooks and most professors rarely progress that far into the material. Unless ungraduates take another course such as public finance, the material may not be systematically covered. Second, those who do get to the material frequently are faced with an array of numbers and tables that often fail to do justice to the concepts that make the Coase theorem so important. In this article, I suggest remedies for these shortcomings.

Treating the subject of externalities as a part of the discussion at the end of the material on perfect competition could help solve the first problem. The Coase theorem provides an interesting perspective on the relationship of markets, externalities, and transactions costs, including information problems. The point at which perfect competition is qualified by the presence of these factors would be an appropriate place to consider the reciprocal nature of externalities. I present a simple graphical model of Coase's findings that is both interesting to students

***James Halteman** is the Hendrickson Professor of Business/Economics at Wheaton College, IL (e-mail: James.Halteman@Wheaton.edu).*

(thereby solving the second problem) and reinforces some of the basic microeconomic concepts that students are internalizing midway through an intermediate micro course.

## GRAPHIC EXAMPLE

The starting point can be any externality problem with which students can identify. I sometimes use a case of music in the dormitory or pollution of a river. The music example is shown in Figure 1, which has the standard treatment of marginal benefits and marginal costs, with decibel levels on the horizontal axis and marginal costs and benefits measured in dollar values on the vertical axis.

In most simple treatments of this situation the problem is viewed as a simple cost-benefit calculation, which will be efficiently solved if the stereo is played at the level 0Y because to go beyond this point would involve a marginal cost higher than the marginal benefit. The general presumption is that any individual does not have the right to disturb others excessively, so by setting the tax per decibel at 0t, Sam will optimize his welfare by playing at the 0Y level. Marginal social costs will equal marginal social benefits and efficiency will be reached.

However, if there is no all-knowing dorm counselor present to set the correct tax rate, things usually deteriorate into some coercive regulatory rule that sets a quiet time or a situation in which no rules or taxes exist. In this case, Sam would have an incentive to play at 20 decibels, irritating Sara. At this point, it would be a simple matter to add two other relevant functions. First, Sam could insulate his walls at some cost. This can be shown as another cost function (see Figure 2). Next, Sara could insulate her walls also or wear earplugs, or both. This can be shown with another cost function on Figure 2 so that three cost functions are now present. Because the total of all marginal values in any given function represents

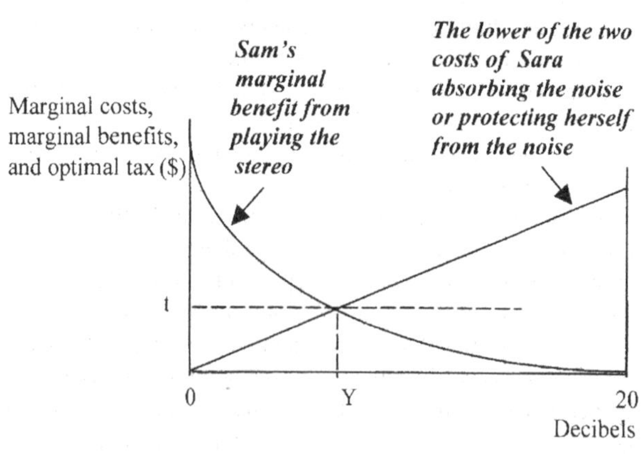


**FIGURE 1. The standard externality presentation, using music as example.**

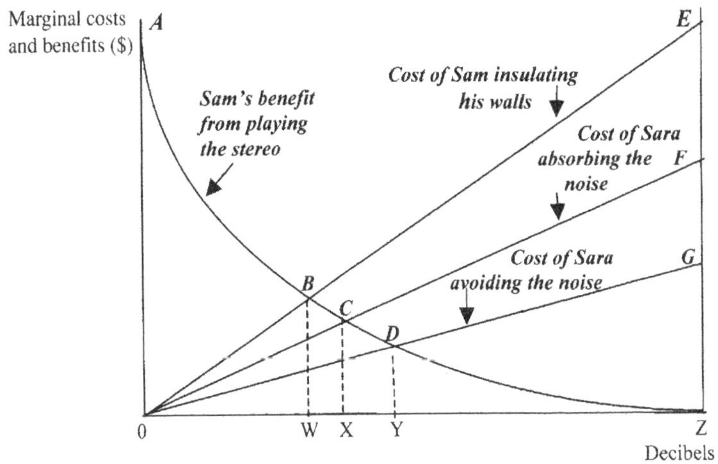


**FIGURE 2. The reciprocal nature of externalities, using music as an example.**

the total value, it will be helpful to identity the areas on the graph with letters. With these additional functions, the full ramifications of the Coase theorem can be explored, and, in the process, some key microeconomic concepts are reinforced.

## POSSIBLE SOLUTIONS

I evaluate six scenarios to illuminate Coase's insights. In each of these cases, assumptions are made about negotiation costs, so it is important to be clear on how those costs are understood. Negotiation costs in the real world involve any impediment that might prevent Sara and Sam from working out mutually agreeable arrangements with which they can live. Any negotiations take some time, and there may be institutional norms or values that make bargaining difficult. Typically, dormitory airwaves are not thought of as negotiable property, and students paying one another for quiet or music time would violate most student's sense of what dorm life should be. These impediments or costs may outweigh any benefits gained from negotiations so, in these situations, I say that negotiation costs prohibit meaningful bargaining. When negotiation costs are not prohibitive, they still will likely be positive, which detracts from the net gains described in the following scenarios. Although these complications reduce the net gains of negotiation, they do not detract from the important contribution of the Coase theorem. Also, these complications help students think through the complex issues that are inevitable as they work from theory to practice. Helping students grapple with why dormitory policy (if it exists) usually relies on coercive regulation will help them understand why Coase solutions are not easy to implement and enforce. Because the starting point for analyzing the externality problem is usually the case of zero or prohibitive negotiation costs, the following six cases use those assumptions. I treat each case in sequence.

1. Sam has the rights to the airwaves, and negotiation costs with Sara are zero.
2. Sara has the airwave rights, and negotiation costs are zero.
3. Negotiation costs are prohibitive, and Sam has the property rights.
4. Negotiation costs are prohibitive, and Sara has the property rights.
5. The airwave rights are auctioned off one decibel at a time.
6. The airwave rights are auctioned off in an all-or-nothing manner.

### Case 1

Because Sam has the airwave rights he will be inclined to play at 20 decibels. Sara will use protective measures costing an amount equal to area *0DY* but, because negotiation costs are zero, will then find it better to pay Sam an amount equal at least to area *DYZ*, so Sam will cut back the stereo to *0Y* (Figure 2). That payment is less than the *DGZY* additional cost that Sara would have needed to protect herself, and Sam is compensated adequately for his loss of listening pleasure. In short, Sam attains the full pleasure of *0AZ* at the minimal social cost of *0DZ*. This level of noise is consistent with the social optimal level in Figure 1.

### Case 2

If Sara has the property rights, Sam is prohibited from making noise, but Sam finds that, by paying Sara an amount at least equal to *0DY*, she can protect herself from the noise while allowing Sam to play to *0Y*. Sam finds additional decibel levels are worth less to him than the cost of compensating Sara to protect herself. Therefore, Sam holds the volume down to *0Y*. Because Sara and Sam can negotiate without cost, the outcome is the same in cases 1 and 2, and efficiency is achieved no matter who is given the property rights. This is the point of the first part of the Coase theorem.

### Case 3

If Sam has property rights and negotiation costs are high, Sam plays to *0Z* decibels, and Sara has no choice but to protect herself at a cost of *0GZ* because to do otherwise would be to absorb the higher cost of listening to the noise. Output of noise is inefficiently high, and an extra cost of *DGZ* is absorbed by society.

### Case 4

If Sara has the property rights and negotiation costs are high, Sam must turn off his stereo as long as it bothers Sara. However, up to point *0W*, Sam's cost of insulating against sound is less than his benefit of listening to music, so Sam plays to that decibel level and installs the proper amount of insulation. The level of music played is less than is socially optimal, and the net benefit to society is only *0AB* compared with *0AD* at the efficient point of *0Y* decibels. The interesting part of this story is that, in case 3, the net social benefit is *0AZ* minus *0GZ*. In case 4, the net social benefit is *0AB*. Therefore, if *DGZ* is greater than *0BD*, it would be preferrable to give the rights to Sara because the net social benefits would be higher. Her costs of alleviating the problem are greater than what Sam must give up to solve the problem. The best allocation of rights will depend on the location of the benefit function and the various cost functions.

### Case 5

In an auction where bidding starts low and moves upward, the winner will need to pay only one cent more than the competitor's last bid. In this case, Sara is willing to bid up to the amount it would cost to insulate against that level of noise. Thus, Sara bids up to her cost of insulating, and Sam takes the bid for a penny more. He buys the rights to cover the decibel level up to *0Y* and then he bids up only to his benefit level, which has now fallen below Sara's insulation costs. Thus, she buys the rights to decibel levels higher than *0Y*. The overall effect is for Sam to play to *0Y* and Sara to spend *0DY* to insulate against the sound. He stops at *0Y* because Sara has rights to the decibel levels beyond that amount for which she paid a total of *YDZ*. This means that the efficient point of *0Y* is attained at the minimum cost of *0DZ* to society.

### Case 6

Finally, if the decibel rights are sold as one block of rights and negotiation costs are zero, Sara will bid up to *0DZ* because that is the most it will cost her if she does not have rights to the airwaves. Sam bids to *0DZ* + 1 cent and gets the rights. Sara then spends *0DY* to insulate and offers Sam *YDZ* to cut the noise level back to *0Y*. Efficiency is reached at the minimum cost of *0DZ*, all of which is borne by Sara. If transactions costs are prohibitive, Sara is willing to bid up to *0GZ* because that is the most it will cost her to protect herself and that is less than the cost of absorbing the noise. Sam compares the area under his benefit curve *0AZ* with the area under his cost of insulating curve *0EZ* and bids to the least of these two alternatives because that will be his loss if Sara wins the bid. In Figure 2, Sam's bid would exceed Sara's bid so he would gain the rights and play at full volume. This scenario cannot be efficient because Sam is playing beyond *0Y*, and Sara will need to spend *DGZ* more than the least-cost solution. The moral of this story is that efficiency in the externality auction markets is reached only when incremental units are auctioned or, lacking that, when negotiation costs are zero.

This analysis can be repeated in many different ways, depending on how the cost functions are drawn. Sam's insulating cost could be much lower, Sara's distaste for the music might be less, or Sara's insulating cost could be much greater. However, the implications will always be the same. Efficiency comes with zero negotiation costs, and, if negotiating is impossible, the correct allocation of property rights will depend on the location of the various cost-and-benefit functions.

In Figure 2, I have also allowed for fruitful discussions on other forms of externality policy. Coercive regulation in the form of a quiet-time curfew is common in many dorms. Finding the optimal noise level $0Y$ may be a process of experimentation with the administration responding to student complaints. Different social norms are sometimes established in different dorms so that a Tiebout (1956) effect takes place in which students who prefer quiet time request placement or move to dorms that are study oriented and others move to the party-oriented dorms.[1] For variety, the cost-and-benefit functions could be turned around to make silence a problem with external effects on those who like music. In this case, the issue of the responsibility of the perpetrator becomes a difficult concept to nail down. Who is the perpetrator is more a question of what value system is espoused.

This framework of analysis reinforces many microeconomics principles in creative ways. The notion that the sum of all the margins equals the total is clear from the way the areas under the marginal functions are used. The auction part of the model illustrates how the winner in an auction pays only one bid above what the second highest bidder is willing to pay, even though this may be considerably below what the winner's willingness to pay curve would allow. Thus, maximizing consumer surplus leads to efficiency.

The formal analysis fits more with a duplex dormitory for two than a dormitory with many students; broader applications must be made with care. However, the broader externality problem does lend itself to discussions of other important related economic concepts. Because buying silence for oneself also provides it for other students for free and because they cannot be excluded from the benefits of silence, some of these scenarios can be an appropriate introduction to the public-good concept and its connection to externality issues. Also, if students act in groups, many game theoretic applications can be introduced along with club theory and the need for enforcement devices. In any case, bringing these theoretical models into the experience of the student in a connected way increases the interest of the student and therefore enhances the learning process.

## CONCLUSION

Almost any other relevant externality issue could be treated graphically like these examples. Some, such as water or air pollution, may have appeal because they may seem more objective. What I hope is clear from this exercise is that when one thinks in the right categories, it is easier to understand the goal of efficiency so that, if departures from it are taken, they will be purposeful and consistent with whatever value system is operative.

### NOTE

1. Although Tiebout intended to explain how various local communities deal with different preferences for services and taxes, his principles and assumptions could readily apply to externality problems where migration away from negative externalities is possible.

### REFERENCES

Coase, R. 1960. The problem of social cost. *Journal of Law and Economics* 3 (October): 1–44.
Frank, R. 2003. *Microeconomics and behavior*. Boston: McGraw-Hill.
Tiebout, C. 1956. A pure theory of local expenditures. *Journal of Political Economy* 64 (October): 416–24.

# [3]



**Coase Theorem.** Anyone who has taught the Coase Theorem to fresh minds has experienced first hand the wonder and admiration which it inspires, yet Coase never wrote it down, and, when others try, it probably turns out to be false or a tautology. The proposition, or propositions, called the Coase Theorem was originally developed through a series of examples (Coase, 1960). Like a judge, Coase steadfastly refused to articulate broad generalizations in his original paper. Like a judge's opinion, for every interpretation of his paper there is a plausible alternative. Instead of trying to arrive at the ultimate answer, I will offer several conventional interpretations of the Coase Theorem and illustrate them with one of his examples. After more than twenty years of debate the conventional interpretations appear to have exhausted its meanings.

A central insight in microeconomics is that free exchange tends to move resources to their highest valued use, in which case the allocation of resources is said to be Pareto efficient. Besides ownership of resources, the law creates many other entitlements, such as the right to use one's land in a certain way, the right to be free from a nuisance, the right to compensation for tortuous accidents, or the right to performance on a contract. Coase can be regarded as having generalized propositions about the exchange of resources to cover propositions about the exchange of legal entitlements. Under this interpretation, the Coase Theorem states that *the initial allocation of legal entitlements does not matter from an efficiency perspective so long as they can be freely exchanged.* In other words, misallocation of legal entitlements by law will be cured in the market by free exchange.

This interpretation suggests that insuring the efficiency of law is a matter of removing impediments to the free exchange of legal entitlements. Legal entitlements often suffer from vagueness, which makes their value difficult to assess. Furthermore, the courts are not always willing to enforce contracts for the sale of legal entitlements. Consequently, under the 'free exchange interpretation', the efficiency of law is to be secured by defining entitlements clearly and enforcing private contracts for their exchange.

Besides freedom of exchange, there are other conditions which economists usually regard as necessary for markets to allocate resources efficiently. One such condition concerns the elusive, but unavoidable, concept of transaction costs. Narrowly conceived, transaction costs refer to the time and effort required to carry out a transaction. In some circumstances these costs can be very high, as when a deal involves several parties at different locations. High transaction costs can block the workings of markets which would otherwise be efficient. Broadly conceived, transaction costs refer to any use of resources required to negotiate and enforce agreements, including the cost of information needed to formulate a bargaining strategy, the time spent higgling, and the cost of preventing cheating by the parties to the bargain. Stressing the 'transaction cost interpretation', the Coase Theorem can be regarded as stating that *the initial allocation of legal entitlements does not matter from an efficiency perspective so long as the transaction costs of exchange are nil.*

Like a frictionless plane in physics, a costless transaction is a logical construction, rather than something encountered in life. Keeping this fact in mind, the policy prescription following from the transaction cost interpretation of the Coase Theorem is to use law to minimize transaction costs, not eliminate them. According to this line of reasoning, rather than allocating legal entitlement efficiently in the first place, lawmakers are more likely to achieve efficiency by lubricating their exchange. Legal procedure is rife with devices whose purpose is to avoid litigation by encouraging private agreements involving an exchange of legal entitlement.

The 'transaction costs' interpretation focuses attention on some obstacles to exchanging legal entitlement, specifically the cost of negotiating and enforcing private agreements. When 'transaction costs' are given a reasonably circumspect definition, there are additional obstacles to private exchange besides transaction costs. The theory of regulation has developed a finer, richer classification based upon deviations from perfect competition (Schultze, 1977). To illustrate, a monopolist can increase his profits by supplying less than the competitive amount of the good and forcing the price up. Thus monopoly is a form of market failure which is usually distinguished from transaction costs. Stressing this 'market failures interpretation', the Coase Theorem can be regarded as stating that *the initial allocation of legal entitlements does not matter from an efficiency perspective so long as they can be exchanged in a perfectly competitive market.*

This interpretation suggests that ensuring the efficiency of law is a matter of ensuring the existence of perfectly competitive markets for legal entitlements. The conditions of perfect competition include the existence of many buyers and sellers, the absence of external effects, full information about price and quality by the participants in the market, and no transaction costs.

The three interpretations can be illustrated by an historical example which Coase made famous. Wood and coal-burning locomotives emit sparks that set fire to farmers' fields from time to time. Each of the parties can take precautions to reduce the damage caused by fires. To illustrate, the farmers can avoid planting and storing crops along the margins of the railroad tracks, and the railroad can instal spark arresters or run fewer trains.

Upon first inspection, it seems that the law controls the incentives for precaution by the parties, and, consequently, determines the amount of damage from fires. To illustrate, injunction is the conventional remedy in property law for a nuisance. If the farmers have a right to enjoin the railroad and shut it down until it stops emitting sparks, it seems that there will be little or no damage from sparks. Conversely, if the railroad has the right to operate trains with impunity, it seems that there will be a lot of damage. According to the Coase Theorem, these appearances are misleading, because while the law creates the initial allocation of entitlements, the market determines the final allocation. To illustrate, if farmers have a right to enjoin the railroad, they can sell this right. Specifically, the railroad could pay a sum of money to the farmers in exchange for a legally binding promise not to enjoin the railroad. Conversely, if the railroad has the right to emit sparks with impunity, it can sell this right. Specifically, farmers could pay a sum of money to the railroad in exchange for a legally binding promise to reduce spark emissions.

Whatever the initial allocation of rights, the farmers and the railroad have an incentive to continue trading entitlements so long as there are potential gains from trade. As with ordinary goods, the gains from trading legal entitlements are not exhausted until each entitlement is held by the party who values it the most. To illustrate, if, say, farmers have a right to be free from sparks, and if the entitlement to emit sparks is worth more to the railroad than the right to be free from sparks is worth to farmers, both parties will benefit from the farmers selling their rights to the railroad. The potential gains from trade are exhausted when entitlements are allocated efficiently. Thus, when the market works, the equilibrium allocation of legal entitlements will be efficient.

The three interpretations of the Coase Theorem give different accounts of the conditions that must be satisfied in order for this market to work. According to the 'free exchange' interpretation, the equilibrium allocation of entitlements will be efficient if entitlements are clearly defined and contracts for their exchange are enforceable. In the example, the conditions of the 'free exchange' interpretation are apparently met when the farmers have the right to enjoin the nuisance, or when the railroad has the right to emit sparks with impunity. Thus, according to the free exchange interpretation of the Coase Theorem, it does not matter from an efficiency perspective whether farmers have the right to enjoin the railroad or the railroad has the right to pollute with impunity.

The conclusion about efficiency is different under the 'transaction cost' interpretation. If there are many farmers, the cost of negotiating and enforcing an agreement among them would be high, especially since individual farmers might hold out for a larger share of the surplus, so inefficiencies in the initial allocation of entitlements would probably persist in spite of opportunities for private agreements. On the other hand, if there are just a few farmers, the cost of negotiating and enforcing an agreement between them and the railroad would be low, so the theorem predicts that the equilibrium allocation of entitlements would be efficient.

Turning to the third version, according to the 'perfect competition' interpretation, the equilibrium allocation of entitlements will be efficient if the conditions of perfect competition are satisfied in the market for legal entitlements. In the example of the railroad and the farmers, there is only one railroad, so the market is characterized by monopoly rather than perfect competition. Furthermore, there may be other types of failure in the conditions of perfect competition. For example, farmers may have more information than the railroad about the harm caused by sparks, whereas the railroad may have more information than the farmers about the technology for reducing spark emissions. In view of these facts, the exchange of legal entitlements between the farmers and the railroad would depart far from the conditions of perfect competition, so the market might fail to cure inefficiencies in the initial allocation of legal entitlements.

Of course, the initial allocation of rights always matters from the perspective of income distribution. To illustrate, if efficiency requires the railroad to be free from injunction, granting the farmers the right to injunctive relief will motivate the railroad to try to buy this right. The purchase is a cost to the railroad and income to the farmers. Conversely, granting impunity to the railroad will save it the cost of purchasing the right and deprive farmers of the income from selling it. Like scarce resources, scarce legal rights are valuable.

IS THE COASE THEOREM TRUE OR FALSE? In economics, a 'proof' is a derivation from generally accepted behavioural assumptions. As I will show, attempts to formulate the Coase Theorem in any of its three interpretations encounter obstacles which suggests that it is probably false or a mere tautology.

The weakest form of the theorem asserts that legal entitlements will be allocated efficiently under perfect competition. When Arrow (1969) examined externalities similar to those discussed by Coase, he showed that the efficiency conditions can be interpreted as the equilibrium conditions in a competitive market for the exchange of externality rights. But, as indicated by Arrow and others (Starrett, 1972), this formal demonstration has little practical value because externalities by their nature have characteristics which prevent the formation of competitive markets.

To illustrate, suppose that pollution is forbidden except by holders of resaleable pollution coupons issued by the government. Each pollutee who holds a coupon thereby prevents pollution from occurring, whereas each polluter who acquires a coupon uses it to increase the amount of pollution. Obviously, the social benefits of an individual pollutee retaining a coupon exceed his private benefits, so pollutees will sell too many of them. Equivalently, the social cost of a polluter acquiring a coupon exceeds his private cost, so pollutees will acquire too many of them. This divergence between private and social costs is itself an externality. So the attempt to eliminate externalities by setting up a market for pollution coupons just gives rise to a new type of externality (for details, see Cooter, 1982.) In reality, there are no perfectly competitive markets for externalities of the type discussed by Coase, and it seems impossible for them to arise spontaneously by private agreement. There might be some way for the government to create a pseudo-market (e.g. Groves, 1976), but none has been implemented.

Turning from the perfectly competitive market interpretation to the transaction cost interpretation of the Coase Theorem, observe that a private solution is likely to be efficient in cases affecting only a few parties, as, say, when contiguous land owners negotiate concerning a nuisance caused by one of them. If only a few parties are involved, the prices of entitlements will be negotiated instead of the parties acting as price-takers, which violates an assumption of perfect competition, but such negotiations often succeed anyway. According to the transaction cost interpretation of the Coase Theorem, externality problems affecting small numbers of people should have efficient solutions.

Although accurate as a rule of thumb, the transaction cost interpretation is not strictly true. It rests upon the proposition that bargaining reaches an efficient conclusion when the costs of negotiating and enforcing agreements is nil (Regan, 1972). In reality, bargaining among small numbers of people sometimes breaks down – unions strike, hijackers kill hostages, realtors lose sales because of disagreements over the price, disputes go to trial, and so forth. The essential obstacle, which has nothing to do with the cost of communicating or enforcing agreements, is the strategic character of bargaining. By definition, a bargaining situation has the characteristic that a surplus can be achieved by agreement, but there is no settled way for dividing it up among the beneficiaries. A self-interested negotiator will press his claim to a share of the surplus as far as he dares without destroying the basis for cooperation. In economic jargon, the rational negotiator demands an additional dollar so long as the resulting increase in the probability of noncooperation creates an expected loss of less than a dollar. When negotiators underestimate an opponent's resolve, they press too hard and the negotiations fail to reach an agreement. Thus bargaining situations are inherently unstable.

Seen in this light, the transaction cost interpretation of the Coase Theorem errs in the direction of optimism by assuming that cooperation will always occur when bargaining is costless. The polar opposite viewpoint, which has been called the 'Hobbes Theorem' (Cooter, 1982), errs in the direction of pessimism by assuming that the problem of dividing the surplus can only be solved by coercive force, not by cooperation. Reality lies in between the poles of optimism and pessimism, because strategic behaviour causes bargaining to fail in some cases, but not in every case.

The challenge to theory and empirical research raised by this interpretation of the Coase Theorem is to predict when legal entitlements will be allocated efficiently by private agreements. To advance this debate, broad labels such as 'transaction costs' and 'free exchange' must yield to substantive, detailed descriptions of the conditions under which private bargaining about legal entitlements succeeds. Fortunately, a more satisfactory bargaining theory has begun to emerge in recent years which adheres more closely to reality. According to this account, bargaining will break down for strategic reasons in a percentage of cases, but in equilibrium no one is surprised by the frequency with which breakdowns occur. (The key concept is the Bayesian Nash equilibrium; see Harsanyi, 1968, and Cooter and Marks, 1982.)

In economics, an 'empirical test' is a comparison between a prediction and facts. Recently, attempts have been made to test the Coase Theorem, for example, by determining the conditions under which bargaining in small groups reaches an efficient conclusion (Spitzer, 1982). The new developments in game theory, combined with the associated empirical research, hold the promise of finally establishing a scientific account of the conditions under which inefficient allocations of legal entitlements will be cured by private agreements.

WHAT IS THE SIGNIFICANCE OF THE COASE THEOREM? Pigou used economics to defend the common law principle that a party who causes a nuisance should be enjoined or required to pay damages. According to Pigou, the common law rules tend to promote economic efficiency by internalizing social costs. In some cases, he found gaps in the common law which require supplementary legislation, such as imposing a tax upon polluters equal to the social cost of pollution.

Coase's paper was framed as an attack upon Pigou's analysis of the law of nuisance. Coase disagreed with the conclusion that government action, through nuisance law or taxation, is typically required to achieve efficiency. The Coase Theorem suggests that the externalities represented by nuisances will sometimes, or perhaps usually, be self-correcting. I have argued that the forms of market failure are too diverse to be subsumed under a reasonably circumspect concept of transaction costs, and, consequently, the transaction cost interpretation of the Coase Theorem should be regarded as false or as a tautology whose truth is achieved by inflating the definition of transaction costs. Although the obstacles to spontaneous, private solutions of externalities are broader than suggested by the Coase Theorem, the role of government in lubricating private agreements, rather than issuing commands, is much favoured in the contemporary economic understanding of regulation.

In the event that government action is required to correct a nuisance, Coase denied Pigou's claim that the common law concept of causality is a useful guide to assigning responsibility. In Coase's view, the fact that someone 'causes' a nuisance, as judged by common law principles, does not imply that holding him liable or enjoining him is efficient. For Coase, the question of efficiency is to be decided by a balancing of cost and benefits in which the role of causality is not decisive. Coase's suggestion that causality should have little bearing upon legal responsibility contradicts countless court decisions and appears to have had little impact upon the practice or theory of law.

Whatever the merits of his arguments, Coase offered a challenge to widely accepted views in public finance. Before his article appeared, not much attention was paid to the possibility that externalities could be cured by private bargains. Thus Coase's claim went to the heart of a major debate in economics. Furthermore, the publication of Coase's article can be regarded as a breakthrough for the subject which has acquired the name of 'law and economics'. Before publication of Coase's article, economic *analysis* (as opposed to economic thought) had received little application to the common law, which is at the core of legal theory and method as taught in law schools. By analysing cases from property law in a lawyerly style, yet drawing upon microeconomics to guide the analysis, Coase demonstrated the fruitfulness of the economic analysis of the common law. He inspired a generation of scholars who pioneered the economic analysis of law, although he did not use the mathematical tools which have come to characterize the subject twenty years later.

ROBERT D. COOTER

*See also* COMMON PROPERTY RIGHTS; ECONOMIC ORGANIZATION AND TRANSACTION COSTS; EXTERNALITY; LAW AND ECONOMICS.

BIBLIOGRAPHY

Arrow, K. 1969. The organization of economic activity: issues pertinent to the choice of market versus non-market allocation. In *The Analysis and Evaluation of Public Expenditure: the PPB System*. US Congress, Joint Economic Committee, Washington, DC: GPO. Reprinted in *Public Expenditure and Policy Analysis*, ed. R. Haveman and J. Margolis, Chicago: Rand McNally, 1977.

**Cobb–Douglas functions**

Coase, R. 1960. The problem of social cost. *Journal of Law and Economics* 3(1), October, 1–44.
Cooter, R. 1980. How the law circumvents Starrett's nonconvexity. *Journal of Economic Theory* 22(3), June, 145–9.
Cooter, R. 1982. The cost of Coase. *Journal of Legal Studies* 11(1), January, 1–34.
Cooter, R. and Marks, S. 1982. Bargaining in the shadow of the law; a testable model of strategic behavior. *Journal of Legal Studies* 11(2), 225–52.
Groves, T. 1976. Information, incentives, and the internalization of production externalities. In *Theory and Measurement of Economic Externalities*, ed. A.Y. Steven, London: Academic Press.
Harsanyi, J.C. 1967–8. Games with incomplete information played by 'Bayesian' players, I–III. *Management Science*, Part I, 14(3), November 1967, 159–82; Part II, 14(5), January 1968, 320–34; Part III, 14(7), March 1968, 486–502.
Pigou, A.C. 1920. *The Economics of Welfare*. London: Macmillan. 4th edn, 1932.
Regan, D. 1972. The problem of social cost revisited. *Journal of Law and Economics* 15(2), October, 427–37.
Schultze, C. 1977. *The Public Use of Private Interest*. Washington, DC: Brookings.
Spitzer, M. 1982. The Coase Theorem: some experimental tests. *Journal of Law and Economics* 25(1), 73–98.
Starrett, D. 1972. Fundamental non-convexities in the theory of externalities. *Journal of Economic Theory* 4(2), April, 180–99.

# [4]



## Coase theorem

Mutuality of advantage from voluntary exchange is one of the most fundamental concepts in economics. The well-known proposition of Ronald H. Coase (1960) – generally known as the Coase theorem – builds on this simple and yet fundamental insight. The law creates many rights and legal entitlements, establishing the initial allocation of rights and liabilities. Whenever there are no legal or factual impediments to exchange, the dynamic of the market will determine the final allocation of such rights.

In this context, Coase suggests that the transferability of rights in a free economy leads toward their best use and an efficient final allocation. Whenever the initial allocation is not optimal, the owners of the rights will have an incentive to transfer them to other individuals who value them more. Such an exchange will continue until there is no further potential for reciprocal profit, which will not be exhausted until each right is in the hands of the highest-valuing individual. The Coase theorem predicts that, in a competitive market environment without legal or factual impediments to exchange, the final allocation of rights will be efficient.

This article discusses the pervasive methodological implications of Ronald Coase's idea to the field of law.

### 1 A brief intellectual history

Coase's assertion that an initial assignment of property rights is often irrelevant to overall welfare has occasioned one of the most intense and fascinating debates in the history of legal and economic thought. Private property is often explained as the unavoidable by-product of scarcity in a world where common pool losses outweigh the sum of contracting costs and enforcement of exclusive property rights. At the turn of the 20th century, the underlying assumption in the economic literature was that private property emerged out of a spontaneous evolutionary process because of the desirable features of private property regimes in the creation of incentives for constrained optimization.

This understanding of the relationship between scarcity and emergence of legal entitlements characterized mainstream property right theory when Coase entered the academic world. Coase began his undergraduate studies at the London School of Economics in 1929, as a candidate for a Bachelor Degree in Commerce. In those years, one of Coase's teachers, Sir Arnold Plant, was re-examining the theme of property rights from a novel perspective. According to Plant, the traditional justification for private property – scarcity – was incapable of serving as the sole intellectual foundation for this institution. Plant showed that incentives, rather than scarcity, lay at the core of the property right problem (Plant, 1974).

Coase's use of legal rules as an object of economic research in his analysis of incentive structure and alternative final resource allocations reveals a remarkable technical affinity with the work of his undergraduate teacher. In his Nobel memorial lecture, Coase acknowledges the importance of his encounter with Plant as a 'great stroke of luck' that cultivated his interest in property rights theory (Coase, 1992, p. 715). For Coase, Plant's teaching that '[t]he normal economic system works itself' (Salter, 1921, pp. 16–17) and that prices in a competitive market lead resources to their highest valuing uses was a revelation into the dynamic of the economic system: 'I was then 21 years of age, and the sun never ceased to shine. I could never have imagined that these ideas would become some 60 years later a major justification for the award of a Nobel Prize. And it is a strange experience to be praised in my eighties for work I did in my twenties' (Coase, 1992, p. 716).

The experience of the following years at the London School of Economics laid the methodological foundations of what would later become Coase's theorem on the problem of social costs. All the ingredients of his revolutionary analysis on the debated theme of social cost had been profiled during his LSE years (see Williamson and Winter, 1991, pp. 34–5). But it is not until the late 1950s that Coase verbalized such a simple and yet ingenious idea. He had first expounded the core of his later theorem in an article published in 1959. In those pages, one grasps what would later become the central theme of Coase's celebrated argument:

> Whether a newly discovered cave belongs to the man who discovered it, the man on whose land the entrance to the cave is located, or the man who owns the surface under which the cave is situated is no doubt dependent on the law of property. But the law merely determines the person with whom it is necessary to make a contract to obtain the use of the cave. Whether the cave is used for storing bank records, as a natural gas reservoir, or for growing mushrooms depends, not on the law of property, but on whether the bank, the natural gas corporation, or the mushroom concern will pay the most in order to be able to use the cave. (1959, p. 25)

The discussion of the rationale of property rights under Coase's highest bidder framework obviously contained an attack on the Pigouvian approach (Pigou, 1920) to the problem. The point was rather self-evident to Coase, but not so for some of the Chicago economists. George Stigler was among Coase's early critics:

> Ronald Coase criticized Pigou's theory rather casually, in the course of a masterly analysis of the regulatory philosophy underlying the Federal Communication Commission's [FCC] work. Chicago economists could not understand how so fine an economist as Coase would make so obvious a mistake. Since he persisted, we invited Coase (he was then at the University of Virginia) to come and give a talk on it. Some twenty economists from Chicago and Ronald Coase assembled one evening at the home of Aaron Director. ... In the course of two hours of argument the vote went from twenty against and one for Coase to twenty-one for Coase. What an exhilarating event! (Stigler, 1988, pp. 75–6)

According to Coase, the objections to his FCC paper are at the origin of his later 1960 article on the problem of social costs. Coase recalls that he was urged to omit that section of his FCC article, something he refused to do. In retrospect, Coase believes that had it not been for the Chicago economists' attacks his full-fledged idea would have never been formulated (1993, p. 250).

## 2 The positive Coase Theorem

The arguments that were refined in the course of such debate were later put together in the form of an article for the *Journal of Law and Economics* in 1960, titled 'The Problem of Social Cost'. This article – later known as the Coase theorem – soon became a milestone in legal and economic literature. In the course of his austere discussion, Coase does not reveal any sign of anticipated realization of the revolutionary power of his insight. Indeed, Coase insists that he never intended to convey his thoughts in the precise and analytical form of a theorem (1988, p. 157).

A few years after the publication of 'The Problem of Social Cost', a sizeable number of commentaries and theoretical elaborations were developed on Coase's newly presented theme. The unpretentious style of Coase's article had thus been crowned by a notoriety rarely attained by legal writings of any sort (Shapiro, 1985, p. 1540). Part of the uproar is explained by the fact that the article challenged an established principle of public finance (see Manne, 1975, pp. 123–6). Before 'The Problem of Social Cost', very little attention had been given to the possibility that the problem of externalities could be resolved through free market exchanges.

Coase boldly attacked the conclusions reached by the Pigouvian tradition by suggesting its influence was in part due to the lack of clarity in its exposition (1960, p. 39). Coase departs from the Pigouvian approach by demonstrating that, in the absence of transaction costs, generators and victims of externalities will negotiate an efficient allocation of resources, independent of the initial assignment of rights among them. In confuting the conclusions of the Pigouvian tradition, Coase gave life to a model with the potential for the evaluation of an unlimited number of legal and social issues.

George Stigler was the first scholar to restate Coase's model in the form of a theorem: '[U]nder perfect competition private and social costs will be equal' (1966, p. 113). Demsetz (1967, p. 349) defined the theorem in the following terms: 'There are two striking implications of this process that are true in a world of zero transaction costs. The output mix that results when the exchange of property rights is allowed is efficient and the mix is independent of who is assigned ownership (except that different wealth distributions may result in different demands)'. Soon thereafter, Guido Calabresi stated the same principle more descriptively: 'Thus, if one assumes rationality, no transaction costs, and no legal impediments to bargaining, all misallocations of resources would be fully cured in the market by bargains' (Calabresi, 1968, p. 68).

The implicit premise of Coase's analysis draws upon a fundamental postulate of microeconomic theory: the free exchange of goods in the market moves goods towards their optimal allocation. The voluntary transfer of individual rights in the marketplace, thus, will cure a non-optimal allocation of legal entitlements.

*2.1 The Coasean methodological revolution*

Coase's article constitutes, according to many commentators, the first example of an economic analysis of law in North American literature. The novelty of his approach inspired an entire generation of scholars – pioneers in this new branch of applied economics. Only a few months prior to receiving the Nobel Prize for economics, in occasion of the First Annual Meeting of the American Law and Economics Association, Ronald H. Coase was recognized, together with Guido Calabresi, Henry G. Manne and Richard A. Posner, as a founding father of Law and Economics. This recognition follows many years of challenging debate. Many of the writings that developed around 'The Problem of Social Cost' tested the premises of Coase's model, seeking to undermine the conditions of his model and stressing the lack of practical reach of his analysis.

Further criticisms pertained to three fundamental points. One group of critics observed that the Coase Theorem disregarded the inter-industrial long-term effects of the system (Calabresi, 1965; Wellisz, 1964). These critics argued that Coase ignored the possible disequilibria which may occur after the negotiation and the likely dynamic changes in the initial equilibrium. In the context of Coase's well-known example, if the right has been assigned to the ranchers, the farmer will have to pay local ranchers until they all relinquish their right of pasture. The entire cost will, thus, burden the farming industry. Farmers will either have to bear the burden of the injury caused by the livestock or agree to pay the price demanded by the ranchers, whichever is less, on the assumption that negotiation is costless. Under this liability rule, the cost of ranching will not reflect the cost imposed on the farmers. The transfer of rights and liability from one group to another will, therefore, result in a shift in the relative wealth and costs associated with the two industries. The criticism claims that, in the long run, every shift of wealth will lead to an inter-industrial disequilibrium.

In 1968, Calabresi, one of the initial proponents of this criticism, reconsidered it, noting that in the presence of determined conditions the conclusions of Coase remain as true in the long run as in the short term (1968, p. 67). Calabresi's later analysis re-established the authority of the Coase Theorem, at least on this point. It became clear that Coase did not ignore the long-term effects of his model. Perhaps not explicitly, he had considered them to their logical extreme. Calabresi observes: 'The reason is simply that (on the given assumptions) the same type of transactions which cured the short run misallocation would also occur to cure the long run ones. ... This process would continue until no bargain could improve the allocation of resources' (1967, pp. 67–8).

In 1972, Harold Demsetz joined this debate, demonstrating with a more systematic analysis that the conclusions reached by Coase are not corroded by the long-term effects of a change in the assignment of property rights. Demsetz's reasoning finds its basis in the principle that the process of allocation of scarce resources among alternative uses is analogous to the process of constrained optimization of the single owner of two conflicting activities.

An additional critique, formulated by Calabresi (1965) and Wellisz (1964), suggests that strategic behaviour in the bargaining process risks compromising Coase's results. These authors observe that the change in the rule of law creates the conditions for possible extortion on the part of the right holders against the other individuals who are bound by the rule. The argument is that individuals are likely to threaten the use of their own rights in a measure which exceeds the optimal level, in order to maximize the gain from the release of their own legal entitlements. By introducing the possibility of strategic behaviour in the negotiation, the result may differ from the optimal equilibrium. Demsetz (1972, p. 21) supplied a convincing answer to this criticism. According to Demsetz, the possibility of strategic behaviour in the negotiations does not alter the efficiency in the final allocation of resources between the two activities. Strategies will be capable of altering the internal distribution of the contractual surplus between the parties, but not the final outcome of the negotiation.

It should be noted, however, that the entire analysis presupposes that the so-called income effect can be ignored. In general, a different allocation of property rights implies a different distribution of wealth between the individuals involved. Different initial endowments generate different final allocations, notwithstanding an equal level of efficiency. In order for the final allocations to be identical, it is necessary that the utility functions of the individuals involved are almost linear. The absence of the income effects implies, in this sense, that the demand functions for the good are independent of the income level.

It should be further observed that the credibility of the threat made in the course of strategic bargaining finds its limits in the market structure in which the Coasean negotiation takes place. In general, the competitive structure of the market eliminates much of the advantage that can be obtained through strategic behavior in the negotiation process. Inasmuch as the market of resources is competitive, strategic bargaining is not capable of bringing about any abnormal return.

The criticism, however, appears to be on the mark when it argues that, in some marginal situations, the curing role of the free exchange may still be impeded. For example, consider reversing the assignment of property rights between the rancher and the farmer. In such a situation, the farmer is likely not to have an equally large number of alternatives. The transfer of a farm from one place to another is costly, and farming unavoidably requires the undertaking of location-specific investments. Since some capital investment is irreversibly locked in that specific location, the farmer has less opportunity to relocate than the rancher. The rancher, consequently, finds himself in a position of local monopoly in the sale of his property right. Demsetz considers the monopoly that affects this feature of the Coasean exchange identical to the standard monopoly of microeconomic analysis (1972, p. 24). According to Demsetz, the concerns for possible monopolistic structures in the market of rights considered by Coase must not, however, be used to raise again the already resolved problem of the initial allocation of rights, since reversing the rule of liability would simply result in the farmer now having monopoly power (1972, pp. 24–5).

A second group of critics concentrated on the distributive effects of the model (Regan, 1972; Nutter, 1968). They argued that a final efficient allocation of resources requires transfers of wealth induced by the changed legal rule. Further, these critics observed that, even if one disregards the distributive effects of the rule, a different assignment of the right could in some cases create the conditions for strategic behaviour in negotiation capable of disturbing the efficiency of the final allocation.

A third group of authors focused on the scarce realism of the no-transaction-cost assumption (see Cooter, 1987, p. 457). According to this criticism, the true Achilles' heel of Coase's analysis was in the unrealistic assumption of absence of costs in the process of negotiation and transfer of the right. These authors observed that the idea of a transaction without cost is a logical fiction cloaking a mere tautology.

## 3 The normative Coase theorem

The utility of models predicting behaviour in a zero transaction-cost world is that they guide the law – whose object is to develop rules which approximate the zero transaction-cost world as closely as possible – in responding to legal problems arising in a positive transaction-cost environment (Epstein, 1993). The vast literature that developed around Coase's theorem formulated important normative corollaries of it, based on the evaluation of the relative costs of alternative assignments of rights.

According to the positive Coase theorem, absent transaction costs, the final allocation of scarce resources would coincide with the use that an individual who is the single owner of different activities would make of his endowments, regardless of the initial assignment of rights and choice of remedial protection. When transaction costs are present, however, an exchange will be pursued only to the point at which its marginal benefit equals the marginal cost of the transaction. If transaction costs exceed the benefits of a contract, no exchange will take place in the market. For a right to be exchanged it is necessary that transaction costs be less than the difference between the demand and supply prices. If this condition is not met, the Coasean bargaining will not be carried out, and both initial assignment of rights and choice of remedies will affect final allocations.

### *3.1 The relevance of transaction costs and the simple normative Coase theorem*

The notion of transaction costs has acquired particular importance in law and economics as the absence of transaction costs represents a fundamental condition for the applicability of the positive Coase theorem. Although at first impression transaction costs play a role analogous to transportation costs in international trade or, more generally, to the contracting costs in the economics of exchange (Demsetz, 1972, p. 20), in Coase's world the role of transaction costs has much greater normative implications.

For purposes of the theorem, the notion of transactions costs should include not only bargaining costs associated with the negotiation and conclusion of the contract but also all costs associated with the strategic behaviour of the parties and the execution and enforcement of the transaction. The notion of transaction costs should thus include *ex ante* costs due to asymmetric information, adverse selection, free riding, and hold-up strategies, as well as *ex post* costs associated with monitoring and enforcing the contracts.

Strategic behaviour may be an important source of transaction costs in a Coasean setting. In Coase's various examples, the property rights which are exchanged are private goods, characterized by their excludability. Difficulties arise when the object of the Coasean bargaining is an entitlement which has the nature of a public good (see Cheung, 1970, pp. 49–70). Due to the well-known problems associated with the supply of public goods, the Coasean bargaining solution may fail to cure a non-optimal allocation of rights that falls within this category. Consider a scenario in which the object of the Coasean negotiation consists of a non-excludable right (for example, the right to enjoy pollution-free air in a residential environment). As well known, individuals will not reveal their own preferences for public goods through the price system, placing public goods among those cases that are most resistant to the Coasean antidote.

A first simple normative reformulation of the Coase theorem focuses on transaction costs and the role that legal systems may play in reducing these impediments to voluntary bargaining. Legal rules can lower obstacles to private bargaining, such as by reducing transaction costs and minimizing other costs associated with transfer (strategic, legal, and so on). For this reason, transactional cost considerations should be fundamental to any analysis of legal regimes and the design of contracting processes, governance mechanisms and institutions.

### *3.2 The complex normative Coase theorem*

The first original formulation of Coase's proposition can be restated as a normative theorem: in the presence of positive transaction costs, the efficiency of the final allocation is not independent of the choice of the legal rule, and that the preferable initial assignment of rights is that which minimizes the effects of such transaction costs. The various normative restatements of the Coase Theorem aim at identifying legal rules and remedies that replicate the outcomes of a hypothetical Coasean bargaining or to mimic the solution that would be chosen by the single owner of interfering resources.

Important normative reformulations of the Coase Theorem focus on two important elements: relevance of initial assignment of rights and relevance of remedial protection. Demsetz (1972) and Calabresi and Melamed (1972) were among the first to discuss systematically the problems resulting from lifting the assumption of zero transaction costs. Articulating the normative core of the Coase theorem, Demsetz observes that the introduction of significant transaction costs into the choice of liability rule analysis does affect resource allocation. One liability rule may be superior to another because the difficulty of avoiding costly interactions is usually different for the interacting parties. Accordingly, the normative predicament indicates that the rule of liability should be based on which party can avoid the costly interaction at the lowest cost.

When two or more parties have conflicting interests in the same resource, the law must decide which party shall prevail, that is, which party shall receive the entitlement. Once the entitlement decision is made, the law must decide how the entitlement is to be protected and whether it may be transferred. Articulating a concept of entitlements protected by property, liability or inalienability rules, Calabresi and Melamed (1972) develop a framework that integrates the approaches of property and tort. Entitlements can be protected by property rules (transfer of the entitlement involves a voluntary sale by its holder), liability rules (the entitlement may be destroyed by another party if he is willing to pay an objectively determined value for it), or rules of inalienability (transfer of the entitlement is not permitted, even between a willing seller and a willing buyer). Calabresi and Melamed allow for a wide range of concerns to be balanced through the assignment of a particular entitlement. Calabresi and Melamed outline how, given the reality of transaction costs, an economic efficiency approach selects one allocation of entitlements over another. Entitlements cannot be enforced solely through property rules because, even if the transfer would benefit all parties, high transaction costs (especially the hold-up problem) may prevent an efficient reallocation. Calabresi and Melamed demonstrate how liability rules often achieve a combination of efficiency and distributive results that would be difficult to achieve under a property rule. Calabresi points out that Coase's analysis offers invaluable instruments for the identification of the areas in which public intervention becomes desirable (Calabresi, 1968, pp. 72–3). In its normative version, the theorem indicates that legal rules that minimize the effects of such costs are to be preferred for being relatively more efficient (Polinksy, 1989, p. 14). In its more complex formulation, the Coase theorem provides, indeed, a guide for such a choice.

The following is a classic illustration (Polinsky, 1989, pp. 11–14). The smoke of a factory soils laundry which is line drying on five neighbouring properties. The losses amount to $150 for each neighbour, for a total of $750. The damage could be eliminated through the installation of a purifying filter on the industrial smokestack or through the acquisition of electric dryers on the part of each one of the neighbouring owners. The cost of the filter would amount to $300, while the dryers would impose a cost of $100 per household, for a total of $500. The first solution is obviously more efficient, since the acquisition of five dryers would require a greater expenditure than the single filter. The Coase theorem predicts that in the absence of transaction costs the efficient solution will be chosen independently of the initial assignment of property rights. Even if we assume an initial allocation of polluting right to the industry (that is, fully legalizing industrial emissions), the landowners would jointly offer to buy the industrial filter at their expense. Sharing the cost of the filter in equal parts, each owner would face a cost of only $60, with a relative saving of $40 compared with the otherwise necessary acquisition of a personal dryer.

If we relax the initial assumption of no transaction costs, the initial allocation of property rights no longer is immaterial. Imagine that each owner has to face a cost of $120 in order to negotiate the contract with his neighbours and with the owner of the industrial plant. If the right is assigned to the industry, each landowner will have to choose whether to bear the loss of his soiled laundry for $150, to acquire the electric dryer for $100, or, finally, to undertake the negotiation process for a total pro-rata cost of $180. Considering these alternatives, each rational landowner would choose to acquire his own dryer, generating a socially non-optimal outcome. However, the assignment of property rights to the neighbouring residents rather than to the polluting industry would minimize the effect of positive transaction costs, since the industry would have incentives to install the filter, without any need for Coasean bargaining with the neighbours.

Two impediments to bargaining (that is, sources of transaction costs) take the form of externalities and hold-up, which Epstein (1993) shows stand in inverse relationship to each other. He defines the optimal legal rule as that which minimizes the sum of these externality and holdout costs in any particular institutional setting. Epstein demonstrates, through examples in property, restitution and tort, how Coase's transaction costs model plays the central organizing role in developing legal responses to many private law problems. Notwithstanding the obvious measurement and information problems, Epstein (1993) stresses the importance of the 'single owner test': where resources are under the command of two or more persons, the legal arrangement should attempt to induce all the parties to behave in the same way that a single owner would. Epstein concludes that, where the single owner test yields a unique result, that result should be adopted as the legal rule. Where the single owner test does not yield clear results, however, no corollary principle will provide a decisive answer to the particular problem.

Further exploring the choice between property and liability rules suggested by Calabresi and Melamed, Kaplow and Shavell (1996) address several factors casting doubt on the equivalence of these alternatives in low transaction-cost environments. Their analysis considers several objections to Coasean costless bargaining, including the inability of a party to ascertain what the other is willing to pay or accept, victims' ability to mitigate harm, the problem posed by one party being judgment proof, and administrative costs. Kaplow and Shavell find a presumption in favour of liability rules over property rules in the context of harmful externalities, but that this may be overcome as a result of one of more of the factors they describe. After considering some of the proffered justifications for the use of property rules to protect possessory interests, the authors find a strong theoretical case for the protection of these interests using property rules. The normative Coase theorem thus underlies the choice of the optimal system to ensure the protection of various types of property rights.

Also bridging the gap between Coase, where liability rules and property rules are equally efficient, and Calabresi and Melamed, where high transaction costs lead to a preference for liability rules, is the work by Ayres and Talley (1995) on private information as a transaction cost. The inefficiency occurs when parties misrepresent their own valuations to gain strategic advantage in the bargaining process. Focusing on the effect of splitting an entitlement between two rivalrous users rather than among buyers or among sellers, these authors find that, when two parties have private information about how much they value an entitlement, endowing each party with a partial claim to the entitlement can reduce the incentive to behave strategically during bargaining by inducing greater disclosure. A bargainer has two Coasean alternatives: buy the other party's claim or sell one's own claim. The normative formulation of Ayres and Talley is that a liability rule regime is preferable because it allows a party's decision to pursue one of these alternative transactions to function as a credible signal of a low or high valuation, thereby encouraging more efficient trade.

Building upon the literature on property fragmentation (Heller, 1998; Buchanan and Yoon, 2000), Parisi (2002) and Schulz, Parisi and Depoorter (2002) suggest that property is subject to a fundamental law of entropy. In the property context, entropy induces a one-directional bias. This bias is driven by asymmetric transaction costs – it is often harder to reunite separated property bundles than to break them apart. Parisi hypothesizes that courts and legislators account for the presence of asymmetric transaction costs and correct for problem through the selective use of remedies and by selecting default rules designed to minimize the total deadweight losses of property fragmentation. Parisi (2006) offers a reformulation of the normative Coase theorem in situations characterized by asymmetric transaction and strategic costs, such as when complementary fragments of property are attributed to different owners. The asymmetry arises from the fact that it is often harder to reunite separated property bundles than to break them apart. This variant of the Coase theorem turns on (*a*) an initial allocation of entitlements that minimizes the effects of the positive transaction costs, and (*b*) the selection of legal rules that reduce social welfare losses by facilitating optimal levels of reunification.

### 4 The Coase theorem and its legacy in law and economics

In 1960 Coase entrusted legal and economic scholars with the challenging task of deriving the implications of his theorem in their areas of research. Coase's invitation was taken up by a number of economists and lawyers who experimented with the unparalleled analytical potential of Coase's theorem in their research. According to Coase, economists in the Pigouvian tradition fail to consider the possible reciprocity of the effects of individual choices. By labelling one agent as injurer and the other as victim, the Pigouvian tradition presumes an initial allocation of rights (Cornes and Sandler, 1986, p. 59). In such a manner this approach falls into a serious methodological error, notwithstanding empirical psychological studies suggesting otherwise (see Kahneman, Knetsch and Thaler, 1990, pp. 1325–48). By taxing the generator of the externality in a measure corresponding to the difference between the private cost and the social cost of his own activity, the followers of Pigou fail to consider the effects of potential victims' behaviour. If the social cost of the industrial emissions is calculated by aggregating the economic disadvantages of the residents who are negatively affected by the smoke, the figure will vary with the number of individuals who fix their residence in that area. If the Pigouvian tax is imposed on the industrial activity only, there will be less incentive for each resident to consider moving into a different neighbourhood. New individuals may actually locate their residence in that area, without considering the potential increase in the costs imposed on the industrial activity.

Through these arguments, Coase's analysis demonstrates the incapacity of the Pigouvian approach to consider the interdependence of the harmful effects generated by individual choices. Coase's analysis occasioned a paradigmatic shift in legal and economic analysis, and, as Henry Manne once observed, 'it is hard to imagine law ever again being free of the influence of the techniques and findings of objective economic analysis' (1993, p. 4). His theorem, short of providing a simplistic formula for the social cost problem, suggests an alternative approach based on the evaluation of the relative costs of alternative assignments of rights and legal protection.

FRANCESCO PARISI

*See also* **hold-up problem; property rights.**

### *Bibliography*

Ayres, I. and Talley, E. 1995. Solomonic bargaining: dividing a legal entitlement to facilitate Coasean trade. *Yale Law Journal* 104, 1027–117.

Buchanan, J. and Yoon, Y.J. 2000. Symmetric tragedies: commons and anticommons property. *Journal of Law and Economics* 29, 1–13.

Calabresi, G. 1965. The decision for accidents: an approach to non-fault allocation of costs. *Harvard Law Review* 78, 713–45.

Calabresi, G. 1968. Transaction costs, resource allocation and liability rules: a comment. *Journal of Law and Economics* 11, 67–8.

Calabresi, G. and Melamed, A.D. 1972. Property rules, liability rules, and inalienability: one view of the cathedral. *Harvard Law Review* 85, 1089–128.

Cheung, S. 1970. The structure of a contract and the theory of a non-exclusive resource. *Journal of Law and Economics* 13, 49–70.

Coase, R.H. 1959. The Federal Communications Commission. *Journal of Law and Economics* 2, 1–40.

Coase, R.H. 1960. The problem of social cost. *Journal of Law and Economics* 3, 1–44.

Coase, R.H. 1988. *The Firm, the Market, and the Law.* Chicago: University of Chicago Press.

Coase, R.H. 1992. The institutional structure of production. *American Economic Review* 82, 713–19.

Coase, R.H. 1993. Law and economics at Chicago. *Journal of Law and Economics* 36, 239–54.

Cooter, R. 1987. Coase Theorem. In *The New Palgrave: A Dictionary of Economics*, vol. 1, ed. J. Eatwell, M. Milgate and P. Newman. London: Macmillan.

Cornes, R. and Sandler, T. 1986. *The Theory of Externalities, Public Goods, and Club Goods.* Cambridge: Cambridge University Press.

Demsetz, H.M. 1967. Toward a theory of property rights. *American Economic Review* 57, 347–59.

Demsetz, H.M. 1972. When does the rule of liability matter? *Journal of Legal Studies* 1, 13–28.

Epstein, R.A. 1993. Holdouts, externalities, and the single owner: one more salute to Ronald Coase. *Journal of Law and Economics* 36, 553–86.

Heller, M.A. 1998. The tragedy of the anticommons: property in the transition from Marx to markets. *Harvard Law Review* 111, 621–88.

Kahneman, D., Knetsch, J.L. and Thaler, R.H. 1990. Experimental tests of the endowment effect and the Coase Theorem. *Journal of Political Economy* 98, 1325–48.

Kaplow, L. and Shavell, S. 1996. Property rules versus liability rules: an economic analysis. *Harvard Law Review* 109, 723–54.

Kuhn, T.S. 1970. *The Structure of Scientific Revolutions*, 2nd edn. Chicago: University of Chicago Press.

Manne, H.G. 1975. *The Economics of Legal Relationships.* St. Paul: West Publishing Co.

Manne, H.G. 1993. *The Intellectual History of George Mason University School of Law.* Arlington, VA: School of Law, George Mason University.

Nutter, G.W. 1968. The Coase Theorem on social cost: a footnote. *Journal of Law and Economics* 16, 503–7.

Parisi, F. 1995. Private property and social costs. *European Journal of Law and Economics* 2, 149–73.

Parisi, F. 2002. Entropy in property. *American Journal of Comparative Law* 50, 595–632.

Parisi, F. 2006. Entropy and the asymmetric Coase Theorem. In *Property Rights Dynamics: A Law and Economics Perspective*, ed. D. Porrini and G. Ramello. London: Routledge.

Polinsky, A.M. 1989. *An Introduction to Law and Economics.* Boston: Little, Brown and Company.

Pigou, A.C. 1920. *The Economics of Welfare.* London: Macmillan.

Plant, A. 1974. *Selected Economic Essays and Addresses.* London: Routledge and Kegan Paul.

Regan, D.H. 1972. The problem of social cost revisited. *Journal of Law and Economics* 15, 427–33.

Salter, J.A. 1921. *Allied Shipping Control.* Oxford: Clarendon Press.

Schulz, N., Parisi, F. and Depoorter, B. 2002. Fragmentation in property: towards a general model. *Journal of Institutional and Theoretical Economics* 158, 594613.

Shapiro, F.R. 1985. The most cited law review articles. *California Law Review* 73, 1540–54.

Stigler, G.J. 1966. *The Theory of Price*, 3rd edn. New York: Macmillan.

Stigler, G.J. 1988. *Memoirs of an Unregulated Economist.* New York: Basic Books.

Wellisz, S. 1964. On external diseconomies and the government assisted invisible hand. *Economica* 31, 345–62.

Williamson, W. and Winter, S.G. 1991. *The Nature of the Firm: Origins, Evolution, and Development.* New York: Oxford University Press.

# Part II
# Coasean Bargaining in the Shadow of the Law

# [5]

# Of Coase and Cattle: Dispute Resolution Among Neighbors in Shasta County

Robert C. Ellickson*

TABLE OF CONTENTS



---


* Robert E. Paradise Professor of Natural Resources Law, Stanford Law School.



My debts are many. Jerry Anderson, Thomas Hagler, and Keith Kelly were able research assistants. Participants in workshops at the Boston University, Harvard, Stanford, and Yale Law Schools provided helpful suggestions. Financial support was received from the Stanford Legal Research Fund, made possible by a bequest from the Estate of Ira S. Lillick, and by gifts from Roderick E. and Carla A. Hills and other friends of the Stanford Law School.

Dozens of people in Shasta County were of immeasurable assistance. I especially thank Bob Bosworth, the President of the Shasta County Cattlemen's Association, and Walt Johnson, the county Farm Advisor, for easing my immersion into Shasta County life.


A few stylistic notes are in order. Except for public figures, the names used are pseudonyms. To reduce clutter, and sometimes to protect privacy, I have generally refrained from footnoting references to individual interviews. The present tense usually denotes the situation in Shasta County in 1982, the year in which I conducted most of my interviews.

This article is part of a forthcoming book to be published by the Harvard University Press. The contents of the book are briefly described in text following note 161 *infra*.

"I think the whole thing is good neighbors. If you don't have good neighbors, you can forget the whole thing."
—Chuck Searle, Shasta County cattleman

"My family believes in 'live and let live.' Have you heard of that?"
—Phil Ritchie, Shasta County farmer

This article reports the results of an investigation into how rural landowners in Shasta County, California, resolve disputes arising from trespass by livestock. The results provide an empirical perspective on one of the most celebrated hypothetical cases in the law-and-economics literature. In his landmark article, "The Problem of Social Cost,"[1] economist Ronald Coase invoked as his fundamental example a conflict between two neighbors—a rancher running cattle and a farmer raising crops. Coase used the Parable of the Farmer and the Rancher to illustrate what has come to be known as the Coase Theorem. This unintuitive proposition asserts, in its strongest form, that when transaction costs are zero, a change in the rule of liability will have no effect on the allocation of resources. For example, the Theorem

1. Coase, *The Problem of Social Cost*, 3 J.L. & ECON. 1 (1960).

predicts that as long as its admittedly heroic assumptions are met, the imposition of liability for cattle trespass would not cause ranchers to reduce the size of their herds, erect more fencing, or keep closer watch on their livestock. The Theorem has become the most fruitful, yet most controversial, proposition in law-and-economics.[2]

Coase himself was fully aware that obtaining information, negotiating agreements, and litigating disputes are all potentially costly, and that thus his Parable might not portray accurately how rural landowners would respond to a change in trespass law.[3] Some law-and-economics scholars, however, assume that transaction costs are indeed often trivial when only two parties are in conflict.[4] Therefore, these scholars might assume that Coase's

2. Some recent landmarks in the Coase Theorem literature are Cooter, *The Cost of Coase*, 11 J. LEGAL STUD. 1 (1982); Hoffman & Spitzer, *The Coase Theorem: Some Experimental Tests*, 25 J.L. & ECON. 73 (1982); Regan, *The Problem of Social Cost Revisited*, 15 J.L. & ECON. 427 (1972). A central theme of these articles is that Coase should have explicitly recognized the possibility that disputants may act strategically and thereby fail to carry out mutually advantageous exchanges. An unusually complete review of the literature is provided by Zerbe, *The Problem of Social Cost in Retrospect*, 2 RESEARCH IN L. & ECON. 83 (1980).

3. *See* Coase, *supra* note 1, at 15–19 (entitled "The Cost of Market Transactions Taken into Account").

Ronald Coase has in fact been a militant for the cause of empiricism. In recent years, he seems to have become increasingly frustrated with the sterility of the abstract debates over his Theorem:

> [W]hile considerations of what would happen in a world of zero transaction costs can give us valuable insights, these insights are, in my view, without value except as steps on the way to the analysis of the real world of positive transaction costs. We do not do well to devote ourselves to a detailed study of the world of zero transaction costs, like augurs divining the future by the minute inspection of the entrails of a goose.

Coase, *The Coase Theorem and the Empty Core: A Comment*, 24 J.L. & ECON. 183, 187 (1981).

The central finding of the present work is that the residents of Shasta County often succeed, without the involvement of the state, in coordinating with one another in a mutually advantageous way. Coase's Parable of the Farmer and the Rancher sounds this same general theme of cooperative interaction. This finding is generally consistent with what Coase found in his own microscopic investigation of the supply of lighthouses in England. *See* Coase, *The Lighthouse in Economics*, 17 J.L. & ECON. 357 (1974).

4. Several of Coase's colleagues at the University of Chicago wedded themselves to this assumption in the 1960s. *See, e.g.*, W. BLUM & H. KALVEN, PUBLIC LAW PERSPECTIVES ON A PRIVATE LAW PROBLEM: AUTO COMPENSATION PLANS 58–59 (1965); Demsetz, *When Does the Rule of Liability Matter*, 1 J. LEGAL STUD. 13, 16 (1972) (transaction costs "would seem to be negligible" when a baseball player negotiates with his club).

The current consensus, even among Chicagoans, is that negotiations in bilateral monopoly situations can be costly because the parties may act strategically. *See, e.g.*, R. POSNER, ECONOMIC ANALYSIS OF LAW 45 (2d ed. 1977); Cooter, Marks & Mnookin, *Bargaining in the Shadow of the Law: A Testable Model of Strategic Behavior*, 11 J. LEGAL STUD. 225, 242–44 (1982) ("The obstacle to agreement is the strategic nature of bargaining, not the cost of communicating"); Landes & Posner, *Salvors, Finders, Good Samaritans, and Other Rescuers: An Economic Study of Altru-*

Parable faithfully depicts how rural landowners resolve cattle-trespass disputes.

To explore the realism of the assumptions underlying the Farmer-Rancher Parable, I searched for a jurisdiction that had imposed varying rules of liability in cattle trespass situations and had changed those rules with some frequency. After briefly surveying a half-dozen candidates in California, I settled on Shasta County. Since 1945, a specific California statute has authorized the Shasta County Board of Supervisors, the county's elected governing body, to determine where in the county an owner of cattle is liable for damages stemming from unintentional cattle trespass on unfenced land.[5] Although most of Shasta County is "open range"—territory where a cattleman is not liable for trespass damages of that sort—the Board has the authority to "close the range" in subareas of the county. A closed-range ordinance makes a cattleman strictly liable for any damage his livestock might cause while trespassing within the area affected by the ordinance.[6] The Shasta County Board of Supervisors has exercised this power to close the range on dozens of occasions since 1945, thus changing the exact rule of liability that Coase used in his famous example.[7] I traveled to Shasta County to determine whether these legal changes had had any impact.[8]

---

*ism*, 7 J. LEGAL STUD. 83, 91 (1978) ("transaction costs under bilateral monopoly are high"). *See also* sources cited at note 2 *supra*.

5. *See* notes 99–103 *infra* and accompanying text.

6. The terms "closed-range" and "open-range" can be a source of confusion. I use the terms throughout this article as they are ordinarily used in Shasta County, to denote the *legal regime* applicable to a particular territory. The potential confusion arises because the terms might be construed as indicating a *method of husbandry*—that is, whether in a particular area it is the custom of cattlemen to run their animals at large or to keep them behind fences. In Shasta County, the correlation between legal regime and method of husbandry is rather weak. For example, most ranchers in the open-range areas of the county keep their herds behind fences.

7. To invoke Calabresi & Melamed's fruitful typology, a closed-range ordinance essentially shifts the legal regime from property-rule protection of the rancher to liability-rule protection of the trespass victim. *See* Calabresi & Melamed, *Property Rules, Liability Rules, and Inalienability: One View of the Cathedral*, 85 HARV. L. REV. 1089, 1105–1115 (1972). Hoffman & Spitzer, *supra* note 2, at 84, deserve credit for noting that Coase had contrasted asymmetrical legal positions. *But cf.* note 112 *infra* and accompanying text (noting the availability of injunctive relief to trespass victims in closed range).

8. A number of other law and economics scholars have investigated empirically the impact of transaction costs on interneighbor coordination. *See, e.g.*, Cheung, *The Fable of the Bees: An Economic Investigation*, 16 J.L. & ECON. 11 (1973); Crocker, *Externalities, Property Rights, and Transactions Costs: An Empirical Study*, 14 J.L. & ECON. 451 (1971). The study closest to mine in its substantive focus, although not its methodology, is Vogel, *The Effect of Changes in Property Rights Entitlements on Production: The Coase Theorem and California Animal Trespass Law*, 15 J. LEGAL

This study presents findings that cast doubt on many of the assumptions undergirding the Coasean Parable. It also strives to help bridge the chasm lying between the law and economics and law and society movements,[9] perhaps the two most significant social-scientific schools of legal research. On the whole, the law and society scholars have gathered the better field data on dispute resolution practices, and the law and economics scholars have developed the more explicit, rigorous, and testable theories of human behavior. Although one might think that members of these two schools would perceive irresistible benefits from collaboration, these two groups have worked largely in isolation from one another. They have separate journals.[10] They gather at separate conferences. They rarely read, much less cite, work by scholars in the other camp. This absence of cross-fertilization stems not only from lack of familiarity with the working language of the other group, but also from a mutual lack of respect, even a contempt, for the kind of work that the other group does. To exaggerate only a little, the law and economics scholars believe that the law and society group is deficient in both sophistication and rigor, and the law and society scholars believe that the law and economics group is not only out of touch with reality but also short on humanity.

In conducting this study, I placed a foot squarely within each of the two camps. Law and economics, the tradition within which I have mainly labored, provided the Parable that inspired the study. By undertaking "microscopic"[11] field research into the

STUD. — (1986) (forthcoming) (regression analysis of effects of various closed-range ordinances on agricultural production in California counties between 1850 and 1877).

In recent years Elizabeth Hoffman and Matthew Spitzer have been the most persistent and creative transaction cost empiricists. *See, e.g.*, Hoffman & Spitzer, *supra* note 2 (report on a series of laboratory experiments in which subjects could achieve gains by cooperating); Spitzer & Hoffman, *A Reply to Kelman's "Consumption Theory, Production Theory, and Ideology in the Coase Theorem,"* 53 S. CAL. L. REV. 1187 (1980) (study of the effect of the elimination of the Reserve Clause on the movement of baseball players between clubs).

9. Any discussion of a chasm between academic subcultures brings to mind C.P. Snow's classic 1959 lecture on "The Two Cultures." Snow used as his polar opposites literary intellectuals and physical scientists, and speculated on whether social scientists represented yet a third culture. C.P. SNOW, THE TWO CULTURES: AND A SECOND LOOK 70–71 (1964). The chasm that I identify is a division *between* groups of social scientists. It suggests that Snow was understandably in a quandary about how to classify members of the social scientific disciplines.

10. The core journals are the JOURNAL OF LAW AND ECONOMICS and the LAW & SOCIETY REVIEW.

11. I borrow the term "microscopic" from Clifford Geertz, an anthropologist noted for his devotion to "thick descriptions" of human interaction. *See, e.g.*, C. GEERTZ, THE INTERPRETATION OF CULTURES 3–30 (1973).

resolution of a narrow class of disputes, however, I followed the methods of pioneering law and society scholars such as Stuart Macaulay and H. Laurence Ross.[12] After reading in both literatures, I confess my disloyal suspicion that law and society scholars would generally be more successful than law and economics scholars in predicting the essentials of the story to come.

The Shasta County evidence indicates that Coase's Farmer-Rancher Parable correctly anticipates that a change in the rule of liability for cattle trespass does not affect, for example, the quality of fences that separate ranches from farms. The Parable's explanation for the allocative toothlessness of law is, however, exactly backward. The Parable's explanation is that transaction costs are low and that parties respond to a new rule by agreeing to an exchange of property rights that perpetuates the prior (efficient) allocation of resources. The field evidence I gathered suggests that a change in animal trespass law indeed fails to affect resource allocation, *not because transaction costs are low, but because transaction costs are high.* Legal rules are costly to learn and enforce. Trespass incidents are minor irritations between parties who typically have complex continuing relationships that enable them readily to enforce informal norms. The Shasta County evidence indicates that under these conditions, potential disputants ignore the formal law. As Coase probably suspected,[13] the Para-

12. In preparing his classic article, *Non-Contractual Relations in Business: A Preliminary Study*, 28 AM. SOC. REV. 55 (1963), Macaulay interviewed business executives and lawyers to find out how Wisconsin manufacturing firms resolve contractual disputes. Ross' best known work is H. ROSS, SETTLED OUT OF COURT (rev. ed. 1980), which describes how insurance adjusters process claims covered under automobile liability policies. Notable also is Ross & Littlefield, *Complaint as a Problem Solving Mechanism*, 12 LAW & SOC'Y REV. 199 (1978), a study of how a large appliance retailer in Denver handles consumer complaints.

Law and society scholars have done relatively little field work on dispute resolution between adjoining landowners. *But see, e.g.*, Baumgartner, *Social Control in Suburbia*, in 2 TOWARD A GENERAL THEORY OF SOCIAL CONTROL 79 (D. Black ed. 1984); Ruffini, *Disputing over Livestock in Sardinia*, in THE DISPUTING PROCESS: LAW IN TEN SOCIETIES 209 (L. Nader & H. Todd eds. 1978) (finding that shepherds in Sardinia rely on self-help, not formal legal processes, to resolve rustling disputes). Economists have also done little field work on relations among neighbors. *But see* sources in the first paragraph of note 8 *supra*.

There is a broad interdisciplinary perception that progress in understanding conflict resolution depends upon more low-level empirical work. *See, e.g.*, R. HARDIN, COLLECTIVE ACTION 229–30 (1982) (comments of a philosopher-game theorist). *See also* Felstiner, *Influences of Social Organization on Dispute Processing*, 9 LAW & SOC'Y REV. 63, 86 n.28 (1974) ("Ironically, we have better data about dispute processing in Indian villages, Mexican towns, and East African tribes than we have about that process in American communities." (comments of a law-and-society scholar)).

13. *See* note 3 *supra* and accompanying text.

ble of the Farmer and the Rancher therefore ill-describes how rural landowners actually interact with one another.

Part I of this article introduces the relevant residents of Shasta County and their techniques of cattle ranching and boundary fencing. Part II narrates the political history of the two closed-range battles that occurred in the area where the study was conducted. Part III explains why I chose this area to study and my field research methods. Part IV, the heart of the article, describes how the rural residents of Shasta County resolve their cattle-trespass disputes. Finally, Part V summarizes the article's principal findings and implications.

## I. Shasta County and Its Cattle Industry

### A. *Physical Environment*

Shasta County lies at the northern end of the 400 mile-long Central Valley of California. The Sacramento River, which drains the northern half of the Central Valley, bisects the county. Redding, Shasta County's county seat and largest city, is situated at an elevation of 500 feet at the spot where the Sacramento River emerges from the mountains north of the Valley to begin its trip south toward San Francisco Bay. High mountain peaks lie within sight of Redding in all directions except south. The Trinity Mountains lie to the west; the towering cone of Mount Shasta stands fifty miles due north, in Siskiyou County; and to the east lie other peaks of the volcanic Cascade Range— notably Mount Lassen, which sits in Shasta County's southeastern corner. To the east, north, and west of Redding, foothills rise irregularly toward these distant mountain peaks.

Weather dictates Shasta County's ranching practices. Like the rest of California, the county has a wet season and a dry season. Redding receives an average annual rainfall of 38.74 inches, most of it concentrated in the winter months.[14] Little rain falls between mid-May and November. During the summer months intense sunlight bakes Redding, and the surrounding mountains block cooling winds.[15] In the spring, the grasslands near Redding are green from the heavy winter rains; by summer, the extreme heat has turned the groundcover brown.

Most of Shasta County's terrain is too mountainous and its

14. Record Searchlight (Redding, Cal.), Aug. 11, 1982, at 15, col. 1.

15. In July, the city's average daily high temperature is 98 degrees. *Id.* at 14, col. 3.

soils too poor to support significant agricultural activity. The majority of the land area in the county is commercial-quality forest, most of which the United States Forest Service and a handful of private timber companies own.[16] Census data describe sixteen percent of the county as "land in farms."[17] The bulk of this agricultural land is unirrigated and used only as seasonal pasture for livestock—principally cattle, the county's major agricultural product. Only one percent of the county's land is used for raising harvested crops,[18] and a majority of this field-crop acreage is devoted to alfalfa or other hay grown as livestock feed.[19]

In 1973, the Shasta County Board of Supervisors voted to "close the range" in a fifty-six square-mile rectangle of territory around Round Mountain, a rural hamlet situated thirty miles northeast of Redding. This ordinance, which county cattlemen now call "Caton's Folly" to embarrass a supervisor who helped pass it, provided the best opportunity in Shasta County to test the effects of an *actual* change in the rule of liability for cattle trespass. Nine years later, in 1982, the Board of Supervisors considered, but rejected, a petition to close the range in the Oak Run area immediately southwest of Caton's Folly.[20] The Oak Run controversy promised to reveal the effects of a *threatened* change in liability rules. Residents of the Oak Run and Round Mountain areas were interviewed to shed more light on these effects. The general area northeast of Redding—what I call the Northeastern Sector—thus warrants closer description.

The Northeastern Sector consists of three ecological zones: grassy plains, foothills, and mountain forest. The elevation of the land largely determines the boundaries of these zones; the higher the terrain, the more rain it receives, and the cooler its summer weather.

The zone between 500 and 1500 feet in elevation, the zone

16. Of the 2.4 million acres of land in Shasta County, 1.3 million have been identified as "commercial forest." Cal. Dep't of Finance, Cal. Statistical Abstract 2, 129 (1983). The United States Forest Service owns 35% of this commercial forest, and forest industry companies own 46%. *Id.* at 129.

17. *Id.* at 111 (citing data from the 1978 U.S. Census of Agriculture).

18. *Id.* at 2, 111.

19. E. Peterson, In the Shadow of the Mountain: A Short History of Shasta County, California 110 (1965).

Coase's Parable involves a pasture adjoining a field of annually harvested crops. These land uses are rarely contiguous in Shasta County. The lessons of the Parable, however, in no way depend on how the Rancher's neighbor uses his land.

20. *See* notes 70-76 *infra* and accompanying text.

FIGURE 1
MAP OF NORTHWESTERN CALIFORNIA

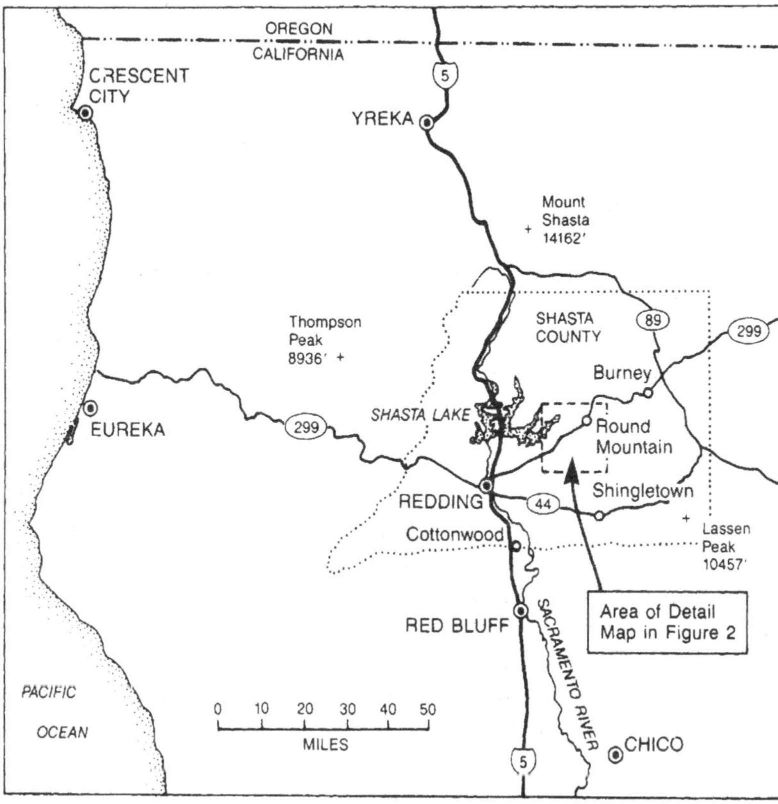


closest to Redding, consists of grassy plains. This idyllic, oak-dotted country provides natural pasture during the spring and, if irrigated, can support a herd year-round. A water supply adequate for irrigation is available, however, only near the streams that flow through the area. Moreover, the soil in much of the grassy plains is infertile hardpan. Because of these natural constraints, the full-time ranchers who operate in this zone typically need at least several square miles of pasture.

The foothills lie between 1500 and 3500 feet in elevation. Both Caton's Folly and the Oak Run area fall within this transition zone. Much of the foothill area has a mixed natural treecover of pine and oak. In open areas the natural ground cover is less likely to be grass than an unpalatable chaparral of manzanita, buckbrush, and like shrubs. To foothill ranchers this brush is almost as repulsive a thought as the importation of Australian beef; the more enterprising foothill ranchers spend much of their energies grappling with this foe.[21]

Mountain forest, the third zone, starts at about 3500 feet. Ponderosa pine, douglas fir, and other conifers that have supplanted the deciduous oaks cover the mountainsides at this elevation. The mountain forests remain green year-round, but most are too cold in winter and too hard to clear to be suitable sites for cattlemen's base ranches. The Roseburg Lumber Company owns much of the mountain forest in the Northeastern Sector.[22] Like other private timber companies in the county, Roseberg has not shown any interest in subdividing its lands for development. For many decades, however, Roseberg and its predecessors in ownership have leased their forests to Shasta County cattlemen for summer range.

### B. *Social Environment*

The volatility of population change may affect how people resolve their disputes. Shasta County has experienced rapid population growth. Between 1930 and 1980, the number of county residents increased ninefold,[23] and in the decade from 1970 to 1980, total County population rose from 78,000 to 116,000.[24] The County's population growth rate of 49.0 percent in the 1970's was substantially higher than the overall state rate (18.5 percent), and was somewhat higher than the aggregate rate for California's nonmetropolitan counties (36.4 percent).[25] Redding's location at the northern end of the Central Valley makes it a natural transportation hub. It serves as the gateway to moun-

21. *See* text accompanying note 46 *infra*.

22. The Roseburg Lumber Company is a closely held corporation based in Roseburg, Oregon. It is controlled by Kenneth Ford, a self-made man whom Forbes Magazine has listed as one of the forty wealthiest persons in the United States. San Francisco Chron., Aug. 28, 1982, at 14, col. 4. When Roseburg purchased its forests in the Northeastern sector in 1979 from the Kimberly-Clark Corporation, it became the fourth timber company to own these lands since the early 1940s.

23. In 1930, the County's population was 13,927. U.S. Dept. of Commerce, Bureau of the Census, 15th Census of the United States, vol. 3, pt. 1, at 284 (1932).

24. U.S. Dept. of Commerce, Bureau of the Census, 1980 Census of Population, vol. 1, pt. 6, ch. A, table 4 (1982). In 1980, 42,000 people lived in the city of Redding. *Id.* By 1984, the city's estimated population exceeded 50,000, and Shasta County achieved the status of a Standard Metropolitan Statistical Area.

25. Calculated from data in the 1980 Census of Population.

FIGURE 2
MAP OF THE OAK RUN/ROUND MOUNTAIN AREA

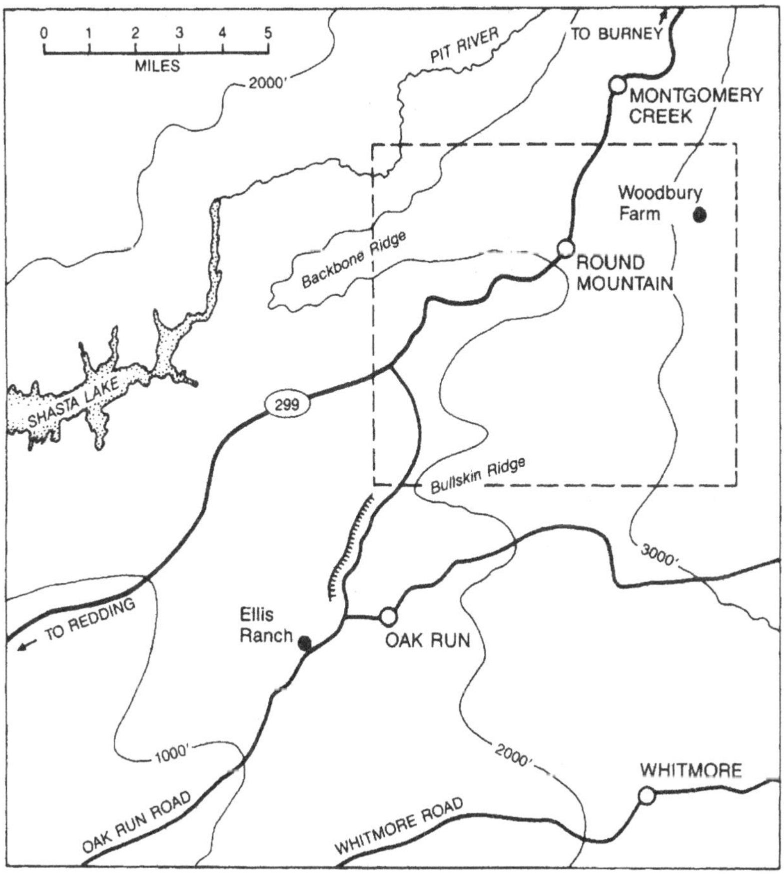


Boundary of Caton's Folly
Fence that Ellis Built at Caton's Request

tain recreation areas lying in three directions, and it has emerged as the major regional center on Interstate 5 between Sacramento, California, and Eugene, Oregon. Many migrants to Shasta County have come from the San Francisco and Los Angeles areas. Indications of social instability have accompanied the influx of migrants. In 1981, Shasta had the highest divorce rate of any county in California,[26] and in 1980, the county's unemployment

26. In 1981, Shasta County had 8.7 dissolutions and nullities of marriage per 1,000 estimated persons, compared to a statewide figure of 5.8 per thousand. STATE OF CAL., DEP'T OF HEALTH SERVS., VITAL STATISTICS OF CALIFORNIA—1981, at 128 (1983).

rate was twice that of the state as a whole.[27]

Precise figures on population trends within the Northeastern Sector are not available. It appears, however, that during the 1970s, the Sector's population grew by an even larger percentage than did the county's.[28] Not surprisingly, the recent demographic histories of the three ecological zones within the Sector are rather different.

Residential patterns in the grassy plains have not changed much in recent years. Beyond the suburbs of Redding most of the acreage in the grasslands and lower foothills remains divided into ranches at least several square miles in size. Approximately half of these ranches are owned by descendants of families that have been in the county for several generations.[29] Although many of these ranches have a current market value of $1,000,000 or more, the ranchers typically have modest annual incomes. For decades, ranchlands in Shasta County have generated an annual cash return of only one or two percent of market value.[30] The cattlemen who own and operate the large family ranches tend to

27. Census data put the County's unemployment rate at 13.8%, compared to the state's 6.5%. U.S. DEP'T OF COMMERCE, BUREAU OF THE CENSUS, 1980 CENSUS OF POPULATION AND HOUSING, ADVANCE ESTIMATES OF SOCIAL, ECONOMIC, AND HOUSING CHARACTERISTICS. The timber industry, an important factor in the Shasta County economy, was in a deep slump in 1980, a factor that no doubt contributed to this disparity.

28. The population of what the Census Bureau calls the Central Shasta division increased from 3,049 in 1970 to 6,784 in 1980, or by 122%. U.S. DEP'T OF COMMERCE, BUREAU OF THE CENSUS, 1980 CENSUS OF POPULATION, vol. 1, pt. 6, ch. A, table 4, n.41 (1982). This division includes both the Northeastern Sector and larger rural territories to the north, south, and southeast.

29. The first pioneers to settle east and northeast of Redding used the grasslands and lower foothills to raise livestock. The descendants of the nineteenth century pioneer families—Coombs, Donaldson, Wagoner—still hold a special place in rural Shasta County society. Oldtimers are quick to identify their roots in the county, and sometimes refer to families who arrived a generation ago as "people who haven't been here very long."

Prior to the 1920s, the Southern Pacific Railroad owned alternate sections in the grassy plains—a reward from the United States for laying track to Redding. The government grant consisted of alternate sections for a distance of 20 miles on both side of the track. S. DAGGETT, CHAPTERS ON THE HISTORY OF THE SOUTHERN PACIFIC 50, 122 (1922). During the 1920s, the Southern Pacific sold off most of its grassland sections at the then market price of $2.50 to $5.00 per acre, thereby enabling the pioneer ranching families to consolidate their holdings. Abandoning their prior practice of running their herds at large, these families erected fences around their multi-thousand-acre spreads, cleared patches of brush, and began to irrigate their better pastures.

30. Interview with Robert Shaw, Redding-based appraiser (July 19, 1982). Mr. Shaw attributed the low returns to tax benefits and psychic income that ranching confers.

Cattle ranching is noted for skimpy financial returns. *See* ARTHUR D. LITTLE, INC., FINAL ENVIRONMENTAL STATEMENT, PROPOSED LIVESTOCK GRAZING PROGRAM, BLM CERBAT/BLACK MOUNTAIN PLANNING UNITS II–139 to –142 (1978) (returns to cattle ranching in Arizona range

follow self-imposed seven-day-a-week work schedules and live in houses less imposing than those one would find in an average American suburb. When estate taxes or property taxes have squeezed them financially, ranching families have either conveyed their entire holdings to other ranchers or to investors seeking tax shelters or, more commonly, they have sold tree-covered pieces of their ranches to developers for subdivision into ranchettes.

The foothills have seen more subdivision activity and absolute population growth than have the grassy plains. Both supply and demand conditions explain this pattern. Because the foothills are somewhat less suited than the grasslands for agriculture, foothill landowners are more likely to consider subdividing their holdings. Most homebuyers would also prefer the foothills to the grasslands as a residential location because the higher elevations are cooler in summer and offer more tree cover. As a result, the foothills within commuting distance of Redding have experienced a multifold increase in population over the past twenty years.[31]

Many of the recent settlers in the foothills are either retirees or younger migrants from California's major urban areas. These newcomers tend to live on minimally improved lots of from five to forty acres, either in owner-built houses or mobile homes. Many of these ranchettes have sprung up near hamlets, such as Oak Run and Round Mountain, that contain a general store, a post office, an elementary school, and other basic community facilities. Despite these clusters of growth, development in the foothills has been rather diffuse. Especially since the mid-1960s, small-scale real estate operatives have subdivided forested areas in every sector of the foothills.[32] Thus virtually all foothill ranch-

from negative to a positive one to two percent; ranchers do it for love); Charlier, *Home on the Range is a Part-Time Deal for Many Cowboys*, Wall St. J., Jan. 8, 1985, at 1, col. 4.

31. Some of the new development has been for second homes. Celebrities such as baseball pitcher Vida Blue, actor Clint Eastwood, country singer Merle Haggard, and ex-Congressman Pete McCloskey are among those who have purchased properties in the rural areas east of Redding.

32. John Williams of the Redding office of the Title Insurance & Trust Co. generously permitted me to use the firm's tract indexes. These indexes showed that in 24 sections near the southern border of Caton's Folly, the number of land parcels increased from 61 in 1930, to 145 in 1972, to 295 in 1982.

Countywide, the number of land parcels quadrupled between 1967 and 1982. Interview with Tony Estacio, Chief, Administrative Services, Assessor's Office of Shasta County (July 8, 1982). These recent rates of parcelization appear atypically high for rural land markets. *See*

ers have some ranchette owners as neighbors. Ranchette owners may keep a farm animal or two as a hobby, but few of them make significant income from agriculture. The ranchette owners nevertheless admire both the cattlemen and the folkways traditionally associated with rural Shasta County.

### C. *Work Environment: Modes of Cattle Ranching*

Despite their long hours of work, few ranchers in Shasta County find raising beef cattle a road to prosperity. The typical rancher runs a cow and calf operation. When his calves are seven to twelve months old, he[33] trucks them a dozen miles south of Redding to the Shasta County Auctionyard at Cottonwood, where each Friday some 3,000 head change hands. Agents for feedlot operators and pasture owners buy the calves, take them to feedlots and pastures outside the county, and feed and fatten them for a few months to prepare them for slaughter. In 1982, a six-hundred pound yearling sold at auction in Cottonwood for about $375, compared to the $500 it would have brought in 1979, the year that nominal beef prices peaked.[34] Not only have beef prices recently failed to match the rate of inflation, but in the 1970s per capita consumption of beef in the United States began to fall.[35] Shasta County is at best marginal cattle country, and some cattlemen there understandably fear that they may be among the casualties in their beleaguered industry's continuing shakeout.

Shasta County cattlemen may be loosely grouped into two categories: the traditionalists and the modernists.[36] Traditional-

R. Healy & J. Short, The Market for Rural Land 22 (1976) (in only one of five counties studied did the number of rural land parcels double between 1954 and 1976).

33. Although women own, manage, and provide most of the physical labor on a number of the ranches in Shasta County, rural culture generally supports the differentiation of sex roles. Thus a woman rancher who wishes to be active in the county Cattlemen's Association is likely to participate only in the CowBelles, the women's auxillary. The National Cattlemen's Association did recently elect its first woman president, JoAnn Smith, but she had come to prominence by serving as president of the Florida CowBelles. N.Y. Times, Apr. 24, 1985, at C1, col. 1.

34. *See* San Francisco Chron., Aug. 26, 1982, at 38, col. 2.

35. Per capita beef consumption peaked at 95.7 lbs. in 1976, and by 1981 had fallen to 78.3 lbs., as consumers shifted toward poultry and pork. N.Y. Times, Aug. 9, 1981, § IV, at 22, col. 3.

36. These categories inevitably oversimplify. For example, Dick Coombs and Chuck Searle employ modernist land-management and husbandry practices, yet continue the traditionalist practice of leasing mountain forest for summer range.

ists tend to be more marginal economically, and have a greater stake in fighting "closed range" ordinances.

1. *The traditionalists.*

Traditional Shasta County cattlemen continue to follow the husbandry practices that were nearly universal in the county as late as the 1920s. A traditionalist's trademark is that he lets his cattle roam, essentially untended, in unfenced mountain areas during the summer.[37] This customary practice evolved in response to the severity of Shasta County's dry season. In the area northeast of Redding, a rancher lacking irrigated pasture needs about ten to twenty acres per animal unit[38] for winter and spring pasture. Thus, to support 200 cattle—a substantial herd by Shasta County standards—a rancher without irrigated pasture needs at least 2,000 acres, or just over three square miles of land. During the dry season the brutal heat makes unirrigated grasslands almost worthless. To feed his animals during the summer, a lowland cattleman must therefore either have access to irrigated pasture or be able to move his animals to the high foothills and mountains where cooler dry season temperatures enable natural forage to survive. The traditionalist solution is a summer grazing lease on a large tract of mountain forest.

The United States Forest Service, the Bureau of Land Management,[39] and major private timber companies, have regularly entered into grazing leases with county cattlemen. Although the timber company grazing leases typically have only a one-year term, the companies have allowed cattlemen to renew them as a matter of course.[40] Federal leases may run for any period up to

37. The classic study of cattlemen operating on unfenced range is E. Osgood, The Day of the Cattleman (1929) (emphasizing practices in Wyoming and Montana during the latter part of the Nineteenth Century). On the history of traditionalist practices in California, see R. Cleland, The Cattle on a Thousand Hills (2d ed. 1951); D. Dary, Cowboy Culture 44–66 (1981).

38. An "animal unit" is a mature cow plus calf, or the equivalent in terms of forage consumption. A horse converts to 1.25 animal units, a sheep to 0.2 animal units, and so on. An "animal unit month" (AUM) is the amount of forage an animal unit consumes in one month of grazing. H. Heady, Rangeland Management 117 (1975).

39. These two agencies manage most of the vast federal holdings in the county. Altogether, federal agencies own 42% of the County's acreage. Walter H. Johnson, *Agriculture as a Competitor for Land,* in Economic Competiton for Land: Shasta County 48 (Univ. of Cal., Agric. Extension Serv. 1966).

40. A specialist in brokering private grazing leases stated that most of his landowner-lessee relationships had endured for decades. Interview with Jim Cochran, Wm. Beatty & Assocs., in Redding, Ca. (July 21, 1982).

ten years,[41] and they also tend to be automatically renewable.[42] A cattleman who has been leasing a tract of forest for summer range thus tends to regard the leased tract as a normal part of his operations. Although the forest areas remain green in summer, they contain too few open meadows to support many cattle. Traditionalists may have to lease 300 acres of forest per animal unit: Thus, a traditionalist with a herd of only 100 animals may lease during the summer a forest equal in area to the city of San Francisco.

The fencing of these far flung forest leaseholds has never been cost-justified in the eyes of either the timber owners or their traditionalist lessees. To reduce the risk of livestock trespassing on contiguous lands, forest leasehold boundaries are often drawn to follow natural barriers such as ridges and gulches. But adroit boundary drawing is hardly a foolproof method for controlling strays. Mountain cattle tend to drift down the drainage areas to lower elevations, especially when the weather turns cold or a drought dries the upland creeks. Lessees occasionally erect drift fences across mountain valleys to block the most obvious migration routes. Because drift fences are easily destroyed by winter snows, however, traditionalists often let their animals roam at will in the mountains. Even a forest lessee who has ridden his leasehold periodically during the summer risks being unable to find part of his herd when he gathers his livestock in mid-October. After the October gathering, a traditionalist returns his animals to a base ranch at a lower elevation, and feeds them hay or other stored feed for a few months until the winter rains revive the natural grasses on the base ranch pastures.[43]

2. *The modernists.*

Modernists among the Shasta County cattlemen keep their livestock behind fences at all times in order to increase their control over their herds.[44] To satisfy the need for summer forage that originally caused traditionalist cattlemen to enter into forest leases, modernists install ditches and sprinklers to irrigate base

41. *See* 43 U.S.C.A. §§ 315b, 1752 (Supp. 1983).

42. Interviews with Terry Brumley of the U.S.F.S., in Redding, Ca. (Aug. 9, 1982), and Paul McClain of the B.L.M., in Redding, Ca. (July 9, 1982).

43. Untimely grazing may damage rangeland. If grazing occurs too early, it may kill immature grass; if it occurs too late, the livestock may eat seeds needed for the following year's forage. Grazing leases therefore regulate entry and exit dates.

44. *See* notes 47–50 *infra* and accompanying text.

ranch pastures. One acre of irrigated pasture can support a cow and calf for an entire summer. A modernist who can irrigate about ten percent of his lands is usually able to run a year-round, fenced operation.[45]

Modernists are more active than traditionalists in managing ranchland vegetation. If not controlled, the native brush that thrives in the foothill zone would consume much of the scarce ground water and soil nutrients that competing grasses need. Modernist foothill ranchers fight the brush by setting controlled burns, spreading herbicides, and dragging chains from tractors to uproot the larger plants.[46] Using these clearing techniques, leading modernist cattlemen have transformed unproductive foothill areas into valuable pasturelands.

Modernists tend to be younger than traditionalists, have more formal education, and be more active in the Cattlemen's Association. Some modernists view the traditionalists as old-fashioned and primitive. Traditionalists, however, see themselves as the "real" cattlemen—the ones who can recognize a cow at half a mile and sleep out under the stars in the tradition of the nineteenth century cowboy.

Despite their stylistic differences, modernists and traditionalists have much in common. Members of both groups believe that the life of the cattleman is the best possible in western America. They enjoy riding horses and regularly wearing blue jeans, cowboy hats, and cowboy boots. They regard the late John Wayne as their kind of guy. Although traditionalists have a much greater stake than modernists do in keeping the Board of Supervisors from closing the range, modernist cattlemen typically join the traditionalists in opposing proposed legal changes that would increase the liabilities of owners of stray cattle.

45. A cattleman needs at least ten acres of unirrigated land per AUM for winter range. If he were to irrigate ten percent of this acreage, he would have enough irrigated pasture for summer range. Instead of irrigating, a modernist who prefers operating behind fences may move his herds to fenced summer grasslands located in the high mountain valleys of Superior California. ("Superior California" is a regionally popular geographical designation that, unlike "Northern California," distinguishes the northmost counties from the Bay Area.)

46. *See generally* H. HEADY, *supra* note 38, at 253–55, 258, 280–329. On controlled burns, see also CAL. PUB. RES. CODE §§ 4475–94 (West Supp. 1981) (delineating the role of the State Department of Forestry); L. STODDART & A. SMITH, RANGE MANAGEMENT 383–94 (1943) (describing the effects of burning upon various types of rangeland).

### D. *The Benefits and Costs of Boundary Fences*

The study of cattle trespass incidents is inevitably a study of fencing. A fence demarcates boundaries, keeps out human and animal trespassers, and keeps in the fencebuilder's own animals. In the Farmer-Rancher Parable, Coase perceived the sole benefit of a fence to be the reduction of trespass damages to crops.[47] In fact, cattlemen enclose their lands largely to prevent damage to their own livestock. Predators, rustlers, winter snows, and poisonous plants such as larkspur all pose potentially lethal threats to cattle roaming unfenced countryside.[48] Cattlemen also worry that a wandering cow will be impregnated by a bull of worthless pedigree. Furthermore, fencing makes it easier for a rancher to provide salt and other useful diet supplements, and to prevent the weight loss likely to occur when cattle walk long distances.

The prices of grazing leases reflect the value that ranchers place on fences. In 1982, fenced land in the Northeastern Sector rented for about $10 per animal unit month, whereas unfenced land rented for about $3.[49] Because both arrangements yield the same quantity of forage, the rent differential provides a rough measure of how much ranchers value the protection and control that boundary fences provide.[50]

Since 1874, the year J.F. Glidden took out the first patent on barbed wire, the barbed wire fence has been the standard American technology for enclosing livestock.[51] California's statutory

47. *See* Coase, *supra* note 1, at 3, 5.

48. Rancher Dick Coombs, the epitome of honor in rural Shasta County, counseled that "[I]f you don't fence, your neighbors get your cattle, and their cattle get your feed."

During the nineteenth century, when cattlemen let their stock loose on the Great Plains during the winter, even the best managers were likely to lose five percent of their mature animals each grazing season. D. BOORSTIN, THE AMERICANS: THE DEMOCRATIC EXPERIENCE 10 (1973). In the Northwest during the same time period, losses ran about 10%. J. OLIPHANT, ON THE CATTLE RANGES OF THE OREGON COUNTRY 240–41 (1968). In Wyoming and Montana, during the disastrous winter of 1885–1886, blizzards killed 85% or more of the livestock in some herds. E. OSGOOD, *supra* note 37, at 216–18.

49. These are rough averages of figures that ranchers and grazing-lease specialists offered in interviews. For the definition of "animal unit month," see note 38 *supra*.

50. The quality of forage of course varies from pasture to pasture, and is apt to be better where a landowner has deliberately tried to cultivate his grasses.

51. D. DARY, *supra* note 37, at 308–31, recounts the impact of the advent of barbed wire on ranching practices nationally. Before barbed wire, the fencing-in of cattle was generally not economical in California. R. CLELAND, *supra* note 37, at 62.

A standard barbed wire fence will not contain sheep or hogs. To fence in those animals, Shasta County landowners use woven wire (which they variously refer to as "netting," "hogwire," or "field fence") for the bottom 39 or 47 inches of fence, and top it off with one to

standard for a "lawful fence" was set at the turn of the century. It calls for three tightly stretched strands of barbed wire stapled to posts situated 16–1/2 feet (one rod) apart.[52] Today, Shasta County ranchers tend to use at least four strands of barbed wire[53] and they employ steel posts instead of the cedar posts customarily used earlier in the century.[54]

In 1982, the materials for a new four-strand, barbed wire fence in Shasta County cost about $2000 per mile. Fence contractors charge at least as much for labor and overhead.[55] Both

---

three strands of barbed wire. Because many ranchers in Shasta County owned sheep and swine a half century ago, many boundary fences there still contain woven wire.

Other types of boundary fences, such as electrified fence, are uncommon. However, an owner of horses may use board fencing, rather than barbed wire, to eliminate the risk that barbs pose to the coats of show animals. A natural barrier such as a gulch or a dense growth of brush may obviate the need for any type of boundary fencing. On fence technology, see generally U.S. DEP'T OF AGRIC., FARMERS' BULL. NO. 2247: FENCES FOR THE FARM AND RURAL HOME (1971).

52. CAL. AGRIC. CODE § 17121 (West 1968). *See also* note 109 *infra*.

53. Because he believed his existing three-strand fence to be inadequate, rancher Dick Coombs persuaded his neighbor Ed Donaldson to join him in adding a fourth strand to their common boundary fence. Walt Johnson, the County Farm Advisor, recommends that barbed wire fences have five strands, and this is what Al Levy installed on the long stretch of new fence on the southern boundary of his mammoth ranch.

A rancher often erects "cross" or "division" fences to subdivide his own pastureland into separate fields. These fences enable a rancher to rest a pasture that would be damaged by further grazing, to control breeding, and to keep livestock away from a controlled burn.

Ranchers tend to invest less time and money in their cross fences than in their boundary fences, in part because a breach in a cross fence is less likely to result in the loss of an animal. Al Levy admitted to using only four strands for his cross fences and to not maintaining them quite as well as his five-strand boundary fences.

54. A half century ago, most Shasta County ranchers made their own fence posts by splitting logs. Should his own ranchland lack an adequate supply of logs, a rancher would contract with a private timber company to obtain the right to split downed cedar trees in the mountain forests.

Today farm supply stores offer ready made steel and wooden posts. Ranchers typically prefer the steel posts because they are less expensive, easier to drive into rocky soil, and more likely to survive a controlled burn. Wooden posts are still essential at corners, gates, stretch panels, and other places where extra strength is needed.

55. Interview with Carl Yokum of Northwest Fence, in Palo Cedro, Cal. (Aug. 11, 1982).

Technological advances—particularly the invention of barbed wire—have made fencing much less expensive relative to land and labor than it was in Abraham Lincoln's log-splitting days. Today, a newcomer to rural Shasta County would spend in the neighborhood of $40,000 to purchase a 40-acre ranchette, but for one-tenth of that sum he could hire a contractor to fence it with barbed wire. In the 1850s, "[i]t was certainly a rare farm-maker who had not to invest more capital—or its equivalent in labor in the case of forested areas—in his fence than in land." Danhof, *Farm-Making Costs and the "Safety Valve": 1850–60*, 49 J. POL. ECON. 317, 345 (1941). Fencing costs in California during the 1850s are estimated to have been $300 to $600 per mile in the currency of the time. *Id.* at 345 n.78. *See also* Meade v. Watson, 67 Cal. 591, 595, 8 P. 311, 313 (1885) (complaint asserted "value" of a stone boundary fence to be $1.75 per rod or $560 per mile). In the latter part of the nineteenth century,

ranchers and ranchette owners customarily build their own fences and thereby drastically reduce out-of-pocket labor expenditures.[56]

Barbed wire fences require periodic maintenance, especially in Shasta County, where many natural forces conspire against fence wire. The extreme summer heat loosens the wire while the winter cold pulls it taut. The deer that migrate through the foothills during the wet season are generally able to jump cattle fences; but when a jumping deer fails to clear a fence cleanly, its hoof may break a tightly stretched top wire.[57] Heavy winter rains, rotting posts, downed trees, unruly bulls, or wayward automobiles may also create a breach. A rancher or his hand therefore must spend a few days each spring, either on horseback or in a pickup truck, riding fence. A conscientious rancher also inspects his fences in the fall after the deer season, in part to see what damage trespassing hunters may have inflicted.[58] With emergency repairs needed frequently, fence maintenance chores weigh constantly on a rancher's mind.[59]

Ranchers believe that the many benefits of perimeter barriers outweigh fence construction and maintenance costs. Cattlemen with permanent ranches in either the grasslands or foothills almost invariably have perimeter fences, as well as cross fences to divide their spreads into separate pastures. A ranchette owner, however, is unlikely to fence the boundary of his land unless he

---

mean family income in the United States was on the order of $600–$800 per year. *See* BUREAU OF THE CENSUS, U.S. DEP'T OF COMMERCE, 1 HISTORICAL STATISTICS OF THE UNITED STATES: COLONIAL TIMES TO 1970 322 (1975). Before the arrival of barbed wire, a mile of fence thus cost about as much as an average family's annual income. In 1981, the mean family income in the United States was $24,000. *See* BUREAU OF THE CENSUS, U.S. DEP'T OF COMMERCE, STATISTICAL ABSTRACT OF THE UNITED STATES 1982–1983, at 435 (1982). That income would have then been sufficient to purchase the installation of at least five miles of barbed wire fence in Shasta County.

56. I found only one rancher, and no ranchette owner, who admitted having contracted out fencing work. The fence contractors of Shasta County agreed that the vast majority of rural fencing is done on a do-it-yourself basis. Walt Johnson, the astute Farm Advisor for Shasta County, could not identify the name of a single fence contractor.

57. To qualify as "lawful," a barbed wire fence in California must have its top strand at least 48 inches above the ground. CAL. AGRIC. CODE § 17121 (West 1968). Farm experts recommend that the top wire of a five-strand fence be elevated 52 inches. *See* FENCES FOR THE FARM AND RURAL HOME, *supra* note 51, at 17. The risk of damage from jumping deer has induced some fence contractors to warn against placing the top strand too high.

58. Veteran rancher and ex-Supervisor Norman Wagoner estimated that a cattleman working alone can inspect and repair a fence at a rate of about two miles per day.

59. Rancher Owen Shellworth estimated that he spent 25% of his work hours on fences, including corral fences.

has livestock. In forest pastures, one observes either no fencing or only an occasional drift fence.[60]

Traditionalists running herds in unfenced mountain forests have provoked most of the closed-range political movements in Shasta County.[61] During the summer months mountain cattle sometimes wander onto rural highways and ravage hay fields and gardens in the settled parts of the foothills. The recent proliferation of ranchettes in the foothills has aggravated these two risks and heightened opposition to the practice of running cattle at large.

## II. The Politics of Cattle Trespass in the Northeastern Foothills

Loose cattle often cause political flaps in Shasta County. Many rural residents know that the Board of Supervisors has the power to adopt closed-range ordinances. They believe that these ordinances increase the civil liabilities of owners of stray livestock not only for trespass damages, but also, and more significantly, for damages stemming from highway collisions between vehicles and domestic animals. When residents and motorists in a particular area of the county suffer a rash of cattle-related incidents, they are likely to report their grievances to their local supervisor, whom they ask to mediate the conflict or to support a closed-range ordinance designed to cure the problem. A closure reduces the number of loose cattle because fear of liability to motorists makes traditionalists reluctant to run cattle at large in closed range.[62]

At least since 1970, the Board of Supervisors has required constituents who propose adoption of a closed-range ordinance to follow a special procedure. The complainants must draw up a petition that identifies a specific territory for closure, gather signatures on copies of the petition, and forward the signed petition to the Board. Although the Board does not insist upon the sub-

60. I did not learn of a single instance in which a forest owner, or a traditionalist cattleman who leased a forest for summer range, had fenced a forest boundary.

61. But they have not provoked all of them. Farm Advisor Walt Johnson could recall several instances in which the trigger had been a rancher, ostensibly operating behind fence, who had deliberately turned out his animals onto neighboring lands.

62. Rural residents in fact exaggerate the impact of a closed-range ordinance on the legal allocation of losses arising out of vehicle-livestock collisions. I do not discuss the highway collision chapter of the Shasta County story in this article, but will treat it at length in my forthcoming book.

mission of a particular minimum number of signatures, closure proponents gather as many as possible. Upon receiving a petition, the Board's staff drafts an ordinance that will implement the closure and publicizes a hearing on the proposed measure.[63] In practice, opponents usually receive sufficient notice of an upcoming hearing to gather signatures on a counterpetition.[64] At the public hearing, the Board hears statements from proponents and opponents and then votes on the measure. The cattlemen have been quite successful in defeating proposed closures. Between 1946 and 1972, the Board approved sixteen closures in various parts of Shasta County, but most of those ordinances only involved lands on Redding's urban fringe.[65]

Prior to the 1973 Caton's Folly ordinance that closed an area near Round Mountain, the Board of Supervisors approved only one closure that affected a significant amount of rural territory east of the Sacramento River. In the early 1960s, mountain cattle began to appear in number along a stretch of State Highway 44 in the Shingletown-Viola area, thirty miles east of Redding. Highway 44 is the major route between Redding and Mount Lassen National Park. In 1965, the Board voted to close the range in a three-mile-wide strip of land straddling the highway for a distance of 12½ miles.[66] This closure affected an area topographically similar to, but south of, the Northeastern Foothills. The Northeastern Foothills remained open range until the Caton's Folly ordinance. The history of that ordinance and of the Board's rejection of the Oak Run closure petition in 1982 helps reveal the role of elected local officials in cattle trespass disputes.

### A. *Caton's Folly: The Closing of the Range at Round Mountain*

The hamlet of Round Mountain lies thirty miles northeast of Redding. Scattered along State Highway 299, the hamlet's main thoroughfare, are a general store, an elementary school, and a substation in Pacific Gas & Electric's hydroelectric power grid.[67]

63. In the early 1980s, the Board held hearings on closed-range petitions no more often than twice a year, on dates in February and July.

64. In 1982, it was the Board's standard practice, upon receiving a closed-range petition, to notify the Shasta County Cattlemen's Association by mail.

65. The county's Department of Public Works periodically prepares and sells to the public a map listing all closed-range ordinances and showing the territories they affect. The statement in the text is based on this map.

66. Shasta County, Cal., Ordinance 459 (Aug. 8, 1966).

67. In March 1984, Round Mountain enjoyed a rare moment of national media attention

The hamlet is 2000 feet in elevation, and is surrounded by higher foothills, the most prominent of which has given the hamlet its name. During the 1960s, the area around Round Mountain, like the rest of the Northeastern Foothills, became increasingly dotted with ranchettes. The frustration of these ranchette owners over the perceived misdeeds of three traditionalists, Paul Totten, Bob Moquet, and Ward Kearney, helped spawn the Caton's Folly ordinance of 1973. The particular activities of these three deserve brief description.

In the early 1970s, Totten, a small-scale traditionalist with a base ranch west of Redding, leased some thirty square miles of Roseburg Lumber Company forest lands for summer range.[68] The western boundary of Totten's leasehold was three miles east of the hamlet of Round Mountain and at a higher elevation. Just west of the boundary was an aging foothill farm with a sixty-acre irrigated field. John Woodbury had acquired this farm in 1966 and over a period of years had converted the irrigated field from natural grass to alfalfa. During the early 1970s, Totten's mountain cattle found and repeatedly used a path that led from the meager offerings of the Roseburg forest to the banquet of Woodbury's unfenced alfalfa field. On occasions when Woodbury would telephone him to complain, Totten would eventually drive the cattle back up into the forest, but neither as promptly nor as irreversibly as Woodbury would have liked.

Bob Moquet's cattle were a more pervasive and longstanding nuisance. A tough and independent leader of a pioneer clan long settled in the Round Mountain area, Moquet aroused particular hostility because he was blatantly unresponsive to his neighbors' complaints. He believed that a cattleman had a divine right to let his cattle loose in the mountains during the summer. Steve Mattingly, a Modernist cattleman who raised registered Galloway cattle on a fenced ranch on Buzzard Roost Road, became particularly concerned that Moquet's hybrid bulls might impregnate his cows.

In the early 1970s, Dr. Arthur Cooley, a Redding physician, obtained a summer grazing lease on a large tract of National For-

when a circuit breaker malfunction in the PG&E substation blacked out parts of six Western states. *See* San Francisco Chron., Mar. 1, 1984, at 1, col. 4.

68. The lessor in the early 1970s was actually the Kimberly-Clark Corporation. Kimberly-Clark sold its forest lands in the northeastern sector to the Roseburg Lumber Company in 1979. *See* note 22 *supra*. For simplicity, the text treats Roseburg as the continuous owner of these lands.

est Service land situated a few miles west of Round Mountain, on Backbone Ridge. To manage his mountain herd of several hundred animals, Cooley hired Ward Kearney, a traditionalist cowboy of exceptional ability. Kearney shared Moquet's view that people who object to stray cattle should fence them out. Consequently, after driving Cooley's cattle to Backbone Ridge, Kearney would allow them to drift down into the ranchette areas and heavily traveled stretches of Highway 299 near Round Mountain.

Cooley, Moquet, and Totten's mountain cattle tipped the political balance in Round Mountain in favor of closure. In early 1973, Mattingly, Woodbury, and a few longtime area residents began meeting to discuss the problem of mountain cattle. These anti-traditionalists eventually drew up and gathered signatures on a petition that asked the Board of Supervisors to convert from open to closed range a seven by eight mile rectangle of territory centered on Round Mountain. It is not clear who drew the exact boundaries of this rectangle. Not surprisingly, all of the activists' lands fell within its perimeter. In the end, 72 persons, mostly Round Mountain residents, signed the closed-range petition.

On March 10, 1973, Mattingly mailed the signed petition to John Caton, the newly elected Board member for the supervisoral district that included the Northeastern Foothills. Caton lived on a ranchette in Montgomery Creek, a hamlet situated three miles northeast of Round Mountain on Highway 299. Caton shared many of the cattlemen's values, yet was aware that mountain cattle had been endangering both residents and motorists. The deepening conflict between traditionalist cattlemen and the residents of the Round Mountain area placed Caton in a delicate political position. He offered to help mediate and asked Mattingly and the other petitioners to wait a few months to see whether the problem would abate. It did not. During the summer of 1973, mountain cattle entered Woodbury's alfalfa field on over a dozen occasions. Woodbury said he telephoned Caton to complain on each occasion.

On December 3, 1973, the Board of Supervisors finally held its hearing on the anti-traditionalists' petition to close the fifty-six square-mile rectangle. The hearing was lightly attended. John Woodbury, pasture owner Phil Ritchie, and ranchette owner Ted Plomeson spoke in favor of the closure. The only significant speaker in opposition was Dr. Cooley, whose protestations of economic hardship elicited little sympathy. The official minutes of the Board's meeting contain no indication that a representative of the Shasta County Cattlemen's Association was present. At the end of the session, the Board voted by a margin of 4 to 1, with Caton in the majority, to declare that the fifty-six square-mile rectangle outlined in the March petition had "ceased to be devoted chiefly to grazing"—the legal language necessary to convert the area from open range to closed range.[69]

With the exception of a few modernists such as Mattingly, Shasta County cattlemen soon came to rue their failure to fight the Round Mountain closure. To chide Caton for supporting what they regarded as a lamentable precedent, they referred to the affected area as "Caton's Folly" or "Caton's Acres." Caton got the point. During the next decade, he successfully persuaded the Board to reject all petitions that would have closed additional territories in the Northeastern Foothills.

### B. *Caton's Repentance: The Defeat of the Oak Run Closure Petition*

Caton's change of heart is best illustrated by his handling of a 1981 petition that asked the Board to close 96 square miles of range in the Oak Run area just southwest of Caton's Folly. The hamlet of Oak Run sits only three miles south of the southwestern corner of Caton's Folly. The hamlet's elevation is 1600 feet, a level where the grassy plains blend with the tangle of brush and trees that typify the foothills. During 1981-1982, only a few months before I conducted most of my interviews, the Oak Run area had been the site of perhaps the most heated closed-range battle in the history of Shasta County. Frank Ellis, a recent entrant into the bigtime cattle business, had singlehandedly provoked the circulation of a petition that sought to triple the area of closed range in the Northeastern Foothills.

#### 1. *Frank Ellis.*

Ellis, accompanied by his wife and school-age children, first moved to Shasta County in about 1973. A rancher and real estate broker by profession, Ellis was then 58 years old. He immediately acquired a functioning 2500-acre ranch astride the Oak Run Road two miles west of Oak Run and just south of an area sprouting ranchettes. The size and prominent location of Ellis' base ranch helped to make him a conspicuous personality in the

69. Shasta County, Cal., Ordinance 498 (Dec. 3, 1973).

Northeastern Foothills. Ellis (who declined my request for an interview) was by all reports a man capable of great charm. But, according to his neighbors, beneath this appealing surface lay a ruthless ambition for wealth and power. Many who dealt with Ellis came to regard him as capricious, spiteful, and not always good for his word. He became the target of numerous lawsuits, and for a time even had an attorney on retainer. One may think of him as the "J.R. Ewing of Shasta County" (although he lived in a style much less luxurious than that of his television counterpart). Although Ellis' aggressive and colorful personality won him a few admirers, his more honorable neighbors and rural acquaintances came to view Ellis as an untrustworthy bully.

During the late 1970s, Ellis built up the largest ranching empire in the Northeastern Foothills. First, he obtained a grazing lease on a section of BLM land to the west of his base ranch. Then in 1978, he persuaded the absentee owners of the largest ranching estate in the area to hire him to manage their scattered grasslands and foothills. By this one stroke, Ellis won control over another 20 square miles of pasture. Ellis eventually purchased hundreds of cattle on credit and hired a band of Mexican *braceros* to tend them.

The various components of Ellis' ranching empire were not physically connected. Ellis knew that all his holdings were within open range, but he erroneously interpreted this to mean that he could legally herd his livestock onto any land that was not fenced. When moving his livestock about, Ellis' cowboys not only deliberately crossed the unfenced private lands of others, but also used those lands as free pasture.[70] By 1981, Ellis' drovers were aggressively running a herd of two to three thousand cattle at large in the grasslands and lower foothills northeast of Redding, an area where virtually all other cattlemen were Modernists who kept their animals behind fences.

2. *Ellis' antagonists.*

Most of the lands that Ellis' livestock invaded were uncultivated and uninhabited tracts held by speculators, who, if anything, appreciated a herd coming through to beat back the brush. Yet in some areas, particularly those near Oak Run itself, Ellis' trespass victims were ranchette owners who had recently moved

70. Although they occurred in open range, these entries were intentional and therefore tortious. *See* text accompanying notes 109–110 *infra*.

to the Northeastern Foothills in search of a pastoral life. Ellis' marauding herds quickly became the bane of these ranchette owners. At least eight built fences at their own expense specifically to keep Ellis' animals off their lands. Although at least two of these ranchette owners saw Ellis as acting within his rights, most of them—in particular, Doug Heinz— did not.

Heinz, a skilled craftsman from southern California, moved to the Northeastern Foothills in 1978 with his wife and small children. The Heinzes acquired a house on a twenty-acre ranchette situated in open range west of Oak Run and about one mile from Ellis' base ranch. As a hobby, Heinz started to raise a few horses and cows on a twelve-acre portion of his ranchette that was enclosed by a five-strand barbed wire fence. The frequent passage of Ellis' herds punctured Heinz's dreams of small-scale squiredom.

According to Heinz, he and Ellis started off on polite terms. On three or four occasions in 1979, several of Ellis' cattle jumped over or broke through Heinz's fence. Heinz reacted to these early trespasses by telephoning Ellis. Ellis' response was to send his drovers to chase the cows within Heinz's field to tire them so they could then be coaxed through the fence. This method of retrieval battered Heinz's fences and Ellis' drovers never repaired the damage. Heinz's patience ran out one snowy day when he discovered that Ellis' hands had dropped hay for 200 cattle in the narrow snowplowed driveway leading to his ranchette. The milling herd that flocked to the hay included cows that had just calved, and these skittish new mothers frightened Heinz's small children.

Although most of Heinz's ranchette-owning neighbors had passively endured indignities from Ellis' livestock, Heinz was relatively short-tempered. He purchased a shotgun and called the county sheriff to protest Ellis' activities. According to what Ellis later told acquaintances, Heinz also began to threaten that Ellis might find "dead cattle." On the next occasion that Ellis' cattle broke through the fence, Heinz seized three animals and held them for three months without notifying Ellis. This incident eventually led to a lawsuit by Heinz to recover boarding costs and to a countersuit by Ellis for mistreatment of Ellis' animals.[71]

71. *See* Heinz v. Ellis, No. 81 SC 7 (Cent. Valley Just. Ct. filed Jan. 8, 1981); Ellis v. Heinz, No. 81 CV 6 (Cent. Valley Just. Ct. filed Jan. 16, 1981). (The names in these citations are pseudonyms). *See also* text accompanying notes 155–158 *infra*.

In early 1981, while his lawsuit against Ellis was still pending, Heinz began a political crusade to stop Ellis' at-large grazing practices.

Heinz anticipated recruiting a host of allies, and not just among his fellow ranchette owners. During 1978-1981, virtually every foothill motorist had reason to be annoyed at Ellis' failure to keep his livestock off the foothill roads. When Ellis' stock were being moved along the highways, motorists were often delayed for up to an hour. On a half dozen occasions, vehicles collided with Ellis' stock on the Oak Run Road. Heinz succeeded in rallying to the anti-Ellis cause dozens of ranchette-owning newcomers, as well as members of at least one respected and long-established ranching family in the Oak Run area.

3. *Caton's mediation and the battle of petitions.*

During 1981, Heinz and his allies peppered their local supervisor, John Caton, with complaints about Ellis' herds. Since his christening at Round Mountain eight years earlier, Caton had become a veteran of political disputes over trespassing cattle. Caton knew that if he supported a closed-range ordinance for the Oak Run area, he would further alienate the powerful cattlemen's lobby, a group had never forgiven him for supporting the Caton's Folly ordinance. On the other hand, if Caton opposed the closure, he would offend a potentially more numerous, if less organized, group comprised of the ranchette owners and motorists that Ellis' herds endangered. Caton sought to defuse the controversy before a formal closure petition surfaced. Working in the spring of 1981 with County Animal Control Officer Brad Bogue, Caton threatened to support a closed-range ordinance for the Oak Run area if Ellis failed to build a fence along a three-mile stretch of the Oak Run Road that Ellis' herds made particularly dangerous. In response, Ellis promised Caton that he would build the fence. But as the summer of 1981 dragged on without any sign that Ellis would perform, Caton began to regard circulation of a closed-range petition as inevitable.

Caton's political instincts proved to be accurate. Some members of the anti-Ellis group preferred to postpone circulating a petition until they had exhausted other types of mediation; this faction, for example, wanted to ask the Shasta County Cattlemen's Association to request Ellis to manage his herds more responsibly. But Heinz decided to force the issue. In the fall of

1981, without consulting some of his leading allies, he drafted and began to circulate a petition designed to close the range in a 96 square-mile area southwest of, and abutting, Caton's Folly. Heinz drew the boundaries broadly in an effort to cast the entire Ellis empire into closed range. The petition did not mention Ellis by name, but it did state that "Our reasons for this stem mostly from the inconsideration and abuse of the open range law of one rancher."[72] Heinz and his allies gathered 42 signatures—an unimpressive total—and delivered their petition to John Caton in late November 1981.

The Board of Supervisors was scheduled to hold its next hearing on closure petitions three months later, in February 1982. The interval enabled Caton to minimize the political risks posed by the Heinz petition. He immediately publicized receipt of the petition, thereby helping the opposition to organize a counter-campaign. Caton showed the Heinz petition to Wayne Thompson, a small-scale sheep rancher who lived on the Oak Run Road. Thompson enlisted his neighbor Larry Brennan, a college graduate who raised a few horses as a hobby on a large ranchette nearby, to draft a counterpetition urging the Board to keep the area open.[73] Thompson tirelessly circulated the counterpetition in the Oak Run area. Prior to the February hearing, Thompson and his associates submitted to the Board the names of 146 persons, mostly residents of the Oak Run area, who had signed their counterpetition. Heinz's temperamental personality and lack of roots in the area limited his own success and aided Thompson's, who outsolicited him by a margin of more than three to one.

---

72. The petition continued:

Our reasons to list a few are:

1. Unsafe roadways due to poorly maintained fences, cows are continually on the roads and jepardizing [sic] the safety of school children.

2. Property destruction of the trespassing cows on private property.

3. Cutting of fences on private property to herd the cows with more ease to other areas of private property.

4. Interference of range cows with private herds.

73. The counterpetition began:

We feel that the "open range" system serves many purposes for the large and small rancher.

1. Limits of liability.

2. Fire protection—through grazing, keeping the grass down.

3. Biological control—through natural fertilization of soil of rangeland, timber production, fuel-wood production.

4. Natural predator control.

5. Prevention of soil erosion due to stronger root system with annual grasses.

The Board also received a second counterpetition. Following standard procedures adopted after the Round Mountain controversy, the Board's staff had automatically informed the Shasta County Cattlemen's Association that the Board had received Heinz's closed-range petition. The Association's leaders then circulated a petition on their own. Their petition to keep the range open attracted only 24 signers, but many were members of well-known ranching families operating northeast of Redding.

Caton's last major step after the Heinz petition surfaced was to remind Ellis that Caton's decision on the closure petition would rest largely on whether Ellis kept his promise to build the three miles of fence along Oak Run Road. Ellis finally responded—grudgingly. By the time of the Board's hearing on February 2, 1982, Ellis' employees had erected three miles of five-strand barbed wire fence, a project that may have cost Ellis as much as $10,000. The fence was positioned on private lands (mostly owned by speculators) on which Ellis had grazed his herds without fee. The new fence helped to reassure motorists; it thus became a conspicuous monument to Caton's effectiveness. The fence offered no relief, however, to ranchette owners such as Heinz whose lands lay between Ellis' ranch and the new fence.

4. *The hearing and its aftermath.*

At the Board's hearing on February 2, 1982, Caton kept his part of his bargain with Ellis. Caton's decision to oppose the closure had become an easy one. Not only had Thompson's counterpetition attracted far more signatories than the Heinz petition had, but Thompson and the cattlemen were also more successful than the Heinz group in turning out supporters at the Board meeting. As ranchette owner and Heinz ally Jeff Marotta stated, "When I saw all those cowboy hats [in the hearing room] I knew we were going to lose." At the hearing, six speakers, including Doug Heinz, spoke in favor of the closure, but thirteen, including Bob Bosworth, president of the Shasta County Cattlemen's Association, spoke against it. Although the hall was packed, Ellis himself was not present. As someone said that night, "He wouldn't dare to be."[74]

Caton was also the beneficiary of a startling stroke of good

74. Just one speaker at the meeting, cattleman Marty Fancher, referred to Ellis by name. Even the members of the anti-Ellis group discreetly spoke only of "one rancher" whose misdeeds had provoked the petition.

fortune: The Ellis ranching empire had just begun to crumble. Ellis had bought hundreds of cattle on credit in anticipation that beef prices would rise. Instead, prices had fallen. This setback, arriving on top of a variety of other financial reverses left Ellis without funds to pay creditors. A week or two before the Board's hearing, Ellis' banks had begun repossessing his cattle and the news immediately circulated within the gossip mills of the Northeastern Foothills.

When the testimony at the hearing came to a close, the other supervisors stated that they would defer to John Caton, the supervisor in whose district the proposed closure lay. Caton recommended that the area remain as open range but added that, if the problem were to continue, the Board should consider closing four sections of land where Heinz and most of the other complaining ranchette owners lived. The Board promptly voted unanimously to deny the Heinz petition. To smooth the waters, Dan Gover, the Board's chairman and a rancher himself, asked Bob Bosworth, president of the county Cattlemen's Association, to meet with Ellis, Heinz, and county animal control officials to see what could be done to control Ellis' herds.[75] Caton had repented for Caton's Folly.

Within a few months of the hearing, both Heinz and Ellis were gone from the Northeastern Foothills. In 1980, Heinz had begun planning the construction of a house in Redding for his family. Only a few days after the Board rejected his petition, he moved out of the ranchette in Oak Run and into his newly completed Redding house. Ellis' stay in Oak Run lasted only three months longer than Heinz's. The banks seized Ellis' cattle, and his creditors were lining up with claims on his ranch. In May 1982, Ellis moved his family 100 miles south to a farm in another California county in the Central Valley. As his parting shot to Shasta County, Ellis ordered his hands to destroy the three miles of fence along the Oak Run Road that he had ordered built just six months before. On the day the Board held its hearing, the two leading players in the drama both knew that they were about to depart from the stage.[76]

75. The proposed meeting was never held, in part because the cattlemen were willing to use only informal sanctions, and, as Bosworth said at the hearing in response to a supervisor's question, this sort of pressure wouldn't work with Ellis because, "He hasn't been in [the County] all that long."

76. This datum is consistent with the widely accepted theoretical proposition that the lack of a prospective long-term future relationship makes disputants less likely to resolve their

## III. Research Methods

I chose the Round Mountain-Oak Run area as the focus for the microscopic study because it had witnessed both an actual and a threatened closure of the range. The area presented opportunities for both longitudinal and cross-sectional analyses. A longitudinal analysis would track the behavior of specific cattlemen and farmers over a span of years in the midst of which an applicable closed-range ordinance had been adopted. A cross-sectional analysis would examine varied locations, rather than time periods, to determine whether on a particular date cattlemen and farmers behaved differently in open-range areas than in closed-range areas. I designed the field study to allow both types of inquiries.[77]

The 56 square-miles in Caton's Folly almost equals the size of Washington, D.C. I decided to concentrate the landowner interviews within the subarea that straddled Caton's Folly's southern boundary. This subarea provided opportunities for cross-sectional analysis because it contained both open-range and closed-range, including some open-range that had recently been subjected to an unsuccessful closure petition.[78]

My research techniques were more similar to those used in anthropology or in-depth journalism than to those used in econometrics or sociometrics. I relied primarily on interviews with two groups of people: (1) landowners in the study area, and

differences without the help of third parties, and hence more likely to resort to legal and political action. *See* text accompanying notes 139–141 *infra.*

77. An ideal research design makes use of time-series data for both experimental and control areas. *See* Lempert, *Strategies of Research Design in the Legal Impact Study: The Control of Rival Hypotheses,* 1 Law & Soc'y Rev. 111, 130–32 (1966).

78. The area around the southern border of Caton's Folly offered several advantages. First, whereas the other three boundaries of Caton's Folly traversed lightly settled private forest, the southern border area was well-settled and thus more likely to be conflict-ridden. Second, only the southern area included some territory that had been threatened with a closure. Third, an investigator conducting a cross-sectional study into the impact of law should pick a situation where the legal boundaries are essentially random with regard to the social and topographic variables that may affect human conduct. Were the boundary not randomly drawn, any differences in landowner behavior that the investigator discovered between the areas might be the result of preexisting conditions (which perhaps caused the line to be drawn where it was), and not the result of differences in legal regimes. The southern boundary of Caton's Folly appeared to be a random line. None of the drafters of the Caton's Folly petition (the persons who selected this boundary) lived near it, and neither did any appreciable number of the petition's signatories. Moreover, the terrain the southern boundary crosses is highly varied, rising from foothills at an elevation of 2100 feet at the western end, to mountain forest at an elevation of 4400 feet at the eastern end. An eight-mile east-west line drawn straight across diverse terrain seems unlikely to have been the product of a gerrymander.

(2) a larger number of "specialists" who were knowledgeable about how rural residents resolve stray cattle disputes. Instead of interviewing many persons who saw the problem from the same perspective, I sought out lesser numbers representing many different perspectives.

Of seventy-three total interviews (most of which were conducted during the summer of 1982), twenty-eight were with persons owning land in the rural area northeast of Redding. Eleven of these twenty-eight owned land inside Caton's Folly; ten owned land outside but within three miles of its southern border, mostly in areas that the Heinz closure petition would have affected; and three more—Hailey, McCall, and Shellworth—owned land both inside and outside Caton's Folly. Of the twenty-eight landowners, eleven could be described as cattle ranchers, four as farmers (whose chief agricultural activity was producing feed for livestock), and thirteen as ranchette owners (some of whom owned farm animals as a hobby). Twenty of the twenty-eight landowners were interviewed face-to-face. Seventeen of these interviews were in-depth sessions lasting one-and-a-half to two hours. The other eight landowner interviews were conducted by telephone; these telephone conversations averaged fifteen minutes in length.

The landowner interviews suffer from several shortcomings as a data source. First, 28 is a small sample. Second, I did not randomly select the people I interviewed; rather, I tended to seek out residents who had either owned cattle, been victims of trespass incidents, or been active in the political battles over closed-range petitions. I also made a particular effort to interview the owners of the largest farms and ranches in the study area. Compared to average foothill landowners, my informants were probably older, wealthier (although still of modest means), longer in residence in northeastern Shasta County, and more active in community affairs. Although most respondents talked without hesitation—indeed, usually with enthusiasm—cooperative people were undoubtedly somewhat overrepresented in the sample. Third, I decided not to use a standardized survey instrument, in part because a formal list of questions might have made respondents ill-at-ease.[79] Fourth, some memories were undoubtedly

79. The authors of many leading microscopic law and society studies have used similar research methods. In his memorable study of contract law, Macaulay interviewed 68 businessmen and lawyers in Wisconsin, apparently without the aid of a standardized questionnaire.

imperfect, and I had reason to suspect that a few landowners had deliberately recast history to place themselves in a better light.[80]

Rather than budget more time to landowner interviews, I chose to mitigate these shortcomings by using government records and interviews with certain specialists to cross-check what the landowners reported. Two types of government records—aerial photographs and court files—contained information relevant to cattle-trespass disputes. Federal agencies had taken aerial photographs of the western portion of Caton's Folly's southern border area in October 1973 and August 1980—that is, two months before, and seven years after, the ordinance had been approved.[81] Although these photos were taken at too high an altitude to indicate the presence of fences or individual animals, they reveal buildings and areas under cultivation. I obtained copies of these photographs in order to have evidence of actual changes in gross land use patterns in and near the study area during the relevant time period.[82] I also searched the records of the state courts that serve the northeastern sector of Shasta County and noted lawsuits arising out of stray livestock incidents.[83]

The other important cross-checks on the landowner interviews were the 50 interviews that I conducted with "specialists,"

*See* Macaulay, *supra* note 12, at 55–56. Ross's interviews with his 67 insurance adjusters were also unstructured. H. Ross, *supra* note 12, at 10. Llewellyn & Hoebel's study of the Cheyenne was based on what sociologists call "memory cases"—tribal legends and tales related by interpreters. K. Llewellyn & E. Hoebel, The Cheyenne Way viii–ix (1941). *See also* Palay, *Comparative Institutional Economics: The Governance of Rail Freight Contracting,* 13 J. Legal Stud. 265, 271 (1984) (study based on 35 field interviews was conducted without the use of a formal questionnaire, in order to encourage the interviewees to be open in their responses).

On methods of what I call "microscopic" field research, see generally Blanck & Turner, *Gestalt Research: Clinical-Field-Research Approaches to Studying Organizations,* in Handbook of Organizational Behavior 109-25 (J. Lorsch ed. 1986).

80. Because I had concentrated my landowner interviews in a subarea, I often heard several interpretations of the same event; I was therefore better able to make an assessment of the credibility of different sources.

81. In October 1973, the Caton's Folly ordinance was pending and landowners might have anticipated its adoption. Thus, aerial photographs taken on an earlier date, had they been available, would have provided better evidence of the *ex ante* situation.

82. I hired a geobotanist skilled in remote sensing to analyze the two sets of aerial photographs. He detected no cross-sectional or longitudinal variations in land use patterns that would cast doubt on the findings presented in Part IV.

83. None of the relevant state courts index their cases by subject matter. To overcome this obstacle, I asked the judges and court clerks if they could recall stray cattle cases, looked for names of likely litigants in the plaintiff and defendant name indexes, and, in the Justice Courts, reviewed all complaints that had been filed during recent eleven-month periods. *See also* note 152 *infra.*

namely, industry and government officials likely to interact with the subjects of the study.[84] Eighty percent of the specialist interviews were conducted in person and the balance were conducted by telephone. The face-to-face sessions averaged 40 minutes in length. As in the landowner interviews, I took detailed handwritten notes during the sessions.[85]

## IV. The Resolution of Animal Trespass Disputes in Shasta County

This Part reports the frequency of cattle trespass incidents in Shasta County, presents relevant California trespass law, and recounts how Shasta County neighbors actually resolve their trespass disputes. In the Coasean Parable of the Farmer and the Rancher, the two neighbors both know and honor applicable legal rules. Much of law and economic scholarship has similarly assumed that law is efficacious in this way.[86] This Part suggests that the assumption of efficacious law is more heroic than certain scholars have realized.

### A. *Animal Trespass Incidents*

Every landowner interviewed, including all thirteen ranchette owners, reported at least one instance in which his lands had been invaded by someone else's livestock. Hay farmers grow what cattle especially like to eat, and thus expect frequent trespasses.[87] Owners of large ranches are also common victims be-

84. The specialists interviewed were: the four state court judges most likely to have been involved in livestock-related cases arising in Shasta County's northeastern sector; six Redding attorneys who had rural landowners as clients; five members of the Board of Directors of the Shasta County Cattlemen's Association; eight adjusters and salesmen employed by the insurance companies that underwrite most of the livestock risks in eastern Shasta County; three real estate appraisers and assessors; eleven county officials (including the Brand Inspector, the Animal Control Officer, the Farm Advisor, a former District Attorney, and several supervisors, including John Caton); four fence contractors and fence material suppliers; six agents of forest owners that lease their lands for grazing; and three grazing lessees. Because several interviewees qualified both as specialists and as landowners, the total number of interviews was 73, not 78.

85. To avoid developing a reputation for undue nosiness, I never asked the landowners about either their religious convictions or their financial situations. Those variables might conceivably affect one's method of resolving low-level disputes; however, the interviewees never volunteered that religion or financial plight affected people's behavior.

86. *See, e.g.*, Calabresi & Melamed, *supra* note 7, at 1090–91 (assuming that the "state" is the sole source of entitlements).

87. John Woodbury suffered almost weekly incursions into his alfalfa field in 1973. *See* text following note 68 *supra*. Although the situation improved when many of the mountain

cause they cannot keep their many miles of aging perimeter fence cattle-tight. Thus, when a rancher gathers his animals on his fenced pastures each spring, he is not startled to find a few head carrying a neighbor's brand.

Because cattle eat almost incessantly, a trespass victim's vegetation is always at risk.[88] Nevertheless, a victim usually regards the loss of grass as trivial so long as the owner removes the animals with reasonable promptness—that is, within a day or two if the animals are easy to corral. Trespassing livestock occasionally do cause more than nominal damage. Several ranchette owners reported incidents in which wayward cattle had damaged their fences and vegetable gardens; one farmer told of the ravaging of some of his ornamental trees.

The most serious trespasses reported were ones involving either at-large cattle or bulls. A ranchette owner narrated how mountain cattle had once invaded his house construction site, broken the windows, and contaminated the creek. A part-time horsebreeder told of buying seven tons of hay and stacking it on an unfenced portion of his fifty-acre ranchette, where it was then eaten by cattle that Frank Ellis had let roam free.

Rural residents especially fear trespasses by bulls. In a modern beef cattle herd, roughly one animal in twenty-five is a bull, whose principal function is to impregnate cows during their brief periods in heat.[89] Bulls are twice as heavy as the other herd animals,[90] and tend to be much more ornery. Several respondents had vivid memories of bull trespasses. A farmer who owned irrigated pasture was amazed at the depth of the hoof marks that an entering bull had made. A ranchette owner and a rancher told of barely escaping goring while attempting to corral invading

lessees subsequently declined to renew their leases, Woodbury was still experiencing a couple of cattle trespasses a year in the early 1980s. Another hay farmer, Phil Ritchie, identified six neighbors whose cattle had trespassed on his lands in recent years.

88. Beef cattle eat feed equal to about 2-1/2% of their body weight each day. DIVISION OF AGRIC. SCI., UNIV. OF CAL., LEAFLET NO. 21184, BEEF PRODUCTION IN CALIFORNIA 12-13 (Nov. 1980).

89. *Cf.* CAL. AGRIC. CODE § 16803 (West 1968) (cattlemen grazing herds on open-range must include at least one bull for every 30 cows). The refinement of artificial insemination techniques has enabled some ranchers to reduce the fraction of bulls in herds kept behind fences.

90. A Hereford bull has a mature weight of 2000 pounds, compared to 1100-1200 pounds for a mature Hereford cow. Steers (castrated male cattle) are typically slaughtered when they weigh between 1000 and 1150 pounds. BEEF PRODUCTION IN CALIFORNIA, *supra* note 88, at 3, 5.

bulls.[91] Because an alien bull often enters in pursuit of cows in heat, owners of female animals fear illicit couplings that might produce offspring of an undesired pedigree. Although no cow owner reported actual damages from misbreeding, several mentioned that this risk especially worried them.

## B. *Animal Trespass Law*

One of the most venerable English common law rules of strict liability in tort is the rule that an owner of domestic livestock is liable, even in the absence of negligence, for property damage that his animals cause while trespassing.[92] This traditional English rule also applies in the closed-range areas of Shasta County.[93]

---

91. I learned of no cattle trespasses that had resulted in personal injury. Two insurance adjusters who frequently had been called upon to settle dog-bite claims could remember, between them, only one personal-injury claim arising from cattle—an instance in which a cow had stepped on someone's foot.

92. The case that has most commonly occurred, and which is most frequently to be found in the books, is as to the obligation of the owner of cattle which he has brought on his land, to prevent their escaping and doing mischief. The law as to them seems to be perfectly settled from early times; the owner must keep them in at his peril, or he will be answerable for the natural consequences of their escape; that is with regard to tame beasts, for the grass they eat and trample upon, though not for any injury to the person of others, for our ancestors have settled that it is not the general nature of horses to kick, or bulls to gore, but if the owner knows that the beast has a vicious propensity to attack man, he will be answerable for that too.

Fletcher v. Rylands, 1 L.R.-Ex. 265, 280 (1866) (Blackburn, J.). *See also* 3 W. BLACKSTONE, COMMENTARIES *211 ("A man is answerable for not only his own trespass, but that of his cattle also").

The operation of this rule in Great Britain is discussed in G. WILLIAMS, LIABILITY FOR ANIMALS 127–99 (1939). *See also* Wigmore, *Responsibility for Tortious Acts: Its History*, 7 HARV. L. REV. 441, 450–52 (1894) (asserting, at 451 n.1, that thirteenth century cases applied a strict liability rule to cattle trespass incidents).

93. *See, e.g.*, Montezuma Improvement Co. v. Simmerly, 181 Cal. 722, 724, 189 P. 100, 101 (1919).

Hornbook law provides a few defenses to, and other limitations on, an animal owner's strict liability for trespass damages. When a cattleman has driven cattle along a highway from which they have strayed and damaged plaintiff's adjoining fields, the plaintiff must prove that the cattleman had been negligent in the management of the herd. *See* RESTATEMENT (SECOND) OF TORTS § 505 (1977). There is authority that trespasses caused by an act of God—for example, an unprecedented windstorm causing a breach in a fence—are not actionable. *See id.* at § 504(3)(c). The Restatement also declines to impose liability for unforeseeable damage. *Id.* at § 504(3)(a); *see also* Williams v. Goodwin, 41 Cal. App. 3d 496, 507, 116 Cal. Rptr. 200, 208 (1974) (recovery granted because personal injury caused by trespassing bull was within the scope of foreseeable harm).

A trespass victim's own misconduct, such as failing to close a cattle gate or breaching a contractual duty to build a fence, may also diminish or bar his recovery. *See* G. WILLIAMS, *supra* note 92, at 178–81; *see also* RESTATEMENT (SECOND) OF TORTS § 504(4) (1977) (trespass

In the open-range areas of the county—that is, in the great bulk of its rural territory—the English rule has been rejected in favor of the pro-cattleman "fencing out" rule that many grazing states adopted during the nineteenth century.[94] In 1850, just after California attained statehood, an open-range rule was adopted for the entire state. In that year, the legislature enacted a statute that entitled a victim of animal trespass to recover damages only when the victim had protected his lands with a "lawful fence."[95] This pro-cattleman policy grew increasingly controver-

---

victim who fails to erect and maintain a fence required by common law or statute is barred from recovery). In California, misconduct by a plaintiff does not typically operate as a complete defense in a strict liability action. *See* Daly v. General Motors Corp., 20 Cal. 3d 725, 575 P.2d 1162, 144 Cal. Rptr. 380 (1978).

94. Many authorities assert that the Western states have been the chief followers of "fencing-out" rules. *See, e.g.*, 2 F. Harper & F. James, The Law of Torts § 14.10 (1956); W. Prosser, J. Wade, & V. Schwartz, Cases and Materials on Torts 706–07 (7th ed. 1982). Nineteenth century treatises on fence law reveal, however, that in that era, "fencing out" was the dominant rule in the United States, particularly in the *Northern* states. *See* W. Thornton, The Law of Railroad Fences and Private Crossings §§ 8–10 (1892) (identifying 13 states as following the English rule and 21 states as having fencing-out regimes); R. Tyler, The Law of Boundaries, Fences, and Window Lights 361–512 (1874) (state-by-state review of fence law, indicating, at 451, that Michigan, for example, enacted a fencing-out statute in 1847); *see also* W. Cronon, Changes in the Land: Indians, Colonists, and the Ecology of New England 134–35 (1983) (the Plymouth and Massachusetts Bay colonies in Massachusetts required planters of corn to fence out livestock).

95. 1850 Cal. Stat., ch. 49, 131. *See* Comerford v. Dupuy, 17 Cal. 308 (1861) (judgment for defendant cattle owners where plaintiff's fence failed to meet lawful fence requirements of 1855 statute); Waters v. Moss, 12 Cal. 535 (1859) (dictum).

In California during that era, the open-range rule was probably more efficient than the English rule. Where there are many cultivated lands, as in England, a livestock owner is typically the cheapest cost avoider in animal-crop interactions because he can best control the whereabouts of his beasts. *See* Calabresi & Hirschoff, *Toward a Test for Strict Liability in Torts*, 81 Yale L.J. 1055, 1060 (1972) (risks should be assigned to the party best able to perform a cost-benefit analysis of accident costs and accident prevention costs and to act on that analysis once it is made). There was little farming in California in the mid-nineteenth century, however, and the grazing of cattle was widespread. *See generally* R. Cleland, The Cattle on a Thousand Hills (2d ed. 1951) (despite the impact of the Gold Rush in northern California, southern California remained a typical cattle frontier for nearly 20 years thereafter). Consequently, it was cheaper to install fencing around the rare field crops than around the ubiquitous grazing areas. Cattlemen running animals at large would have incurred high transaction costs in organizing to erect fences that would reduce their common risk of tort liability; in contrast, because a single farmer could decide on his own whether or not to fence, he would incur lower transaction costs. If efficiency-minded frontier lawmakers assumed that actors knew and honored the legal rules, they therefore would have imposed the risk of trespass across an unfenced boundary on the farmer, the cheaper avoider of trespass damages to isolated fields of crops.

Lawful-fence statutes, still found in many western states, adopt an even more sophisticated approach to the allocation of animal trespass risks. The statutes identify specific fence technologies that farmers can employ to revive their rights to recover for trespass damages. *See* note 109 *infra*. When a trespass has occurred despite the presence of a lawful fence, the

sial as California became more settled and field crops became more common. During the latter part of the nineteenth century, the California legislature enacted a series of statutes effectively closing the range in designated counties and thereby granting more protection to farmers who had not built fences.[96]

The closed-range exceptions began to swamp California's traditional open-range rule and eventually triggered a comprehensive legislative response. In the Estray Act of 1915,[97] the legislature adopted for most of California the traditional English rule that the owner of livestock is strictly liable for trespass damage.[98] This statute, however, retained the open-range rule for six counties in the lightly populated northern part of the state where the tradition of running cattle at large remained strong. The Estray Act of 1915 thus specifically excepted all of Shasta, Del Norte, Lassen, Modoc, Siskiyou, and Trinity Counties from the closed-range regime.[99]

---

statutes place the loss on the cattleman, the person who is usually the cheaper avoider of this sort of trespass, because he can best discover whether any of his animals are prone to break through or jump over fences and can best act on that knowledge.

Because lawful-fence rules provide rather bright-line standards, compared to negligence rules, they are relatively easy to communicate and apply. Lawful-fence statutes are thus suited to enforcement by lay "fence viewers"—private individuals whom some states have authorized to judge the quality of fencing and to assess trespass damages or fence construction costs. *See* note 111 *infra.*

96. *See* 3 CAL. JUR. 3D *Animals* § 55, at 676 n.42 (1973) (citing 14 county-specific fencing statutes that the California legislature enacted between 1863 and 1878 and repealed in the 1930s); Note, *Torts: Trespass by Animals upon Unenclosed Lands in California,* 7 CALIF. L. REV. 365 (1919).

97. 1915 Cal. Stat. 636 (current version at CAL. AGRIC. CODE §§ 17,001–17,128 (West 1968)).

98. Although the 1915 statute nominally dealt only with a trespass victim's rights to take up estrays, California case law has consistently held that a statutory right to seize estrays in the absence of a lawful fence carries with it the right to recover trespass damages under the traditional common law rule of strict liability. *See* Montezuma Improvement Co. v. Simmerly, 181 Cal. 722, 189 P. 100 (1919); Hahn v. Garratt, 69 Cal. 146, 10 P. 329 (1886); Williams v. Goodwin, 41 Cal. App. 3d 496, 116 Cal. Rptr. 200 (1974) (dictum).

99. 1915 Cal. Stat. 636 (current version at CAL. AGRIC. CODE §§ 17,123–17,126 (West 1968)). Subsequent amendments deleted the exemptions applicable to all of Del Norte County, and parts of Shasta and Trinity Counties. *See* CAL. AGRIC. CODE §§ 17,123–17,126 (West 1968).

The California code authorizes the board of supervisors of *any* county to declare by ordinance that part or all of the county is "devoted chiefly to grazing." *See* CAL. AGRIC. CODE § 17,124 (West 1968). A declaration of this sort converts the designated area to an open-range regime—that is, it takes from trespass victims who lack lawful fences their preexisting entitlement to seize estrays and to recover trespass damages. *See* Williams v. Goodwin, 41 Cal. App. 3d 496, 503 n.8, 116 Cal. Rptr. 200, 205 n.8 (1974) (dictum); 39 Op. Cal. Att'y Gen. 75 (1962).

Responding in part to lobbying efforts by local cattlemen's associations, an increasing

In 1945, the Legislature enacted two amendments that dealt exclusively with Shasta County, the least rural of the six exempt counties. The first stated that a prime agricultural area just south of Redding was "not . . . devoted chiefly to grazing"—a declaration that the legislature had decided to close the range in that small area of the county.[100] The second amendment empowered the Board of Supervisors of Shasta County to adopt ordinances designating additional areas of the county as places no longer devoted chiefly to grazing. This legal designation would make cattlemen strictly liable for trespass damage occurring in those locations.[101] For the next 29 years, Shasta was the only California county to possess this special authority.[102] Today, Shasta County has a crazy-quilt of open- and closed-range areas unmatched by any other California county.[103]

The distinction between open-range and closed-range has formal legal significance in Shasta County trespass disputes. In closed-range, the English rule governs and an animal owner, with rare exceptions,[104] is strictly liable for trespass damage to prop-

number of California's foothill counties have converted parts of their mountain forest to open range. *See, e.g.*, Amador County, Cal., Ordinance 590 (Apr. 26, 1977); Calavaras County, Cal., Ordinance 179 (June 3, 1940) (opening range in entire county), *repealed by* Ordinance 411 (Nov. 7, 1967) (referendum measure); Calavaras County, Cal., Ordinance 779 (Dec. 29, 1975) (townsite of Sheep Ranch); El Dorado County, Cal., Code §§ 16,501–16,505 (adopted Feb. 3, 1976); Mariposa County, Cal., Ordinance 128 (May 7, 1945) (the first of several ordinances opening the range in the National Forest areas of the county); Placer County, Cal., Ordinance 2017-B (June 29, 1976).

100. 1945 Cal. Stat. 1538–39 (current version at CAL. AGRIC. CODE § 17126 (West 1968)).

101. 1945 Cal. Stat. 1539 (current version at CAL. AGRIC. CODE § 17,127 (West 1968)).

102. The state legislature granted the board of supervisors of Trinity County, Shasta's neighbor to the west, similar authority in 1974. 1974 Cal. Stat. 409 (current version at CAL. AGRIC. CODE § 17,127 (West Supp. 1985)). Any closed-range county that exercises its statutory power to open the range in a particular area undoubtedly also has the power to switch that same area back to a closed regime. At least one California county has flip-flopped in this way. See note 99 *supra* (describing legal events in Calaveras County).

A number of western states that generally adhere to an open-range regime also authorize substate entities to selectively "close" parts of their range. *See, e.g.*, Ricca v. Bojorquez, 13 Ariz. App. 10, 473 P.2d 812 (1970) (Arizona procedure entitling landowners to close range by petition to the county board of supervisors unconstitutionally delegates power to private parties); Maguire v. Yanke, 99 Idaho 829, 590 P.2d 85 (1978) (describing Idaho procedure whereby landowners can petition to close range on a district by district basis); WASH. REV. CODE ANN. § 16.24.010 (1962) (option to close range granted to counties without townships).

103. A map issued by the Shasta County Department of Public Works in 1981 showed 28 separate areas the Board of Supervisors had closed by ordinance since 1945. Although most of the closed areas were located near Redding, there were areas of closed-range in the hinterland in every direction from the city.

104. See note 93 *supra*.

erty. In open-range areas, by contrast, even a livestock owner[105] who has negligently managed his animals is generally not liable[106] for trespass damage to the lands[107] of a neighbor.

Even in open range, however, there remain three important pockets of trespass liability. First, owners of goats, swine, and vicious dogs are subjected to the English rule throughout Shasta County.[108] Second, when a cattleman's livestock have trespassed

105. Persons other than the animal's owner could conceivably be held liable for an animal's damage. Livestock owned by one person often permissively graze on the lands of another. For example, both grazing leases and agistment arrangements—contracts to feed and care for the livestock of another—are common in cattle country. The California courts, as expansive as any state's in imposing tort liability, would likely hold a grazing landlord liable were he negligently to abet trespasses by a lessee's livestock. *Cf.* Uccello v. Laudenslayer, 44 Cal. App. 3d 504, 118 Cal. Rptr. 741 (1975) (residential landlord who knew of tenant's vicious dog and had the power to have it removed owed a duty of care to tenants' invitees and could be liable for negligence to dog-bite victim). *But cf.* Blake v. Dunn Farms, Inc., 274 Ind. 560, 413 N.E.2d 560 (1980) (landlord not liable for damages stemming from escape of tenant's horse that he knew little about). *See also* RESTATEMENT (SECOND) OF TORTS § 504 comment d (1977) (only a "possessor" of livestock, not the owner of the land from whence the animals escaped, is strictly liable for trespass damages); Annot., 21 A.L.R.4th 123 (1983) (liability of nonowner of livestock in highway collision cases). Because of this risk, the agent for many timberland owners in Shasta County includes a "hold harmless" clause in his standard grazing lease to entitle the lessor to indemnification from the lessee.

106. Prosser asserts that a trespass victim who lacks a lawful fence required by statute can still prevail against a cattle owner who was "at fault." *See* W. PROSSER, HANDBOOK OF THE LAW OF TORTS 498 n.58 (4th ed. 1971); *see also* W. PROSSER, J. WADE & V. SCHWARTZ, *supra* note 94, at 707. This implies that a fencing-out statute only deprives trespass victims of the right to proceed on a theory of strict liability; it lets them proceed on a theory of negligence.

In California, the weight of legal authority does not support the Prosser view. Except when the defendant intended that his cattle trespass, a plaintiff's proof of the presence of a lawful fence has been regarded as a prerequisite for recovery in open range. *See, e.g.*, Logan v. Gedney, 38 Cal. 579 (1869); Comerford v. Dupuy, 17 Cal. 308 (1861). *See also* RESTATEMENT (SECOND) OF TORTS § 504 comment k (1977); 2 F. HARPER & F. JAMES, *supra* note 94, § 14.10, at 829. To use a phrase that seems almost quaint in the current era of comparative negligence, in open range a California landowner without a lawful fence essentially "assumes the risk" that neighbors will negligently handle their cattle.

107. Other rules may apply when the injury has been to person or chattels. In closed-range, a cattle owner is strictly liable for foreseeable personal injuries that his livestock cause. *See* Williams v. Goodwin, 41 Cal. App. 3d 496, 116 Cal. Rptr. 200 (1974) (owner of trespassing bull strictly liable for trampling of night watchman in closed-range); Annot., 88 A.L.R.2d 709 (1963). *But cf.* RESTATEMENT (SECOND) OF TORTS § 504 (1977) (denying possessor of unfenced land in open-range recovery for personal injuries on a strict liability theory).

In both open- and closed-range, the owner of a trespassing animal would be strictly liable if that animal were to kill animals belonging to the owner of the premises invaded. *See* CAL. CIV. CODE § 3341 (West 1970); *cf.* CAL. AGRIC. CODE § 31501 (West 1968) (owner of trespassing dog is liable for twice the value of damages to livestock and poultry).

108. *See* CAL. AGRIC. CODE. § 17128 (West 1968) (excepting owners of "goats, swine, or hogs" from benefits of open-range rule); Shasta County Ordinance Code § 3306 (declaring it "unlawful" to permit "any vicious dog or other dangerous animal" to run at large).

The California Agricultural Code provides that "[a] person in charge of any stallion, bull,

through, or over, a "lawful fence" that entirely encloses the victim's premises, the cattleman remains strictly liable for trespass damages. (A California statute, unamended since 1915, defines the technological standard that a fence must meet to be "lawful."[109]) Third, common law decisions make a livestock owner in open range liable for trespass when he *intentionally* causes his animals to enter the unfenced lands of another. Thus when Frank Ellis actively herded his cattle across the lands of his neighbors, he was liable for trespass. According to some precedents, he would have been liable for trespass had he merely placed his cat-

---

boar, ram, or male goat shall not turn out or permit such animal to be turned out or to run at large." CAL. AGRIC. CODE § 16702 (West 1968). This provision is not compatible with CAL. AGRIC. CODE § 16803 (West 1968) (*requiring* the presence of one purebred bull for every 30 cows run at large). Brad Bogue, Shasta County's Animal Control Officer, interprets the latter section as controlling the former.

109. Section 17122 of the Agricultural Code reads:

> In any county or part of a county devoted chiefly to grazing and so declared pursuant to this article, a person shall not have the right to take up any estray animal found upon his premises, or upon premises to which he has the right of possession, nor shall he have a lien thereon, *unless the premises are entirely enclosed with a good and substantial fence.*

CAL. AGRIC. CODE § 17122 (West 1968) (emphasis added). Judicial decisions construe this sort of provision as also denying a person without such a fence the right to recover damages for cattle trespass. *See* note 98 *supra*. *See also* CAL. AGRIC. CODE § 17128 (West 1968).

Section 17121 describes the quality of fencing necessary to meet this standard:

> A lawful fence is any fence which is good, strong, substantial, and sufficient to prevent the ingress and egress of livestock. No wire fence is a good and substantial fence within the meaning of this article unless it has three tightly stretched barbed wires securely fastened to posts of reasonable strength, firmly set in the ground not more than one rod [16–1/2 feet] apart, one of which wires shall be at least four feet above the surface of the ground. Any kind of wire or other fence of height, strength and capacity equal to or greater than the wire fence herein described is a good and substantial fence within the meaning of this article . . . .

CAL. AGRIC. CODE § 17121 (West 1968).

This statutory definition of a lawful fence remains essentially unchanged since 1919. *Compare with* 1919 Cal. Stat. 1150. The definition is technologically obsolete because, at least in Shasta County, cattlemen customarily use at least four strands of barbed wire in their boundary fences. *See* note 53 *supra*. A fence that fails the statutory standard for "lawfulness" may be deemed to have been negligently built, thereby exposing the fencebuilder to liability for damage caused by the fence. *See* Loveland v. Gardner, 79 Cal. 317, 21 P. 766 (1889) (plaintiff can recover for damage his horses suffered when they encountered defendant's negligently stretched barbed wire fence).

California's statutory definitions of lawful fences before the invention of barbed wire are described in R. TYLER, *supra* note 94, at 482–84 (some samples: stone walls 4-1/2 feet high; rail fences 5-1/2 feet high; a five-foot high hedge). W. THORTON, *supra* note 94, at 201–23, provides a state-by-state review of statutory standards for the adequacy of fences in the late nineteenth century.

Other states' current statutory definitions of lawful fences vary from California's. *See, e.g.*, ARIZ. REV. STAT. ANN. § 24–501 (1971); NEV. REV. STAT. § 569.450(1) (1979); WASH. REV. CODE ANN. § 16.60.010 (1962). Many of their provisions seem equally antiquated.

tle on his own lands in a way that would make it substantially certain that they would venture onto his neighbors' pastures.[110]

When the law of either open- or closed-range entitles a trespass victim to relief, the remedy is usually an award of compensatory damages.[111] A plaintiff who has suffered from continuing wrongful trespasses may also be entitled to an injunction against future incursions.[112] Moreover, California's Estray Act entitles a landowner whose premises have been wrongly invaded by cattle to seize them as security for a claim to recover boarding costs and other damages. A trespass victim who invokes this procedure must provide proper notice to the Director of Agriculture; if certain statutory requirements are met, the animals can be sold

110. State courts have rather uniformly imposed tort liability on any cattleman who has actively herded his livestock onto the lands of another, even when the victim's land was situated in open-range. In some states, a cattleman has been held liable only when he has deliberately transported animals across the boundary line. *See, e.g.*, Garcia v. Sumrall, 58 Ariz. 526, 121 P.2d 640 (1942); Richards v. Sanderson, 39 Colo. 270, 89 P. 769 (1907). In other states, the entry of a cattleman's livestock has also been regarded as intentionally tortious when he has left them on a range from which it was substantially certain that they would enter the plaintiff's lands. *See, e.g.*, Lazarus v. Phelps, 152 U.S. 81 (1894); Mower v. Olsen, 49 Utah 373, 164 P. 482 (1917). *See generally* Annot., 158 A.L.R. 375 (1945).

Two reported California decisions deal with the issue of intentional trespass by livestock owners; in both, applicable statutes prohibited the "herding" of livestock on the lands of others. The more recent decision, Cramer v. Jenkins, 82 Cal. App. 269, 255 P. 877 (1927), supports the proposition that leaving animals in a range from which they are substantially certain to trespass constitutes tortious misconduct. *But cf.* Logan v. Gedney, 38 Cal. 579 (1869) (implying that active herding may be required). The California Supreme Court's current pro-plaintiff predilections would incline it to follow the *Cramer* approach.

111. Because evidence of damage to forage is fleeting, some states (although currently not California) authorize the appointment of disinterested residents of the area to serve as "fence viewers" to assess the amount of the damages. *See, e.g.*, WASH. REV. CODE ANN. § 16.60.015 (Supp. 1986) ("damages [shall be] assessed by three reliable, disinterested parties and practical farmers, within five days next after the trespass has been committed . . . ."). *See generally* 35 AM. JUR. 2d *Fences* §§ 24-32 (1967). The practice of delegating the valuation of damages to fence viewers was widespread in the nineteenth century and before. *See* R. TYLER, *supra* note 94, at 395, 399, 459 & 476 (describing statutes in New York, Maine, Wisconsin, and Kansas); W. CRONON, *supra* note 94, at 135 (colonial Massachusetts). At least one of the early California fence statutes provided for the appointment of fence viewers. *See* 1860 Cal. Stat. 142 (viewers' role is to assess the contributions that would be needed from the landowners on each side to build a sufficient partition fence).

Some early California statutes authorized cattle-trespass victims to recover double damages in certain situations. *See, e.g.*, 1850 Cal. Stat. 131 (victim enclosed by lawful fence can recover double damages for defendant's second offense). The Estray Act of 1915 contained no double damages provisions, and no reported California decision has granted this remedy in a cattle-trespass case. *But see* NEV. REV. STAT. § 569.440(1) (1979) (entitling trespass victim situated behind a lawful fence to recover double damages for second offense if the animal owner had been negligent).

112. *See* Montezuma Improvement Co. v. Simmerly, 181 Cal. 722, 189 P. 100 (1919); Blevins v. Mullally, 22 Cal. App. 519, 135 P. 307 (1913).

to satisfy the claim.[113]

The formal law provides trespass victims with only limited self-help remedies. A victim can use reasonable force to drive the animals off his land.[114] In addition, a trespass victim willing to give the animals proper care can seize estrays and bill the costs of their care to their owner. But a victim is generally not entitled to kill or wound the offending animals.[115] For example, a fruit-grower in Mendocino County (a closed-range county) was recently convicted for malicious maiming of animals when, without prior warning to the livestock owner, he shot and killed livestock trespassing in his unfenced orchard.[116] We shall see that in this respect the formal law diverges from Shasta County mores.[117]

The distinction between open-range and closed-range has

---

113. *See* CAL. AGRIC. CODE §§ 17041, 17042, 17091–95, 17122 (West 1968 & Supp. 1985). The animal owner may contest the propriety of the victim's invocation of this self-help remedy. *See* Wigmore v. Buell, 122 Cal. 144, 54 P. 600 (1898) (construing Estray Act of 1878); Yraceburn v. Cape, 60 Cal. App. 374, 212 P. 938 (1923) (victim wrongly invoked power to seize animals). The distraint procedure also poses potentially thorny state action and due process issues. *Cf.* Flagg Brothers, Inc. v. Brooks, 436 U.S. 149 (1978) (warehouseman's sale of entrusted goods).

The "right to distrain animals damage feasant" has deep roots in the English common law. *See* 3 W. BLACKSTONE, COMMENTARIES *211; G. WILLIAMS, *supra* note 92, at 7–123.

114. People v. Dunn, 39 Cal. App. 3d 418, 114 Cal. Rptr. 164 (1974) (dictum).

Shasta County trespass victims sometimes follow the time-honored self-help strategy of herding the intruding stock to a distant and inconvenient location. *See* text accompanying note 145 *infra*. On the issue of whether this represents a reasonable exercise of self-help, compare Gilson v. Fisk, 8 N.H. 404 (1836) (trespass victim who drove herd three miles away held liable in damages for death of eight sheep), with Wells v. State, 13 S.W. 889 (Tex. Ct. App. 1890) (victim of intentional trespass did not violate criminal statute when he drove cattle 3–4 miles afield).

115. *See* Crawford v. Crawford, 88 Ga. 234, 14 S.E. 609 (1891) (statute entitled owner of slain cattle to treble damages); Bruister v. Haney, 233 Miss. 527, 102 So. 2d 806 (1958) (trespass victim held liable in damages for intentionally poisoning entering cattle); Ford v. Taggart, 4 Tex. 492 (1849) (killer of trespassing mules civilly liable to their owner). *But see* Hummel v. State, 69 Okla. Crim. 38, 99 P.2d 913 (1940) (rancher was privileged to castrate a bull that threatened to impregnate pure-bred cows that were grazing on open-range). *See generally* J. INGHAM, THE LAW OF ANIMALS § 45 (1900); Annot., 12 A.L.R.3d 1103 (1967) (liability for accidentally or intentionally poisoning trespassing stock).

116. People v. Dunn, 39 Cal. App. 3d 418, 114 Cal. Rptr. 164 (1974).

117. *See* text accompanying notes 145–146 *infra*.

Self-help justice—occasionally organized on a group basis as vigilante justice—was a tradition in the nineteenth century American West. "The laws [in Wyoming] appeared to require that a farmer fence his land to keep cattle out, but many a farmer preferred to save the cost of a fence, then wait until cattle came in his land, and with a shot or two secure a winter's supply of beef." D. BOORSTIN, THE AMERICANS: THE DEMOCRATIC EXPERIENCE 30 (1973). *See also* E. OSGOOD, *supra* note 37, at 157–60 (lynching of horse thieves), at 242 (killing of trespassing cattle) & at 252–53 (describing how large cattle companies mobilized an army to invade Johnson County, Wyoming, to prevent small ranchers from using violent self-help against the companies' cattle).

formal relevance in public as well as private trespass law. Shasta County's law enforcement officials are entitled to impound cattle found running at large in closed range, but not those found in open range.[118] Brad Bogue, the county Animal Control Officer, relies primarily on mediation and warnings when responding to reports of loose animals. Regardless of whether the trespass has occurred in open or closed range, Bogue's first priority is to locate the owner of the offending animals, and to ask him to retrieve the livestock promptly. For example, if the owner of a ranchette situated in open range were to complain of trespassing mountain cattle, Bogue would inform the complainant of the cattleman's rights in open range, but he would also find the owner of the animals and explain why it would be in the owner's interest to take better care of the livestock. Bogue asserts that little else is required in the usual case. In most years, Bogue's office does not impound a single head of cattle[119] or issue a single criminal citation for failure to prevent cattle trespass.[120]

### C. *Knowledge of Animal Trespass Law*

Before examining how Shasta County landowners actually resolve their cattle trespass disputes, I describe their working knowledge of the formal rules of trespass law. The extent of their knowledge is relevant for at least two reasons. First, Coase's Parable is set in a world of zero transaction costs, where everyone has perfect knowledge of legal rules. In reality, legal knowledge is imperfect because legal research is costly and

118. *See* SHASTA COUNTY ORDINANCE CODE § 3306 (habitual animal trespasses declared to be a public nuisance, "provided that this section shall not apply to livestock upon the open range").

119. The Shasta County Animal Control Office's Monthly Reports for 1980–1982 indicate that the office impounded one "bovine" during that period—a stray animal that Bogue said was found within one block of the office's animal shelter. This figure understates the number of public impoundments, because the Brand Inspector on occasion may ship stray cattle to the Cottonwood Auction Yard, which is better equipped than the animal shelter to board livestock.

120. Robert Baker, the County District Attorney from 1965 to 1979, could not recall a single criminal prosecution for cattle trespass on private lands. Gary Glendenning, the livestock specialist in the Detective's Division of the County Sheriff's Office, affirmed that criminal trespass actions were "never" brought, and that law enforcement officials mainly endeavored to identify and return the trespassing stock.

Criminal proceedings have been initiated against owners of stray livestock, however, when the stray animals have repeatedly posed serious risks to *motorists*. *See, e.g.*, State v. Whitlach, No. 82 CR 324 (Central Valley Just. Ct., Cal.) (misdemeanor action prompted by 26 telephone calls about cattle on roadways).

human cognitive capacities are limited. The following overview of the working legal knowledge of Shasta County residents provides a glimpse at how people behave in the face of these constraints. Analysts interested in designing legal rules to achieve specific instrumental goals must heed data of this sort, because rules cannot have instrumental effects unless they are communicated to the relevant actors. Second, most residents resolve trespass disputes by applying lower-level norms that are consistent with an overarching norm of cooperation among neighbors. To the extent that residents understand that their lower-level norms are inconsistent with formal legal rules, the more notable it is that the norms prevail.

1. *Laymen's knowledge of trespass law.*

To apply formal legal rules to a specific trespass incident, a Shasta County resident would first have to know whether it had occurred in an open-range or closed-range area of the county. Ideally, the resident would either have or know how to readily locate the map of closed-range areas published by the county's Department of Public Works. Second, a legally sophisticated person would have a working command of the rules of trespass law that were presented in the prior subpart, and know how they vary from open to closed range.

I found no one in Shasta County—layman or professional—with a complete working knowledge of the formal trespass rules just described. The persons best informed are, interestingly enough, two public officials without legal training: Brad Bogue, the Animal Control Officer, and Bruce Jordan, the Brand Inspector.[121] Their jobs require them to deal with stray livestock on almost a daily basis. Both have striven to learn applicable legal rules, and both sometimes invoke formal law when mediating disputes between county residents. Both Bogue and Jordan possess copies of the closed-range map and relevant provisions of the California Code. What they do *not* know is the case law; for example, neither is aware of the rule that an intentional trespass is always tortious, even in open-range. Nevertheless, Bogue and Jordan, both familiar figures to the cattlemen and (to a lesser extent) the ranchette owners of rural Shasta County, have done

121. Bogue is a Shasta County employee; Jordan is an employee of the California Bureau of Livestock Identification.

more than anyone else to educate the populace about formal trespass law.

What do ordinary rural residents know of that law? To a remarkable degree the landowners I interviewed did know whether their own lands were within open- or closed-range. Of the 25 I asked to identify whether they lived in open or closed range, 21 provided the correct answer, including two who were fully aware that they owned land in both.[122] This level of knowledge is probably atypically high.[123] Most of the landowner interviews were conducted in the Round Mountain and Oak Run areas. The former was the site in 1973 of the Caton's Folly closed-range battle. More importantly, Frank Ellis' aggressive herding had provoked a furious closed-range battle in the Oak Run area just six months before I conducted the interviews. Two well-placed sources—the Oak Run postmaster and the proprietress of the Oak Run general store—estimated that this political storm had caught the attention of perhaps eighty percent of the area's adult residents. In the summer of 1982, probably no populace in the United States was more alert to the legal distinction between open- and closed-range than the inhabitants of Oak Run.[124]

What do laymen know of the substance of trespass law? In particular, what do they know of how the rules vary from open- to closed-range? Laymen tend to conceive of these legal rules in black-and-white terms: Either the livestock owners or the trespass victims "have the rights." We have seen that the law of animal trespass in open-range is quite esoteric. Even there, an animal owner is liable, for example, for intentional trespass, trespass through a lawful fence, or trespass by a goat.[125] Only a few rural residents of Shasta County know anything of these subtleties. "Estray" and "lawful fence," central terms in the law of animal trespass, are not words in the cattlemen's everyday vocabulary. Neither of the two most sophisticated open-range ranchers that I interviewed were aware that enclosure by a lawful fence

122. Eleven correctly stated they lived in open-range; eight correctly stated they lived in closed-range; one gave a flatly wrong answer; one, a partially wrong answer; and two "didn't know."

123. My interviewees were disproportionately active in local politics; two had obtained copies of the Department of Public Works closed-range map in conjunction with their political endeavors.

124. Of 11 respondents asked, only three stated that they had known when they bought their land what kind of "legal range" it lay in.

125. *See* text accompanying notes 108–110 *supra*.

elevates a farmer's rights to recover for trespass. A traditionalist, whose cattle had often caused mischief in the Northeastern Foothills, thought estrays could never be seized in open-range, although a lawful fence gives a trespass victim exactly that entitlement. No interviewee believed that Ellis' intentional herding on his neighbors' lands in open-range might have been in excess of his rights.

As most laymen in rural Shasta County see it, trespass law is clear and simple. In closed-range, an animal owner is strictly liable for trespass damages. (They of course never used, and would not recognize, the phrase "strict liability.") In open-range, their basic premise is that an animal owner is never liable. When I posed hypothetical fact situations designed to put their simple rules under stress, the lay respondents sometimes backpedaled a bit, but they ultimately stuck to the notion that cattlemen have the rights in open-range and trespass victims the rights in closed-range.

2. *Legal specialists' knowledge of trespass law.*

The laymen's penchant for simplicity enabled them to identify correctly the substance of the English rule on cattle trespass that formally applies in closed-range. In that regard, the laymen outperformed the "legal specialists"—the judges, attorneys, and insurance adjusters. Although I sought out specialists who I had reason to believe would be knowledgeable about rural legal problems, I found that in two important respects the legal specialists had a worse working knowledge of trespass and estray rules than did the lay landowners.[126] First, in contrast to the landowners, the legal specialists immediately invoked *negligence* rules when asked to analyze rights in trespass cases. In general, they thought that a cattleman would not be liable for trespass in open-range (although about half seemed aware that this result would be affected by the presence of a lawful fence), and that he would be liable *only when negligent* in closed-range. The negligence approach has so dominated American tort law during this century that legal specialists—insurance adjusters in particular—may fail to identify narrow pockets where strict liability rules,

126. This startling finding can be attributed to the fact that trespass and estray claims are virtually never processed through the formal legal institutions of Shasta County. *See* text accompanying notes 151–160 *infra*.

such as the English rule on cattle trespass, formally apply.[127]

Second, unlike the lay rural residents, the legal specialists knew almost nothing about the location of the closed-range districts in the county.[128] For example, two lawyers who lived in rural Shasta County and raised livestock as a sideline, were ignorant of these boundaries; one incorrectly identified the kind of range in which he lived, and the other admitted he did not know what areas were open or closed. The latter added that this did not concern him because he would fence his lands under either legal regime.

I interviewed four insurance adjusters who settle trespass-damage claims in Shasta County. These adjusters had little working knowledge of the location of closed-range and open-range areas or of the legal significance of those designations. One incorrectly identified Shasta County as an entirely closed-range jurisdiction. Another stated that he did not keep up with the closed-range situation because "closed-range" just signifies places where there are fences, and the fence situation changes too rapidly to be worth following. The other two adjusters knew a bit more about the legal situation. Although neither possessed a closed-range map, they were able to guess how to locate one. On the other hand, both implied that they would not bother to find out whether a trespass incident had occurred in open- or closed-range before settling a claim. The liability rules that these adjusters apply to routine trespass claims seemed largely independent of formal law.[129]

### D. *The Settlement of Trespass Disputes*[130]

If Shasta County residents were to act like the farmer and the

127. Some legal specialists conceivably may also believe that the negligence principle is in every application normatively superior to the principle of strict liability.

128. Additionally, neither of the two fence contractors interviewed had any notion of these boundaries. The county tax assessor assigned to the Oak Run-Round Mountain area was equally unfamiliar with the closed-range map.

129. In his study of the settlement of automobile-liability claims, Ross found the law-in-action to be simpler and more mechanical than the formal law, but he did not find it to be quite as disconnected as I found it in trespass cases. *See* H. Ross, *supra* note 12, at 134–35, 237–40. One might expect formal liability law to be particularly toothless when it applies to situations—such as animal trespass incidents—that generate few insurance claims, and for which the claims are almost always for paltry monetary amounts.

130. The scholars involved in the Civil Liability Research Project have attempted to standardize the vocabulary of dispute resolution. They use "grievance" to describe a perceived entitlement to pursue a claim against another, "claim" to describe a demand for

rancher in Coase's Parable, they would settle their trespass problems in the following way.[131] First, they would look to the formal law to determine who had what entitlements. They would then regard those substantive rules as beyond their influence ("exogenous" to use the economists' adjective). When they faced a potentially costly interaction, such as a trespass risk to crops, they would resolve it "in the shadow of"[132] the formal legal rules. Because transactions would be costless, enforcement would be complete: No violation of an entitlement would be ignored. For the same reason, two neighbors who interacted on a number of fronts would resolve their disputes front-by-front, rather than globally. My findings cast doubt on the realism of each of these implications of the Parable. Because Coase himself was fully aware that transactions are costly and thus that the Parable was no more than an abstraction, my findings in no way diminish his monumental contribution.[133] The findings may, however, serve as a valuable caution to other law-and-economics scholars who may have underestimated the impact of transaction costs on how the world works.[134]

1. *Norms, not legal rules, are the basic sources of entitlements.*

In rural Shasta County, trespass conflicts are generally resolved not "*in* the shadow of the law" but, rather, *beyond* that shadow. Most rural residents are consciously committed to an overarching norm of cooperation among neighbors.[135] In tres-

---

redress, and "dispute" to describe a rejected claim. *See, e.g.*, Miller & Sarat, *Grievances, Claims, and Disputes: Assessing the Adversary Culture*, 15 LAW & SOC'Y REV. 525, 527 (1980–1981). I am less precise and employ these terms loosely, as they tend to be employed in ordinary speech.

131. *See* Coase, *supra* note 1, at 15.

132. This now-familiar phrase originated in Mnookin & Kornhauser, *Bargaining in the Shadow of the Law: The Case of Divorce*, 88 YALE L.J. 950 (1979).

133. *See* notes 3, 13 *supra* and accompanying texts.

134. Law-and-economics scholars often employ models that explicitly assume that actors have perfect knowledge of legal rules. *See, e.g.*, A. POLINSKY, AN INTRODUCTION TO LAW AND ECONOMICS 37–49 (1983) (assuming drivers and pedestrians know personal injury law); Shavell, *An Analysis of Causation and the Scope of Liability in the Law of Torts*, 9 J. LEGAL STUD. 463, 471 (1980).

135. Although the rural landowners were emphatic about the importance of neighborliness and could offer many specific examples of neighborly behavior, they never articulated a general formula for how a rural resident should behave. In my forthcoming book on Shasta County I hypothesize that the specific norms they honored were wealth-maximizing, and explore how wealth-maximizing norms might evolve. *See also* text following note 161 *infra*.

For other discussions of the role of nonlegal norms in dispute settlement, see Eisenberg, *Private Ordering Through Negotiation: Dispute-Settlement and Rulemaking*, 89 HARV. L. REV. 637, 638–65 (1976); Macaulay, *supra* note 12, at 61–62.

pass situations, their salient lower-level norm, adhered to by all but a few deviants, is that an owner of livestock is responsible for the acts of his animals. Allegiance to this norm seems wholly independent of formal legal entitlements. Most cattlemen believe that a rancher should keep his animals from eating a neighbor's grass, regardless of whether the range is open or closed. Cattlemen typically couch their justifications for the norm in moral terms:

> Marty Fancher: "Suppose I sat down [uninvited] to a dinner your wife had cooked." Dick Coombs: It "isn't right" to get free pasturage at the expense of one's neighbors. Owen Shellworth: "[My cattle] don't belong [in my neighbor's field]." Attorney-rancher Pete Schultz: A cattleman is "morally obligated to fence" to protect his neighbor's crops, even in open range.

The next several pages describe in greater detail how the norms of neighborliness operate and how deviants who violate these norms are informally controlled. These pages also identify another set of deviants: trespass victims who actually invoke their formal legal rights.

2. *Incomplete enforcement: the live-and-let-live philosophy.*

The norm that an animal owner should control his stock is modified by another norm that holds that a rural resident should "lump" minor damage stemming from isolated trespass incidents. The neighborly response to an isolated infraction is an exchange of civilities. A trespass victim should notify the animal owner that the trespass has occurred and assist the owner in retrieving the stray stock. Virtually all residents have telephones, the standard means of communication. A telephone report is regarded not as a form of complaint, but rather as a service to the animal owner, who, after all, has a valuable asset on the loose. Upon receiving a telephone report, a cattleman who is a good neighbor will quickly retrieve the animals (by truck if necessary), apologize for the occurrence, and thank the caller. The Mortons and the Shellworths, two ranching families in the Oak Run area particularly esteemed for their neighborliness, are known for promptly and apologetically responding to their neighbors' notifications of trespass.[136]

136. A trespass victim who cannot recognize the brand of the intruding animal—a quandary more common for ranchette owners than for ranchers—may telephone county authorities. Calls of this sort are eventually referred to the Brand Inspector or Animal Control

Several realities of rural life in Shasta County help explain why residents are expected to lump trespass losses. First, it is commonplace for a country landowner to lose a bit of forage or to suffer minor fence damage. The area northeast of Redding lies on a deer migration route. During the late winter and early spring thousands of deer and elk move through the area, easily jumping the barbed wire fences.[137] Because wild animals trespass so often, most rural residents come to regard minor damage from alien animals not as an injurious event, but as an inevitable part of life.

Second, most residents expect to be on both the giving and receiving ends of trespass incidents. Even the ranchette owners have, if not a few hobby livestock, at least several dogs, which they keep for companionship, security, and pest control. Unlike cattle, dogs that trespass may harass, or even kill, other farm animals. If trespass risks are symmetrical, and if residents lump all trespass losses, accounts balance in the long run. Under these conditions, the advantage of reciprocal lumping is that each person is made whole without having to expend time or money to settle disputes.

The norm of reciprocal restraint that underlies "live-and-let-live" also calls for ranchers to lump the costs of boarding another person's animal, even for months at a time. A cattleman often finds in his herd an animal wearing someone else's brand. If he recognizes the brand he will customarily inform its owner, but the two will often agree that the simplest solution is for the animal to stay put until the trespass victim next gathers his animals, an event that may be weeks or months away. The cost of "cutting" a single animal from a larger herd seems to underlie this custom. Thus, ranchers often consciously provide other people's cattle with feed worth perhaps as much as $10 to $100 per animal. Although Shasta County ranchers tend to regard themselves as financially pinched, even ranchers who know that they are legally entitled to recover feeding costs virtually never seek monetary compensation for boarding estrays. The largest

Officer, who, as mentioned, then regard their main priority to be return of the animal to its owner.

137. One rancher reported that during the winter he expects to find 30–40 deer grazing in his hayfield each night. The owner of a particularly large ranch estimated that about 500 deer winter there—a condition he likes, because deer are "part of nature." John Woodbury, a key lobbyist for the passage of the Caton's Folly ordinance, stated that elk and deer had eaten more of the grass in his alfalfa field than mountain cattle ever had.

ranchers northeast of Redding who were interviewed reported that they had never charged anyone, or been charged by anyone, for costs of that sort. Even when they do not know to whom a stray animal belongs, they put the animal in their truck the next time they take a load of animals to the auctionyard at Cottonwood, and drop it off without charge so that the Brand Inspector can locate the owner.[138]

3. *The complexity of interneighbor relations: comprehensive mental accounts of who owes whom.*

Residents with few animals may of course not perceive any average reciprocity of advantage in a live-and-let-live approach to animal trespass incidents. What if, for example, a particular rancher's livestock repeatedly caused minor mischief in a particular farmer's fields? In that situation, Shasta County norms call for the farmer to keep track of those minor losses in a mental account. Eventually, the norms entitle him to act to remedy any imbalance.

A fundamental feature of rural society makes this enforcement system feasible: *Rural residents deal with one another on a large number of fronts, and most residents expect those interactions to continue far into the future.* In sociological terms, their relationships are "multiplex," not "simplex."[139] They interact on water supply, controlled burns, fence repairs, social events, staffing the volunteer fire department, and so on. Where population densities are low, each neighbor looms larger. Thus any trespass dispute with a neighbor is almost certain to be but one thread in the rich fabric of a continuing relationship.

A person in a multiplex relationship can keep a rough mental

138. Brand Inspector Bruce Jordan estimated that ranchers drop off approximately 300 head of stray livestock at the auctionyard each year, and that these ranchers typically decline to seek compensation from the owners of the strays.

139. *See* R. Kidder, Connecting Law and Society 70–72 (1983). The law and society literature has long emphasized that law is not likely to be important to parties enmeshed in a continuing relationship. For example, Marc Galanter has observed:

> In the American setting, litigation tends to be between parties who are strangers. Either they never had a mutually beneficial continuing relationship, as in the typical automobile case, or their relationship—marital, commercial, or organizational—is ruptured. In either case, there is no anticipated future relationship. In the American setting, unlike some others, resort to litigation is [usually] viewed as an irreparable breach of the relationship.

Galanter, *Reading the Landscape of Disputes: What We Know and Don't Know (and Think We Know) About Our Allegedly Contentious and Litigious Society*, 31 U.C.L.A. L. Rev. 4, 24–25 (1983) (brackets in original).

account of the outstanding credits and debits in each aspect of that relationship.[140] Should the aggregate account fall out of balance, tension may mount because the net creditor may begin to perceive the net debtor as an overreacher. On the other hand, so long as the aggregate account is in balance, neither party need be concerned that particular subaccounts are not. For example, if a rancher were to owe a farmer in the trespass subaccount, the farmer can be expected to remain content if that imbalance were to be offset by a debt he owed the rancher in, say, the water-supply subaccount.[141]

The live-and-let-live norm also suggests that neighbors should put up with minor imbalances in their aggregate accounts, especially when they perceive that their future interactions will provide adequate opportunities for settling old scores. Creditors may prefer having others in their debt. For example, when Larry Brennan lost six to seven tons of baled hay to Frank Ellis' cattle in open range, Brennan (although he did not know it) had a strong legal claim against Ellis for intentional trespass. Brennan estimated his loss at between $300 and $500, hardly a trivial amount. When Ellis learned of Brennan's loss he told Brennan to "come down and take some hay" from Ellis' barn. Brennan declined this offer of compensation, partly because he thought he should not have piled the bales in an unfenced area, but also because, to paraphrase his words, he would rather have Ellis in debt to him than be in debt to Ellis. Brennan was willing to let Ellis run up a deficit in their aggregate interpersonal accounts because he thought that as a creditor he would have more leverage over Ellis' future behavior.

4. *The control of deviants: the key role of self-help.*

The rural Shasta County population includes deviants who do not adequately control their livestock and do not adequately bal-

140. *Cf.* A. Vidich & J. Bensman, Small Town in Mass Society 34 (rev. ed. 1968):

> To a great extent these arrangements between friends and neighbors have a reciprocal character: a man who helps others may himself expect to be helped later on. In a way the whole system takes on the character of insurance. Of course some people are more conscious of their premium payments than others and keep a kind of mental bookkeeping on "what they owe and who owes them what," which is a perfectly permissible practice so long as one does not openly confront others with unbalanced accounts.

141. *See* O. Williamson, Markets and Hierarchies 256–57 (1975) (a party to a continuing relationship seeks to achieve a favorable balance in the overall set of interactions, not in each separate interaction).

ance their informal accounts with their neighbors. Frank Ellis, for example, seemed to care little about his reputation among his neighbors. In general, the traditionalists who let their animals loose in the mountains during the summer are less scrupulous than the modernists are in honoring the norms of neighborliness, perhaps because the traditionalists have less complex, and shorter-lived, interrelationships with the persons who encounter their range cattle.

To discipline deviants, the residents of rural Shasta County use the following four types of countermeasures, listed in escalating order of seriousness: (1) self-help retaliation; (2) reports to county authorities; (3) claims for compensation informally submitted without the help of attorneys; and (4) formal legal claims to recover damages. The law starts to gain bite as one moves down this list.

*Self-help.* Because most trespass disputes in Shasta County are resolved according to extralegal rules, the fundamental enforcement device is also extralegal. A measured amount of self-help—just enough to "get even," to invoke a marvelously apt phrase—is the predominant and ethically preferred response to someone who has not taken adequate steps to prevent his animals from trespassing.[142]

The mildest form of self-help is negative gossip.[143] This usually works because only the extreme deviants are immune from the general obsession with neighborliness. Although the Oak Run-Round Mountain area is undergoing a rapid increase in population, it remains distinctly rural in atmosphere. People tend to know one another, and they value their reputations in the community. Some ranching families have lived in the area for several generations and plan to stay indefinitely. Members of these families seem particularly intent on maintaining their reputations as good neighbors. Should one of them not promptly and courteously retrieve an estray, he might fear that any resulting gossip would permanently besmirch the family name.

Residents of the Northeastern Foothills seem quite conscious of the role of gossip in their system of social control. One long-time resident, who had also lived for many years in a suburb of a

142. *See generally* Black, *Crime as Social Control,* 48 AM. SOC. REV. 34 (1983) (a trenchant assessment of the phenomenon of self-help).

143. *See* Merry, *Rethinking Gossip and Scandal,* in 1 TOWARD A GENERAL THEORY OF SOCIAL CONTROL 271 (D. Black ed. 1984).

major California urban area, observed that people in the Oak Run area "gossip all the time," much more than in the urban area. Another reported intentionally using gossip to sanction a traditionalist who had been "impolite" when coming to pick up some stray mountain cattle; he reported that application of this self-help device produced an apology, an outcome itself presumably circulated through the gossip system.

The furor over Frank Ellis' loose cattle in the Oak Run area induced area residents to try a sophisticated variation of the gossip sanction. The ranchette residents who were particularly bothered by Ellis' cattle could see that he was utterly indifferent to his reputation among them. On the other hand, they thought that a large rancher such as Ellis would worry about his reputation among the large cattle operators in the county. They therefore reported Ellis' activities to the Board of Directors of the Shasta County Cattlemen's Association. This move proved unrewarding, for Ellis was also surprisingly indifferent to his reputation among the cattlemen. As the Association President later explained in a hearing before the county Board of Supervisors, the problem was that Ellis, a county resident for a decade, "hasn't been [in the County] all that long."[144]

When milder measures such as gossip fail, a person is regarded as being justified in threatening to use, and perhaps even actually using, tougher self-help sanctions. Particularly in unfenced country, a victim may respond to repeated cattle trespasses by herding the offending animals to a location extremely inconvenient for their owner.[145] Another common response to repeated trespasses is to threaten to kill a responsible animal should it ever enter again. Although the killing of trespassing livestock is a crime in California,[146] six landowners—not noticeably less civilized than the others—unhesitatingly volunteered that they had issued death threats of this sort. These threats are credible in Shasta County, because victims of recurring trespasses, particularly if they have first issued a warning, feel justified in killing or injuring the mischievous animals. Despite the criminality of the conduct (a fact not necessarily known to the

144. *See* note 75 *supra*.

145. Two respondents admitted that they had done this. For some scattered precedents on the legality of this practice, see note 114 *supra*.

146. CAL. PENAL CODE § 597(a) (West Supp. 1985); People v. Dunn, 39 Cal. App. 3d 418, 114 Cal. Rptr. 164 (1974).

respondents), I learned the identity of two persons who had shot trespassing cattle. Another landowner told of running the steer of an uncooperative neighbor into a fence. The most intriguing report came from a rancher who had had recurrent problems with a trespassing bull many years ago. This rancher told a key law enforcement official that he wanted to castrate the bull—"to turn it into a steer." The official replied that he "would have deaf ears" if that were to occur. The rancher asserted that he then carried out his threat.

It is difficult to estimate how frequently rural residents actually resort to violent self-help. Nevertheless, fear of physical retaliation is undoubtedly one of the major incentives for order in rural Shasta County. Ranchers who run herds at large freely admit that they worry that their trespassing cattle might meet with violence. One traditionalist reported that he is responsive to complaints from ranchette owners because he fears they will poison or shoot his stock. A judge for a rural district of the county asserted that a vicious animal is likely to "disappear" if its owner does not control it. A resident of the Oak Run area stated that some area residents responded to Frank Ellis' practice of running herds at large by rustling Ellis' cattle. He suggested that Ellis prepare a teeshirt with the following inscription: "Eat Ellis Beef. Everyone in Oak Run Does!"

*Complaints to public officials.*[147] The long-time ranchers of Shasta County pride themselves on being able to resolve their problems on their own. Except when they lose animals to rustlers, they do not seek help from public officials. Although ranchette owners also use the self-help remedies of gossip and violence, they, unlike the cattlemen, sometimes respond to a trespass incident by contacting a county official who they think will remedy the problem. These calls are usually funneled to the Animal Control Officer or Brand Inspector, who report that most of their callers are ranchette owners with limited rural experience. As already discussed, these calls do produce results. The county officials typically contact the owner of the animal, who then arranges for its removal. Brad Bogue, the Animal Control Officer, reported that in half the cases the caller knows whose animal it is. This suggests that callers often think that requests

147. *Cf.* Engel, *Cases, Conflict, and Accommodation: Patterns of Legal Interaction in an American Community*, 1983 AM. B. FOUND. RESEARCH J. 803, 821 (role of complaints to public officials in a rural Illinois county).

for removal have more effect when issued by someone in authority.

Mere removal of an animal may provide only temporary relief if its owner is a mountain lessee whose cattle repeatedly descend upon the ranchettes. County officials therefore use mild threats to caution repeat offenders. In closed-range, they may mention both their power to impound the estrays and the risk of criminal prosecution. These threats appear to be bluffs; the County never impounds stray cattle when it can locate an owner, and it rarely prosecutes cattlemen (and then only when their animals have posed risks to motorists).[148] In open-range, county officials may deliver a more subtle threat: not that they will initiate a prosecution, but that, if the owner does not mend his ways, the Board of Supervisors may face insuperable pressure to close the range in the relevant area. Because cattlemen perceive that a closure significantly diminishes their legal entitlements in situations where motorists have collided with their livestock, this threat can catch their attention.

A trespass victim's most effective official protest is one delivered directly to his elected county supervisor—the person best situated to change stray-cattle liability rules. Many Shasta County residents are aware that traditionalist cattlemen fear the supervisors more than they fear law enforcement authorities. Thus in 1973, alfalfa farmer John Woodbury made his repeated phone calls about mountain cattle not to Brad Bogue but to Supervisor John Caton.[149] When a supervisor receives many calls from trespass victims, his first instinct is to mediate the crisis. Former supervisor Norman Wagoner's standard procedure was to assemble the ranchers in the area and advise them to put pressure on the offender or else risk the closure of the range. Wagoner's successor, Supervisor John Caton, similarly told Frank Ellis that he would support a closure at Oak Run unless Ellis built three miles of fence along the Oak Run Road. If a supervisor is not responsive to a constituent's complaint, the constituent may respond by circulating a closure petition.[150]

*The rarity of claims for monetary relief.* Because Shasta County residents tend to settle their trespass disputes beyond the

148. *See* notes 119–120 *supra* and accompanying text.

149. *See* text following note 68 *supra.*

150. This was how Doug Heinz goaded Supervisor John Caton into action at Oak Run. *See* text accompanying note 72 *supra.*

shadow of the law, one might expect that the norms of neighborliness would include a norm against the invocation of formal legal rights. And this norm is indeed strongly established.[151] Owen Shellworth: "I don't believe in lawyers [because there are] always hard feelings [when you litigate]." Tony Morton: "[I never press a monetary claim because] I try to be a good neighbor." Norman Wagoner: "Being good neighbors means no lawsuits." Although trespasses are frequent, *Shasta County's rural residents virtually never file formal trespass actions against one another.* John Woodbury, for example, made dozens of phone calls to Supervisor John Caton, but never sought monetary compensation from the traditionalists whose cattle had repeatedly marauded his alfalfa field. Court records and conversations with court clerks indicate that in most years not a single private lawsuit is filed in the county's courts seeking damages for either trespass by livestock or the expense of boarding estrays.[152] The residents of the Northeastern Foothills not only refrain from filing formal lawsuits, but they are also strongly disinclined to submit informal monetary claims to an owner of trespassing animals or that owner's insurance company.[153]

The landowners who were interviewed clearly regard their restraint in seeking monetary relief as a mark of virtue. When asked why they did not pursue meritorious legal claims arising from trespass or fence-finance disputes, various landowners replied: "I'm not that kind of guy;" "I don't believe in it;" "I don't like to create a stink;" "I try to get along." The landowners who attempted to provide a rationale for this forbearance all implied the same one, a long-term reciprocity of advantage. Ann Kershaw: "The only one that makes money [when you litigate] is the lawyer." Al Levy: "I figure it will balance out in the long run."

151. Investigators have found norms against litigation in other social environments. *See* Engel, *supra* note 147, at 816–22, 851–56 (rural Illinois county); Macaulay, *supra* note 12, at 64 (Wisconsin businessmen).

152. In the Burney Justice Court, the 1980 small claims files showed no animal trespass cases, and the clerks could recall no such cases in their four years on the job.

In the Central Valley Justice Court, no small claims for the 8/81 to 6/82 period involved animal trespass, and the civil clerk who had worked there for 11 years could not remember any. The index of defendants for the 1975–82 period indicated that Frank Ellis was the only large rancher to become the target of any kind of legal action. *See* text accompanying notes 155–160 *infra*.

153. I did hear several secondhand reports of informally settled claims for the costs of boarding estrays. Only one rancher told of paying such a claim; he regarded the claimant's pursuit of the money as a "cheap move."

Pete Schultz: "I hope they'll do the same for me." Phil Ritchie: "My family believes in 'live and let live.' "

Mutual restraint saves parties with long-term relationships the costs of going through the formal claims process. Adjoining landowners who practice live-and-let-live are both better off whenever the negative externalities from their activities are roughly in equipoise. Equipoise is as likely in closed-range as in open. Landowners with property in closed-range—the ones with the greatest formal legal rights—were the source of half of the quotations in the prior two paragraphs.

Shasta County landowners regard a monetary settlement as an arms-length transaction that symbolizes an unneighborly relationship. Should your goat happen to eat your neighbor's tomatoes, the neighborly thing for you to do would be to help replant the tomatoes; a transfer of money would be too cold and too impersonal.[154] When Kevin O'Hara's cattle went through a break in a fence and destroyed his neighbor's corn crop (a loss of less than $100), O'Hara had to work hard to persuade his neighbor to accept O'Hara's offer of money damages. O'Hara insisted on making this payment because he "felt responsible" for his neighbor's loss, a feeling that would not have been in the least affected had the event occurred in open- instead of closed-range. There can also be social pressure against offering money settlements. Bob Bosworth's father agreed many decades ago to pay damages to a trespass victim in a closed-range area just south of Shasta County; other cattlemen then rebuked him for setting an unfortunate precedent. The junior Bosworth, currently President of the Shasta County Cattlemen's Association, could recall no other out-of-pocket settlement in a trespass case.

Trespass victims who sustain an unusually large loss are more likely to take the potentially deviant step of making a claim for monetary relief. I interviewed adjusters for the two insurance companies whose liability policies would be most likely to cover losses from animal trespass. The adjusters' responses suggest that in a typical year these companies receive fewer than ten trespass damage claims originating in Shasta County. In the paradig-

154. A donor who wishes to symbolize an intimate relationship typically gives, not currency, but a gift that apparently required special effort to prepare. *See* Landa, *The Enigma of the* Kula Ring: *Gift-Exchanges and Primitive Law and Order*, 3 INT'L REV. L. & ECON. 137, 152 (1983) (Melanesians return armshells for necklaces because to return a necklace for a necklace would be interpreted as a rejection of friendship). *See generally* M. MAUSS, THE GIFT (1967).

matic case, the insured is not a rancher, but rather a ranchette owner whose family's horse escaped and trampled a neighboring homeowner's shrubbery. The claimant is typically not represented by an attorney—a type of professional these adjusters rarely encounter. The adjusters also settle each year two or three trespass claims that homeowners or ranchette owners have brought against ranchers. Ranchers who suffer trespasses virtually never file claims against others' insurance companies. An adjuster for the company that insures most Shasta County ranchers stated that he could not recall, in his twenty years of adjusting, a single rancher's claim for compensation for trespass damage.

The landowners, particularly the ranchers, express a strong aversion to hiring an attorney to fight one's battles. To hire an attorney is to escalate a conflict. A good neighbor does not do such a thing because the "natural working order" calls for two neighbors to work out their problems between themselves. The files in the Shasta County courthouses reveal that the ranchers who honor norms of neighborliness—the vast majority—are simply not involved in cattle-related litigation of any kind.

My field research uncovered two instances in which animal trespass victims in the Oak Run-Round Mountain area had turned to attorneys. In one of these cases the victim actually filed a formal complaint. Because attorney-backed claims are so unusual, these two disputes deserve elaboration.

The first dispute involved Tom Hailey and Curtis McCall. For three generations, Hailey's family has owned a large tract of foothill forest in an open-range area near Oak Run. In about 1978, Hailey discovered McCall's cattle grazing on some of Hailey's partially fenced land. Hailey suspected that McCall had brought the animals in through a gate in Hailey's fence. When Hailey confronted him, McCall, who lived about a mile away, acted as if the incursion had been accidental. Hailey subsequently found a salt block on the tract—an object he could fairly assume that McCall had put there to service his herd. Hailey thus concluded that McCall had not only deliberately trespassed, but had also aggravated the offense by untruthfully denying the charge. Hailey seized the salt block and consulted an attorney, who advised him to seek compensation from McCall. The two principals eventually agreed to a small monetary settlement.

Hailey is a semi-retired government employee who spends much of his time outside of Shasta County; he is regarded as reclusive and eccentric—certainly someone outside the mainstream of Oak Run society. McCall, a retired engineer with a hard-driving style, moved to Shasta County in the late 1970s to run a small livestock ranch. The Haileys refer to him as a "Texan"—a term that connotes someone who is both an outsider and lacks neighborly instincts.

The second dispute involved Doug Heinz and Frank Ellis. As already noted, Heinz had the misfortune of owning a ranchette near Ellis' ranch.[155] After experiencing repeated problems with Ellis' cattle, Heinz unilaterally seized three of the animals that had broken through his fence. Heinz boarded these animals for three months without notifying Ellis. Heinz later asserted he intended to return them when Ellis next held a roundup. According to Heinz, Ellis eventually found out that Heinz had the animals and asked for their return. Heinz agreed to return them if Ellis would pay pasturage. When Ellis replied, "You know I'm good for it," Heinz released the animals and sent Ellis a bill. Ellis refused to pay the bill, and he further infuriated Heinz by calling him "boy" whenever Heinz brought up the debt.

On January 8, 1981, Heinz filed a small-claims action against Ellis to recover $750 "for property damage, hay and grain ate [sic] by defendant's cattle, boarding of animals."[156] Acting through the attorney he kept on retainer, Ellis responded eight days later with a separate civil suit against Heinz.[157] Ellis's complaint sought $1,500 compensatory and $10,000 punitive damages from Heinz for the shooting deaths of two Black Brangus cows that Ellis had pastured on BLM lands; it also sought compensation for the weight loss Ellis' three live animals had sustained during the months Heinz had been feeding them. The two legal actions were later consolidated. Heinz, who called Ellis' allegation that Heinz had killed two cows "100 percent lies" and "scare tactics," hired a bright young Redding attorney to represent him. This attorney threatened to pursue a malicious prosecution action against Ellis if Ellis persisted in asserting that Heinz had slain the Black Brangus cows. In December 1981, the parties agreed to a settlement under the terms of which Ellis paid Heinz $300 in damages and $100 for attorney fees. Ellis' insurance company picked up the tab. By that time Heinz was

155. *See* text following note 70 *supra*.

156. Heinz v. Ellis, No. 81 SC 7 (Cent. Valley Just. Ct. filed Jan. 8, 1981).

157. Ellis v. Heinz, No. 81 CV 6 (Cent. Valley Just. Ct. filed Jan. 16, 1981).

spearheading a political campaign to close the range Ellis had been using.[158]

The Heinz-Ellis and Hailey-McCall disputes share several characteristics. Although both arose in open range, in each instance legal authority favored the trespass victim: Hailey, because McCall's trespass had been intentional; and Heinz, because Ellis' animals had broken through an apparently lawful fence.[159] In both instances, the victim, before consulting an attorney, had attempted to obtain informal satisfaction but had been rebuffed. Each victim perceived that the animal owner had not been honest. Each dispute was ultimately settled in the victim's favor. In both instances, neither the trespass victim nor the cattle owner was well-socialized in rural Shasta County norms. Thus other respondents tended to refer to the four individuals involved in these two claims as "bad apples," "odd ducks," or otherwise as people not aware of the natural working order. Ordinary people, it seems, do not often turn to attorneys to help resolve disputes.[160]

## V. Summary and Implications

Coase's Parable of the Farmer and the Rancher, like most writing in law and economics, implies that disputants look solely to formal legal rules to determine their entitlements. In rural Shasta County, California, residents instead typically look to informal norms to determine their entitlements in animal trespass situations. In open-range areas, the norm that a livestock owner should supervise his animals dominates the legal rule that a cattleman is not legally liable for unintentional trespasses on unfenced land. Trespass victims mainly employ negative gossip and physical reprisals against trespassing stock to discipline cattlemen who violate this norm.

In Shasta County, the law of trespass had no apparent feed-

158. *See* text accompanying notes 71–76 *supra.*

159. Heinz had technically imperiled his statutory claim for damages under the Estray Act when he failed to notify the proper public authorities promptly that he had taken up Ellis' animals. *See* Cal. Agric. Code §§ 17042, 17095 (West 1967).

160. *See also* W. Nelson, Dispute and Conflict Resolution in Plymouth Colony, Massachusetts 1725–1825 (1981) (Plymouth's particularly litigious individuals during the 1725–1774 period tended to be people who were poorly socialized); Todd, *Litigious Marginals: Character and Disputing in a Bavarian Village*, in The Disputing Process: Law in Ten Societies, *supra* note 12, at 86, 118 (socially marginal people were disproportionately represented in civil and criminal litigation).

back effects on trespass norms. In no instance did the legal designation of an area as open (or closed) range affect how residents resolved a trespass or estray dispute. Thus Rancher Kevin O'Hara paid a neighbor for the loss of a corn crop because he "felt responsible," a feeling he said would not have been influenced by formal trespass law. Being located in closed range did not appear to make a trespass victim more likely to perceive a grievance or to exercise self-help. Insurance adjusters paid virtually no attention to the distinction between open-range and closed-range when settling trespass claims.

Other findings suggest the unreality of other literal features of the Coasean Parable. Victims of stray cattle did not treat the formal legal rules as exogenous; they were aware that one way to use limited resources is to lobby for legal change. Victims' enforcement of their norm-based entitlements was far from complete; they ignored some trespasses altogether and used others to offset outstanding informal debts. Victims tended to shun monetary settlements and instead preferred in-kind transfers, including ones effected through self-help. Although these findings are at odds with the literal features of the Coasean Parable, they are fully consistent with Coase's central idea that, regardless of the specific content of law, people tend to structure their affairs to their mutual advantage.

The Shasta County evidence suggests that law and economics scholars need to pay more heed to how transaction costs influence the resolution of disputes. Because it is costly to carry out legal research and to engage in legal proceedings, a rational actor often has good reason to apply informal norms, not law, to evaluate the propriety of human behavior. Contracts scholars have long known that norms are likely to be especially influential when disputants share a continuing relationship.[161] A farmer and a rancher who own adjoining lands are enduringly intertwined, and therefore readily able to employ nonlegal methods of dispute resolution. Law-and-economics scholars misdirect their readers and students when they invoke examples—such as the Parable of the Farmer and the Rancher—that greatly exaggerate the domain of human activity upon which the law casts a shadow.

This article will be incorporated into a forthcoming book on

161. *See, e.g.*, Macaulay, *supra* note 12; Macneil, *The Many Futures of Contracts*, 47 S. CAL. L. REV. 691, 715 (1974).

dispute resolution among neighbors. Other parts of the book will describe how Shasta County residents resolve disputes over both the financing of boundary fences and the allocation of losses stemming from vehicle-livestock collisions on highways. The book will explain why proposed closed-range ordinances generate so much political heat in Shasta County even though trespass law is itself practically irrelevant. Finally and more ambitiously, in the book I will use the Shasta County data as a springboard to develop a theory of the content and role of norms. Building on recent work in game theory, I hypothesize that, in the absence of identified "social imperfections," the norms that govern the relations among members of a group tend to maximize the aggregate wealth of group members. The book will explore the normative and positive implications of this theory for the interplay between the legal system and more informal systems of social control.

# [6]

# THE COASE THEOREM AND CALIFORNIA ANIMAL TRESPASS LAW

*KENNETH R. VOGEL**

## I. Introduction

THE modern study of law and economics is often the study of transaction costs.[1] Sometimes the inquiry is normative, and the question is which assignment of rights will minimize transaction costs and thus promote overall social welfare. Sometimes the inquiry is positive and asks what effect different rights assignments have had on the behavior of the parties whose conduct the law governed. In his pathbreaking paper "The Problem of Social Cost,"[2] Ronald Coase used the classic conflict between the rancher and the farmer to illustrate the central role that these transaction costs played. In this paper I return to this problem not only from a normative—analytical—but also from a positive—historical—point of view.

Until 1960, when Coase published "The Problem of Social Cost," causation was a fairly settled issue for lawyers and economists interested in

* Associate Professor of Law and Leonard Cohen Research Fellow in Law and Economics, Loyola Law School, Los Angeles. This work was supported in part by a grant from the National Science Foundation (DAR-80-11904). The analyses, opinions, and conclusions are those of the author and not of the Foundation. I would like to thank Robert Ellickson, Matthew Spitzer, Mitchell Polinsky, and Victor Goldberg as well as participants in the Conference on Property Rights of the Verein für Socialpolitik in Basel for their helpful criticisms and comments. I am also indebted to Frances Maloy and David Gianturco for their valuable assistance in carrying out the empirical analysis and to Erich Luschei for all his invaluable help.

1 The term "transaction costs" is used here in the broadest possible sense as any technical market failure or public good that would prevent the attainment of an internal social optimum. Often transaction costs are defined to be only those costs that increase the costs of negotiating or enforcing a contract. For a thorough development of the concept of transaction costs, see Oliver E. Williamson, Markets and Hierarchies: Analysis and Antitrust Implications (1975).

2 Ronald Coase, The Problem of Social Cost, 3 J. Law & Econ. 1 (1960). For an extensive list of the literature that has analyzed the Coase theorem, see Elizabeth Hoffman & Matthew L. Spitzer, The Coase Theorem: Some Experimental Tests, 25 J. Law & Econ. 73 (1982).

[*Journal of Legal Studies*, vol. XVI (January 1987)]
 0047-2530/87/1601-0009$01.50

the problem of externalities. It seemed clear that a generator of externalities would be the cause of resulting harm. For example, if a firm manufacturing steel also emitted smoke that damaged the laundry next door, the smoke from the steel mill was said to cause harm to the laundry. It was also agreed that the proper party for the law to influence, if there were a significant enough reason for the state to be involved, would be that generator, although there was some disagreement whether the proper means was regulation, prohibition, or taxation.[3]

Coase changed the nature of the discussion by his far-reaching insight that the nature of causation is a reciprocal phenomenon, so that either the generator or the receptor could be considered to be the cause of the harm. In the previous example, the laundry also caused the damage by operating its business in proximity to the steel mill. To avoid the harm, the steel mill could shut down or adopt antipollution measures. Alternatively, the laundry could move or do all its work in an enclosed space. In principle, if causation is reciprocal, it becomes equally appropriate for the government to assign rights, or taxes and subsidies, to either party. In fact, Coase went so far as to postulate that in a well-functioning market system[4] identical production would result regardless of the original assignment of rights. Coase showed that, except for income or wealth effects in consumption,[5] it would be a matter of complete indifference to whom the rights are assigned, except to the affected parties' wealth.

The next section of the paper, through a discussion of nonconvexities and transactional asymmetries, examines the circumstances in which an original assignment of rights can prevent the parties from bargaining incrementally to a social optimum. The third section presents a historical analysis. It examines the way in which the assignment of rights between farmers and cattle ranchers influenced their behavior in a discrete time and place: California in the last half of the nineteenth century. It contains a discussion of the various types of laws that were used to regulate the conflict between farmers and ranchers and demonstrates the shift with time toward greater protection of farmers. The third section reports the results of a standard regression analysis to confirm the central theoretical

[3] For the original discussion of the use of taxation in controlling externalities, see A. C. Pigou, The Economics of Welfare, 172 *et seq.* & 192–96 (1952). For an application of the three rules to the assignment of rights when externalities occur, see also A. Mitchell Polinsky, Controlling Externalities and Protecting Entitlements: Property Rights, Liability Rule, and Tax-Subsidy Approaches, 8 J. Legal Stud. 1 (1979).

[4] This has been interpreted as a system with no transaction costs by the voluminous post-Coasean literature; see, for example, Richard O. Zerbe, Jr., The Problem of Social Cost in Retrospect, 2 Research in L. & Econ. 83 (1980).

[5] When the income of consumers changes, they will purchase a different bundle of goods. More wealthy consumers are more likely to consume meat and less likely to eat potatoes.

point: the original assignment of rights does matter in a consistent foreseeable way. The assignment of rights toward the farmer tended systematically to increase the overall levels of production.

## II. Nonconvexities and Transactional Asymmetries in the Bargaining Process

Given Coase's assumptions, the search for ideal property right configurations[6] becomes a search for entitlements that advance overall efficiency (defined as some Pareto superior state in which one person has been made better off without making anyone worse off). Yet, apart from minimizing transaction costs, there appear to be no accepted criteria for directing the behavior of government in the design of property rights systems. Because it is not clear when transaction costs will be minimized, it is difficult to justify any general legal entitlements.

Applied to the example of the steel plant and the laundry, Coase's views make it problematic whether the sound legal regime allows the steel mill the unbridled right to pollute or entitles the laundry to be free from the pollution. In yet another classic example close to the historical concerns of this paper, it becomes unclear whether the rancher should have the privilege of allowing his cattle to wander on the farmer's land or whether the farmer should have the right to exclude everyone, including cattle ranchers, from using his land without his permission. Both situations do have this parallel. The harm inflicted by the steel mill or the rancher on the laundry or the farmer is a direct consequence of the acts of the mill or the rancher. In contrast, if the legal entitlement is given to the farmer or the laundry, the harm inflicted on the steel mill or the rancher requires the intervention of the legal system.

The essence of Coase's hypothesis is that, in the absence of transaction costs, the parties will trade for the right to interfere more (to emit more smoke over the laundry or to have more cattle trespass over more of the farmer's land) or to be freer from interference (to have less smoke or to have fewer cattle trespassing over less land). By taking this right, whichever way it is defined, into account, its full opportunity cost will be realized. If Coase is correct, the parties will trade until the final, equilibrium allocation of rights and duties between them is efficient. Efficiency means some Pareto optimal state in which no one can be made better off without making someone worse off.

[6] The conditions for an efficient system of property rights are universality, transferability, and exclusivity, according to Posner. See Richard A. Posner, Economic Analysis of Law, ch. 2 (2d ed. 1977). For the limits on transferability, see Richard A. Epstein, Why Restrain Alienation? 85 Colum. L. Rev. 970 (1985).

There have been a number of criticisms of this hypothesis, three of which are useful for testing its limits. The first comes from ordinary language theorists like Epstein. Epstein (among others) has suggested that efficiency is at best a second-stage consideration. It should be considered only after decisions on fairness have been reached.[7] Epstein criticizes Coase's concept of causation, which implies that a joint condition of the two parties is usually necessary for the creation of any harm. He uses Coase's own language, which differentiates between the causing agent (subject of the sentence) and the harmed party (object of the sentence): "[A] confectioner the noise and vibration from whose machinery *disturbed* a doctor"; "straying cattle which *destroy* crops on neighbouring land." He then notes that it is only by the use of the legal system that the doctor could harm the confectioner or the farmer could harm the rancher; therefore the situations do not truly exhibit the causal reciprocity that Coase insists they have. However, Epstein does not then give a "simple semantic equivalent to the concept of causation." Rather he gives four distinct paradigmatic cases: "A hit B"; "A frightened B"; "A compelled B to hit C"; and "A created the dangerous condition that resulted in harm to B."[8]

What ties Epstein's cases together can best be understood as the liberty enhancing goals of freedom from force and from falsehood.[9] Epstein believes that an animal trespass rule should allow a cause of action on the grounds of "your cattle ate my crops," although it is not clear what kind of assumption of risk defense would be allowed for failure to fence or from planting too close to the fence.[10] Unfortunately, Epstein's theory does not lend itself to any simple general theory of nonreciprocity, which is needed to define the limits of Coase. Therefore, in an attempt to make the ordinary language criticism of Coase more explicit, an analysis of two additional sources of development, from the law-and-economics literature, may be useful.

The second view comes out of the transaction costs approach. It was propounded by Coase and developed by Wittman.[11] Wittman added the

[7] Richard A. Epstein, A Theory of Strict Liability, 2 J. Legal Stud. 151, 152 (1973).

[8] *Id.* at 164–77. For criticisms of Epstein's paradigmatic analysis, see John Borgo, Causal Paradigms in Tort Law, 8 J. Legal Stud. 419 (1979); Richard W. Wright, Causation in Tort Law, 73 Calif. L. Rev. 1735, 1750–58 (1985).

[9] Richard A. Epstein, Causation and Corrective Justice: A Reply to Two Critics, 8 J. Legal Stud. 477, 489 (1979).

[10] Richard A. Epstein, Charles O. Gregory, & Harry Kalven, Jr., Cases and Materials on Torts, 566–67 (4th ed. 1984).

[11] See, for example, Donald Wittman, Liability for Harm or Restitution for Benefit? 13 J. Legal Stud. 57 (1984).

concept that transaction costs may be asymmetrical depending on who is assigned the entitlement. Wittman argues that the assignment of entitlements serves as a "baseline" from which one can measure the extent of relevant harm or benefit. He shows that, in the presence of administrative (transaction) cost asymmetries, the choice of a baseline may affect the equilibrium. Any baseline that has relatively high transaction costs, making it difficult to measure the proper compensation, will ordinarily be inappropriate. Wittman's method for assigning property rights then turns out to be rather straightforward: "One first asks what is the most efficient outcome; then one asks which liability scheme involves the lowest court administrative costs."[12]

Note that this method does have the disadvantage that the policymaker (judge or legislator) must know which is the most efficient outcome in order to assign initial entitlements (the baseline). Where the original baseline is inappropriate, inefficient outcomes will be the consequence. The likelihood of finding the right baseline will be further clouded once the class of permissible baselines is allowed to include intermediate positions. One must know not only who the proper party should be but also what the appropriate standard of care should be before deciding on the efficient entitlement. For example, when a railroad emits sparks while it travels near a farm with stacked hay, the decision maker (judge) must decide not only whether the farmer has a right to be free from sparks or the railroad has the right to emit sparks but must also pass on the intermediate rules (such as recovery only under negligence or recovery unless the farmer has been contributorily negligent) to determine which outcome is preferred. All this analysis is needed just to decide to whom the entitlement should be given (to decide what is the cause of harm).

There is no way in the Wittman methodology to separate the proper person to be given the right from the proper standard to be used. One cannot first decide that the farmer should have a right to be free from sparks and then decide that that right should be limited to circumstances of railroad negligence because of the possibility of high transaction costs. Many hidden pitfalls may beset the Wittman methodology notwithstanding its seeming theoretical appeal and simplicity. It is therefore apparently not a likely candidate for explicating Epstein's ordinary language criticism of Coase.

The third criticism of the application of the Coase hypothesis also uses the possibility of asymmetries to explain the reasons for assigning entitlements to one party rather than the other. Rather than conventional bargaining or informational transaction costs, this theory is developed from

[12] *Id.* at 65.

the concept of nonconvexity. Nonconvexities arise in the presence of externalities and public goods. In geometrical terms a space is convex if one can draw a line between any two points within the space without leaving the space. Similarly, the space is said to be nonconvex when there is a set of points within the space that can be connected only by leaving the space. The importance of the distinction between convex and nonconvex spaces is this: where the space is nonconvex, a barrier against optimal trades may arise. Stated otherwise, in the absence of convexity in its production function, a firm that is willing to make marginal adjustments may not realize that an alternative use of its resources will ultimately increase its production. This result occurs because the information the firm receives from comparing the price of a purchase or sale with its marginal rate of transformation between input and product will give the false information that further marginal adjustments toward the optimum will decrease profits. The decision maker will, thus, never get the proper information from marginal prices, which is what microeconomic theory assumes.[13] Only if a firm operates in the convex part of its production set will it receive the proper signals from prices. Similar results will be true for a consumer if his consumption set is nonconvex.

In the typical case used by economists—a trade of market goods between two parties—the trading space will be convex. Nonconvexities arise in the presence of externalities. A common example of an externality resulting in a nonconvex trading space is the case of the steel mill and the laundry. As the steel mill marginally increases its production from zero, adding smoke to the atmosphere, it begins marginally to decrease the quality (value) of the output of a neighboring laundry. The smoke is considered an externality for two reasons. The first is that normally there is no market for smoke: no consumer would pay to be able to consume more. All that is required to eliminate this aspect of the problem is to assign an entitlement to the smoke. Then either the mill will pay to produce more, or consumers (the laundry) will pay to consume less. The second reason is that the market may fail to reach an optimum even once the right has been assigned.

There are two reasons for this market failure. The first is that bargaining (transaction) costs may be higher in this market than in the typical market. These costs could arise, for example, because of costs of negotiations necessitated by having only two parties and a unique situation or difficulty in exchanging information (on the quantity of smoke emitted). The second reason for market failure, the one with which I am concerned, arises because there is no logical limit to the amount of smoke that can be

[13] Harold Varian, Microeconomic Analysis 158 *et seq.* (1978).

produced. The mill can increase its production, which will eventually lead to the degradation of the quality of the laundry's service until no one will want to purchase the laundry's service at any price. The mill may even produce more smoke than that. It is this characteristic of the externality that is termed a "nonconvexity."

Where nonconvexities are present, the original assignment of rights becomes critical in determining whether a series of voluntary exchanges can exhaust all the gains from trade.[14] The right must be initially assigned so that the trading takes place in the convex parts of the sets. Otherwise, not even the market system will have low enough transaction costs to achieve the efficient solution. It will be shown that to achieve this condition it is necessary to grant the entitlement to the party whose production function is made nonconvex by interactions with the other party. It is that party who is normally termed the "victim" or the "receptor."

Nonconvexities in production are associated with the existence of externalities or other "public goods." Whenever there is a significant externality due to the interaction of two or more parties, the production (or consumption) space of the receptor (victim) will be nonconvex.[15] Also, when the fundamental nature of a good is public, the normal market system will not achieve optimality.[16] It is only when the market system can achieve optimality that the invariance portion of the Coase theorem will be valid. Then the assignment of entitlements would be irrelevant to efficiency. When the nature of the good can be characterized as public, associated with a nonconvex production or consumption space, then the assignment of rights will matter as the market system will fail to achieve

[14] For the first recognition of this result, see David Shapiro, A Note on Rent and the Coase Theorem, 7 J. Econ. Theory 125 (1974). See also Editorial Addendum to David Shapiro, "A Note on Rent and the Coase Theorem," 14 J. Econ. Theory 221 (1977); and Robert Cooter, How the Law Circumvents Starrett's Nonconvexity, 22 J. Econ. Theory 499 (1980).

[15] David Starrett, Fundamental Nonconvexities in the Theory of Externalities, 4 J. Econ. Theory 180 (1972). Starrett demonstrated that the existence of externalities implies that the production space of the externality receptor will be nonconvex.

[16] This is because the normal optimality condition for a market system is for $MRS_i =$ MRT. For public goods and externalities the optimality condition is $\Sigma_i MRS_i =$ MRT (where $i$ is a consumer). The problem with public goods is thus not simply the part of the free-rider problem where parties may have incentives to hide their true preferences (which is a clear transaction costs problem). Rather it derives from the nature of the good itself. Even if preferences are truthfully revealed, it may still not be possible to achieve Pareto optimality. For instance, it may be impossible to exclude nonpaying consumers. But even if it were possible, it would be inefficient to do so. This is because there is no additional cost to provide the good to nonpayors. For example, it is possible to scramble satellite broadcasts of cable television, but utility would be increased by not scrambling, as the nonpayors would get a benefit with no loss to any other party. Varian, *supra* note 13, at 207. See also Anthony B. Atkinson & Joseph E. Stiglitz, Lectures on Public Economics 482–89 (1980).

optimality. Thus the legal system becomes most relevant when the nature of the interaction is public. Most of the instances in which public law (rather than private contract) sets the entitlements will probably be in this class of "public goods."

To see how the existence of nonconvexities complicates the process of mutually beneficial exchange, a diagrammatic exposition will be used. We contrast the situations set out in Figure 1, where there is no nonconvexity, with that in Figure 2, where there is one. In Figure 1, the potential gains from trade will be exhausted no matter what the original endowments because the production space is convex. For instance, if producers A and B are both using one input $L$ (land), in fixed supply between them, in order to produce two outputs, $X$ and $Y$, respectively, they will trade that input as long as their marginal revenue products with respect to that good differ. Equilibrium will occur when the marginal revenue products of A and B for the input $L$ are equal. In Figure 1, with a fixed amount of $L$, $L_0$, A and B will trade until total profit $(P_xF_x + P_yF_y)$ is maximized, at $L^*$. At that point the terms of trade are along the lines $rL$ and $-rL$, where $r$ is the price for the input $L$ (agreed on between A and B in the market process), $P_x$ is the net price of $X$, and $P_y$ is the net price of $Y$ (that is, the price net of all input cost except that of $L$). Thus $P_xF_x$ is the profit from producing $X$ having taken all costs other than shared $L$ (land) into account. In the example, as the "production" spaces, defined as the areas under the net profit functions $P_xF_x$ and $P_xF_y$, are strictly convex, it will not matter to the equilibrium allocation what the initial endowments of $L$ were. Equilibrium will always be achieved at $L^*$. The only difference is to the parties' wealth.

If A (producing $X$) has the entitlement, the baseline is on the right of Figure 1. A could use all of $L$ to produce $X^{\sim}$ and to achieve a profit of $P_xX^{\sim}$. He could do better by trading with B. If he trades $(L_0 - L^*)$ to B, he will receive a side payment (in the market for $L$) of $r(L_0 - L^*)$. He will also make a profit (not counting the opportunity cost of land) of $P_xX^*$ for a total profit of $\rho_x$.[17] A will make this trade as the $rL$ price line is greater than his $P_xF_x$ profit function. B is similarly willing to make this trade. He will improve his condition from zero profit, as there is zero production of $Y$ $(P_yF_y = 0$ at $L_0)$, to $\rho_{xy}$ profit[18] on the $-rL$ price line. B achieves this profit by producing $Y^*$ (at $L^*$) while paying $r(L_0 - L)$ for the use of $(L_0 - L^*)$.

On the other hand, if B has the entitlement to $L$, then the baseline is on the left of Figure 1. B would use all the land to produce $Y^{\sim}$ and receive a profit of $P_yY^{\sim}$. B also could do better by trading some land with A. By

[17] $\rho_x = P_xX^* + r(L_0 - L^*)$.

[18] $\rho_{yx} = P_yY^* - r(L_0 - L^*)$.

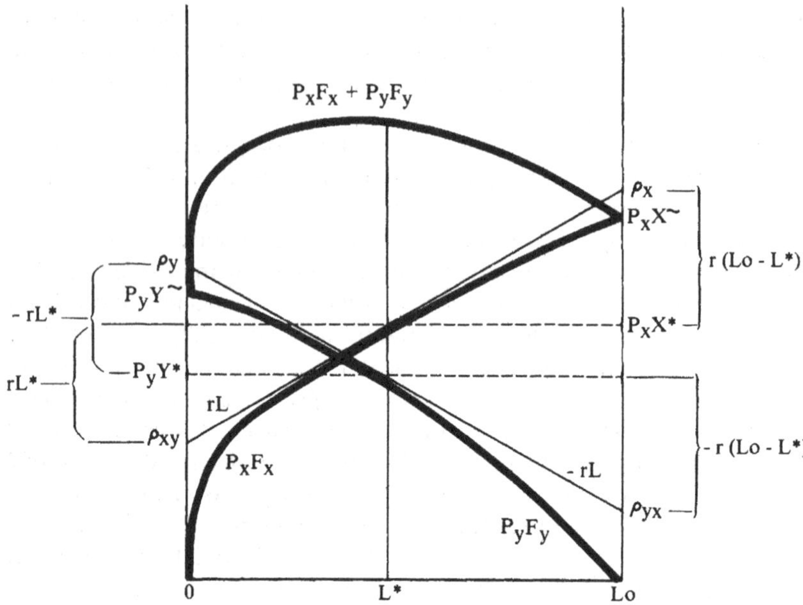


FIGURE 1

trading $L^*$ to A, B will still receive a profit of $P_y Y^*$ from producing $Y$; and B will also receive a payment of $rL^*$ from A for A's use of $L$. B therefore has a profit of $\rho_y$,[19] which is greater than $P_y Y^{\sim}$. The treatment of A is similar to the treatment of B when A had the right to $L$. As can be seen from this discussion, parties are willing to trade whenever the price line is above their profit function.

Figure 2 shows the impediments to trade when the externality gives rise to a nonconvexity in the production space. This situation can arise whenever the rancher makes a partial use of the farmer's land that is sufficient to prevent economical crop production. Any more intensive use of the land by the rancher will not result in further financial loss to the farmer, yet it will continue to benefit the rancher.

In Figure 2, if $F$ is the production function of the farmer, it reaches (or asymptotically approaches) zero before all the land is used extensively by the rancher. If this is an accurate description of the production process, then a trade between the farmer and the rancher will yield different equilibria depending on the initial endowments of the rights of the two parties. If all the rights were owned by the farmer, the negotiation process would begin with the status quo baseline at the far left side of Figure 2.

[19] $\rho_y = P_y Y^* + rL^*$.

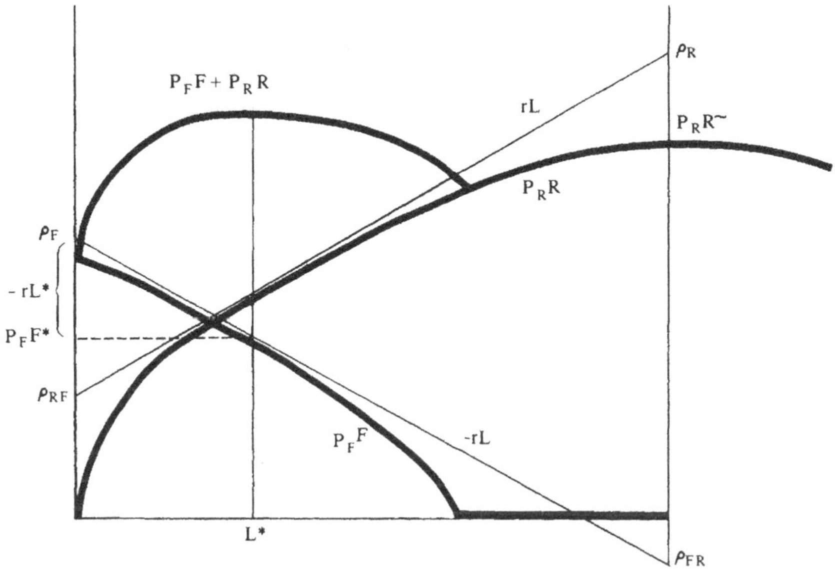


FIGURE 2

The farmer would be willing to trade with the rancher (and vice versa) at the same price of land as before ($r$), and they would reach equilibrium at $L^*$. Both parties will have improved their profit by the trade. The farmer will have increased his profit from $P_F F^{\sim}$ (where $P_F F$ reaches its maximum at the right side of Fig. 2) to $\rho_F$.[20] The rancher will also have increased his profit from zero to $\rho_{RF}$.

However, if the rancher had the right, his no-trade status quo point would be at the far right side of Figure 2, where his profit is maximized. This is shown as the point at which the $P_R R$ production function reaches its maximum, at $P_R R^{\sim}$. The farmer will be unwilling to trade as any trade must cost him more than he will profit from farming. For example, suppose trade were conducted on the efficient $rL$ and $-rL$ price lines as before. While the farmer would profit $P_F F^*$ from farming, he must make a side payment of $r(L_0 - L^*)$ for the use of the land. The profit of the farmer would thus be negative ($\rho_{FR}$).[21] In this case the side payment exceeds the profit from farming because of the fact that the production function reached zero (and thus became nonconvex) before the externality (the use of land by cattle) reached its most internally profitable amount for the generator. In this case the price line lies below the profit function; thus the

[20] $\rho_F = P_F F^* + rL^*$.

[21] $\rho_{FR} = P_F F^* - r(L_0 - L^*)$.

TABLE 1

RELATION BETWEEN NUMBER IN HERD AND CROP LOSS

| Number in Herd (Steers) | Total Herd Value ($) | Value per Additional Steer ($) | Total Crop Loss ($ or Tons) | Crop Loss per Additional Steer ($ or Tons) | Total Value ($) |
|---|---|---|---|---|---|
| 1 | 5 | 5 | 1 | 1 | 24 |
| 2 | 9 | 4 | 3 | 2 | 26 |
| 3 | 12 | 3 | 6 | 3 | 26 |
| 4 | 15 | 3 | 10 | 4 | 25 |
| 5 | 17 | 2 | 15 | 5 | 22 |
| 6 | 19 | 2 | 20 | 5 | 19 |
| 7 | 20 | 1 | 20 | 0 | 20 |
| 8 | 21 | 1 | 20 | 0 | 21 |
| 9 | 20 | −1 | 20 | 0 | 20 |

farmer would not be willing to make the trade. Therefore the only way to ensure that the optimal equilibrium will be reached is to give the party with the nonconvexity in its production space, here the farmer, the right to be free from the externality.

A similar and simpler example of the farmer and the rancher in the presence of externality, leading to a nonconvex production function, can be demonstrated by extending Coase's arithmetic example (see Table 1).

As in Coase's example, whether the farmer has the right to exclude or the rancher has the right to use, the optimal number of steers will be three (which is the point at which the additional damage done by the steers equals the additional value of raising an additional steer). As Coase shows, that number will be reached along either bargaining path, from either two or four steers. This solution is identical with the optimal equilibrium that would be reached along either bargaining path in Figure 1 from $P_yY^{\sim}$ if the farmer has the right or from $P_xX^{\sim}$ if the rancher has the right. If the rancher has the right to trespass and is raising four steers, the fourth steer is worth an additional three dollars to him. However, that steer would cause an additional four dollars in damage to the farmer, who would therefore be willing and able to pay the rancher up to that four dollars to reduce his herd to three. Thus the price of the side payment is greater than the profit for both the farmer and the rancher. Say the side payment price is \$3.75. For the rancher, receiving the payment, \$3.75 > \$3.00. For the farmer, making the payment, −\$3.75 > −\$4.00.

If the farmer has the right to exclude and the number of steers is one, the second steer would cause two dollars in damage yet would be worth an additional four dollars to the rancher, so the farmer would accept an offer from the rancher to increase cattle use of his land. Similar marginal moves from zero or five steers can be shown using the same method.

Once the number of cattle goes from six to seven, there is a significant change in the effect of the steers on the farmer. The additional (or marginal) damage caused by additional cattle is zero, as the entire economically recoverable crop has been destroyed.

If the rancher has the right to use all the land (his own and the farmer's), the baseline would be eight steers, as that would maximize the net value of the herd to the rancher at twenty-one dollars. To reduce the herd to seven he would require a payment of at least one dollar, as his value would decrease to twenty dollars; yet the farmer would not be willing or able to pay anything, as he would still have twenty dollars in damage and zero net gain. As in Figure 2, the farmer is unwilling (or unable) to make a trade when the price received is less than the profit increase. In this case the price received would be negative and the profit increase zero.

On the other hand, if the farmer has the right, the baseline would be zero steers, but the farmer would be willing to accept one, two, and then possibly three, as each trade would yield a net increase in the profits of both parties. The nonconvexity prevents bargaining along the marginal bargaining path to reach the optimal allocation if the starting point (the baseline) is in the nonconvex region where the rancher has the privilege to use the land. Yet if the farmer has the right, the parties need trade only in the region where the production function is convex and can bargain to achieve the optimal allocation. Thus nonconvexities due to the presence of externalities may cause suboptimal production if the right is assigned to the externality generator.[22]

Another source of nonconvexity, which may lead to asymmetry of result with different assignments of rights, may be due to large numbers of potential traders. For example, if there are many cattle ranchers, one may think of the trading axis (the *X*-axis in Figures 1 and 2) as being in number of cattle; then a contract with one rancher does not solve the problem of potential nonconvexities if the entitlement is assigned to the ranchers. Any other rancher may still come onto the land and spoil the bargain. On the other hand, large numbers of farmers do not pose a problem even when the farmers hold the entitlement. Any agreement concerns one rancher and one farmer; and if farmer A agrees to allow rancher B to use a portion of his land to depasture B's cattle, then B will enjoy the benefit of that bargain even if farmer C refuses to let B's cattle come onto C's land. Therefore the asymmetry that occurs because of nonconvexity in the two-party contracting situation may be amplified when there are many parties.

[22] For a more rigorous explication of the importance of nonconvexities in the assignment of liability, see Kenneth R. Vogel, Nonconvexity and Causation (in press).

## III. A History of California Animal Trespass Law

There is probably no instance in American legal history that better approximates the conditions of the Coase theorem, in which transaction costs were insignificant barriers to bargaining, than the example of cattle trespass. There is also probably no example of cattle trespass law more suitable for an analysis of the predictive power of the Coase theorem than the situation that emerged in nineteenth-century California. The legislature essentially carried out an experiment in the efficacy of various forms of laws concerning the wandering of animals. It varied the statutes concerning animal trespass on a county-by-county basis, slowly proceeding from a statewide rule that allowed animals to trespass to one that gave landowners the right to prohibit trespassing animals and to collect damages, in all but four "grazing" counties.

From 1850 to 1890, over 150 local laws were enacted to adjust the conflicting rights, duties, and desires of farmers and ranchers. An analysis of the developments in agricultural production that occurred after those statutory enactments is consistent with the hypothesis articulated above: the efficiency of a system of entitlements is affected by the "baseline" chosen. It is also shown that, in this study at least, it is more efficient to grant a right to exclude to the receptor of externalities, that is, to the farmer, than it is to grant a privilege of use to the externality producer, the rancher.

The conflict as to the appropriate rule to use continues even today. Elsewhere in this volume Ellickson presents an example of these laws in action in the twentieth century. He extends the notion of rules from formal laws to include informal group norms. One of the results that he presents shows that even when the law permits animal owners to let their cattle trespass, the ranchers in Shasta county have come to the informal norm of behavior that it is inappropriate or unneighborly[23] for this use to occur. Apparently, they are willing to keep the legal rule so that it can be used in a system of strict liability when cattle are damaged in accidents with strangers, as in automobile accidents.[24] Many of Ellickson's criticisms of the "law-and-economics" scholars' "legal centralism" are undoubtedly true. However, it is worth noting that, contrary to the modern evidence in Shasta, not only did the trespass law have significant effects

[23] For the development of the concept of "normalcy" in neighborhood activity regulation, see Robert G. Ellickson, Alternatives to Zoning: Covenants, Nuisance Rules, and Fines as Land Use Controls, 40 U. Chi. L. Rev. 681 (1973). This is similar to what I mean by "unneighborly."

[24] Robert C. Ellickson, A Critique of Economic and Sociological Theories of Social Control, J. Legal Stud. (in this issue).

on behavior, but it was also an issue of political significance matched only by water rights during the nineteenth century. If it had not been as central to economic and hence political discourse, it is probably true that the law alone would be much less important in its effects on behavior. This would probably be due to the cost to most people of learning the law. Clearly, there remains much need for research to discover the boundaries of when the formal rule of law will be more important as a behavior regulator than those less formal rules, norms, and ethics.[25]

The experiment in the assignment of property rights by the California legislature is investigated because it illustrates an example of a situation in which the assignment of property entitlements appears to have made a difference in the amount of production of the underlying products: crops and animals.

California became a state of the Union in 1850, having developed rapidly because of the Gold Rush of 1849. Before it became a territory of the United States in 1848, California was a territory of Mexico (and, before Mexico existed, a province of Spain). Under Mexican rule the predominant form of economic activity was raising cattle on large tracts of land known as *ranchos*.[26] The products derived from the cattle were numerous. In addition to selling the cattle for beef, the ranchers slaughtered the cattle for tallow and hide and produced dried beef, also known as *carne seca* or jerky. The Gold Rush drastically boosted the population in the northern cities and the mines. For tallow and hide, a steer had been previously worth only $4.00 a head. The sudden demand for beef increased the price of a head to as high as $75. The prices beckoned southern ranchers, who undertook drives of five and six hundred miles with a thousand cattle. Indian attacks were not uncommon, cattle rustling was a constant risk, and a sudden storm on the open range could scatter the cattle for miles. A subsequent glut in the cattle market and increased competition from sheep herders drove cattle prices down to their former levels.[27]

The cattle grazed on the vast unfenced range of land, frequently becoming mixed together with neighboring owners' herds. This commingling necessitated rodeos in order to separate the various owners' stock from each other. The procedure for the rodeo was quite formalized.[28] A landowner was required to give four days notice to his neighbors of the time and place of the rodeo so that they could come to collect their cattle.

[25] *Id.*

[26] See generally Robert Glass Cleland, The Cattle on a Thousand Hills: Southern California, 1850–1870 (1941).

[27] *Id.* at 88–91, 137–42.

[28] *Id.* at 74–80.

Calves that had no brands and that did not follow a mother belonged to the owner of the land on which the rodeo was being held. In addition to roving herds of cattle, large bands of both wild and trained horses grazed on the open range. On occasion, hundreds of the unbroken horses were killed to save the grasses for cattle. Sheep also used the pastures. As sheep raising grew in prominence in the state, sheep occasionally displaced cattle as the stock of the *ranchos*. In 1850, less that 18,000 sheep were reported in California. By 1860 that number had reached 1 million.[29]

After California entered the Union, its first legislature passed an act to enact the common law as the law of the state.[30] It also passed an act that made an exception to the common law in the case of animal trespass. The California legislature largely retained the rules favoring the cattle industry that existed under Mexican rule.[31] The Trespass Act of 1850[32] defined a lawful fence[33] and gave an owner of land who had enclosed his premises with such a fence the right to collect damages that grazing or other animals caused. For a second trespass double damages could be collected. However, if an owner or occupier of land did not fence those animals out with a lawful fence, he had no rights against the owner of the animals or against the animals themselves. Moreover, if the landowner "killed, maimed, or materially hurt" an animal, he was liable for all damage sustained by the animal and for the costs accruing from the suit.[34]

The issue of animal trespass was to become one of the two most bitter in the California legislature in the nineteenth century.[35] The privilege given to animal owners was perhaps the greatest grievance of the farmers and their allies in the San Francisco Chamber of Commerce,[36] who fought

[29] *Id.* at 186–92.

[30] An Act Adopting the Common Law, ch. 41, 1850–53 Compiled Laws Cal. 186.

[31] An Act to Regulate Rodeos, ch. 92, 1850–53 Compiled Laws Cal. 337. Cleland, *supra* note 26, at 74–80, provides an excellent description of these rules in operation.

[32] Ch. 142, 1850–53 Compiled Laws Cal. 793.

[33] "Every inclosure shall be deemed a lawful fence, which is four and a half feet high, if made of stone; and if made of rails, five and a half feet high; if made upon the embankment of a ditch three feet high from the bottom of the ditch, the fence shall be two feet high; said fence to be substantial and reasonably strong, and made so close that stock cannot get their heads through it, and if made to turn small stock, sufficiently tight to keep such stock out. A hedge fence shall be considered a lawful fence if five feet high and sufficiently close to turn stock." *Id.*

[34] *Id.*

[35] The other was water rights. See generally Appendices to the Journals of the Senate and Assembly 1850–90.

[36] The mercantile interests favored the farmers in this dispute because of the type of product that the two agricultural groups produced. Farmers were producing wheat, corn, and other grains as well as vegetables, which were fairly easy to export. Only the tallow and hides of the cattle were exportable, and therefore cattle probably could not yield as high a value per acre as grain. *Id.*

for its repeal from the 1850s through the 1870s. In fact, from 1851 to 1890 well over 150 separate acts changing the property rights regime were enacted by the California legislature. The acts can be categorized in three ways: by county, by animal,[37] and by enforcement mechanism.[38]

The changes were usually enacted for a small group of counties at one time. However, some acts had a statewide scope, while others were limited only to certain townships or portions of a county. Geographically, the scheme of enactments became chaotic. Acts passed concerning a limited area could prejudice farmers on nearby, unprotected land. If a change in law affected only a portion of the county, ranchers could move to another portion with little difficulty. Farmers whose lands were not within the geographic boundaries protected were made to bear the greater burden of subsidizing the cattle industry.

The original enforcement mechanism was the Trespass Act of 1850, a fence-out (hereinafter "fence") law that required landowners to erect a lawful fence to protect their property; without such a fence there would be no liability. The earliest alternative rules allowed the finder of an estrayed animal to "take up" animals found on his land whether or not the land was enclosed by a lawful fence. Under this rule, which will be called a "trespass" law, the landowner would receive only the expenses for caring for the animals until the owner was found or the animal was sold at a public auction.[39] Another type of statute, which will be called an "estray" law, also gave the finder of an estray on his property the right to recover damages that the animal had caused in addition to the expenses granted by the trespass acts.[40]

[37] Separate statutes were passed for each of the grazing animals. Grazing animals included horses, mules, jacks, jennies, hogs, sheep, goats, and cattle (horned and neat). Some statutes concerned only a single class of animal, while others were more general in their application.

[38] These five types of legal rules span much of the range of possible relationships between the parties. In the terms of Calabresi and Melamed, either the property rule or the liability rule is assigned to either the generator or the receptor of the externality. Guido Calabresi & A. Douglas Melamed, Property Rules, Liability Rules, and Inalienability: One View of the Cathedral, 85 Harv. L. Rev. 1089–1128 (1972). The original property rule was the privilege that owners of animals had of letting their stock roam at large. Polinsky, *supra* note 3, has extended this categorization to include tax-subsidy rules, such as the criminal law.

[39] The earliest example of such a statute is An Act concerning Estray Animals, ch. 33, 1851 Cal. Stat. 299, which stated: "§ 1. Every person finding a stray horse, mare, colt, mule, jack, or jenny . . . upon his farm . . . shall, within 5 days, if said animal or animals remain on his farm . . . go before some Justice of the Peace . . . and give . . . a full description . . . and . . . information that will lead to the cause of said animal or animals coming to his farm. . . . *Provided* no animal shall be considered an estray, if the owner is known. § 2. [A]ny person claiming and proving said stray animal or animals that have been posted by this Act shall have restitution of the property so claimed by paying *all costs and such charges* [my emphasis] as may be awarded to the taker up by the Justice of the Peace of his county."

[40] The earliest example of an estray law is An Act concerning Hogs found Running at

There were two further categories of statutes that gave the power to take up to the local government. The first of these was a "pound" law under which the municipality or county could appoint an officer to take up and impound estrays. Under these laws the government collected the expenses of caring for the animals.[41] The alternative law gave the local justice of the peace the power to levy a fine in addition to the statutory expenses as an additional "criminal" deterrent to an animal owner who allowed his stock to run at large or to trespass on the lands of another.[42]

### A. *Description of Entitlements*

*Fence laws* gave a privilege to the rancher to allow his cattle to wander. To prevent damage to his crops, the farmer either had to purchase that privilege from the rancher(s) or had to enclose his own land with a fence meeting the standard set by law. The Trespass Act of 1850 was a strict nonliability statute. If the farmer did not meet all the conditions for a lawful fence, for whatever reason, he could not recover for damaged crops. *Comerford v. Dupuy*[43] illustrates the strictness of the law. Comerford owned a parcel of land that was under cultivation and that was enclosed by a fence on three sides, the fourth side being a steep bluff overlooking the ocean. It was found that the plaintiff's fence on the south side, where the defendant's cattle broke through, was as strong and sub-

---

Large in the Counties of Marin, Sacramento, San Francisco, Alameda, Stanislaus, Yuba and Santa Clara, ch. 148, 1856 Cal. Stat. 229: "§ 3. If the owners of such hogs come forward within five days after the time such notices were posted and prove them to be their property, the person taking them up shall deliver them to such owner upon their paying all costs, charges and *damages* [my emphasis], sustained by reason of their trespassing."

[41] The first pound law enacted was An Act to Prevent Certain Animals from Running at Large in Napa City, ch. 192, 1862 Cal. Stat. 210: "§ 2. If any animals . . . shall be found running at large within the surveyed limits of Napa City . . . it shall be lawful, and it is hereby made the duty of the Sheriff or any Constable of said county, upon being notified thereof by any resident of said town, to take up and impound and keep such animal. . . . § 3. The officer taking up any horse, mule, or horned cattle, shall be entitled to a fee of two dollars each, and one dollar for each day such officer keeps such animal, one dollar for taking up each hog or goat, and fifty cents per day for keeping the same, in each case to date from the time of posting said animals, hogs, or goats."

[42] The first criminal law was An Act Restricting the Herding of Sheep to Certain Pastures in the Counties of Sonoma and Marin, ch. 194, 1857 Cal. Stat. 227: "§ 1. It shall not be lawful for any person, or persons, owning or having charge of any sheep . . . to herd the same, or to permit them to be herded on the land or possessory claim of other than the land or possessory claim of the owner or owners of such sheep. § 2. The owner or owners, or the agents of such owners of sheep, violating the provisions of section first of this Act, on complaint of the party or parties injured, and on conviction thereof before any justice of the peace for the township where either of the interested parties may reside, shall be liable to a fine of not less than twenty-five dollars, nor more than two hundred dollars."

[43] 17 Cal. 308 (1861).

stantial as the statute required.[44] However, twenty feet of the fence was not three feet high, as the statute mandated, and in some places the fence had broken down and had been patched back up. There was a judgment for the defendant under an instruction that, even if the cattle had entered where the fence was lawful, the plaintiff still could not recover[45] if any part of the fence was below the statutory height. The judgment was affirmed on appeal: "We think a party cannot recover for injuries done by cattle of defendant breaking into plaintiff's close, unless the land entered be inclosed by a fence of the character prescribed in the statute, or at least, by an inclosure equivalent to that described in the statute in its capacity to exclude cattle."[46]

However, this did not mean that animal owners had all the rights to use others' land at all times. For instance, there was no strict liability for damages done to animals while they were trespassing, at least not on railroad property. In one case a locomotive struck and killed plaintiff's cow while traveling twenty to twenty-five miles per hour without slowing or blowing the whistle before striking the animal. In spite of the fact that the cow could be seen for a half mile before it was struck, the plaintiff could not recover on strict liability principles. The court used a balancing test, applying normal contributory negligence principles. While the plaintiff had the right to let the cow run at large, the defendant had a right to run cars at their usual times and rates of speed. Therefore, if the plaintiff were to allow his cattle to roam in a place that was extrahazardous, he must exercise an extra degree of care.[47]

*Trespass and estray laws* are types of liability rules in favor of the farmer, the receptor, who receives a right to protect his land and to collect statutory damages for injury done to his right to exclude.[48] Trespass laws allowed the farmer to collect only the expenses he incurred while caring for an estrayed animal. Estray laws allowed those expenses and also permitted recovery for lost crops and damage to the land.

In *Hahn v. Garratt*[49] the plaintiff sought to recover damages caused to his crops by the trespassing of the defendant's cattle under an estray law.

[44] In this case that meant a fence in a ditch. The ditch was three to four feet wide and three feet deep. The fence was on posts eight feet apart with two rails. It was seven feet from outside the ditch to the top rail and five to six feet from the bottom of the ditch to the top rail.

[45] Comerford sued for the value of 407 dozen cabbages and other injuries, totaling $2,500.

[46] 17 Cal. at 310.

[47] Richmond v. Sacramento Valley R.R. Co., 18 Cal. 351 (1861).

[48] There is no liability rule in favor of the ranchers, except to the extent that farmers who injure animals while taking them up must pay damages under either the trespass or the estray act.

[49] 69 Cal. 146 (1886).

The defendant requested a jury instruction that the plaintiff could not recover unless he showed that the land was enclosed by a fence strong enough to prevent ingress by cattle or that the defendant had intentionally herded his stock on the plaintiff's land. The plaintiff's land was not enclosed; however, an estray act applied to Santa Clara County.[50] The trial court refused the defendant's instruction and instead instructed the jury that in Santa Clara County the owner of land was not required to fence in his land in order to recover damages for injuries caused by trespassing cattle. Rather, in that county the owner of the cattle had the obligation to prevent the trespasses. On appeal, the judgment for the plaintiff was affirmed.[51] The court traced the history of California animal trespass law:

> It is claimed for appellant that the rule of the common law of England, which required every man to keep his cattle within his own close, and made him liable in damages for all injuries resulting from their being permitted to range at large, has never prevailed in this state. . . . When the common law was adopted, in 1850, it was made the rule of decision in all the courts of this state. . . . At that time the principal industries of the state were mining and cattle-raising. To encourage and promote these industries, acts were passed by the legislature, before the adoption of the common law, which have been held to be inconsistent with some of its rules. . . . Since then farming and fruit-raising have become important industries, and to encourage and protect them, special acts have been passed for some of the counties, which in effect restored the rules of the common law.[52]

*Pound and criminal laws* also provided some relief for farmers and the citizenry but held it at a distance through tedious procedures and various exceptions to the rule.[53] For instance, in "An Act Supplementary to An Act to Prevent the Trespassing of Animals upon Private Property,"[54] the owner of "trespassed" land had to give the animal's owner five days notice to remove it. If after five days the animal remained, the landowner had to register a complaint with the justice of the peace and give proof of the animal's presence. The justice would then issue an order of removal. If the animal's owner still did not remove it, the justice could impose a fine at his discretion of not less than ten dollars and not more than $100.

[50] As previously mentioned, many of the acts relating to cattle and land were passed on a county-by-county basis. See text around note 37 *supra*. In this case the applicable statute was An Act concerning Estrays, and Animals Found Running at Large in the County of Santa Clara, ch. 393, 1863 Cal. Stat. 581; *amended by* ch. 411, 1871–72 Cal. Stat. 580.

[51] 69 Cal. 146 (1886).

[52] *Id*. at 147.

[53] Two possible "taxation" schemes are implicit in the pound and criminal laws. However, once again both rules give the right to be free from trespass to landowners and the citizenry and the duty to restrain the animals to the animal owners.

[54] Chapter 411, 1861 Cal. Stat. 474.

The act excepted two categories of animal owners from its operation. The first class exempted was persons driving animals to the market. They had a privilege to linger for two days, after which the landowner could give them their five days' notice. The second group of animal owners excluded from the act was those who owned grazing farms and whose lands were proportionate to the number of their cattle and horses.[55] The minimum statutory proportion of land to animals was 1,200 large cattle and horses to a square league of land.[56] There are no reported cases interpreting these acts. This may imply that they were rarely used or were not of significant importance.

### B. *Effect of Land Use Entitlements on Use*

The Trespass Act of 1850 was unsatisfactory in the eyes of farmers. They were unable to protect their property unless they strictly adhered to the rules for legal fences. The laws perpetuated the domination of land use by ranchers and hindered the development of farming. In a description of a trip from San Diego to Los Angeles in 1858, the Visiting Committee of the State Agricultural Society found

> rolling hills covered with wild oats, and with the remains of a heavy crop of clover . . . most perfect succession of hill and valley. . . . [H]ills rise from 100 to 500 feet high with sides sufficiently sloping and tops sufficiently rounding to admit the use of a team and plow almost universally. . . . The soil is generally a rich dark mold, interspersed with districts of volcanic scoria, yellow sand, dark gravel, etc. In the rainy season, and for months succeeding, nothing can exceed the rich green of the growing oats and the fragrance of clover in bloom.[57]

In spite of that glowing report of the possibilities of the land, the committee found many cattle and horses but very few acres under cultivation. Documenting their trip through California, they write of an area about thirty-six miles from San Diego called Guapemita, where of 7,260 acres eighty were enclosed and under cultivation. Further north, they pass the Valley of San Mateo, owned by Pio Pico, containing about fourteen square miles with a large band of cattle and horses. Then follows the Mission of San Juan Capistrano, with "few gardens and small fields." Then they mentioned the Santa Anna Ranch, "a good piece of ground, in ruins, with several acres of corn." Only when they get close to Los

[55] The legislature seemed concerned that animal owners who had a great number of stock but very little land might intrude on their neighbors.

[56] A square league of land equals approximately ten square miles or 6,000 acres.

[57] California State Agricultural Society, Transactions during 1858, Appendix to the Journal of the Senate of California, 10th Sess. (1859) (hereinafter cited as Transactions 1858).

Angeles do they encounter much cultivation, but most of the land is clearly used as open range.[58]

The reason that all farmers and the commercial interests of the state gave for this state of land use was the fence law. In a report of the Agricultural Society in 1863, the problem was clearly posed:

> If two adjoining tracts of land, one occupied for stock growing and the other for grain farming, are considered, it will be seen that either one or the other must be fenced, or the grain field will be encroached upon and destroyed by the stock. It is needless, at this point of the illustration, to state that the grain field is incapable of going over upon the stock range and committing depradations. . . . The greatest obstacle to profitable farming in this State has been the costliness of fences, not only at the outset but for constant repairs.[59]

Wilson Flint estimated that in the central district of the state it would cost approximately ten dollars per acre to fence land. There were at that time 1,959,490 acres under fence in the thirteen counties[60] that he studied; the fencing enclosing those farms thus cost over $19.5 million. The market value of all stock in those counties (horses, mules, cattle, sheep, and hogs) was only $8.8 million. "Thus showing that the fences have cost ten million seven hundred and ninety thousand one hundred and twenty-six dollars more than the total value of stock in the district. By this it appears that grain growers could well have afforded to have bought all the stock and given it away for exile and thereby saved [over $10 million], if they could by doing so have escaped the necessity of erecting fences to protect their grain fields."[61]

It was estimated that "[t]he expense of building and maintaining fences in repair in California . . . are [*sic*] probably greater than any other country in the world." In New York, Erza Cornell estimated that the cost of rail and stake fence was thirty cents a rod or ninety-six dollars per mile. In California, the cheapest fencing (post and plank) cost $2.19 per rod or

[58] *Id.*

[59] Wilson Flint, California State Agricultural Society, The Fence Question, in Transactions during 1863, 2 Appendix to the Journals of the Senate and Assembly of California, 15th Sess., (1864), at 146, 150.

[60] Alameda, Colusa, Contra Costa, Napa, Sacramento, San Joaquin, San Mateo, Santa Clara, Santa Cruz, Solano, Sonoma, Sutter, and Yolo counties.

[61] Flint, *supra* note 59. An obvious question is why the farmers did not do just that, assuming low transaction costs. The answer is obviously that purchasing cattle from the ranchers would only encourage the ranchers to purchase, breed, or otherwise procure cattle for a second round of deals. Even agreement by the rancher to cease the practice of ranching could not forestall new entrants and would be more expensive to negotiate. Only if the ranchers' land could be burdened by a covenant, forbidding future owners from raising animals, would the farmer be protected.

about $700 per mile. At the same time, owing to the location of markets, wheat earned $2.50 per bushel in New York as compared with $1.20 in California.[62]

The enormous cost of fencing kept the issue of animal trespass in the political arena.[63] Fencing was in fact in such close proportion to the receipts from growing crops that it prevented people from farming. The extra labor and material required to erect and maintain the fences was considered simply as a tax:

> It is hardly necessary to state that this enormous . . . tax upon the agricultural interests . . . is thought to be necessary in order that the horses and cattle may be allowed to roam at large upon the public commons as the monarchs of all they survey. Sheep and hogs must be left out of consideration in these estimates, they not being among the privileged classes of quadrupeds. . . . The strangest part of the whole subject is the fact that a very small portion of this stock, or but a little of this field—the commons—around which this fence is built and maintained, belongs to the people whose money and time goes to build and maintain it. And yet, from force of habit, they persistently continue to impose this tax upon themselves in the vain attempt to surround the people's cattle with a *lawful* fence and thus relieve the owners of the expense of a herder, and prevent the cattle from doing damages.[64]

The availability of fencing varied with the region of the state. In northern California near the mountains, wooden fencing was available: "In 7 days we have made 18 hund. [*sic*] Rails & Slats. . . . Mr. McNeil agreed with me to take 2000 Slats at $8 per hund. and 500 Posts at $6 per hund."[65] Wooden fences were the superior choice in that area. "Several landholders in Napa Valley are making Wrie [*sic*] fences. . . . But told George that they cost more than a Redwood fence if this be the case I think few will be made as they can't be as good They must be a poor defence [*sic*] versus hogs."[66]

The amount of fencing purchased by Mr. McNeil would construct a

[62] California State Board of Agriculture, Report for the Years 1864–65, 2 Appendix to the Journals of the Senate and Assembly of California, 16th Sess. (1866), at 16 (hereinafter cited as Report).

[63] However, some of the initial changes in the law relating to grazing animals did not come because of the complaints of the grain growers. Rather, the cattle and horse ranchers pressured the legislature during the session of 1857 to pass an act to forbid sheep from being herded or grazed on the lands or possessory claims of others than the owners of such sheep, in the counties of Marin and Sonoma. An Act Restricting the Herding of Sheep to Certain Pastures in the Counties of Sonoma and Marin, ch. 194, 1857 Cal. Stat. 227.

[64] Report, *supra* note 62, at 18.

[65] Anancias Rogers Pond Journal, 1852–62, p. 30, March 25, 1853, Huntington Library, MS HM19384 (hereinafter cited as Pond Journal).

[66] *Id.* at 39, April 30, 1853.

fence approximately one mile long; this would be sufficient to enclose a square parcel of about forty acres at a cost of $190. However, in southern California, wood was very expensive, and therefore it would not be the fencing material of choice. As an alternative to a wooden fence, a hedge fence was planted by a community of Germans who settled in Anaheim in 1857. From a purchase of 1,200 acres of the Rancho San Juan Cajon de Santa Ana, the community set aside 200 acres for a town and divided the rest into twenty-acre farms: "Forty thousand willow poles, planted eighteen inches apart, were used to make a live fence about the property. The upright cuttings projected six feet above ground; they were 'strengthened by three horizontal poles, and defended by a ditch four feet deep, six feet wide at the top, sloping to a breadth of one foot at the bottom.' The barrier thus formed was so impenetrable that even herds of starving cattle, in times of drought, could not break through it."[67]

It is important to note that one fence surrounded these 1,200 acres inhabited by fifty families. By enclosing the entire property by one fence, the total fence was much shorter and the cost per family much lower.[68]

Even with fencing, there was a limit to its efficacy in restraining large herds. In times of drought thousands of thirst-crazed cattle would press in against the willow fence of Anaheim. Some would break through and have to be shot for the protection of the citizens. Other measures taken to stop the animals included planting thorned shrubs on the outside of the fence and having a mounted guard patrol the perimeter to prevent the intrusions.[69]

In addition to the cost of fencing and patrols and to the economic loss from damages resulting from cattle, the situation in which the farmer had the obligation to protect his land was considered inequitable:

> It certainly should be the right of an individual who is in tenancy of a piece of land to enjoy its undisturbed use, particularly when, as an evidence of his good faith and honest intentions toward his neighbors he should give them notice that they need apprehend no encroachment on their domain from himself or anything under his control and with which assurance his neighbor is relieved of the necessity of erecting barricades. Ought not the statute to provide for a mutual pledge between the parties that neither should encroach on the other? Not so in its practice. It

[67] Cleland, *supra* note 26, at 211.

[68] A fence of approximately six miles is required to enclose 1,200 acres in one parcel; even at $200 per mile that would be $1,200. On the other hand, enclosing fifty parcels of twenty acres requires approximately fifteen miles of fence or two and one half times as much fence as enclosing the entire area as one cattle-free zone. Anaheim was virtually unique as a large farming settlement in southern California in the 1860s. See Transactions 1858, *supra* note 57.

[69] Lucile E. Dickson, The Founding and Early History of Anaheim, California, 11 Hist. Soc'y S. Cal. Q. 26, 31 (1919).

compels the party who voluntarily takes a position where he can do no wrong to others to erect costly barricades to protect his own industry, on his own premises, from the wanton aggressions of his neighbors.[70]

Following the enactment of the fence-in laws beginning in the 1860s, wheat farming expanded rapidly. From the late 1860s through the next two decades this change has been described as the most significant agricultural development of the period.[71] In particular, the reference was to the Sacramento and the San Joaquin valleys. Writing in 1875, I. N. Hoag, former secretary of the California State Agricultural Society, describes the agricultural transition that occurred in that region:

These elevated shelves, or plains were originally covered throughout the whole length of the State with a most luxuriant growth of wild oats, frequently standing from eight to ten feet high, through which roamed the year round countless herds of wild cattle. . . . They are now covered each year with vast fields of wheat and barley, and dotted over with villages, and farm houses, and farm establishments. . . . Still back of these plains come the rolling or foothill lands, lying at the feet of the mountain ranges which hem in the great inland valley. . . . Millions of acres of these hills are now occupied as sheep walks and Winter homes for stock cattle and dairies.[72]

The picture presented shows a movement of wheat farming into the valleys and a movement of the stock interests up into the foothills. Keeping in mind that under the fence-out law cattle could graze freely on the lands of others, there are several possible reasons that would explain how wheat farming could develop in an area dominated by cattle ranching. First, the greater availability of lumber in the northern counties may have permitted farmers to enclose their lands. Second, the farmers may have contracted with the ranch owners to keep their cattle more effectively under control. Third, the legislature, by passing a statute that forced ranchers to pay for damages to crops destroyed by wandering cattle, may have given the farmers incentives to plant crops, contrary to the implications of the Coase hypothesis.[73]

[70] Flint, *supra* note 59, at 151. Flint draws an analogy between the rancher and a thief who trains a raven to fly into open windows to seize jewels: "Will it be pretended that it should be obligatory on the owners of these valuables to erect such barriers as would prevent the thieving raven from obtaining access to the coveted articles, and that it would be no felony for the party employing the raven . . . to receive the fruits of the robbery and convert to his own use the proceeds."

[71] Robert Glass Cleland, From Wilderness to Empire 324 (1944).

[72] I. N. Hoag, California State Agricultural Society, Agricultural Review, in Transactions during 1874, 1 Appendix to the Journal of the Senate and Assembly of California, 21st sess. (1875), at 245, 251.

[73] As mentioned in the text at note 39 *supra*, the legislature also provided other types of

The theory that increased availability of lumber for fencing may have lead to increased production of wheat in the San Joaquin and Sacramento valleys has some credibility. Although barbed wire was not available until 1874,[74] both those valleys are in the northern part of the state, close to the California forests. Lumber would have been easier to acquire there than in most parts of southern California. Still, even with a greater availability of lumber, the costs of erecting fences were extremely high.[75] In addition to the cost of carrying wood by comparatively primitive methods (by some form of animal driven cart), labor costs were also high. The fences had to be "substantial" to meet legal requirements, meaning that they had to be sufficiently strong to turn stock.[76]

Furthermore, the initial cost of constructing the fences did not end the matter. The fences had to be kept in repair. Wood has a natural tendency to rot, and the fences were subject to the stress of cattle pressing against them. A lamentation of the period illustrates the degree of stress that the cattle could impose: "Common fences are no defense against wild and starving cattle. As the time of harvest approaches, fields require guarding day and night."[77] Journal entries for 1856 from Rancho Azusa illustrate how much effort could be required of a landowner to keep a fence in repair: "[C]arried stakes for Vineyard fence in Small Cart, the Cattle having entered and broken down a peach tree" (November 14);[78] "[c]attle getting into the Vineyard" (November 23);[79] "again cattle in large numbers in the Vineyard, Shut them up in Corral, destroyed a peach tree" (November 25);[80] "people engaged in cutting and hauling stakes for fence of Vineyard" (November 27);[81] "people all engaged in cutting & hauling, Stake and cutting ditch for Vineyard fence" (December 3).[82] This cattle

---

enforcement mechanisms to encourage the farming interests or to discourage ranchers from allowing their animals to roam wildly on the lands of others. A criminal law might not give farmers as much of an incentive to plant crops as a liability rule would. Although ranchers would be punished to some extent for failing to keep their animals under control, the fine did not return the crop value to the farmers.

[74] Cleland, *supra* note 26, at 87 n.28. See also Ernest Bogart and Ronald Kemmerer, Economic History of the American People 500 (1942).

[75] See text at note 59 *supra*.

[76] This requirement was strictly enforced. See the discussion of Comerford v. Dupuy in the text at notes 43–46 *supra*.

[77] Kern County Weekly Courier (Bakersfield) (April 29, 1871), cited in John Ludeke, The No Fence Law of 1874: Victory for San Joaquin Valley Farmers, 59 Cal. Hist. Soc'y Q. 98, 108 (1980).

[78] Henry Dalton, 2 Daily Occurances of Azusa 7, Huntington Library, MS DL 1139.

[79] *Id.* at 8.

[80] *Id.*

[81] *Id.*

[82] *Id.* at 10.

invasion at Rancho Azusa continued through December 13. Fence building at Azusa was an ongoing enterprise, with three men constantly engaged in building and repairing fences.[83]

Although there are documented instances of large grain holdings in the valleys,[84] there was also a trend toward the development of small farms.[85] Small farmers were less able to afford the high costs of fencing.[86] Therefore the availability of fencing alone probably does not explain the growth of farming. As the cost of fencing was less per acre for large farmers than it was for small,[87] there must be an alternative explanation for the growth of farming and especially of small farms.

Next I consider the possibility that farmers may have contracted with ranchers to have the ranchers keep their cattle away from crops. In situations in which there was only one owner of stock in a locality, the possibility of such contracts may have existed. One example of such a contract was a lease between Henry Dalton and Jose Ochoa: "[T]he party of the 2 part further covenants that he will not at any time during the existence of the lease permit any Stock whatsoever in quantities over the number of 5 to run on the lands of the Rancho Azusa belonging to the party of the first part."[88]

However, this contract came into existence after the law applying to Los Angeles county had changed to give the entitlement to the farmer. In other situations Dalton was more likely to use the law to protect his lands. Even when he did not have the legal power, Dalton attempted to warn trespassers off his ranch. In a newspaper notice in 1852, Dalton complains: "[P]ersons are in the habit of running cattle and other animals . . . also plundering timber . . . on the lands of Santa Anita and San Francisquito"; he therefore warns that he will "henceforth prosecute without distinction all persons found trespassing . . . and allow no permission to be granted except under his own signature."[89]

83 See generally *id.*

84 Cleland, *supra* note 71, at 324–29.

85 Statewide the number of small farms nearly doubled from 1860 to 1880. In 1860, nine million acres were devoted to farming and the average size of a farm was 466 acres. In 1880, seventeen million acres were devoted to farming and the average size of a farm was 462 acres. From 1860 to 1880 the number of farms rose from approximately nineteen thousand to thirty-six thousand. N. P. Chipman, California State Agricultural Society, Annual Address in Transactions during 1886, 3 Appendix to the Journals of the Senate and the Assembly, 27th sess., 187, 197 (1887).

86 See text at note 68 *supra.*

87 The size of a farm goes up as the square compared with the length of fence. For example, a 100-acre farm can be enclosed by a 9,000-foot fence, while a ten-acre farm may require 5,000 feet of fence to enclose it.

88 Henry Dalton, 3 Daily Occurances of Azusa 7, June 19, 1861, Huntington Library, MS DL 1140.

89 Los Angeles Star (February 14, 1852).

These warnings did not apparently work as long as cattle owners had the right to allow their animals to trespass.[90] Once the law in Los Angeles county favored the farmer,[91] Dalton had more power to use: "Some months since I called the attention of M. Corbitt to the fact of your sheep grazing on my land of S. Francisquito. . . . If perchance you will have no objection to make one a fair compensation for the pasture allready consumed and I shall have no objections to making arrangements for their pasturage hereafter, provided we can agree on terms."[92]

One typical situation seems to have been that in which there were numerous cattle ranchers. In such a case, the ability of farmers to contract with cattle ranchers was severely limited. For instance, in Kern County, which is in the southern part of the San Joaquin valley, cattle ranchers from outside the county often pastured their herds within the county. In 1871 it was estimated that there were over 60,000 head of cattle in Kern County that had been driven there by ranchers living in other counties[93] or outside California.

The reason that there were few agreements between farmers and cattle raisers when the cattle raisers had the privilege to trespass can again be traced to nonconvexities. While the large number of ranchers will increase the transaction costs, this is not simply an example of transaction costs that remain high regardless of the original assignment of rights. All that is required to return to the zero transaction costs condition is to change the law to give the right to exclude to the farmer. Then each farmer may negotiate (or not) with one rancher if that rancher considers it to be profitable to use a farmer's land. The nonconvexity in this example comes about as the number of ranchers (not just the number of cattle) may increase without bound, just as there was a nonconvexity in Figure 2 when the number of cattle could increase without being bounded by the convex portion of the production set.

The fence law in essence allowed the land of the state to be held as a commons.[94] As no one needed to own land to raise cattle, many ranchers

[90] For the numerous instances when cattle trespassed on Rancho Azusa, see generally Dalton, *supra* note 78.

[91] See An Act Supplementary to An Act to Prevent the Trespassing of Animals upon Private Property, ch. 411, 1861 Cal. Stat. 474.

[92] Dalton, *supra* note 78.

[93] Ludeke, *supra* note 77, at 108.

[94] The inefficiency of the commons form of ownership is well-known. Garrett Hardin, Tragedy of the Commons, 162 Sci. 1243 (1968), gives the example of overgrazing in Africa to show the ecological problems that result from a regime under which anyone who wishes to use a resource may do so. John Umbeck, Might Makes Rights: A Theory of the Formation and Initial Distribution of Property Rights, 19 Econ. Inquiry 38 (1981), in explaining the formation of "property" rights during the Gold Rush of 1849, shows that, when force (might) is used as the allocation mechanism, the resource so assigned is appropriated by the

became nomadic, with no need to worry about using the land efficiently or even paying taxes: "[T]he country has been greatly injured by being overstocked. A great share are owned by persons never intending to either Squat or settle in the state. They should be called Sliders, I am of the opinion that but half or not more than that have ever been assessed I know of parties owning thousands of cattle (& not one acre of land) And have heard them say they were scattered from Colusa to Petaluma in other word in six different Counties."[95]

The fence law is one instance of bargaining costs increasing because of the assignment of entitlements. Clearly, the administrative costs are asymmetrical with respect to the entitlement. A large number of ranchers are potentially users of any plot of land. If a farmer fails to contract with the rancher who actually uses his land, all the payments made to the other ranchers are useless. On the other hand, if the farmer has the entitlement, while cattle may (if a rancher is negligent) wander over the lands of many farmers, every contract made will benefit the rancher who has paid for the right to trespass. They each decrease the damages that must be paid for violating the farmers' entitlements. Changing the right from the rancher to the farmer changes the negotiations from one (farmer) to *N* (ranchers) to a simple one (farmer) to one (rancher). Therefore it is not side payments from farmers to ranchers that explain the growth of grain growing in the valleys in the absence of changes in the laws.

Thus we must consider the third theory that can explain the development of the valleys as grain producers: the legislature provided rules giving farmers legal protection against trespassing animals. In an area where mixed use is appropriate, it is more efficient to give the entitlement to the farmer.[96] This is not necessarily because farming is a more appropriate use, but rather because the costs of negotiating rents or calculating damages when the farmer has the entitlement are lower than the costs of calculating lost potential "use value" with *N* ranchers, potential users of a plot of land, when the ranchers have the entitlement. To see how changes in the law may have accelerated the development of crop growing

user who has the comparative advantage in the use of force rather than the use of the resource. Therefore, under that scheme, less of the resource will be allocated to the user with the comparative advantage in productive use, so society has fewer products.

[95] Pond Journal, *supra* note 65, at 74, February 4, 1862.

[96] If ranching (or farming) were the only economically efficient use of land, it would not matter who had the entitlement as (by assumption) there would be no competition between uses. For example, even if farmers had the entitlement to be free from trespassing animals, if it were uneconomical to farm grazing land, farmers would not choose to farm there. If perchance one made the mistake of trying, either ranchers could pay him his expected profit (zero) or would compensate him his expected profit (zero) if they happened to trespass. With no gain from farming or from side payments no one would farm grazing land.

in California, two methodologies are used. First in Section III*C*, a history of the legislative enactments for the counties of Sacramento and San Joaquin[97] is presented in an attempt to convey the extent of changes in the law. Then in Section IV a regression analysis of the effect of changes in the laws on agricultural production is presented to show the relation between the statutory enactments and the changes in agricultural production in a more formal way.

### C. *Changes in the Central Valley*

As early as 1851, the California legislature enacted a trespass law covering the counties of Sacramento and San Joaquin.[98] Farmers could take up stray cattle[99] and receive expenses for their care. However, if the person who took up an animal put it to use,[100] no expenses were permitted for caring for the animal. In addition, farmers had a duty to report estrayed cattle within three months to a justice of the peace, even if they had not taken up the animals. A breach of the duty subjected the farmer to a fine not exceeding the value of the estrayed stock.[101] In 1856, the act was repealed and replaced by a similar enactment that was slightly more favorable to the farmers' interests.[102] If after a year's time the animal had not been claimed, the farmer acquired full rights to it on payment of half the animal's appraised value into the county treasury. Landowners were also relieved of their duty to report estrays that they had not taken up. They continued to have the responsibility of posting notice or notifying the owner if they "took up" an estray.[103]

In 1858, the legislature brought both counties within the scope of an 1857 criminal law forbidding the owners of sheep to herd them on the lands of others.[104] The mandatory fine for herding sheep on another's land

[97] Sacramento and San Joaquin were used as sample counties from the Sacramento and San Joaquin valleys. The acts concerning animal trespass law were passed on a county-by-county basis. Sometimes only certain portions of a county were involved, and sometimes only certain townships were covered by the acts.

[98] An Act concerning Estray Animals, ch. 160, 1850–53 Compiled Laws Cal. 854.

[99] Farmers were not the only class of people entitled to take up cattle, and cattle were not the only class of animal mentioned in the statute. Horses, mules, goats, sheep, and other animals were among those that could be taken up, and nonfarmers could take up an animal if it was found wandering on their premises.

[100] For instance, an estrayed cow could be harnessed to a plow, or it could be milked.

[101] An Act concerning Estray Animals, ch. 160, § 5, 1850–53 Compiled Laws Cal. 854–55.

[102] An Act concerning Estray Animals, ch. 128, 1856 Cal. Stat. 186.

[103] *Id.* at 187.

[104] An Act Restricting the Herding of Sheep to Certain Pastures in the Counties of Sonoma and Marin, ch. 194, 1857 Cal. Stat. 227, *amended by* ch. 207, 1858 Cal. Stat. 165.

ranged from twenty-five dollars to \$200.[105] In addition, the injured party was awarded a minimum of twenty-five dollars for each day the violation continued. Sheep found trespassing could also be taken up in accordance with the estray laws relating to cattle.[106]

In 1862, the legislature enacted a liability rule[107] in favor of farmers in certain parts of Sacramento County during certain seasons of the year.[108] Farmers could collect damages for all injuries done to their land by trespassing cattle regardless of whether the land was enclosed by a lawful fence. This act protected farmers only from trespasses on cultivated fields during the sowing, planting, growing, and harvesting seasons and until the crops were removed.[109] The legislature applied this rule only to the valley portions of the county: "[T]his Act shall only apply to that portion of Sacramento County lying south of the American River, on the east bank of the Sacramento, and extending from the Sacramento River to the high lands, or to the line of overflow, as designated on the map of Swamp and Overflowed Lands of Sacramento County."[110] In 1866, other portions of Sacramento County received legislative protection from trespassing cattle by an additional estray law that provided for a system of arbitration to determine damages and that stipulated the sums that farmers could collect as expenses for taking up and safely keeping cattle.[111]

Farmers in San Joaquin County, which lies just south of Sacramento County in the Central Valley, received a slightly different system of protection from that afforded farmers in Sacramento County. In 1864, the legislature authorized the county to impound animals wandering in a farmer's enclosure.[112] In addition to receiving damages for injuries to

[105] For Sacramento County a new law dealing with sheep was enacted some years later. It provided a minimum fine of twenty dollars and a maximum fine of fifty. The injured party received at least five cents a head for every day the violation continued. An Act to Restrict Sheep from Being Herded or Running at Large in Sacramento County, ch. 231, 1875–76 Cal. Stat. 305.

[106] *Id.*

[107] An estray law in the terminology of this paper.

[108] An Act for the Better Protection of Farmers in Certain Portions of Sacramento County, ch. 311, 1862 Cal. Stat. 425.

[109] *Id.*

[110] *Id.* The legislature repeatedly amended the laws to change the geographic areas protected. For Sacramento County this amendment process was particularly hectic. Not all the amendments are mentioned in the text. The important legal developments are noted above, but it should be kept in mind that different parts of Sacramento County were covered by different laws at different times.

[111] An Act to Protect Agriculture, and to Prevent the Trepassing of Animals upon Private Property, ch. 361, 1865–66 Cal. Stat. 440.

[112] An Act to Establish and Maintain Public Pounds, for the Better Securing of Estrays and Other Stock, in the County of San Joaquin, ch. 372, 1863–64 Cal. Stat. 418 (hereinafter referred to as Pound Act). Note that the estray laws were still in effect at this time. 1856 Cal.

crops within an enclosure, farmers also were granted expenses of ten cents a mile for driving estrays to the pound and ten cents per estray if the drive to the pound was further than one mile (if less than a mile, it was five cents per head).[113] Farmers were required to post an impound notice in a public place, for which they received twenty-five cents. An additional twenty cents per mile was awarded for transportation from the pound to wherever the notice was posted.[114] An animal owner who attempted to retake his stock while the animals were being driven to the pound or who attempted a pound breach could be fined up to $100 and could be imprisoned for up to three months.[115]

In 1866, the legislature eliminated the fencing requirement of the impound laws.[116] Farmers could collect damages for injuries to their crops without having first fenced their lands. In addition, the legislature permitted farmers the same fees that the pounds received if the farmer chose to impound an animal on his own property.[117] The amendment applied only to that part of the county north of the Mokelumne River.[118]

In 1872, the legislature gave farmers in San Joaquin County additional protection by eliminating the need for impounding entirely.[119] Farmers could take up animals they found trespassing on their lands and could receive compensation for their keep. Alternatively, they could bring an action for the damage sustained because of the trespass.[120]

Finally, in 1876, both Sacramento and San Joaquin counties were brought within the provisions of an authentic "no fence" law.[121] The legislature made it unlawful for any animal belonging to a given landowner to trespass on the land of another landowner. For such a trespass, the

Stat. 186. Pound laws relieved the farmer of the burden of caring for estrays. If the farmer did not choose to undertake the drive to the pound, however, he could impound the animal or animals in his own barn or corral.

113 Pound Act, *supra* note 112, at 420.

114 *Id.*

115 *Id.*

116 An Act Amendatory of and Supplemental to an Act Entitled An Act to Establish and Maintain Public Pounds for the Better Securing of Estrays and Other Stock in the County of San Joaquin, ch. 456, 1865–66 Cal. Stat. 588.

117 This provision of the act would be brought into play in the event that the county authorities failed to set up a system of pounds. *Id.* at 589. This amounted to fifty cents for each animal impounded, except for sheep, for which only ten cents was allowed. 1863–64 Cal. Stat. at 186.

118 *Id.* at 589.

119 An Act to Protect Agriculture and to Prevent the Trespassing of Animals upon Private Property, ch. 407, 1871–72 Cal. Stat. 563.

120 *Id.* at 565.

121 An Act concerning Trespassing of Animals upon Private Lands in Certain Counties in the State of California, ch. 136, 1877–78 Cal. Stat. 176.

landowner could recover damages and court costs. Attachment procedures were provided in order to give the plaintiff better security for the payment of a judgment,[122] and no animal was exempt from attachment.[123] Additionally, more effective procedures for actions *in rem* against the animals were established. If an injured party brought an action *in rem* and no interested party answered, a default judgment could be entered ten days from the posting of the summons on the courthouse door.[124]

Changes in the law in Sacramento and San Joaquin counties typified the changes made throughout California. Originally, the laws relating to animals favored the cattle ranchers. As time passed, the legislature recognized that the privilege granted ranchers impeded the development of the state's agricultural resources. To encourage agriculture, the legislature experimented with a variety of rules each of which had differing effects on the production of stocks and crops. It should be clear that it requires a more formal analytic approach to understand the effects of this enormous complexity of statutory enactments. The next section details an econometric model that is used to test whether these enactments had the effect of encouraging more efficient agricultural production.

## IV. Empirical Analysis

When California became a territory of the United States in 1848, it was primarily a place where cattle were raised. With the huge increase in population caused by the Gold Rush of 1849, the economic, social, and political processes underwent rapid and radical transformation. California changed from ranching territory into a mining, farming, and mercantile state. The possible causes of the transformation were increases in population, changes in technology, and changes in the law. The question that I am investigating here is the extent to which it was the changes in the law that effected changes in the economic productive life of the area.

Clearly, these adjustments took place as a feedback process. Not only did the law effect the way in which economic production was transformed, but the economic conversions also caused changes in the law. Farming and mercantile interests[125] lobbied the legislature to enact rules that were more favorable to farmers. The statutory enactments pertained to places where there was the most political pressure to change and the least political resistance.[126] This political pressure occurred in large part

[122] *Id.* at 177.
[123] *Id.*
[124] *Id.* at 177–78.
[125] See text at note 36 *supra*.
[126] Ludeke, *supra* note 77.

in those areas where there was increased population of farmers. Given that the production process of ranching in the middle of the nineteenth century allowed cattle to run at large on vast acreages without fences, only in farming would any sizable population produce enough to make profitable use of small plots of land. Therefore increases in population were a cause of both the changes in the law and increases in agricultural production.[127] There is no question that increases in agricultural population encouraged the legislature to change the law.[128]

There is perhaps no real-world example that will come closer to the idealized well-functioning market system envisioned by Coase[129] than this example of the trespass of grazing animals on farmland. The externality is visible, the parties are, at least post hoc, easily identifiable, and it is easy to measure, or use proxies to estimate, the damages. If models based on Coasean analysis are accurate, changes from the Trespass Act[130] to estray laws[131] would have had no significant effect on the relative growth of production of farmers and ranchers.

On the other hand, if changing the negotiating baseline has a significant effect, then changes from fence-out to fence-in laws should increase the production of farm production and the production of all agricultural products.[132] Thus if raisers of stock have the privilege to use land they will not consider the full value of the land. Because of the possible nonconvexity in the production space of the farmer or of some other asymmetry in transaction costs, ranchers will not normally be paid by the farmer to limit their trespass.[133] In fact this was observed as early as 1867: "Instances

[127] The changes in the law also probably occurred against those animals whose owners had the least political power and against those animals that were most likely to cause damage. For an example of the problems that hogs caused, see Pond Journal, *supra* note 65, at 39, April 30, 1853.

[128] For a theoretical explanation of the changes in legislation due to the preferences of the electorate, see James M. Buchanan & Gordon Tullock, The Calculus of Consent: Logical Foundations of Constitutional Democracy (1962).

[129] Coase, *supra* note 2.

[130] The Trespass Act (a fence-out law) gave a privilege of use to the rancher. See text at notes 43–47 *supra*.

[131] Estray laws give the right to exclude to the landowner and allow the possessor of land to "take up" stray animals. See text at note 48 *supra*.

[132] If the change to the fence-in regime is more efficient than the fence-out regime, not only should the production of crops increase (which could occur merely because of a change in the entitlement if transaction costs were too high to have further trades), but the total production should also increase as land is (by assumption) being devoted to a higher valued use. Therefore, if either total production or the production of crops does not increase following a change in the law, the baseline hypotheses are refuted.

[133] The example of a contract giving a limited right of animals to trespass was limited to a landowner's lease, where the landowner had the statutory right to exclude. See Dalton, *supra* note 88. No contracts were found under the legal regime under which the animal owners had the privilege to use.

can be cited where the rancher who owns cattle by the thousands has purchased of the public domain from eighty to one hundred sixty acres . . . surrounded by thousands of acres of good agricultural land . . . which . . . he uses and enjoys as absolutely as if he had obtained a patent for the whole tract. . . . The herding of large bands of cattle on the unenclosed lands has a tendency to prevent its settlement by permanent farmers."[134]

An understanding of the complexity of factors that were described in the historical materials can be furthered by the use of econometric techniques. To test whether changes in the law had the effect of increasing total and crop production, the following model was estimated:

$$\text{Production} = F[\text{Inputs, costs, legal variables, growth factor, technology (fertility, weather, interaction)}].$$

As the model is attempting to explain whether changes in statutes that apply to individual counties changed the production of agricultural products in each of the counties, all data are collected annually by county.[135]

Annual data were collected by county on the thousands of bushels of each crop harvested.[136] These are the statistics used as a measure of production. The measure of input of land is the number of acres of land cultivated for each crop. Annual data on the number of head of cattle and sheep[137] are also reported and compiled by county as the gauge of production of stock. Most changes in the law are reported as "dummy" variables with a value of zero if the type of law has not been enacted or one if it has.[138]

The measure of the interaction between competing land uses is the density of use within a county. The more intensely that land is used, the more probable it will be that competing uses will be neighbors. Estimation of the effect of growth of population is achieved through the use of time as a variable.[139] Annual data on climate and fertility were not available, so density of crop production was also used as a proxy for fertility and

[134] Committee on Agriculture, Report in Relation to Fencing Agricultural Lands, California Senate, 17th Sess. (1868).

[135] Assessors of the several counties of California collected yearly taxes on land, improvements, personal property, and production. They reported their assessments, or estimates of value and quantity produced, annually to the legislature. The assessments were published annually in appendices to the proceedings of the legislature. All the statutory changes took place from 1850 to 1887; this therefore is the period studied.

[136] The two principal crops were wheat and barley; therefore they are the ones studied.

[137] Cattle and sheep were the two dominant animals raised in California in the nineteenth century.

[138] If the statute applied to only a part of a county, a fraction less than one is used. Unfortunately, as all the other data are reported by county, it is impossible to see the microeffects of the statutes within a county using this methodology.

[139] Other annual measures of population growth were not available.

TABLE 2

EXPLANATION OF VARIABLES

| | | |
|---|---|---|
| WHMA | = | Wheat in thousands of bushels, moving averaged |
| BAMA | = | Barley in thousands of bushels, moving averaged |
| CATMA | = | Cattle in thousands of head, moving averaged |
| SHMA | = | Sheep in thousands of head, moving averaged |
| WPAC | = | Wheat per acre, moving averaged |
| BPAC | = | Barley per acre, moving averaged |
| VPAC | = | Assessed value per acre, moving averaged |
| YEAR | = | Calendar year, 1854–90 |
| LHT | = | Hog Trespass Law |
| LHE | = | Hog Estray Law |
| LHP | = | Hog Pound Law |
| LHC | = | Hog Criminal Law |
| LST | = | Sheep Trespass Law |
| LSE | = | Sheep Estray Law |
| LSC | = | Sheep Criminal Law |
| LCT | = | Cattle Trespass Law |
| LCE | = | Cattle Estray Law |
| LCC | = | Cattle Criminal Law |
| LAT | = | All Animal Trespass Law |
| LAE | = | All Animal Estray Law |

climate factors. In addition, assessed value serves as the measure for the cost of the primary input, land.[140] Because of variability in data collection,[141] all production data are reported as five-year moving averages,[142] which are used to reduce the unexplained variability in the production information (for a list of variables, see Table 2).

The estimated model is a simple linear multiple regression model in which each of the explanatory variables will explain a portion of the variability in the production of $X$, where $X$ is one of the crops or animals studied. The estimated model was a linear model of the form

$$\begin{aligned} X\mathrm{MA} = {} & b_1 + b_2\mathrm{LHE} + b_3\mathrm{LHP} + b_4\mathrm{LHC} + b_5\mathrm{LST} + b_6\mathrm{LSC} \\ & + b_7\mathrm{LCT} + b_8\mathrm{LCE} + b_9\mathrm{LCC} + b_{10}\mathrm{LAE} \\ & + b_{11}\mathrm{YEAR} + b_{12}\mathrm{VPAC} + b_{13}\mathrm{WPAC} + b_{14}\mathrm{BPAC}, \end{aligned}$$

[140] This value also takes other inputs into account, such as fencing, corrals, and farm buildings, since they are counted as improvements. It also accounts for the difference in the costs of farm- and rangeland, as farms had a higher assessed value per acre.

[141] This may be due to the fact that assessors apparently used the previous year's assessment over again, or it may be caused by real microchanges in climate or other unexplained factors.

[142] Moving averages were calculated by the formula

$$X\mathrm{MA}_t = .1X_{t-2} + .2X_{t-1} + .4X_t + .2X_{t+1} + .1X_{t+2},$$

where $X$ refers to one of the animals or crops studied. This formula weights the present year ($t$) very strongly (by 40 percent) but allows the years before and after the year studied to smooth some of that unexplained variation.

where *X*MA is the moving average for each of the four products studied: wheat, barley, cattle, and sheep production.[143] This equation was estimated using as an observation each of the fifty-four counties that existed in California for up to thirty-seven years, during 1850–87.[144] The estimation results for the complete model are presented in Table 3.

These results are consistent with models that predict that changes in the baseline will affect the equilibrium outcome and are inconsistent with the Coasean hypothesis. Uniformly, the significant coefficients on the legal variables are positive, which implies that changes from fence-out to fence-in laws encouraged the growth of the crop-growing industry. For instance, the coefficient of 170 on LHE, in the equation explaining WHMA, means that a change from the Trespass Act of 1850 to a Hog Estray Law tended to increase the annual production of wheat in a county by 170,000 bushels.

The effect on wheat is quite striking. In a typical county that had all the significant statutes in effect,[145] the production of wheat would have increased by over 1,270,000 bushels. Barley, a less important crop, would have had its annual production increased by a total of over 270,000 bushels in a typical county if every statute that had a significant effect was in force. It must also be noted that there was no trend attributable merely to growth. That is, the effect of YEAR on both crops was negative and for wheat insignificant. These results suggest that the growth of the agricultural sector in California in this period of strong growth can be explained by the efficacy of the changes in animal trespass law.

The results of the equations estimating the effect of the law on cattle production is also consistent with the hypotheses that fence-in laws (the trespass, estray, and criminal statutes) would increase the efficiency of land use in the total of crop growing and animal raising. For cattle there were three statutes that had a significant effect on production: the cattle estray laws and criminal laws regarding cattle and sheep. The total effect of the three laws was to increase the number of cattle in a typical county by about 3,000 head.

[143] A number of the possible legal variables were dropped from the equation because of the high degree of collinearity with other variables: $R_{\text{LHT.LHE}} = .712$; $R_{\text{LSE.LCE}} = .680$; and $R_{\text{LAT.LAE}} = .748$. Also, there were separate acts for horses, but they were essentially coterminous with laws relating to cattle: $R_{\text{LHorseT.LCT}} = 1.00$; $R_{\text{LHorseE.LCE}} = 0.973$; and $R_{\text{LHorseC.LCC}} = 1.00$.

[144] Not every county existed for the entire period, and many observations had one or more missing values. Any observation with a missing value for any of the included variables was dropped. These two reasons account for about two-thirds of the potential sample of 1,828 observations; therefore there are only 619 complete observations. The model was estimated using ordinary least squares regression, with a pooled cross-sectional time series.

[145] The variables LHE, LHC, LCT, LCE, and LAE were all significant at the 5 percent level or better.

TABLE 3

REGRESSION RESULTS

| EXPLANATORY VARIABLES | DEPENDENT VARIABLES | | | |
|---|---|---|---|---|
| | WHMA | BAMA | CATMA | SHMA |
| LHE | 170.49 | 82.31 | −1.19 | −15.97 |
| | (3.72)** | (5.25)** | (−1.32) | (−2.86)** |
| LHP | −296.99 | −45.59 | −4.77 | −81.34 |
| | (−.95) | (−.43) | (−.78) | (−2.14)** |
| LHC | 81.01 | 22.28 | −.79 | −4.74 |
| | (2.66)** | (2.14)* | (−1.32) | (−1.28) |
| LST | −1.49 | −1.77 | −.35 | −1.16 |
| | (−.05) | (−.19) | (−.64) | (−.35) |
| LSC | 2.53 | 1.20 | .08 | −.17 |
| | (1.60) | (2.22)* | (2.48)* | (−.88) |
| LCT | 580.26 | 97.17 | −.88 | 35.62 |
| | (4.19)** | (2.05)* | (−.32) | (2.11)* |
| LCE | 140.02 | 35.12 | 2.77 | −.27 |
| | (1.98)* | (1.47) | (1.99)* | (−.036) |
| LCC | −2.20 | 3.71 | .35 | 2.13 |
| | (−.98) | (4.85)** | (7.96)** | (7.81)** |
| LAE | 303.02 | 68.00 | −1.11 | 23.92 |
| | (5.54)** | (3.63)** | (−1.04) | (3.59)** |
| YEAR | −4.30 | −2.96 | −.12 | 1.47 |
| | (1.11) | (−2.27)* | (−1.55) | (3.11)** |
| VPAC | −.00009 | −.00003 | −.000003 | .000008 |
| | (−.63) | (−.50) | (−1.17) | (.45) |
| WPAC | .86 | ... | −.03 | −.08 |
| | (1.44) | | (−2.40)* | (−1.05) |
| BPAC | ... | .002 | .00004 | .0002 |
| | | (1.63) | (.52) | (.46) |
| Constant | 7930.51 | 5545.54 | 234.05 | −2682.18 |
| | (1.10) | (2.27)* | (1.65)* | (−3.05)** |
| $R^2$ | .154 | .164 | .131 | .168 |
| $F$ | 10.388** | 11.120** | 8.175** | 10.594** |
| df | 12,606 | 12,606 | 13,605 | 13,605 |

NOTE.—The numbers in parentheses are *t*-statistics. For an explanation of the variables, see Table 2.
* Significant at the 5 percent level.
** Significant at the 10 percent level.

The laws did not have a consistent effect on the production of sheep. The pound and estray laws that applied to hogs (LHE and LHP) had a negative relation with sheep production. They were associated with a decrease in sheep production of almost 100,000 head in the average county to which they apply. On the other hand, cattle trespass and cattle criminal laws and estray laws that applied to all animals were associated with increases in sheep production. The total increase that can be traced to these laws was approximately 60,000 head. In addition there was a significant positive trend associated with the sheep industry: every year was associated with an additional 1,500 sheep per county.

Changes in the animal trespass laws would be associated with increases in the production of animals if the new laws encouraged ranchers to adopt more efficient techniques. It is clear that the technology of ranching did change during this period of time and that the changes seem to have corresponded to the changes in the law.[146]

A possible explanation of the negative effect of several statutes on sheep production is the expected one (from the "baseline" hypotheses) that laws that sheep raisers viewed as increasing their costs would lead them to decrease production in those areas with higher costs. The efficacy of the laws relating to cattle tended to increase the number of sheep, as cattle and sheep were competing users of pastureland. Those statutes that made it more expensive for cattle ranchers caused them either to decrease production or to decrease their use of open land and substitute hay and fenced pastures. With these changes, the availability of range for sheep would increase.

As the analysis of the regression equations in this section has demonstrated, the simple Coase theorem does not form the basis of an empirically verifiable hypothesis regarding the efficiency of property rights entitlements. Clearly in a zero transaction cost world the Coase theorem would be verified, as it is tautologically true. Any failure of the theorem would always be due to the existence of transaction costs. We are obviously not in that world, so the zero transaction cost version of the theorem is simply not empirically verifiable. Rather, that version of the theorem that posits that the assignment of rights is irrelevant can be rejected in favor of "baseline" theories. These theories acknowledge that the assignment of rights sets the negotiating baseline that affects the equilibrium allocation.

Changes in the law had very consistent positive effects on the production of crops, which is clearly in accord with the theory that giving rights to the receptor would increase its production. Regarding animal production, changes in the law often allowed the production of animals to grow. Otherwise animal production decreased so that agricultural production could increase. This is exactly what one would have expected from theories of property rights entitlement that accept the significance of baselines.

The strong effects of the law on production, shown by the econometric results, thus should be interpreted as a refutation of that application of the Coase theorem that implies that changes in the legal rights of the parties in

[146] See generally Cleland, *supra* note 26, at 87 n.28. See also Ludeke, *supra* note 77, at 109–11, where some ranchers were found to have begun the process of fencing in even before the law encouraged it by giving rights to the farmer.

a property rights dispute have no effect on the equilibrium production of the parties. There are two possible reasons for this result.

The first reason derives from the more commonly held view that in large number bargaining situations the transaction costs become high enough to prevent an efficient bargain from resulting. If this theory is correct, then one must go through a search for the efficient outcome, as detailed by Wittman, to determine how entitlements must be assigned. As mentioned earlier, this procedure is ordinarily very difficult, as the decision maker will ordinarily not have all the correct information or even the correct incentives.[147]

The second reason is derived from the observation that when a significant externality exists the production (or consumption) function of the receptor will be nonconvex. The nonconvexity will also result in a failure of the market system to achieve an optimal result; but this problem occurs only when the generator of the externality is assigned the right. Under this theory it is quite easy to correct the problem: simply assign the entitlement to the externality receptor. While it may still be true that high transaction costs may prevent the optimal equilibrium from being achieved even in this circumstance, we know that the market system cannot achieve optimality as long as the right is assigned to the externality generator. Only if the decision maker is able to use Wittman's methodology is there a reason to depart from the prima facie rule that the right should be assigned to the receptor. This result is much the same as what ordinary language theorists, like Epstein, have argued. Only now there is also a technical economic verification for the instance in which the Coase theorem fails.

[147] See text at note 12 *supra*.

# [7]

# The Coase Theorem, Free Agency, and Major League Baseball: A Panel Study of Pitcher Mobility from 1961 to 1992*

TIMOTHY R. HYLAN
*Eli Lilly and Company*
*Indianapolis, Indiana*

MAUREEN J. LAGE
*Miami University*
*Oxford, Ohio*

MICHAEL TREGLIA
*Miami University*
*Oxford, Ohio*

## I. Introduction

A great deal of conceptual and empirical work in the economic analysis of the law and property rights has been directed towards resolving a controversy surrounding the Coase Theorem. Many economists and legal scholars interpret the theorem as containing two propositions. The first is that, in the absence of transactions costs and wealth effects, parties will bargain to an efficient outcome. The second holds that the *same* outcome will be achieved regardless of the distribution of property rights. The latter is known as the invariance thesis and it has been a source of dispute among scholars and between economic theorists and owners of economic enterprises (e.g., owners of professional sports teams) [5; 11; 16; 23; 24; 25; 26; 28; 29].[1] This paper provides an econometric test of the invariance proposition. Major League Baseball presents a natural experiment consisting of an industry in which there has been an explicit change in the assignment of property rights. Beginning in 1879, the reserve clause gave monopsony power to team owners; a player could negotiate salary only with the team that owned his contract and the team could trade or sell the player as management saw fit. In 1976 this system was replaced by the institution of free agency whereby a player with at least six years of Major League experience acquired

*Thanks to Don Cymrot, James Dunlevy, Rodney Fort, John Heywood, Richard Thaler and an anonymous referee for comments and suggestions on earlier drafts of this paper. In addition, we thank workshop participants at the CNA Corporation, Miami University, the University of Illinois College of Law, the Pennsylvania State University, and West Virginia University for their helpful comments as well.

1. It should be noted that Rottenberg [24] first discussed the invariance proposition, which is a particular application of the Coase Theorem.

the right to sell his services to prospective buyers.[2] One implication of the invariance thesis is the testable hypothesis that the mobility decisions made by players after the introduction of free agency would be the same as those made by the owners in the pre-free agency era.

The abundance of data from professional baseball provides an excellent opportunity for testing many propositions from economics. Detailed measures of an individual player's productivity are collected annually as well as output measures of team performance. Also, one can clearly identify the team where each player is employed and can readily trace the mobility of players over time. Hence, there exist previous empirical examinations of the Coase Theorem, free agency, and the mobility decisions of Major League Baseball players. However, there does not appear to be agreement upon what constitutes an appropriate test of the invariance thesis in the case of baseball free agency. Previous examinations of this issue have used data that differed in terms of the period under analysis, the subset of the population of baseball players used for analysis, measures of labor mobility behavior, and measures of the outcomes of that behavior. The level of sophistication of the statistical tests has also varied widely.[3] A significant contribution of this paper is that it provides an econometric analysis of the mobility behavior of *all* pitchers who played in Major League Baseball during the 1961–92 period.

The results of this paper lead to a rejection of the invariance thesis of the Coase Theorem. The empirical analysis shows that after the introduction of free agency, the pitchers with greater longevity in the major leagues are less likely to move relative to their mobility in the pre-free agency period. The results also indicate that, in general, better pitchers are less likely to move and that pitchers playing on teams with higher winning percentages or in large market cities were less likely to move.

The rest of the paper is organized as follows: Section II provides brief reviews of the labor mobility decision and the Coase Theorem to motivate the expected effect of the introduction of free agency on labor mobility. It also critically examines previous empirical tests of the invariance thesis. Section III discusses the empirical model while section IV briefly describes the creation of the data set and relevant variables. The results of the empirical analysis are presented and discussed in section V. Section VI concludes and outlines an agenda for future research.

## II. Labor Mobility, Baseball and the Coase Theorem

### *Conceptual Issues*

Labor mobility can be broadly classified as *involuntary* or *voluntary*. Involuntary labor mobility is the result of workers being forced to leave their current employment. In general, this may be due to dismissal for poor performance, structural changes in the economy, or shifts in the demand for labor. Player mobility in Major League Baseball during the pre-free agency period would be classified as involuntary mobility. A player would cease to be a member of the team if management released the player from his contract or assigned that player to another team.[4] As the owner of the rights to the player's contract, the team has an incentive to realize the maximum value of that asset. Thus, it is expected that owners will trade players so as to achieve a distribution of

2. Dworkin [13] and Scully [26] provide description and analysis of the institutional details.

3. These issues are critically discussed in the following section.

4. Note that a player being traded might desire such a change in employers. Nevertheless, the terminology reflects that team management has the power in the mobility decision during the pre-free agency period.

player talent that equalizes marginal revenue product (MRP) across teams. If a player on Team A had a higher MRP with, say, Team B, the owners of the two teams would have an incentive to negotiate a deal sending the player to Team B for suitable compensation.

Voluntary mobility occurs when workers choose to change jobs because they are dissatisfied with their current position or because they expect to find a better one elsewhere. The mobility decision in this scenario depends upon the acquisition of information about alternative opportunities, the costs of moving, and the increase in earnings expected from moving. The attainment of free agent status would allow a player the opportunity to voluntarily move to a team from which he could extract a better offer than he currently possessed.[5] The expected outcome is that a player will move to the team where his MRP is highest. However, this will result in the same distribution of talent that obtained when the owners moved the players. That is, the player distribution will be the one that maximizes league revenues, although in this case it would be the player receiving the rents associated with his provision of labor services.[6]

The existence of transactions costs and wealth effects may lead to observance of results that are inconsistent with the predictions of the Coase Theorem. The assumption of negligible transactions costs is central to the efficiency version. Should they be large, transactions costs may completely erode the gains from trade and inhibit the exchange of entitlements from lower-valued users to higher-valued users. Thus, the assignment of rights will have efficiency implications when transactions costs are relatively high. Whether transactions costs are significant in Major League Baseball is not clear. Agent fees and league conventions against sales of players are potentially important sources of transactions costs. Agent fees represent perhaps the biggest transactions costs players face in negotiating a salary with a team. Often the agent's fee is a fraction of the total compensation package and the size could be larger than the cooperative surplus. While player salaries generally increased in absolute terms following free agency, it is not clear whether agent fees or other kinds of transactions costs became larger in relative terms to the overall compensation package or even whether they are large enough to affect exchange. League agreements not to sell players for cash might also be a source of transactions costs. A well known example is that of Commissioner Kuhn blocking several player sales by Charley Finley of the Oakland A's during 1976. The action was justified as being in "the best interests of baseball."[7] Fan opposition to the selling of favored players might be a source of transactions costs that could lead owners to agreements not to make such sales. Ultimately, the role of transactions costs is an empirical issue.[8] However, while the absence of transactions costs is important for the efficiency version of the Coase Theorem, the invariance prediction does not necessarily depend upon this issue. Although transaction costs might impair some trades, if the level of transaction costs is roughly the same before and after free agency, then the degree of labor mobility need not have been altered.

The relevance of wealth effects is the second issue concerning the applicability of the Coase Theorem. In contrast to transactions costs, the absence of wealth effects is crucial for the invariance proposition. Wealth effects are potentially important in the baseball setting because free

5. In the first year of free agency, 1977, the average salary rose from $51,501 to $76,066. At the start of the 1994 season, the average player's salary was $1.2 million. A partial list of studies on the effect of free agency on player salaries includes Sommers and Quinton [27], Hill and Spelman [17], Noll [20], Scully [26], Quirk and Fort [21], and Fort and Quirk [14].

6. Scully [26] and Fort and Quirk [14] contain graphical analyses of the distribution of player talent.

7. This episode is discussed in Scully [26].

8. It should be noted that a strand in the literature views the Coase Theorem as a tautology rather than an empirical proposition. To the tautologists, if an inefficient outcome is observed, it *must* be due to the presence of transactions costs [3; 25].

agency shifts bargaining power previously held by the owners to the players. Assuming the team is a profit-maximizing firm, it will value a player the same regardless of whether the team or the player has the mobility entitlement. However, receiving the entitlement may affect the behavior of a utility-maximizing player [28]. For example, a preference to play for a championship team or a team near the player's home may manifest itself if the player is feeling wealthier after the change to free agency. As a specific example, when Kirby Puckett re-signed as a Minnesota Twin in December 1992, he reportedly turned down a higher paying offer from the Boston Red Sox, citing his ties to the community and to the Twins organization.[9] Thus, in general, a player's mobility decision could be affected by the change in assignment of property rights.

Assuming the absence of wealth effects and that the level of transactions costs did not change significantly after the introduction of free agency, the above considerations suggest that Major League Ballplayers will move to teams where their marginal revenue product is highest. During the period before free agency, team management has the incentive to find such a team for the player. Post-free agency, the player has the incentive to find the team where his skills are valued highest.[10] The invariance thesis predicts that the mobility decisions are not affected by the ownership of the property rights; i.e., controlling for player quality, the likelihood of a particular type of player moving from one team to another before the advent of free agency should not differ from the probability of that type of player changing teams in the post-free agency era.

*Empirical Issues*

A wide range of evidence has been brought to bear in examinations of the applicability of the invariance thesis to Major League Baseball. These include: casual observations of the baseball labor market; measures of aggregate labor mobility before and after the introduction of free agency; and, in an indirect attempt to get at the issue of invariance in behavior by focusing on the outcomes of that behavior, researchers have examined if competitiveness in baseball has been altered due to the institutional change. First have been the simple presentations of situations wherein a number of free agents failed to re-sign with their current team [19] or the assertion that the proportion of free agents re-signing with their current team is virtually insignificant [29]. This evidence is adduced to indicate the failure of the invariance thesis under the supposition that the free agents were already at the team that valued their services most highly. We return to this point below.

The second approach examined the aggregate flows of player talent in an attempt to discern if players moved themselves in the post free-agency period in the same manner as the team owners had moved them previously. Comparing the *rate* of player transfers in the years before the introduction of free agency with that occurring in the following years, Spitzer and Hoffman [28] and Besanko and Simon [1] find the institutional change had no significant effect on the rate at which players switched teams. On the other hand, there have been mixed results about player mobility behavior vis-à-vis owner movement of players when team and market characteristics are included in the analysis. Rottenberg [24] was the first to point out that team winning percentage and market size were important factors determining the mobility of player talent. Assuming diminishing returns to player talent, Rottenberg's analysis implied that good players should move from better teams to worse teams because their marginal contribution would be greater on the weaker team.

9. *Baseball Tonight*, ESPN, 30 July 1995.

10. Fort and Quirk [14] indicate that although the player goes to the team where his MRP is highest, he is paid only the MRP at the next highest team. Cassing and Douglas [4] suggest that the auction mechanism leads to bias and that free agents may be paid "too much."

Also, since marginal revenue would be greater in large cities than small cities, ceteris paribus, players would be expected to move from small market teams to large market teams. Besanko and Simon [1] provide some evidence reporting no change in the correlation between player mobility and either team winning percentage or market size after the introduction of free agency. However, their result is sensitive to the correlation measure.[11] Drahozal [12] analyzed the subset of players signing long-term contracts between 1977–81 and reports that players entering the free agent draft and non-reentrants tend to come from same size cities. However, in his sample, players entering the free agent draft do not move from smaller to larger cities, a result contradicting a prediction made by Rottenberg.[12] Note that by basing the analysis upon data from 1977–81, Drahozal's study of the invariance thesis is a test of whether the owners move non-free agent eligible players the same way the free agent eligible players move themselves *in the post-free agency era*. Cymrot, Dunlevy and Even [9] also exploit the dual nature of the post-free agency Major League Baseball labor market. Using salary data on hitters from 1979–80, they find that free agent eligible players tend to move in response to estimated salary gains similarly to the mobility of non-free agent eligibles.

The third type of evidence marshaled in examinations of the invariance thesis was indirect evidence pertaining to team competitiveness. Since Rottenberg's analysis pertaining to the movement of good players from better to worse teams would hold under any institutional arrangement regarding property rights, this implied that competitive balance in baseball should be unaffected by changes in the ownership of property rights to players' services. Using measures of between-season competitiveness and within-season competitiveness, Besanko and Simon [1] fail to detect a change in the level of competitiveness in Major League Baseball after the introduction of free agency. Drahozal [12] calculates the standard deviations of winning percentages in the National and American Leagues before and after the introduction of free agency. Although a statistical test is not presented, he claims a failure to see a clear difference in the dispersion of winning percentages lends support to the invariance proposition. Scully [26], using a similar test but more data, finds that free agency led to increased competition in the National League.

The data and methodology employed in the above examinations of the invariance thesis, while suggestive, can be improved upon. First, the introduction of free agency into Major League Baseball was an important institutional change that might have disrupted the market and led to disequilibrium outcomes while agents were adjusting to the new environment. Ideally, a test of the invariance thesis as applied to the institutional change of free agency would focus on the mobility of individual players, encompass a period of time long enough to allow the market to adjust to the institutional change, and compare the movement of players before the change to player movement after the introduction of free agency. For the most part, the papers cited above were written when only a few years of data from the post-free agency period were available. By contrast, the analysis in this paper is based upon a period of time long enough so that a presumption exists that equilibrium behavior is being captured.[13] Also, while the analysis of data

11. Besanko and Simon [1] reject the Coase Theorem using the Pearson correlation coefficient but fail to reject using the Spearman coefficient.

12. Cymrot [7] showed that good teams tend to lose "non-marginal" free agents. While this supports Rottenberg's prediction, it does not shed light on the invariance proposition.

13. It should be noted that by using the period of 1961–1992 in this paper, any possible disequilibrium period is included in the analysis. As a test of robustness, our results were re-estimated, omitting the sample period 1976–1980 (i.e., immediately after the implementation of free agency). The results remain unchanged. Note that this does not rule out the possibility that using data *only* from such a period might lead to different results.

exclusively from the post-free agency era may not be revealing any current differences between the mobility behavior of free agent eligible and non-free agent eligible players, it is obvious that this strategy will fail to capture any inter-period differences. Since the test employed in this paper is based on panel data over an extended period, it does capture changes in mobility behavior across regimes.

Second, it is not clear that focusing on aggregate mobility patterns or the outcomes of those patterns constitutes an appropriate test of the invariance thesis as applied to the introduction of free agency. For example, even if the aggregate rate at which players moved in the pre-free agency period did not differ from the rate in the post-free agency era, if the types or quality of players transferring has been altered, then the invariance thesis would not hold. Similarly, the research examining team winning performance and competitiveness did not control for player quality and, hence, ignored this aspect of the invariance thesis. The analysis in this paper is based upon the complete player statistics of all pitchers from 1961–1992 as well as a number of team performance measures and institutional variables. Use of this rich data set and econometric techniques to control for player quality, team characteristics and other institutional factors provides a sharper analysis of the impact of free agency on pitcher mobility than has been obtained heretofore.

Note that by focusing on the mobility behavior of *all* pitchers, this paper's approach differs from those which examine the invariance thesis by considering only the mobility behavior of free agents [19; 29] or that of free agents that moved [10].[14] We believe that observing a number of free agents that fail to re-sign with their current team is beside the point in an evaluation of the invariance proposition. Our interpretation of the Coase Theorem's invariance thesis is that, ceteris paribus, the mobility behavior of players in the free agency period should be no different from that mobility in the pre-free agency era. The invariance proposition does not predict whether a particular player *will* move to another team, but only that he would be *no more or less likely* to move after free agency; the likelihood of moving would not be affected by the assignment of rights to the mobility decision.

## III. Econometric Specification

The empirical test of the invariance thesis employed in this paper focuses on the decision regarding a player's mobility. A player moves to another team if the expected net benefits from moving to another team are positive. The net benefits to moving are specified as:

$$Y^*_{i,t} = \beta \mathbf{X}_{i,t-1} + \gamma Z_{i,t} + \epsilon_{i,t} \tag{1}$$

where $Y^*_{i,t}$ is a variable reflecting the net benefits of individual $i$ moving to another team in period $t$, $\mathbf{X}_{i,t-1}$ is a vector of explanatory variables, $\beta$ is a vector of parameters to be estimated, $Z_{i,t}$ is a variable controlling for whether the period is before or after free agency, $\gamma$ is a parameter to be estimated, and $\epsilon_{i,t}$ is an independent and identically distributed error term. The invariance thesis implies that $\gamma$ equals zero and the slope coefficients, $\beta$, are not significantly different in the pre- and post-free agency periods.

The net benefits to a player of moving are unobservable in practice. However, an indicator variable measuring whether the player moved to another team can be defined as follows:

14. In this regard, the paper is following the literature on migration which recognizes that some people move while others stay put. See Cymrot and Dunlevy [8] for an application of this literature to the baseball players labor market.

$$Y_{i,t} = 1 \text{ if } Y^*_{i,t} > 0;$$
$$Y_{i,t} = 0 \text{ if } Y^*_{i,t} \leq 0. \qquad (2)$$

Substitution of $Y_{i,t}$ as a proxy for $Y^*_{i,t}$ allows maximum likelihood estimation of equation (1) using a probit analysis.

The empirical analysis exploits the panel nature of the dataset. In particular, repeated observations across individuals allow unobserved individual heterogeneity to be controlled for in the analysis. Important sources of heterogeneity in baseball pitchers may be the player's natural ability, his "heart," or team leadership characteristics. For example, Jack Morris (a three-time, twenty game winner) was recently signed by the Cincinnati Reds for the 1995 season. In response to a reporter's question, he said ". . . but the bottom line is that I've always been able to win. It's something I strive for. I hope my attitude can rub off."[15] Such traits are thought to be important in building winning teams and could affect mobility. To test for potentially important individual effects, a random effects probit model was estimated.[16] However, estimation of this model revealed that individual heterogeneity was not a significant determinant of pitcher mobility. Although not expected, given this result, it is more efficient to estimate the model treating the sample as a pooled cross section/time series data set.[17] These results are reported below.

## IV. Data

The data in this study are the records of Major League Baseball pitchers who played between 1961 an 1992.[18] There were three main reasons for the choice of this data set. First, the data covers *all* pitchers over the period of analysis. By including the entire sample of pitchers, this paper differs from previous studies of baseball player mobility which were based upon more restricted subsets of the baseball player population. Second, the choice of pitchers allows for control over player heterogeneity across different positions. This dispenses with the need to control for positional differences through a large number of indicator variables. Third, by choosing a time frame of thirty-two periods, a balanced data set was obtained relative to the introduction of free agency. Free agency was instituted in November 1976; the data set extends both sixteen years before and sixteen years after that date. For these reasons, the panel data set used in this study is a much richer basis for an evaluation of the invariance hypothesis than has been utilized in previous analses of the effects from free agency.

The total number of pitchers in Major League Baseball between 1961 and 1992 is 2,403 which represents approximately thirty-eight per cent of all pitchers who ever played. Of the pitchers in this sample, 766 have at least six years of experience in the major leagues.[19] The final panel data set contains 11,699 pitcher-year observations.

15. *Washington Post*, 9 April 1995.

16. The individual effect may be modeled as a fixed effect or a random effect. However, fixed effects probit estimation is not possible with panel data. Since the maximum likelihood estimation jointly determines the parameter estimates and the individual effects, the individual specific effects cannot be removed. The random effects specification was estimated using the Butler-Moffitt quadrature procedure [2].

17. Greene [15] contains a review of the literature and an accessible introduction to random effects probit procedures. Diagnostic checking revealed that adding team performance measures rendered the individual effects insignificant.

18. Unless otherwise indicated, all statistics are taken from Thorn and Palmer [30].

19. Pitchers with at least six years of experience represent approximately thirty-two per cent of the sample. The average tenure in the major leagues of the pitchers in the sample is 4.87 years.

The discrete choice analysis focuses on whether or not a player moved during a particular period. In the model, the start of a period is defined as the beginning of the off-season and the period runs through the end of the ensuing regular season. The dependent variable in the probit estimation is an indicator variable that is coded "1" if a player moved to another team during the period in question. For example, the period denoted 1990 would begin with the off-season following the 1989 regular season and extend to the end of the 1990 season. If a player remained with the same team throughout this period, the dependent variable would be coded as "0." Otherwise, the indicator would be coded "1."

Three classes of explanatory variables are included in the analysis to control for the effects of individual performance, team characteristics, and institutional effects. The measures of an individual's performance consist of the following: winning percentage (*PCT*); a dummy variable coded "1" if the pitcher was a twenty game winner, "0" otherwise (*TWENT*); opponents' batting average (*OAV*); adjusted earned run average (*ERAPLUS*); and an indicator variable coded "1" if the pitcher won the Cy Young award during the previous season and "0" otherwise (*CYYOUNG*). In addition, the number of games started divided by total number of appearances (*GS*) and the number of games saved divided by total number of appearances (*SV*) are also used as independent variables. These last two variables are intended to capture any differences between relief pitchers and starting pitchers, given the increasing importance of relief pitching over the duration of the sample period.

Since information about the productivities of the players becomes available over time and, in the post-free agency era, a player's tenure in the Major Leagues is a critical factor determining eligibility for contract rights, several controls are included to capture the effect of player longevity on mobility. Relatively inexperienced pitchers with zero to two years of service in the Major Leagues are treated as the base case. If a pitcher had three to five years of service in the league, then *YRSLG0* is coded "1" and "0" otherwise; *YRSLG1* is coded "1" if a pitcher has six years of service in the Majors, "0" otherwise; *YRSLG2* is "1" for veteran players with seven to ten years of service; and *YRSLG3* is coded "1" for pitchers with eleven or more years in Major League Baseball.

The team performance measures include the team's prior year winning percentage (*TPCT*) as well as an indicator variable if the player was on a team that won their divisional pennant in the previous season. *PW* is coded "1" for a player on such a team and "0" otherwise. Also, a control was added to capture differences between National and American League teams. Baseball aficionados view the strike zone in the National League to be smaller than in the American League which is considered to favor hitters relative to pitchers in the National League (and vice-versa in the American). In addition, the American League adopted the Designated Hitter Rule in 1973 while this is not a part of the National League game. The variable *NATL* was coded "1" for players on teams in the National League and "0" otherwise.

One of the controls for changes in the institutional arrangements of the game captured the effect of league expansion on player mobility. The variable *ROSTER* is constructed by multiplying the number of roster spots per team by the total number of teams in MLB in a given year. This variable captures the effect of having an increasing number of players in Major League Baseball. For example, a player who was not good enough to play in the majors prior to expansion would not show up in the data set, while ceteris paribus, after an increase in the number of roster spots or the number of teams in the league, a player with equivalent skills may be able to make a team. If these players are marginal, they may be more likely to change teams as they try for an opening as a reserve player. Therefore, we might expect *ROSTER* to be positively related to mobility.

The introduction of free agency ushered in an era of rising player salaries. In an effort to control their costs, team owners apparently resorted to collusive practices after the 1980 players strike. A professional arbitrator found baseball team owners guilty of collusion in the free agent market during the 1985 and 1986 seasons. Since collusive behavior on the owners part meant restricted offers for player services and this could affect player mobility, the variable *COLLUS* is coded "1" for the years 1985–86 and is "0" otherwise.[20]

A third institutional change which occurred in Major League Baseball during the period of analysis is the increasing importance of television as a source of revenues. For example, between 1965 and 1987 the fees from the sale of broadcast rights for the average team rose over one thousand percent [26]. Furthermore, Scully [26, 110] has argued that ". . . the value of the local rights more or less is determined by the size of the broadcast market." Therefore, we have included the variable *POP*, which is equal to the population of the metropolitan area (measured in millions) divided by the square root of the number of teams in the city.[21] This variable also captures any differences between "big city" and "small city" teams.[22]

The final variables used to control for institutional changes are those which measure the effect of free agency on player mobility. Since free agency did not begin formally until November 1976, the indicator variable *FREE* is coded "1" for the 1977 through 1992 seasons and "0" otherwise. Also, *FREE* is interacted with each of the longevity variables to test if player mobility in the free agency period differs from the pre-free agency period depending upon the type of player. In particular, since free agency is a right limited to players with six or more years of experience, the interaction of *YRSLG*1 with *FREE* (*YRSLG*1*F*) will identify the effect of attaining the minimum service requirement for free agent eligibility on pitcher mobility. The interactions of *YRSLG*2 with *FREE* and that of *YRSLG*3 with *FREE* is designed to capture any changes in the mobility behavior of veteran players after free agency.[23] Finally, although players with zero to five years of experience are generally not eligible for free agency, those with three to five years are eligible for salary arbitration. This is a right not held by the players with only zero to two years of service. Furthermore, if the team does not agree to salary arbitration, the players in the former category may become free agents. The interaction of *YRSLG*0 with *FREE* captures any differences in the mobility between pitchers with zero to two years in the major leagues and those with three to five years of service in the post-free agency era.[24]

The variable *AGENT* was included to control for those pitchers who declared themselves

20. See Scully [26] for discussion of the collusion amongst the owners. Some evidence suggests that the collusion era lasted much longer than 1985–1986. For example, Marvin Miller testified before Congress in 1982 about the possibility of clubs colluding. Scully has argued that, "There is no prospect of solution to the (collusion) dispute . . . until the current labor-management agreement expires on 31 December 1989" [26, 42]. In order to allow for the possibility of a lengthier collusion era, we also set *COLLUS* equal to one during the entire period of the 1981–89 labor-management agreement. Results reported are not sensitive to alternative specifications of *COLLUS*.

21. Source for this variable is *The Statistical Abstract of the United States*, various editions. Division of the population by the square root of the number of teams is consistent with Coffin [6], who argues that this is the best way to account for the cities which have more than one major league team. This variable was also calculated as simply the population of the metropolitan area and as the population divided by the number of teams in the city. Results reported are not sensitive to alternative specifications.

22. We thank the referee for suggesting the use of population data.

23. The choice of ten years of service as the break between *YRSLG*2 and *YRSLG*3 was somewhat arbitrary. Experimenting with other choices for this break point did not affect the results.

24. The 1976 Basic Agreement and subsequent agreements provide for a number of circumstances in which a player with fewer than six years of service may become a free agent. See Wong [31] for details. Also, arbitration eligibility has been determined by two years of service for most of the period in the dataset. The 1986 Basic Agreement raised the arbitration eligibility requirement to three years of service but the 1990 lockout led to compromise on this issue and 17% of players with two years of service again became eligible for arbitration. Diagnostic checks using zero to three years of service as the omitted category did not affect the magnitude nor the significance of the results.

**Table I.** Descriptive Statistics

| Variable | Mean | Standard Deviation |
|---|---|---|
| *PCT* | 0.174 | 0.167 |
| *TWENT* | 0.018 | 0.135 |
| *GS* | 0.407 | 0.414 |
| *SV* | 0.048 | 0.098 |
| *SO* | 2.014 | 1.440 |
| *OAV* | 0.267 | 0.068 |
| *ERAPLUS* | 98.318 | 48.911 |
| *CYYOUNG* | 0.005 | 0.074 |
| *YRSLG0* | 0.250 | 0.433 |
| *YRSLG1* | 0.060 | 0.238 |
| *YRSLG2* | 0.156 | 0.363 |
| *YRSLG3* | 0.090 | 0.287 |
| *YRSLG0F* | 0.141 | 0.348 |
| *YRSLG1F* | 0.033 | 0.179 |
| *YRSLG2F* | 0.086 | 0.280 |
| *YRSLG3F* | 0.056 | 0.230 |
| *NATL* | 0.477 | 0.499 |
| *PW* | 0.079 | 0.271 |
| *POP* | 3.171 | 1.689 |
| *TPCT* | 0.492 | 0.089 |
| *ROSTER* | 600.15 | 56.834 |
| *COLLUS* | 0.071 | 0.257 |
| *FREE* | 0.562 | 0.496 |
| *AGENT* | 0.046 | 0.210 |

free agents.[25] *AGENT* is coded "1" if the player was declared a free agent during the previous year and "0" otherwise. This proxies for "true" eligibility to move since some pitchers may have signed long term contracts. Thus, although some individuals may have the requisite number of years of service to be eligible for free agent status, a long term contract binding them to a certain team would preclude those individuals from exercising this right.

The invariance proposition of the Coase Theorem holds that the institutional change (*FREE*) should have no effect on player mobility taken by itself, that players of different service levels should not move differently due to this change (the interaction between *YRSLG** and *FREE* should be insignificant for all variables *YRSLG*0, *YRSLG*1, *YRSLG*2, *YRSLG*3) and, additionally, the slope coefficients should not statistically differ before and after free agency.

## V. Results

Table I presents the descriptive statistics of all variables used in the regression. Of all the pitchers covered in the sample, 56.2% played in the post-free agency era while only 4.6% declared themselves free agents.

The main results are presented in Table II. The first results show that "better" pitchers were less likely to move. Pitcher winning percentage, games started, saves, strikeouts, and winning

25. The source for the *AGENT* variable is various issues of the *Official Baseball Guide* [22].

**Table II.** Maximum Likelihood Regression Results

| Variable | Coefficient | $t$-statistic[a] | Marginal Effects |
|---|---|---|---|
| *INTERCEPT* | −0.3500 | −1.486 | −0.0840 |
| *PCT* | 0.3878 | −2.460*** | −0.0931 |
| *TWENT* | −0.1362 | −1.106 | −0.0327 |
| *GS* | −0.3660 | −5.420*** | −0.0879 |
| *SV* | −1.2811 | −7.636*** | −0.3075 |
| *SO* | −0.0719 | −3.744*** | −0.0173 |
| *OAV* | 0.2053 | 0.916 | 0.0493 |
| *ERAPLUS* | −0.0002 | −0.649 | −0.0001 |
| *CYYOUNG* | −0.6884 | −2.601*** | −0.1652 |
| *YRSLG0* | 0.8324 | 15.940*** | 0.1998 |
| *YRSLG1* | 0.8966 | 10.727*** | 0.2151 |
| *YRSLG2* | 0.9780 | 16.310*** | 0.2348 |
| *YRSLG3* | 1.2795 | 17.015*** | 0.3071 |
| *ROSTER* | 0.0007 | 1.783* | 0.0002 |
| *COLLUS* | 0.0340 | 0.618 | 0.0082 |
| *NATL* | −0.0120 | −0.726 | −0.0048 |
| *PW* | 0.0424 | 0.755 | 0.0102 |
| *TPCT* | −1.8640 | −11.676*** | −0.4474 |
| *POP* | −0.0151 | −1.848* | −0.0036 |
| *FREE* | −0.0030 | −0.052 | 0.0007 |
| *YRSLG0F* | −0.1244 | −1.800* | −0.0495 |
| *YRSLG1F* | −0.0196 | −0.174 | −0.0471 |
| *YRSLG2F* | −0.2109 | −2.630*** | −0.0506 |
| *YRSLG3F* | −0.6608 | −6.674*** | −0.1586 |
| *AGENT* | 1.2477 | 18.852*** | 0.2995 |

a. *, **, and *** represent significance at the 10, 5 and 1% level, respectively.

the Cy Young award all had negative coefficients that were statistically significant. The results also show that pitchers become more likely to move as their longevity increases. Taking pitchers with zero to two years of experience as the base case, the coefficients on *YRSLG*0, *YRSLG*1, *YRSLG*2 and *YRSLG*3 are positive, increasing and highly significant. The last column of Table II shows the contribution to the probability of moving of each of the variables, i.e., the marginal effects.[26] These show that the longevity variables, as well as *CYYOUNG* and *SV*, had much higher contribution to the likelihood of moving than did the other variables which captured individual performance; the former variables were generally two to three times the magnitude of the latter.

League expansion and/or increases in the team's roster size (*ROSTER*) had the expected positive effect on pitcher mobility. However, the results indicate that the collusion era was not a significant determinant of mobility. In addition, playing on National League teams or a team that won its divisional pennant did not appear to be a significant determinant of mobility. On the other hand, the variables capturing team winning percentage and city population size show significant negative effects on player mobility. The negative sign on *POP* shows that pitchers are

26. For continuous variables, the marginal effects were calculated by computing $\Phi(\mathbf{X}, B)$ for each observation, summing up over all observations, and dividing the sum by the number of observations in the data set. Each variable was separately increased by one standard deviation from the mean and $\Phi(\mathbf{X}, B)/N$ was computed. The difference is the marginal effect. For dichotomous variables, the marginal effect was calculated in a similar fashion with the variable set to 0 for all observations and then set to 1.

less likely to leave large city teams. This result complements both Rottenberg's [24] prediction that players would move to large city teams and Cymrot's [7] empirical results that free agents move to large market teams. However, the negative sign on *TPCT* (indicating that better teams are less likely to lose players) contrasts with another of Cymrot's results. He found that good teams did lose free agents.

Turning to the invariance proposition, the coefficient on the *FREE* variable is positive but insignificant. Taken by itself, this might be interpreted as lending support to the invariance thesis. However, our broad interpretation of the Coase Theorem is that the mobility behavior of all players must not change due to an institutional change. This does not occur in the data. Seasoned pitchers (those with seven or more years of service) have significantly lower likelihood of moving during the post-free agency era as is shown in the interaction of the *YRSLG** variables with the *FREE* variable; i.e., *YRSLG2F* and *YRSLG3F* were negative and significant.[27] The invariance thesis is rejected on this basis. In particular, *YRSLG3F* shows that the probability of moving for the pitchers with the most years of service is reduced by approximately 50% in the post-free agency era. Interestingly, *YRSLG1F* was not significantly different from zero. This means that the pitchers with six years of service in the majors, the minimum requirement to attain free agent status, were not any less likely to move after the introduction of free agency than before.

To emphasize the above, recall that free agency applies to all those with six years of experience and who are not under long-term contracts. Recognizably, free agency could increase the value of long-term contracts and potentially reduce the mobility of players who sign such a contract. The issuance of long-term contracts may be more likely under free agency as teams attempt to buy back the property rights to the player.[28] The invariance thesis would view the long-term contract as just another mechanism for moving the right to its highest valued use.

The data shows that pitchers who declare themselves to be free agents have a strong likelihood of moving; the coefficient on the *AGENT* variable is positive and significant. Kelman [19] and Thaler [29] would reject the invariance proposition on this basis. However, since the *AGENT* variable is controlling for players who have signaled a desire to change teams, this may be capturing self-selection. Since there is no way of knowing if these players would have moved in the absence of free agency, we believe that the *FREE* variable and the interaction of *FREE* with the longevity variables (*YRSLG0*, *YRSLG1*, *YRSLG2*, *YRSLG3*) provides the correct basis for evaluating the invariance thesis. A fair test of the invariance thesis would consider the mobility behavior of all players and not just that of declared free agents.[29]

## VI. Conclusion

The invariance thesis of the Coase Theorem holds that a change in the distribution of property rights will not affect the allocation of resources. In this paper, the mobility behavior of all pitchers

27. Note that all pitchers with more than two years of experience have negative coefficients on the interaction term.

28. Kahn [18] found that free agency raised contract duration.

29. One caveat in interpreting the results is the advent of final-offer arbitration in 1973. Given the timing of this policy, it is difficult to completely disentangle any possible effects that arbitration as opposed to free agency may have on player mobility. Examination of *YRSLG0F* shows that pitchers with years of service which make them eligible for arbitration but not free agency are significantly less likely to move during the free agency era. As a diagnostic check, we estimate Table II for the years 1971–76, setting *ARB* equal to "1" during the era of final-offer arbitration (after the 1973 season) and "0" otherwise. Results indicate that arbitration had a minimal effect on player mobility. It should be noted however, that such results may be biased due to any possible disequilibrium effect which might have occurred immediately after the implementation of final-offer arbitration.

playing in Major League Baseball from 1961–1992 is examined to shed light on the invariance proposition. The evidence shows that, while controlling for player ability, team characteristics, and self-selection by the players, the mobility behavior of veteran pitchers changed after the introduction of free agency in 1976. Specifically, those pitchers with seven or more years of service in the Major Leagues were less likely to move than had been the case when team owners had the rights to the rents from the player's services. These results lead to a rejection of the invariance proposition of the Coase Theorem.

One obvious extension of this methodology would be to extend the analysis to hitters. Cymrot and Dunlevy [8] postulate that mobility behavior should not differ between offensive and defensive players. This remains to be seen. In addition, obtaining measures of wealth effects and transactions costs would be useful variables. It may be argued that this paper's rejection of the invariance thesis for the veteran pitchers could reflect the presence of wealth effects. The fact that previous studies failed to reject the invariance proposition implies that wealth effects, if present, were not significant in the past. This may no longer be true given the escalating salaries in Major League Baseball.

## References

1. Besanko, David A. and Daniel Simon, "Resource Allocation in the Baseball Players' Labor Market: An Empirical Investigation." *Review of Business and Economic Research,* Fall 1985, 71–84.

2. Butler J. and R. Moffitt, "A Computationally Efficient Quadrature Procedure for the One Factor Multinomial Probit Model." *Econometrica,* May 1982, 761–64.

3. Calabresi, Guido, "Transaction Cost, Resource Allocation and Liability Rules—A Comment." *Journal of Law and Economics,* April 1968, 67–73.

4. Cassing, James and Richard W. Douglas, "Implications of the Auction Mechanism in Baseball's Free Agent Draft." *Southern Economic Journal,* July 1980, 110–21.

5. Coase, Ronald H., "The Problem of Social Choice." *Journal of Law and Economics,* October 1960, 1–44.

6. Coffin, Donald A. "Understanding Attendance in Major League Baseball, 1976–1979," Working Paper, Indiana University Northwest, 1995.

7. Cymrot, Donald J., "Migration Trends and Earnings of Free Agents in Major League Baseball, 1976–1979." *Economic Inquiry,* October 1983, 545–56.

8. ——— and James A. Dunlevy, "Are Free Agents Perspicacious Peregrinators?" *Review of Economics and Statistics,* February 1987, 50–58.

9. ———, ———, and William E. Even. " 'Who's on First?' An Empirical Test of the Coase Theorem in Baseball," Working Paper, Miami University, 1995.

10. Daly, George and William J. Moore, "Externalities, Property Rights and the Allocation of Resources in Major League Baseball." *Economic Inquiry,* January 1981, 77–95.

11. Demsetz, Harold, "When Does the Rule of Liability Matter?" *Journal of Legal Studies,* January 1972, 13–28.

12. Drahozol, Christopher, "The Impact of Free Agency on the Distribution of Playing Talents in Major League Baseball." *Journal of Economics and Business,* May 1986, 113–21.

13. Dworkin, James. *Owners versus Players: Baseball and Collective Bargaining.* Boston: Auburn House, 1981.

14. Fort, Rodney and James Quirk, "Cross-Subsidization, Incentives, and Outcomes in Professional Team Sports Leagues." *Journal of Economic Literature,* September 1995, 1265–99.

15. Greene, William H. *Econometric Analysis.* Englewood Cliffs, N.J.: Prentice Hall, 1993.

16. Grier, Kevin B. and Robert D. Tollison, "The Rookie Draft and Competitive Balance: The Case of Professional Football." *Journal of Economic Behavior and Organization,* October 1994, 293–98.

17. Hill, James and William Spelman, "Professional Baseball: The Reserve Clause and Salary Structure." *Industrial Relations,* Winter 1983, 1–19.

18. Kahn, Lawrence, "Free Agency, Long-Term Contracts and Compensation in Major League Baseball: Estimates from Panel Data." *The Review of Economics and Statistics,* February 1993, 157–64.

19. Kelman, Mark, "Consumption Theory, Production Theory, and Ideology in the Coase Theorem." *Southern California Law Review,* March 1979, 669–98.

20. Noll, Roger, "The Economics of Sports Leagues." *The Law of Professional and Amateur Sports,* edited by Gary Uberstine. New York: C. Boardman Co., 1988.

21. Quirk, James and Rodney Fort. *Pay Dirt: The Business of Professional Team Sports*. Princeton, N.J.: Princeton University Press, 1992.

22. The Sporting News. *Official Baseball Guide*. St. Louis, Missouri: The Sporting News, 1977–92.

23. Regan, Donald H., "The Problem of Social Cost Revisited." *Journal of Law and Economics*, October 1972, 427–37.

24. Rottenberg, Simon, "The Baseball Players' Labor Market." *Journal of Political Economy*, June 1956, 242–58.

25. Schwab, Stewart, "Coase Defends Coase: Why Lawyers Listen and Economists Do Not." *Michigan Law Review*, May 1989, 1171–98.

26. Scully, Gerald W. *The Business of Major League Baseball*. Chicago: The University of Chicago Press, 1989.

27. Sommers, Paul M. and N. Quinton, "Pay and Performance in Major League Baseball: The Case of the First Family of Free Agents." *Journal of Human Resources*, Summer 1982, 426–36.

28. Spitzer, Matthew L. and Elizabeth Hoffman, "A Reply to Consumption Theory, Production Theory, and Ideology in the Coase Theorem." *Southern California Law Review*, March 1980, 1187–214.

29. Thaler, Richard, "Toward a Positive Theory of Consumer Choice." *Journal of Economic Behavior and Organization*, March 1980, 39–60.

30. Thorn, John and Pete Palmer, eds. *Total Baseball*. New York: Harper Collins, 1993.

31. Wong, Glenn M., "Major League Baseball's Grievance Arbitration System: A Comparison with Nonsports Industry." *Employee Relations Law Journal*, Winter 1987, 464–90.

# Part III
# Coase Theorem and the Constitution

# [8]

# THE COASE THEOREM AND THE THEORY OF THE STATE*

JAMES M. BUCHANAN**

Things were really quite simple in the post-Pigovian world of microeconomic policy, a world characterized by possible divergencies between private and social marginal cost (or product). The classically nefarious factory might be observed to spew its smoke on the neighboring housewife's laundry, and in so doing impose costs that were not reckoned in its presumed strict profit-maximizing calculus. The remedy seemed straightforward. The "government" should impose a corrective tax on the factory owner, related directly to the smoke-generating output (or, if required, a particular input) and measured by the marginal external or spillover cost. Through this device the firm would be forced to make its decisions on the basis of a "socially correct" comparison of costs and revenues. Its profit-mazimizing objective should then lead it to results that would be "socially optimal."

Things have not seemed nearly so simple since R. H. Coase presented his analysis of social cost.[1] Coase's central insight lay in his recognition that there are two sides to any potential economic interdependence, two parties to any potential exchange, and that this insures at least some pressure toward fully voluntary and freely negotiated agreements. Moreover, such agreements tend to insure the attainment of efficiency without the necessity of goverrmental intervention beyond the initial definition of rights and the enforcement of contracts. Applied to the example in hand, if the damage to the housewife's laundry exceeds in value the benefits that the firm derives from allowing its stacks to smoke, a range of mutual gain exists, and utility and profit-maximizing behavior on the part of the two parties involved will result in at least some reduction in the observed level of smoke damage, a reduction that can be taken to be efficient in terms of total product value. No governmental remedy may be called for at all, and indeed Coase argued that attempted correction by government might create inefficiency. Such intervention might forestall or distort the negotiations between the affected parties. As a further aspect of his analysis, Coase advanced the

*I am indebted to my colleagues Winston Bush, Dennis Mueller, and Gordon Tullock for helpful suggestions.

**Director, Center for the Study of Public Choice, Virginia Polytechnic Institute and State University.

1. Coase, *The Problem of Social Cost,* 3 J. Law & Econ. 1-44 (1960).

theorem on allocational neutrality that now bears his name. This states that under idealized conditions when transactions costs are absent and where income-effect feedbacks are not relevant, the allocational results of voluntarily negotiated agreements will be invariant over differing assignments of property rights among the parties to the interaction.

Much of the discussion since 1960 has involved the limitations of this theorem in the presence of positive transactions costs. In this setting, differing assignments of rights may affect allocative outcomes. Furthermore, the transactions costs barrier to voluntarily negotiated agreements that can be classified as tolerably efficient may be all but prohibitive in some situations, notably those that may require simultaneous agreement among many parties. The generalized transactions costs rubric may be used to array alternative institutional structures, with the implied objective being that of minimizing these costs.

My purpose in this paper is not to elaborate these extensions and/or limitations of the Coase analysis, many of which have become familiar even if an exhaustive taxonomy of cases has not been completed. My purpose is almost the opposite. I want to extend the Coase analysis, within his assumptions of zero transactions costs and insignificant income-effect feedbacks, to differing institutional settings than those that have normally been implicitly assumed in the discussions of the neutrality theorem. This approach leads to the question: Why did Coase suggest that the Pigovian prescriptions might produce inefficient results? Or, to put this somewhat differently, why does the theorem of allocational neutrality stop short at certain ill-defined institutional limits? Why can it not be extended to encompass all possible institutional variations, variations that may be broadly interpreted as differences in the assignments of property rights? What is there in the implied Pigovian institutional framework that might inhibit the voluntary negotiations among parties, always assuming zero transactions costs? If the neutrality theorem holds, why should the political economist be overly concerned about institutional reform, as such?

There is a paradox of sorts here between the theorem of allocational neutrality, interpreted in its most general sense, and Coase's basic policy position. One implication of the theorem, so interpreted, would be that the thrust of classical political economy may have been misdirected. Adam Smith's central message points toward institutional reform and reconstruction as means of guaranteeing overall efficiency in resource usage, and, as noted, we can always interpret institutions as embodying specific property rights. Governmental authorities were to be stripped of their traditionally established rights to interfere in the workings of the market economy; or, stated conversely, individual traders were to be granted rights to negotiate on their own terms. The central theorem of classical economies might be summarized as the demonstration of the differences in allocational results under divergent institutional structures. I do not think that Coase would disagree with my statements here, and I think that he shares with me an admiration for Adam Smith and that Coase, too, places Smith's emphasis on institutional-structural reform above the modern policy emphasis on detailed and particularistic manipulation of observed results.

The apparent paradox may be resolved when we take account of the theory of the state or of government that is, perhaps surprisingly, shared by Adam Smith, Pigou, and Coase. My argument proceeds in several steps. First, it is necessary to distinguish carefully between property rights and liability rules. Secondly, I shall demonstrate that governmental or collective action, if conceived in the Wicksellian framework or model, does not modify the applicability of the neutrality theorem. Thirdly, I shall show that government, conceived in a non-Wicksellian model, need not modify the applicability of the theorem, but that, in such case, property rights are explicitly changed with the introduction of governmental action. Finally, I shall suggest that the theory of government decision-making implicit in both classical and neoclassical economics, and carried over in Coase's analysis, offers the source of the seemingly paradoxical limits on the neutrality theorem.

## PROPERTY RULES AND LIABILITY RULES

In his basic paper, Coase did not carefully make a distinction between the assignment of rights to particular individuals and the rules determining the liability of particular individuals for damage that their behavior might impose on others. His example, the now-familiar one of the interaction between the rancher and the farmer, was discussed in terms of alternative rules for bearing liability for damages. Either the rancher, whose cattle strayed onto the neighboring croplands, was liable for damages that the farmer might suffer, or he was not liable. If both cattle and grain were marketed competitively, the neutrality theorem showed that the same allocative outcome would be generated, regardless of which set of liability rules should be in existence. In the former case, the rancher, knowing in advance that he would be liable for damages caused by his straying animals, would include these payments as an anticipated cost in making his size-of-herd decisions. In the latter case, the farmer, knowing that he can collect no damages from the rancher (and that he must respect the property rights of the rancher to cattle), will find it advantageous to initiate payments to the latter in exchange for agreements limiting the size of herd, if indeed the value of crop damage at the margin exceeds the value of the additional grazing to the rancher.

Coase overlooked the fact that the institutional structure was significantly different in the two cases. In the second case, the shift toward an efficient outcome takes place through an ordinary market or exchange process, in which none other than the two parties need get involved. In the first case, however, as presented by Coase, there must be third-party interference by a "judge" to assess charges for damage that has been done. In the context of his discussions, this institutional difference does not matter, since the third-party can, presumably, measure and assess damages with complete accuracy. The difference is nonetheless important in the more general setting. Consistency should have dictated that the first case be presented, not as one where the rancher was liable *ex post* for damages caused by his straying animals, but as one where the farmer held enforceable property rights in his croplands, rights that were inviolate except on his own agreement. In this framework, the rancher would have had to negotiate an agreement with the farmer in advance of any actual straying of cattle. This converts the institutional setting on this side into one that is parallel to the converse case. No third party, no judge, is required to intervene and to assess damages *ex post.*

We may define this setting as one in which property rules are established and enforced, as opposed to liability rules.[2] This setting calls direct attention to the motivation that both parties have to exploit the potentially realizable surplus by moving from the initial inefficient position. This setting also allows for an extension of the neutrality-efficiency theorem beyond those strictly objectifiable circumstances suggested to be present in the Coase example. If the precise degree of damage caused by external imposition is ambiguous, the third party must necessarily exercise his own best judgment in making a settlement. By contrast, if property rules are defined, with

2. This terminology is adopted from the discussion by Calabresi and Melamed, whose paper clarifies the distinction between these two. As they state, a property rule "is the form of entitlement which gives rise to the least amount of state intervention." *See* Calabresi & Melamed, *Property Rules, Liability Rules, and Inalienability: One View of the Cathedral,* 85 Harv. L. Rev. 1089-146 (1972); *see also* Demsetz, *Some Aspects of Property Rights,* 9 J. Law & Econ. 64-5 (1966).

In a paper to be published, I have also called attention to the distinction between these two institutional arrangements, noting in particular the necessary resort to third-party action under liability rules. *See* Buchanan, *The Institutional Structure of Externality,* Pub. Choice (forthcoming).

the necessity of prior agreement on the part of the potentially damaged party, the latter's own subjective assessment of potential damage becomes controlling in determining the range over which final outcomes may settle. This assessment is, of course, a better measure of actual value lost than the estimate made by any third party.

## WICKSELLIAN UNANIMITY

For my purposes in this paper, the specification that parties to an interaction are defined by property rather than liability rules facilitates relating the Coase theorem on allocational neutrality to the underlying conception or theory of government or of the State. In the simplest possible model, we may conceive of a polity that is limited in membership to the parties directly involved in the potential interaction. The interacting group can be made coincident in membership with the political unit. On this basis, we can interpret the "trades" among the parties as being analogous to collective or governmental decisions reached under the operation of a Wicksellian rule of unanimity.[3] Consider either the earlier factory-housewife example, or Coase's familiar rancher-farmer one. In either illustration, we can think of the two-party group as comprising the all-inclusive membership in the political community, in which case agreement between the two parties on any matter is equivalent to unanimous accord. Resort to third-party adjudication is impossible for the simple reason that no third party exists.

From this context, it becomes easier to conceive "the State" merely as the instrumental means or device through which individuals attempt to carry out activities aimed at securing jointly-desired objectives. This is, of course, the traditional framework for all theories of social-contract origins of government. In this setting, all activities of the public sector are explained in exchange terms, even if it is recognized that the exchange process is significantly more complex than that which makes up the central subject matter of orthodox economic theory. There is at least no conceptual or logical necessity to think of "the State" as an entity that exists separate from and apart from citizens.

If we remain within the strict contractarian conception of collective action, where all decisions require unanimous consent by all

3. Collective decision-making under a rule of unanimity is associated with the name of Knut Wicksell in modern public-finance theory analysis because he proposed institutional reforms that embodied unanimity in the reaching of tax and expenditure decisions. *See*, K. Wicksell, *Finanztheoretische Untersuchungen* (Jena: Gustav Fischer, 1896). The central portion of this work appears in English translation as, *A New Principle of Just Taxation*, in Classics in the Theory of Public Finance 72-118 (R. Musgrave & A. Peacock ed. 1959).

members of the political community, and if we retain the assumption that transactions costs are absent, the Coase theorem on allocational neutrality may be applied beyond those limits within which it has normally been discussed. In this model, collective or governmental decision-making remains equivalent to freely-negotiated voluntary exchange. Hence, there is little or no cause for concern about "governmental intervention" as such, because any action that might properly be classified as "governmental" would not emerge unless all parties agree on the contractual terms.

Differences in the assignment of rights might, as in the standard simple exchange cases, generate differences in distributional outcomes, but the contractual process would lead to allocational results that are both efficient and invariant. Consider a classic example, that introduces what we may appropriately call collective or public goods, David Hume's villagers whose utility would be increased by drainage of a meadow. The neutrality theorem, applied to this example, demonstrates that an efficient and unchanged allocational result will emerge from freely-negotiated contract whether the postulated initial position should be one in which individuals own separate plots of land through which the swampy stream flows or whether the whole meadow is defined as communal property, accessible to all parties. With an effective unanimity rule, and with zero transactions costs, the complex exchange that is required for efficiency would be worked out under any initial structure of individual rights. The sharing of the gross gains-from-trade among separate persons would, of course, be infiuenced by the particular property assignment in being. If the sharing of such gains modifies individual demands for the common good, at the margin, that is, if income effects are present, differing assignments can produce slight differences in allocational results, but, under the assumptions here, those results produced will continue to be efficient.

## SIMPLE MAJORITY VOTING

When the unanimity requirement for collective decisions is abandoned, governmental action no longer represents a complex equivalent of a voluntary exchange process.[4] If decisions that are to be binding over the inclusive group can be made by a subset of this group, there is no guarantee that a particular individual holds against the

4. It is possible to use the analogue to voluntary exchange at the level of constitutional, as opposed to day-to-day choice. That is to say, we might analyze the selection of a political constitution, the rules for the reaching of collective decisions, under a postulated unanimity rule. It is then possible to derive a logical basis for non-unanimity rules from unanimous agreement at the constitutional level. This is the approach taken in J. Buchanan & G. Tullock, The Calculus of Consent (1962).

imposition of net harm or damage. Once his own contractual agreement to the terms of governmental or collective action is dropped as a requirement, an individual can no longer be certain that he will share in the gross gains that governmental action will, presumably, generate. From this it seems to follow that collective action, motivated by improvement in the positions of members of a decisive coalition smaller than the totality of community membership, need not produce results that are efficient, even with zero transactions costs.[5] Any nonunanimity voting rule, for example, that of simple majority voting, would seem to produce results that may be, in the net, inefficient.

The neutrality theorum is, however, more powerful than might be suggested by cursory attention to this example. Efficient outcomes will tend to emerge from the contractual process, even under less-than-unanimity voting rules for collective action, if the modified structure of property rights consequent on the departure from unanimity is acknowledged, and if individuals are allowed freely to negotiate trades in these rights. Economists have not fully incorporated the property-rights structure of less-than-unanimity voting rules into their orthodoxy, and they tend to stop short of the extension of the neutrality theorem herein suggested.

Consider a situation in which individuals hold well-defined rights, which are acknowledged by all parties, and which are known to be enforceable without costs. If no collective action is undertaken, individuals trade such rights among themselves in simple exchanges, insuring mutuality of gain. If collective action is undertaken, but only on the agreement of all parties, mutality of gain (or, at the limit, absence of loss) is insured. If this requirement is dropped, and individuals may be subjected to damage or harm through collective action, the value of their initial holdings is necessarily changed, again on the assumption of zero transactions costs. Individuals no longer hold claims that are inviolate against imposed reductions in value. A new and ambiguous set of rights is brought into being by the authorization of governmental action taken without the approval of all parties. Any potentially decisive decision-making coalition, a simple majority of voters in our example here, possesses rights to the nominal holdings of the minority. These rights are, in this instance, ambiguous because they emerge only upon the identification of the majority coalition that is to be decisive with respect to the issue under

5. With zero transactions costs, any departure from unanimity voting rules for collective action would hardly be acceptable at the constitutional level. But this modification is introduced here for purposes of developing the exposition of the argument, not for descriptive relevance.

consideration for collective action. Once identified, however, members of the effective majority hold potentially marketable rights. These may be exchanged, directly or indirectly, and the contractual process will again insure that the efficient allocative outcome will be achieved, and that this will be invariant, given the appropriate assumptions about transactions costs and income effects.

We may illustrate this in a highly-simplified three-person example. Consider a community that includes three men: A, B, and C. Collective decisions are to be made by simple majority voting. Initial holdings of units of an all-purpose and numberable consumption good are, let us say, 100 for A, 60 for B, and 30 for C. In this environment, let us suppose that a governmental project is proposed, one that promises to yield benefits of 30 units, distributed equally among the three persons. The gross costs of this project are, however, 40 units; clearly, the proposal is inefficient. Despite this, if B and C can succeed in organizing themselves into a majority coalition, and if they can impose the full tax costs of the proposal on A, they can make net gains. In this case, the results would appear as follows:

| Person | Benefits | Costs | Net |
|---|---|---|---|
| A | 10 | 40 | –30 |
| B | 10 | 0 | 10 |
| C | 10 | 0 | 10 |

Once B and C are identified as the decisive members of the coalition, however, individual A can negotiate trades, or side payments, that will be mutually beneficial to all parties, and which will keep this inefficient outcome from being achieved. Individual A can, for example, offer either B or C a net gain of 15 units to join a different majority coalition that will disapprove the project. Or, if both B and C hold firm, they can exact from A a payment of 10 units for their agreement to withhold the project. The side payments, which must be allowed to take place under our assumption of zero transactions costs, will insure that all inefficient projects are forestalled, and, similarly, that all efficient projects will be carried out.[6]

The values to individuals of the "property rights in franchise"

6. It is often erroneously argued that individuals with the superior economic power, A in our example, can exercise more influence in the formation of dominant coalitions than individuals with inferior economic power, C in our example. If, however, C fully recognizes the exploitation potential available in the situation described, he can offer B precisely the same terms as those offered by A. In the basic arithmetic here, there is no more likelihood that the net gains from not undertaking the project, 10 units, will be shared by A rather than by B or C. In effect, the Von Neumann-Morgenstern solution set of imputations to the simple majority game becomes:

(5,5,0) (5,0,5) (0,5,5).

For an elaboration of this analysis, *see*, Buchanan & Tullock *supra* note 4, at chs. 11 and 12.

embodied in a majority-voting regime depend critically on the constitutional limits within which majorities are allowed to take collective-political action. These values will also depend on the technological possibilities for potential coalition gains within the given set of constitutional constraints defined. Detailed exploration of these interesting and mostly unresolved issues would not be suitable in this paper. For present purposes, the points to be recognized are, firstly, that any departure from unanimity in collective decision processes modifies the structure of rights from that which is defined exclusively by private-sector claims and obligations, and, secondly, that even with this modified set of rights, the theorum on allocational neutrality remains valid within the required, and highly restricted, assumptions concerning transactions costs and income effects.[7]

## ADMINISTRATIVE AUTHORITY

In traditional economic-policy discussions, the arguments for and/or against governmental intervention in the private sector rarely take place under explicitly defined models for collective decision making. For the most part, those who propose "corrections" to the outcomes of voluntary exchange processes, like those who oppose them, are content to treat governmental decisions as exogenous to the valuations of the persons in the economy itself. If, however, these arguments are interpreted consistently within any collective decision-making framework, the structure that can most readily be inferred is neither that of unanimity nor simple majority voting. The model of government that accords most closely with economic policy discussions is one in which authority to take collective action is vested in an administrator, a bureaucrat, an expert, who chooses for the community, presumably on the basis of his own version of the "public interest," or, in technical economist's jargon, some "social welfare function."

It is useful, therefore, to extend our analysis of the theorem on allocational neutrality to this administrative-decision model of public choice. Probably because the model is essentially implicit rather than explicitly postulated, little or no attention has been paid to the alternative means through which the single decision-maker for the collectivity may be selected. Nor need this concern us here. Strictly

7. In another paper, I have developed somewhat more fully some of the possible implications of the modified rights structure that majority voting rules embody. *See* Buchanan, The Political Economy of the Welfare State, Center for the Study of Public Choice Research Paper No. 808231-1-8 (June, 1972). This paper was prepared for the Conference on Capitalism and Freedom, in honor of Milton Friedman, in Charlottesville, Virginia, October 1972; it will be published in the volume of conference proceedings.

speaking, the conclusions developed below follow whether the decision-maker be divinely ordained, democratically elected, arbitrarily appointed, selected in competitive examination, or hereditarily determined.[8] I want to examine a model in which a single person has been empowered to make decisions for a whole community. This defines a specific structure of rights, an assignment, and the problem is to determine the allocative results that will emerge in comparison with those predicted under alternative structures. The first point to be noted is the same as that made with respect to simple majority voting. The delegation of decision-making power to the single person modifies the set of rights in existence, even prior to the onset of any imposed governmental action. The designated chooser for the community holds potentially valued claims that were nonexistent before he is constitutionally authorized to act.

Consider again Hume's drainage of the village meadow. Instead of operating through a rule of unanimity, we now assume that the village has empowered a single person to act on behalf of all persons in the group and, furthermore, it is acknowledged that his decisions will be enforced. Formally, it does not matter whether the decision-maker is chosen from within or from outside the group. For expositional simplicity, however, we shall assume that he is selected from outside the village. We now assume that a drainage project, lumpy in nature, will yield symmetrically distributed benefits to villagers valued at 1000 units of the numeraire commodity. The project will cost a total of 800 units and the taxing institution requires symmetrical sharing. The project is clearly Pareto-efficient, and, as indicated earlier, under an operating rule of unanimity, the project will be undertaken, given our zero transactions costs assumption, and including all free-rider behavior under the transactions costs rubric. The question becomes: Would this project necessarily be selected by the single decision-maker, the alternative structure of property rights under consideration?

It is illegitimate to assume that the single administrator knows the preferences of the citizens, or, even should these be estimated with accuracy, that he would necessarily embody individual values dollar-for-dollar in his own choice calculus. The administrator or bureaucrat will select the project if the costs that he bears are less than the benefits that he, personally, secures. But these costs and benefits are not, and cannot possibly be, those of the community of citizens. Apparently, there is nothing in this model to insure correspondence

8. The method of selection may affect the motivation of the decision-maker and, in this way, modify the likelihood that the behavioral hypotheses implicit in the orthodox conceptions will be corroborated.

between the bureaucrat's choices and those results that are to be classified as efficient by orthodox economists' criteria. This suggests that the theorem of allocational neutrality breaks down.

If, however, we move beyond this naive model of administrative behavior, the applicability of the neutrality theorem may be restored. By acting in accordance with his own subjective evaluation, the bureaucrat may be failing to maximize the value of the property right that has been assigned to him constitutionally. To show this, let us assume that, naively, the decision-taker decides against the project noted. In this decision, he deprives the citizenry of benefits valued at 1000 units and, at the same time, avoids the imposition of tax costs of 800 units on the community. In a setting with zero transactions costs, where large numbers can readily reach contractual agreements, the citizenry, as an inclusive group of taxpayer-beneficiaries, would be willing to offer side payments up to a total of 200 units to secure a change from negative to positive action on the project.[9] If the decision-maker, the administrator or bureaucrat, uses these side payments, either indicatively or actually, to determine his final choice, the drainage project will be carried out. The theorem of allocational neutrality is apparently validated in this more sophisticated model for bureaucratic behavior. So long as the decision-maker acts to maximize the potential rent on the property right delegated to him, the right to make the final decision for the whole community, the allocative result will be identical to that forthcoming under alternative rights structures, with, of course, the transactions-costs, income-effect assumptions postulated. As in all property-assignment shifts, the distributional results may be quite different under differing assignments. If the bureaucrat maximizes the potential rent on his right to choose for the group, and, furthermore, if he collects this in the form of a personal side payment, there is an income transfer from members of the original group to the "outsider" selected as decision-taker.[10]

9. In the numerical example, the potentially-capturable rent seems to be 200 units because of the assumptions that both benefits and costs of the drainage project are shared symmetrically among all of the villagers. If these assumptions are relaxed, the decision-maker can collect a larger sum in rent. His potential gain, will, in all cases, be the sum of the *larger* of the *positive* or the *negative* differences between benefits and costs, the sum being taken over all members of the community.

10. This modifies the standard economist's treatment of the distinction between allocational and distributional results. The latter may, for certain purposes, be neglected if the zero-sum aspects are confined to a stable group of "members." If, however, a new rights assignment, such as that discussed, generates distributional transfers outside the original group, the effects, for this group, are negative-sum. Applied to the realistic setting in which transactions costs are present, this suggests that a community may, under certain conditions, find it advantageous to put up with allocative inefficiency rather than to secure its removal at the expense of distributional transfers to delegated decision-takers.

Objection may be raised to rent-maximizing as the appropriate norm for bureaucratic behavior, even if we neglect ethical considerations (these will be introduced in Section V). To postulate that the designated decision-maker maximizes the potential side payments that he can receive from taxpayer-beneficiaries, as a group, implies that the decision-maker, himself, is indifferent as among the choice alternatives, that he places no personal evaluation on the differences among these opportunities available to him. If, in fact, the bureaucrat or administrator is external to the affected group of persons in the community, this assumption may seem plausibly realistic. If, however, he is chosen from within the community itself, his own evaluation must be taken into account. Whether the decision-taker is selected from within or without the original group of members, his own evaluation can be, and must be, included in any correct assessment of costs and benefits.

We may return to the numerical illustration introduced above. Suppose that the gross benefits of the proposed drainage project, to all persons other than the decision-taker, amount to 1000 units of a numeraire good (we may call these "dollars"), and that the gross costs, to all persons other than the decision-taker, amount to 800. Suppose, however, that the decision-maker, himself, places a monetary value of, say, 400 dollars on the "natural beauty" of the swampy and undrained meadow. Even should he be required to pay no part of the tax costs of the project, this 400 units of value necessarily becomes a component in the total opportunity cost of the drainage scheme. Under these conditions, the bureaucrat will refuse the proffered side payment of 200 units. The project will not be undertaken.

Does this result suggest that the theorem of allocational neutrality breaks down? The question of whether the decision-taker is selected from within or without the initial membership of the group becomes critical at this point. If the selection is internal, the project is inefficient under the conditions suggested, and it will not be undertaken under any rights assignment. This is because the person's negative evaluation would be an input in any internal contractual negotiations that might produce an allocative outcome. In this case, the neutrality theorem remains valid. Suppose, however, that the bureaucrat is not in the initial group of members. In such case, his own personal evaluation of the project alternatives will not enter and will not affect allocative outcomes when the assignment of rights is limited to initial members. This decision-maker's evaluation will, however, enter as a determinant when he is assigned the rights to choose for the group. The neutrality theorem would not hold valid under these conditions unless the decision-maker should be, in fact, wholly indifferent as among the choice alternatives.

This result should not be at all surprising. The theorem on allocational neutrality, even under its restricted set of required assumptions, should hardly be expected to extend to rights assignments that embody differing memberships in the group. For fixed memberships, the theorem remains fully valid. Even when the decision-maker is selected from outside, the theorem suggests that any change in rights assignments, once the additional member is included, among this new membership will produce identical allocational results.

## THE THEORY OF THE STATE

It is possible to interpret both the policy implications of Coase's theorem on allocational neutrality and Pigovian corrective policy prescriptions in terms of the underlying conceptions, models, or theories of government. As the analysis above has suggested, under certain conceptions of governmental process, neither Coase nor the Pigovians should have been greatly concerned about institutional change as means of generating allocative efficiency. If distributional considerations are neglected, and if decision-makers for the community are chosen from within the group, the structure of rights will modify allocative outcomes only because of differentials in levels of transactions costs, provided that the decision-takers are motivated by economic self-interest. The policy thrust of Coase's discussion is, however, to the effect that governmental or collective intrusion into the negotiation processes of the market economy tends to retard rather than to advance movement toward allocative efficiency. Conversely, the policy thrust of the whole Pigovian tradition is that governmental or collective intrusion into the market economy tends to be corrective of distortions and leads toward rather than away from those results that might satisfy agreed-on efficiency criteria.

The Pigovian model of the state may be examined first. The decision-taker, the person or group empowered to impose the corrective taxes and subsidies, is presumed to act in accordance with rules laid down for him by the welfare economist. His task is that of measuring social costs and social benefits from alternative courses of action, a task that he is presumed able to carry out effectively. On the basis of such measurements, the decision-taker is to follow the rules laid down, quite independently of the personal opportunity costs that he may face in refusing side payment offers. The Pigovian policy-maker must be an economic eunuch. The idealized allocative results are, of course, identical with those that would emerge under a regime where the decision-maker is wholly "corrupt" in the sense of strict maximization of the potential side payments or rents on his rights to make decisions. If he is expected to behave as a rent-maximizer, however, there would be no need for elaborated and detailed instruction in the form of rules or norms, as derived from the theorems of welfare economics. Within this Pigovian conception, the decision-maker for the group does not and/or should not maximize the rental value of the rights of decision that he is granted. This may be treated either as a positive prediction about bureaucratic behavior or as a normative proposition for bureaucratic behavior.

In the Coase conception,[11] an interpretation that is similar in certain respects seems to follow. If, in fact, governmental decision-makers act as strict rent-maximizers, the neutrality theorem suggests that there should be little or no concern about allocative results, per se. The evidence of such concern must, therefore, indicate some denial of the rent-maximizing behavioral hypothesis. Again, this may be taken as positive prediction or normative statement. The governmental decision-maker, the bureaucrat, empowered to act on behalf of the group, either does not maximize rents on the rights that he commands or he should not do so on moral-ethical grounds. In either case, the Coase concern for allocational efficiency returns since the negotiating pressure toward optimality is removed once the decision-making power is shifted from the market to the public sector.

It is perhaps surprising to find common elements in the basic conceptions of political process held by the proponents of essentially opposing policy positions. But in both the Pigovian framework and in that imputed here to Coase, the governmental decision-maker, either singly or as a member of a choosing group, is and/or should be "incorruptible." In this respect, the two conceptions of governmental process seem identical, despite the sharp differences in information possibilities attributed to the governmental authority in the two models. In the Pigovian tradition, the bureaucrat is both informed and incorruptible; in the Coase framework, he is ignorant and incorruptible.

Agreement on this "incorruptibility" characteristic of governmental decision-makers, and indeed the introduction of the term "corruptible" in this familiar usage, suggests that there exist widely-shared ethical presuppositions concerning the inalienability of the delegated rights to make collective choices. That is to say, some shift away from the unanimity rule for collective decisions may be accepted as

11. For an explicit statement of the Coase-Chicago position, *see* Demsetz, *The Exchange and Enforcement of Property Rights*, 7 J. Law & Econ. 21-2 (1964).

necessary, with the accompanying acknowledgment that new and previously nonexistent "rights of decision" are brought into being, rights that have economic value that is potentially capturable by the subset of the citizenry empowered to take decisions on behalf of all. Such rights may, however, be considered to be inalienable; that is, the holder is not entitled to sell them or to exploit his possession of them through collection of personal rewards, either directly or indirectly.[12] It would be inappropriate in this paper to examine in detail the validity of such ethical presuppositions, although this opens up many interesting and highly controversial topics for analysis.[13]

The existence of such presuppositions can scarcely be denied. The pejorative content of such terms as "vote-trading," "logrolling," "political favoritism," "spoils system," "pork barrel legislation" —these attest to the pervasiveness of negative attitudes toward even minor attempts on the part of possessors of political decision-making rights to increase rental returns. If these attitudes are sufficiently widespread, prohibitions against bureaucratic and political rent-maximization may extend beyond the mere promulgation of ethical norms for behavior. The rewards and punishments that are consciously built into the governmental structure may be specifically aimed at making such rent-maximization unprofitable for any person empowered to take decisions on behalf of the whole group. The designated bureaucrat who is assigned authority over one specific aspect of public policy may not be morally or ethically inhibited from accepting side payments. But he may face harsh legal penalties should he accede to monetary temptations. To the extent that these constitutionally-determined constraints insure that the economic self-interests of governmental decision-makers dictate behavior unre-

12. In the paper previously cited, Calabresi and Melamed discuss the inalienability of rights at some length, and particularly they draw attention to several examples where inalienability is accepted. *See* Calabresi and Melamed, *supra* note 2.

The precise location of "inalienability" in the situation discussed may be questioned. In delegating decision-making authority to an agent, citizens may not be considered to be transferring the economic value inherent in the "right to choose." In this framework, it is the rights of the citizenry which are "inalienable" in some fundamental sense, and the agent could scarcely transfer a "right" which he does not possess. In my discussion, I have equated the empirically observed delegation of decision-making authority with an effective transfer of a valuable "right" which is then supposed to be "inalienable."

13. The ethical bases for such widely-shared attitudes may be challenged when the economic analysis is carefully developed. In the case of marketing rights to make decisions for the community, the relative undesirability of the distributional results provide a sufficient reason for inalienability. Conceptually, the decision-maker can capture *all* of the potential surplus from constitutionally-authorized action. In this limit, those who presumably make the constitutional delegation of authority, the citizenry, find themselves with zero net gains from collective action. So long as the delegation of decision rights along with inalienability is predicted to generate positive net gains, the citizenry's economic position is enhanced. The possible inefficiency in the standard allocative sense is more than offset by the distributional gains.

sponsive to proffered side-payments (direct or indirect) it may be argued, almost tautologically, that any outcomes chosen for the community by the "incorruptibles" must be, by definition, classified as "efficient." This would produce the paradoxical conclusion that the conditions for efficiency depend critically on the institutional structure and that, even with unchanged personal evaluations, solutions which are deemed efficient under one set of institutions may be inefficient under another.

The avoidance of this paradox becomes possible if we are content to define as allocationally efficient only that set of possible outcomes that could emerge from the contractual negotiation process among persons in the community, on the assumption that no rights are inalienable. In this case, the introduction of inalienability in the rights of governmental decision-takers clearly makes the theorem of allocational neutrality invalid. Under the highly restricted assumptions of zero transactions costs, any activity will be efficiently organized in the absence of governmental intervention, and, absent income effect feedbacks, the allocational outcome will be invariant over differing assignments of private and alienable rights. Under such conditions as these, it is the inalienability of rights that the shift to the public sector introduces which removes the guarantee that outcomes will be efficient, not the shift to governmental decision-taking per se. If we avoid the apparent paradox in this manner, however, the implication is left that the constitutional shift of activities to the public sector is an almost necessary source of inefficiency. When other considerations are accounted for, however, this implication need not follow. When transactions costs are recognized, and especially when distributional implications are considered, efficiency "in the large" may dictate the governmental organization of activities along with the inalienability of the rights delegated necessarily to bureaucratic decision-makers. There is no final escape from the requirements that each particular institutional change proposed must be examined on its own merits, on some case-by-case procedure, with the interdependence among separate organizational decisions firmly in mind.

# [9]

# COMMENT

## THE INVERSE COASE THEOREM AND DECLARATIONS OF WAR

J. GREGORY SIDAK*

Relying on constitutional text, history, and the theorem for which Ronald Coase won the Nobel Prize,[1] I argued in this *Journal* that Congress should formally declare war when authorizing the use of military force on the scale of the Persian Gulf War.[2] Professor Harold Hongju Koh of the Yale Law School replied that my "ill-advised ambition to marry constitutional originalism with law-and-economics should be killed before it spreads."[3] Although flattered to play Salman Rushdie to Koh's Ayatollah, I suggest that the professor call off the jihad.

I agree that "the Constitution no more enacts the Coase Theorem than it does Herbert Spencer's *Social Statics*."[4] That does not mean, however, that economics cannot illuminate the compelling logic of the Framers' design. Far from arguing that the Framers "enacted" as a matter of original intent what we now call the Coase Theorem, I offered a normative interpretation of the War Clause that built upon a positive economic analysis of the separation of powers.

Coase observed that in the absence of transaction costs, the ultimate use of a resource will be determined not by the initial assignment of property rights between two parties, but rather by which of the two parties can put the resource to its highest-valued use, and thus will have the means and incentive to induce the other party to exchange his rights to that resource. Normatively, the Coase Theorem implies that legal rules

---

* A.B. 1977, A.M., J.D. 1981, Stanford University. Member of the California and District of Columbia Bars. I thank Fred S. McChesney, Geoffrey P. Miller, Richard A. Posner, Melinda Ledden Sidak, Thomas A. Smith, and Matthew L. Spitzer, who were kind enough to read this paper in draft. The views expressed here are solely my own.

1. *See* Ronald H. Coase, *The Problem of Social Cost*, 3 J.L. & ECON. 1 (1960).

2. *See* J. Gregory Sidak, *To Declare War*, 41 DUKE L.J. 27 (1991).

3. Harold H. Koh, *The Coase Theorem and the War Power: A Response*, 41 DUKE L.J. 122, 125 (1991).

4. *Id.* at 128-29.

should facilitate such bargaining by reducing transaction costs.[5] However, as James Buchanan has argued, when the Theorem is extended to a theory of the state, "new and previously nonexistent 'rights of decision' are brought into being, rights that have economic value that is potentially capturable by the subset of the citizenry empowered to make decisions on behalf of all."[6] Monitoring the officials who exercise rights of decision is costly. The diverse output of government is not amenable to expression in a few statistics (as are the profitability and risk of a public corporation, for example), and, as presentment shows, many government decisions are joint products of several agents in separate branches—a distribution of responsibilities that invites shirking.[7]

Monitoring costs are reduced, and political accountability enhanced, by prohibiting bargains that alter the Constitution's formal allocation of rights of decision among political actors.[8] One might describe this proposition as the "Inverse Coase Theorem." Koh apparently has misunderstood my basic point; he claims that constitutional controversies cannot satisfy the Coase Theorem's underlying assumptions.[9] If only this were true, I would be the last to complain. It would be desirable if an absence of necessary conditions in addition to zero transaction costs thwarted the reallocation of rights of decision.[10] But obviously the executive and legislative branches *do* make bargains that reallocate constitutional rights of

5. *See* Robert Cooter & Thomas Ulen, Law and Economics 101 (1988); Robert Cooter, *The Cost of Coase*, 11 J. Legal Stud. 1, 14-20 (1982).

6. James M. Buchanan, Explorations into Constitutional Economics 397 (Robert D. Tollison & Viktor J. Vanberg eds., 1989).

7. *See* Armen A. Alchian & Harold Demsetz, *Production, Information Costs, and Economic Organization*, 62 Am. Econ. Rev. 777, 779-81 (1972); Morris Fiorina, *Group Concentration and the Delegation of Legislative Authority*, *in* Regulatory Policy and the Social Sciences 175, 179 (Roger Noll ed., 1985).

8. Such rights are inalienable so that their holder may not "sell them or . . . exploit his possession of them through collection of personal rewards, either directly or indirectly," and this inalienability "clearly makes the [Coase] theorem of allocational neutrality invalid." Buchanan, *supra* note 6, at 398.

9. *See* Koh, *supra* note 3, at 129.

10. Only if I were arguing that bargains between the branches *should* occur would I need to ask when they *can* occur. *See id.* at 129-30 nn.39 & 40 (citing Elizabeth Hoffman & Matthew L. Spitzer, *The Coase Theorem: Some Experimental Tests*, 25 J.L. & Econ. 73 (1982); Elizabeth Hoffman & Matthew L. Spitzer, *Experimental Tests of the Coase Theorem with Large Bargaining Groups*, 15 J. Legal Stud. 149 (1986)).

Koh also states that "analogizing constitutional powers to 'property rights' oversimplifies to the point of distortion" because "separation of powers principles do not draw sharp boundaries between congressional and presidential authorities in foreign affairs." Koh, *supra* note 3, at 130. One could say the same about the use of the air by one party to dry laundry and by another to dispose of sooty exhaust. Why should it be harder to define the war powers (and duties) of the President and Congress than to define property rights in the electromagnetic spectrum (which Coase was studying when he had the insight for *The Problem of Social Cost*, *see* Coase, *supra* note 1, at 1 n.1 (discussing Ronald H. Coase, *The Federal Communications Commission*, 2 J.L. & Econ. 1 (1959)))? For a more

decision. Curiously, after Koh says that this practice is impossible, he lauds the occasions where it does happen—an interesting position in that it is both empirically false and logically self-contradictory.[11] Koh's hypothetical, in which the President's trespassing cattle damage Congress's crops, also shows how he has missed my point.[12] My point is that there are agency costs associated with some kinds of cooperative behavior between the branches. If the President (ranch manager) and the Congress (farm manager) were mutually to agree to share something that belonged to the People (landowner), then the hypothetical would be relevant. In the Persian Gulf War, Congress and the President mutually agreed to ignore the constitutionally required formality of declaring war when in fact initiating full-scale offensive war, all to the detriment of the principal—"We the People"—of whom both the President and Congress are supposed to be agents.

If the branches do trade rights of decision, it becomes more difficult for a citizen to know which branch is responsible for a particular decision. He therefore incurs higher cost in petitioning government. Moreover, the locus of a decision can alter the decision itself. Such factors as the different discount rates for assessing policy options implied by the

critical analysis of the limits of analogizing the separation of powers to property rights, see Geoffrey P. Miller, *Rights and Structure in Constitutional Theory*, 8 SOC. PHIL. & POL'Y 196, 201-05 (1991).

11. Koh asserts: "To argue that Congress may only approve war by formal declaration makes about as much sense these days as a claim the Congress may only approve an international commitment by a treaty ratified by two-thirds of the Senate," because an executive agreement approved by joint resolution "has become viewed as effectively interchangeable with an Article II treaty for forging our international commitments." Koh, *supra* note 3, at 126 & n.24. Far from supporting Koh's position, this example demonstrates why the inalienability of rights of decision matters.

Calling a treaty a congressional-executive agreement could produce a different decision—either because it would disable one-third plus one members of the Senate from vetoing a treaty, or because Congress may usurp the President's control of the agenda in the treaty-making process by negotiating a treaty and then overriding the President's veto of the joint resolution enacting it as an international agreement.

With respect to the second possibility, although a congressional-executive agreement supposedly "can be concluded only by the President, who alone possesses the constitutional power to negotiate with other governments," that rule is violated if the agreement can substitute for a treaty "in *every* instance." RESTATEMENT (THIRD) OF THE FOREIGN RELATIONS LAW OF THE UNITED STATES § 303 cmt. e (1987) (emphasis added). In 1987, for example, Speaker of the House Jim Wright discussed arms reductions directly with Mikhail Gorbachev. *See* J. Gregory Sidak, *The President's Power of the Purse*, 1989 DUKE L.J. 1162, 1212; *see also* Statement on Signing the Departments of Commerce, Justice, and State, the Judiciary, and Related Agencies Appropriations Act, 1992, 27 WEEKLY COMP. PRES. DOC. 1529 (Oct. 28, 1991) ("The Constitution . . . vests exclusive authority in the President to control the timing and substance of negotiations with foreign governments and to choose the officials who will negotiate on behalf of the United States.").

Rather than explain why we should no longer care about the President's control over treaties and the prerogative of a minority of the Senate to veto them, Koh cites the Necessary and Proper Clause, U.S. CONST. art. I, § 8, cl. 18, as if it empowers Congress to strike outmoded words from the Constitution. *See* Koh, *supra* note 3, at 126-27.

12. *See* Koh, *supra* note 3, at 131.

differing tenure of judges, senators, presidents, and representatives; the different constituencies represented through different modes of election for each branch (and each house of Congress); the different degrees to which vote cycling is implied by the different methods of agenda control in the three branches; and the influence on the speed and secrecy of decisions caused by the relative unity or plurality of the decision process, can all affect the content of a particular decision.

Nonetheless, Koh views the phrase "To declare War" as outmoded. Although the United States and its allies killed as many as 150,000 Iraqi soldiers during the six-week Persian Gulf War,[13] Koh calls it "nothing less than bizarre" and an instance of "mindless originalism" to insist that lethal force of such magnitude must be authorized by the declaration of war for which the Constitution expressly provides.[14] He urges that "formal declarations of war [be] left to their special historical place."[15] What that place is, and how killing 25,000 persons per week is an illustration of Congress using the "scalpel" of a limited authorization of war rather than the "meat cleaver" of a formal declaration of war,[16] are questions that Koh does not attempt to answer.

13. *See* Caryle Murphy, *Iraqi Death Toll Remains Clouded*, WASH. POST, June 23, 1991, at A1, A17 (reporting Defense Intelligence Agency estimates).

14. *See* Koh, *supra* note 3, at 127, 128.

15. *Id.* at 132.

16. *See id.* at 128.

# Part IV
# Coase Theorem and Political Markets

# [10]

*Economica*, **54**, 517–520

# The Coase Theorem and Coalitional Stability

By Varouj A. Aivazian,[1] Jeffrey L. Callen[2] and Irwin Lipnowski[3]

[1] *University of Toronto*; [2] *Hebrew University of Jerusalem and McMaster University*; [3] *University of Manitoba*

Final version received 2 December 1986. Accepted 21 January 1987.

It is the contention of this paper that the Coase theorem has yet to be formulated and proved in a rigorous manner. The problem addressed is that of strategic coalitional behaviour when more than two agents are involved in the externality. It is shown that there are examples for which non-efficient allocations are stable in the sense of Aumann–Maschler bargaining sets, thereby vitiating the Coase theorem. Hence a proper formulation of the Coase theorem must exclude bargaining set stability.

It is our contention that the Coase theorem—which asserts that, with zero transaction costs and zero income effects, the identical Pareto-efficient allocation of resources will emerge regardless of the initial assignment of property rights—has yet to be formulated and proved in a rigorous manner.[1] The problem addressed here is that of strategic coalitional behaviour when more than two agents are involved in the externality. For the Coase theorem to hold in such situations, two conditions are important. First, assuming that the maximum joint payoff can be effected only by the formation of the grand coalition (e.g. by the merger of all parties involved in the externality), the grand coalition must be stable. Second, *only* the grand coalition must be stable; for if some other coalition is also stable, then the latter may form instead of the grand coalition so that a Pareto-optimal allocation need not obtain.

The point of this note is to show that a rigorous statement of the Coase theorem must exclude bargaining set notions of coalitional stability because, for both $M_1^{(i)}$ and $M_1$ bargaining set stability, the Coase theorem is violated.[2]

## I. Bargaining Sets and the Coase Theorem

Following Aivazian and Callen (1981), we consider two factories (firms 1 and 2) polluting a neighbourhood laundry (firm 3). Let the characteristic function $V$ denote profits per day where it is assumed that $V(1)=1$, $V(2)=2$, $V(3)=3$, $V(1,2)=8$, $V(1,3)=9$, $V(2,3)=10$, $V(1,2,3)=12$. The characteristic function is strictly superadditive, since only the grand coalition can maximize joint profits. Thus, with no transaction costs all three firms have an incentive to negotiate (i.e. to form coalitions) and internalize the externality. For example, if firms 1 and 3 were to merge, they could realize a net gain of 5.[3] However, if the grand coalition were to form, thereby internalizing the externality completely, the joint gain would be one more than for any other potential coalition structure.

As originally noted by Aivazian and Callen in a similar example, if the polluters are liable, then the grand coalition would result, the polluters would discontinue operations, and a Pareto-optimal allocation of resources would obtain. However, suppose there is no liability for polluting. Then the allocation of resources depends on bargaining among the three firms, and thus on coalitional stability.[4]

Let us first adopt the $M_1^{(i)}$ definition of bargaining set stability. The superscript ($i$) denotes that any allocation (payoff configuration) must be individually rational. That is, if $x_i$ defines the allocation of profits to firm $i$ in a specific coalition structure, then $x_i \geq V(i)$, all $i$. The bargaining set is based on the notions of 'objections' and 'counter-objections'. Specifically, suppose two firms $k$, $l$ are in the same coalition. Then $k$ has an objection against $l$ if $k$ can form another coalition excluding $l$ in which $k$ and all other members of the new coalition earn more than in the original coalition. On the other hand, $l$ has a counter-objection against $k$ if $l$ can form another coalition excluding $k$ in which: (1) $l$ and the other members of the new coalition are no worse off than in the original coalition and (2) any member of $l$'s (counter-objection) coalition who is also a member of $k$'s potential (objection) coalition can do as well in $l$'s coalition as in $k$'s. The bargaining set $M_1^{(i)}$ is the set of all individually rational allocations which are coalitionally stable in the sense that every objection by an individual has a counter-objection.

Applying the $M_1^{(i)}$ concept to the above example yields the following bargaining set:[5]

(i) $\{1, 2, 3; (1), (2), (3)\}$ (ii) $\{3{\cdot}5, 4{\cdot}5, 3; (1, 2), (3)\}$

(iii) $\{3{\cdot}5, 2, 5{\cdot}5; (1, 3), (2)\}$ (iv) $\{1, 4{\cdot}5, 5{\cdot}5; (2, 3), (1)\}$

(v) $\{3, 4, 5; (1, 2, 3)\}$

Each element denotes the allocation and the coalition structure that is in the bargaining set. For example, element (iv) states that the coalition of firms 2 and 3 will be in the bargaining set provided firm 1 receives 1, firm 2 receives 4·5 and firm 3 receives 5·5 in profits, respectively. To see that element (iv) is in the bargaining set, suppose firm 2 proposes an objection against firm 3 of $\{3{\cdot}5-\varepsilon, 4{\cdot}5+\varepsilon, 3; (1, 2), (3)\}$ where $\varepsilon > 0$. In other words, firm 2 threatens to form a coalition with firm 1 which excludes firm 3 and which in the process makes 1 and 2 better off and 3 worse off by comparison with the original coalition structure (iv). Note that firm 2's objection is reasonably strong in the sense that 2 is only $\varepsilon > 0$ better off under the new coalition as compared with (iv). Nevertheless, the original coalition in (iv) is stable because firm 3 has a counter-objection to 2, namely, $\{3{\cdot}5, 2, 5{\cdot}5; (1, 3), (2)\}$. Hence, firm 3 can respond to firm 2's objection by forming a coalition with firm 1 in which both members of the coalition are better off by comparison with the objection and no worse off by comparison with (iv). Similarly, if firm 3 should threaten the objection $\{3{\cdot}5-\varepsilon, 2, 5{\cdot}5+\varepsilon; (1, 3), (2)\}$ to firm 2, the latter can respond by the counter-objection $\{3{\cdot}5, 4{\cdot}5, 3; (1, 2), (3)\}$. Therefore, the payoff configuration (iv) is stable in the sense that, if firms 2 and 3 form a coalition with the appropriate allocation given by (iv), neither firm in the coalition has a credible threat against the other that could lead to the dissolution of the coalition.[6]

From the perspective of the Coase theorem, the bargaining set $M_1^{(i)}$ definition of coalitional stability is problematic. Every coalition structure, including no coalition at all, is potentially stable.[7] This means that the attainment of the grand coalition is not assured. Far from it. In our example, there are four other possible stable allocations and coalition structures, any one of which will *not* result in a Pareto-optimal allocation of resources.[8] A proper formulation of the Coase theorem should exclude by assumption the bargaining set $M_1^{(i)}$.

Even more problematic to the Coase theorem is the bargaining set concept $M_1$, which differs from $M_1^{(i)}$ by the imposition of an additional requirement, namely, coalitional rationality. Coalitional rationality here means that no proper subset of any coalition is able to obtain more for itself than its allocation in the coalition. It turns out that the bargaining set $M_1$ for the above example is the same as $M_1^{(i)}$ except that it excludes the grand coalition. That the grand coalition does not belong to $M_1$ is easily seen by noting that the sub-coalition of firms 1 and 2 earn only 7 in the grand coalition. This is less than the 8 they would have earned by forming their own coalition. Indeed, every two-firm sub-coalition earns less in the grand coalition allocation (v) than it would by forming a separate coalition, thereby violating coalitional rationality. In the case of $M_1$, not only is the grand coalition not stable, but every other coalition arrangement is potentially stable. Therefore, if the polluters are not liable for damages, bargaining will not yield a Pareto-optimal allocation of resources. Again, a proper formulation of the Coase theorem must preclude the bargaining set $M_1$.

## II. Conclusion

We showed that there are examples for which non-efficient allocations are stable in the sense of Aumann–Maschler bargaining sets, thereby vitiating the Coase theorem. Although there may be alternative negotiating mechanisms, such as that considered by Harsanyi (1977) in his construction of the Harsanyi–Nash–Shapley value, which yield a Pareto-optimal allocation of resources, nevertheless, we have shown that a proper formulation of the Coase theorem must exclude bargaining set stability.

## ACKNOWLEDGMENTS

We wish to thank Professors Leonid Hurwicz and Bezalel Peleg for helpful discussions. Not having seen the final product, they can hardly be blamed for its inadequacies. We also wish to thank the anoymous referees for helpful comments.

## NOTES

1. See Coase (1960, 1981). Implicit in discussions of the Coase theorem is the assumption that agents have complete information about one another's production opportunities or preference functions. We shall retain this assumption.
2. See Aumann and Maschler (1964) on bargaining set theory.
3. In this example, the two factories also have an incentive to negotiate with each other since $V(1,2) > V(1) + V(2)$. This is either because one factory also pollutes the other, or because of any type of synergy in their production processes; e.g. they can economize on fixed costs after they merge.
4. In Aivazian and Callen (1981), the core is empty when there is no liability for polluting and thus the Coase theorem is violated.
5. The following set of linear inequalities, involving $x_1$, $x_2$ and $x_3$ as unknowns in the example, determines (see Aumann and Maschler, 1964, Theorem 2.1) the bargaining set $M_1^{(i)}$ imputation for the grand coalition. For $k$ not to have a justified objection against $l$, at least one of the three conditions must obtain in each row $k/l$ ($k, l = 1, 2, 3$):

1/2: $x_1 + x_3 \geq 9$ or $x_2 = 2$ or $10 - x_2 \geq 9 - x_1$

1/3: $x_1+x_2 \geq 8$ or $x_3=3$ or $10-x_3 \geq 8-x_1$
2/1: $x_2+x_3 \geq 10$ or $x_1=1$ or $9-x_1 \geq 10-x_2$
2/3: $x_1+x_2 \geq 8$ or $x_3=3$ or $9-x_3 \geq 8-x_2$
3/1: $x_2+x_3 \geq 10$ or $x_1=1$ or $8-x_1 \geq 10-x_3$
3/2: $x_1+x_3 \geq 9$ or $x_2=2$ or $8-x_2 \geq 9-x_3$

Solution: $x=(x_1, x_2, x_3)=(3, 4, 5)$.

6. One might object to this process by arguing that the excluded party might make simultaneous offers to both parties in the coalition to enter. This will not change the stability relationships. For example, suppose element (ii) obtains and firm 3 offers 0·25 to both members of the coalition to enter. Suppose in fact that firm 3 reaps all the benefits from the grand coalition yielding the allocation {3·75, 4·75, 3·5; (1, 2, 3)}. Nevertheless, the latter allocation is not stable for two reasons. First, two potential breakway coalitions—namely {2, 3} and {1, 3}—could do better than under the terms proposed by player 3, since under the proposed imputation (3·75, 4·75, 3·5) we have $x_1+x_3=7{\cdot}25<V(1,3)=9$ and $x_2+x_3=8{\cdot}25<V(2,3)=10$. Thus player 3 can do better in either of these two-player coalitions, as in elements (iii) or (iv) of the bargaining set. The potential gain for a breakway coalition involving either {1, 3} or {2, 3} creates instability in the proposed imputation, which plagues any imputation in this example because of the empty core. A second source of instability for proposed imputation is that, unlike the payoff configurations in the bargaining set, there is no constraining factor neutralizing a threatened breakaway ('objection') by a 'counter-objections'. See also note 8.
7. This is a general result for the bargaining set $M_1^{(i)}$ and does not depend on the specific example. See Peleg (1963).
8. Note that the example was constructed so that every coalition structure containing two parties provides a return to all participants of 11 whereas the grand coalition obtains 12. Thus, there is a large number of grand coalition structures that are Pareto-superior to a stable two-party coalition structure; e.g. {3·75, 4·75, 3·5; (1, 2, 3)} is Pareto-superior to {3·5, 4·5, 3; (1, 2) 3}. The point of our example is that, unless the Coase theorem is to be a tautology, stability and Pareto optimality must be defined independently of each other. Given the Aumann–Maschler definitions of stability, an imputation such as (ii), namely {3·5, 4·5, 3; (1, 2) 3}, is stable despite the fact that it is Pareto-dominated by many grand coalition structures. Intuitively, although 3 may offer more to both 1 and 2 than they get in (ii), 1 and 2 may still prefer to have their own coalition and exclude 3, provided neither has a credible threat to break away and form a *separate* coalition with 3. Notice that the proposed grand coalition allocation is unstable since two potential breakaway coalitions, {2, 3} and {1, 3}, could do better (as explained in note 6) *and* that the player left out of a potential breakaway coalition with 3 would be worse off than in (ii).

## REFERENCES

AIVAZIAN, V. A. and CALLEN, J. L. (1981). The Coase theorem and the empty core. *Journal of Law and Economics*, **24**, 175–81.

AUMANN, R. J. and MASCHLER, M. (1964). The bargaining set for cooperative games. In M. Dresher, L. S. Shapley, and A. W. Tucker (eds), *Advances in Game Theory*, Princeton: Princeton University Press.

COASE, R. H. (1960). The problem of social cost. *Journal of Law and Economics*, **1**, 1–44.

—— (1981). The Coase theorem and the empty core: a comment. *Journal of Law and Economics*, **24**, 183–7.

HARSANYI, J. C. (1977). *Rational Behavior and Bargaining Equilibrium in Games and Social Situations.* Cambridge: University Press.

PELEG, B. (1963). Existence theorem for the bargaining set $M_1^{(i)}$. *Bulleting of the American Mathematical Society*, **60**, 109. 109–10.

# [11]

ELSEVIER

European Journal of Political Economy
Vol. 13 (1997) 419–442

European Journal of
POLITICAL
ECONOMY

# Property rights, contracts, cyclical social preferences and the Coase theorem: A synthesis

Peter Bernholz *

*Universitat Basel, Wirtschaftswissenschaftliches Zent., Petersgraben 51, 4003 Basel, Switzerland*

**Abstract**

In earlier work I demonstrated the relationship between contracts and cyclical social preferences and also that (negative) externalities are a necessary condition for the presence of cyclical social preferences. In this paper I define negative externalities broadly to include effects on members within the same group or organization 'outvoted' in a collective decision-making process by a 'majority'. The Coase theorem states that negative externality problems can be resolved efficiently by contracts, whatever the assignment of property rights, provided there are no transaction costs. Transaction costs are notably neglected in the social choice literature. Thus one might ask whether the Coase theorem might not also hold for the more general case of Arrow's general impossibility theorem, which includes all decisions by political bodies, organizations, groups and individuals and is not limited to decisions related to market participants. If this were so, there would be no need to be concerned about Arrow's general impossibility theorem, since all inefficient outcomes would be removed by contracts. The same would be true for Sen's 'impossibility of a Paretian liberal'. Also, if such contracts could be enforced, outcomes would be stable, thus removing the instability and inconsistency implied by social preference cycles in which each outcome is dominated by another one. In the present paper I ask whether and under which conditions the Coase theorem can be applied to this general case. In doing so, I shed new light on implicit assumptions of the theorem. © 1997 Elsevier Science B.V.

*JEL classification:* D23; D62; D70; D71

* Tel.: +41-61-2673341/44; fax: +41-61-2673340; e-mail: bernholzp@ubaclu.unibas.ch.


*PII* S0176-2680(97)00027-X

## 1. Introduction

The Coase theorem (Coase, 1960) states that negative externalities will be removed by bargaining in a market economy, whatever the initial assignment of property rights, if transaction costs are absent. This claim has been rightly challenged years ago (Aivazian and Callen, 1981) for situations involving more than two persons and (or) issues. In this paper the Coase theorem will be generalized to cover such more complex situations. This implies that more stringend assumptions have to be made to ensure the validity of this generalized version. In the process of presenting the critique of the theorem and in developing the proof, it will also turn out that the generalized theorem implies remarkable consequences for the debate on the importance of the Arrow (1963) impossibility theorem as expected (Bernholz, 1986), and of the Sen (1976) theorem of the 'impossibility of a Paretian liberal'.

The paper is organized as follows. In Section 2 a critique of the Coase theorem and the possibility to overcome the problems exposed by it with the help of *binding contracts*, will be discussed. Section 3 takes up the meaning of the generalization of the theorem proposed in this paper and analyzes some of its implications. In Section 4 the definitions and general assumptions necessary for the proof are presented. Section 5 contains the proof of the generalized Coase theorem. The proof is further illustrated with the help of examples in Section 6. Section 7 concludes the paper with some further comments on the meaning and the implications of the result.

## 2. The Coase theorem: Problems, solutions and generalization

It is well-known that according to the Coase theorem (Coase, 1960) negative externalities can be efficiently removed by bargaining of the parties concerned in the absence of transaction costs. As a matter of fact, however, this claim is only warranted in the case of only two persons trying to remove one externality. Already sixteen years ago, Aivazian and Callen (1981) demonstrated with an example that the Coase theorem may not hold if three agents are faced by negative externalities produced by two of them. We will not present their example here since it is expressed in game theoretical terms and uses additive money values, whereas we will use ordinal individual preference orderings. But the gist of their argument can be presented with the help of the example of Table 1 and Fig. 1.

In Table 1 the ordinal ranking of outcomes $x_1, x_2, \ldots, x_8$ is given for three individuals 1, 2 and 3. Each of them has the right to decide among the two alternatives of one issue. Assume that individual $i$ has been assigned the rights to decide issue $M_i$ ($i = 1, 2, 3$). An outcome $x_j$ ($j = 1, 2, \ldots, 8$) is thus brought about by the decisions of all individuals. In Fig. 1 (as in all subsequent figures) the corner points of the rectangles represent outcomes, the dimensions $M_i$ ($i = 1, 2, 3$)

Table 1

| | Members of society | | |
|---|---|---|---|
| | 1 | 2 | 3 |
| Strong, separable individual preference orderings | $x_8$ | $x_1$ | $x_5$ |
| | $x_4$ | $x_2$ | $x_7$ |
| | $x_2$ | $x_3$ | $x_3$ |
| | $x_3$ | $x_5$ | $x_6$ |
| | $x_6$ | $x_6$ | $x_1$ |
| | $x_1$ | $x_4$ | $x_8$ |
| | $x_7$ | $x_7$ | $x_2$ |
| | $x_5$ | $x_8$ | $x_4$ |

issues. The number of corner points on a line in one dimension shows the number of alternatives of the respective issue, in this case two for all three issues. Thus, $x_3$ is different from $x_1$ only in an alternative of the first issue, $x_8$ from $x_4$ only in an alternative of the third issue. But since $x_7$ is different from $x_6$ in the first and the second dimension, they contain different alternatives both in the first and second issues, but not in the third issue. Similarly $x_8$ is different from $x_1$ concerning the alternatives of all three issues. Note also that, for example, $x_6$ and $x_8$ contain the same alternative of the third issue $M_3$, or $x_1$ and $x_2$ of the first issue $M_1$.

Now consider, for example, a decision by 3 on $M_3$ to move from $x_3$ (the present status quo) to $x_7$ which is preferred by him. Then this clearly involves negative externalities to individuals 1 and 2, since they both prefer $x_3$ to $x_7$. A move from $x_1$ to $x_5$ by 3 would imply similar externalities. Other decisions by the three individuals also imply externalities for the other two.

In Fig. 1 an arrow points from the outcome preferred by the individual(s) who has (have) the right to make the decision to that outcome to which it is preferred. For $M_i$ this is always individual $i$. Diagonal arrows, however, are related to the preferences of all individuals who together control the issues involved. To move,

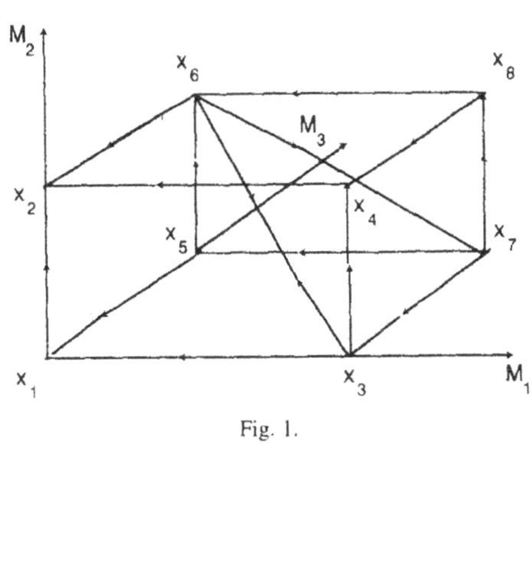


Fig. 1.

for example, from $x_7$ to $x_6$, an agreement, a contract among 1 and 2 is necessary, since changes in both dimensions $M_1$ and $M_2$ are required, i.e. in issues which are decided by 1 and 2, respectively. Thus both 1 and 2 prefer $x_6$ to $x_7$.

It is obvious from Fig. 1 that without any contracts $x_7$ would be the resulting stable outcome. With contracts allowed, however, 1 and 2 would agree on $x_6$ which they both prefer to $x_7$. Thus they would remove the negative externalities which they inflicted on each other by selecting $x_5$ over $x_6$ or $x_7$ over $x_8$ and $x_7$ over $x_5$ or $x_8$ over $x_6$. This result is quite in line with Coasean analysis. But $x_6$ is not Pareto-optimal, since $x_3$ is preferred to it by all individuals. Thus they would conclude a contract with the aim to move $x_3$.

So far so good. But from $x_3$ individual 3 can bring about $x_7$ which is preferred by him. This is exactly the critical argument made by Aivazian and Callen: Each outcome is dominated by another one, or in the game theoretical language they use, the core is empty. Thus no stable Pareto-optimal outcome results, contrary to the Coase theorem.

Put in another way, we may also say that cyclical social preferences exist, which is consistent with an earlier result that cyclical social preferences can only occur if (negative) externalities are present (Bernholz, 1982).

Is this the end of the story? I believe not. For if *contracts* were *binding* individual 3 could not move from $x_3$ to $x_7$, since this would imply a breach of contract. For in concluding the agreement with 1 and 2 to move from $x_6$ to $x_3$, individual 3 incurred the obligation to change $M_3$ from the second to the first alternative. But moving from $x_7$ to $x_3$ would reverse this change and thus violate the contract. As a consequence, with binding contracts Pareto-optimal outcome $x_3$ would be stable, the Coase theorem would be valid.

Until now we have only considered the case in which only individuals have the right to decide issues. But what happens if also subsets of society comprising more than one individual have the right to decide issues? Unfortunately things get more complicated under such conditions and the Coase theorem may not hold even if the kinds of contracts considered above are binding. We will prove this in a moment.

Before doing so, however, let us introduce some definitions. First, call any subset of society having the right to control an issue with more than one member an *organization*. Second, define as *external contracts* all contracts concluded by an individual or an organization controlling an issue with other organizations or(and) individuals controlling different issues. Third, let us define an *internal contract*. Internal contracts are contracts among members of an organization who have, according to the governing rules of the organization, the right to take decisions in its name on the issue(s) the organization controls. Such rules may be simple majority voting by all members of the organization, or by the shareholders according to the number of shares they hold, or even unanimity.

Now we will show that not only *binding external* but also *binding internal contracts* are necessary for the validity of the Coase theorem. Consider the

Table 2

| | Members of society | | |
|---|---|---|---|
| | 1 | 2 | 3 |
| Strong, separable individual preference orderings | $x_3$ | $x_5$ | $x_8$ |
| | $x_4$ | $x_6$ | $x_2$ |
| | $x_1$ | $x_3$ | $x_7$ |
| | $x_2$ | $x_4$ | $x_1$ |
| | $x_7$ | $x_1$ | $x_4$ |
| | $x_5$ | $x_2$ | $x_6$ |
| | $x_8$ | $x_7$ | $x_3$ |
| | $x_6$ | $x_8$ | $x_5$ |

example of Table 2 and Fig. 2. In Table 2 the preferences of individuals 1, 2 and 3 are given. And as shown by the two dimensions of Fig. 2, this time two issues $M_1$ and $M_2$ have to be decided. But now we assume that both issues are controlled by organizations whose decisions are taken by simple majority rule. And both organizations comprise all members of society, namely individuals 1, 2 and 3. To visualize things we may, for example, think of identical shareholders of two firms, all holding the same number of shares in both firms. The arrows in Fig. 2 thus represent majority preferences and decisions. Note that $M_2$ has two, whereas $M_1$ has three alternatives, and that $x_7$ is the only Pareto-inferior outcome.

Now, without contracts allowed, $x_3$ would be the stable Pareto-optimal outcome. But with contracts among the two organizations allowed it would be dominated by $x_6$, which is also Pareto-optimal. For $x_6$ is preferred to $x_3$ by both 2 and 3, who form a decisive majority in both organizations and can thus act in the name of their organizations. But $x_6$ is also not stable, since $x_7$ is preferred by 1 and 3, which also constitute a winning coalition for both organizations. Note that in this case no *external* contract is broken, since 1 and 3 can unanimously dissolve the contract binding their organizations to bring about $x_6$ since they have the right

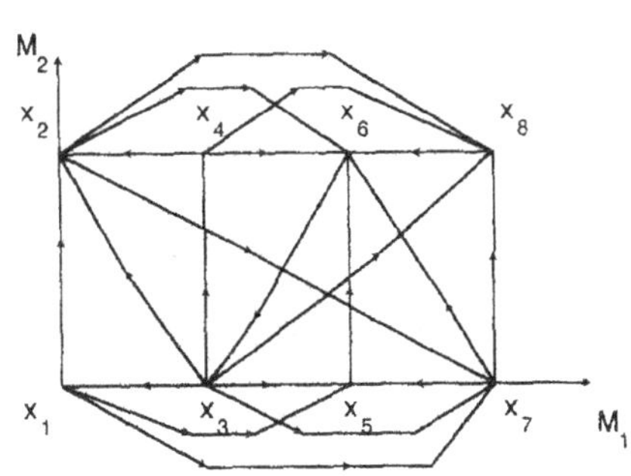


Fig. 2.

to act for their organizations. But $x_7$ is not stable in a similar way, since it is dominated by $x_2$, which is again dominated by $x_3$. Thus, no stable outcome exists, but we have cyclical social preferences among outcomes all different in two issues to which Pareto-inferior outcome $x_7$ belongs. Again the Coase theorem does not hold and this in spite of *binding external contracts*, since they can be dissolved unanimously. It thus follows that the Coase theorem can only be saved if not only *external* but also *internal contracts* are binding. For if both 2 and 3 are bound by their internal contract to bring about $x_6$, 3 cannot conclude the contradictory contract with 2 to move to $x_7$.

## 3. Generalizing the coase theorem and its implications

We have shown that problems arise with the Coase theorem as soon as it is meant to refer to more than two people and (or) issues and if organizations have the right to decide issues. It has also been pointed out that these problems may be solved and thus the validity of the generalized Coase theorem be demonstrated, if *binding and thus enforceable external* and *internal contracts* are assumed. In Section 5 we will present a corresponding proof, depending however additionally on the assumption of separable individual preference orderings (compare A1 in Section 4).

It thus turns out that strong additional assumptions are necessary to prove the generalized Coase theorem. On the other hand, it is important to realize the very broad range of relationships to which the Theorem can be applied after such a generalization. Let us first consider the notion of an assignment of rights to decide issues to individuals or organizations. In a sense, we have already generalized the concept of property rights by assigning the rights to decide issues. Subsequently we will assume that such rights will be assigned for each issue to one and only one individual or organization. We thus assume that these rights include, for example, all kinds of rights to use and to transform property, to provide and to make use of services, if the respective individual or organization owns them. Such rights also include rights of political or administrative organizations like parliaments, bureaucratic agencies and councils to decide on the building, let's say, of roads and bridges, or the provision of police or of social welfare services, if they are entitled to take such decisions. Excluded, however, are all meta-rights to change the existing assignment of rights. Thus parliaments are not entitled to change property rights.

Secondly, the notion of contracts does not only refer to contracts among agents in the private sphere. Thus, besides contracts referring to market exchange and barter, political contracts like logrolling contracts are also included. Finally, as already mentioned, the concept of organization includes not only private organizations like business firms and clubs, but also parliaments, political parties and bureaucratic agencies of the state.

The generalized Coase theorem thus refers to a very broad range of applications. As a consequence, the proof of its validity implies that the problems implied by the Arrow (1963) impossibility theorem and by the Sen (1970) theorem of the 'impossibility of a Paretian liberal' (Compare the example of Table 4 and Fig. 4 in Section 6), can be solved if the assumptions are met which are necessary to prove the generalized Coase theorem. For cyclical social preferences including two or more issues can only occur if negative externalities are present (Bernholz, 1982). But now the generalized Coase theorem tells us that with binding internal and external contracts and separable individual preference orderings, a stable Pareto-optimal outcome will result. Thus such an outcome will also be selected in the presence of cyclical social preferences.

This result is not surprising, since already years ago the theorem that the possibility of logrolling over several issues implies cyclical social preferences (Bernholz, 1974) was generalized. In this generalization it was shown that for any decentralized assignment of rights to subsets of society (including political rights) to decide issues, cyclical social preferences are implied by beneficial contracts among decisive coalitions having the right to control these issues (Bernholz, 1980; Schwartz, 1981, 1986). This result means that *contracts* are a necessary condition for cyclical social preferences apart from one-issue cycles. As a consequence, if contracts are made *binding* obviously some stable Pareto-optimal outcome will be selected.

Two points should, however, be kept in mind. First, negative externalities are here very broadly defined. They include besides traditional all negative externalities brought about in organizations for 'outvoted minorities' by collective decision-making (Buchanan, 1962; Buchanan and Tullock, 1962, 43–62). Second, our statement is not meant to assert that the theorems derived by Arrow and Sen are not correct. Quite the contrary. For our assumption of separable individual preference orderings (A1 in Section 4) clearly implies a violation of Arrow's axion of unrestricted domain. And Sen's 'impossibility' is only overcome because we allow binding *external* contracts (A4 and A7 in Section 4).

## 4. Definitions and general assumptions

The following definitions and assumptions describe the broad class of institutions, distributions of rights and decision rules for which the generalization of the Coase theorem to be derived is valid. They also introduce the conditions under which this generalization can be proved.

$V$: Set of all members of society, with $|V| \geq 2$.

$V_i \subseteq V$: Set of members of society having the right to decide issue, $M_i$ ($i = 1, 2, \ldots, n$; $n \geq 2$), $1 \leq |V_i|$.

$M$: Set of $n \geq 2$ issues $M_i$; $M_i$ comprises $m_i \geq 2$ alternatives.

$x_j \in U = M_1 x M_2 x \ldots x M_n$ is called an outcome. It is an $n$-dimensional vector with one and only one component (alternative) out of each issue.

$C_i \subsetneq V_i$ is a decisive coalition, which can, according to some decision rule (see A3), take decisions for $V_i$ on issue $M_i$, i.e. select one of its $m_i$ alternatives. Such coalitions are called one-issue coalitions.

$C^k$ is a decisive coalition formed by contract among $k$ one-issue coalitions $C_i$ which control the respective $k$ issues $(1 < k \leq n)$.

$C^{K_j}$ is used to denote such a decisive $C^k$ coalition formed by a contract referring to a specific set of issues $K_j \subsetneq M(j = 1, 2, \ldots, r)$ where $|C^{K_j}| \equiv k_j$ is the number of these issues.

$P$, $R$: Assume that a decisive coalition $C_i$ or $C^k$ exists, all of whose members prefer $x_i$ to $x_j$, i.e. $x_i P_h x_j$, all $h \in C_i$ or $C^k$, $x_i$, $x_j \in U$. Then $x_i P x_j$ and we may say, 'society prefers $x_i$ to $x_j$'. Similarly, if there exists no such decisive coalition, we describe this by $x_j R x_i$.

Let us explain the meaning of these definitions.

To make our problem not trivial since $V$ comprises all members of society, the number of such members has at least to be two, $|V| \geq 2$.

No such restriction applies to the number of individuals in $V_i$. This number can range from one individual to all members of society and can, but need not, be different for all $V_i$. Note that organizations like joint stock companies, bureaucracies and parliaments are covered by our notation, since the $V_i$ can also refer to such organizations. Three extreme cases included in our definitions are $|V_1| = |V_2| = |V_3| = \ldots = |V_n| = 1$ and $V_1 = V_2 = V_3 = \ldots = V_n = V$. In the latter case, all members of society together have the right to decide each issue. We might call such an organizational setting of society a total direct democracy if the decision rule applied were simple majority voting (see A3). The former case covers pure liberalism if the individuals having the right to decide the $M_i$'s are different, but also dictatorship of individual $v$ if

$$V_1 = V_2 = V_3 = \ldots = V_n = \{v\}$$

It should be obvious that each outcome $x_j$ comprises one alternative out of each issue. Otherwise it would not be a complete description of the world. Each state of the world is, however, also influenced by natural events, which are not issues in our notation if they cannot be influenced by human actions. As far as this is the case, they have to be considered as constants and are neglected in our definition of outcomes. Since there exist $m_i$ alternatives for issue $M_i (i = 1, 2, \ldots, n)$ there $m_1 \cdot m_2 \cdot m_3 \cdot \ldots \cdot m_n$ are combinations of them. Thus, this is also the number of outcomes. Note that a decision by $V_i$ concerning $M_i$ influences an outcome only in its $i$th component.

Let us now make the following assumptions:

A0: The members of society have weak, complete and transitive ordinal preference orderings over the outcomes.

A1: The members of society have separable preference orderings.

It seems to be appropriate to recall the definition of separable individual preference orderings. Consider two pairs of outcomes (vectors), each containing alternatives of $n$ issues (components). Assume that outcomes $x_i$ and $x_j \in U$ are defined by their components as follows:

$$x_i = (x_{i1}, x_{i2}, x_{i3}, \ldots, x_{in}), \qquad x_j = (x_{j1}, x_{j2}, x_{j3}, \ldots, x_{jn}).$$

Assume further that $x_i$ and $x_j$ contain identical components for $k$ issues $(1 \le k < n)$ such that $x_{ik} = x_{jk}$ and that $x_i^*$ and $x_j^*$ differ from $x_i$ and $x_j$ only in these components but in the same way. They thus contain the same components $x_{ik}^* = x_{jk}^* \neq x_{ik} = x_{jk}$ in the $k$ issues. Then individual preference orderings are separable if

$$x_i R_h x_i^* \text{ implies } x_j R_h x_j^* \text{ and } x_i P_h x_i^* \text{ implies } x_j P_h x_i^* .$$

An example of separable individual preferences is given in Table 3 together with Fig. 3.

A2: The right to decide issue $M_i$ is assigned to one and only one $V_i$. This is true for each issue $M_i$ $(i = 1, 2, \ldots, n)$ so that the assignment of rights is complete.

We thus exclude the possibility that an issue $M_i$ is not assigned to any $V_i$ or that it is assigned to several $V_i$ (i.e. a lack of rights or a conflict of rights to decide $M_i$). Note also that rights to decide meta-issues in the sense of rights to change the assignment of rights to decide issues are excluded. This means, for example, that a parliament in a democratic institutional setting does not have the right to reassign by legislation rights to decide issues. This implies, of course, that the existence of a constitution is implied by our assumptions.

A3: Each $V_i$ takes its decision concerning issue $M_i$ according to some non-stochastic decision rule having the following properties [1]:

(1) There exists at least one decisive coalition $C_i \subseteq V_i$ such that if $x_i P_h x_j$, for all $h \in C_i$, then $x_i P x_j$ for society.

(2) $V_i - C_i$ is not a decisive coalition.

(3) For any $C_i$ and $g (C_i \subseteq V_i, g \in V_i)$, $C_i \cup \{g\}$ is also a decisive coalition, if $x_i P_h x_j$ and for all $h \in C_i$ and $x_i P_g x_j$.

Assumption A3 allows a very broad class of decision rules: Majority voting, qualified majority voting, majority voting with a majority of shares (i.e. also unequal voting rights of individuals), unanimity voting, etc. The assumption is also consistent with abstention by those individuals who are indifferent between alternatives. Obviously there generally will be, but need not be different decision rules for the $V_i$'s. It is also clear that each $V_i$ which does comprise more than one individual can contain several decisive coalitions $C_i$, $C_i'$, $C_i''$, .... But because of A3, 2 there must be members of $V_i$ who belong to each of such decisive coalitions. Thus, for example, $C_i \cap C_i' \neq \emptyset$.

[1] This definition does not exclude some rather absurd decisions rules. We do not exclude them since Theorem 1 is valid for them, too.

A4: A number $k$ of $C_i$'s with one decisive coalition for each of $k$ issues ($1 < k \leq n$), can conclude an *external* contract agreeing on distinctive alternatives to be selected for each of these issues. The union of the $k$ $C_i$'s is called a $C^k$ coalition, since this decisive coalition can control the $k$ issues.

Note that such a contract is called an *external* contract since it is concluded by a decisive coalition controlling one issue with other decisive coalitions (one other decisive coalition) controlling other issues. Thus an external contract is an agreement of $k$ one-issue coalitions to form a $C^k$ coalition. It should also be clear that *external* contracts are concluded by each $C_i$ for (the whole of) $V_i$. The members having the right by the internal decision rule of $V_i$ to conclude contracts thus oblige the whole organization by such contracts.

A5: The members $h \varepsilon C_i$ of any $C_i$ can conclude an *internal* contract to select some alternative or to conclude external contracts and only to cancel or to change them by unanimous agreement.

*Internal* contracts oblige the members of decisive coalitions. They can be important since individual members of a decisive coalition $C_i$ may want to become members of another decisive coalition $C_i'$ and thus destroy $C_i$ [2].

A6: Each external contract agreed on by some $C_i$'s is combined with an internal contract for those $C_i$'s for which $|C_i| > 1$.

A7: All external and internal contracts are *binding*, i.e. enforceable. They can only be changed or annulled if all partners agree *unanimously*.

A8: There exists no dictatorship.

A9: Each contract concluded is executed before the next contract is concluded.

For simplicity let us assume finally:

A10: If more than one contract is concluded, this is done sequentially. The sequence is determined by a chance mechanism.

## 5. Proof of the theorem

Before stating the theorem let us define what is meant in this paper by the stability of an outcome: An outcome is said to be stable if no $C^k$-coalition can be formed ($k = 2, \ldots, n$) all of whose members prefer another outcome and can bring it about without at least one of ist members breaking an external or internal contract.

[2] If several $V_i$ with $|V_i| > 1$ are identical, the delimitation between external and internal contracts becomes blurred (as e.g. a logrolling contract within a parliament). In legal terms one would speak of external contracts only if each $V_i$ were a separate legal entity (like corporations). Only then would the contracts concluded by a decisive majority be binding for all members of $V_i$. For the subsequent proof this problem of delimitation is, however, unimportant since we have assumed that both kinds of contracts are binding for the members of decisive coalitions.

We now turn to the formulation of Theorem 1.

*Theorem 1.* *Assume that strong and separable individual preferences are given. Then if no one-issue social preference cycles exist and if (only) binding internal and external contracts can be concluded by any number of k of $C_i \subseteq V_i$ coalitions ($i \in \{1, 2, \ldots, n\}$, $1 < k \leq n$), a stable Pareto-optimal outcome will result from their decisions.*

The assumptions of strong and separable individual preferences, and of the absence of one-issue social preference cycles will be relaxed or discussed, respectively later on.

Let us first use assumption A8 to exclude dictatorship, i.e. the case in which one individual has the right to decide all issues. For in this case the theorem would be trivially true even without the assumptions of separable individual preferences and of binding contracts.

We begin the proof without loss of generality by considering a situation in which no contract on more than one issue has been concluded. Thus from the assumption in Theorem 1 a stable outcome exists, since no one-issue social preference cycles are present. We call this outcome $x_0$. Any contract comprising a set of $K_j$ issues by a $C^{K_j}$ coalition ($1 < |K_j| \leq n$) leads then to a new outcome (A4 and A9). Since contracts are concluded and executed sequentially (A9 and A10) we may call without loss of generality the outcomes brought about by such coalitions starting from $x_0$: $x_1, x_2, x_3, \ldots$. We call the respective sets of issues to which the contracts refer $K_1, K_2, K_3, \ldots$. Note also that $k_j \equiv |K_j|$.

Now consider first the contract leading from $x_0$ to $x_1$. Here the members of the $k_1$ $C_i$'s participating in the respective $C^{K_1}$ coalition according to assumptions A2, A3 and A4 are not bound by any earlier contracts. They thus will select the alternatives out of the $k_1$ issues they control which are most preferred by all of them and preferred at least to $x_0$. Thus we get

$$x_1 P_h x_0 \text{ for all } h \in C^{K_1} \text{ and consequently by } A_2, A_3 \text{ and } A_4, x_1 P x_0.$$

Moreover, there exists no $x_s$ such that $x_s P_h x_1$ for all $h \in C^{K_1}$ and which is different from $x_0$ in the same set of $K_1$ issues.

Next let us discuss a contract concluded by $k_r$ ($r > 1$, $1 < k_r \leq n$) $C_r$'s forming a $C^{K_r}$ coalition respective to a set of $K_r$ issues leading from outcome $x_{r-1}$ to outcome $x_r$. Obviously such a contract implies again that

$$x_r P_h x_{r-1} \text{ for all } h \in C^{K_r}, \text{ such that } x_r P x_{r-1},$$

and also that no better outcome for all $h \in C^{K_r}$ can be reached by this coalition. But the contract may imply an additional condition, namely if the issues in one or more of the earlier contracts are *overlapping* with the issues contained in this $r$th contract, i.e. if

$$\bigcap_{j=1}^{r} K_j \neq \emptyset.$$

For in this case of *overlapping contracts*, some or all people and organizations participating are bound by external and internal contracts concluded earlier (A5, A6, A7). This, however, means that each individual who has been a partner in an earlier overlapping contract enjoys a veto power concerning the conclusion of the new $r$th contract. For assume, for example, that $K_g \cap K_r \neq \varnothing (1 \leq g < r)$, then first all $C_g$'s in $C^{K_g}$ have to agree to changes of the alternatives in the overlapping issues because *external* contracts are binding. Note that this is also true for $C_g$'s participating in the $g$th contract who control issues which are not overlapping with those in $K_r$. Second, it is also not sufficient that some $k_g$ coalitions $C'_g$ which are different from the $C_g$'s concluding the $g$th contract agree to the new $r$th contract.

For since $C'_g \cap C_g \neq \varnothing$ because of A3, at least one individual out of $C'_g$ belonged also to $C_g$ and is thus bound by the internal contract implied by the $g$-th contract (A6). If we take these conditions together, it follows that each $h \in C^{K_g} \cup C^{K_r}$ has to prefer $x_r$ to $x_{r-1}$ to make the $r$th contract possible. And this is true for each set of issues $K_g$ $(g = 1, 2, \ldots, r-1)$ which overlaps with $K_r$.

It follows from the above that a sequence of contracts, in which the issues comprised by each later contract overlap with the issues of all contracts concluded before, leads to a better situation for all individuals who were participating in earlier contracts. Thus, there is no reason for them to decide in favor of an earlier outcome. Thus $x_r$ is a stable outcome as far as coalitions $C^{K_1}, C^{K_2}, \ldots, C^{K_r}$ are concerned.

It remains to consider the case in which, let's say, $K_r$ does not intersect with one, some or all $K_j (1 \leq j < r)$. Assume, for example, that $K_r \cap K_j = \emptyset$ for some $j$. Then the conclusion of the $r$th contract would not imply a violation of the $j$th contract, since it would only relate to issues not involved in this contract. As a consequence $x_j P_h x_r$ for all $h \in C^{K_j}$ would be a possibility. But because of assumption A1 (separable individual preferences) coalition $C^{K_j}$ cannot reach a better outcome than $x_r$ by changing its contract, as will be shown subsequently.

Consider first $x_r$ and $x_{r-1}$ (i.e. $j = r-1$). Define without loss of generality

$$x_r \equiv \left({}^1x_r^k, {}^{k+1}x_r^q, {}^{q+1}x_{r-1}^n\right),$$

$$x_{r-1} \equiv \left({}^1x^k, {}^{k+1}x_{r-1}^q, {}^{q+1}x_{r-1}^n\right),$$

$$x_{r-2} \equiv \left({}^1x_{r-1}^k, {}^{k+1}x_{r-1}^q, {}^{q+1}x_{r-1}^n\right),$$

$$x_g \equiv \left({}^1x_{r-1}^k, {}^{k+1}x_r^q, {}^{q+1}x_{r-1}^n\right);$$

with

$${}^1x_r^k \equiv (x_{r1}, x_{r2}, \ldots, x_{rk}),$$

$${}^{k+1}x_r^q \equiv (x_{rk+1}, x_{rk+2}, \ldots, x_{rq}),$$

$${}^{q+1}x_r^n \equiv (x_{rq+1}, x_{rq+2}, \ldots, x_{rn}).$$

Then $C^{K_{r-1}}$ has agreed on a contract such that $x_{r-1} P x_{r-2}$, since

$$x_{r-1} P_h x_{r-2} \text{ for all } h \in C^{K_{r-1}}.$$

Now after the execution of this contract $C^{K_r}$ agrees on a contract (A9) bringing about $x_r$. Then because of A1 and the definitions just given

$$x_r P_h x_g \text{ for all } h \in C^{K_{r-1}}.$$

Note that in this case $K^{r-1}$ comprises issues 1, 2, ..., $k$ and $K^r$ issues $k+1$, $k+2$, ..., $q$. It follows that $C^{K_{r-1}}$ has no reason to change its contract. Obviously the same is true if we consider any other $j(1 \leq j \leq r-1)$. There is no reason to change a contract concluded by $C^{K_j}$ in the $K_j$ issues because of the non-overlapping contract agreed on by $C^{K_r}$. Thus $x_r$ is stable as far as all those $C^{K_j}(1 \leq j \leq r)$ are concerned which have concluded earlier contracts which are not overlapping with the contract to bring about $x_r$.

Taking this result together with the earlier one it follows that the sequence of contracts leading from $x_0$ by way of $x_1$, $x_2$, ... to $x_r$ brings about a contract $x_r$ which is stable relative to all ealier coalitions independent of whether $K_r$ overlaps with $K_1$, $K_2$, ..., $K_{r-1}$ or not.

But from this, the proof of Theorem 1 is easily completed. For since only a finite number of outcomes exists (A0) we conclude that by adding more and more contracts profitable to participating individuals (by increasing $r$) a stable outcome will be finally reached. This is the outcome from which no longer a new coalition can be formed, all of whose members prefer another outcome. For all the older coalitions have no reason to change this final outcome.

After having shown that a stable outcome results, let us prove its Pareto-optimality. It should be clear that the final outcome cannot be Pareto-inferior. For given the assumption of strong individual preferences in Theorem 1 a Pareto-inferior outcome would imply the existence of a coalition who would prefer and could realize another outcome since this outcome would be preferred by all individuals in society. Thus the Pareto-inferior outcome would not be stable contradicting our result that the final outcome is stable. This completes the proof of Theorem 1.

Let us note, however, that it is obvious from the above argument that the resulting stable Pareto-optimal outcome is path dependent, i.e. the sequence of contracts is important for the members of society from a distributional point of view.

Finally in this section let us remove the assumption of strong individual preferences. Then we have obviously a problem with the above proof. For assume that there exist two outcomes $x_i$ and $x_j$ such that $x_i$ is Pareto-better than $x_j$ and also Pareto-optimal. Thus,

$$x_i R_h x_j \text{ for all } h \in V.$$

But now only for a few or even only one individual $s \in V$

$$x_i P_s x_j$$

may hold. And these individuals (this individual) may not be able to form decisive coalitions $C_i$ concerning all issues $M_i$ in which $x_i$ and $x_j$ are different. But then Pareto-inferior outcome $x_j$ would be stable if a sufficient set of the indifferent people would not agree to conclude a contract favoring the individual(s) preferring $x_i$. Now one might argue that all people who were indifferent would abstain, so that in the extreme a decisive coalition could be formed by just one individual. But even this assumption would not be sufficient, since there may be some $V_i$'s with no member preferring $x_i$.

Thus we need additional assumptions for Theorem 1 to be extended to the case of weak individual preference orderings. Such assumptions could be first that one or more issues refer to goods which are finely divisible and which are valued by all members of society such that they prefer more of them to less. Secondly, that there exists a close neighbourhood of $x_i$ containing outcomes with slightly smaller amounts of these goods than $x_i$ that are also preferred to $x_j$ by those who prefer $x_i$ to $x_j$. Thirdly, that those individuals own at least a small amount of one of these goods.

Without formalizing this idea, it is obvious that then some $x_r$ would exist in the neighbourhood of $x_i$ such that

$$x_i P_s x_r P_s x_j \text{ and } x_r P_h x_i I x_j$$

for the respective members of society. But then it follows that Pareto-inferior $x_j$ is not stable and our above proof could be applied.

## 6. Intuitive logic of the proof and examples illustrating the theorem

It may be helpful to sketch the intuitive logic of the proof of Theorem 1 and then to illustrate it with some further examples. We have considered a finite number of issues which have to be resolved, each of which is assigned to an individual or organization to decide. These issues are decided sequentially, some of them together with the help of contracts. The assumption of a finite number ensures that an end of the sequence of decisions is reached. The further assump-

Table 3

| | Members of society | | |
|---|---|---|---|
| | 1 | 2 | 3 |
| Strong, separable individual preference orderings | $x_3$ | $x_6$ | $x_4$ |
| | $x_5$ | $x_5$ | $x_3$ |
| | $x_4$ | $x_4$ | $x_2$ |
| | $x_1$ | $x_2$ | $x_1$ |
| | $x_6$ | $x_3$ | $x_6$ |
| | $x_2$ | $x_1$ | $x_5$ |

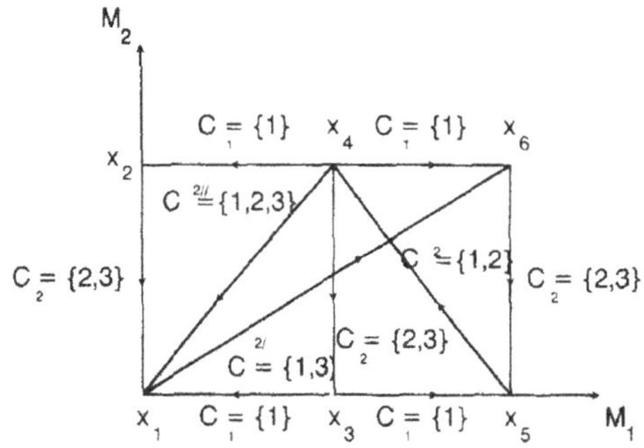


Fig. 3.

tions of *binding internal* and *external contracts* prevent that the sequence does turn back on itself, since cycles require defections from external or internal contracts. Finally, the assumption of separable individual preferences ensures that no decisons made earlier are later resented and thus changed. The final outcome must be Pareto-optimal, since the entire society comprises all subsets of its members who have the right and are willing to write a contract to move to a Pareto-better outcome if the final outcome were Pareto-inferior.

Let us now consider some examples to illustrate the theorem. Consider first the example of Table 3 and of Fig. 3, where strong and separable individual preference orderings have been assumed. We will show again with this example that external contracts have to be binding.

The example comprises two issues, $M_1$ and $M_2$ ($n = 2$; $k = 2$), with three and two alternatives, respectively [3]. The assignment of rights is as follows: $V_1 = \{1\}$, $V_2 = \{1,2,3\}$. $M_2$ is decided by simple majority voting of the three members of society. Note that $V_1 \cup V_2 = V = \{1, 2, 3\}$.

From Table 3 $x_4 P_h x_2$ and $x_4 P_h x_1$ for all $h \in V$. $x_1$ and $x_2$ are thus Pareto-inferior. All other outcomes are Pareto-optimal. All points in Fig. 3 should be connected by arrows. But we have omitted several diagonal arrows to simplify the picture. For all arrows drawn, the decisive coalitions have been mentioned. The arrows are pointing to the dominated outcome.

Let us first note that separable individual preferences imply that all arrows which are parallel, point into the same direction. This is true for individual preferences as can be seen by setting, e.g. $x_2 = x_i, x_1 = x_i^*$ and $x_6 = x_j, x_5 = x_j^*$ in the above definition. But parallel arrows for the individuals of a decisive

[3] Note that in this, as in all other examples, the issue structure of the $x_i$ cannot be seen from the notation and thus from the table. It is only made evident in the figures belonging to the tables. Both have thus to be considered together.

Table 4

| | Members of society | |
|---|---|---|
| | 1 | 2 |
| Strong, separable individual preference orderings | $x_1$ | $x_4$ |
| | $x_2$ | $x_2$ |
| | $x_3$ | $x_3$ |
| | $x_4$ | $x_1$ |

coalition necessarily imply parallel arrows for collective decisions made by these coalitions. This is reflected by the parallel arrows of Fig. 3.

Now, if no 2-issue contracts were allowed $x_4$ would be a stable outcome. In fact, it is a Nash-equilibrium for $C_1 = \{1\}$ and $C_2 = \{2, 3\}$ and it is also Pareto-optimal. But it can and will be overturned if a contract establishing $C^2 = \{1, 2\}$ is concluded among $C_1\{1\}$ and $C_2' = \{1, 2\}$ to establish $x_5$. Now it is obvious that $x_5$ is not stable if external contracts were not binding for $V_1$ and $V_2$, since $x_3 P_1 x_5$ and $x_6 P_2 x_5$, $x_6 P_3 x_5$. In fact, as has been shown in an earlier paper (Bernholz, 1980), contracts are the only reason of cyclical social preferences if no one-issue cycles exist. This is also the case in Fig. 3. It thus follows that only *binding* external contracts, contracts concluded by $C_1$ and $C_2'$ for $V_1$ and $V_2$ lead to a stable outcome $x_5$ which is also Pareto-optimal.

Without contracts, $x_4$ was a stable Pareto-optimal outcome. But the stable outcome can also be Pareto-inferior in this case. Look, for example, at the simple example of Table 4 and Fig. 4. We assume $V_1 = \{1\}$ and $V_2 = \{2\}$, $V = \{1, 2\}$. The stable outcome without contract, $x_3$, is Pareto-inferior. If we allow now a contract between $C_1$ and $C_2$, $C^2$ will be formed since both members of society prefer $x_2$ to $x_3$. But again Pareto-optimal outcome $x_2$ is only stable if the external contract is binding. Let me note in passing that our example models Sen's example of reading or not reading 'Lady Chatterley's Lover' by mother and daughter. It is thus clear that there exists no paradox of a Paretian liberal if binding external contracts can be concluded.

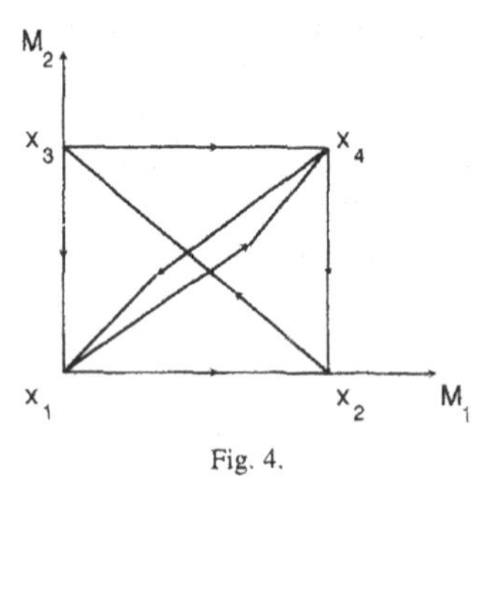


Fig. 4.

Table 5

| | Members of society | | |
|---|---|---|---|
| | 1 | 2 | 3 |
| Strong, separable individual preference orderings over outcomes | $x_3$ | $x_2$ | $x_6$ |
| | $x_1$ | $x_1$ | $x_8$ |
| | $x_4$ | $x_6$ | $x_2$ |
| | $x_7$ | $x_4$ | $x_4$ |
| | $x_5$ | $x_5$ | $x_5$ |
| | $x_8$ | $x_8$ | $x_1$ |
| | $x_6$ | $x_7$ | $x_7$ |
| | $x_2$ | $x_3$ | $x_3$ |

We return to our discussion of problems involved in the proof of Theorem 1 and observe that with two issues a Pareto-inferior outcome can never be stable if there exists a Pareto-superior outcome which is different from it in both issues. But it also turned out that only *binding external contracts* stabilized the Pareto-optimal outcomes $x_5$ and $x_2$ in the two examples. We have already shown with the help of the example of Table 2 and Fig. 2 (Section 2) that *binding internal contracts* are also needed to stabilize a Pareto-better and (finally) a Pareto-optimal outcome. Thus, we can now turn to show why separable individual preferences are a necessary condition for the validity of Theorem 1.

Even with binding internal and external contracts problems may be caused by the fact that a Pareto-optimal outcome which was stable when contracts comprising up to $l$ issues were concluded, may become unstable if $k$ is increased to a number greater than $l(k \geq l)$. This follows since contracts refer to issues and not to outcomes, so that additional outcomes may only differ in the $k - l$ issues on which no contracts have been concluded until now. Members of the respective $V_i$'s are thus not bound concerning these issues. These relationships will become clear

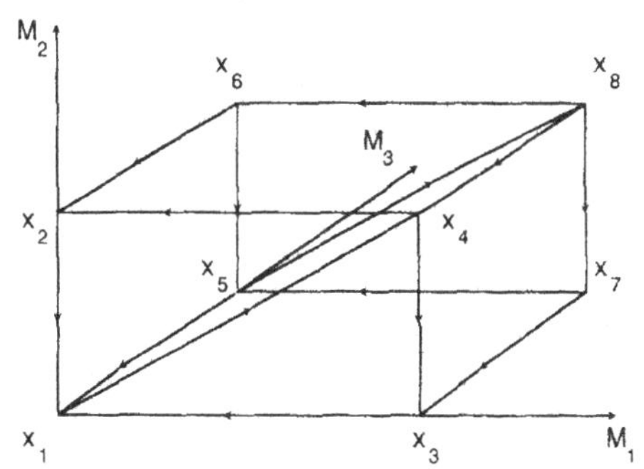


Fig. 5.

by looking at the example of Table 5 and Fig. 5. We assume $V_1 = \{1\}$, $V_2 = \{1, 2, 3\} = V$ with simple majority voting and $V_3 = \{3\}$.

In Fig. 5 we have again omitted several arrows for clarity of presentation. For our later argument it is important that $x_4 P x_5$, since for all $h \in V\, x_4 P_h x_5$, so that a $C^k = C^n = V$ coalition (with $k = n = 3$) can be formed by concluding a binding contract. The corresponding arrow is missing in Fig. 5.

All members of society have separable preferences as can be seen by comparing Table 5 and the three issue-dimensions given by Fig. 5. We repeat that separable individual preferences imply that all arrows which are parallel point into the same direction. This is true for individual preference orderings as can be seen by setting, for example, $x_4 = x_i^*$, $x_1 = x_i$ and $x_8 = x_j^*$, $x_5 = x_j$. But parallel arrows for the individuals of a decisive coalition necessarily imply parallel arrows for decisions made by these coalitions. This is reflected by the arrows of Fig. 5.

Now assume that no external contracts are allowed for the moment and consider only issues $M_1$ and $M_2$ with outcomes $x_1$, $x_2$, $x_3$ and $x_4$. Then obviously $x_4$ will be selected. In fact, we have a prisoner's dilemma for 1 and 2 who both prefer $x_1$ to $x_4$. Allowing 2-issue contracts so that a $C^2$ coalition can be formed, results in $x_1 P x_4$, where $x_1$ is Pareto-optimal and stable because of the binding external contract concerning the respective two issues on which it has been concluded. But outcome $x_1$ is not stable as soon as we take the third issue (dimension) into account which is controlled by $C_3 = V_3 = \{3\}$. For $x_5 P_3 x_1$ so that $x_5 P x_1$.

Now we see at once that the members of $C^2$ have no reason to change their contract referring to issues $M_1$ and $M_2$. For because of the assumption of separability of individual preferences all arrows connecting $x_5$ with other points of Fig. 5 in these dimensions, point into the same direction as those connecting $x_1$. It is true that all $h \in C^2$ prefer $x_1$ to $x_5$ but they have no right to take a decision concerning $M_3$. Also, member 3 of $V_3$ cannot move to an outcome better for him by his decision alone in the example. More generally, he might be able to move to an outcome, say $x_{10}$, but for it the same would be true for the $C^2$ coalition. So, even in the general case some point would be reached which would be stable also for individual 3 and for $C^2$.

It might be profitable however, as in the example, to form a 2-issue coalition relative to $M_2$ and $M_3$, to reach $x_2$ which is better than $x_5$ for its members 2 and 3. But such a coalition could only be formed if the other coalition partner of $C^2$ would also agree, since external and internal contracts are binding. Thus, if this should happen, a stable outcome better for all $h \in V^2 \cup \{3\}$ would result. In our example this is not the case.

There is still another case to be considered, namely a 3-issue coalition $C^3$ might be formed in our example. If $x_5$ has been reached before, we see that a coalition could agree on such a contract, namely $C^3 = \{1, 2, 3\} = V$, since $x_4 P_h x_5$ for all $h \in C^3$. But $x_4$ is Pareto-optimal and stable since contracts are binding. Note, however, that $x_4$ need not be Pareto-better than $x_5$ as in the example. If we reversed, for example, the preference ordering between $x_4$ and $x_5$ for member two, there would still exist a $C^{3\prime} = \{1, 3\}$ which would prefer $x_4$ and could bring it about. But since member 1 is a partner in the $C^2$ coalition necessary to bring about $x_1$ against $x_4$ or $x_5$ against $x_8$, $C^{3\prime}$ (recall that contracts refer to issues) could then not be formed because the internal contract among the members of $C_2 = \{1, 2\}$ is binding. On the other hand, this would not matter, for $x_5$ is now also Pareto-optimal. This confirms again our earlier statement that a Pareto-inferior point will never be stable.

## 7. Meaning and implications of the result

We have shown that a generalized Coase theorem is valid and that thus with negative externalities present stable Pareto-optimal outcomes will result in decentralized political-economic systems with the help of *binding internal and external contracts*, whatever the assignment of political and economic rights, *if separable individual preferences are present.* The setting analyzed allows not only all kinds of contracts like purchase and exchange of goods, but also the exchange of votes and of all kinds of services and actions. The analysis covers also any possible decentralized assignment of rights to individuals and organizations in the broadest sense like parties, cities, parliaments, bureaucracies, joint stock companies, cooperatives and electorates. Here we call any $V_i$ an organization if $|V_i| > 1$. The approach also comprises an extremely broad range of decision rules.

The greater generality of our theorem compared to the Coase theorem has been bought at the expense of strong additional assumptions, which will be discussed below. This is, however, not true for the additional assumptions extending our theorem to the case of weak individual preference orderings. The discussions of the Coase theorem always imply the existence of at least one finely divisible good (like money) which is valued and owned by everybody and the existence of a neighborhood of outcomes also preferred to the outcomes implying unabated negative externalities.

The next assumptions to be discussed are binding internal contracts and the absence of one-issue social preference cycles. *Binding internal contracts* are necessary to prevent the problems implied by social preference cycles or to stabilize outcomes at the $k \geq 2$ level. (Compare the example of Table 2 and Fig. 2 with the cycle $x_2 P x_7 P x_6 P x_3 P x_2$.) Now such cycles arise *similar to one-issue cycles* because of shifting one-issue coalitions $C_i$, $C_i'$, $C_i''$ ($i = 1, 2, \ldots, k$). The example of Table 6 and Fig. 6 demonstrates this for the simplest well-known case of a one-issue cycle.

Here $n = 1$, $V_1 = V = \{1, 2, 3\}$ and simple majority voting is assumed.

Now the Coase theorem does not consider such problems and perhaps it appears that it need not be concerned with one-issue cycles, since binding external contracts relate to at least two issues and thus stabilize one-issue cycles if

Table 6

| | Members of society | | |
|---|---|---|---|
| | 1 | 2 | 3 |
| Strong, individual preference orderings | $x_1$ | $x_2$ | $x_3$ |
| | $x_2$ | $x_3$ | $x_1$ |
| | $x_3$ | $x_1$ | $x_2$ |

contracts are concluded. But, in fact, these problems cannot be excluded. For what would happen if with contracts concluded comprising up to $k-1$ issues no beneficial contract on $k$ issues would be concluded and if a $k$th issue would show a one-issue cycle? Obviously no stable outcome might result and a Pareto-inferior outcome could be a member of the cycle. It is also obvious that Pareto-inferior outcomes contained in social preference cycles cannot be excluded without *binding internal contracts*, even if no one-issue cycles exist (see example of Table 2 and Fig. 2). Thus the absence of one-issue cycles seems to be a necessary condition not only for our theorem but also for the more limited Coase theorem.

In this connection it may be important to stress another fact. If it were always possible to form one-issue coalitions agreeing on binding *internal* contracts preferring one alternative of the issue, then we could drop our assumption of the absence of one-issue cycles. For such internal binding contracts would select a stable outcome of the one-issue cycles (Bernholz, 1978). Thus a binding internal contract by the members of $C_1 = \{1, 3\}$ would lead to stable outcome $x_1$ in the above example.

Perhaps the most critical assumption we made to prove Theorem 1 concerned separable individual preference orderings. Without it there can be cases in which earlier contracts on sets of $K_j$-issues have to be renegotiated because a new contract on a set of $K_r$ non-overlapping issues has brought about an outcome $x_r$ which is worse for $C^{K_j}$ than another one which can be reached by this coalition.

Now it seems that there exists some justification for assuming separable individual preference orderings. For individuals usually cover by contracts the issues which are most important to them. Thus a non-overlapping contract concluded by others later on will leave undisturbed their ordering of outcomes

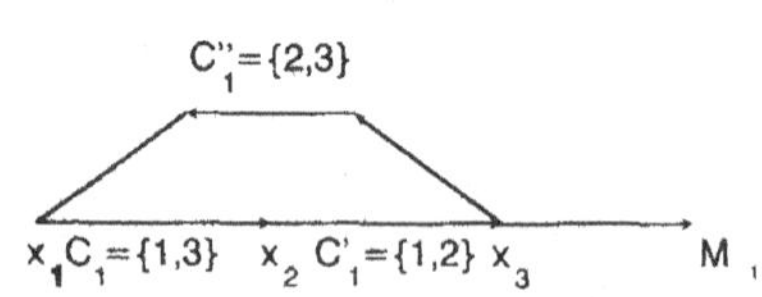


Fig. 6.

even if they are changed in issues of little concern to them. On the other hand, the separability condition may be considered to be pretty strong. For according to our proof of Theorem 1, decisions are taken sequentially. And in this context the separability assumption prevents any regret over decisions taken in the past and any revision of them after other agents have changed perhaps drastically the situation by their decisions on other issues.

Another very critical assumption necessary for the validity of the generalized Coase theorem is the assumption of a fixed assignment of rights to decide issues. For it is obvious that some people might wish to switch organizations, to form new ones or to get a reassignment of rights after they have observed part of the sequence of decisions or find out what the final outcome might be. In a sense it may thus be considered quite illiberal to have a fixed assignment of decision rights as well as of organization membership. This again points to important problems which should be analyzed. One could, e.g. try to find out the consequences of a right to exchange membership in organizations or of a meta-right of the whole of society to change the assignment of rights by some decision rule.

Another critical assumption we made were external and internal contracts which are *binding*. This was necessary to reach a stable Pareto-optimal outcome. Already Aivazian and Callen (1981) showed that the Coase theorem may not hold for three or more partners who can conclude contracts, since there may exist no core. In this case, each proposed coalition (and thus contract) is defeated by another one. This problem was solved in the present paper by assuming *binding* contracts. Historically, the evolution of contract law with enforcement of contracts has possibly much to do with this fact, that otherwise no stability can be reached.

Non-binding contracts provide no basis for rational behavior which has to rely on trustworthy relationships and predictable actions of others. For non-binding contracts are only stable in repetitive situations under certain conditions, as shown by game theory.

It may be asked further why in deriving the Coase theorem only *binding external* and *not binding internal* contracts have been discussed in earlier contributions. The explanation is probably that one has thought only of *individuals* and not of organizations agreeing on contracts. In this case, which we may call 'pure liberalism', only single individuals have the right to decide issues, i.e. all $V_i$ contain only one individual. In such a setting, internal contracts would not occur at all. Also one-issue social preference cycles could not take place because of transitive individual preferences. Thus the condition of binding *external* contracts would be sufficient.

Note, however, that we should additionally postulate for 'pure liberalism' that each member of society has the right to control at least one issue, which implies $n \geq m$. Otherwise oligarchy or even the case of dictatorship would be covered by the definition.

It follows that *for a purely liberal society, the assumptions of binding internal contracts and of the absence of one-issue social preference cycles can be dropped,* since they are not needed. Thus one can argue that in the absence of transaction costs, a purely liberal assignment of all rights to decide issues together with the possibility to conclude binding external contracts would lead to Pareto-optimal stable outcomes. But already in this highly abstract and unrealistic case, the importance can be seen of the evolutionary development of contracts and of mechanisms to enforce them. Thus it is not surprising that besides social norms contract law, courts to adjudicate them and law enforcement to enforce contracts and to safeguard property rights evolved historically.

We have pointed out that our result is also relevant for the evaluation of Arrow's impossibility theorem. Under the assumptions necessary for the proof of Theorem 1 a stable Pareto-optimal outcome results in a decentralized political economic system whether this outcome is a member of cyclical social preferences or not. It can thus be argued that Arrow's theorem is only relevant in cases in which one or more of these assumptions are not fulfilled.

The reasons why the Arrow theorem may not be relevant are obviously the existence of *binding* contracts and the separability of individual preference orderings. The former allow to remove negative externalities and prevent people inflicting new negative 'political' externalities on the partners with whom they have concluded the contract by violating it. And the separability assumption ensures that no new negative externalities are created by a revision of earlier decisions. And we know that cyclical social preferences can only occur if negative externalities are present (Bernholz, 1982).

The assumption of separable individual preference orderings clearly violates Arrow's postulate of unrestricted domain. Thus we are in a sense following a similar approach to that taken by Bailey (1979), though our approach is much more general. Bailey wanted to show that Arrow's claim that even the market violates his axioms was wrong. Bailey demonstrated that under the usual assumptions made in economics, exchange brings about a solution on the Pareto frontier. This is certainly correct, but the usual assumptions like a negatively sloped demand curve violate Arrow's postulate, a fact not seen by Bailey.

We have shown in this paper that up to $n$-issue contracts may be necessary to get stable Pareto-optimal outcomes. But if transaction costs are no longer neglected, it is clear that they generally increase with the number of issues and of people involved. It follows that this is already a sufficient condition for the evolution of organizations in history, of organizations which control one or more issues, so that the number of people participating in negotiating contracts and thus contract costs are reduced. From this conclusion it follows that we cannot agree with Williamson's statement (1981, p. 1545): "that but for the *simultaneous* existence of *bounded rationality and opportunism*, all economic contracting problems are trivial and the study of economic institutions is unimportant. Thus, but for bounded rationality, all economic exchange could be effectively organized by contract". For even if rationality were not bounded and no opportunism existed, it would be efficient to reduce the number of participants in negotiating contracts by forming organizations to save transaction costs. Thus even with unchanging issues, alternatives and outcomes there would exist an additional motivation to create organizations.

The evolution of organizations leads, however, as shown by our additional assumptions, to new problems, which we may describe by the term 'politics'. The emergence of organizations brings with it new negative externalities to 'outvoted' members (Buchanan, 1962, Buchanan and Tullock, 1965, 60–62) and the problems thus created are related to the stability of coalitions. They divide into two questions, namely which coalitions will be formed at all and whether they will be binding. If we look at the example of Table 6 and Fig. 6, it is not clear which coalition will be formed. This may depend on the agenda determining the sequence of voting. Also whether one contract concluded by the members of such a coalition will be stable may depend on externally imposed rules of the game cutting the decision process or whether the decisions taken are repetitive so that they form a repeated game of indefinite length ending only with a certain low probability (Bernholz, 1978). With more than one issue, phenomena like logrolling (Bernholz, 1974), vote trading and instability of government (Downs, 1957, 55–62) can occur, which all imply cyclical social preferences. All this is well-known from public choice theory (see Mueller, 1989), but it is important to stress that the *absence of binding internal contracts* is not only a problem for parties, communities and parliaments, but also of companies, cooperatives, their boards etc. Since all these 'political' problems can only be overcome by binding internal contracts, it is an important question how far legal systems have already evolved to solve such problems, or what could be done to move them towards such solutions.

On the other hand, we should not forget that our analysis has been confined to the case of perfect information concerning outcomes, issues and decision rights of subsets of society. No meta-rights of individuals or organizations (like parliaments) to change the assignment of rights were included in our assumptions. Also, no changes of the number of possible outcomes, of issues and alternatives and of available information have been allowed. Now it is obvious that, given imperfect and changing information and the possibility of changes in the number of outcomes, issues and alternatives, it may well be that binding contracts and especially binding political internal contracts, may have negative consequences. This can be the case since binding contracts can only be adapted to changing conditions and information by unanimous consent of all participants. It is clear that in such a setting these disadvantages of binding contracts would have to be weighed against their advantages analyzed above.

Our concluding remarks should have made it clear that though our approach has solved some important problems it has also brought other problems into the open which are as important as the well-known neglect of transaction costs by the Coase theorem and which need much analytical effort to be successfully included into the analysis.

## Acknowledgements

I am grateful to James M. Buchanan, Hans Gersbach, Malte Faber, Dennis Mueller and three unknown referees for helpful comments.

## References

Aivazian, V.A., Callen, J.L., 1981. The Coase Theorem and the empty core. The Journal of Law and Economics 24 (1), 175–181.

Arrow, K.J., 1963/1951. Social Choice and Individual Values. John Wiley & Sons, New York.

Bailey, M.J., 1979. The possibility of rational social choice in economics. Journal of Political Economy 87 (1), 37–56.

Bernholz, P., 1974. Logrolling, Arrow-paradox and decision rules: A generalization. Kyklos 27, 49–62.

Bernholz, P., 1978. On the stability of logrolling outcomes in stochastic games. Public Choice 33 (3), 65–82.

Bernholz, P., 1980. A general social dilemma: Profitable exchange and intransitive group preferences. Z. Nationalökon. 40, 1–23 (reprinted in: Buchanan, J.M., Tollison, R.D. The Theory of Public Choice. II. University of Michigan Press, Ann Arbor, pp. 361–381).

Bernholz, P., 1982. Externalities as a necessary condition for cyclical social preferences. The Quarterly Journal of Economics 47 (4), 699–705.

Bernholz, P., 1986. A general constitutional possibility theorem. Public Choice 51, 249–265.

Buchanan, J.M., 1962. Politics, policy and Pigovian margins. Economica NS 29, 17–28.

Buchanan, J.M., Tullock, G., 1962. The Calculus of Consent. University of Michigan Press, Ann Arbor.

Coase, R.H., 1960. The problem of social cost. Journal of Law and Economics 3, 1–44.

Downs, A., 1957. An Economic Theory of Democracy. Harper and Row, New York.

Mueller, D.C., 1989. Public Choice II. Cambridge University Press, Cambridge, New York.

Schwartz, T., 1981. The universal-instability theorem. Public Choice 37, 487–501.

Schwartz, T., 1986. The Logic of Collective Choice. Columbia University Press, New York, ch. 11.

Sen, A.K., 1970. The impossibility of a paretian liberal. Journal of Political Economy 78, 152–157.

Williamson, O.E., 1981. The modern corporation: Origins, evolution, attributes. Journal of Economic Literature 19, 1537–1568.

# [12]

ELSEVIER

European Journal of Political Economy
Vol. 15 (1999) 331–335

European Journal of
POLITICAL
ECONOMY

# The generalized Coase Theorem and separable individual preferences: an extension

Peter Bernholz *

*University of Basel, Basel Center for Economics and Business, Postfach, Petersgraben 51, CH-4003 Basel, Switzerland*

Received 1 August 1997; received in revised form 1 July 1998; accepted 1 September 1998

**Abstract**

In a recent article [Bernholz, P., 1997. Property rights, contracts, cyclical social preferences, and the Coase Theorem: A synthesis. European Journal of Political Economy, 13, 419–442] it was shown that the Coase Theorem can be generalized to all cases of assignments of rights, including political and bureaucratic rights. At the same time, however, additional assumptions besides the absence of transaction costs had to be introduced to assure the validity even of the original Coase Theorem limited to market phenomena. The assumptions are that external and internal contracts must be binding, that a finely divisible good like money must be present and be valued by all, and that individual preference orderings are separable. In the present extension this latter rather restrictive assumption will be removed. I will thus demonstrate the conditions under which the generalized Coase Theorem holds without the assumption of separable individual preference orderings. © 1999 Elsevier Science B.V. All rights reserved.

*Keywords:* Coase Theorem; Rights; Individual preference ordering

## 1. Sketch of notations and assumptions

I show first by using an example that problems arise with the Coase Theorem if individual preference orderings are not separable. In doing so, I assume *strong* individual preference orderings, three issues, and a society consisting of three

* Fax: +41-61-267-3340; E-mail: bernholzp@ubaclu.unibas.ch


PII: S0176-2680(99)00009-9

Table 1
Members of society

| | 1 | 2 | 3 |
|---|---|---|---|
| Strong | $x_3$ | $x_2$ | $x_6$ |
| Individual | $x_1$ | $x_1$ | $x_4$ |
| Preference | $x_4$ | $x_6$ | $x_2$ |
| Orderings | $x_7$ | $x_4$ | $x_8$ |
| over | $x_8$ | $x_8$ | $x_5$ |
| Outcomes | $x_5$ | $x_5$ | $x_1$ |
| | $x_6$ | $x_7$ | $x_7$ |
| | $x_2$ | $x_3$ | $x_3$ |

individuals, i.e., $V = \{1,2,3\}$. Individual preference orderings over the outcomes $x_1, x_2, \ldots, x_8$, are given by Table 1.

Each outcome comprises three alternatives, one out of the three issues. The three issues $M_1$, $M_2$ and $M_3$ are represented by the three dimensions of Fig. 1, where each issue contains only two alternatives. Thus, for example, outcome $x_8$ is different from $x_1$ in the alternatives of all three issues, $x_3$ only in those of the first issue $M_1$.

All rights refer to issues and are assigned to subsets of society. In the example the right to decide the first and the third issue is assigned to individuals 1 and 3, respectively. All individuals together have the right to decide $M_2$. Thus we have $V_1 = \{1\} \subset V$, $V_2 = \{1,2,3\} = V$, $V_3 = \{3\} \subset V$. We assume further that $M_2$ is decided by simple majority vote.

It is obvious that externalities are present in the example. A decision by 1 to move from $x_5$ to $x_7$ implies negative externalities for 2 and 3. But 1 has the right to do so, since the first issue has been assigned to it. And it can do so, if $x_5$ happens to be the status quo. Similarly externalities are present in other cases, for

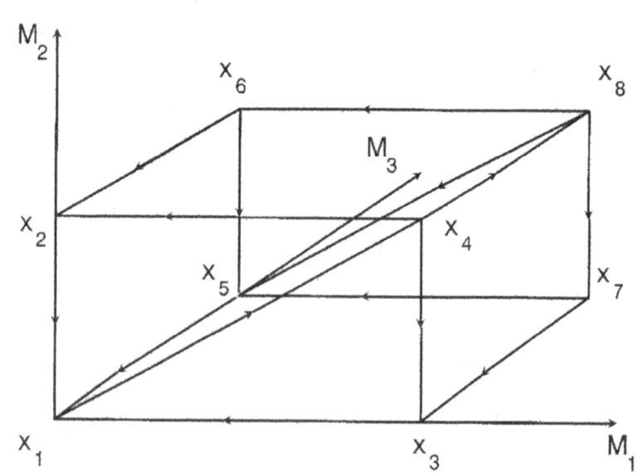


Fig. 1.

example if a majority {2,3} decides concerning issue 2 to move from $x_1$ to $x_2$. For this implies a negative externality to the outvoted minority, voter 1. Note further that there are inseparabilities in individual preference orderings. Consider the preference ordering of individual 3 in Table 1. He prefers $x_6$ to $x_2$ and at the same time $x_4$ to $x_8$. But the two outcomes of both pairs differ among each other only in the same alternatives of the same issue $M_3$ (Fig. 1). Thus separability would require that the ordering between the outcomes of one of the pairs be reversed.

The arrows in Fig. 1 point from the dominating to the dominated outcome. Thus, since 1 has the right to decide $M_1$, the arrows in that dimension correspond to his preference ordering.

The right to decide $M_2$, however, has been assigned to $V_2 = \{1,2,3\}$ who decide by simple majority. Now 2 and 3 form such a majority, for example, for the decision between $x_4$ and $x_3$. As a consequence the arrow points to the latter, since it is worse for both of them. Finally, we have to mention that a move, for example, from $x_5$ to $x_8$ or $x_4$ can only be accomplished with the help of a contract among $V_1$ and $V_2$ or $V_1$, $V_2$ and $V_3$, respectively, since rights refer only to issues.

## 2. Problems with the Coase Theorem given non-separable individual preference orderings

It follows directly from looking at Fig. 1 that if contracts are not allowed, $x_4$ is the only stable outcome. But 1 and 2 prefer $x_1$, and 1 controls the first and they both together as a majority control the second issue. Thus they conclude a binding *external* and *internal* contract to bring about $x_1$. But in spite of the fact that the contract is *binding* for them, this is not a stable outcome. For 3 is not a partner to the contract, and he prefers not only $x_5$ but can realize it, since he has the right to decide issue $M_3$. But this outcome is Pareto-inferior, since all members of society prefer $x_8$ to it and can realize this outcome by a binding contract implying the first two issues. But it again is Pareto-inferior to $x_4$, which can be brought about by 3. As a consequence a cycle is present. We have cyclical ‘social preferences’. No stable Pareto-optimal outcome exists. Or, put differently, the existing *negative externalities* cannot be removed even by *binding contracts*. The latter statement is directly related to the fact that *cyclical social preferences implying two or more issues* can only occur if *negative externalities* are present (Bernholz, 1997).

The reason for the existence of cyclical social preferences and no stable Pareto-optimal solution as asserted by the Coase Theorem is clearly the *existence of non-separable individual preference orderings*. In the example the cycle mentioned would, for example, not exist, if individual 3 had a separable preference ordering, so that $x_8$ would be preferred by him to $x_4$ (the general proof is given in Bernholz, 1997). Now cyclical social preferences would not be of any concern if they contained only Pareto-optimal outcomes. But as shown by the example, this is clearly not the case. On the other hand, the assumption of *separable individual preference orderings* is rather strong and restrictive. We intend thus to show subsequently that the validity of the generalized Coase Theorem can be maintained in the absence of this assumption under certain conditions.

## 3. Proof of the generalized Coase Theorem with non-separable individual preference orderings present

Let us first consider the cycle mentioned for the above example. We have seen that of the four outcomes in the cycle, two are not Pareto-optimal, whereas $x_1$ and $x_4$ are. Can this situation be solved with the help of *binding contracts*? This is indeed the case in the sense that all Pareto-inferior outcomes can be excluded.

If the cycle were the only one, all its outcomes would recur regularly with a certain frequency or probability, where we may call the probability with which $x_i$ occurs $p_i$. With only the above cycle considered, we might reasonably set all $p_i$ equal to 1/4. Now consider first $x_8$, which is dominated by Pareto-optimal $x_4$. Since we have assumed strong individual preferences, the latter is better than the former for all three members of society. They could thus conclude a profitable contract agreeing that they would no longer bring about $x_8$, but instead limit themselves to move to the other outcomes in the former cycle with probabilities $p_1 = p_5 = 1/4$ and $p_{4'} = 1/2$. The frequency of $x_8$ would thus be added to that of the Pareto-superior outcome. But since $x_4$ is also Pareto-superior to $x_5$, a similar reasoning applies to these two outcomes. Consequently the *binding* contract will state that its partners will bring about the two Pareto-optimal outcomes of the former cycle with frequencies $p_{4''} = 3/4$ and $p_1 = 1/4$. But then the cycle is broken, negative externalities are removed and a stable Pareto-optimal solution alternating between $x_1$ and $x_4$ is reached.

It is obvious that a similar result can be easily proved for the general case with many issues and members of society and with many, possibly, interlocking cycles. For assume that there exist one or more possibly interlocking social preference cycles. Then the system might become stuck in one of them. In this case assign the observed frequencies $p_i$ with $\Sigma p_i = 1$ to all outcomes $x_i$ in the (interlocking) cycle(s). Next select all Pareto-inferior outcomes $x_j$ within the (interlocking) cycle(s) and substitute for them in the contract to be agreed on Pareto-superior outcomes from within or without the cycle(s). Add to the frequencies of these outcomes those of the outcomes for which they have been substituted. Note that for Pareto-superior outcomes selected from outside the cycle(s) the original frequency is zero. It follows from this argument that the *binding* contract concluded contains only Pareto-optimal outcomes which will be brought about by the partners with different frequencies. Thus a stable solution comprising only Pareto-optimal outcomes emerges. Finally, since the argument holds true for any (possibly connected) social preference cycle(s) in which the system may become stuck, such an outcome will always be reached by a binding contract.

## 4. Concluding remarks

The argument can be easily extended to the case of weak individual preference orderings by assuming that at least one finely divisible good is present, which is positively valued by all individuals (see Bernholz, 1997).

More importantly, however, the above proof shows that, without the assumption of separable individual preference orderings, the generalized and even the limited Coase theorem is only valid, if distributional considerations are taken into account when concluding a contract of the type discussed above. In the example, member 3 would only agree to the contract if the Pareto-optimal outcome $x_4$ would be brought about three times as often as $x_1$ by the partners.

It follows that potential partners who have the right to decide issues or are necessary members of a decisive coalition $C_i \subset V_i$ can insist on higher frequencies for the Pareto-optimal outcomes favouring their interests.

In this paper I have, moreover, neglected bargaining problems which may arise because there can exist several outcomes which are Pareto-preferred to a given Pareto-inferior outcome in a cycle. For in this case there may arise a conflict because of different individual preference orderings about which of these outcomes to substitute. We have thus implicitly assumed that such conflicts are always solved because of the interest of all partners to move to a better solution.

## References

Bernholz, P., 1997. Property rights, contracts, cyclical social preferences, and the Coase Theorem: a synthesis. European Journal of Political Economy 13, 419–442.

# [13]

*Public Choice* **115:** 1–36, 2003.




## Political Coase theorem

FRANCESCO PARISI*
*School of Law, George Mason University, Arlington, VA 22201-4498, U.S.A.; e-mail: parisi@gmu.edu*

Accepted 22 December 2002

**Abstract.** This article considers the applicability of the Coase theorem (in both its positive and normative formulations) to the political market. The article analogizes the choice of decision rules in the political market to the choice of legal rules in the traditional Coase theorem and further analogizes alternative initial coalitions to the different initial allocations of entitlements considered by Coase (1960). On the basis of these analogies, the paper examines the relevance (or lack thereof) of alternative voting rules and initial coalitions on the final political outcome. The article further shows that, if all voters are allowed to enter into Coasian bargaining over the policy outcome to be adopted by the majority coalition (i.e., if political bargains are possible and are enforceable), uniqueness and stability are obtained. The analysis of the axiomatic Nash bargaining equilibrium yields an interesting geometric intuition. If voters have similar utility functions centered around different ideal policy points, the Coasian bargaining will be conducive to the "center of mass" of the policy space, which weighs the agents' preferences as revealed in the bargaining process. Such ideal equilibrium satisfies most criteria of social welfare. The article concludes considering the various practical limits of this ideal political market, whenever collective action and agency problems affect the political bargaining in a representative or direct democracy.

*With all side payments prohibited, there is no assurance that collective action will be taken in the most productive way.*

James M. Buchanan and Gordon Tullock (1962)

### 1. Introduction

In most legal systems of the world, the wholesale market for votes is constitutionally protected. Interest groups are allowed to influence policy outcomes through campaign contributions which are in turn used to obtain larger political support through advertising (Levinson, 1999). Yet, vote buying is prohibited at the retail level. Anti-trafficking laws, in fact, generally prohibit "offering, making, soliciting, or receiving payments in return for voting or withholding a vote" (Karlan, 1999).

* I would like to thank Henry Hansmann, Dennis C. Mueller, Charles K. Rowley and Gordon Tullock for insightful comments and guidance in this research. Carlo Lancellotti, Dario Fusato and Richard Souther provided valuable research assistance.

2

The different legal treatment of wholesale and retail vote trading has enjoyed occasional rationalizations in legal and economic theory.[1] On this point, the intellectual split between political scientists, political economists and public law scholars is most evident. For political scientists, vote trading is such a natural component of real life politics that they make no effort at rationalizing, justifying or challenging such reality. Common names, such as "horse trading" or "deal making," are generally used by political scientists to describe the general phenomenon of vote trading. Political economists are equally at ease with the idea of an implicit market for political consensus and develop and actively utilize politics-like-market metaphors that unveil the implicit market mechanisms that drive political dynamics.[2]

Public law scholars remain among the few who evaluate the normative implications of market for votes. These latter scholars occasionally object to the "commodification" of political consensus. It is argued, the commodification of the vote would undesirably encourage citizens to bring their own self-interest into the process, at the expense of the aspirational and expressive qualities of the political exchange and to the detriment of the community at large.[3] The objections and institutional analysis of vote trading usually focuses on vote trading in legislative settings, with little or no consideration of the buying of the votes of individual voters. While such lack of attention may be justified by pragmatical reasons (given the practical difficulties of monitoring and enforcing vote trading at the individual level), we should nevertheless consider that individuals and groups with strong preferences for particular policy outcomes may use alternative, in-kind means of vote buying. They donate money to the campaigns of favored candidates, finance the advertising of political messages, distribute cigarettes and other items to marginal voters on election day, offer to transport them to and from the polls, and so on. These practices and institutions, while in many ways falling short of the necessary attributes of the first-best exchange and enforcement mechanisms considered in this paper, nevertheless should not be ignored.

Objections to institutionalized vote trading are also raised with respect to logrolling at the representatives' level. Public law scholars suggest that such political exchanges should be discouraged because they undermine political accountability and because imperfections in the market for votes are likely to engender costs that outweigh the benefits of a free market in votes (Karlan, 1999).

These arguments, while sensible in their own turf, seem to treat indistinctly the question of agency problems in political representation with the understanding of the effects of an explicit market for votes on the resulting political outcome. This article wishes to shed some light on the issue of logrolling and political representation, giving separate attention to the two dimensions of the problem.

Building on the results of my previous paper on the market for votes (Parisi, 1998), I will focus preliminarily on the properties of a market for votes in the absence of agency problems, e.g., in a direct democracy or in a world where the representatives' preference profiles faithfully reflect the preferences of the people. In such ideal world of perfect representation, the incentives of the legislatures are perfectly aligned with those of the voters, so that we can interchangeably think of the aggregation of the politicians' policy preferences as the aggregation of the preferences of society at large. These assumptions are later relaxed, considering the different impact of vote exchange mechanisms in the presence of agency and collective action problems. In particular, this Article examines the potential role of bargaining and side-payments among voters subject to a majoritarian decision-rule, in inducing stable and socially desirable policy outcomes. Revisiting the conclusions reached by Bernholz (1980), I show that, under fairly standard assumptions, majoritarian outcomes with bargaining are unique and stable as long as minority voters are allowed to influence the majority policy-making through side payments and as long as political bargains are enforceable. The results in turn provide an argument for enforcing political bargains.[4] In addition, this Article provides an alternative explanation for Tullock's (1981) puzzle as to why there is so much stability in the political process. By reconceptualizing Arrow's (1963) theorem using voters' utility functions rather than mere preference profiles (i.e., ordered preferences), the approach adopted in this Article allows voter preferences to be continuous and differentiable, without imposing any stringent condition relative to cardinality and interpersonal comparability of preferences.[5]

Section 2 discusses the considerations that motivated this research and formulates claims on the properties of a market for votes. Section 3 presents a basic Pareto optimization model as a benchmark to evaluate a Coasian bargaining result. The model is used to explore the implications of Coasian assumptions for the bargaining outcome. If agency problems in representation are assumed away, bargaining and side payments among voters will yield Pareto-optimal outcomes, reaching results similar to those of an ideal unanimity rule, yet avoiding the hold-ups and transaction costs often occasioned by such rules.[6] Section 4 discusses the geometry of the market for votes, identifying the conditions under which bargaining and side-payments will yield a unique and stable majority outcome. Section 5 explores the welfare implications of the market for votes. This analysis shows that if voters have utility functions with similar curvatures, centered around equidistant ideal points, the bargaining outcome will satisfy the Benthamite[7] and Nash[8] cri-

4

teria of social welfare. Conversely, if voters' utility functions have different curvatures or are centered around ideal points that are not equidistant from one another, then the competing criteria of social welfare are likely to be satisfied at different points and the bargaining outcome will fulfill only the Benthamite criterion of social welfare. Section 6 discusses some implications of the market for votes in the real-world political marketplace. This Article concludes by considering possible extensions and welfare implications of the political bargaining model once the assumption of symmetric preferences is relaxed.

## 2. Majority voting and inter-coalition bargaining

One of the main insights of social choice theory is that the correlation between preference and choice is weaker for groups than for individuals.[9] According to Arrow's possibility theorem, it may indeed be too much to expect methods of collective decision making to be at the same time rational and egalitarian. (Arrow, 1963: 46–60) Arrow's theorem shows that any social decision that is adopted must violate at least one of six self-evident axioms of normative political theory, commonly described by the following terms: range, universal domain, unanimity, nondictatorship, independence of irrelevant alternatives, and rationality.[10] Arrow's conclusion and its various corollaries pose a dramatic threat to the legitimacy of political decisions given the absence of any guarantee that the optimal collective choice will be obtained through a stable political process.[11] The heart of Arrow's theorem states that there are no non-dictatorial rules or procedures for collective decision-making that reflect the combined preferences of voters to a consistent collective outcome.[12] This Article considers the implications of Arrow's theorem where there are cyclical majorities which are capable of repealing any resolution that has been adopted previously.

As this Article will demonstrate, if all voters are allowed to enter into Coasian bargaining over the policy outcome to be adopted by the majority coalition, and if political bargains are enforceable, collective preferences in a multi-dimensional policy space will be transitive as long as individual preferences are single-peaked. This result runs contrary to the common thought in public and social choice theory. Most of the literature on the stability implications of log-rolling[13] considers the context of bargaining for the formation of coalitions where side-payments are only instruments for entering the majority coalition, and no side-payments are made by those who are not part of the majority.[14] Furthermore, the conclusions that logrolling situations imply voting cycles assume that every voter at every step of the logrolling sequence can betray a previous coalition agreement to enter into a new coalition with other parties.

This Article considers a broader role for bargaining and side-payments. Bargaining is permitted, with exchanges taking place among all voters and all coalitions. This assumption more accurately reflects the bargaining that takes place during the legislative process.[15] Additionally, voters' agreements (whether under the form of explicit vote trades or implicit logrolling) are assumed to be enforceable. In such a scenario, where bargained-for exchanges take place among all voters and coalitions and where there are enforceable political agreements, the intransitive result of Arrow's (1963) paradox holds true only under implausible conditions.

### 2.1. *One man, one vote, and the limits of democracy*

In situations in which no strong political consensus is reached on a given issue, intransitivity may result. This intransitivity implies that a different order in the decision-making process may affect the outcome, and that any winning coalition may be undermined by the reintroduction of an alternative it previously defeated. The structure of the voting process does not allow the cycle to be broken by looking at the intensity of voters' preferences. The outcome is arbitrarily determined by the order of motions, with no guarantee that the ultimate result will yield a higher level of social welfare than that potentially afforded by any other defeated policy alternative.

Democratic voting allows no expression of intensity of preferences, but only ordering among alternative outcomes. The inability of the democratic process to capture the intensity of the voters' preferences is a by-product of the generally espoused principle that every individual is entitled to one – and only one – vote. This effect of the "one man, one vote" rule is exacerbated by the fact that individual voters do not face the opportunity cost of casting their vote. Whether their preference is strong or weak, voters will cast their vote in favor of their favored option. Even if specifically designed to allow voters to indicate the intensity of voters' preferences, the voting ballot could not possibly capture such intensity. Absent a mechanism to extract the true intensity of their preferences, individual voters would tend to overstate their cardinal preferences in order to maximize the impact of their votes.

Democracy gives equal weight to all votes when they are counted, regardless of how strongly or weakly the voters feel about the issue.[16] In this way, numerically equal groups have equal political say in the process. However, if the distribution of sentiments on an issue is not symmetrical, and the minority holds strong preferences, the outcome would be inefficient.

6

### 2.2. *Introducing vote trading and the opportunity cost of voting*

By introducing the possibility of bargaining and vote-trading in the process, the intensity of preferences is reflected in the decision-making process. With bargaining and side-payments, the "one man, one vote" rule would provide the initial entitlement for each voter-trader. The exchange mechanism would then reveal the relative strength of individual preferences.[17] Once voters have an opportunity to trade their votes, they will face the opportunity cost of casting their vote. In the case of non-tradeable votes voters would cast their vote for their favored option regardless of the intensity of their preference. Once vote trading is permitted, however, voters may be inclined to utilize their vote only on issues for which they feel strongly about. They would, instead, prefer to transfer their vote in support of less preferred policies in exchange for payments or in-kind concessions. This sort of behavior, to some extent observable in real life legislative settings, creates an "opportunity cost" in casting a vote. Put it differently, the presence of exchange opportunities allows the voting system to capture intensity (as well as ordinal ranking) of voters' preferences.

In this way, political bargaining may provide a solution to the intensity problem, and at the same time correct for the cyclicality problem. Politicians know well that under certain conditions the outcome may depend on the sequence of decisions and therefore on agenda-setting. For example, in a situation with intransitive preferences, the agenda-setter may influence the process in favor of his preferred policy by determining the sequence of decisions.[18] Agenda-setting increases the internal predictability of the outcome for those who are involved in the process and have full information about it. Voters (or legislators) sharing similar information on their respective prospects will have an opportunity to bargain under conditions of symmetric information, trading votes for issues on which they hold weak preferences in exchange for votes on issues which have more value for them. Economic theory teaches that bargaining between politicians will continue until the marginal utility of gaining one vote on a certain issue equals the marginal cost of giving up one vote for another issue.

Generalized bargaining yields a Pareto-optimal policy outcome. If cycling majorities still occur, it may be for either of two reasons. First, bargaining among politicians may not be perfect if strategic gate-keepers are still capable of influencing the outcome.[19] In such cases, a solution must be found in eliminating the barrier to Pareto-improving trades.

Alternatively, the intensity of preferences may be identical across voters, so that there is no surplus to pursue through political bargaining and vote trading. In this latter case, cycling produces unpredictability but not inefficiency. The situations left to cycling would be those that leave deciding voters indifferent. In these rather marginal cases, there are no social welfare losses from the cyclicality of the outcome.

One should further expect the competitive nature of the market for votes to cure some of the problems that have been identified in the social choice literature.[20]

## 3. Coasian bargaining and collective decision-making

This section considers whether the outcome selected by majorities in a Coasian environment can be said to maximize the combined welfare of the platforms. The analysis suggests that both stability and efficiency are obtained through Coasian bargaining: a result which is partially at odds with some of the conclusions of the social choice and public choice literature.

Previous attempts to study the stability and efficiency properties of logrolling include Buchanan and Tullock (1962), Coleman (1966), Mueller (1967), Park (1967), Mueller, Philpotts and Vanek (1972) and Koford (1982), among others. Buchanan and Tullock (1962) are generally recognized as the first public choice scholars expressly to discuss the issue of vote trading in a multi-dimensional policy space. The issue, treated in Chapter 10 of their *Calculus of Consent*, rests on the insightful and well-known assertion of efficiency of vote trading, expressed in the following terms: "Permitting those citizens who feel strongly about an issue to compensate in some way those whose opinion is only feebly held can result in a great increase in the well-being of both groups, and the prohibition of such transactions will serve to prevent movement toward the conceptual social optimality surface, under almost any definition of this term." (Buchanan and Tullock, 1962: 133). Buchanan and Tullock's contribution left its mark, not so much for the exposition of the efficiency or stability properties of the outcome (results that, in the context of their monographic treatment, were asserted more as intuitions than proofs), but rather for having postulated a framework of exchange in collective decisions that could operate just like an exchange of economic goods.

In subsequent years, Coleman (1966) first tackled a formal analysis of a hypothetical vote trading in the context of Arrow's impossibility theorem in search for a method that would allow voters to express the relative intensity of their preference and differences between utility levels associated with alternative policies. Coleman contemplates sequential decisions in a legislative body, where actors have an opportunity to express the intensity of their preference, even if imperfectly and incompletely. Through this hypothetical mechanism political behavior can be viewed as a generalization of market behavior and political institutions can be viewed as an extension of the market. Coleman (1966: 1122) interestingly points out that unlike the atomistic market of neoclassical economics, each political actor has only partial control over any given outcome, rather than complete control over a specific result. This requires the use of expected values in all political trades and the more complex consideration of rational behavior under uncertainty and possible risk aversion. Coleman's (1966) paper provided an important contribution to the conceptualization of vote trading, but triggered some debate and criticism. Among others, Mueller (1967) criticized Coleman's (1966) model for the lack of a mechanism for voters to actually exchange votes. The absence of an actual market mechanism with enforceable promises induced two major shortcomings. First, the hypothetical agreements failed to reveal the voter's true preferences because of the voters' incentive to conceal their true preferences in order to increase their bargaining power. Second, because voting decisions are made sequentially, there is the temptation for the second voter to violate the agreement once the first voter has delivered his end of the bargain. By replacing the set of agreements with a systems which allows votes actually to be exchanged, both of these weaknesses could be eliminated, but Mueller (1967: 1310) concluded his critique of Coleman suggesting that "the resulting set of policy decisions will fall far short of being in any sense socially optimal." A different attack to Coleman's results was moved by Park (1967) who disputes Coleman's (1966) apparent assertion that there is ordinarily a stable equilibrium outcome to a vote trading situation with many decisions and many voters. Park (1967: 1301) argued, instead, that no such stable outcome would exist and if it did, "it must be exactly the same as the outcome without vote trading."

In later years, Mueller, Philpotts and Vanek (1972) revisited the issue of vote trading with a computer simulation. The simulation established a market for votes, allowing actual exchanges of votes and adjusting prices until markets cleared. Once equilibrium was established, the votes are cast in accordance with the preferences and number of votes held by each voter in the final equilibrium state. The results are then compared to the likely outcome of a simple majority rule without vote trading, revealing two substantial improvements of vote trading over simple majority rule: (a) the computer simulation generated results that indicated gains in efficiency, with higher aggregate social utility that simple-majority voting; and (b) vote trading improved the equity of the voting process by narrowing the dispersion of utility gains of the participants. Even though the interesting results of Mueller, Philpotts and Vanek (1972) are consistent with the general intuition of my paper, I shall resist the temptation to generalize the interpretation of their results, which necessarily rest on the specifications of their computer simulation.

9

More recently, Koford (1982) presents a model of legislative vote-trading contemplated to fit to American institutional realities. To keep number of traders low, the model assumes that legislators trade only with party leaders, who set prices for political support of proposed bills. Each legislator trades away votes on bills of little importance to his constituency and of high concern to others in exchange for promises to support (or oppose) particular bills of high concern to his constituency. This model is focused on replicating the features of actual logrolling and political exchange mechanisms rather than studying the general welfare attributes of a market for votes.

### 3.1. *The basic model*

Consider the simplest case of a two-dimensional policy space ($G_1, G_2$) with three voters (1, 2, 3) who are allowed to bargain and offer side-payments in a generic consumption good (Y) in exchange for policy concessions from the other voters.[21] The existence of concave and well-behaved[22] utility functions for all voters guarantees the existence of a single policy outcome which satisfies the Pareto criterion of efficiency[23] and the Benthamite criterion of social welfare.[24]

Consider three voters 1, 2 and 3, with utility functions $U_i = u(G_1, G_2, Y_i^0 - Y_i)$ for all $i = 1 \ldots 3$, where $G_1$ and $G_2$ are publicly provided goods and $Y_i^0$ is the initial endowment of Y for voter i, and $Y_i$ is the individual contribution to the public good. Further, consider a public sector production function $F = f(G_1, G_2, Y)$ where $G_1$ and $G_2$ are the production outputs and Y is a generic input, equal to the sum of the individual contributions, such that $Y = \sum_{i=1}^{3} Y_i$. One can study the conditions for Pareto optimality for this problem by setting up a Lagrange equation[25] of the following fashion:

$$\mathcal{L} = U_1(G_1, G_2, Y_1^0 - Y_1) + \sum_{i=2}^{3} \lambda_i [U_i(G_1, G_2, Y_i^0 - Y_i) - U_i^0] + \delta_1(Y_1 + Y_2 + Y_3 - Y) + \delta_2 f(G_1, G_2, Y) \quad (1.1)$$

One can then study the first order conditions by setting all partial derivatives equal to zero and solving the system of equations.

$$\partial\mathcal{L}/\partial G_1 \equiv U_{1G1} + \lambda_2 U_{2G1} + \lambda_3 U_{3G1} + \delta_2 F_{G1} = 0 \quad (1.2)$$

$$\partial\mathcal{L}/\partial G_2 \equiv U_{1G2} + \lambda_2 U_{2G2} + \lambda_3 U_{3G2} + \delta_2 F_{G2} = 0 \quad (1.3)$$

$$\partial\mathcal{L}/\partial Y_i \equiv -U_{1Y1} + \delta_1 = 0 \quad (1.4)$$

$$\partial \mathcal{L}/\partial Y_2 \equiv -\lambda_2 U_{2Y2} + \delta_1 = 0 \quad (1.5)$$

$$\partial \mathcal{L}/\partial Y_3 \equiv -\lambda_3 U_{3Y3} + \delta_1 = 0 \quad (1.6)$$

$$\partial \mathcal{L}/\partial Y \equiv \delta_2 F_Y - \delta_1 = 0 \quad (1.7)$$

Further consider that all partial derivatives with respect to the Lagrangian multipliers are set equal to zero. From equation (1.4) one can find the value of $\delta_1$ which can be substituted into equations (1.5), (1.6) and (1.7). This substitution allows one to solve for $\lambda_2$, $\lambda_3$ and $\delta_2$. Substituting these values into equations (1.2) and (1.3), one finds (1.8):

$$\begin{aligned} &U_{1G1}/U_{1Y1} + U_{2G1}/U_{2Y2} + U_{3G1}/U_{3Y3} + F_{G1}/F_Y = \\ &U_{1G2}/U_{1Y1} + U_{2G2}/U_{2Y2} + U_{3G2}/U_{3Y3} + F_{G2}/F_Y \end{aligned} \quad (1.8)$$

Assuming identical production functions for $G_1$ and $G_2$, and equal marginal utility of wealth across voters (i.e., assuming away wealth effects), such that the following is true:

$$F_{G1} = F_{G2} \quad (1.9)$$

$$U_{1Y1} = U_{2Y2} = U_{3Y3}, \quad (1.10)$$

equation (1.8) collapses to the following proposition, as characterizing the solution to our optimization problem:

$$\sum_{i=1}^{3} U_{iG1} = \sum_{i=1}^{3} U_{iG2} \quad (1.11)$$

Equation (1.11) yields very interesting results. First, given strict concavity of all $U_i$'s, in equation (1.1) the optimization point is unique. This uniqueness follows from a very simple geometrical intuition.[26] If all $U_i$'s are concave, their sum must be concave, as the maximum of a concave function is unique. The countour of points that maximizes equation (1.1) will collapse into a single point given its nature as a maximum in a two-dimensional plane. Second, if $U_i$'s have equal curvatures around different ideal points, equation (1.11) implies that the bargaining outcome will be conducive to a policy outcome which is at the interior of the policy triangle shown in Figure 1 below. As shown in Section 4, the optimization point will be equally distant from the voters' ideal points. Again one can invoke the geometrical intuition behind this proposition. Given the uniqueness result, symmetry requires that such

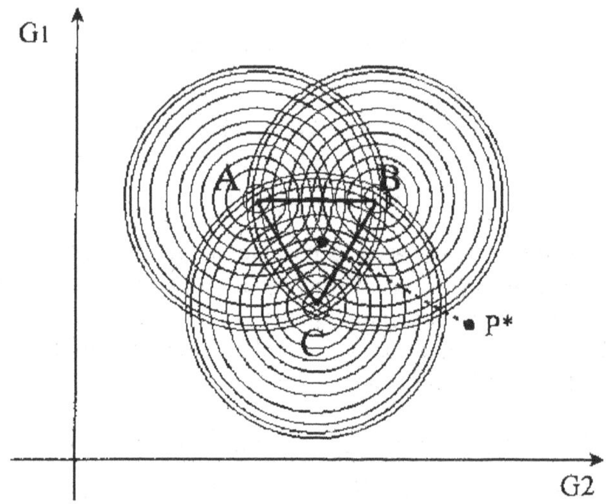


*Figure 1.*

point be equidistant from the voter's ideal point, as shown in equations (2.8), (2.9), (3.8) and (3.9) derived below. This condition of equal distance will be met at the center of the policy space. This implies that the bargaining result will generate moderate and centrist policy determinations with outcomes that will approach the "center of mass" of the policy space.

The greater the steepness of the utility hill for one voter, the closer the policy outcome comes to her ideal point. Thus, more politically-sensitive voters can be viewed as having a greater bargaining power in the political exchange process.[27]

### 3.2. *Toward a (positive) political Coase theorem*

We can now articulate some implications of a Coasian result in the context of the political market. As for the general case, rights and initial entitlements need to be established,[28] and contracts or exchanges need to be costlessly enforceable.[29]

The results are far-reaching and can be articulated in the following three propositions and corollaries.

*Proposition 1*: If the conditions for the Coase theorem are present for all voters, different initial majority coalitions will lead to the same final policy outcome.

12

Proposition 1 is the political analogue of a core result of the traditional Coase theorem according to which the efficient final allocation of resources is achieved independently of the initial assignment of rights.[30] The implicit premise of this proposition draws upon a fundamental postulate of microeconomic theory: the free exchange of goods in the market moves goods towards their optimal allocation, such that, only when every possibility of beneficial exchange is satisfied, resources will reach their stable final allocation.[31]

The political system creates many entitlements that are also susceptible of implicit or explicit exchange. Applying by analogy the idea of the free exchange of goods in the market, this suggests that the transferability of votes in a free political market leads towards efficient final policy allocations. Any socially sub-optimal majoritarian policy would be cured by the voluntary bargaining between majority and minority parties in the political marketplace.

Different initial coalitions – like different initial assignment of rights in the traditional Coase theorem – will obviously change the direction of side payments. But such distributional effects will have no impact on the final policy outcome.

This result should not be surprising. After all, Buchanan and Tullock (1962: 60–62) have shown that majoritarian decision-making can impose negative externalities on the outvoted minority. Like for its original case of externalities among farmers and ranchers, the Coasian bargaining solution fulfills its mission, correcting the externality problem of majoritarian democracy.

The Coasian bargaining assumption[32] implies that all vote promises are enforceable.[33] The coexistence of zero-transaction cost and full enforceability assumptions may in some way be seen as contradictory: contract enforcement is a cost of transacting. But such "costless enforcement" also provides the basis for the traditional formulations of the Coase theorem, as it applies to the exchange of legal entitlements. The enforceability assumption further necessitates that, once entered into, contracts can be modified only with the consent of all the parties. Minority voters can join the coalition and have a marginal effect on the policy outcome by out-bidding or "bribing"[34] members of the pre-existing majority.[35] With enforceable contracts, majority members cannot cheat on each other. Collectively, they will entertain offers made by minority voters who will influence the status quo with their side payments. In the real-world market for votes, legislators sometimes have to be creative to make contracts enforceable.[36] Many real-life instruments often concur to induce such result. Reputation associated with seniority and past voting record, relational contracts, political hands-tying and bonding mechanisms, etc. often contribute to making the fulfilment of political promises more attractive than their breach. Some of these institutions are discussed in Crain et al. (1986).[37]

Assuming continuous policy options which allow incremental moves, consider the following. If there is a socially superior option, parties left out from the initial majority will be able to bribe all majority voters and induce them to move closer to that point. The new bribers will now be part of the expanded majority coalition. If the new policy is not yet at the social maximum, there will still be an additional voter willing to bribe all contracting parties to move closer to their ideal point. As we learn from microeconomic theory, the potential for reciprocal benefit in the exchange will not be exhausted until the policy with the highest social value is implemented. In the political context, this predicts that, in a competitive market for votes without transactional impediments, the resulting policy outcome would be globally efficient. This intuition is verified in Section 5, where it is shown that the bargaining outcome will be obtained at the Benthamite social optimum point and, under conditions of initial symmetry, it will at the same time satisfy the Nash criterion of social welfare.

Once the contracting parties have reached the social optimum policy, there will be no occasion for further instability. No voter or group of voters will be able to bribe all others to alter the ultimate policy outcome. The key for this result is that contracts are enforceable (i.e., contracts can be revised only with the consent of the contracting parties).

The zero transaction cost version of the Political Coase theorem is uninstructive with respect to the choice of optimal decision rules. As the following proposition and corollaries point out, if political bargaining is possible and costless, the same policy outcome is obtained regardless of the decision rule chosen for policy deliberations.

*Proposition 2*: In a world of zero transaction costs, the choice of alternative decision rules has no effect on the policy outcome.

The absence of transaction costs guarantees that the final policy outcome will not depend upon the choice of decision rules. As easily recognizable, Proposition 2 is the political analogue of another important result of the traditional Coase theorem, according to which, in a world of zero transaction costs, the choice of remedies is irrelevant for the efficient final allocation of resources.

The logic of this result is relatively straightforward. Building upon the conclusions of Proposition 1, consider again that in the political context, an initial majority coalition with globally suboptimal policies has an incentive to shift the policy outcome away from the majority contract curve towards the minority ideal point, as long as political contracts with side payments between minority to majority voters are allowed and enforceable.[38] Such an exchange will continue until there is no further room for reciprocal net benefits for majority and minority voters. The same bargaining will take place regardless of the initial size of the majority coalition and regardless of the voting majority requirements. Different decision rules – like different remedies in the original context of the Coase theorem – will have no effect on the final policy outcomes.

In the political context, this proposition has two explanatory corollaries that can be formulated as follows.

*Corollary 2.1*: At the limit, in a world with zero transaction costs, dictatorship and unanimity rules would be conducive to identical policy outcomes.

*Corollary 2.2*: Likewise, the choice of different majority or super-majority decision rules would have no impact on the final outcome.

In the absence of transaction costs, the same logic explains the irrelevance of alternative decision rules. If decisions are initially made by a single dictator, all individuals (except the dictator himself) can be thought as the "minority" group. In the absence of transactional impediments, any socially sub-optimal dictatorial policy would be cured by the voluntary bargaining between the dictator and his subjects, until the resulting policy outcome is globally efficient.

The above irrelevance propositions, obviously, lose their grasp in a world of positive transaction costs. We could thus use some of the normative corollaries to the Coase theorem in order to obtain some insight for the choice of optimal decision rules. For example, if, in the absence of transaction costs, unanimity rules and dictatorship lead to identical policy outcomes, which should be the default decision rule in the presence of positive transaction costs? Should the decision rule be one of unanimity (putting the burden on the sponsors of a new policy to acquire the consent of all other voters) or should the decision power be granted to a single dictator (shifting the burden on the citizens to bribe their dictator for desirable policy outcomes)? One can realize that the above question is qualitatively similar to the question we are used to pose with respect to the allocation of rights and choice of remedies in the traditional context of the Coase theorem. In the presence of transaction costs, different decision rules not only have distributive effects (i.e., changing the direction of payments from one group to the other) but may also have significant allocative (i.e., efficiency) consequences. In the political context, the answer to this question should be found considering the tradeoff between direct and external decision making costs, along the lines of Buchanan and Tullock (1962).

Furthermore, if transaction costs are high, the normative extension of the Coase theorem would suggest that rights should be allocated in such a way as to minimize the impact of such transactional impediments. In the political context, if there is a strong asymmetry between the intensity of preferences of the various members of society (e.g., a minority would suffer a great loss while a majority would receive only a small benefit as a result of a civil rights violation) supermajority or unanimity requirements may be appropriate. This, indeed, is the logic that explains the constitutional protection of civil rights.[39] Likewise, in cases of unequal group size with a systematic difference in the group's effectiveness to carry out collective action, the burden of political bargaining should be placed on the more effective group.[40]

This interpretation of the Coasian assumptions in the context of a market for votes may also require some additional discussion. As for the general Coase theorem, wealth effects need to be assumed away (Coase, 1960: 15–16). To the extent that there are binding wealth constraints which influence the bargaining process, such constraints matter because they influence the market allocation of resources. The "wealth effect" objection applied to the Coase (1960) theorem is in no way avoided in the context of the market for votes.

As with the general case (Coase, 1960: 15), transaction costs need to be assumed away for the irrelevance propositions to hold. In the context of coalition exchanges, however, individual voters face a public good problem in revealing their true policy preferences. Individuals' true willingness to pay for a "public good" policy may not be reflected in the Coasian bargaining, since each voter has an incentive to free-ride on the side payments offered by other voters in the same coalition.[41]

In the framework of the Coase (1960) theorem, the public good problem can be viewed as imposing substantial transaction costs in the bargaining process. In order to study the features of the market for votes in the absence of strategic hold-ups, this Article considers a case with only three individuals, each with full knowledge of the other parties' preferences. By assuming away transaction costs of a strategic nature, the analysis shows that the Pareto optimal policy outcome will be reached, consistent with the Coasian prediction, where the utility for all parties is maximized. The bargaining result will maximize the aggregate welfare of the parties and, given strict concavity of the parties' utility functions, it will be unique. One can thus synthesize another important claim as follows.

*Proposition 3:* If the Coase (1960) theorem holds, voters' preferences are strictly concave, and vote-exchange agreements are enforceable, cycling in a multi-dimensional policy space is excluded.

This uniqueness and stability proposition suggests that, if Coasian exchange is possible at no cost and political agreements are enforceable, the result will occur at a point of (global) social maximum. The enforceability of coalition agreements avoids the usual cyclicality problems associated with re-shuffling majorities. Any point other than the global maximum will be unstable, since there will always be enough surplus to allow for side payments to voters in exchange for policy concessions. Once the socially optimal point is reached, there will be no opportunity to destabilize the policy arrangement.

This proposition is consistent with Bernholz's (1982) theorem according to which externalities are a necessary condition for cyclical social preferences.[42] In our context, Coasian political bargaining allows to correct the externality problem and, in turn, eliminates a necessary condition for intransitive collective choices.

The critical assumptions for this result are obviously that policy preferences be concave and political agreements be enforceable, so that any attempt to modify the bargained for policy choice would have to be accepted by all parties (i.e., the standard assumption that valid contracts can be resolved only with the consent of the contracting parties).[43]

If agreements among voters are enforceable, Coasian bargaining will continue – and possibly occasion transitional cycling until all gains from trade are exploited. Once the optimal policy point is reached, no majority coalition will be capable of buying out the vote of all other parties and destabilize such a policy outcome. In this way, the bargaining will tend to produce a Pareto-optimal and stable outcome. Allowing for side payments and strict concavity of each voter's utility function, the uniqueness of the Coasian bargaining result is guaranteed. Section 4 shows that under such conditions, the policy outcome will maximize the aggregate welfare of the parties, according to a Benthamite criterion of welfare. Section 5 further shows that if the voters' utility functions have identical curvatures, and have equidistant ideal points, the Coasian result will also satisfy the Nash criterion of welfare.

## 4. The geometry of a market for votes

Some interesting properties of the bargaining result may be found by studying the geometry of the model. The intuition behind the result reached in Section 3 is indeed relatively straightforward and can be illustrated through the following geometrical example.

In this example, I utilize standard win-set analysis[44] The circles represent political "indifference curves" for the various voters – the set of points that the equidistant from each voter's ideal policy, A, B, and C, which generates a constant level of utility. I assume (a) concavity of the voters' preferences over policy alternatives; (b) the availability of continuous policy options in the relevant policy space; and (c) the existence of a sufficiently large area of intersection between the indifference curves of the voters (i.e., I am assuming away voters' alienation). The policy space is in the $G_1 - G_2$ plane, i.e., the various combinations of publicly provided goods, $G_1$ and $G_2$. The dotted triangle delimits the Pareto set: policy options that fall outside the triangle can be improved upon with no prejudice to any voter.

In a simple majority system without enforceable coalition contracts, the likely policy outcomes would take place along the sides of the policy triangle, which represent the policy contract curves for all feasible majorities (i.e., the aggregate of the best possible combinations of $G^1$ and $G_2$ for any two out of the three voters). If it were not like this, the possibility of different wealth-improving policy changes would remain open, with the reciprocal advantage for each of the contracting parties.

In the following pages, I will show that, in the presence of enforceable political agreements between majority and minority voters, the contract curves along the perimeter would no longer constitute the limits of majoritarian politics. Any point along the sides of the policy triangle could, in fact be improved upon, since any movement towards the center of the triangle would give rise to utility gains for the non-coalition voters that more than compensate for the utility losses occasioned by the policy change for the coalition members.

Figure 1 considers three voters 1, 2, and 3 with concave utility functions $F_i(G_1, G_2) = f[(G_1^* - \alpha_i)^2, (G_2^* - \beta_i)^2]$ and circular indifference curves around their ideal policy points A, B, and C, such that $\alpha_i$ and $\beta_i$ represent the distance for each voter from a hypothetical central policy point $P^* = (G_1^*, G_2^*)$. For the purpose of this illustration, I assume that the voters' ideal points A, B, and C lie at an equal distance from the policy point $P^*$, so that the radius connecting each voter's ideal point to $P^*$ will be $(\alpha_i + \beta_i)^2$ with an equal value for each voter. The equal distance assumption will not eliminate the differences between the ideal policies (i.e., the actual values of the voters' $\alpha_i$ and $\beta_i$ are different). The above simplification will facilitate the study of the first order conditions of our maximization problem.

Consider any policy point along the three sides of the triangle formed by the voters' ideal points $A = (G_1 - \alpha_1, G_2 - \beta_1)$; $B = (G_1 - \alpha_2, G_2 - \beta_2)$; and $C = (G_1 - \alpha_3, G_2 - \beta_3)$. Given concavity for all utility curves $U_1$, $U_2$, and $U_3$, any point which is internal to the triangle will yield a greater summation height and multiplication height than any point along the sides. The proof for this claim can be found by considering how the sum of the heights of the three functions varies in relation to the sides of the triangle.[45] Any movement away from the sides of the policy triangle toward its center point $P^* = (G_1^*, G_2^*)$ will increase the sum and the product of the heights of the three utility curves $\sum_{i=1}^{3} U_i$. Any such movement will indeed give rise to utility gains that more than compensate for the utility losses occasioned by the transition.

One can use a simple argument *a contrario* to illustrate this point. Consider $P^* = (G_1^*, G_2^*)$ as a starting point and evaluate the welfare implications of any move away from $P^*$. Given concavity, any move away from $P^*$ will reduce the summation height $\sum_{i=1}^{3} U_i$. A move in any direction will increase the sum of utility for the favored voters at a decreasing rate, while the sum of utility losses for the other voters will increase at an increasing rate. The geometrical representation suggests that any move away from the center of the policy space would generate utility losses for the losers that exceed the utility gains obtained by the winners in violation of the Kaldor-Hicks criterion of welfare.[46]

In the absence of transaction costs, bargaining will continue until there is no surplus to be exploited from further trade. Interestingly, due to the ability of the voters to enter into binding contracts with one another, the contract curves for the various parties are no longer represented by the segments connecting the voters' ideal points (i.e., segments AB, AC and BC in Figure 1) but will converge toward the center of the policy triangle.[47] The reason for such peculiarity is that, just like standard agreements in contract law, coalition contracts, once they are formed, can only be dissolved with the consent of all coalition members. This implies that any non-coalition voter will have to contract with the coalition as a unitary group, rather than attempting to destabilize the existing coalition by inducing some of its members to breach the preexisting political agreement. At any point in time, the contract curves will be those connecting existing coalitions (as a weighted group) and individual non-coalition members attempting to change the policy outcome.

The bargaining equilibrium leads to an insightful geometrical result. In a frictionless political system, the market for votes leads to the "center of mass" of the policy triangle.[48]

Section 5 will formally prove the above intuition, evaluating the welfare properties of our hypothetical market for votes.

## 5. The welfare properties of the market for votes

The intuition behind the result in Section 4 is relatively straightforward. The geometry of the model can be illustrated with a functional example, which

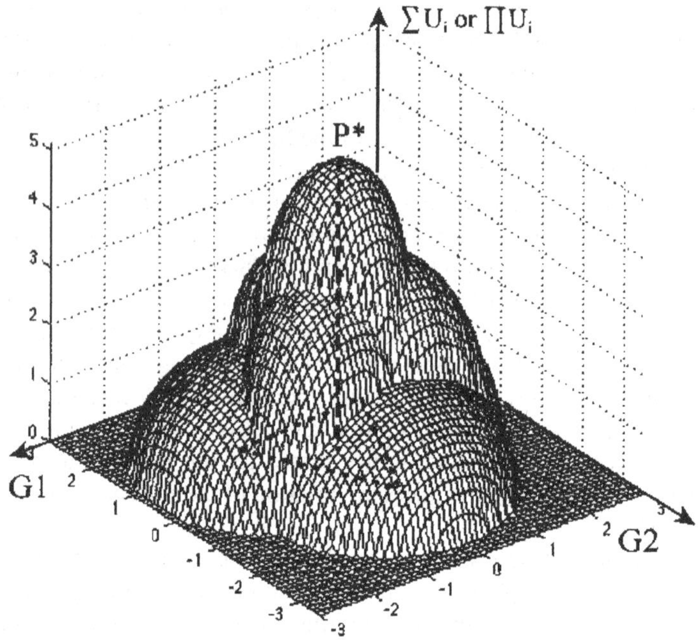


*Figure 2.*

allows the study of other interesting properties of the bargaining result as it relates to the Benthamite and Nash standards of social welfare.

In Figure 2, I plotted the voters aggregate preferences, using the Benthamite form of aggregation (i.e., with a summation of the voters' preferences). Qualitatively similar results would be obtained with a Nash-type aggregation (i.e., with the product of voters' preferences). As Figure 2 illustrates, there is a global maximum which characterizes the social welfare properties of the Coasian bargaining result. Such maximum is found at the center of the policy triangle, $P^*$. These uniqueness and centrality results are robust to different forms of preference aggregation, as shown in the following sections.

### 5.1. *Benthamite social welfare and the market for votes*

To examine the welfare implications of the Coasian bargaining result in Section 3 under the Benthamite criterion of social welfare,[49] consider again the three voters 1, 2, and 3 with concave utility functions $F_i(G_1, G_2) = f[(G_1^* - \alpha_i)^2 + (G_2^* - \beta_i)^2]$. To simplify the notations, the arguments of the function are renamed $w = [(G_1^* - \alpha_i)^2 + (G_2^* - \beta_i)^2]$. For the purpose of this illustration, assume that the voters' ideal points A, B, and C are equidistant

20

from the policy point P*. The squared radius connecting each voter's ideal point to P* will thus be $(\alpha_i^2 + \beta_i^2)$ for all voters, in spite of the possible differences between the respective $\alpha_i$ and $\beta_i$. This allows one to drop some unnecessary notations from the first order conditions found below.

The summation of these functions is denoted as:

$$Z(G_1, G_2) = \sum_{i=1}^{3} f_i(G_1, G_2) \tag{2.1}$$

The partial derivatives with respect to the two variables $G_1$ and $G_2$ are:

$$\partial Z/\partial G_1 \equiv 2\sum_{i=1}^{3}(G_1^* - \alpha_i)f_w[(G_1^* - \alpha_i)^2 + (G_2^* - \beta_i)^2] = 0 \tag{2.2}$$

$$\partial Z/\partial G_2 \equiv 2\sum_{i=1}^{3}(G_2^* - \beta_i)f_w[(G_1^* - \alpha_i)^2 + (G_2^* - \beta_i)^2] = 0 \tag{2.3}$$

For simplicity, consider the case in which the policy point is found in $P^*(G_1^* = 0, G_2^* = 0)$, as represented in Figure 1. Then, equations (2.2) and (2.3) become respectively:

$$\partial Z/\partial G_1 \equiv -2\sum_{i=1}^{3} a_i f_w[\alpha_i^2 + \beta_i^2] = 0 \tag{2.4}$$

$$\partial Z/\partial G_2 \equiv -2\sum_{i=1}^{3} b_i f_w[\alpha_i^2 + \beta_i^2] = 0 \tag{2.5}$$

Solving for all $i = 1, 2, 3$ and assuming equally shaped utility functions centered around different ideal points, there will be a central point P*, such that the voters' ideal points will lie along the $[\alpha_i^2 + \beta_i^2]$ radius. One can simplify the first order conditions above, to obtain:

$$\partial Z/\partial G_1 \equiv -2f_w[\alpha_1 + \alpha_2 + \alpha_3] = 0 \tag{2.6}$$

$$\partial Z/\partial G_2 \equiv -2f_w[\beta_1 + \beta_2 + \beta_3] = 0 \tag{2.7}$$

The first order conditions[50] will be satisfied by equations (2.8) and (2.9), or alternatively by setting all $f_w = 0$:[51]

$$\sum_{i=1}^{3} \alpha_i = 0 \tag{2.8}$$

$$\sum_{i=1}^{3} \beta_i = 0 \tag{2.9}$$

Equations (2.8) and (2.9) need to be interpreted in conjunction with the simplifying assumptions made previously. If voters have similarly shaped utility functions (in this case, spherical curvatures), centered around different ideal policy points, then the Benthamite social optimum is to be found in the locus of points that satisfies equations (2.8) and (2.9), which, in the specific case, occurs at the "center of mass" of the policy triangle ABC. As it happens, the result that was generated by the Coasian bargaining in Section 3 satisfies the Benthamite criterion of social welfare. If voters have utility functions with different curvatures, the result would differ algebraically. The properties of the derived Benthamite equilibrium – uniqueness and centrality in the policy space – however, would remain, subject only to the strict concavity of the voters' preferences.

### 5.2. *Nash social welfare and the market for votes*

One can now study the welfare implications of the Coasian bargaining result of Section 3 in conjunction with the Nash criterion of social welfare.[52] Consider again the three voters 1, 2, and 3 with concave utility functions $F_i(G_1, G_2) = f[(G_1^* - \alpha_i)^2 + (G_2^* - \beta_i)^2]$, and denote the arguments of the function $w = [(G_1^* - \alpha_i)^2 + (G_2^* - \beta_i)^2]$.

The multiplication of these functions may be expressed as:

$$H(G_1, G_2) = \prod_{i=1,2,3} f_i[(G_1 - \alpha_i)^2 + (G_2 - \beta_i)^2] \tag{3.1}$$

The short-hand for the partial derivatives with respect to the two variables $G_1$ and $G_2$ is:

$$\partial H/\partial G_1 \equiv f_{1G1} f_2 f_3 + f_{2G1} f_1 f_3 + f_{3G1} f_1 f_2 = 0 \tag{3.2}$$

$$\partial H/\partial G_2 \equiv f_{1G2} f_2 f_3 + f_{2G2} f_1 f_3 + f_{3G2} f_1 f_2 = 0 \tag{3.3}$$

As with the Benthamite discussion, consider the case in which the policy point is found in $P^*(G_1^* = 0, G_2^* = 0)$, as represented in Figure 1. Revealing the arguments hidden in the short-hand notations, the equations (3.2) and (3.3) become respectively:

$$\partial H/\partial G_1 \equiv -2\sum_{i=1}^{3}\alpha_i f_w[f(w)]^2 = 0 \tag{3.4}$$

$$\partial H/\partial G_2 \equiv -2\sum_{i=1}^{3}\beta_i f_w[f(w)]^2 = 0 \tag{3.5}$$

Solving for all $i = 1, 2, 3$ and assuming equally-shaped utility functions, one can simplify to obtain the first order conditions:

$$\partial H/\partial G_1 \equiv -2f_w[f(w)]^2[\alpha_1 + \alpha_2 + \alpha_3] = 0 \tag{3.6}$$

$$\partial H/\partial G_2 \equiv -2f_w[f(w)]^2[\beta_1 + \beta_2 + \beta_3] = 0 \tag{3.6}$$

The first order conditions[53] will be satisfied by equations (3.8) and (3.9), or alternatively by setting $[f(w)]^2 = 0$, or $f_w = 0$:[54]

$$\sum_{i=1}^{3}\alpha_i = 0 \tag{3.8}$$

$$\sum_{i=1}^{3}\beta_i = 0 \tag{3.9}$$

Thus if voters have identically shaped utility functions centered around different ideal policy points, the Nash social optimum is to be found in the locus of points that satisfies equations (3.8) and (3.9), which coincides with the Benthamite social optimum studied above. Given the assumed "symmetries," Coasian bargaining in a market for votes satisfies both the Benthamite and the Nash criteria of social welfare. Conversely, if voters have differently-shaped utility functions, the Pareto-optimal point achieved through Coasian bargaining will not simultaneously satisfy the Benthamite and Nash criteria of social welfare. Indeed, the Benthamite and Nash social welfare functions would have different critical values. Given the different curvatures, the grand-sum and the grandproduct of voters' utility would be maximized at different points of the policy space. However, even assuming voters with different ideal points and differently shaped utility functions, the Benthamite and Nash optima – reached at different points in the policy space – will share the same properties of uniqueness and centrality, subject only to the strict concavity of the voters' utility functions. It is interesting to note that, in the absence of transaction costs, the Benthamite optimum, rather than the Nash optimum, will be reached through Coasian bargaining.

## 6. Implications and corollaries of the market for votes

In real politics, legislative and political bodies seldom work like markets. Cooter (2000) points out three main challenges to the politics-like-market analogy. The first reason why political markets do not function like ordinary markets is that the value of a legislator's vote often depends upon how other legislators vote. There are pervasive externalities and resulting free riding incentives in political action. The second reason is that real life politics has too many political actors for each one to bargain with everyone else. Unlike the atomistic marketplace of traditional economics, bilateral negotiations would be prohibitively expensive in real life politics. Third, Cooter points out the diffuse hostility to a rationalization of politics as a market for consensus. Ordinary citizens with little information about legislative bargains would resist any institutionalization of political bargaining, objecting to their representatives participating in open log-rolling.

The results derived in Sections 4 and 5 lay a foundation for the study of the determinants and welfare implications of political bargaining once the ideal conditions of the Political Coase theorem are relaxed. Accordingly, the results of the model presented in this Article should be assessed in light of the real world limitations of the political environments. The following points are illustrative in this regard. They consider: (A) discrete policy choices and discontinuities; (B) issue bundling; (C) free riding and bargaining failures; and (D) agency problems and the political dilemma.

### 6.1. *Discrete policy choices and discontinuities*

The results presented in Sections 4 and 5 were derived from a model where voters could carry out policy exchanges in a continuous policy space. Namely, as discussed above, the model assumes that the policy choices are continuous, not discrete or "lumpy." Likewise, policy concessions between voters could be made continuously. In the context of our bargaining game, the assumption was rendered necessary by the techniques of marginal optimization utilized in the algebraic setup.

The nature of real-life politics, however, often presents discontinuities. Policy choices are often binary and there is no practical opportunity for the voters to transform such policy choice into a continuous space. Discontinuities are often induced by the exogenous reality of the policy choice (e.g., build a bridge versus do not build a bridge, etc.) but may also be institutionally created (e.g., a reappointment in office is for a fixed term and voters do not have the option to bargain for a half-term reappointment, even when it may be efficient to do so). While in most situations the efficiency result of the market for votes is likely to hold (albeit constrained) also in the case of discrete choices, the result cannot be generalized. This is not because market mechanisms only work in a continuous space (indeed, many transactions in the market for goods involve discrete choices), but because there is no guarantee that the discrete policy choices will allow gains from potential trade.

If the potential gain from policy bargaining is generated by the concavity of voter's preferences in the relevant policy dimensions, a "balanced" policy package would likely maximize the voters' aggregate utility. But, if exogenous discontinuities prevent such convergence towards balanced policy outcomes (e.g., no opportunity to negotiate a half-term reappointment of a controversial candidate), the surplus from trade may no longer be achievable. Furthermore, discrete policy choices may often generate a zero-sum conflict: one party's gain may correspond to the other parties' loss. In spite of the assumed concavities in the underlying policy preferences, voters may be faced with a zero-sum political struggle. In the presence of such discontinuities, Coasian bargaining would not ameliorate the situation and would not lead to a Pareto improvement.

### 6.2. *Issue bundling*

In the real world of politics, there are transaction costs. As a way to minimize the effect of transaction costs, policy "packages" are traded and voted upon in the usual course of dealing. In this manner, political deals are characterized by the bundling of different issues. Congressional voting normally requires a binomial vote on legislation supplying a bundle of bargained-for provisions. Legislative rules are unable to prevent amendments that are unrelated to the subject matter of the bill at issue.[55] For example, when Congress sent President Clinton the 1997 appropriations bill that funds White House operations, it included legislative riders ranging from the repeal of a law allowing states to share in federal price discounts from the pharmaceutical industry, to a provision to clarify that imports manufactured by indentured child labor are prohibited.[56] Although the item veto enabled President Clinton to remove particular items from such bundles, at least for a time,[57] he utilized that power narrowly and selectively.[58]

From an efficiency perspective, bundling – just like tying in a commodity market – may generate suboptimal outcomes.[59] In order for a vote exchange process to work at its best, all dimensions of the policy space should be the potential object of bargaining and trade. Bundling reduces the dimensions of the bargaining space. At the limit, all policy dimensions may collapse down to a one-dimensional policy space (e.g., size of government), limiting the domain of the optimization process.

In an ideal world with no transaction costs, no bundling should exist, in order to maximize the beneficial functioning of the political market. In a real world with positive transaction costs, a positive amount of bundling is to be expected and may well be desirable in the design of a second best optimization process. Professor Elhauge has noted that where there is issue bundling, "diffuse interests can be systematically underrepresented even if voters face no collective action problem" (Elhauge, 1991: 41). But the market will adjust to reach the optimal tradeoffs between the savings on transaction costs and the inefficiencies of tying.

### 6.3. *Free riding and bargaining failures*

An important assumption of the Coase (1960) theorem is the absence of transaction costs. A costless transaction requires the absence of strategic behavior in the bargaining process. This condition is highly problematic in the context of multi-party voting. The opportunity for individual strategic behavior is elevated where two polar groups seek compromise. In the real-world market for votes, the term "triangulation" has been used to describe the result of efforts to legislate in the middle ground between ideological extremes, where vote-trading transaction costs are high.[60]

All cyclicality problems require the presence of at least three voters. Bargaining among three voters in a two-dimensional space is highly sensitive to free riding and other forms of strategic preference revelation.

The free riding problem is exacerbated by an increase in the ratio of number of voters over the number of dimensions of the policy space (e.g., it would be worst with a large number of voters in a two-policy space). Refer back to Figure 1 to illustrate the point. Any movement in the policy space will generate benefits or losses for at least two parties. In the great majority of cases, all three parties will be affected by a potential policy change. Under such conditions, any bargaining carried out by one voter has the potential of creating side benefits for another voter. Any policy change "purchased" by one voter is potentially a free good (or a free bad) for another voter. In three-party bargaining, voters are thus faced with a collective action problem. The problem is exacerbated by an increase in the number of voters. In a multi-voter setting, strategic behavior may indeed plague the bargaining process.[61]

Note, however, that collective action problems are no more of a challenge to the Political Coase theorem than Dixit and Olson's (1997) argument was a challenge to the traditional Coase theorem.[62] The collective action problem described above, in fact, is not different from any other free-riding problem in a Coasian setting. If the object of one individual's bargaining generates benefits for other individuals who are not involved in the bargain, the bargaining generates positive externalities. As a result, the incentives to undertake the bargaining may be seriously undermined. Every individual wishes to be the free rider, having somebody else pay the price of the common good. Thus, similar to any public good situation, there will be a sub-optimal level of bargaining for the common interest.[63]

### 6.4. *Agency problems and the political dilemma*

The analysis of the hypothetical market for votes considered in this Article takes the will of the voters as a given. Just as the efficient market hypothesis assumes that decisions are taken directly by the interested individuals, without the institutional interface of democratic representation, likewise the political market result of this Article applies to forms of direct democracy or other forms of democratic representation that are not chronically affected by pervasive agency problems in representation. Accordingly, the results of the model presented in this Article should be assessed in light of the real world limitations, considering the effect of agency problems in the bargaining mechanism. In the real world of politics, most collective decisions are carried out by political representatives, who undertake collective decisions as agents of the represented individuals and are able to engage in a limited amount of side-bargaining over votes. Political representation is often undermined by serious agency problems.[64] Such discrepancies are most visible when an agency problem in political representation occurs at the margin of a crucial vote.[65] If bargaining is carried out in the absence of agency problems, the bargaining result maximizes the voters' utility, as illustrated above. But where the bargaining is carried out by interested representatives, the opportunity is present for departures from the optimal outcome. This problem is exacerbated because the voters themselves cannot bargain, and bargaining takes place through the action of representatives, or agents, that can exploit the bargaining surplus to their own personal advantage with only partial consideration of the underlying voters' interests.

In general terms, if market mechanisms are allowed to operate in political contexts, the collective decision-making mechanism is lubricated. In the absence of representation failures, the collective outcome will approximate the allocative outcome of a competitive market. If bargaining is carried out by agents whose underlying incentives differ from those of their principals, the market mechanism may generate greater discrepancies between the ideal and the real political outcomes. Bargaining has been known to induce agents in Congress to abandon their principals' core values. This brings us back to the recently voiced concern that vote-buying may undermine the concept of electoral accountability, transforming "what should be a relational agreement and ongoing conversation between elected official and citizen into a discrete contract between candidate and voter" (Karlan, 1999: 1711).[66]

The market for votes, in other words, lubricates the dynamics of politics and accentuates the features of the underlying political system. In a world of good politics, it allows for better outcomes. In a world of political failures, it may exacerbate the existing problems comprehensively illustrated by the extensive public choice literature.[67]

## 7. Conclusion

This Article has developed a theoretical model showing that, if votes are alienable and vote-trading contracts are enforceable, bargaining (i.e., logrolling) will exploit gains from trade. Collective decision-making will have desirable social properties under these assumptions and, moreover, voting outcomes will be invariant to the operative voting rule: the same collective choices will be taken under dictatorship, a rule of unanimity, or anything in between. Furthermore, the geometry of the Political Coase theorem shows that political bargaining yields unique policy outcomes under generally plausible conditions, even in settings that would otherwise be characterized by intransitive group preferences. The fact that in a frictionless world outcomes are as ideal as outcomes in ordinary markets poses the question as to why in the real world one can buy bread but not votes. The first and most obvious answer is that the real world of politics is not a frictionless world. Certainly, institutional and legal reforms may reduce such transaction costs, by facilitating the formation and enforcement of political contracts, but no matter how well the exchange mechanism could be lubricated, transaction, monitoring and enforcement costs would remain daunting. Second, the real world of representative democracy is affected by agency problems. The observability of politicians' voting records constitutes an effective constraint on their political action. The market for votes would render such voting record hardly tractable and this would compromise the effectiveness of political accountability.

In spite of the existing gap between the frictionless world of the Political Coase theorem and the real world of politics, the results of this article provide an important stepping stone for the formulation of relevant corollaries, applicable to the case of positive transaction costs. The normative corollaries of the Political Coase theorem recognize that in the presence of positive transaction costs or with imperfect enforcement mechanisms for political contracts, different decision rules would most likely generate different policy outcomes. Likewise, given the frictions of political exchange, different initial coalitions are likely to affect the final policy outcome. The understanding of these normative corollaries would allow a deeper understanding of the costs and benefits of alternative decision rules.[68] Inasmuch as political bargains are feasible but transaction costs are positive, the choice of alternative decision

28

rules could contribute to minimizing the social harm induced by such frictions. Additionally, once the abstract conditions of frictionless bargaining are relaxed, the criterion of choice among alternative decision rules articulated by Buchanan and Tullock (1962: 97–116) might further be extended to account for the potential gains from trade promoted by alternative voting rules. The optimal choice would balance the traditional costs of the calculus of consent (i.e., direct costs and external decision costs) with the opportunity to bring the policy outcome closer to the ideal, yet unobtainable, outcome of the Political Coase theorem.

## Notes

1. It has been suggested that, in this respect, the American political system is flawed, since it invites "wholesale" vote buying, but prohibits vote buying at the "retail" level (Levinson, 1999: 1749). The exchange of campaign contributions for favorable governmental policy outcomes from political office-holders, is an uncontested reality of the political market, yet there is a substantial intellectual hostility in the recognition, let alone the enforcement, of explicit transactions for political consensus. Most recently, Karlan (1999: 1711) explains the fact that legal systems prevent the buying of votes and, at the same time, they permit implicit vote-buying through campaign promises with the argument that wholesale campaign promises differ from the purchase of votes because they "serve informational role that enables voters generally to choose more intelligently among candidates."
2. The politics-like-markets analogues form an established foundation of much of the work in public choice and political economy. Stigler (1971); Becker (1983) and Peltzman (1990), among others, have provided seminal formulations of the efficiency hypothesis of politics. The trust of this foundational hypothesis is that political markets are generally clearing, at least in the sense that, in equilibrium, no individual can improve his wealth (or utility) without reducing the wealth (or utility) of at least one other individual. For an outsider's review essay on the Chicago perspective on political markets, see Rowley (1993: 11–14)
3. According to Karlan (1999: 1711), there is a methodological tension in the current conceptualization of the right to vote: "On the one hand, the right to vote serves a powerful expressive function. . . . On the other hand, the functional point of voting is to aggregate individuals' preferences and to allocate political power (and ultimately the benefits and burdens the government confers) among groups." Karlan (1999: 1713) further notes that the presence of money could change voters' preferences: " If voters think of their votes as simply something to be auctioned to the highest bidder, they are likely to see the sole purpose of the political process as maximization of their own short-term self-interest."
4. The desirability of allowing enforceable political contracts in a direct democracy could also be examined through the following Rawls-type or Buchanan-type arguments. In the original position meta-bargain among the three agents, there are three reasonable 2 person solutions (1/2,1/2,0),(1/2,0,1/2),(0,1/2,1/2) given zero bargaining costs and the typical axiomatic bargaining specifications which leads to the fair split of the voter's surplus. In that setting if voters had an opportunity to agree *ex ante* on a procedure (this could be formulated as a Rawlsian original position choice or as contractarian choice of the "rules of the game" a-lá-Buchanan). However, given the voters' concave utility functions, by

Jenson's Inequality, each player prefers U(1/3) > 2/3U(1/2), therefore each is willing to bind himself to a system of enforceable political contracts as opposed to taking the chance that he will be the excluded party (each party has a 1/3 chance of this happening, under symmetric initial bargaining positions).

5. The cardinality and interpersonal comparability of preferences is regarded as one of the main problems of social welfare analysis. Two individuals, A and B, can say if they prefer X to Y (ordinal preferences), but nobody can say if A likes X more than B likes Y (cardinal preferences with interpersonal comparability). The use of utility curves in this paper avoids the problems associated with straight cardinal comparisons. This approach appears to have become rather common in the social choice literature. See, e.g., Roemer (1996).
6. As indicated above, for the purpose of this exercise, I assume away agency problems in representation. This condition could materialize in the limit case of direct democracy, but would also be met if we imagine that reelection or reputational constraints of legislators guarantee that the trading process takes some account of the preferences of the platform-voters.
7. According to the Benthamite criterion, the measure of social welfare is given by the sum of the utility of the various members of society. See Mueller (1989), attributing the additive form of the social welfare function to Jeremy Bentham.
8. According to the Nash criterion, social welfare is given by the product of the utility of the members of society. See Mueller (1989: 379–382), attributing the multiplicative form of the social welfare function to John Nash. See also Nash (1950).
9. The insight in this formulation is attributable to a well-known game-theorist, Shubik (1982).
10. See, e.g. Mueller (1989: 385–386); Stearns (1994: 1247–1252); and Vikrey (1960).
11. The observation that the likelihood of cycling majorities decreases in situations where the number of decision-makers is much greater than the number of choices does not affect the practical relevance of Arrow's analysis applied to the political process, where the large number of decision-makers is actually concentrated into a restricted number of interest groups with "group" votes.
12. For the proof of these propositions, see Arrow (1963); see also Stearns (1994: 1249) and Stearns (1995).
13. See, e.g., Bernholz (1973); Miller (1977); Schwartz (1977).
14. Such bargaining does not require any relaxation of Arrow's axioms, although it may at times be perceived as interfering with the irrelevance axiom in that parties could attach value to otherwise irrelevant options.
15. Such cross-coalition exchanges are not uncommon and often occur in a flurry. For example, in anticipation of a congressional vote on fast-track trade authority in November 1997, President Bill Clinton and House Speaker Newt Gingrich (R-Ga.) engaged in a "frenzied round of deal-making" in an attempt to acquire enough votes to support the measure (Yang and Pianin, 1997). The White House offered what the late Rep. Sonny Bono (R-Cal.) called "a sale like I've never seen before," (Gugliotta, 1997) and House Republican leaders similarly offered to support "specific spending projects for Democratic lawmakers" (Yang and Pianin, 1997) who agreed to vote in favor of the legislation.
16. See *Davis* v. *Bandemer* (1986).
17. From an efficiency perspective, in fact, weight should be given to intensive preferences.
18. Judge Easterbrook (1983) has noted that "someone with control of the agenda can manipulate the choice so that the legislature adopts proposals that only a minority support." See also Levine and Plott (1977); Levmore (1989).

30

19. For example, in September 1997, Senator Jesse Helms (R-N.C.), as Chairman of the Senate Foreign Relations Committee, was able to block the committee from considering President Clinton's nomination of William F. Weld to be ambassador to Mexico. Although committee Democrats were able to garner the votes of two Republicans to establish a majority and force Helms to call a meeting, Senate rules enabled him to act as a strategic gate-keeper and leave consideration of Weld's nomination off of the agenda. See Dewar (1997).
20. For the reasons explained above, however, this expectation is at odds with the common thought in the public and social choice literature, specifically the results reached by Bernholz (1980).
21. The existence of a numeraire different from the object of the bargaining is essential for any of the bargaining to take place. The Coasian bargaining for a change in the distribution of tax burdens, for example, will not be conceivable if money is the only thing that can be used as a numeraire for the exchange. It is, in fact, impossible to buy money with like money, since there would be no surplus from the trade.
22. The assumption of well-behaved utility obviously refers to the functions being smooth and continuous to allow for differentiability. In the context of this Article, they carry the additional implication of single-peakedness of the individual preferences.
23. In this setting, the Pareto criterion is satisfied because nobody can be made better off without someone else being made worse off. Any policy move from the central equilibrium will be prejudicial to the interest of at least one voter.
24. See Mueller (1989).
25. See Chiang (1984).
26. The mathematical proof of the uniqueness under strict concavity is omitted, given the geometrical intuitiveness of the proposition.
27. This notion was probably reflected in the Fall 1997 fast-track trade authority vote-bargaining. The Senate "overwhelmingly favor[ed] fast track," primarily because senators "can balance adverse trade effects in one part of [their] state against boom times elsewhere, and catastrophe is easier to absorb. But in House districts, a member's political future may depend on the tariff structure of a single agricultural commodity." (Gugliotta, 1997). Thus, it was in the House of Representatives where the bargaining frenzy took place, and the most politically sensitive representatives were able to bargain for the biggest payoffs (Gugliotta, 1997).
28. As Cooter (1987) observes, one of the most relevant impediments to the working of the Coase theorem is the existence of uncertainties regarding the content and enforceability of the rights. An imprecise definition of which political bargains could enjoy legal protection and which other agreements would only be supported by the threat of informal political sanctions renders the actual working of a market for votes problematic. In order for the conditions for the free exchange to be verified in the Political Coase theorem, it is necessary to define ex ante the content of the rights without ambiguity, and to specify the legal or political means to enforce their transfer.
29. E.g., a side payment given in consideration for a policy amendment needs to grant an enforceable right to the amendment itself.
30. Stigler (1966: 113) was the first scholar to restate Coase's argument in the form of a theorem. Coase (1988) recognizes Stigler's merit in this respect. The following year, Demsetz (1967: 349) provided a more extensive formulation of the theorem: "There are two striking implications of this process that are true in a world of zero transaction costs. The output mix that results when the exchange of property rights is allowed is efficient and the mix is independent of who is assigned ownership (except that different wealth

distributions may result in different demands)." Soon thereafter, Guido Calabresi (1968: 68) stated the same principle in the following terms: "Thus, if one assumes rationality, no transaction costs, and no legal impediments to bargaining, all misallocations of resources would be fully cured in the market by bargains."

31. In his recent *Notes on the Problem of Social Cost*, Coase (1988) cites Edgeworth (1881) as the principal source of inspiration for the formulation of this important part of his theorem.
32. See generally Coase (1960).
33. Among the transaction costs that the Coase theorem assumes away are those associated with "monitoring and enforcing any bargain struck." (Elhauge, 1991: 96 n. 247).
34. "[G]roups with lower costs of organizational and collective action are likely to be those which can mount the most effective bribe, as public choice theory presumes in the political context." (Kahn, 1990).
35. Note that the Coasian result requires that contracts are binding. Thus, any change away from a policy supported by a majority coalition requires the agreement of all members of the coalition. If any bargaining or side-payment is made by a minority member, it should be directed to all members of the current coalition, not just to a subset of decisive voters.
36. In the Fall 1997 bargaining for fast-track trade authority votes, many representatives willing to trade votes to President Clinton and Speaker Gingrich still "insisted on cementing Clinton's promises in print in an omnibus Ways and Means Committee amendment that [would have been] inserted into the fast-track bill when it came to the floor."

    (Gugliotta, 1997). After support fell short and the vote was postponed, the White House attempted to signal the enforceability of its bargains (and ensure its influence against the status quo) in a future vote by publicly stating that it would not "go back and undo the things that we pledged that we would do." (Gugliotta, 1997) (quoting presidential spokesperson Michael McCurry).
37. Even though the legal system offers no enforcement mechanism for explicit political exchanges, there are may non-legal enforcement mechanisms, comparable to those examined by Kronman (1985) that are at work in the context of political exchange. Furthermore, there is an extensive literature on structure-induced equilibrium that in many ways may be relevant to the point.
38. In this context, globally suboptimal policies would be those that fail to take into proper account the intensity of preferences (or willingness to pay) of minority voters.
39. Buchanan and Tullock (1962) utilize a dramatic example of logrolling to illustrate the potential benefits of a free market for political consensus. The example was narrated in a retrospective essay by Tullock (1998: 131) along the following lines: "It is fairly clear logrolling can generate benefits. ... Long ago when Buchanan and I were working on the *Calculus of Consent* we discussed the situation of the Jews in Germany. If there had been a well functioning democratic legislature, it seems fairly certain that the Jews by trading their votes for a number of other projects could have prevented severe discrimination against themselves even if the majority of those in Germany favored it, because they would not favor it enough so that they would not accept compensation." Considering the rent-seeking and transaction costs of real politics, the same dramatic illustration can be utilized to explain the modern use of *ius cogens* (unanimity) or constitutional (super-majority) constraints to prevent discrimination and to protect human rights.
40. These propositions follow as a mere extension of the normative corollaries of Coase's (1960) theorem, formulated by Calabresi and Melamed (1972) for the case of positive transaction costs and by Parisi (2001) for the case of asymmetric transaction costs.

32

41. Again, the Fall 1997 bargaining over fast-track trade authority legislation provides a useful illustration. Representative E. Clay Shaw (R-Fla.), who lobbied for concessions and side-payments in favor of Florida interests, lamented that "I don't think any of this won any more votes" (Gugliotta, 1997) from Florida's twenty-three member House-delegation – many of whom refused to stake a position in advance of the vote, yet were able to free-ride on Shaw's bargaining efforts.
42. Bernholz convincingly proved that the presence of externalities is a necessary condition for Arrow's (1963) general impossibility theorem. Externalities are defined in the Pareto sense, according to the Buchanan and Tullock (1962) definition of political externalities.
43. As Stearns (1992: 399–422) suggests, "there is no obvious way to maintain the benefits of allowing minority interests to force compromises in their favor without incurring the costs." The item veto (Line Item Veto Act, 1996) might be mistaken as Congress' consent to having its own vote-trading contracts modified by the President, at least to the extent necessary to limit pork-barrel bribery. But even if congressional intent could be read in this regard, the item veto seemingly produces political-market failure by granting the President power to modify "legitimate compromises that a bill's supporters need in order to gain majority support." (Stearns, 1992) (discussing the expected impact of proposed conferral of item veto power to the President on executive and legislative bargaining). See also Sidak and Smith (1990) (discussing alternative forms for proposed item veto legislation).
44. See Ordeshook (1997) (discussing use of spatial analysis to study democratic politics). See also Shepsle and Weingast (1984).
45. The formal proof of this claim is developed in Section 5 of this Article.
46. Under the Kaldor-Hicks efficiency criterion, "only those changes are recommended in which at least one person is made better off and no one is made worse off. That criterion requires that gainers explicitly compensate losers in any change". Cooter and Ulen (1997).
47. This implies that the equilibrium will be found in a point that does not fall along any of the contract curves between any two of the voters.
48. For the more general case with asymmetric voters' ideal points, the equilibrium will be reached at orthocenter (i.e., the intersection of the heights of the policy triangle). Given the initial symmetry, such point coincides with the center of mass of the policy triangle in our example.
49. See Mueller (1989).
50. The second order conditions for a maximum will be verified if the Hessian $H = f_{11} + f_{22} + f_{12}^2 > 0$, with $f_{11} < 0$.
51. This latter possibility is excluded by the fact that the three voters reach their bliss point in different points on the policy space. Thus they will not simultaneously satisfy the $f_w = 0$ condition.
52. See Mueller (1989: 379–382); see also Nash (1950).
53. The second order conditions fora maximum will be verified if the Hessian $H = f_{11} + f_{22} + f_{12}^2 > 0$, with $f_{11} < 0$.
54. Similar to the Benthamite case, the $f_w = 0$ possibility is excluded because the three voters have their respective bliss points in different locations of policy space, so that there is no policy combination that satisfies simultaneously the $f_w = 0$ condition. The other alternative $[f(w)]^2 = 0$ obviously would not satisfy the second order conditions for a maximum.
55. See Dixon (1985); Riggs (1973).
56. See Rogers (1997).
57. See *New York* v. *Clinton* (1998) (holding that the Line Item Veto Act violates the constitutional principles of bicameralism, presentment, and separation of powers).

33

58. See Penny (1997) (urging President Clinton to "put Congress on notice that he will aggressively-not randomly or reluctantly-exercise the [item] veto").
59. See Robinson (1988). Cf. *Jefferson Parish Hosp. Dist. No. 2* v. *Hyde* (1984) (holding that tying arrangements are presumptively anti-competitive).
60. Broder (1997), attributing the "triangulation" concept as used here to former Clinton-advisor Dick Morris.
61. Here too, the Fall 1997 bargaining for votes in favor of fast-track trade authority provides a useful example. While other Florida congressmen served as "honest brokers" for substantive concessions and side payments favoring their state, strategic holdouts such as Rep. Michael Bilirakis (R-Fla.) and Rep. Peter Deutsch (D-Fla.) refused to reveal their preferences and claimed to be "formally undecided" and "undecided to the bitter end", respectively (Gugliotta, 1997).
62. Avinash Dixit and Mancur Olson have discussed the collective action problem in the context of Coasian bargaining, questioning the practical validity of the Coasian proposition in a multi-party context. See Dixit and Olson, Jr., (1997) (unpublished manuscript on file with the *George Mason Law Review*).
63. But see generally Coase (1974); Coase (1988); Parisi (1995).
64. Public choice theory provides ample analysis of misaligned incentives, including rational abstention, rational ignorance, and special interest advantages. See Becker (1985); Macey (1997: 1137–1139).
65. Examples of this sort, unfortunately, are uncountable. To mention one example, we can think of former Rep. Marjorie Margolies-Mezvinsky (D-Pa.) in 1993. The first-term congresswoman "cast the deciding vote for President Clinton's 1993 tax increase – after promising her constituents she would vote against it". (Heidorn Dec. 1994). Her "budget vote quid pro quo" was the President's attendance at a local event in her district (Heidorn Nov. 1994). And while she told her constituents that "she favored the elimination of political action committees, she was among the biggest recipients of PAC money in the country." (Heidorn Dec. 1994). In the 1994 election, her principals responded by ousting her as their agent in Congress in favor of the same Republican opponent she had defeated at the polls in 1992 (Heidorn Dec. 1994).
66. On the side dealing which preceded the anticipated fast-track trade authority vote in the Fall of 1997, Rep. Sonny Bono (R-Cal.) said that "You should do as much as you can for your district . . . If the game is going to be played, you just have to ride the waves and prepare to max it". (Gugliotta, 1997) But Rep. Timothy J. Roemer (D-Ind.) warned that "if a congress member gets a bridge for a vote, and the vote is not popular back home, the bridge may not stand long". (Yang and Pianin, 1997).
67. See, e.g., Epstein (1984); Eskridge, Jr. (1988); Macey (1986); Stout (1992).
68. On the tradeoff between transaction costs and losses from minority exploitation, see Buchanan and Tullock (1962: 97–116).

## References

### Cases and Statutes

*Davis* v. *Bandemer*, 478 U.S. 109, 124 (1986).
*Jefferson Parish Hosp. Dist. No. 2* v. *Hyde*, 466 U.S. 2, 9 (1984).
*Line Item Veto Act*. Pub. L. No. 104–130, 110 Stat. 1200 (1996) (codified at 2 U.S.C.A. § 691 (West 1997)).
*New York* v. *Clinton*, 985 F. Supp. 168 (D.D.C. 1998).

34


**Books and Journal Articles**

Arrow, K. (1963). *Social choice and individual values.* New Haven: Yale University Press.

Becker, G.S. (1983). A theory of competition among pressure groups for political influence. *Quarterly Journal of Economics* 98: 371–400.

Becker, G.S. (1985). Public policies, groups, and dead weight costs. *Journal of Public Economics* 28: 329.

Bernholz, P. (1973). Logrolling, arrow paradox and cyclical majorities. *Public Choice* 15: 87.

Bernholz, P. (1980). A general social dilemma: Profitable exchange and intransitive group preferences. *Zeitschrift für National Ökonomie* 40: 1.

Bernholz, P. (1982). Externalities as a necessary condition for cyclical social preferences. *Quarterly Journal of Economics* 97: 699.

Broder, D. (1997). Catatonic politics. *Washington Post* (Nov. 11).

Buchanan, J. and Tullock G. (1962). *The calculus of consent: Logical foundations of constitutional democracy.* Ann Arbor: University of Michigan Press.

Calabresi, G. (1968). Transaction costs, resource allocation and liability rules. A comment. *Journal of Law and Economics* 11: 67.

Calabresi, G. and Douglas, M.A. (1972). Property rules, liability rules and inalienabilty: One view of the cathedral. *Harvard Law Review* 85: 1089–1128.

Chiang, A. (1984). *Fundamental methods of mathematical economics.* New York: McGraw-Hill.

Coase, R. (1960). The problem of social cost. *Journal of Law & Economics* 3: 2.

Coase, R. (1974). The lighthouse in economics. *Journal of Law and Economics* 17: 357–376.

Coase, R. (1988). Notes on the problem of social cost. In: Coase, R. (Ed.), *The firm, the market, and the law.* Chicago: University of Chicago Press.

Coleman, J. (1966). The possibility of a social welfare function. *The American Economics Review* 56: 1105.

Coleman, J. (1967). The possibility of a social welfare function: Reply. *The American Economics Review* 57: 1311.

Cooter, R. (1987). Coase theorem. In: J. Eatwell, M. Milgate and P. Newman (Eds.), *The new Palgrave. A dictionary of economics* 1: 457.

Cooter, R.D. (2000). *The strategic constitution.* Princeton, NJ: Princeton University Press.

Cooter, R. and Ulen, T. (1997). *Law and economics.* Reading, Mass.: Addison-Wesley.

Crain W.M., Leavens, D.R. and Tollison, R.D. (1986). Final voting in legislatures. *American Economic Review* 76: 833–841.

Demsetz, H. (1964). The exchange and enforcement of property rights. *Journal of Law and Economics* 7: 11.

Demsetz, H. (1967). Toward a theory of property rights. *American Economics Review* 57: 347.

Dewar, H. (1997). Sen. Helms' Gavel leaves Weld nomination in Limbo. *Washington Post* (Sept. 13).

Dixit, A. and Olson, M., Jr. (1997). Does voluntary participation undermine the Coase theorem? Unpublished manuscript.

Dixon, A. (1985). Line-item veto controversy. *Congressional Digest* 64: 282.

Easterbrook, F. (1983). Statutes' domains. *University of Chicago Law Review* 50: 547.

Edgeworth, F.Y. (1881). *Mathematical psychics.*

Elhauge, E. (1991). Does interest group theory justify more intrusive judicial review? *Yale Law Journal* 101: 41.

Epstein, R. (1984). Toward a revitalization of the contract clause. *University of Chicago Law Review* 51: 703.

Eskridge, W., Jr. (1988). Politics without romance: Implications of public choice theory for statutory interpretation. *Virginia Law Review* 74: 275.

Gughotta, G. (1997). Wheeling and dealing and keeping score on the 'fast track'. *Washington Post* (Nov. 26).

Heidorn, R., Jr. (1994). Fateful vote stays at center stage. *Philadelphia Inquirer* (Nov. 2).

Heidorn, R., Jr. (1994). Margolies-Mezvinsky: Voted out of office but hardly defeated. *Philadelphia Inquirer* (Dec. 24).

Kahn, P. (1990). The politics of unregulation: Public choice and limits on government. *Cornell Law Review* 75: 306 n. 101.

Karlan, P. (1999). Symposium commentary: Politics by other means. *Virginia Law Review* 85: 1697.

Koford, K. (1982). Why so much stability? Centralized vote trading. *Public Choice* 39: 245.

Kronman, A. (1985). Contracts and the state of nature. *Journal of Law, Economics and Organization* 1: 3.

Levine, M. and Plott, C. (1977). Agenda influence and its implications. *Virginia Law Review* 63: 561.

Levinson, D. (1999). Symposium commentary: Market failures and failures of markets. *Virginia Law Review* 85: 1745.

Levmore, S. (1989). Parliamentary law, majority decisionmaking, and the voting paradox. *Virginia Law Review* 75: 971.

Macey, J. (1986). Promoting public-regarding legislation through statutory interpretation: An interest group model. *Columbia Law Review* 86: 223.

Macey, J. (1997). Public and private ordering and the production of legitimate and illegitimate legal rules. *Cornell Law Review* 82: 1137–1139.

Miller, N. (1977). Logrolling, vote trading, and the paradox of voting: A game of theoretical overview. *Public Choice* 30: 51.

Mueller, D. (1967). The possibility of a social welfare function: Comment. *American Economics Review* 57: 1304.

Mueller, D. (1989). *Public choice II*. Cambridge, UK; New York: Cambridge University Press.

Mueller, D., Philpotts, G. and Vanek, J. (1972). The social gains from exchanging votes: A simulation. *Public Choice* 13: 55.

Nash, J. (1950). The bargaining problem. *Econometrica* 18: 155.

Ordeshook, P. (1997). The spatial analysis of elections and committees: Four decades of research. In: D. Mueller (Ed.), *Perspectives on public choice: A handbook*. Cambridge, U.K.; New York: Cambridge University Press.

Parisi, F. (1995). Private property and social costs. *European Journal of Law and Economics* 2: 149.

Parisi, F. (1998). The market for votes: Coasian bargaining in an Arrovian setting. *George Mason Law Review* 6: 745.

Parisi, F. (2001). The asymmetric Coase theorem: Dual remedies for a unified property. *George Mason University Law and Economics Working Papers # 01*.

Park, R. (1967). The possibility of a social welfare function: Comment. *American Economics Review* 57: 1300.

Peltzman, S. (1990). How efficient is the voting market? *Journal of Law and Economics* 33: 27–63.

Penny, T. (1997). Pork is safe from this president's line-item vetoes. *Wall Street Journal* (Nov. 13).

Riggs, R. (1973). Separation of powers: Congressional riders and the veto power. *University of Michigan Journal of Law Reform* 6: 743.

36


Robinson, G. (1988). Public choice speculations on the item veto. *Virginia Law Review* 74: 407.

Roemer, J. (1996). *Theories of distributive justice*. Cambridge, Mass.: Harvard University Press.

Rogers, D. (1997). Clinton warns he's prepared to veto spending bills if changes aren't made. *Wall Street Journal* (Oct. 2).

Rowley, C.K. (1993). *Public choice* (3 Vols.). Edward Elgar Publishing.

Schwartz, T. (1977). Collective choice, separation of issues and vote trading. *American Political Science Review* 71: 999.

Shepsle, K. and Weingast, B. (1984). Uncovered sets and sophisticated voting outcomes with implications for agenda control. *American Journal of Political Science* 28: 49.

Shubik, M. (1982). *Game theory in the social sciences: Concepts and solutions*. Cambridge, Mass.: MIT Press.

Sidak, J. and Smith, T. (1990). Four faces of the item veto: A reply to Tribe and Kurland. *Northwestern University Law Review* 84: 437.

Stearns, M. (1992). The public choice case against the item veto. *Washington & Lee Law Review* 49: 399.

Stearns, M. (1994). The misguided renaissance of social choice. *Yale Law Journal* 103: 1219.

Stearns, M. (1995). Standing back from the forest: Justiciability and social choice. *California Law Review* 83: 1384.

Stigler, G.J. (1966). *The theory of price* 113 (3d ed.).

Stigler, G.J. (1971). Economic competition and political competition. *Public Choice* 13: 91–106.

Stigler, G.J. (1972). The law and economics of public policy: A plea to the scholars. *Journal of Legal Studies* 1: 1.

Stout, L. (1992). Strict scrutiny and social choice: An economic inquiry into fundamental rights and suspect classifications. *Georgetown Law Journal* 80: 1787.

Tullock, G. (1981). Why so much stability? *Public Choice* 37: 189.

Tullock, G. (1998). *On voting: A public choice approach*. Cheltenham, U.K.: Edward Elgar Publishing.

Vikrey, W. (1960). Utility, strategy, and social decision rules. *Quarterly Journal of Economics* 74: 507.

Yang, J. and Pianin, E. (1997). Final push for fast trade. Washington Post (Nov. 8).

# Part V
# Does Liability Matter? Coase Theorem in the Long-Run

# [14]



# On External Diseconomies and the Government-Assisted Invisible Hand[1]

STANISLAW WELLISZ

## I. THE MODERN-OLD APPROACH AND ITS LIMITATIONS

The areas of economics in which theory is tailored to the theorist's political beliefs are steadily shrinking. Gone are the days of the " dismal science " and of theories protesting against the " exploitation of man by man ". Even the Keynesian controversies have simmered down.

The gloom which descends upon us with the passing of the colourful era in which theory was pregnant with policies is still occasionally dispelled by welfare economics controversies. Welfare economics, more than any other field, lends itself to wishful theorizing. As Buchanan put it so aptly:

> If, as J. de V. Graaff suggests, " *laissez faire* welfare theory " was " largely concerned with demonstrating the optimal properties of free competition and the unfettered price system," it is surely equally accurate to suggest that modern welfare theory has been largely concerned with demonstrating that these conclusions are invalid; that is, that competitive markets do not satisfy the necessary conditions for optimality.[2]

Much of modern welfare economics is indeed concerned with the problem of market failure, and the analysis of market failure appears to imply the desirability of administrative intervention. Until recently everybody agreed that where there are externalities, market allocation is bound to be non-optimal; the only point of controversy concerned the frequency and the severity of the external effects and the urgency of administrative action.[3]

The apparent unanimity of modern welfare economists has been shattered in the last few years by modern-old welfare economists who launched a vigorous attack on the logic of the modern treatment, and an equally vigorous defence of the old virtues of the market. It now seems that the modern theory is dead and that the modern-old triumphs all along the line.

What is somewhat puzzling in the modern-old vs. modern controversy is that all the protagonists apparently agree on the incapacity of theorists to say anything meaningful about welfare problems. J. de V. Graaff, one of the finest exponents of the " modern " school, was widely known

[1] To all intents and purposes Lester Telser is a co-author of this paper. I also wish to thank Harry Johnson, Harold Demsetz and Merton Miller for their generous help.

[2] J. M. Buchanan, " Policy and the Pigovian Margins ", *Economica*, vol. 29 (1962), p. 17, n. 3.

[3] For a summary of the controversy preceding the modern-old attack, see Francis Bator, " The Anatomy of Market Failure ", *Quarterly Journal of Economics*, vol. 72 (1958).

for his scepticism concerning the field. Little states that " economic welfare is a subject in which rigour and refinement are probably worse than useless. Rough theory, or good common sense, is, in practice, what we require."[1] Little also voices his preference for intelligent administrative decisions over static analysis.[2] Buchanan, a modern-old theorist, apparently subscribes to the " widely acknowledged " notion " that welfare economics, as such, can provide few guides to policy-making in a specific sense,"[3] while Turvey, in a survey of the recent controversy, buries the administrative interventionist and the economic theorist under a common tombstone: " When negotiation [between the units creating externalities and those suffering from or benefiting from them] is possible, the case for government intervention is one of justice, not of economic efficiency; when it is not, the theorist should be silent and call in the applied economist."[4]

In the face of the prevailing opinions, I would like to consider whether we should put our entire trust in the market or whether administrative and judicial intervention is called for where there are externalities. I shall also discuss whether the economist with theoretical training ought to yield his role to Mr. Little's administrator or to Mr. Turvey's applied economist.

The strongest reason for the theorist's concern with the problem of externalities is that " practical men " work on the dual assumption of the prevalence of externalities and of the necessity of radical steps to improve our imperfect world:

> In a world of rapidly increasing population and of material growth, the problems economists associate with external diseconomies—the inevitable treading on each other's toes—are pushed to the forefront of public controversy. Sooner or later one form or another of external diseconomy becomes recognized as a major social problem and the hands of central or local authorities are forced by the clamour of the public that something be done. Unless economists are prepared to give advice in such cases, initiative will pass into the hands of the " planners," the engineers and the administrators, with results that may well be as irreversible as they are, sometimes, deplorable.[5]

It is painfully clear that administrators and planners frequently avail themselves of the opportunity of interfering with resource allocation. It is possible, of course, that they are the possessors of specialized knowledge which economists do not have. If this is so, their science is hermetic, for it does not appear in any of the writings of the " practical planners ". For the time being it is wise to assume that despite all

[1] I. M. D. Little, *A Critique of Welfare Economics*, 2nd ed., 1957, p. 279.

[2] *Ibid.*, p. 184.

[3] Buchanan, *loc. cit.*, p. 17, n. 3.

[4] R. Turvey, " On Divergences between Social Cost and Private Cost ", *Economica*, vol. 30 (1963), p. 313.

[5] E. J. Mishan, " Welfare Criteria for External Effects ," *American Economic Review*, vol. 51 (1961), p. 594.

protestations economists do have a comparative advantage in dealing with economic problems.

Let us now pass to the main question which is whether economists should advocate that specific action be taken to deal with external economies and diseconomies, or whether they should insist that the problem be left to the market mechanism.

The Pigovian tradition, accepted by modern welfare economists, claims that whenever private and social costs diverge, steps should be taken to equalize the two. For instance, if sparks and smoke from a steam railway damage the surrounding land, it is appropriate to impose upon the railway costs equal to the amount of the damage. Unless such action is taken, the railway will disregard the social diseconomy and it will expand beyond the social optimum. Conversely, an activity which yields positive external effects should be encouraged to expand beyond the individual optimum which does not take into account such effects.

The modern-old economists, and especially Coase and Buchanan, challenge the established position: they claim that the private market *can* lead to a Pareto optimum despite externalities since it is possible to establish a market in externalities. Administrative measures, on the other hand, may cause divergences from the optimum.[1] An even stronger case is presented by Davis and Whinston.[2] The two authors consider two types of externalities (to be defined later): in one type, "separable externalities," it is "difficult" to reach an optimum by instituting Pigovian taxes and subsidies, while in the other, more general type, "non-separable externalities," the task is " impossible."[3]

Coase's vigorous and original article provides an excellent starting point for a critical appraisal of the attacks on the Pigovian tradition.

Where Pigou was anxious to compensate the victims of diseconomies, Coase concentrates his attention on the conditions under which the largest social product can be achieved:

> When an economist is comparing alternative social arrangements, the proper procedure is to compare the total social product yielded by those different arrangements. The comparison of private and social costs is neither here nor there.[4]

Coase carries his challenge right into the enemy's camp: he takes up and expands Pigou's example of a railway damaging nearby fields, and unlike Pigou, he concludes that the market is likely to yield the correct allocative solution while judicial and administrative interference is unlikely to achieve the task. The Pigou-Coase example deserves re-

[1] Buchanan, *loc. cit.*; J. M. Buchanan and W. C. Stubblebine, " Externality ", *Economica*, vol. 29 (1962); R. H. Coase, " The Problem of Social Cost ", *Journal of Law and Economics*, vol. 3 (1960).

[2] O. A. Davis and A. Whinston, " Externalities, Welfare, and the Theory of Games ", *Journal of Political Economy*, vol. 60 (1962).

[3] *Ibid.*, p. 261.

[4] Coase, *loc. cit.*, p. 34.

examination so that we can see where the strength and the weakness of Coase's argument lie.[1]

According to Coase, " if the railway could make a bargain with everyone having property adjoining the railway line and there were no costs involved in making such bargains, it would not matter whether the railway was liable for damage caused by fires or not."[2] If the damage suffered by the landowners is greater than the benefits reaped by the railway, the landowners will be able to pay a sum sufficient to induce the railway to curtail operations. If the damage is less than the benefit, it would be unwarranted to prevent the railway from operating because total product would thereby be diminished. Coase takes great care to show that if courts award excess damages, they are likely to curtail useful activities in order to protect the interests of the victims of external diseconomies.

The adjustment is, of course, discontinuous where the activity is discrete, but in the case of divisible activities, bargaining will lead to a true Pareto optimum. " In full Pareto equilibrium ... [the] internal benefits measured in terms of some numéraire good, net of costs, must be just equal, at the margin, to the external damage that is imposed on other parties."[3] As long as there is disequilibrium, it pays one of the sides to offer compensation to the other to achieve a modification of the position. By contrast, an administrative imposition of costs will not necessarily produce an adjustment of the level of production leading to the Pareto optimum.

To clarify the reasoning underlying his conclusions in the railway case, Coase constructs the following numerical example. Assume, says Coase, that a railway faces the choice of running one or two trains per day.

> Suppose that the running of one train per day would enable the railway to perform services worth $150 per annum and running two trains a day would enable the railway to perform services worth $250 per annum. Suppose further that the cost of running one train is $50 per annum and two trains $100 per annum. Assuming perfect competition, the cost equals the fall in the value of production elsewhere due to the employment of additional factors of production by the railway. Clearly, the railway would find it profitable to run two trains per day. But suppose that running one train per day would destroy by fire crops worth ... $60 and two trains a day would result in the destruction of crops worth $120. In these circumstances running one train per day would raise the value of total production but the running of a second train would reduce the value of total production.[4]

The second train increases the railway's net return by $50 but causes

[1] Coase builds up his case almost exclusively on the basis of diverse court cases concerned with problems of external economies. While this makes for fascinating reading, I shall limit myself to a few examples, and proceed along more theoretical lines, thus sacrificing some realism for the sake of generality of the argument.

[2] Coase, *loc. cit.*, p. 31.

[3] Buchanan and Stubblebine, *loc. cit.*, p. 381.

[4] Coase, *loc. cit.*, p. 32.

destruction of $60 worth of crops, hence the total product is diminished by $10. Thus " the conclusion that it would be better if the second train did not run is correct ".[1]

To prevent the second train from being run, Coase says Pigou would make the railway liable for damages. Coase cautions us, however, that if damage liability is imposed, the farmer might intensify production in order to suffer greater damages and collect greater compensation. If he does so, it might not be worthwhile for the railway to run even one train per day. For instance, if the farmer intensifies his production to such an extent that even one train per day causes $110 worth of damage, and two trains per day cause $300 worth of damage, and if the railway has to pay compensation, no trains will be run. Thus if there is no liability, and the market is not permitted to operate, the diseconomy-producing activity is likely to be pushed beyond the Pareto-optimal point, but if there is liability, it will be curtailed below the Pareto-optimal level.[2]

In a no-liability regime the Pareto optimum will be achieved if the farmer(s) enters (enter) into a free bargain with the railway. Since the second train would cause a damage of $60 above and beyond the damage caused by the first train, the farmer(s) will be willing to pay the railway up to $60 for *not* running the second train. Since the railway gains only $50 by running the second train, it will accept any sum above $50 for not running it. Any bargain reached between the limits of $50 and $60 benefits both sides and leads to a Pareto optimum.

To appraise the correctness of reasoning underlying the railway example (and some of the other examples used to illustrate the modern-old approach), it is necessary to specify carefully the market setting within which the bargaining takes place. It is clear that the modern-old bargaining solution does not apply to monopolies, and that the output reached in isolation by a monopolist may be socially preferable to the output level which will pertain after the monopolist strikes a bargain with the units which suffer external diseconomies.[3] To

[1] *Ibid.*, p. 32.

[2] Coase, *loc. cit.*, pp. 32–3.

[3] Let $dd'$ be the demand curve facing the railway and $mm'$ the marginal revenue curve. As in Coase's example, let us assume that the average cost of running trains is constant, so that $CC'$ represents the average and the marginal cost curve.

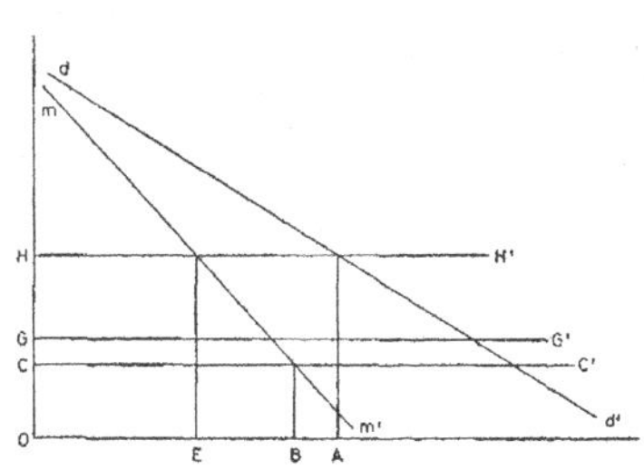

fix a monopolist's output at an optimal level, one must—for better or for worse—attack the problem along Pigovian lines.

To keep within the spirit of the modern-old argument, I shall limit myself from now on to external inter-relations of firms imbedded in the competitive system. Coase's railway, I shall assume, is managed along purely competitive lines, and it faces a perfectly elastic demand curve. This assumption may be difficult to reconcile with reality and also with Coase's own figures,[1] but it is essential for the modern-old argument.

Having specified that the externalities which are under discussion arise among competitive price-takers, let us consider briefly what is meant by an externality in a competitive regime: if the firms make zero profits before external costs are imposed on them, how can they bribe the would-be externality-creating-units to eliminate the externality? Clearly, a brief digression on private and social costs is called for at this point.

In a perfectly competitive industry in which there are no Ricardian rents, external diseconomies result in factor-use changes without creating any social costs. In such a setting, every firm operates at a zero profit level, and all the factors are paid their opportunity cost. If external costs are imposed upon one of the competitive units, that unit will make losses and, in the long run, it will go out of business. As output is curtailed and ultimately abandoned, the displaced factors find employment in alternate uses. In the initial situation the factors were employed at opportunity cost, hence the alternate-use output has the same value as the original output.[2] Thus there is a change in production pattern but no social loss. Moreover, since the unit displaced by the external cost operated initially at zero profit, it has neither the incentive nor the means to bribe the externality-producing unit.

---

Let *OG* be the marginal cost imposed by the railway on the farmers, and *OH* be the social marginal cost obtained by summing the railway's marginal cost and the marginal external cost. The Pareto-optimal output *OA* is determined by the intersection of the social marginal cost with the demand curve. In the absence of bargains with the farmers, the railway's maximum profit output *OB* is determined by the intersection of the railway's marginal cost with the marginal revenue curve. If the farmers offer the railway compensation in exchange for a reduction in output, the railway will be willing to reduce output to *OE*, at which point the marginal social cost equals the railway's marginal revenue. In the case shown the output which will obtain in the absence of bargains, i.e., *OB*, is socially preferable to output *OE*.

[1] Coase's arithmetic suggests that the railway is a monopolist with constant marginal costs ($50 per train) facing a downward sloping demand curve. Under this interpretation it appears to be useful to run a second train because the marginal social cost of $110 ($50 being the marginal cost to the railway, and $60 being external costs) is less than the average revenue from the two trains ($125). The apparent decrease in the total product under the two-train regime is caused by the neglect of the consumers' surplus. Harold Demsetz disagrees with this interpretation of the railway example and claims that the railway is meant to be a perfectly discriminating monopolist, in which case Coase's one-train solution would be correct. It is a little difficult to accept this interpretation, however, since the perfectly discriminating monopolist violates the Pareto conditions in distribution, since arbitrage among consumers could improve some consumers' welfare without decreasing the welfare of any consumers.

[2] This statement is not strictly true, but in dealing with individual firms in a competitive setting (which is in keeping with the level of discourse of Pigou's critics), it is legitimate to disregard effects of second-order magnitude.

To re-create the modern-old reasoning in a competitive setting, it is necessary to postulate the existence of non-transferable resources giving rise to Ricardian rents. Consider, for instance, a case in which a smoke-stack is erected next to a farm field, and imagine that the smoke reduces the crops. If all the factors were employed at their opportunity cost, the farmer would move elsewhere, and the land would remain fallow, or it would be put to some alternative use bringing the same rate of return to the land as the initial use. If, however, the land stays under the (now reduced) crop, or if it is put to a use in which it brings a marginal product of lesser value, a reduction of land rent will occur. The external loss caused by the smoke is measured not by the amount of the crop destroyed but by the decline in the difference between the value of the field's product and the opportunity cost of the movable factors, i.e., by the decline in the Ricardian rent. Thus changes in the Ricardian rent measure the external effects of firms imbedded in a competitive setting. The net returns used in Coase's examples can thus be interpreted as net rents.[1]

Let us now return to Coase's railway example and concentrate on the problem of losses to farmers. Coase apparently assumes that the farmers have no foreknowledge of the damage which will be done by the second train. If they had such foreknowledge, they could reduce the damage in most cases—say, by switching to crops which are less affected by smoke or by planting or sowing more sparsely.

Table 1 gives a hypothetical example of net rents accruing to farmers who have three alternative courses of action, A, B and C, with the railway running 0, 1, 2, 3 and 4 trains daily. By stretching our imaginations we can assume that the railway operates in a competitive regime and that its net returns represent net rents. Coase's " net returns " to 1 and 2 trains are thus interpreted in Table 1, and additional numbers are made up for 3, 4 and 5 trains. Column C is consistent with Coase's assumption that no crop-switching will take place (and the figures for the damage caused by 1 and 2 trains are his), while columns A and B show the hypothetical result of crop-switching to reduce the damage:

TABLE I

| *Number of trains* | *Net rents to the factors employed by the railway* | *Net rents to the factors employed by alternative cropping methods* | | |
|---|---|---|---|---|
| | | A | B | C |
| | $ | $ | $ | $ |
| 0 | 0 | 50 | 100 | 150 |
| 1 | 100 | 40 | 80 | 90 |
| 2 | 150 | 30 | 50 | 30 |
| 3 | 170 | 25 | 20 | −30 |
| 4 | 160 | 10 | 0 | −30 |
| 5 | 0 | 0 | 0 | −30 |

[1] The formal profit-maximization conditions under perfect competiton are not affected, of course, by inclusion of the rent.

If the farmers have no foreknowledge of any damage, they will adopt alternative C, and if two trains are run per day, they will suffer $60 worth of damage (as in Coase's example) and have a net rent of $30, as shown in Table 1. If, however, they know that two trains will be run per day, they will adopt alternative B. This alternative would be less profitable than alternative C if no trains were running, but it is more profitable in a two-train regime because of the lesser damage to crops.

Acting in isolation, the railway would find it profitable to run three trains per day and collect a rent of $170. The farmers would find it best to switch to alternative A, with a net rent of $25 under the three-train regime. Notice, however, that the railway would gain only $20 by running the additional train, and the farmers would lose $25. If bargaining were opened, the railway would reduce the number of trains to 2 if it received compensation larger than $20, and the farmers would be willing to pay up to $25 in exchange for a reduction of train runs from 3 to 2. Thus it is in the interest of all parties concerned to reach a Pareto-optimal solution.

The modern-old solution as presented above is technically unexceptionable, but one may wonder whether it is a mere curiosity or whether it is broadly applicable to externality problems. To obtain the solution it was necessary to assume that (1) bargaining concerns the *marginal* unit and (2) that the bargaining limits are well defined. These assumptions may or may not be satisfied in actual situations.

Consider again the railway example. To obtain the best bargain with the farmers, the railway might threaten to run five trains per day and thus destroy the entire crop. To avoid this possibility and to obtain a reduction in train runs to two a day, the farmers would be willing to pay up to $50. Conversely, if the railway company were seeking permission to run a railway, the farmers would seek to appropriate the entire rent accruing to the railway under the optimal regime, i.e., $150, even though the damage would equal only $100. Thus the bargaining limits are set by the rents accruing to the two parties under the optimal regime, and not by the marginal rents.

It is conceivable, of course, that the modern-old economists think of situations in which large numbers of potential external-diseconomy producers compete for a large number of potential sites so that the bargaining limits are narrowed down through competition to the marginal units. If this is so, the solution is correct, but the assumptions which must be made to achieve the solution are out of harmony with the examples examined by Coase and, what is more serious, have only a faint bearing on reality.[1]

[1] When in the absence of zoning, a factory is erected, it is not usual for the factory owner to notify the nearby farmers about the amount of smoke which he intends to produce, so that the bargaining, if any, takes place after the factory is built. It is still more unusual for a number of factories to compete not only for a site but for the privilege of smoking on to nearby fields. The ex-ante bargaining would require rather unusual property relationships which would, in effect, internalize the externality.

Bargaining for the entire rent accruing to the opposite party does not, in itself, preclude the possibility of reaching a Pareto optimum, for it is to the advantage of both parties to reach a level of joint maximum rent. Moreover, the process opens up magnificent business prospects: any activity can be turned to profit as long as it is sufficiently annoying to someone else. As long as the activity absorbs no resources, i.e., as long as the blackmailers maintain amateur standing, the economist who refrains from social judgment can find no fault with the situation.[1]

A more crucial assumption made by the modern-old school is that the parties to the bargain know how much it pays them to offer in order to induce a change in the output of the other unit. The assumption is reasonable in cases in which unit(s) " 1 " has (have) an external effect on unit(s) " 2," but unit(s) " 2 " does (do) not affect externally the costs of unit(s) " 1." In such situations the unit(s) determines (determine) in isolation the optimal output. The payments are determined by the benefits reaped by the " 2 " unit(s) when " 1 " output changes from the isolation equilibrium level, and the costs to " 1 " of such output changes. If there is a mutual externality between " 1 " unit(s) and " 2 " unit(s), neither the " 1's " nor the " 2's " may be able to achieve an individual optimum; hence it may not be possible to determine the size of payments leading to a joint optimum. As Davis and Whinston have shown, the continuous case corresponds to a two-person, non-zero sum game which, in general, has no saddle point,[2] and, therefore, neither simple nor mixed strategies will yield an individual optimum.[3] Thus a bargain may never be reached, and even when it is reached, there will be temptation to improve one's position by violating the agreement.

The bargaining solution also breaks down, as Turvey notes, when the group suffering through (or benefiting from) an externality is too large for the members to " get together ". In such cases, there is " a case for collective action to achieve optimum allocation ".[4] Buchanan also recognizes the case for collective action in the case of goods which are not privately divisible, though he warns us that any political solution

[1] Pigou took a rather dim view of the " costless bargaining " assumption: " Of bargaining proper there is little that need be said. It is obvious that intelligence and resources devoted to this purpose, whether on one side or on the other, and whether successful or unsuccessful, yield no product to the community as a whole . . . These activities are wasted. They contribute to private, but not to social net product." *The Economics of Welfare*, 4th ed., 1938, p. 201. Pigou is too harsh in his judgment: insofar as the bargaining process changes the pattern of resource use and provided that it is imbedded in a competitive setting, it does contribute to social product. It is quite possible, however, that just as with public regulation, the absorption of resources may be so great as to nullify the beneficial effects of improved resource use.

[2] Davis and Whinston, *loc. cit.*, p. 259 ff. Curiously enough, the numerical example given by the authors is one in which there is a stable equilibrium which will be reached with each firm acting in isolation. It is very simple, however, to construct plausible cases which do not have such an equilibrium.

[3] For a discussion of the vicissitudes of a bargaining solution in variable threat situations, see R. L. Bishop, " Game-Theoretic Analyses of Bargaining ", *Quarterly Journal of Economics*, vol. 77 (1963).

[4] Turvey, *loc. cit.*, p. 312.

involves the imposition of some externalities as long as the goods are not entirely indivisible.[1]

The large-group difficulty lies in that it is to the advantage of any member of the group to refuse to bear any part of the cost of a settlement, while reaping the advantages. If there are n farmers affected by the smoke from a train, it pays any farmer to let the remaining (n-1) bribe the railway and to enjoy cost-free the results of the bargain. Moreover, if the externality does not affect all the firms in a fixed proportion, it pays to form coalitions. For instance, the construction of a higher smokestack might reduce the pollution of nearby fields but increase that of more distant areas. If this be so, one can foresee the formation of separate pressure groups, and the larger the number of possible combinations of interests, the smaller the possibility of Pareto-optimal solutions.[2]

The discussion of conditions under which the modern-old solution is valid leads to the conclusion that far from being a universal panacea, the private bargain solution to external diseconomies applies only to exceptional cases. Such cases are, moreover, of little interest to the policy maker. If a private bargain can be made to everybody's satisfaction, there is no reason for judicial or administrative interference. The policy maker must cope with situations in which " payment cannot be exacted from the benefited parties or compensation enforced on behalf of the injured parties ",[3] that is, with situations where private bargains fail. Moreover, the policy maker cannot be restricted to perfect competition but must also deal with monopolies, and private bargains involving monopolies may, as we have seen, aggravate resource misallocation instead of achieving a social optimum. It is therefore of crucial importance to determine whether it is possible to devise a Pigovian system of taxes and subsidies which will help the market's " invisible hand " in achieving socially optimal results.

## II. The Pigovian Solution to the Problem of Externalities

The Pigovian prescription for externalities is: devise a system of taxes and subsidies which will modify the cost function of an externality-creating firm in such a fashion that the firm must produce at the socially optimal level if it wishes to maximize profits.

The Pigovian approach may be attacked on the grounds of practicability: the cost of devising and administering a tax-subsidy scheme may exceed the benefits. Recently Davis and Whinston have attacked the

[1] Buchanan, *loc. cit.*, p. 29.

[2] To find a way out of this difficulty, one is tempted to search for a sub-set of units, all of which are willing to co-operate on a voluntary basis. Such a solution has no legitimate place in a purely competitive setting for it is a basic assumption of the theory of perfect competition that all units behave exactly alike. In a large group it is in the interest of every unit to refuse to pay and to let the other units bear the entire cost; in any sub-set of units the same behaviour must pertain.

[3] Pigou, *op cit.*, p. 183.

solutions on the grounds of theoretical feasibility, and their conclusions appear to be taken as authoritative by the modern-old economists.[1]

The question whether the Pigovian solutions are practical is one of immense importance, for many a beautiful scheme of economic theorists has failed to pass the test of applicability. Precedence must go, however, to the problem of the theoretical possibility of reaching a solution, for if a solution cannot be found, there is no point in searching for it. If Davis and Whinston are right, the economist has nothing to say where the market fails.[2]

Davis and Whinston make a distinction between " separable " externalities which can, though with " difficulty," be handled through the Pigovian method and completely intractable (except through mergers) " non-separable " externalities. If the output level of unit(s) " 1 " affects the total cost *but not the marginal cost* of unit(s) " 2 " (and/or if there is a linkage of this kind in the reverse direction), the externality is separable. If the output level of unit(s) " 1 " affects the marginal cost of unit(s) " 2 " (and/or there is such a linkage in the reverse direction), the externality is non-separable.[3]

As it turns out, the problem of devising a Pigovian solution for the " separable " case does not arise for, as can be readily demonstrated, the " separable externalities " do not affect the pattern of resource allocation. After showing the irrelevancy of the " separable " case, we shall proceed to construct a Pigovian solution to the " insoluble " problem.

The output level of a firm in a competitive industry is determined by the marginal cost and by the product price which is parametrically given to the firm. As long as the price remains constant and the marginal costs do not change, the optimum output level of the firm will not change. Since " separable " externalities have no effect on marginal cost, they do not alter the firm's optimal output level. As a consequence " separable " externalities have no influence on the allocation of productive resources though they do affect product distribution.[4]

It may seem that " separable " externalities affect resource allocation in the long run, through their effect on the total (produce or shutdown) decisions of the affected firms. A firm's optimal output level may not

[1] See especially Turvey, *op. cit.*, p. 312 and *passim.*

[2] As will be shown, the type of externalities which, according to Davis and Whinston, can be handled through the Pigovian method, is of no consequence in resource allocation problems.

[3] Let $C_1$ and $C_2$ represent the total cost functions of firms " 1 " and " 2 " respectively, and $q_1$, $q_2$ be the respective output levels. If the two firms are externally linked, $C_1 = f_1(q_1, q_2)$ and $C_2 = f_2(q_1, q_2)$ where $\partial C_1/\partial C_2 \neq 0$ and/or $\partial C_2/\partial q_1 \neq 0$. Separability means that $\partial^2 C_1/\partial q_2 \partial q_1 = 0$ and $\partial^2 C_2/\partial q_1 \partial q_2 = 0$, while in cases of non-separability $\partial^2 C_1/\partial q_2 \partial q_1 \neq 0$ and/or $\partial^2 C_2/\partial q_1 \partial q_2 \neq 0$.

[4] As Davis and Whinston rightly observed, the cost functions used in the literature to demonstrate the effect of externalities on the Pareto conditions are invariably of the " separable " type. For instance, J. M. Henderson and R. E. Quandt in their *Microeconomic Theory*, 1958, p. 216, discuss the following cost functions:

$C_1 = 0{\cdot}1q_1^2 + 5q_1 - 0{\cdot}1q_2^2$; $C_2 = 0{\cdot}2q_2^2 + 7q_2 + 0{\cdot}025q_1^2$ .The Henderson-Quandt example is especially unfortunate, for the cost functions used by them are incompatible with a long-run competitive equilibrium.

change as long as the firm remains in production, but as a consequence of the imposition of external costs, the firm may find it most profitable to go out of production altogether. This argument is spurious, however. In considering the total (produce or shutdown) decision, the firm treats *all* the costs as if they were variable, even those costs which are fixed in the short run. The decision to produce or to discontinue production is based on considerations of long-run marginal costs. If an externality modifies the long-run marginal cost of a firm, it must be classified as " non-separable " in the long run.

A different argument purporting to show the impact of " separable " externalities on resource allocation in a competitive setting is based on an apparent analogy with the " prisoner's dilemma."[1] Imagine a residential neighbourhood in which the returns on individual houses are affected by the general condition of other houses. As long as the entire neighbourhood is run down, there is a certain (marginal) return on the improvement of every house. If the general level of maintenance is raised in the neighbourhood as a whole, the rate of return on the improved as well as on the unimproved properties will go up. It is possible for the return on the improved houses and on the (few remaining) unimproved houses to go up by the same amount so that the marginal return from improving an individual property will be the same as before. It is also readily conceivable that as long as the neighbourhood is run down, there will be no incentive to individual improvement but that everybody would benefit from concerted action. We thus have what seems to be a case of separable externalities affecting resource use and calling for a Pigovian tax-subsidy scheme which will benefit all the producers.

The " prisoner's dilemma " argument on which the neighbourhood example is built runs as follows. Imagine there are two individuals accused of committing a joint crime. If neither of them confesses, both will be set free. If one of them confesses, both will be sentenced, but the one who confesses will receive a lighter sentence. Individual behaviour (based on the principle of minimaxing the penalty) calls for confession, but concerted action calls for denial of guilt. It is clearly in the best interest of both prisoners to engage in concerted action. But is it in the interest of society that they should be set free? This somewhat facetious question applies to the neighbourhood example as well as to the prisoners. The fact that the property owners in a given neighbourhood benefit through concerted action does not permit us to conclude that the concerted action benefits the community as a whole. The concerted action is beneficial to the property owners because it increases the demand for their product. This increase in demand can only occur if there is a decrease in demand for property in other neighbourhoods and/or for other goods and services. The *ceteris paribus* assumption underlying

[1] See Davis and Whinston, *loc. cit.*; also the same authors' " Economics of Urban Renewal ", *Law and Contemporary Problems*, Winter 1961, pp. 108–110.

partial equilibirum analysis can no longer be made, and the discussion of externalities in a competitive setting (no product variation, price takers' equilibrium) fails to apply.

To remain within the analytical framework of the discussion between the modern-old and the modern welfare economists, we must confine our attention to cases of " non-separable " externalities, that is, to cases where the output of a firm (or firms) affects the marginal cost of another firm (or firms). In such cases it may not be possible for a firm to determine in isolation its optimal output. Davis and Whinston thereby conclude that it is impossible to devise a tax-subsidy scheme which will induce each firm to move to a joint optimum and that the joint optimum objective can be achieved only through merger.[1]

The Davis-Whinston argument appears to be based on the notion that the Pigovian tax-subsidy scheme can only function if the firms involved start from a well-defined equilibrium position. The argument applies to the bargaining solution since it is difficult to strike a bargain unless one knows how much one will gain from it. There is no such requirement for the Pigovian scheme. For the scheme to function it is not necessary to start from any set point; what is required is that there be taxes and subsidies which internalize the external effect. If such taxes and subsidies can be imposed, each firm will move toward the Pareto optimum simply by attempting to equate its marginal costs (including tax) to the price. It will be shown that, contrarily to the Davis-Whinston assertion, such a scheme can be devised where there are " non-separable " externalities.[2]

Consider two perfectly competitive firms, 1 and 2, which seek to maximize their total profits,[3] i.e., to equate marginal costs and marginal revenues:

$$p_1 = \partial C_1/\partial q_1 \quad ; \quad p_2 = \partial C_2/\partial q_2$$

where $p_1$ and $p_2$ are the prices facing Firm 1 and Firm 2, with $q_1$, $q_2$ being their respective outputs and $C_1$, $C_2$ their respective cost functions. If the two firms are linked by non-separable external effects, the marginal cost of each firm is a function of the output of the other firm, i.e.,

$$C_1 = f_1(q_1,q_2); \; C_2 = f_2(q_1,q_2)$$

and

$$\partial^2 C_1/\partial q_2 \partial q_1 \neq 0; \; \partial^2 C_2/\partial q_1 \partial q_2 \neq 0.$$

As a consequence, the individual optimum output of the two firms $\hat{q}_1$ and $\hat{q}_2$ (i.e., the output which yields maximum profit under the given circumstances) is a function of the output level of the other firm:

$$\hat{q}_1 = g_1(q_2) \quad ; \quad \hat{q}_2 = g_2(q_1).$$

[1] Davis and Whinston, *loc. cit.*, pp. 253–6. The Davis-Whinston assertion also implies that it is impossible to devise a pricing scheme for a divisionalized firm if there are non-separable externalities between the divisions.

[2] I owe this proof to Lester Telser.

[3] The costs are defined here as being net of rent in order to make the analysis consistent with perfectly competitive conditions.

The individual optimization process is represented graphically in Figure 1, in which the curve $\hat{q}_1$ represents the optimal output of Firm 1 as a function of $q_2$, the output of Firm 2, and curve $\hat{q}_2$ shows the optimal output of Firm 2 for various output levels of Firm 1. In the diagram Firm 1 creates external diseconomies to Firm 2, and Firm 2 to Firm 1. As drawn, the equilibrium point given by the intersection of curves $\hat{q}_1$ and $\hat{q}_2$ is unstable (though in some cases it may be stable), and it differs from the socially optimal output $E$.[1] The purpose of the Pigovian tax-subsidy scheme is so to modify the cost functions faced by the two firms as to induce the two firms to produce at $E$, i.e., to have a stable equilibrium point at $E$.

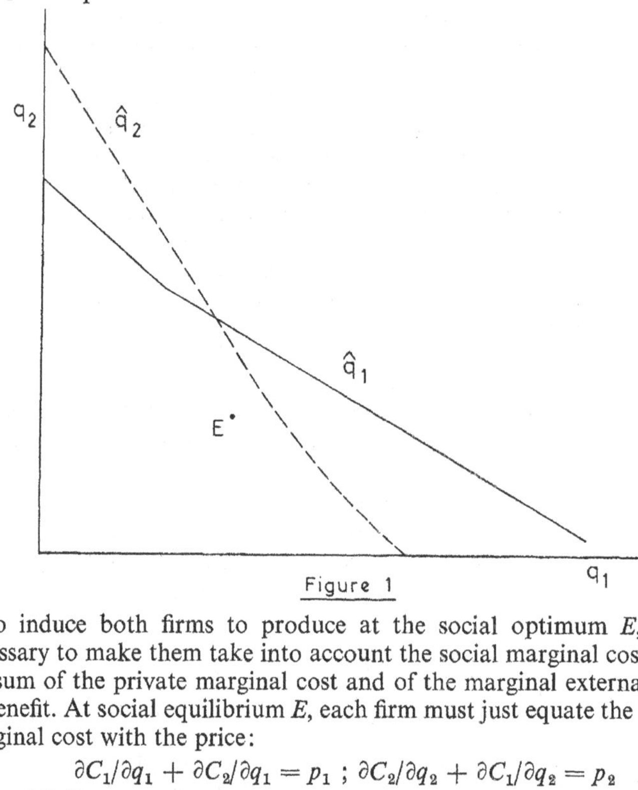


Figure 1

To induce both firms to produce at the social optimum $E$, it is necessary to make them take into account the social marginal cost, i.e., the sum of the private marginal cost and of the marginal external cost or benefit. At social equilibrium $E$, each firm must just equate the social marginal cost with the price:

$$\partial C_1/\partial q_1 + \partial C_2/\partial q_1 = p_1 \ ; \ \partial C_2/\partial q_2 + \partial C_1/\partial q_2 = p_2$$

where $\partial C_2/\partial q_1$ represents the marginal cost imposed by 1 upon 2, and $\partial C_1/\partial q_2$ the effect of 2 upon 1.

The Pigovian problem is to impose upon each firm a tax which internalizes the external effects so that each firm will choose the socially optimal output by considering its price and its own marginal costs

[1] For a discussion of conditions under which the equilibrium point resulting from individual optimization yields a social optimum in spite of external effects, see Buchanan and Stubblebine, *loc. cit.*, p. 375. Such cases are exceptions rather than a rule, however.

(including the tax) without taking into account any other factors. Consider, for instance, a Pigovian tax to be imposed upon Firm 1. The new cost function which will include the tax must have the following two properties: (1) the new cost function must equal the sum of internal costs of 1 and of the external costs imposed by 1 on 2, for all values of $q_1$, and (2) the new cost function must be a single-valued function of $q_1$. Writing $C'_1$ for the new cost function of Firm 1, conditions (1) and (2) will be satisfied if:

$$\partial C'_1(q_1)/\partial q_1 \equiv \partial C(q_1 q_2)/\partial q_1$$

where $C(q_1 q_2) = C_1(q_1 q_2) + C_2(q_1 q_2)$.
An analogous condition can be written for the tax to be imposed on Firm 2:

$$\partial C'_2(q_2)/\partial q_2 \equiv \partial C(q_1 q_2)/\partial q_2.$$

Since the new cost function for which we are searching is a function of a single variable it follows that:

$$\partial C'_1/\partial q_1 \equiv dC'_1/dq_1, \text{ and } \partial C'_2/\partial q_2 \equiv dC'_2/dq_2.$$

The problem, then, is to find functions $g_1$ and $g_2$ such that $q_2 = g_1(q_1)$ and $q_1 = g_1(q_2)$ where $g_1$ and $g_2$ are the solutions to the differential equations

$$\partial C/\partial q_1 = dC_1/dq_1 \text{ and } \partial C/\partial q_2 = dC_2/dq_2.$$

Writing in extenso the above equations we have:

$$\frac{\partial C_1}{\partial q_1} + \frac{\partial C_2}{\partial q_1} = \frac{\partial C_1}{\partial q_1} + \frac{\partial C_1}{\partial q_2}\frac{dq_2}{dq_1}; \text{ and } \frac{\partial C_1}{\partial q_2} + \frac{\partial C_2}{\partial q_2} = \frac{\partial C_2}{\partial q_2} + \frac{\partial C_2}{\partial q_1}\frac{dq_1}{dq_2};$$

and simplifying:

$$\frac{\partial C_2}{\partial q_1} = \frac{\partial C_1}{\partial q_2}\frac{dq_2}{dq_1}; \text{ and } \frac{\partial C_1}{\partial q_2} = \frac{\partial C_2}{\partial q_1}\frac{dq_1}{dq_2};$$

and by re-arranging terms

$$\frac{dq_2}{dq_1} = \frac{\partial C_2}{\partial q_1}\Big/\frac{\partial C_1}{\partial q_2} = F_1(q_1 q_2); \frac{dq_1}{dq_2} = \frac{\partial C_1}{\partial q_2}\Big/\frac{\partial C_2}{\partial q_1} = F_2(q_1 q_2).$$

The solutions to the last two equations are $q_2 = g_1(q_1)$ and $q_1 = g_2(q_1)$. The solutions exist whenever $F_1$ and $F_2$ are continuous functions with continuous partial derivatives $\partial F_1/\partial q_2$ and $\partial F_2/\partial q_1$. The two firms will thus face new cost functions which are respectively $C'_1 = C'_1(q_1, g_1(q_1))$ and $C'_2 = C'_2(q_2, g_2(q_2))$ where $g_1$ and $g_2$ are the Pigovian taxes internalizing the external effect.[1]

The formal proof that a Pigovian system of taxes can be designed[2] does not prove that such taxes are easy to design or that their adminis-

[1] The tax on Firm 1 is a function (possibly a highly complicated one) of the output of Firm 1, and similarly for Firm 2. Taxes proportioned to the output will only be appropriate if it is reasonable to give linear approximations of the cost functions in respect to both variables.

[2] For a discussion of the integrability conditions which must be satisfied in the case of more than two units, see H. Wold and L. Juréen, *Demand Analysis*, 1953, pp. 90–94. The proof, developed by Wold for utility analysis, applies to cost analysis as well.

tration is practicable. In some cases it might be preferable to use outright prohibition of certain activities (such as zoning laws) whereas in others it might be less costly to ignore the externalities and let the market function without any interference. The choice of course of action must be dictated by weighing the costs and the benefits of the alternative arrangements.

The Pigovian tax-subsidy scheme, unlike the modern-old bargains, applies to the broad spectrum of externality cases. The scheme is, nevertheless, repugnant to the modern-old economists.

Buchanan's objections to the Pigovian method are based on the observation that any administrative measure is likely to impose externalities of its own.[1] Thus Mr. X might not feel personally threatened by fire (or he lives in an entirely fireproof building); yet he is forced to pay taxes to support the fire department. The objection is valid, alas: there is no way of constructing a non-dictatorial social welfare function,[2] and there is no way of devising an equitable system of payment for public goods.[3] These points are well worth keeping in mind, and one should continuously be reminded of the dangers of administrative meddling in economic affairs. Unfortunately, however, the policy maker must choose between imperfect alternatives, and it might be well worth the economists' while to design the best available system of Pigovian taxes instead of making indignant noises when the policy makers adopt silly measures for want of expert advice.

The cost of administration and the possibility of imposition of excessive burdens on the externality-producing unit cause concern to Coase. It is true, of course, that the cost of regulation may outweigh its benefits, and that governments in general shy away from this kind of cost-benefit analysis. Public welfare would doubtless increase if we dropped the unreasonable expedient of valuing government services at cost, and if we probed into their actual value. Fear of excessive bounties is less warranted. Excessive damages work against the interests of the aggrieved parties as much as against the interests of society. If a socially useful activity is eliminated because damages are too high, no compensation will accrue to the damaged party. Farmers adversely affected by smoke are better off if they receive a steady stream of compensation from a smoke-producing factory, i.e., if they appropriate part of the rent accruing to the factory,[4] than they are if the factory is forced to move away. Thus whether cost allocation is done through bargaining or whether it is done through the judicial-administrative process, it is in the interests of all the parties to reach a social optimum, for at that

[1] See Buchanan, *loc. cit.*, pp. 25 ff.

[2] On this point see Kenneth J. Arrow, *Social Choice and Individual Values*, 1951.

[3] See J. Wiseman, "The Theory of Public Utility Pricing—An Empty Box", *Oxford Economic Papers*, vol. IX (1957).

[4] I assume here that the factory collects some Ricardian rent and that it prefers to share the rent with the farmers rather than to move away. If there is no Ricardian rent accruing to the factory, it is socially indifferent whether the factory moves away or not.

point the spoils are the greatest. The problem, in either case, is how to divide the spoils; it is always in everybody's interest to make the spoils as large as possible. Unfortunately, in most types of external relations the market does not lead to a social optimum; hence, whether we like it or not, we must try to design a workable Pigovian system of taxes or subsidies, or we must live with the externalities in our non-optimal world.

## III. Conclusions

The critics of the Pigovian tradition have done us a great service by pointing out the ambiguities and the lack of clarity in the orthodox treatment of externalities. They have done well, too, to point out how important it is to reckon the administrative cost of action taken to remedy situations in which there are externalities. Externalities may well be permitted to persist if the administrative action absorbs more resources than are lost through a deviation from a Pareto optimum. This is just common sense, but it is good to put common sense into scientific language every so often. It was also useful to point out (as Kenneth Arrow did before) that any collective action imposes the will of some on others; hence, it too creates externalities of its own.

The mutual bargain solution proposed by the modern-old economists lacks, unfortunately, the necessary generality to be of policy importance. Pigou, as we know, was concerned with externality situations "of such a sort that payment cannot be exacted from the benefited factor or compensation enforced on behalf of the injured factors".[1] To be more precise, he should have also included cases where private bargains cannot be reached, and cases where private bargains are contrary to public interest. In the former category we must include bargains with variable-threat limits, in the latter, bargains in which monopolies are involved.

Even in the rare instances where externalities are a private matter between two parties, the superiority of private bargains over judicial arbitration is hard to accept. Whether it is reached by direct bargaining or by a judicial process, the solution to the conflict is most satisfactory to both sides if the final situation is Pareto optimal. It is clear, moreover, that even if provision is made for judicial recourse, the parties concerned may, if they wish, strike a private bargain. The fact that arbitration and other judicial methods of settling disputes is so prevalent gives proof that it is not always easy, or cheap, to reach a private bargain.

Finally, there is the problem of equity. To be sure, economists abandon their scientific detachment when they start moralizing. It is worth pointing out, however, that while the judicial process, rightly or wrongly, tends to compensate the victim, the bargaining process compensates the threat-making party, and one can hardly claim that threat-making deserves reward.

[1] Pigou, *op. cit.*, p. 183.

The attempt to prove the impossibility of devising a Pigovian scheme in cases of " non-separable " externalities was potentially the most dangerous of the attacks on the Pigovian tradition. Luckily for the " modern " welfare economics, the proof demonstrates only that where externalities are " non-separable," it may be impossible to reach a " modern-old " bargain. The Pigovian solution withstood the attack.

The practical problem of devising Pigovian tax-subsidy schemes may be exceedingly complex. Pigou hoped to leave resource allocation to the " invisible hand " and to help guide that hand through taxes and subsidies. He recognized, however, that " when the interrelations of the various private persons affected are highly complex, the Government may find it necessary to exercise some means of authoritative control in addition to providing a bounty ".[1] In some cases, too, as the " modern-old " economists remind us, it is best for the government to adopt a hands-off policy.

To sum up, the modern-old counter-attack has left us just about where we were before it was made. Since the counter-attack was thickly hedged with disclaimers concerning the economists' ability to say anything useful about welfare problems, the lack of concrete results cannot come as much of a surprise. Yet this lack of results must be disappointing to those of us who are dissatisfied with the " solutions " to externalities put into effect by " intelligent administrators " and by " applied economists." Perhaps, after all, the welfare economists could do better than the " practical men " if only they were able to apply their skills to the practical problems which cry for solutions.

*Columbia University.*

[1] Pigou, *op. cit.*, p. 194.

# [15]

# THE COASE THEOREM ON SOCIAL COST: A FOOTNOTE*

*G. WARREN NUTTER*
*University of Virginia*

UNTIL recently, orthodox economic theory, following Pigou, had maintained that the cost of a nuisance would not be properly evaluated in the market-place unless, among other things, the agent "producing" it were made responsible for damages. In his article on social cost,[1] R. H. Coase proved Pigou wrong by demonstrating the symmetry of marginal costing under alternative assignments of property rights. Specifically, he showed that, whenever the cost of market transactions can be neglected, the "damaging agent" will make the same calculation of marginal cost whether charged with responsibility for damages or not. He went on to argue that assignment of property rights would have no effect on allocation of resources.[2]

George Stigler has since cast the Coase theorem in a more general form: under perfect competition and any assignment of property rights, market transactions between a firm "producing" a nuisance and one "consuming" it will bring about the same composition of output as would have been determined by a single firm engaged in both activities.[3] That is, market transactions will have the same consequences as internal management no matter what the property structure, provided only that costs of transactions are negligible.

Questions have been raised, however, as to whether the Coase theorem applies to the allocation of resources in the long run. If cattle ranchers are responsible for damage caused to grain crops by straying cows, it has been argued, there will be fewer cattle ranchers and more grain farmers than if farmers are responsible. As Guido Calabresi has put it: "The short of the matter is, liability rules do affect the amount of money people make—in the short run; and in the long run people will enter those activities where they make more money."[4]

* I am grateful to R. H. Coase, Milton Friedman, and George J. Stigler for helping to get my thinking straight on the problem discussed here.

[1] R. H. Coase, The Problem of Social Cost, 3 J. Law & Econ. 1 (1960).

[2] *Id.* at 8.

[3] George J. Stigler, The Theory of Price 113 (3d ed. 1966).

[4] Guido Calabresi, The Decision for Accidents: An Approach to Nonfault Allocation of Costs, 78 Harv. L. Rev. 713, 730 (1965). For a similar argument in a rather different

The purpose of this note is to show that the liability rule has no effect on the alternative costs of either the "nuisance-generating" enterprise (the rancher) or the "nuisance-consuming" enterprise (the farmer). Hence the Coase theorem applies to the long-run as well as the short-run allocation of resources.

Let us follow Coase in examining the case of the straying cattle. Imagine a wheat farm and a cattle ranch situated on adjoining plots of land. If the cattle are not attended or restrained, they will stray into the wheat fields and trample crops, creating a nuisance for the wheat farmer. (We ignore incidental benefits to the cattle from eating crops and to the crops from droppings.) Let us consider first how a single entrepreneur would arrange the planting of wheat and the growing of cattle if he owned the two enterprises jointly and sold their products (wheat and meat) in highly competitive markets.

For convenience, let the marginal cost of producing wheat or meat on an isolated plot be an increasing linear function of output, as illustrated by the point values in Table 1.[5] Let the price be \$5.00 for wheat and \$10.00 for meat. Let the amount of wheat trampled daily be directly proportional to the daily outputs of both wheat and meat. Specifically

$$d = 0.1\,mw,$$

where $d$ is the amount of wheat damaged, $m$ the output of meat, and $w$ the output of wheat.[6]

TABLE 1
COST OF PRODUCING WHEAT AND MEAT ON ISOLATED PLOTS

| Wheat | | | Meat | | |
|---|---|---|---|---|---|
| Daily Output | Marginal Cost | Total Cost | Daily Output | Marginal Cost | Total Cost |
| 1 | \$1.50 | \$ 1.00 | 1 | \$ 6.50 | \$ 6.00 |
| 2 | 2.50 | 3.00 | 2 | 7.50 | 13.00 |
| 3 | 3.50 | 6.00 | 3 | 8.50 | 21.00 |
| 4 | 4.50 | 10.00 | 4 | 9.50 | 30.00 |
| 4.5 | 5.00 | 12.38 | 4.5 | 10.00 | 34.88 |
| 5 | 5.50 | 15.00 | 5 | 10.50 | 40.00 |

context, see David F. Bramhall and Edwin S. Mills, A Note on the Asymmetry Between Fees and Payments, 2 Water Resources Research 615 (1966). Calabresi has since argued that this view is incorrect. See his Transaction Costs, Resource Allocation and Liability Rules—A Comment, 11 J. Law & Econ. 67 (1968).

5 The cost functions are as follows: $C_w = 0.5w(1+w)$ and $C_m = 0.5m(11+m)$, where $C_w$ represents total cost of wheat, $C_m$ total cost of meat, $w$ output of wheat, and $m$ output of meat.

6 Coase does not take account of the effect of the wheat crop on damage in his nu-

If the cattle could somehow be kept from wandering onto the wheat land at no cost to the enterprise, costs of production would be as given in Table 1. On the basis of the specified prices, the optimum output would be 4.5 for both meat and wheat, so that the quasi-rent would be $10.12 for each plot of land or $20.24 for both together.

If the cattle are allowed to roam, the entrepreneur must take account of the damage to crops in determining the optimum outputs of wheat and meat. In the case of each product, he must add marginal damage to marginal cost of production to derive the full marginal cost relevant for a decision on output. In our simple example, marginal damage attributable to the one product (say, wheat) is constant for any given output of the other (say, meat), but varies directly with the latter (see Table 2). On the basis of full marginal cost (see Table 3), a combined output of 3 units each of wheat and meat will be optimum.[7] The production is worth $45.00, from which must be subtracted production costs of $17.00 (Table 1) and total damage of $4.50, so that quasi-rent for both plots of land together is $13.50.[8]

TABLE 2
MARGINAL DAMAGE TO WHEAT CROP IN THE CASE OF ADJOINING WHEAT AND CATTLE PLOTS

| Daily Output of Wheat | Marginal Damage to Wheat for Meat Output of | | | Daily Output of Meat | Marginal Damage to Wheat for Wheat Output of | | |
|---|---|---|---|---|---|---|---|
| | 2 | 3 | 4 | | 2 | 3 | 4 |
| 1 | $1.00 | $1.50 | $2.00 | 1 | $1.00 | $1.50 | $2.00 |
| 2 | 1.00 | 1.50 | 2.00 | 2 | 1.00 | 1.50 | 2.00 |
| 3 | 1.00 | 1.50 | 2.00 | 3 | 1.00 | 1.50 | 2.00 |
| 4 | 1.00 | 1.50 | 2.00 | 4 | 1.00 | 1.50 | 2.00 |
| 5 | 1.00 | 1.50 | 2.00 | 5 | 1.00 | 1.50 | 2.00 |

There might be some way of keeping the cattle off the wheat land—for example, a fence—that would yield a higher quasi-rent than $13.50, but whether there is or not will not affect the main line of argument about to be made. Therefore, let us suppose that there is not.

The interesting thing is that the entrepreneur will charge marginal dam-

merical example (R. H. Coase, *supra* note 1, at 3), but he discusses at some length the dependence of damage on the presence of persons to be damaged in the case of the factory emitting smoke (*id.* at 41-42).

[7] For the reason given in the preceding footnote, Coase argues that the wheat crop will not change (*id.* at 3-4).

[8] Alternatively, the damaged wheat (0.9 unit) could be subtracted from gross output to yield a net output of 2.1. Total receipts would be $40.50, total costs $27.00, and quasi-rent $13.50. Damage is taken instead as a cost in order to facilitate the line of argument to follow.

TABLE 3

MARGINAL COST[a] OF PRODUCING WHEAT AND MEAT ON ADJOINING PLOTS

| Daily Output of Wheat | Marginal Cost for Meat Output of | | | Daily Output of Meat | Marginal Cost for Wheat Output of | | |
|---|---|---|---|---|---|---|---|
| | 2 | 3 | 4 | | 2 | 3 | 4 |
| 1 | $2.50 | $3.00 | $3.50 | 1 | $ 7.50 | $ 8.00 | $ 8.50 |
| 2 | 3.50 | 4.00 | 4.50 | 2 | 8.50 | 9.00 | 9.50 |
| 3 | 4.50 | 5.00 | 5.50 | 3 | 9.50 | 10.00 | 10.50 |
| 4 | 5.50 | 6.00 | 6.50 | 4 | 10.50 | 11.00 | 11.50 |
| 5 | 6.50 | 7.00 | 7.50 | 5 | 11.50 | 12.00 | 12.50 |

[a] Marginal cost from Table 1 plus marginal damage from Table 2.

ages against *both* wheat and meat in calculating his optimum combination of output, whereas the damage is in fact a joint cost that needs to be covered only once by the total value of the joint product. Marginal damage as calculated by the producer is not an alternative cost to him since it does not reflect the value of resources that can be put to some alternative use. It is instead a purely internal cost to this joint venture. It is most properly considered as a charge against economic rent, not as a cost in the normal sense.

We may see why this is so by considering the question: Under what conditions will the entrepreneur grow wheat and cattle on the adjoining plots? The answer is, of course, that he will do so only if each plot, taken separately, would yield a quasi-rent of no more than $3.38 ($13.50 minus $10.12) in the best alternative use to which it could be put without imposing a joint cost on both activities—that is, without generating a nuisance. He might, for example, grow wheat on the wheat land and corn on the cattle land. Since the quasi-rent on the wheat land would be $10.12, he would engage in the wheat-corn enterprise if the quasi-rent on the cattle land exceeded $3.38 when used to grow corn, so that the total quasi-rent exceeded $13.50, the amount in the wheat-cattle enterprise. Similarly, he would undertake a cattle-horse enterprise if growing horses on the wheat land would yield a quasi-rent on that land of more than $3.38.

Let the alternative cost of each plot taken separately be exactly $3.38. The one plot then has an economic rent of $6.74 ($10.12 minus $3.38) in growing wheat, and the other has the same economic rent in growing cattle.[9] The existence of rent for each plot is a necessary condition for the undertaking of the cattle-wheat venture. With an alternative cost of $3.38 for each plot, it is a matter of indifference to both the entrepreneur and the economy whether these two plots are used for cattle and wheat, for cattle and the

[9] It is an accident of our example that rent turns out to be the same in either case. In general, in order for the wheat-cattle enterprise to be undertaken, the rent for that joint use of land has to be at least equal to the higher of the two rents on wheat and cattle land taken separately.

next best "non-nuisance-generating" alternative to wheat, or for wheat and the next best "non-nuisance-generating" alternative to cattle. Each would involve an economic rent of $6.74, attributable in the first case to both plots jointly, in the second to the cattle plot, and in the third to the wheat plot.

The decision of whether to engage in the cattle-wheat enterprise or of how much wheat and meat to produce will not be affected by the way in which the joint cost of damaged wheat is distributed between the two parts of the enterprise. The gross economic rent attributable to each plot of land will be calculated as follows:

| | Wheat | Meat |
|---|---|---|
| Value of output | $15.00 | $30.00 |
| Minus cost of production | | |
| Inputs except land | 6.00 | 21.00 |
| Land | 3.38 | 3.38 |
| Gross economic rent to land | $ 5.62 | $ 5.62 |

To derive the net rent of $6.74, total damage of $4.50 in the form of trampled wheat must be charged against the total gross rent of $11.24. If the damage is charged to wheat, the net rent is distributed as $1.12 to wheat land and $5.62 to cattle land. If the damage is charged to cattle, the figures are reversed. The alternative ways of accounting for the damage affect the distribution of rent alone. They do not affect the allocation of resources.

It is clear that the same reasoning applies to separate enterprises growing wheat and meat on these adjoining plots. If the sum of managerial and transaction costs are lower for two enterprises than managerial costs are alone for a joint enterprise, the former will prevail over the latter under competitive conditions. The legal rule defining which firm is to be responsible for the (joint) nuisance will affect nothing but the distribution of economic rent between the two plots of land.

This conclusion does not appear so strange when we recognize that a combination of activities generating a nuisance will not be introduced into a perfectly competitive economy unless that combination yields at least as large a net value of output as any other uses of the same resources would yield. Put another way, the nuisance will come into existence only if output rises by at least enough to compensate for it. In order for this to be the case, each of the activities in the combination must impart an economic rent to some resource employed by the combination of activities.

The necessary prior existence of rent ensures, then, that the Coase theorem applies to the long as well as the short run.

# [16]

# TRANSACTION COSTS, RESOURCE ALLOCATION AND LIABILITY RULES—A COMMENT*

*GUIDO CALABRESI*
*Yale Law School*

IN his article on "The Problem of Social Cost" Professor Coase argued that (assuming no transaction costs) the same allocation of resources will come about regardless of which of two joint cost causers is initially charged with the cost, in other words regardless of liability rules.[1] Various writers—including me—accepted that conclusion for the short run, but had doubts about its validity in the long run situation. The argument was that even if transactions brought about the same short run allocation, liability rules would affect the relative wealth of the two joint cost causing activities, and in the long run this would affect the relative number of firms and hence the relative output of the activities.[2]

Further thought has convinced me that if one assumes no transaction costs—including no costs of excluding from the benefits the free loaders, that is, those who would gain from a bargain but who are unwilling to pay to bring it about—and if one assumes, as one must, rationality and no legal impediments to bargaining, Coase's analysis must hold for the long run as well as the short run. The reason is simply that (on the given assumptions) the same type of transactions which cured the short run misallocation would also occur to cure the long run ones. For example, if we assume that the cost of factory smoke which destroys neighboring farmers' wheat can be avoided more cheaply by a smoke control device than by growing a smoke resistant wheat, then, even if the loss is left on the farmers they will, under the assumptions made, pay the factory to install the smoke control device. This would, in the short run, result in more factories relative to farmers and lower relative farm output than if the liability rule had been reversed. But if, as a result of this liability rule, farm output is too low relative to factory output those who lose from this "misallocation" would have every reason

* I am particularly indebted to Professor R. H. Coase of Chicago, and Professor Ward Bowman, of Yale, with each of whom I have discussed parts of this comment.

1 Coase, The Problem of Social Cost, 3 J. Law & Econ. 1 (1960).

2 See, for example, Calabresi, The Decision for Accidents: An Approach to Nonfault Allocation of Costs, 78 Harv. L. Rev. 713, 730 n.28, 731 n.30 (1965) and Calabresi, Fault, Accidents and the Wonderful World of Blum and Kalven, 75 Yale L.J. 216, 231-232 and accompanying footnotes (1965).

to bribe farmers to produce more and factories to produce less. This process would continue until no bargain could improve the allocation of resources.

The interesting thing about this analysis, however, is that there is no reason whatsoever to limit it to joint cost causers. Thus, if one assumes rationality, no transaction costs, and no legal impediments to bargaining, *all* misallocations of resources would be fully cured in the market by bargains.[3] Far from being surprising, this statement is tautological, at least if one accepts any of the various classic definitions of misallocation. These ultimately come down to a statement akin to the following: A misallocation exists when there is available a possible reallocation in which all those who would lose from the reallocation could be fully compensated by those who would gain, and, at the end of this compensation process, there would still be some who would be better off than before.

This and other similar definitions of resource misallocation merely mean that there is a misallocation when a situation can be improved by bargains. If people are rational, bargains are costless, and there are no legal impediments to bargains, transactions will *ex hypothesis* occur to the point where bargains can no longer improve the situation; to the point, in short, of optimal resource allocation.[4] We can, therefore, state as an axiom the proposition that all externalities can be internalized and all misallocations, even those created by legal structures, can be remedied by the market, except to the extent that transactions cost money or the structure itself creates some impediments to bargaining.[5]

It may be that this welfare economics analogue to Say's law has always been quite obvious to economists, although if it has its relevance has too frequently been ignored. In any event, lawyers who use economics have in

[3] See note 5 *infra.*

[4] Any given individual qua individual might well be richer or poorer as a result of the liability rules in force at the beginning of the bargaining process. But this difference in distribution of wealth would *ex hypothesis* not be one which would affect total social product.

[5] By transaction costs, I have in mind costs like those of getting large numbers of people together to bargain, and costs of excluding free loaders. But one may properly ask the question: in what way are these qualitatively different from the cost of establishing a bargain between two parties, i.e., the cost of walking over and dickering? And if they are not, then how are they different from common selling costs, which we all assume the market normally handles optimally? Perhaps the difference is a qualitative one which escapes me. If it is not, it may be that as to normal selling costs, or costs of one-for-one dickering we readily accept the probably justifiable empirical conclusion that no substitute for the market can achieve a similar result as cheaply. But see e.g., Calabresi, The Decision for Accidents, 78 Harv. L. Rev. 713, 725-729 (1965), and Calabresi, Fault, Accidents and the Wonderful World of Blum and Kalven, 75 Yale L.J. 216, 223-231 (1965) (suggesting that liability rules may occasionally be crucial even in these cases). With the kinds of costs which Coase seems to call transaction costs, that conclusion, though possibly often still valid, cannot be accepted without more data. See Coase, *supra* note 1.

virtually every case been hopelessly confused on the subject.[6] For this reason, if no other, it is worthwhile elaborating on the practical implications of the proposition.

The primary implication is that problems of misallocation of resources and externalities are not theoretical but empirical ones. The resource allocation aim is to approximate, both closely and cheaply, the result the market would bring about if bargaining actually were costless.[7] The question then becomes: Is this accomplished most accurately and most cheaply by structural rules (like anti-trust laws), by liability rules, by taxation and governmental spending, by letting the market have free play or by some combination of these? This question depends in large part on the relative *cost* of reaching the correct result by each of these means (an empirical problem which probably could be resolved, at least approximately, in most instances), and the relative *chances* of reaching a widely *wrong* result depending on the method used (also an empirical problem but one as to which it is hard to get other than "guess" type data). The resolution of these two problems and their interplay is *the* problem of accomplishing optimal resource allocations.

Two points are implied in the foregoing discussion. The first is that since transactions do cost money, and since substitutes for transactions, be they taxation, liability rules, or structural rules, are also not costless, the "optimal" result is not necessarily the same as if transactions were costless. Whatever device is used, the question must be asked: Are its costs worth the benefits in better resource allocations it brings about or have we instead approached a false optimum by a series of games which are not worth the candles used? This does not mean, though, that the actual optimum is necessarily the one an unaided market would reach. Further market improvements may well be prohibitive at a stage where laws and their enforcement are still a relatively cheap way of getting nearer the goal.[8]

The second point is that both the unreachable goal of "that point which would be reached if transactions were costless," and the gains which reaching nearer the goal would bring are not usually subject to precise definition or

[6] One notable recent exception is Professor Frank I. Michaelman. See Michaelman, Property, Utility and Fairness: Comments on the Ethical Foundations of "Just Compensation" Law, 80 Harv. L. Rev. 1165, 1172-1176 (1967).

[7] Professor Harold Demsetz in a very provocative article has recently suggested that the institution of private property and its protection by the law can be explained in these terms. Demsetz, Toward a Theory of Property Rights, 57 Am. Econ. Ass'n. Pap. & Proc. 347 (1967). Surprisingly, he does not suggest that one of the examples which he gives of externalities not internalized by private property, that of factory smoke pollution, might also be handled by a change in property rights, that is, by making the factory owner liable for the smoke, *id.* at 357. This might resolve the problem if transaction costs were significantly lower if the factory owner were initially liable than if homeowners bore the loss, a not unlikely hypothesis.

[8] See Demsetz, *supra* note 7.

quantification. They are, in fact, largely defined by guesses. As a result, the question of whether a given law is worth its costs (in terms of better resource allocation) is rarely susceptible to empirical proof. This does not mean, of course, that the best we can do is adopt a laissez faire policy and let the market do the best it can. It is precisely the province of good government to make guesses as to what laws are likely to be worth their costs. Hopefully it will use what empirical information is available and seek to develop empirical information which is not currently available (how much information is worth *its* costs is also a question, however). But there is no reason to assume that in the absence of conclusive information no government action is better than some action. This is especially so if the guesses made take into account two factors. The first is: Action in an uncertain case is more likely to be justified if the market can correct an error resulting from the proposed action more cheaply than it could an error resulting from inaction. The second is: Action in an uncertain case is more likely to be justified if goals *other* than resource allocation (like proper income distribution) are served by the action. In effect the first factor says, in uncertainty increase the chances of correcting an error, while the second says, the achievement of other goals is accomplished very cheaply where the most that can be said about the resource allocation effect of a move is that we cannot be *sure* that it will be favorable.[9]

The relevance of the foregoing analysis may be seen in various areas of government intervention. I shall briefly mention three because they have brought forth different governmental responses: (1) the monopoly area, (2) highways or parks, (3) automobile accidents.

(1) Why should we have laws which attempt to control monopolies? Assuming no transaction costs, those who lose from the relative underproduction of monopolies could bribe monopolists to produce more. We know, however, that such market action is usually unrealistic—that is, it would be too expensive relative to the benefits it would bring. The problem of excluding free loaders, would—absent any other problems—suffice to make it so. We believe that a series of structural rules, a series of laws in this

[9] Some may argue that other goals, like income redistribution, are best achieved not through *ad hoc* decisions but rather as part of a general policy implemented through devices (like some forms of progressive taxation) chosen with the goal specifically in mind. Even if this position is accepted, it is possible that a general policy in favor of a particular distribution of income could be arrived at and its implementation be intentionally left to particular cases where no provably adverse resource allocation effects would come about. This would be especially attractive to those who accept the view that most forms of progressive taxation misallocate resources.

The mention of other goals may suggest that their benefits can be established with substantial certainty. That obviously is not so, but the process of deciding whether to accomplish these goals does not, in our society, seem to depend on the ability of social scientists to prove their desirability with substantial certainty.

case, are cheaper than market correction would be, and more important, we believe they are cheap enough to be worth having. This last belief involves certain guesses about what a "costless" market would do, and what the gains of approaching that goal by legislation are. Even if we assume that these guesses are in large terms fairly supported by empirical information, we certainly reach a point where the putative gains of further more stringent legislation or of more stringent enforcement are hard to justify in terms of the costs of such programs. In such a situation how far we go cannot help but be affected, and properly so, by what other goals—like dilution of power, or income redistribution—we think a further step will accomplish. Far from being irrelevant, these factors may be made an integral part of the law, if not the economics, of antitrust.[10]

(2) The question of why we have public highways is not totally dissimilar. One can view the decision to have public highways as the product of certain assumptions about what people would do if there were no transaction costs. These assumptions are largely guess work—perhaps even more guess work than in the monopoly case. As in the monopoly situation, government intervention is believed to bring us nearer, and more cheaply, to what a costless market would establish than would the real market. The reason may be that exclusion of free loaders seems substantially more expensive than compulsion of payment by all putative gainers, including would-be free loaders. The result is taxation, in part, of those who supposedly gain from the presence of a better highway system. I say in part, because here again the guesses made are inevitably affected by other goals. "Free" parks can be analyzed in the same way. The validity of the assumptions, the availability of empirical information and the effect of other goals may be quite different. But the basic analysis remains the same.

(3) The case of automobile accidents is somewhat more complex. It presents in fairly typical fashion the problem of multiple cost causers. As such it raises quite clearly the issue of short and long run misallocations, and the issue of which governmental interventions are, if incorrect, more subject to market corrections.

Assume that the cheapest short run way of minimizing the sum of accident costs and of the costs of avoiding accidents involving pedestrians and cars is to have rubber bumpers rather than to have pedestrians wear fluorescent clothes. In a world of costless transactions rubber bumpers would become established in the market regardless of liability rules, regardless of whether

10 Obviously there are also many cases where these other goals are pursued without regard to possible adverse resource allocation effects. My object in this comment is not to criticize or even to discuss such situations. Mine is a minimalist position and suggests only that taking such other goals into account is justified where doing so gives rise to no provable adverse resource allocation effects.

cars or pedestrians bore the loss initially. Since transactions cost money, the short run effect would in fact be quite different, depending on who was held liable. Making the car owner liable would establish the proper number of rubber bumpers. This would be the desired short run resource allocation, unless, of course, the cost of establishing car owner liability were too great relative to the gains it brought about.[11] But making the car owner liable also has long run effects affecting the relative number of cars and pedestrians. Our assumption as to the best short run liability bearer does not carry with it any guarantee that the car owners are the best long run bearers. It might be that in a world of no transaction costs rubber bumpers would be established, but more cars relative to pedestrians would be desired than would come about if liability were placed on car owners.

Depending on how sure we are of our long and short run guesses, this problem can be handled by using different devices. For example, the short run allocation could be accomplished by a car-owner liability rule, while the long run hypothetical misallocation could be corrected by a subsidy to car makers raised from taxes on pedestrians. But the sureness necessary to justify this subsidy, in the absence of nonresource allocation goals which might support it, seems very hard to come by.

The automobile accident situation also raises the point that different devices for accomplishing seemingly "optimal" resource allocation vary in desirability depending on their relative costs and on the relative likelihood of error in our guess work. Returning to the rubber bumper example, if we are perfectly sure that rubber bumpers are always the cheapest way of minimizing the sum of car-pedestrian accident costs and the costs of avoiding such accidents, it seems likely that the cheapest way of getting rubber bumpers is by a law that requires them, rather than by liability rules. It is quite a different thing if the "cheapest way" is more complex and involves some rubber bumpers, and some more careful driving by owners without rubber bumpers.

This in turn suggests another factor in the decision. Suppose we are not sure whether rubber bumpers or wearing fluorescent clothing is the "cheapest way" of handling the car-pedestrian accident problem. In this case it may become necessary to consider the following question: Is an erroneous placing of liability on car owners or an erroneous placing of liability on pedestrians more likely to be corrected in the market? Whether car owners (or car makers) can bribe pedestrians more cheaply than pedestrians can bribe car owners or makers, becomes the relevant issue. Similarly, it becomes crucial to

[11] This caveat has a long history in torts law and is in large part the basis of Holmes' famous justification of the fault system. See Holmes, The Common Law, 94-96 (1881). Needless to say, the caveat is perfectly valid even if it fails, as I believe it does, to justify the fault-liability system today.

decide whether an error brought about by a "liability rule" is more subject to market correction than an error resulting from a law requiring a particular type of rubber bumper.

Clearly this sketchy description of the automobile accident problem (like those of monopoly and highways) can only indicate the range and complexity of the issues involved in deciding whom to hold liable, and what safety devices to require. A full analysis of the resource allocation issue in auto accidents has, to my knowledge, not yet been attempted. A fully adequate decision would clearly require immense amounts of empirical data. But here (as in the monopoly and highway cases) the lawyer cannot wait for near certainty. He must propose solutions which seem to be the best on the basis of data and impressions currently available. And here too he will be aided in making practical proposals by the fact that goals other than optimal resource allocations may give clear indications of the desirable course in situations where resource allocations policy gives only a hint. One such goal may well be the often mentioned goal of "adequate" loss spreading (which is, in fact, closely analogous to the income distribution policy).

The conclusion is that Coase's analysis, read as a kind of Say's law of welfare economics, gives us an admirable tool for suggesting what kind of empirical data would be useful in making resource allocation decisions, and for indicating what kinds of guesses are likely to be justifiably made in the absence of convincing data. Some may take Coase's analysis to suggest that little or no government intervention is usually the best rule. My own conclusions are quite different. His analysis, combined with common intuitions or guesses as to the relative costs of transactions, taxation, structural rules and liability rules, can go far to explain various types of heretofore inadequately justified governmental actions. This is especially so if one considers the relevance of goals other than resource allocations to those situations where inadequate data makes resource allocations an unsatisfactory guide. Perhaps more precise data will some day prove some of these interventions to be improper from the standpoint of resource allocation. Then we shall have to choose, as we often do, between the bigger pie and other aims. Coase's analysis certainly suggests situations where this has been done. Its principal importance lies, however, in helping to delineate those areas of uncertainty where more facts would help us make better resource allocation judgments, and where, at least in the absence of more facts, the lawyer must be guided by guess work as to what the facts are and by goals other than resource allocations in suggesting workable solutions for problems which cannot wait till all the facts are in.

# [17]

# WHEN DOES THE RULE OF LIABILITY MATTER?

*HAROLD DEMSETZ**

THE active interface between law and economics has been limited largely to antitrust and regulation, but recent work, primarily in economics, has revealed a much wider area of common interest. The new development, which deals with the definition and structure of property rights, has implications for central areas of the law, such as real property, torts, and contracts, although it originated in an economic analysis of the divergence between private and social cost. While still in its embryonic stage, the analysis has proceeded far enough for it to be called to the attention of a wider audience.

The questions with which we shall be concerned are whether and under what conditions a legal decision about liability affects the uses to which resources will be put and the distribution of wealth between owners of resources. If ranchers are held liable for the damage done by their cattle to corn fields, how will the outputs of meat and corn be affected? If drivers or pedestrians, alternatively, are held liable for automobile-pedestrian accidents, how will the accident rate be affected? What implications for extortion (an extreme form of wealth redistribution) are found in the decision about who is liable for damages?

## I.

Recent developments in this area began with an article by Professor R. H. Coase.[1] Coase's work presented a penetrating criticism of the conventional treatment by economists of divergences between private and social cost. The social cost of furthering an economic activity is the resulting reduction in the value of production that is obtainable from other activities. Such reductions occur because the resources required to further an activity are scarce and must be diverted from other possible uses. According to the view that Coase challenged, social cost, being the sum total of the costs incurred to carry on any activity, might very well differ from private cost. For example, the so-

* Professor of Business Economics, Law School and Graduate School of Business, University of Chicago. The author wishes to thank the Charles R. Walgreen Foundation for financial aid through its grant to the University of Chicago, and, also, the Lilly Endowment through its grant to the University of California.

[1] R. H. Coase, The Problem of Social Cost, 3 J. Law & Econ. 1 (1960).

cial cost of running steam locomotives properly includes the fire damage done to surrounding farm crops by sparks from the locomotive. If the railroad is not required to pay for these damages, perhaps through a tax per train, then, according to the conventional analysis, the railroad would not take account of crop damage costs in deciding how many trains to run. In the absence of a specific public policy to intervene, the rate at which an activity is carried forth, which is determined solely by private cost, would diverge from the optimum rate, which is determined by social cost. In the present example, the private cost of running additional trains, being less than the social cost because crop damage is not taken into account, would encourage the railroad to run too many trains per day. The conventional economic analysis called for the levy of a tax per train, equivalent to the damages, in order to bring social cost and private cost into equality.

Coase demonstrated that the imposition of such a tax could, in some circumstances, aggravate the difficulty, but two other aspects of his work are of more concern to us. Coase (1) showed that powerful market forces exist that tend to bring private and social cost into equality without the use of a tax, and (2) discussed the conditions under which the legal position toward liability for damages would and would not alter the allocation of resources. Coase discusses an interaction between two productive activities, ranching and farming, in the context of a competitive regime in which the cost of transacting (or negotiating) is assumed to be zero.[2] His analysis concludes that social cost and private cost will be brought into equality through market negotiations—and this regardless of which party is assigned the responsibility for bearing the cost that results from the proximity of ranching and farming.

The law, reasoning that crops *stand in the way* of a neighbor's cattle, can leave the farmer to bear the cost of crop damage; alternatively, reasoning that cattle *stray errantly* across farm fields, the law can assign liability for crop damages to ranchers. Coase's work demonstrates that either legal position will result in the same resource allocation—*i.e.*, in the same quantities of corn and meat—and, also, that negotiations between the parties to the damage will, with either legal position, eliminate any divergence between private and social cost. If the law favors ranchers by leaving farmers to bear the cost of crop damage, then there exist incentives for farmers to pay ranchers to reduce the sizes of the herds, or to take other measures that will reduce the amount of damage. A summary arithmetic example reveals how such market transactions lead to Coase's results.

Suppose that the net return to an owner of ranchland would be increased by $50 if herd size were increased by one head of cattle but that the additional

[2] *Id.* at 2-8.

head of cattle would impose corn damage on the owner of neighboring farmland that reduced his net return by $60. If the law did *not* require the rancher to compensate the farmer, the farmer would offer to pay the rancher a sum up to $60, the damage he would suffer if the rancher increased his herd by one head. The rancher would accept the offer since any amount above $50 would be more than ample compensation for the reduction in net returns associated with the smaller herd size.

Negotiations would continue until the net return to the rancher of a head of cattle exceeded the reduction in net return to the farmer associated with the damage done by that head of cattle. Such negotiations would bring the total value of corn and beef produced to a maximum since herd size would be reduced only when the consequent increase in the net value of corn output ($60 in the above example) exceeded the decrease in the net value of beef output ($50 in the example) required to reduce crop damage.

If the rule of liability were the reverse, requiring the owner of ranchland to compensate the farmer for the crop damage, the same equilibrium would be reached. Since the rancher earns a net return of only $50 and must pay damages of $60 if he raises an additional head of cattle, he would find it in his interest not to increase the size of his herd. Moreover, he would reduce the size of his herd as long as the net return forgone was smaller than the resulting increase in the net return to farming since this would be the liability to him if he did not reduce herd size by another unit. He would be led to settle upon the same herd size, with the same consequence for crop size, as he would have chosen in the absence of liability. The mix of output is not changed[3] because negotiations between the parties eliminate all divergence between private and social cost.

The resulting equality between social and private cost is important enough to warrant a few more words. The conventional analysis of the farmer-rancher interaction would have concluded that in the absence of liability for damage (or of an appropriate tax per head of cattle) the social cost of increasing herd size would have exceeded the rancher's private cost by the $60 damage done to the neighboring farmer's crops. The rancher, if he were neither held liable nor taxed, would have no reason to take account of this damage and would

[3] I ignore other possibilities such as building a fence. These are discussed by Coase (*id.* at 3). Consideration of them changes the exposition but not the results.

One further assumption is required for the mix of output to remain unchanged. Any redistribution of wealth resulting from a change in the rule of liability is assumed to have no consequences for the demands for the products produced. Owners of farmland and ranchland should be vegetarians in equal proportions, for otherwise a redistribution of wealth between these two groups would alter the market demands for corn and beef and thereby indirectly alter the mix of output produced. The wealth redistribution problem will be discussed later when we turn to the subject of extortion.

therefore be led to raise too many cattle and impose too much damage on farm crops. It is the supposed existence of this gap between private and social cost that seems to call for a tax per head of cattle or for an assignment of liability to the rancher. Coase's reasoning shows this logic to be in error. Even in the absence of a tax or liability for damage, the harmful effects of his activities on surrounding crops would be brought to bear on the private calculations of the owner of ranchland, for he must reckon as a true (but implicit) cost of increasing herd size the payment from the farmer that he must forgo if he refuses to agree to the farmer's request for a reduction in herd size. Market negotiations bring the full cost of his decision to bear on him through the offers made by the farmer and thereby eliminate any difference between private and social cost. This, as Coase recognized, would not be true if the cost of negotiating could not be assumed to be negligible. We shall return to this problem later.

It is not generally appreciated that Coase's reasoning has legal applications that extend beyond problems of the divergence between social and private cost as these typically are conceived. What is at issue in the farmer-rancher case is which party has a particular property right. In the one case the farmer has the right to allow or prohibit cattle grazing on certain specified lands, while in the other case it is the rancher who has the right. Private property takes the form of a bundle of rights, of which different components may be held by different persons. In the absence of significant negotiating cost, the use to which these property rights is put is independent of the identities of the owners since each owner will be given market incentives to use his property right in the most valuable way. Just what is the most valuable way depends on market conditions and not owner identities.

The analysis can be extended to many types of property right problems. One that is of current interest to lawyers is the continuing litigation about the legal status of the reserve clause in organized baseball. An important defense of the reserve clause has been the assertion that it prevents wealthy baseball clubs from acquiring too large a share of the good players. By applying the above analysis to this problem it is possible to refute the assertion, especially since the cost of negotiations would seem to be negligible in this case. For what is at issue is whether the identity of the owner of a player's baseball services will alter the location of his playing activities. An application of Coase's analysis to this problem suggests that the reserve clause should have no effect on the identity of the team for which a player plays.

When signing initially with a major league organization, a player owns his baseball talent in the sense that he has the right to offer his services for sale to any ball club. But once he signs with a major league club, he can no longer negotiate with other clubs for the sale of his services, although he retains the right to refuse to play. The reserve clause, which is written into every major league contract, requires major league clubs who wish to acquire the services of a player who is already under contract to purchase his contract from the club currently owning it. Thus, once a player signs with a major league organization, part of the bundle of property rights to his services are transferred from the player to the club with which he signs. The right to play on various teams passes via the reserve clause from the player to the club owning his contract, and this club can reserve the player for its own use even though other teams might be willing to pay the player more than he is receiving.

The question considered here is *not* whether there exists a correlation between the wealth of a club and the quality of its players. The relevant question is whether the distribution of players among teams would change were the reserve clause to be declared illegal. Would wealthier clubs acquire more good players if the right to negotiate with other teams always resided with the player?[4]

In the absence of the reserve clause, a player would change clubs only if he found it in his interest to do so. With the reserve clause, a player will change clubs only if the club that owns his contract finds it in its interest. It appears that a different pattern of player migration between clubs might exist with the reserve clause than without it. But the appearance is deceptive. No matter who owns the right to sell the contract for the services of a baseball player, the distribution of players among teams will remain the same.

To see why this is so, assume that a player *not* subject to the reserve clause receives a $15,000 per annum wage from club A for which he currently plays. Club B offers him $16,000 to play for them. If this amount exceeds the value of the player to club A, the club will not find it in its interest to make a counteroffer large enough to retain the player's services and he will join club B. However, if his services are worth more than $16,000 to club A, the club will find it in its interest to make a counteroffer large enough to retain his services. With no reserve clause the player plays for the club that most highly values[5] his services.

Let us now suppose that the reserve clause is effective and, as before, that

[4] The reserve clause and other aspects of organized baseball are discussed in Simon Rottenberg, The Baseball Players' Labor Market, 64 J. Pol. Econ. 242 (1956). The reasoning employed by Rottenberg is similar but not identical to the above argument. Rottenberg's argument is based partly on the premise, not used here, that it takes two fairly well matched teams to produce a good game.

[5] Nonpecuniary aspects of his employment are discussed later, but it should be noted that the argument for retention of the reserve clause is not based on nonpecuniary job amenities.

the player is currently paid $15,000 by club A. Club B now offers club A $1,000 per annum (or its present value equivalent) for the player's contract, so that if the negotiations succeed club B will pay $16,000 for the player's services of which $15,000 is paid to the player under the terms of the purchased contract and $1,000 is paid to club A. If $1,000 per annum exceeds the player's net value to club A after it pays his $15,000 annual salary, then it will be in club A's interest to sell his contract to club B, but if the player is worth more to club A than $16,000 (equal to the $1,000 offer from club B plus the player's $15,000 salary), it will refuse to sell his contract.

The condition under which the player is transferred to club B when he is subject to the reserve clause is precisely the condition under which he will elect to transfer to club B when he is not subject to the reserve clause. He transfers to club B if club B finds his services more valuable than does club A whether or not the reserve clause is in effect. The reserve clause, therefore, cannot be expected to result in a different distribution of players among teams than would prevail in its absence.

The reader may object, suggesting that nonpecuniary considerations might make the distribution of players different depending on the legal status of the reserve clause. But this objection also would be in error. Suppose that the player, presently owned by a California club, has developed a preference for working in California. If there were no reserve clause, his preference would lead him to ask at least $1,000 more to play ball with a Chicago club than he earns playing for a California club; and, in the absence of a reserve clause, a Chicago club would need to bid $1,000 more than a California club to obtain his services. But this is also true with the reserve clause. Under reserve clause arrangements, suppose that the Chicago club offers the California club only $500 more than the player's net value to the California club. The California club, indeed, will be tempted to sell the player's contract to Chicago. It appears that the $500 increment, which would be too small to move the player were there no reserve clause, is large enough to move him if there is a reserve clause. This is incorrect because the player, when working under the reserve clause arrangement, would be willing to offer a sum of up to $1,000 (the value of the nonpecuniary amenities to him of California) to the California club to induce it to refuse to sell his contract to Chicago. Any amount above $500 would be sufficient to make the California club reject Chicago's offer since Chicago is offering only $500 more than the player is worth to the California club. (The player can "offer" such an amount by accepting a pay reduction.) With or without the reserve clause, then, the player will locate where the value he places on amenities plus the value of his baseball talent is greatest.

## II

The significance of Coase's work quickly led to critical responses by Wellisz,[6] Calabresi,[7] and others, although Calabresi withdrew his criticism in a later paper.[8] The criticism centered around two allegations—that the Coase theorem neglects long-run considerations that negate it and that the spirit of the work endorses the use of resources for the undesirable purpose of "extortion." The long-run issue is discussed here and the "extortion" problem in Part III. In Part IV, I discuss the problems introduced when the assumption of negligible transaction cost is dropped.

The question of long-run considerations has been raised because it would seem that different liability rules would alter the profitability of remaining inside or outside each industry. It is alleged that if farmers are left to bear the cost that arises from proximity to cattle, the rate of return to farming will fall and resources will therefore leave the farming industry. Alternatively, if ranchers are left to bear the cost, the resulting reduction in rate of return to ranching will lead to the exit of resources from that industry. Hence, even if transaction cost is zero, the market will allocate resources differently in the long run depending upon which rule of liability is chosen.

But short-run versus long-run considerations should have no bearing on the Coase theorem, which is based on the proposition that an implicit cost (the forgone payment from the farmer) is just as much a cost as is an explicit cost (the liability damage), and this proposition surely must hold in the long run as well as in the short run. One way of demonstrating this is by allowing the two activities to be merged under a common owner. A detailed example of this is given by G. Warren Nutter.[9] If there is no special cost to operating a multiproduct firm, the costly interaction between farming and ranching will be fully brought to the owner's attention in his operation of a farming-ranching enterprise. The mix of output that he produces will be that which maximizes his earnings. The rule of liability that is chosen can have no effect on his decisions because the owner of such a firm must bear the interaction cost whichever legal rule is adopted. The cost interdependence is a technical-economic interdependence, not a legal one. Since such merged operations are possible, the rule of liability is rendered irrelevant to the

[6] Stanislaw Wellisz, On External Diseconomies and the Government Assisted Invisible Hand, 31 Economica (N.S.) 345 (1964).

[7] Guido Calabresi, The Decision for Accidents: An Approach to Nonfault Allocation of Costs, 78 Harv. L. Rev. 713 (1965).

[8] Guido Calabresi, Transaction Costs, Resource Allocation and Liability Rules—A Comment, 11 J. Law & Econ. 67 (1968).

[9] G. Warren Nutter, The Coase Theorem on Social Cost: A Footnote, 11 J. Law & Econ. 503 (1968).

choice of output mix. But a refutation of the criticism that is based on the use of the joint product enterprise gives rise to the (incorrect) suspicion that the basic problem has been begged, since the rule of liability that is chosen cannot in this case alter the wealth of the owner of a farming-ranching enterprise. The spirit of the argument can be preserved, while the suspicion is allayed, by assuming that the advantages offered by specialization of ownership are so great that it is uneconomic to merge the two activities into a single ranching-farming firm.

If owners of farmland bear the cost of crop damage, what must be the cost conditions that are associated with an equilibrium allocation of land to farming, ranching, and other uses? For such damage to arise there must be a sufficient scarcity of land to force farms and ranches into proximity. Marginal farm acreage (acreage that just "breaks even") must earn revenue sufficient to cover all cost, including the cost of crop damage done by straying cattle. Suppose the proximity of ranching and farming reduces the net return to the owner of farmland by $100 as compared with what could be earned were there no neighboring ranch. If ranching continues on the neighboring acres, it must be true that the net return to the owner of the ranchland exceeds $100, for otherwise the farmer would have been able to purchase the removal of cattle from neighboring land by offering $100 to the neighboring ranchers. The reduction in net return to farming brought about because of crop damage is thus implicitly taken into account by the owner of the ranchland when he refuses the offer of the owner of the neighboring farmland. The money offered by the farmer is refused by the rancher precisely because the continued use of the land for grazing brings in additional net revenue in excess of $100.

Land that is submarginal as farm or ranchland (land that cannot be profitably farmed or ranched) is unable to earn revenue sufficient to cover the explicit $100 damage cost if it is put to the plough or the $100 implicit cost if it is employed in ranching. Were this land to be employed in farming, its owner would suffer losses attributable in part to the damage done to his crops by straying cattle, whereas if it were employed in ranching its owner would suffer the implicit loss of forgoing a $100 payment from the neighboring farmer (the owners of farmland bearing the cost of crop damage). Submarginal land by definition can be neither farmed nor ranched profitably.

Now let the rule of liability be changed so that ranchers become liable for crop damage. If there is to be a long-run effect, it must be true that the cost interrelationships change in a manner that causes either the conversion of ranchland to farmland or submarginal land to farmland. But neither conversion can be made profitable by the change in liability.

Acreage that was marginally profitable in ranching must remain ranchland because it had been earning net revenues in excess of the $100 damages done by cattle to surrounding farmland. If a producing ranch were to be switched from ranching to farming to avoid the new liability its owner would forgo revenues (in excess of $100) that exceeded the resulting reduction in liability ($100). The owner of what was marginal ranchland, therefore, will continue to employ his land in ranching under the new liability rule.

The land that previously was submarginal must remain submarginal. The changed liability rule will not attract this land into farming. Submarginal lands under the original rule of liability earned insufficient revenues in farming to cover the $100 cost of crop damage. Under the new rule of liability, neighboring ranchers will succeed in negotiating with the owners of this land to keep it out of farming. Operating ranches, under the old rule of liability, had been yielding net revenues in excess of $100; therefore it will be possible and profitable for ranchers, in order to avoid the $100 crop damage that otherwise would result, to offer an amount to the owners of submarginal land that is sufficient to keep the land out of farming.

There is a temptation at this point in the argument to believe that an error has been made. Suppose that the farmer suffers damages equal to $100 and the rancher enjoys a net return equal to $110. If the rancher is not liable he will choose to continue ranching and to refuse a payment from a neighboring farmer of $100 to stop ranching. But if the rule of liability is reversed, he will continue ranching only if his $110 net return is sufficient to cover the cost imposed on the farmer ($100) *plus* the payment required to keep submarginal land (which can be assumed to border on another boundary of the ranch) out of farming. There has been no error in the argument, but there is an error in introducing the second neighbor halfway through the analysis. With the rancher not liable, he would have elected to remain in ranching only if the net return to ranching exceeded the payments to leave ranching offered to him by *both* his neighbors. If the rancher finds it remunerative to remain in ranching in the face of both these offers he must earn a sufficient net return from ranching, after the rule of liability is changed and he is held liable, to be able to pay damages to his neighboring farmer *and* to pay the owner of neighboring submarginal land to keep that land out of production.

The change in the rule of liability does not lead to a conversion of ranchland or submarginal land to farming. The use of land that maximized returns before the change in liability rule continues to maximize returns after the new rule is adopted, and the mix of output is unaffected by the choice of liability rule even when long-run considerations are analyzed. To understand the effect of altering the rule of liability it is important to recognize that the owner of a resource who finds it in his interest to employ that resource in a particular way when he bears the cost of an interaction will be paid to employ that resource ***in the same way*** when the rule of liability is reversed. What can happen, and in this case does happen, when the rule of liability is changed is that present owners of land having a comparative advantage in ranching suffer a ***windfall*** loss in the value of their land while owners of farmland enjoy a ***windfall*** gain. But this redistribution of wealth cannot alter the uses of these lands.

## III

The problem of "extortion" is part of the larger problem of wealth redistribution that may accompany a change in the rule of liability. Our concern here is with situations in which such a redistribution takes place. However, it should be noted that, when there is no restriction on contracting, a change in the rule of liability need not be accompanied by wealth redistribution. If owners of firms are made liable for industrial accidents, for example, then the equilibrium wage will move downward to reflect the shifting of this explicit cost from workers to employers. Employers no longer will need to cover the cost of industrial accidents in the wages they pay since this cost will be paid by them in the form of industrial accident insurance or self-insurance required by the new rule of liability. The general effect of shifting accident liability directly to firms will be merely to change the classification, not the amount, of remuneration. What under no employer liability were simply wages become under employer liability wages plus accident benefits. No redistribution of wealth accompanies the change in liability. Workers who, when they had to bear the cost of accidents directly, received $X in wages will, under the new rule of liability, receive part of the $X in the form of accident compensation and the remainder in wages, but there will be no change in their total income after taking account of expected accident costs under the two systems.

This holds strictly only if workers and employers are allowed to enter into voluntary contractual arrangements for reshifting the explicit cost back to workers, a matter that need not be discussed in detail here. If such agreements are disallowed by the law—*i.e.*, if the costs of making such agreements is prohibitively high because of their illegality—then some wealth may be redistributed from those workers who would have found it advantageous to self-insure to workers who find it advantageous to buy insurance; such a law would force workers, in the wage reductions they must accept, to purchase insurance for industrial accidents from their employers.

The problem of "extortion" arises when a change in liability gives rise to a redistribution in wealth. In the farmer-rancher case, the relative values of nearby farm and ranchlands will be changed when the rule of liability is altered. Under one rule of liability, with farmers required to bear the cost of crop damage, farmers will need to pay ranchers to reduce herd size; under the other rule ranchers will have to pay farmers for damages or for any alteration in the quantity of corn grown nearby. The change in the direction of payments must affect the rents that can be collected by owners of these lands and thus the market values of these lands.

In these cases the owner of the specialized resource, ranchland or farmland, that is not required to bear the cost of the interaction may threaten to increase the intensity of the interaction in an attempt to get his neighbor to pay him a larger sum than would ordinarily be required to obtain his cooperation in adjusting the intensity of the interaction downward. The owner of ranchland, if he is not liable for crop damage done by straying cattle, might, in the absence of a neighboring farmer, raise only 1,000 head of cattle. With proximity between farming and ranching, a neighboring owner of farmland might be willing to pay the rancher the sum required to finance a 200-head reduction in herd size. However, if the owner of ranchland *threatens* to raise 1,500 head, he may be able to secure more than this sum from the farmer because of the additional crop damage that would be caused by the larger herd size. With or without this "extortion" threat, the size of the herd will be reduced to 800 because that is the size, by assumption, that maximizes the total value of both activities. Given the interrelationship between the two activities, that is the herd size that will maximize the return to the farmer and, indirectly, the sum available for possible transfer to the rancher. What is at issue is the sharing of this maximum return.

To the extent that there exist alternative farm sites, the ability of the owner of ranchland to make such a threat credible is compromised. Competition among such owners will reduce the payment that farmers make to ranchers to that sum which is just sufficient to offset the revenue forgone by ranchers when herd size is reduced. No rancher could succeed in a threat to increase herd size above normal numbers because other ranchers would be willing to compete to zero the price that farmers are asked to pay to avoid abnormally large herd sizes. Abnormally large herd size, in itself, will generate losses to owners of ranchland and, for this reason, competition among such owners will reduce the price that owners of farmland must pay to avoid such excessive herd sizes to zero.

But if a ranchland owner has a locational monopoly, in the sense that there are no alternative sites available to farmers, then the rancher may succeed in acquiring a larger sum from his neighboring farmer in order to avoid abnormally large herd sizes. The acquisition of a larger sum by the owner of ranchland generally will require him to incur some cost to make his threat credible, perhaps by actually beginning to increase herd size beyond normal levels. If the cost of making this threat credible is low relative to the sum available for transfer from the owner of farmland, the rancher will be in a good position to accomplish the transfer. The sum available for transfer will be the amount by which the value of the neighboring land when used as farmland exceeds its value in the next best use. If the rancher were to demand a larger payment from his neighbor, the neighboring land would be switched to some other use.

The temptation to label such threats extortion or blackmail must be resisted by economists for these are legal and not economic distinctions. The rancher merely attempts to maximize profits. If his agreements with neighboring farmers are marketed in competition with other ranchers, profit maximization constrained by competition implies that an agreement to reduce herd size can be purchased for a smaller payment than if effective competition in such agreements is absent. The appropriate economic label for this problem is nothing more nor less than monopoly. It takes on the cast of such legal classifications as extortion only because the context seems to be one where the monopoly return is received by threatening to produce something that is not wanted—excessively large herds. The conventional monopoly problem involves a reduction or a threat to reduce the output of a desired good. In the unconventional monopoly problem presented here, there is a threat to increase herd size beyond desirable levels. But this difference is superficial. The conventional monopoly problem can be viewed as one in which the monopolist produces more scarcity than is desired, and the unconventional monopoly problem discussed here can be considered one in which the monopolist threatens to produce too small a reduction in crop damage. Any additional sum that the rancher succeeds in transferring to himself from the farmer is correctly identified as a monopoly return.

The temptation to resolve this monopoly problem merely by reversing the rule of liability must be resisted. Should the liability rule be reversed and the owner of ranchland now be held liable for damage done by his cattle to surrounding crops, the specific monopoly problem that we have been discussing would be resolved. But if the farmer enjoys a locational monopoly such that the rancher has nowhere else to locate, the shoe will now be on the other foot. The farmer can threaten to increase the number of bushels of corn planted, and hence the damage for which the rancher will be liable, unless the rancher pays the farmer a sum greater than would be required under competitive conditions. The potential for monopoly and the wealth redistribution implied by monopoly is present in principle whether or not the owner of ranchland is held liable for damages. Both the symmetry of the problem and its disappearance under competitive conditions refute the allegation that Coase's analysis implicitly endorses the use of resources in undesirable activities.

Should the law treat such classes of monopoly problem as "extortion" or "blackmail"? It may not be useful for the law to take this step because the threat is made credible by increasing the output of an economic good—cattle if the rancher is not liable, corn if he is. Because it is difficult to sort desirable from undesirable increases in herd or crop size, there is a real danger of penalizing desirable increases in herd or crop size by mistake if such wealth transfers are treated as extortion. Activities to which anti-extortion laws normally apply typically involve the use of violence or the threat to take some action that falls within a general class of actions considered socially undesirable. The application of anti-extortion legal measures in such cases is less likely to penalize socially desirable actions by mistake. In other cases, it may be possible for the courts to limit the amount of payments to levels that are reasonable compensations for costs incurred (or profits forgone), although it is not clear how easily such determinations can be made by courts. Alternatively, it is possible to attempt to eliminate the source of the problem—monopoly—but the wisdom of relying on antitrust in this context is a matter on which the author is unprepared to speak.

## IV

The costly interaction between farming and ranching is not properly attributed to the actions of either party individually, being "caused," instead, by resource scarcity, the scarcity of land and fencing materials. If transaction cost is negligible, it would seem that the choice of liability rule cannot depend on who "causes" the damage since both jointly do, or on how resource allocation will be altered, since no such alteration will take place, but largely on judicial or legislative preferences with regard to wealth distribution.

Once significant transacting or negotiating cost is admitted into the analysis, the choice of liability rule will have effects on resource allocation, and it no longer follows that wealth distribution is the main or even an important consideration in choosing the liability rule. The assumption of negligible transacting cost can be only a beginning to understanding the economic consequences of the legal arrangements that underlie the operations of the economy, but little more can be done here than to illustrate the nature of the considerations.[10]

The most obvious effect of introducing significant transacting cost is that

10 Other considerations that arise when the cost of transacting is positive are discussed in Harold Demsetz, Some Aspects of Property Rights, 9 J. Law & Econ. 61 (1966).

negotiations will not be consummated in those situations where the expected benefits from exchange are less than the expected cost of exchanging. Exchange opportunities will be exploited only up to the point where the marginal gain from trade equals the marginal cost of trade. Of course, there is nothing necessarily inefficient in halting exchange at this point. If this were all that could be said on the subject, there would be little more to do than call the reader's attention to the similar analytical roles of transport cost in international trade and transacting cost in exchange generally. But there is more to say.

Significant transacting cost implies that the rule of liability generally will have allocative effects (as Coase recognizes). Consider the problem of liability for automobile-pedestrian accidents. To the extent that "accident" has any economic meaning it must mean that circumstances are such that voluntary negotiations between the driver and the pedestrian are prohibitively costly in many driving situations. The parties to an accident, either because of the speed with which the accident occurs or because of a failure to notice the presence of a competing claimant for the right-of-way, cannot conclude an agreement over the use of the right-of-way at costs that are low enough, *ex ante*, to make the effort worthwhile.

Partly as a consequence of the costliness of such negotiations, rules of the road are developed. Speed limits, traffic signals, and legal constraints on passing are substituted for the development of saleable private rights. In a specific case it may be possible to assign private rights to use the road in a way that makes the exchange of these rights feasible, but, in general, if these rules make economic sense it is precisely because the cost of transacting is expected to be too high in most cases to warrant the development of saleable private rights to the use of roads.

The practicality of such rules is not an argument for or against government action, but a rationale for the substitution of rules for negotiation. The use of rules to eliminate costly negotiations can be found in the management of privately owned parking lots and toll roads as well as in those that are publicly owned.

Such rules notwithstanding, accidents do take place. Assuming that the cost of transacting is too high to make negotiated agreements practical in such cases, we can compare the effect on resource allocation of the rule of liability that is chosen. If drivers are held liable in automobile-pedestrian accidents, the incentives for pedestrians to be careful about how and where they cross streets will be reduced. The incentives for drivers to be careful will be increased. Indeed, if each pedestrian could be guaranteed *full* compensation for all financial, physical, and psychological costs suffered in an accident, then pedestrians would become indifferent between being struck by an auto and not being struck. Drivers, however, would actively seek to avoid accidents since they would always be liable, whereas if it were possible to have a system of complete and full pedestrian liability it would be the drivers who became indifferent between accidents and no accidents and it would be the pedestrians who actively sought to avoid accidents.

In a regime in which transacting cost was zero, either system of liability would generate the same accident-avoiding behavior, as the Coase analysis suggests. With driver liability, drivers would themselves avoid accidents or, if such avoidance could be purchased at lower cost from pedestrians, drivers would pay pedestrians to avoid accidents. Under a scheme of pedestrian liability it would be the pedestrians who took direct action to avoid accidents or indirect action by paying drivers to avoid accidents. Under either rule of liability those accidents are avoided for which the accident cost exceeds the least cost method of avoiding accidents, where the least cost is the lesser of either the driver or pedestrian cost of avoiding accidents. Both rules of liability, assuming zero transacting cost, yield the same accident rate and the same accident-avoiding behavior. The effect of switching from one rule of liability to another is limited to wealth redistribution.

In a situation in which transacting cost is prohibitively high, driver liability leads to the avoidance only of those accidents for which the cost of avoidance to the *driver* is less than the expected accident cost, and pedestrian liability leads to the avoidance of only those accidents for which the cost of avoidance to the *pedestrian* is less than the expected accident cost. In general, the accident rate that results will differ under these two systems since the cost of avoiding accidents will not be the same for drivers and pedestrians. Both systems will lead to higher accident rates than would be true if transacting costs were zero. The effect of positive transacting cost is to raise the cost of avoiding accidents through the foreclosure of the use of possibly cheaper cost-avoidance techniques when these can be employed only by the other party to the accident. A similar conclusion can be reached for all liability problems when transacting cost is prohibitive and when the law cannot particularize the rule of liability to take account of who is the least-cost damage avoider in every instance.

One liability rule may be superior to another if transacting costs are more than negligible precisely because the difficulty of avoiding costly interactions is not generally the same for the interacting parties. It may be less costly for pedestrians to avoid accidents or for farmers to relocate their crops than it is for drivers to avoid accidents or ranchers to reduce the number of cattle they raise. If information about this were known, it would be possible for the legal system to improve the allocation of resources by placing liability on that party who in the usual situation could be expected to avoid the costly interaction most cheaply.

The use of words such as "blame," "responsible," and "fault" must be treated with care by the economist because they have no useful meanings in an economic analysis of these problems other than as synonyms for the party who could have most easily avoided the costly interaction. Whether the interaction problem involves crop damage, accidents, soot, or water pollution, the qualitative relationship between the interacting parties is symmetrical. It is the *joint* use of a resource, be it geographic location, air, or water that leads to these interactions. It is the demand for scarce resources that leads to conflicting interests.

The legal system does produce rules for determining *prima facie* "fault," but in this context "fault" means only according to some acceptable and applicable legal precedent. In an accident involving a rear-end collision, the court generally will place the burden for proving the absence of negligence on the party driving the following car. If a car strikes a person running across a fenced expressway at night the burden of proving the absence of negligence is likely to be placed on the pedestrian. In treating such cases differently, the law bases its decisions on acceptable and appropriate precedents, but the acceptability of these precedents should not be confused with the morality of the interacting parties. A deeper analysis of these precedents may reveal that they generally make sense from the economic viewpoint of placing the liability on that party who can, at least cost, reduce the probability of a costly interaction happening. Less care need be taken by the driver of the following car in a rear-end collision than would need to be taken by the lead driver to avoid the accident, and less care is needed by a pedestrian to refrain from running across an expressway than is needed by a driver to avoid striking the pedestrian. Nor need the acceptability of such precedents be based on restitution since, as these precedents become known, their long-run effect is to deter accidents at least cost. If courts are to ignore wealth, religion, or family in deciding such conflicts, if persons before the courts are to be treated with regard only to the cause of action and available proof, then, as a normative proposition, it is difficult to suggest any criterion for deciding liability other than placing it on the party able to avoid the costly interaction most easily.

# [18]

# THE PROBLEM OF SOCIAL COST REVISITED

*DONALD H. REGAN*
*University of Michigan Law School*

SOME years ago, in a paper entitled "The Problem of Social Cost,"[1] Professor Ronald Coase asserted and argued for a proposition which has since acquired the convenient sobriquet "the Coase Theorem." The proposition is: That in a world of perfect competition, perfect information, and zero transaction costs, the allocation of resources in the economy will be efficient and will be unaffected by legal rules regarding the initial impact of costs resulting from externalities. Note that there are two claims being made, which it is well to separate for purposes of discussion. The first claim is that, under the conditions described, *some* efficient allocation of resources will be achieved, whatever the legal rule. The second claim is that, under those conditions, the *same* efficient allocation will be achieved, whatever the legal rule. I shall refer to the first claim as the "efficiency" thesis and to the second claim as the "invariance" thesis of the Coase Theorem. I shall argue that neither thesis can be deduced from the traditional assumptions about individual economic behavior which are the foundation of neoclassical price theory and contemporary welfare economics.[2]

Let me be quite clear (or as clear as I can be in advance of presenting my argument)—my primary point is not that the Coase Theorem is false, but that the truth of the Coase Theorem can only be deduced from an assumption or assumptions which differ in kind from the usual assumptions we make about economic agents. The most traditional sort of assumption, and the assumption which is part of every rigorous proof I am familiar with concerning the existence or efficiency of competitive equilibria, is the assumption that each economic agent maximizes something (utility or profit) in the face of prices he takes as given. We depart from this most traditional sort of assumption in the case of the monopolist or the monopsonist—but even the monopolist and the monopsonist operate in an economic environment

[1] R. H. Coase, The Problem of Social Cost, 3 J. Law & Econ. 1 (1960).

[2] I should note at some point, and this seems as good a point as any other, that I do not contest the correctness of the Coase Theorem, or its analogue, in certain cases which do not involve a genuine externality at all, such as the case of products liability, with attention focused on accidents to users of the product. (Accidents to "innocent bystanders" are a genuine externality.)

which responds in a particular known way to each possible choice of the agent under consideration. The next step—to the consideration of oligopoly, duopoly, bilateral monopoly, or whatever—takes us into the realm of strategic behavior and the theory of games. My basic thesis in this essay is that the Coase Theorem is a proposition in the theory of games, and not a proposition about traditional markets or competitive equilibrium. My secondary thesis is that the Coase Theorem even as a proposition in the theory of games is open to doubt.

## I

Instead of beginning with Coase's explicit argument for the Coase Theorem, let us consider an argument which is implicit in Coase's original paper, but which has been stated most clearly by Calabresi:

> The interesting thing about this [Coase's] analysis, however, is that there is no reason whatsoever to limit it to joint cost causers. Thus, if one assumes rationality, no transaction costs, and no legal impediments to bargaining, *all* misallocations of resources would be fully cured in the market by bargains. Far from being surprising, this statement is tautological, at least if one accepts any of the various classic definitions of misallocation. These ultimately come down to a statement akin to the following: A misallocation exists when there is available a possible reallocation in which all those who would lose from the reallocation could be fully compensated by those who would gain, and, at the end of this compensation process, there would still be some who would be better off than before.
>
> This and other similar definitions of resource misallocation merely mean that there is a misallocation when a situation can be improved by bargains. If people are rational, bargains are costless, and there are no legal impediments to bargains, transactions will *ex hypothesis* occur to the point where bargains can no longer improve the situation; to the point, in short, of optimal resource allocation. We can, therefore, state as an axiom the proposition that all externalities can be internalized and all misallocations, even those created by legal structures can be remedied by the market, except to the extent that transactions cost money or the structure itself creates some impediments to bargaining.[3]

I call this the "*a priori* argument" for the Coase Theorem—"*a priori*" because it reaches a conclusion about the result of individuals' economic behavior without any model of how individuals behave. What Calabresi is saying may be rendered briefly as follows: If it cost nothing to get all the individuals in an economy together and to get them to reach an agreement about how the economy's resources should be employed, and if all these in-

[3] Guido Calabresi, Transactions Costs, Resource Allocation, and Liability Rules—A Comment, 11 J. Law & Econ. 67, 68 (1968). [Footnotes in original omitted.]

dividuals were rational, then necessarily, they would agree on a Pareto-efficient allocation.[4]

Whether this statement is a tautology, as Calabresi says it is, depends on the meanings of the terms used. While Calabresi is careful to tell us what he means by "misallocation," he says nothing about what he means by "rational," a chameleon among words. In varying contexts the rational man has been taken to be (*inter alios*): one who maximizes utility (or profit) in the face of given prices and economic conditions; one who maximizes *expected* utility (or profit )in the face of risk; or one who adopts a maximin strategy if he is playing a two-person constant-sum game. All of these are standard meanings of "rational," but none of them suffices to make Calabresi's statement a tautology, because the bargaining situation he envisages is an *n*-person, variable-sum game, where *n* is likely to be very large indeed. For participants in *n*-person, variable-sum games we do not, so far as I know, have any real satisfactory concept of rational behavior. In particular, what we do not have (which we do have in the simpler situations mentioned above) is a model of behavior which seems to be "rational" both for the individual and with regard to the overall outcome for the community.

To illustrate the problem: In a variable-sum game the players have something to gain from cooperation, but there are usually a variety of ways in which the fruits of cooperation can be divided up. Each individual will wish to see not only that the benefits of cooperation are achieved, but that he gets as large a share of the benefits as possible. He will likely be led to threats of non-cooperation as a device to increase his share. Clearly the threats will be ineffective if they are not believed, and it is unlikely that threats will be generally believed unless they are occasionally carried out. But whenever a threat is carried out, the outcome of the game will be sub-optimal, in the Pareto sense.[5] In other words, what appears to be rational individual behavior will occasionally lead to an "irrational" overall outcome.

Two possible ways of avoiding the force of this suggestion come rapidly to mind. One thing Calabresi might do is to define "transaction costs" to

[4] As I observe in the text below, the *a priori* argument would not establish the invariance part of the Coase thesis even if it did establish the efficiency part. Calabresi apparently regards it as establishing both parts because of an implicit assumption that there is a unique efficient allocation.

[5] Support for the suggestion that it is part of the nature of a threat that it results in inefficiency if it is carried out may be found in Thomas C. Schelling, The Strategy of Conflict (1960) and R. Nozick, Coercion, in Philosophy, Science, and Method: Essays in Honor of Ernest Nagel (Sidney Morgenbesser, Patrick Suppes & Morton White, eds., 1969). Note that what we are suggesting is that the carrying out of a threat results in inefficiency as compared to the original set of possible outcomes. It does not necessarily result in inefficiency within the set of outcomes available after the maker of a threat becomes irreversibly committed to the behavior he has threatened.

include the social cost of individual bargaining tactics. This would be a clever move, but if we are correct in arguing that rational individual bargaining may not always lead to socially optimal outcomes, then this definition would make the assumptions of zero transaction costs and individual rationality inconsistent. Alternatively, Calabresi might define "rational" implicitly by requiring it to mean whatever is necessary to make his claim tautological. In other words, to say that individuals were rational would mean precisely that in a costless negotiation situation, they would come out with a Pareto-efficient agreement.[6]

This approach has considerable appeal. If we watched the parties to a variable-sum game make threats and counter-threats and finally end up in an inefficient situation, we might be tempted to think at least one of them must have cut off his nose to spite his face. Of course, if we accept the conclusion that rational individual bargaining tactics involve some unavoidable social cost, this is not necessarily true. We might also reflect that this implicit definition is too symmetrical. As far as the definition is concerned, ***both*** parties must have cut off their noses to spite their faces. Each has contributed to the failure to reach an optimum. But that impartial judgment has not nearly the same intuitive appeal. Our intuitive reaction is that at least one party must have behaved badly, but not necessarily both. This suggests that we do have some notions of rational (or perhaps reasonable) individual behavior in this kind of situation at an intuitive level. The problem is to formalize those notions and then consider whether rational individual behavior does or does not guarantee collective rationality.[7]

[6] This interpretation of Calabresi might even be suggested by his statement that the efficiency part of the Coase Theorem can be treated as an "axiom." The word "axiom" has at least two ordinary senses, however. In one sense, an axiom is merely an assumption of a deductive system. In another sense, an axiom is an assumption which is supposed to be self-evident. In the text we are considering the possibility of taking the efficiency claim of the Coase Theorem as an axiom in the first sense, and we are arguing against this on the ground that it is certainly not an axiom in the second sense—that is, it is not self-evident. Calabresi, since he views the efficiency claim as tautological and understands it, presumably does regard it as self-evident.

[7] There is an assumption which might be useful in some contexts which is not unlike the Calabresi axiom. It is the assumption that the expected magnitude of the inefficiency which will remain after negotiation in any situation decreases as transaction costs decrease. We will not investigate the consequences of this assumption, but we note two points. First, this assumption definitely does not entail the Calabresi axiom. It does not entail that when transaction costs are zero, the expected magnitude of the inefficiency is zero. Second, even this assumption is by no means self-evident. Transaction costs may be such as to make communication not worthwhile or impossible. But to say communication is not worthwhile is to say threats are not worthwhile. If this is true it may be easier for the parties concerned to reach an efficient position which, for one reason or another, is salient, than it would be if communication were possible and there was some prospect of a threat's being effective. This argument closely parallels Schelling's observation that

I do not mean to assert categorically that rational individuals faced with zero transaction costs will fail to reach a Pareto-optimum, although I have suggested what I consider a good reason for thinking this might often be the case. What I do emphasize is that we have no basis for the claim that a Pareto-optimum will be achieved, since we are offered no model of individual behavior. There are some bargaining models we might consider, such as Harsanyi's,[8] but to investigate them would take us considerably afield. I am not aware of any bargaining model which has the features that have made the competitive market model the main tool of price theorists and welfare economists, namely that the existence and efficiency of equilibria can be deduced from assumptions about technology and individual behavior which are fairly plausible on the whole.

So far we have discussed one highly abstract argument for the efficiency thesis of the Coase Theorem. More specific arguments, including Coase's original argument, generally purport to establish the efficiency claim and the invariance claim together, and will be considered in a moment. Since I shall attempt to show that every more specific argument somewhere includes an implicit appeal to the *a priori* argument which we have just considered, it is worth pausing to note the connection between the *a priori* argument and the invariance thesis. More specifically, what we should note is that the *a priori* argument lends no support whatever to the invariance claim. Even if the *a priori* argument is accepted, it allows us to say only that in a world of zero transaction costs and rational individuals, some efficient allocation of resources will be achieved whatever the legal rules. Will the allocation be the same, whatever the legal rules? This question we cannot answer, on the basis of the *a priori* argument, since the *a priori* argument says nothing about what efficient allocation will be achieved in any bargaining situation, and since it gives us no explicit model of individual behavior from which we might hope to find out. If we adopt the *a priori* argument for the Coase Theorem, part of the Theorem becomes undecidable, since *the* allocation of resources resulting from any given legal situation is incompletely specified.

Of course, if instead of the *a priori* argument we were operating with a specific bargaining model, then we might decide the truth or falsity of the invariance claim. It could be suggested that in a plausible bargaining model

---

inability to send or receive communications may redound to the benefit of a party thus incapacitated. Thomas C. Schelling, *supra* note 5, *passim*. The laws against extortion might be interpreted as an effort selectively to increase transaction costs, in order to promote efficiency.

[8] John C. Harsanyi, A General Theory of Rational Behavior in Game Situations, 34 Econometrica 613 (1966). See also John C. Harsanyi, Bargaining and Conflict Situations in the Light of a New Approach to Game Theory, 55 Am. Econ. Rev. No. 2, at 477 (Papers & Proceedings, 1965).

the outcome of any negotiation ought to reflect to some extent our intuitive evaluation of the strength of the parties' bargaining positions; and it could also be suggested that legal rules are an important determinant of the strength of the parties' bargaining positions;[9] in which case we would expect the invariance claim to be false. In other words, one of the criteria for the plausibility of a bargaining model might be that it falsify the invariance thesis (at least if the model is sufficiently sophisticated so that the invariance thesis can be investigated). The main point, though, is that without a model, the *a priori* argument tells us nothing about the invariance claim one way or the other.

## II

Now let us shift the focus of our attention to the invariance claim specifically, and let us begin with a simple and obvious argument against the invariance claim. We incorporate Coase's rancher-farmer example and discussion by reference. Even if Coase's argument is good in the short run, and a change of legal rule does not alter the efficient allocation of resources, there will be changes in the long run. If the original legal rule specified that the rancher was liable, and the new legal rule specifies that the farmer is liable, then after the change of rule the rancher will not be paying some damages he was paying before, and the farmer will be paying a bribe he was not paying before. The rancher, then, will be earning a positive profit, and the farmer a negative profit (since by assumption the original position was a perfectly competitive equilibrium). The ordinary consequence of this profit disequilibrium will be the allocation of new resources to ranching, and the exit of resources from farming. In the long run, then, the allocation of resources will change.

The argument I have just made is not novel. It was put forward by Calabresi some years ago.[10] Unfortunately, Calabresi recanted in the later comment on the Coase Theorem from which we have already quoted. His answer to his own original argument was, essentially, that, given Coase's assumptions, "the same type of transactions which cured the short run misallocation would also occur to cure the long run ones."[11] This implicitly assumes that the long-run changes brought about by the alteration of the legal rule are "misallocations," which require to be cured. But on the face of it we have no reason for

[9] Specifically, we would expect the legal rules to influence the outcome of a bargaining or arbitration session by influencing the "conflict point," the outcome which prevails if no agreement is reached.

[10] Guido Calabresi, The Decision for Accidents: An Approach to Nonfault Allocation of Costs, 78 Harv. L. Rev. 713, 730 n.28 (1965).

[11] Guido Calabresi, *supra* note 3, at 67.

thinking they are anything of the kind. It is well known that different efficient competitive equilibria correspond to different distributions of wealth. Even granting, then, that the allocation before the change of legal rule was efficient, and that the allocation after the change must also be efficient, there is no reason to assume they must be the same, if the change of legal rule effected a redistribution of wealth, as there is every reason to suppose it did.

Perhaps it would be more enlightening to speak of "distribution of welfare" than "distribution of wealth." If we do that, then it is plain that we should expect a change in legal rule which shifts certain costs from ranchers to farmers to redistribute welfare away from people who consume farm products or supply factors to farms and in favor of people who consume ranch products or supply factors to ranches. Of course, in the usual model of a competitive economy, the "initial distribution of wealth" refers to the initial distribution of stocks of goods, shares in the profits of firms, and ability to supply factors. There is no reference to legal rules. But then, in the usual model of a competitive economy, externalities are not admitted.

So far we have presented the straightforward argument against the invariance claim, and we have pointed out the fallacy of Calabresi's answer to that straightforward argument. A different answer to the straightforward argument is suggested by Professor Nutter in a recent comment.[12] Essentially, Nutter argues that a change of legal rule will not cause a reallocation of resources, but only a redistribution of rents. What Nutter offers by way of argument is simply an arithmetical example, and his example does fall (or may be interpreted to fall) into the one class of cases where his conclusion is plausible —that is, where the change in legal rule might merely redistribute rents. That is the class of cases where ranching and farming both use factors (in this case land) which, when their activity is favored by the legal rule (that is, when their activity is not liable) command rents at least equal to the total damage caused by the externality. In such cases, the cost of damage may come out of the rents earned by factors used in the activity held liable. But this is hardly the general case. In the general case, there may be no factor which is earning any rent at all in the favored activity. All factors may be earning only their opportunity cost of employment in that activity. Plainly, if no factor is earning any rent in the favored activity, then a change of legal rule which makes that activity disfavored cannot merely redistribute rents.

At this point Nutter, or another defender of the invariance thesis, might argue that the factors employed in the favored activity *must* be earning some rent, on the ground that a situation in which the factors in the favored

[12] G. Warren Nutter, The Coase Theorem on Social Cost: A Footnote, 11 J. Law & Econ. 503 (1968).

activity were earning zero rent could not persist. Suppose farming is the favored activity. Now, if the factors employed in farming are earning zero rent (the argument goes), then the rancher, instead of paying damages, will bribe the factors currently employed in farming to go elsewhere, and will pay out less in this process, since the total bribes need only exceed the total rents, which, being zero, are less than the current damage payment. Therefore the situation will not persist, and an equilibrium will be reached (or so the argument might continue) only when the total damage is less than the rents being earned in the favored activity and the rancher has no further opportunity for profitable bribes.

First, I should like to observe that this argument, like Coase's original argument, depends explicitly on the possibility of bribes, and therefore introduces non-market behavior. We are sliding back in the direction of the *a priori* argument. Still, the appeal to non-market behavior may not seem objectionable—the model may not seem implausible—in the context of a fairly specific example such as this one. Let us then admit the possibility of non-market behavior, and consider the next step.

The farmer, who suddenly finds that his units of factors have been bribed out from under him by the clever rancher, is not going to sit still. His first thought might be to hire other indistinguishable units of factors, but the rancher will have forestalled that by bribing not merely the units which were originally employed by the farmer but *all* units of those factors not to work for the farmer. After all, when one can accomplish his purpose with an infinitesimal bribe, he can afford to bribe widely. The farmer's second thought will be better. He will realize that the rancher has turned a tidy profit by bribing his factors away instead of paying damages, and that he (the farmer) can get a share by the simple expedient of threatening to go back into business by offering higher bribes to the required units of factors. To be sure, if he goes back into business on the same scale he will lose money. (Not much, since a bribe which needs only to exceed an infinitesimal competing offer can afford to be quite small. The farmer also has a natural advantage, in that the rancher must bribe all units, while the farmer must bid only for an insignificant fraction of all units.) But he will collect damages from the rancher, and the rancher will lose more than he will. Plainly, therefore, the rancher will see the light and turn over to the farmer some of his saving. How much? Well, we can't say. As a matter of fact, the rancher is in a very touchy position. Just as he had to bribe *all* the units of those factors which the farmer employed (and not just the particular units originally employed by the farmer), he will now notice that he is open to precisely the same threat the farmer has just made from all potential farmers! We could pursue this line of speculation, but the point is clear enough. The result is at best indeterminate, and it seems not unlikely the rancher will finally just stay at the original equilibrium, paying out his damages to a farmer whose factors earn zero rent.[13]

There is a final argument in favor of the Coase Theorem which has been suggested by a number of writers.[14] The argument is essentially that in a world of perfect information and zero transaction costs, there would not be any external effects between or among firms for legal rules to deal with. If there were two or more firms which were failing to internalize between them an externality which connected their production functions (the argument runs), then it would be profitable for these two firms to merge. The externality would be internalized, efficient production would be achieved, and the joint profit would be greater than the sum of the profits of the original firms. The legal rule is left with nothing to operate on, unless it is supposed to govern the distribution of rewards within the firm, which we assume it is not.

The first thing to observe about this argument is that, like Coase's original argument, it assumes successful bargaining and therefore assumes the truth of the Coase Theorem, at least in a limited context. We are offered no explicit model of the process by which appropriate firms are created. It is simply asserted that in a world of perfect information and zero transaction costs, the right organization of the economy into firms would appear. In other words, it is asserted that a bargaining problem among indeterminate numbers of potential entrepreneurs will be "solved" in an efficient fashion. This assertion may seem fairly plausible if we concentrate on externalities which involve only two or three firms before the merger movement, and if we concentrate only on the two or three entrepreneurs associated with those firms. But we have no license thus to limit our vision. For one thing, many external effects operate among many firms. If we allow complete internalization by merger it is likely that we will end up with non-competitive market structures in many

13 Actually, once we have opened up the possibility of bribes and threats, we observe that the rancher may be susceptible to threats by potential farmers even when the original farmer is in the market and collecting damages. As long as there is some land around the rancher not being used for farming, any potential farmer is in a position to damage the rancher by going into farming, and therefore in a position to attempt to extort from the rancher a bribe for not going into business. This is true despite the fact that the potential farmer, if he went into business, would lose money. The outcome is, of course, indeterminate. This suggests that one reason we have legal rules against extortion and "spite fences" and so on, is that in addition to being mean-spirited, such devices are incompatible with the market system. Compare *supra* note 7.

14 For example, George J. Stigler, The Theory of Price 113 (3rd ed. 1966); Otto A. Davis & Andrew Whinston, Externalities, Welfare, and the Theory of Games, 70 J. Pol. Econ. 241 (1962); Harold Demsetz, Toward a Theory of Property Rights, 57 Am. Econ. Rev. No. 2, at 347, 349 n.2 (Papers & Proceedings, 1967); G. Warren Nutter, *supra* note 12.

industries. For that matter, if we allow internalization of "pecuniary" externalities as well as technological ones—that is, if we allow firms to merge for the purpose of becoming monopolies, as it will be in their interest to do—then we should expect a non-competitive market structure in every industry. Of course, we could appeal to the Coase Theorem again, and rely on bargains to cure misallocations resulting from monopoly, but now we have lost the defense of our original appeal to the Coase Theorem, which was that we were assuming it only in a limited context, where it was plausible, to prove it in a broader context. There is another difficulty with this appeal to the Coase Theorem in a "narrow context." Even if we have an externality which affects only a small number of actual firms before the merger movement, it may affect many more potential firms. As we observed in connection with the rancher-farmer case, it may not be enough for the rancher to buy off (or merge with) an individual farmer. So long as farming is the favored activity, it may be necessary to include every potential farmer in the deal, since every potential farmer is in a position to inflict damage on the rancher or on the merged rancher-farmer combination. To sum up, the appeal to mergers or "appropriate" firms does not allow us to deduce the Coase Theorem from traditional and plausible assumptions. We need to assume the Coase Theorem in some contexts, and fairly broad contexts at that.

## III

The upshot of all this is that Pigou was right after all, in a very important way. Pigou at least recognized that if we wish to rely on the *market* to produce an efficient result—that is, if we are going to attempt to deduce the efficiency of the result from the traditional assumptions about individual behavior—then some government intervention is required in order to equate marginal private and marginal social cost. On the other hand, Pigou overlooked, or at least did not draw attention to, a very important feature of the problem, which Coase did draw attention to. That feature is that most externalities are, in Coase's words, "reciprocal." Which is to say, it is very likely that the damage done is affected not by the decisions of one individual alone, but by the decisions of many. The reciprocal nature of most externalities means that Pigou considerably underestimated the difficulty of finding regulatory (tax-subsidy) schemes which would guarantee internalization. In the rancher-farmer case, it will not do just to have the rancher pay damages to the farmer, because then the farmer will have no incentive to take into account the effect of his own decisions on the damage. In general to set up an appropriate tax-subsidy scheme might require as much information on the part of the regulating agency as would be required for centralized decision-making. The market-mechanism-plus-regulation, then, is no certain high road to efficiency.[15] As to invariance, if we do rely on the market-mechanism-plus-regulation, and if we are fortunate enough to achieve an efficient equilibrium, then there is every reason to believe that different regulatory schemes will produce different efficient equilibria.

Finally, a word to the reader who wonders what difference it all makes. After all, even those who assert the Coase Theorem as a deducible proposition about competitive equilibria never seriously claim that the assumption of zero transaction costs is realistic, so they always admit, as Coase himself pointed out, that we need legal rules, and that what the rules are is important. Aside from the simple matter of theoretical correctness, I think my conclusions are important for two reasons. First, the assumption of zero transaction costs, though it is unrealistic in general, might in certain cases, where the externality is localized, be thought no more unrealistic than the other simplifying assumptions economists work with regularly. In such cases, one who believed the Coase Theorem might claim that having a legal rule really was a matter of indifference, whereas if the Coase Theorem is false, or depends on novel and dubious assumptions, this claim would be without foundation. Second, and more important, once we realize that the legal rule affects (or, if we rely on bargaining, presumably affects) the allocation of resources and the distribution of welfare even granting Coase's assumptions, we will not be tempted to speak as if the only function, or even the primary function, of legal rules when there are transaction costs is to help us approach some uniquc optimum which would exist if only transactions were costless. If there are externalities, then there are decisions to be made about the distribution of welfare even if we assume an "initial distribution of wealth" which is specified in every other respect than the rules concerning externalities.

15 An illuminating foray into the difficulties of devising an appropriate tax-subsidy scheme is provided by Otto A. Davis & Andrew Whinston, *supra* note 14.

# [19]

# The Coase Proposition, Information Constraints, and Long-Run Equilibrium

*By* WILLIAM SCHULZE AND RALPH C. D'ARGE*

Ronald Coase in his now famous paper on social costs asserted that, given the initial " . . . delimitation of rights . . . the ultimate result (which maximizes the value of production) is independent of . . . [the choice of a liability or nonliability rule] . . . if the pricing system is assured to work without cost" (p. 8). Guido Calabresi recently restated the Coase proposition more succinctly as follows: "The same allocation of resources will come about regardless of which of two joint cost users is initially charged with the cost, in other words, regardless of liability rules" (1968, p. 67). Of course, Calabresi also presumed zero transactions costs. In addition, Calabresi reiterated the Coase conclusion that liability rules do not influence the efficient allocation of resources in either the short or long run.[1]

A major logical problem with the Coase proposition is in introducing a perturbation into an otherwise perfect system and then asserting that regardless of legal rules, the system will regain its perfection. Coase, by introducing a perturbation, negates one of the assumptions necessary for asserting that the allocation of resources will be efficient regardless of liability rules in both the short and long run, namely perfect information.[2] A perturbation occurs which is not known in advance, i.e., information is lacking; but there is apparently complete information at zero cost for all future actual and potential exchanges.[3]

Much of the confusion on externalities and legal rules, we submit, has arisen because writers in the field have not made clear their assumptions on transactions costs.

Applying a competitive model of two industries with an externality and allowing for entry and exit we find that a liability rule will lead to a misallocation of resources in the long run, given the acceptance of a particular set of assumptions on transactions costs which are commonly accepted in the economics literature. We also find that a nonliability rule leads to misallocation. A Pigovian tax, alternatively, leads to a local optimum in resources allocation provided the system is stable and receptors are not compensated.

## I

In this section we undertake a comparison of the Coase proposition and Pigovian taxes in the long run where particular positive transactions costs are introduced. That effort is concentrated on external diseconomies of

* Assistant professor of economics, University of New Mexico, and professor of economics, University of California, Riverside, respectively.

[1] See Guido Calabresi (1968, p. 68). Coase states "... the long-run equilibrium position . . . is the same whether or not the cattle-raiser is held responsible for the crop damage brought about by his cattle" (p. 8).

[2] In the short run, bargaining solutions with or without a liability rule are Pareto efficient. However, a number of writers including Calabresi, and indirectly David Bramhall and Edwin Mills, have raised questions as to the conclusion by Coase that long-run allocation of resources will be the same regardless of liability rules. As noted earlier, Calabresi recently reversed his opinion and concluded that long-run as well as short-run resource allocation would be the same. See Calabresi (1968), and Bramhall and Mills.

[3] The question arises as to the nature and meaning of perturbations. There appear to be two categories of causes for such perturbations: purely random events much like accidents; and forms of designed coercion. For example, if farmer *A*'s cows enter farmer *B*'s corn field, Coase never analyzes why the cows entered. Did farmer *A* inadvertently allow entry or was it by design, i.e., *A* herded them close to the field so the cows would be attracted by the corn? Most of the literature on externalities takes it as given that the externality (or perturbation) results from unexpected or inadvertent behavior of one party. But, again, inadvertent behavior is suggestive that there *are* gaps in information and transactions costs are not zero. And coercion by design, other imprefections aside, cannot occur unless at least one party has less than perfect information.

production with firm entry where there are some implicit assumptions on transactions costs normally presumed in the literature on perfect competition. One such assumption is that firms and consumers are price takers. Also, it is taken as given that atomistic firms enter or exit a particular industry on the basis of expected future profits which equal, by assumption, current profits. Thus there is assumed to be an informational barrier (very high transactions costs) associated with knowledge of future profits. Further, it is assumed firms in both emitter and receptor industries can costlessly negotiate, but that third parties are barred from such negotiation. Finally, it is assumed that there is a government agency in the Pigovian tax case that can enforce tax payments and distribute revenues costlessly. These assumptions, while semi-inconsistent as regards transactions costs (i.e., some transactions costs are presumed to be extremely high and others virtually zero), underlie most studies of competitive behavior of firms.

It has been widely demonstrated that the Coase proposition is essentially valid, given the assumption of zero transactions costs after the appearance of an externality, in the short run. However, the "wealth effect" coupled with transactions costs which Coase, Calabresi, and others ignore is particularly significant when one considers competitive long run equilibrium in production. Here, since the structure of industry is not fixed but is subject to a kind of Malthusian law of entry, not only are resources allocated most efficiently among firms, but the most efficient combination of firms is also assured in the long run under perfect competition with no externalities. The question to be resolved is whether or not negotiations between producers exploiting the gains from trade made available by an externality in production will result in an efficient solution not just in the short run but in the long run as well. Since profitability of firms determines entry (presumed to be costless), and since the allocation of property rights with respect to an externality will affect relative profitability of emitters and receptors, it is clear that the structure of industry will not be invariant to the configuration of property rights.[4] Further, free entry may be inconsistent with stability of a negotiated solution arising under a nonliability rule because new entrants can act as free riders, a possibility excluded by a liability rule or a Pigovian tax.

Consider a two-industry partial equilibrium model with a diffuse externality such that the output of industry 2 adversely affects the production of every firm in industry 1 in a like manner.[5] An example might be the release of air pollutants with instantaneous horizontal mixing by industry in an airshed which also contains agricultural producers. The question would then be to determine how many industrial firms and how many farmers should locate in the airshed. Where there are $n_1$ identical firms, each producing output $y_1$ in industry 1, and $n_2$ identical firms, each producing output $y_2$ in industry 2, we can write inverse demand functions (price $P_i$ as a function of industry output $n_iy_i$) for industry 1 as $P_1(n_1y_1)$ where $P_1'(n_1y_1)<0$ and for industry 2 as $P_2(n_2y_2)$ where $P_2'(n_2y_2)<0$.[6] The total production cost for each firm in industry 1 is given as $C_1(y_1)+D_1(n_2y_2)$ where $C_1(y_1)$ is the direct cost of production for each firm in industry 1 and $D_1(n_2y_2)$ is the damage incurred by each firm in industry 1 as the result of the emissions of industry 2. Note that we are presuming damages are separable. However, some of our results concerning the optimality of various policy measures are not dependent on this assumption. Total cost for each firm in industry 2 is $C_2(y_2)$. We assume $C_1'$, $C_2'$, $C_1''$, $C_2''>0$ and $D_1'$, $D_1''>0$ in the relevant regions of production for each industry.

The conditions for a social optimum in a partial equilibrium framework are generated by maximizing net benefits ($NB$) which can be defined as the difference between willingness to pay for the output of both industries

[4] This has been pointed out by Bramhall and Mills.

[5] We have also considered a two-industry general equilibrium model which gives essentially identical results. The approach used here facilitates the use of graphs and simplifies dynamic analysis.

[6] Primes denote differentiation.

and the total cost of production in both industries. Thus we seek a maximum of

$$(1)\quad NB=\int_0^{n_1y_1} P_1(s_1)ds_1+\int_0^{n_2y_2} P_2(s_2)ds_2 - [n_1(C_1(y_1)+D_1(n_2y_2))+n_2C_2(y_2)],$$
$$y_1,\ y_2,\ n_1,\ n_2 \geq 0$$

where $s_1$ and $s_2$ are dummy variables of integration in the demand functions for total output of each industry. Assuming an interior solution, the first-order conditions are:

$$(2)\quad \partial NB/\partial y_1 = n_1(P_1 - C_1') = 0$$

$$(3)\quad \partial NB/\partial y_2 = n_2(P_2 - C_2' - n_1D_1') = 0$$

$$(4)\quad \partial NB/\partial n_1 = P_1y_1 - (C_1 + D_1) = 0 = \overset{*}{\pi}_1$$

$$(5)\quad \partial NB/\partial n_2 = P_2y_2 - (C_2 + n_1D_1'y_2) = 0 = \overset{*}{\pi}_2$$

The interpretation of (2) and (3) is quite straightforward and implies, where $n_1, n_2>0$, that for each firm in industry 1 price should be equal to marginal cost ($C_1'$), and that for each firm in industry 2 price should equal marginal cost ($C_2'$) plus marginal damages to industry 1 ($n_1D_1'$). These are the usual short-run conditions with a unidirectional externality between firms. The conditions for a long-run optimum, (4) and (5), are more interesting since they should correspond to the definition of zero profits for firms in industries 1 and 2, respectively (assuming firms enter until profits are zero). Equation (4) implies that $\pi_1^*=0$ is the optimum level of profits where receptor firms bear the full cost of the externality $D_1$ at the optimum. This result suggests that compensation for damages will distort long-run equilibrium in the receptor industry. Equation (5) implies that $\pi_2^*=0$ is the optimum level of profits where the emitters must bear an additional cost of $n_1D_1'$ per unit of output $y_2$ produced. This can be interpreted as an optimum long-run Pigovian tax equal to marginal damages on the output of the emitter industry. We note then that the optimal policy barring renegotiation after taxation is to do nothing with respect to the receptor firms, allowing them to bear the cost of the externality after the optimal tax on output has been applied to firms in industry 2.[7] This will assure the optimum number of firms in each industry. However, to prevent further distortion, the tax revenue must be distributed in the form of lump sums to consumers. Tax revenue *cannot* be used to compensate receptors unless it is unrelated to their view of damages.

The relationship between the optimal Pigovian tax case (denoted *), the unadjusted externality case (denoted $E$), and the liability case (denoted $L$) can be best demonstrated with the aid of Figures 1 (a firm in industry 1) and 2 (a firm in industry 2). In Figure 1, the optimal long-run equilibrium point for receptor firms is * at the lowest point of the average total cost curve *including* optimal damages suffered ($AC_1^*$). This point is defined by the intersection of the marginal cost curve ($C_1'$) with the adjusted average total cost curve ($AC_1^*$). As damages ($D_1$) increase with increasing output of industry 2, the average total cost curve of firms in industry 1 including damages shifts upward. We presume that where the optimum tax is applied to firms in industry 2 and free entry exists for both industries, there will be a convergence to $D_1^*$ the optimal long-run level of damages, and optimal price $P_1^*$ and quantity $y_1^*$ will result from the long-run equilibrium point (*). The dynamic stability of the Pigovian tax system will be examined later.

The optimum equilibrium point in Figure 2 for firms in industry 2 is also denoted *. This can be defined by the intersection of the average total cost curve including the tax ($AC_2^*$) with marginal social cost ($C_2' + n_1D_1'$). Note that this point corresponds to the zero profit condition for firms in industry 2 where $AC_2^E$ is the adjusted average cost and the area $P_2^E E * P_2^*$ is the optimal long-run tax collected from each firm in the emitter industry. This implies that, if through some mechanism not involving a tax or levy, the

[7] See Allen Kneese and Blair Bower, p. 100, and Ralph Turvey.

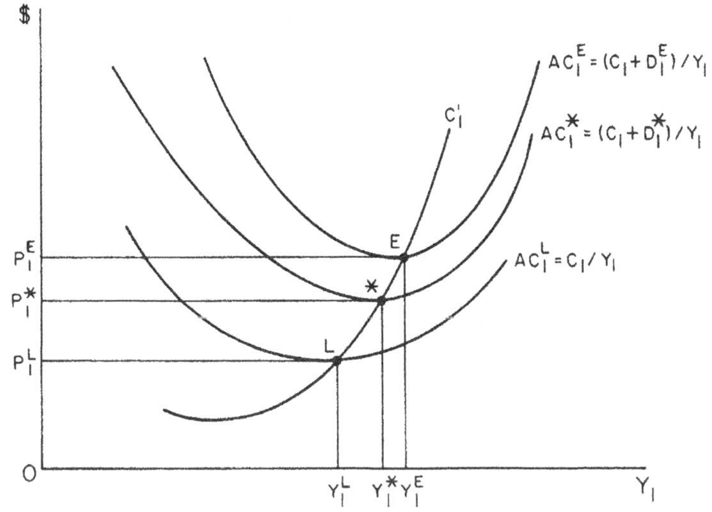


FIGURE 1

two industries reach the optimum point * in Figures 1 and 2, positive profits equal to the area $P_2^E E * P_2^*$ times $n_2^*$ will be obtained. Since positive profits will induce more firms to enter, the optimum points * cannot be a stable equilibrium under free entry. Thus the Pigovian tax serves to remove these destabilizing profits which explains the asymmetry (taxes without compensation) which so bothered Coase.[8]

The uncompensated externality case results in a long-run equilibrium at point $E$ in Figure 1 for firms in industry 1. Here, since damages received ($D_1^E$) will be greater than optimal ($D_1^*$), the average cost curve ($AC_1^E$) will lie above $AC_1^*$. Since the externality is separable, the marginal cost function ($C_1'$) does not shift so entry or exit occurs until profits are zero resulting in a long-run price of $P_1^E$ and output per firm of $y_1^E$. This implies, where the demand function for industry 1 as a whole is downward sloping ($P_1' < 0$), that total industry output and number of firms will be less than optimal in the unadjusted externality case for receptors, since externality price and output for each firm are both greater than optimal price and output per firm, respectively. This occurs because at the higher (nonoptimal) price, industry demand is less. In Figure 2 the long-run externality equilibrium point $E$ for firms in the emitter industry occurs where average private cost ($AC_2^E$) equals private marginal cost ($C_2'$) resulting in a price ($P_2^E$) lower than the optimum price ($P_2^*$). However, firm size is still optimal since output ($y_2^E$) in this case is identical to the case under taxation ($y_2^*$). The intuitive explanation of this result, which is not dependent on separability, is simply that in spite of the externality, social product is still maximized by producing each unit of $y_2$ as cheaply as possible. This implies that in the unadjusted externality case, there will be too much total output from the emitter

[8] Coase in fact proposed a double tax system, one tax on emitters equal to *total damages*, and another to regulate entry, p. 41. The optimum tax is of course determined by *marginal damages*, and this is the source of his confusion. More recently, William Baumol has attempted to demonstrate that a single Pigovian tax is needed to achieve a local optimum in terms of location and efficiency. Baumol's finding reinforces the conclusions identified here. F. Trenery Dolbear, Jr., p. 99, criticizes marginal taxes where there is an externality in consumption because emitters pay more taxes than damages induced. In production with free entry or in consumption where a location decision is involved, this *must* be the case to achieve the optimum externality.

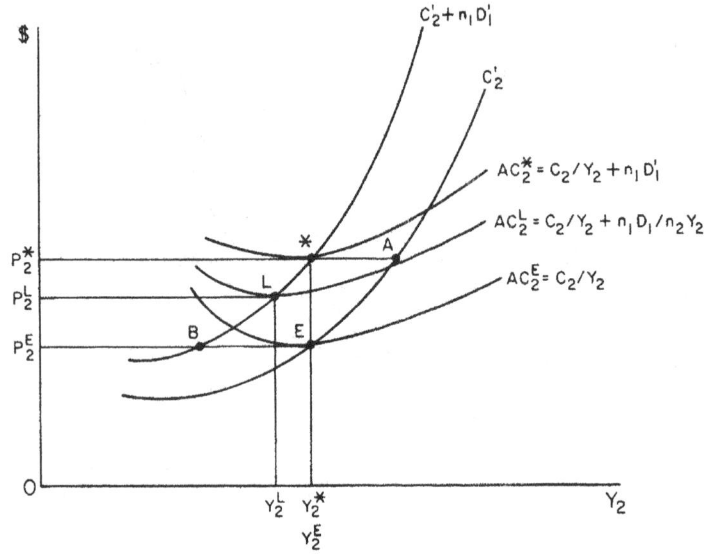


FIGURE 2

industry and too many firms, because the demand curve for the entire industry is assumed to be downward sloping ($P_2' < 0$) even though each firm perceives demand as infinitely elastic. Thus, in the unadjusted externality case, there is an underallocation of resources to the receptor industry and an overallocation of resources to the emitter industry.

In the liability case discussed here we assume that firms in industry 1 are compensated for damages and that potential entrants into the industry are aware that they too will be compensated. Firms in industry 2 including potential entrants are responsible for damages done to industry 1 and we assume, since the externality is diffuse and the firms are taken as identical, that each must bear the cost of compensation equally. With liability, profits for firms in industry 1 and 2 can then be written as:

$$(6) \quad \pi_1 = P_1 y_1 - C_1(y_1) - D_1(n_2 y_2) + [D_1(n_2 y_2)]$$

$$\pi_2 = P_2 y_2 - C_2(y_2) - [n_1 D_1(n_2 y_2)/n_2]$$

where the terms in brackets are compensation or liability payments by firms in each industry, respectively. The first-order conditions for maximum profits in each firm, assuming an interior solution, are

$$(7) \quad \partial \pi_1/\partial y_1 = P_1 - C_1' = 0$$

$$(8) \quad \partial \pi_2/\partial y_2 = P_2 - C_2' - n_1 D_1' = 0$$

which imply that the conditions for short-run optimality are satisfied.[9] However, if it is assumed that firms enter until profits are zero, compensation to industry 1 results in a long-run equilibrium (position $L$ in Figure 1), the lowest point on the average cost curve without damages ($AC_1^L$) for firms in the receptor industry. Again the marginal cost function ($C_1'$) does not shift since damages are separable and the resulting price ($P_1^L$) and output for each firm ($y_1^L$) under the liability case are less than optimum. Thus both *total* industry output and the number of firms will be too large for the receptor industry in

[9] A comparison of (7) and (8) with (2) and (3) will verify this statement when it is assumed that there is no entry or exit in the short run.

the liability case since demand for the industry's output will be greater at the lower price.

Turning to Figure 2, firms in industry 2 will reach an equilibrium point ($L$) in the long run under a liability rule which is the lowest point of the average total cost curve including each firm's share of damages to be paid ($AC_2^L$). Note that because total damages increase at an increasing rate, marginal damages ($n_1D_1'$) are greater than average damages ($n_1D_1/n_2y_2$) so $AC_2^L$ lies below $AC_2^*$ and the intersection of the marginal social cost function ($C_2'+n_1D_1'$) and $AC_2^L$ lies below and to the left of the optimum (*). This is the point of zero profits including liability for damages for the emitter industry. Both price ($P_2^L$) and output ($y_2^L$) are too low for each firm in industry 2. However, total industry output will be too high and there will be too many firms in the emitter industry under a liability rule since, given the lower price, aggregate industry demand will be too high. Thus, there results a long-run *overallocation* of resources to *both* industry 1 and 2. This sheds additional light on what Coase has called the Pigovian tradition, or in more modern form, the advocacy of taxation to correct external diseconomies by adjusting prices to equal marginal social costs. Taxation is necessary to prevent a misallocation of resources in long-run production even if there are well-defined property rights with respect to the externality such as in the liability case above. A liability solution *could* be adjusted to the optimum equilibrium point by taxing receptors an amount equal to the difference between marginal damages and average damages, a procedure sufficiently inefficient as regards information and enforcement costs to make a liability solution unattractive.

The nonliability case can best be explained in two steps. First, we will demonstrate that a negotiated solution under a nonliability rule cannot sustain the optimum points (*) assuming that the number of firms in each industry is constrained to be less than or equal to the optimum ($n_1 \leq n_1^*$, $n_2 \leq n_2^*$). As will be seen later, this assumption prevents a free rider problem from upsetting the potential equilibrium point (*) in Figures 1 and 2. Assume that firms in both industries are initially at *. We now observe that * for firm 1 in Figure 1 is a point of zero profits. However, in Figure 2 it is clear that firms in industry 2 could earn profits greater than those obtained under * by moving to point $A$. Thus, for * to be achieved by negotiation for firms in industry 2, firms in industry 1 must offer to pay a bribe at least equal to the difference between profits at * and profits at $A$ to existing firms in industry 2. Clearly firms in industry 1 are making zero profits at * in Figure 1 and cannot pay the bribe. Thus, the optimum points * in Figures 1 and 2 are not feasible under a nonliability bargaining solution even ignoring the destabilizing effects of entry on coalitions since firms in industry 2 must be made at least as well off at market price $P_2^*$ as they would be by not adjusting for the externality. Thus, firms in industry 2 would be unwilling to remain at *. It is conceivable, with the number of firms fixed by controlling entry through some licensing process, to achieve a short-run optimum with a solution somewhere along the marginal social cost function ($C_2'+n_1D_1'$) in Figure 2. However, the number of firms in industry 1 must be fixed ($n_1 \leq n_1^*$) such that profits sufficient to cover bribes to industry can be obtained. Clearly, without some taxation policy, even by controlling entry, the long-run optimum solution is not attainable under nonliability since receptors cannot initially afford to bribe emitters.

If free entry is allowed, potential entrants always have a valid threat of entry in the nonliability case if market prices are above $P_2^E$ in industry 2 or above the lowest point of the current average cost plus average damages in industry 1. It is clearly impossible to bribe potential firms to stay out of an industry as long as they could earn earn positive profits by entering, because under perfect information regarding current profitability, an indefinitely large number of potential firms would eventually threaten to enter. In Figure 2, entry would result in an eventual price of $P_2^E$ for firms in industry 2 with a short-run optimum position at point $B$, implying negative profits for emitter firms. However, this point cannot be stable because firms in industry 1 must earn sufficient profits to compensate firms in industry 2 for their losses. But free entry into industry 1 will tend to force profits in that industry to zero by a free rider process where receptors will enter (given a level of emissions reduced by negotiations between existing firms), join the coalition, but find profits eventually reduced to the point where firms in industry 2 can no longer be bribed to reduce output. Note that this process assumes that firms are price takers, i.e., perceived demand for each firm or potential entrant is infinitely elastic. Thus, potential entrants cannot realize that entry must lower price, destabilizing existing solutions. This sketch of events implies that under a nonliability rule with free entry negotiated solutions are unstable. One can again imagine a sufficiently complicated set of regulations and/or taxes to allow an optimal solution to be obtained under a nonliability rule, but these take on a Rube Goldberg character similar to the liability case.

Although we have excluded negotiation costs from this analysis, it is difficult to imagine any set of circumstances in which firms are competitive (free entry is of course a necessary condition for the existence of competitive firms), an externality exists between industries, and long-run optimality is achieved without taxation. The Coase proposition then reduces to an intuitive result. It may be preferable to allow courts to settle two-party disputes between private individuals over nuisances such as motorcycle noise by the allocation of rights. However, since it is a priori impossible to discover if a liability solution is Pareto superior to the unadjusted externality state in long-run production, policy makers would be well advised to rely on taxation or optimal standards where emitters bear the cost of meeting those standards.[10] Negotiations after taxation must involve a transfer of funds between industries and can be treated as collusive behavior.

## II

So far, the analysis has implicitly assumed that the second-order conditions for a maximum of net benefits can be satisfied by a Pigovian tax and that the optimal long-run equilibrium point is dynamically stable. We will now demonstrate under quite general conditions that if the second-order conditions are satisfied, the optimal point is locally stable, and that under additional assumptions (essentially those underlying the previous comparative static analysis) local stability implies that the second-order conditions are satisfied. The latter is clearly the more significant in that it assures us a Pigovian tax is optimal if the dynamic equilibrium solution is an interior point. However, the optimal solution may be on the boundary, i.e., one of the industries might cease production. The possibility of boundary solutions should be considered because the presence of an externality will tend to make the long-run production frontier convex rather than concave. This implies that the second-order conditions are significant even where diminishing marginal productivity (increasing marginal cost) for each industry, taken separately, is assured. Further, it is also conceivable that only a local optimum will be achieved by corrective policies. (See Baumol and David Bradford.)

To assure at least the local optimality of an interior point, the first-order conditions (2)–(5) can be totally differentiated to give a matrix equation of the form shown as equation (9). The second-order conditions for a maximum of (1) require that the matrix $A$ be negative definite or that $|A|>0$, $|A_{44}|<0$, $|A_{44.33}|>0$, and $|A_{44.33.22}|<0$.[11] Note that $A$ (assuming the optimal tax is applied to correct for externalities that are present in production) will quite generally be a symmetric matrix ($A=A'$). In the specific case where damages are separable, the optimal tax on output of industry 2, ($n_1D_1'$) can be calculated solely from the form of the damage function ($D_1(n_2y_2)$) and a knowledge

[10] An optimal standard where entry is considered must specify both allowable emissions for each firm and also regulate the number of emitters.

[11] The notation $|A_{hi.jk}|$ indicates the determinant of the matrix derived from $A$ with rows $h$ and $j$ and columns $i$ and $k$ excluded.

$$
(9)\qquad \begin{bmatrix} & & & \\ & A & & \\ & & & \end{bmatrix}\begin{bmatrix} dy_1 \\ dy_2 \\ dn_1 \\ dn_2 \end{bmatrix} = \begin{bmatrix} 0 \\ 0 \\ 0 \\ 0 \end{bmatrix}
$$

where

$$
A = \begin{bmatrix} n_1(n_1P_1' - C_1'') & 0 & n_1P_1'y_1 & 0 \\ 0 & n_2(n_2P_2' - C_2'' - n_1n_2D_1'') & -n_2D_1' & n_2y_2(P_2' - n_1D_1'') \\ n_1P_1'y_1 & -n_2D_1' & P_1'y_1^2 & -D_1'y_2 \\ 0 & n_2y_2(P_2' - n_1D_1'') & -D_1'y_2 & y_2^2(P_2' - n_1D_1'') \end{bmatrix}
$$

of the number of firms in each industry. However, to check a priori if a true optimum is achieved by a solution of equations (2)–(5) we must be able to determine the elements of the $A$ matrix. This clearly involves additional knowledge of the form of all cost functions and of the demand curves for each industry. Fortunately, an analysis of the dynamics of firm entry will allow us to dispense with this problem in the separable case and further demonstrate at least the theoretical validity of outcomes under Pigovian tax policies.

The dynamic model of entry applied here follows the work of Vernon Smith and others for the competitive case.[12] If we assume that output is adjusted instantaneously with the optimal tax applied, the conditions for a short-run profit maximum for $n_1$ firms in industry 1 and $n_2$ firms in industry 2 will be, respectively:

$$(10)\qquad n_1(P_1 - C_1') = 0$$

$$(11)\qquad n_2(P_2 - C_2' - n_1D_1') = 0$$

Profits for firms in each industry will then be

$$(12)\qquad \pi_1 = y_1P_1 - (C_1 + D_1)$$

$$(13)\qquad \pi_2 = y_2P_2 - (C_2 + n_1D_1'y_2)$$

This system of four equations can be solved to eliminate $y_1$ and $y_2$, so profits in each industry can be written as a function of the number of firms in both industries:

$$(14)\qquad \pi_1 = \pi_1(n_1, n_2) \qquad (\pi_1(\overset{*}{n}_1, \overset{*}{n}_2) = 0)$$

$$\pi_2 = \pi_2(n_1, n_2) \qquad (\pi_2(\overset{*}{n}_1, \overset{*}{n}_2) = 0)$$

Entry equations are assumed to take the form:

$$(15)\qquad \dot{n}_1 = H_1(\pi_1) \qquad (H_1' > 0,\ H_1(0) = 0)$$

$$\dot{n}_2 = H_2(\pi_2) \qquad (H_2' > 0,\ H_2(0) = 0)$$

where a dot above the variable indicates the time derivative. To determine if the system is stable about the equilibrium point $(n_1^*, n_2^*)$, linearization proceeds as shown in equation (16).

$$
(16)\qquad \begin{bmatrix} \dot{n}_1 \\ \dot{n}_2 \end{bmatrix} = \begin{bmatrix} H_1'(0)\partial\overset{*}{\pi}_1/\partial n_1 & H_1'(0)\partial\overset{*}{\pi}_1/\partial n_2 \\ H_2'(0)\partial\overset{*}{\pi}_2/\partial n_1 & H_2'(0)\partial\overset{*}{\pi}_2/\partial n_2 \end{bmatrix} \cdot \begin{bmatrix} n_1 - \overset{*}{n}_1 \\ n_2 - \overset{*}{n}_2 \end{bmatrix} + \begin{bmatrix} H_1(0) \\ H_2(0) \end{bmatrix}
$$

Local stability is assured if the trace of the matrix of partial derivatives is negative,

$$(17)\qquad H_1'(0)\partial\overset{*}{\pi}_1/\partial n_1 + H_2'(0)\partial\overset{*}{\pi}_2/n_2 < 0$$

and if the determinant of that matrix is positive,

$$(18)\qquad H_1'(0)H_2'(0)(\partial\pi_1/\partial n_1\partial\pi_2/\partial n_2 - \partial\pi_1/\partial n_2\partial\pi_2/\partial n_1) > 0$$

Given the second-order conditions for a social optimum, the dynamic model of entry,

[12] For dynamic models of firm entry see Smith, E. Philip Howrey and Richard E. Quandt, and Myron G. Myers and E. Richard Weintraub.

and the condition for local stability as defined above we can state the following proposition:

PROPOSITION 1: *Given an objective criterion similar to that in equation (1) above (we can additionally allow interdependent demand functions, nonseparable externalities, and/or reciprocal externalities between the two industries) and assuming the first-order conditions (10) and (11) can be achieved by a Pigovian tax policy, the optimal equilibrium point will be locally stable if the second-order conditions are satisfied (i.e., the system is at a local optimum).*

Where output is adjusted instantaneously (9) can be rewritten as

$$\begin{bmatrix} & & & \\ & A & & \\ & & & \end{bmatrix}\begin{bmatrix} dy_1 \\ dy_2 \\ dn_1 \\ dn_2 \end{bmatrix} = \begin{bmatrix} 0 \\ 0 \\ d\pi_1 \\ d\pi_2 \end{bmatrix}$$

Solving this system for $\partial\pi_i/\partial n_j$ $(i, j=1, 2)$ and applying Jacobi's Theorem on determinants[13] gives

(19)

$$\partial\pi_1/\partial n_1 = \frac{|A_{44}|}{|A_{44.33}|} \qquad \partial\pi_1/\partial n_2 = \frac{|A_{43}|}{|A_{44.33}|}$$

$$\partial\pi_2/\partial n_1 = \frac{|A_{34}|}{|A_{44.33}|} \qquad \partial\pi_2/\partial n_2 = \frac{|A_{33}|}{|A_{44.33}|}$$

Condition (17) can now be rewritten in terms of the $A$ matrix by again applying Jacobi's Theorem to the second term in brackets as

$$(20)\quad H_1'(0)\left(\frac{|A_{44}|}{|A_{44.33}|}\right) + H_2'(0)\left(\frac{|A|}{|A_{44}|} + \frac{|A_{34}||A_{43}|}{|A_{44.33}||A_{44}|}\right)$$

By assumption $H_1'(0), H_2'(0) > 0$ and since $A$ is symmetric $|A_{34}|\ |A_{43}| > 0$. Thus, if the second-order conditions are satisfied ($|A| > 0$, $|A_{44}| < 0$, $|A_{44.33}| > 0$, $|A_{44.33.22}| < 0$), expression (20) must be less than zero, satisfying the first of the stability conditions.

[13] Only one case of Jacobi's Theorem is needed throughout: $|A|\ |A_{44.33}| = |A_{33}|\ |A_{44}| - |A_{34}|\ |A_{43}|$.

Using (19) and applying Jacobi's Theorem once more, condition (18) can be rewritten in terms of the $A$ matrix as:

$$(21)\qquad H_1'(0)H_2'(0)\frac{|A|}{|A_{44.33}|}$$

which by assumptions on $H_1'(0)$ and $H_2'(0)$ and fulfillment of the second-order conditions must be positive, satisfying the second condition for local stability.

This proposition implies that if the system is at or near a local optimum point it will tend to remain there, or more succinctly, that an optimum point is a point of stable equilibrium. Unfortunately, global optimality is more difficult to demonstrate.

PROPOSITION 2: *Given the objective criterion defined in (1) above and assuming the first-order conditions (10) and (11) can be achieved by a Pigovian tax if the following conditions are met: $P_1'$, $P_2' < 0$ and $C_1''$, $C_2''$, $D_1'$, $D_1'' > 0$, then local stability implies local optimality.*

Note that Proposition 2 includes the assumption of separability on demand functions *and* on damages.

By inspection of the $A$ matrix we note that all of the nonzero elements are negative by our assumptions on the signs of the relevant partial derivatives. This implies that $|A_{44.33.22}| < 0$ and $|A_{44.33}| > 0$. The signs of the higher order determinants can now be derived from the stability conditions.

From the second condition for local stability (21) we have

$$H_1'(0)H_2'(0)\frac{|A|}{|A_{44.33}|} > 0$$

which implies that $|A| > 0$ since $H_1(0)$, $H_2(0)$, $|A_{44.33}| > 0$. The first condition for local stability (17) gives

$$\left(\frac{H_1'(0)}{|A_{44.33}|}\right)|A_{44}| + \left(H_2'(0)\left(|A| + \frac{|A_{34}||A_{43}|}{|A_{44.33}|}\right)\right)\frac{1}{|A_{44}|} < 0$$

which implies $|A_{44}|<0$ since the terms in brackets are positive by previous arguments.

This proposition assures us that, at least in separable cases, if a Pigovian tax policy yields a stable equilibrium point, then that point is a local optimum in the long run with free entry.

## REFERENCES

**W. J. Baumol,** "On Taxation and Control of Externalities," *Amer. Econ. Rev.*, June 1972, *62*, 307–22.

——— **and D. F. Bradford,** "Detrimental Externalities and Non-Convexity of the Production Set," *Economica*, May 1972, *39*, 160–76.

**D. F. Bramhall and E. S. Mills,** "A Note on the Asymmetry Between Fees and Payments," *Water Resources Research*, Third Quarter 1966, *2*, 615–16.

**G. Calabresi,** "The Decision for Accidents: An Approach to Nonfault Allocation of Costs," *Harvard Law Rev.*, Feb. 1965, *78*, 713–30.

———, "Transactions Costs, Resource Allocation, and Liability Rules—A Comment," *J. Law Econ.*, Apr. 1968, *11*, 67–73.

**R. H. Coase,** "The Problem of Social Cost," *J. Law Econ.*, Oct. 1960, *3*, 1–44.

**F. T. Dolbear, Jr.,** "On the Theory of Optimum Externality," *Amer. Econ. Rev.*, Mar. 1967, *57*, 90–103.

**E. P. Howrey and R. E. Quandt,** "The Dynamics of the Number of Firms in an Industry," *Rev. Econ. Stud.*, July 1968, *35*, 349–52.

**A. V. Kneese and B. T. Bower,** *Managing Water Quality: Economics, Technology, Institutions*, Baltimore 1968.

**M. G. Myers and E. R. Weintraub,** "A Dynamic Model of Firm Entry," *Rev. Econ. Stud.*, Jan. 1971, *38*, 127–30.

**V. L. Smith,** "Economics of Production from Natural Resources," *Amer. Econ. Rev.*, June 1968, *58*, 409–31.

**R. Turvey,** "On Divergences Between Social Cost and Private Cost," *Economica*, Aug. 1963, *30*, 309–13.

# Part VI
# Other Theoretical Critiques

# [20]

ELSEVIER

Japan and the World Economy 7 (1995) 1–7

Japan and the WORLD ECONOMY

# Some uneasiness with the Coase Theorem

Paul Samuelson *

*Department of Economics, MIT, E52-383-C, Cambridge, MA 02139-4307, USA*

Received March 1993; accepted April 1993

**Abstract**

Allocation of property rights – and how they are to be defined – has important economic implications. Only in certain Santa Claus situations – constant returns to scale, infinite divisibility, free entry, dispersed ownership of each grade of factor, shared knowledge, complete markets – only then will Smithian self-interest be compelled to achieve Pareto-Optimality. To try to capture all that which contributes to deadweight loss under the verbal rubric of "transactions costs" weakens a useful concept without gaining understanding of incompleteness of markets, asymmetries of information, and insusceptibilities of various technologies to decentralized pricing algorithms.

*Keywords:* Coase Theorem; Optimality

*JEL classification:* B15

The Coase Theorem, I learn from The New Palgrave Dictionary (1987, Vol. I, p. 504), inspires wonder and admiration in "fresh" minds. Yet Ronald Coase never wrote IT down. When rash folk do try, Palgrave tells me, it "probably" turns out to be "false" or a "tautology"; and the something called "Coase Proposition" is to be apprehended by a series of examples.

If at first you don't succeed, try again. When I look up the see-also reference for Coase Theorem and read about Common Property Rights in Palgrave, I learn that non-dissipation of rent is what efficient societies need – and, by this stage, I have too little reward to go on reading.

* Tel. (617) 253-3362. Fax: (617) 253-0560.


*SSDI* 0922-1425(94)00040-9

Perhaps I can do better reading George Stigler's Memoirs of an Unregulated Economist (Stigler, 1988)? George, whom we miss and revere in memory, devotes a chapter entitled "Eureka!" to the 1960 evening when Ronald Coase converted 20 Chicago-School skeptics to become believers in (what Stigler was to christen) the Coase Theorem. Stigler presumed to define what IT was: "When there are no transaction costs the assignments of legal rights have no effect upon the allocation of resources among economic enterprises" – Stigler goes on to say that this is a "reasonable and possibly even obvious [proposition] once it is explained." But I cannot find where Stigler has presented the explanation.

Something called "transaction costs" are part of the argument. In the 1960 evening's example, zero transaction costs meant that information was perfect for everyone. (Already this is a strange use of language. And substantively bad transaction-cost economics.) Ranchers A had cattle with a known propensity to wander and to trample Farmers B's crops. If one firm, GM or Mitsubishi, owned all farm and ranch lands, their operations-research experts could work out the maximum-net-profit configuration of geographical beef–cotton production. Considering only these lands and only the laborers on them, the collectivity that owns GM would maximize the $P_1Q_1 + P_2Q_2 - C_{12} = \Pi$ profit at its optimality point. For this subset of the world, it is the only Pareto-Optimal point: any other point produces less swag to divvy up among this subset of producers; more swag can bribe resisters to go along to unanimous agreement; and then the MaxSwag of $(\Pi_R + \Pi_F = \Pi^*)$ gets somehow divided between Ranchers and Farmers as $(\Pi_R^*, \Pi_F^*)$.

Follow the bare-bones logic of the above discussion and nothing institutional matters in economics. Always when you specify technology and tastes, out of the vast infinity of feasible vectors of economic variables, infinitely-most of the feasible configurations are Pareto-Non-Optimal. They involve "deadweight loss," in the sense that from what they mete out to all $N$ persons, there exist possible vectorial movements that can make each one better off without hurting anyone – or, more weakly, can make some person(s) better off without hurting any other person. Property rights don't matter. If knowledge is perfect, by definition of our talking about "rational persons" they will somehow agree to end up at some (generically unpredictable?) Pareto-Optimal point.

Did 21 savants buy this palaver? Transaction Costs are indeed important. But there is much more in their absence than symmetries of knowledge among all economic agents. The usual boilerplate about the Coase Theorem and about Property Rights I find seriously defective in the analysis of transaction costs. My major critique cuts much deeper than this, however. But on the way to that let me tarry with some illuminating examples.

The Tragedy of the Commons is an economic parable about how, in the absence of land ownership and the levying of rent for land use, free-entry labor will push and shove until on every acre average labor productivity is the same. But mathematical calculation tells that this will be a Non-Pareto-Optimal configuration in comparison with an allocation of labor that equalizes everywhere marginal labor productivity.

Is it obvious that propertyless laborers in an egalitarian utopia should vote to abolish a common land, turning over to others a rent collecting right? In the economists' version of the problem – where your work never tramples on mine – Samuelson (1974, 1990, 1992, 1993) and Weitzman and Cohen (1975) have shown that the extra production made possible by rent collection falls short of the product lost to the rent collectors – and that partway privatization can be worse than none. Workers would prefer a social compact in which regulators by fiat allocated laborers to achieve Equi-Marginal-Products; and then divvied up equally the total production, keeping "explicit rents at zero."

This example shows why transaction costs involve more than ignorance and knowledge. If I have knowledge of all technology and tastes, do I have perfect knowledge? Yes if I am God or Frank Ramsey. I can know all the mathematical functions needed for calculating the Newtonian maximum; but, as the old writers used to say, doing the algorithm may be work not fitting for a human. Hayek, or Lerner–Lange, could agree in this land case that the algorithm of laissez-faire is a dandy parallel-computation method for allocating resources. Pragmatically, property rights do affect resource allocations.

But what if we faced increasing returns to scale and integer-programming technology? At no stage in our early lives could Ronald or Paul know how to compute independently of property rights what Coase's unique Pareto-Optimum configuration is: we wait for a Ralph Gomory to teach us how. In real life what we can actually get to divide up will depend crucially on what the property and power relations happen to be and side payments are usually not present to obfuscate this. The Civil War was not aborted by purchase of the slaves and setting them free. If I go the road of buying off those who would burglarize me, I soon evoke a new supply of threatening burglars.

Rather than pursue a better handle on what it is that is involved in "transaction costs," let me use my limited time to identify and reject the dubious major premise of Coase argumentation.

## 1. Major doubt

Recall two Cournot producers of $q_1$ and $q_2$, who can each produce costlessly 0,1,2,... units. Their combined supplies, $q_1 + q_2 = Q$, can be auctioned to myriad consumers at a price of $P$ in accordance with a known demand function: $P = f(Q) = f(q_1 + q_2)$, where each collects $Pq_1$ and $Pq_2$. For simplicity let demand be linear: $f(Q) = 2 - Q$ so that the cost-free monopolist will best exploit consumers by selling $Q^* = 1$ unit. Cournot correctly believed that each duopolist would be motivated to supply more than their quota under monopoly and would receive in profit less than one-half of the monopoly swag achievable when each brings only one unit to market. Coase and Stigler have to insist that together the duopolists will decide that only two units are to be produced. Why will these two free spirits agree on that? Stigler and Coase have to reply: "Because you are not rational if you don't agree in advance to achieve maximum profits obtainable for both of you."

Note that ex ante I have no way of knowing how you and I will share. Equally? Who guarantees that, even if we each have one nose? Am I a fool to hold out? My nuisance value is great: if willing to bear pain myself, I can guarantee that you will bear unlimited pain. Rather than get nought, you may acquiesce in my selling more than you.

Mathematically speaking, a one-time, two-person, non-cooperative, non-zero-sum game is indeterminate in solution. Its Cournot–Nash solution is only one possible solution. Generally speaking, that is not a Pareto-Optimal solution. Moreover, if Duopolist B could find out that Duopolist A follows a Cournot–Nash strategy, B's optimal $q_1^*$ would not be that of the Cournot–Nash solution. (Caveat: when the same $[q_1 f(q_1 + q_2), q_2 f(q_1 + q_2)]$ game is played over and over again, the new game in the $[q_1(t), q_1(t+1), \ldots, q_2(t), q_2(t+1), \ldots]$ space may converge toward a Nash–Solution that is more nearly Pareto-Optimal.)

I doubt that one can usefully capture the content of the game-theoretic interactions between ranchers and farmers or parent and child under the rubric of "transaction costs." Is there some coherent proof that, without transaction costs, real-life rivals must find their way to Pareto-Optimal frontiers?

## 2. Discussion

Ronald Coase is, of course, better than is Stigler on Coase. Many disciples cheerfully agree: There is no Coase Theorem. The case of Zero Transactions Cost is a polar parable, and the great value of the new revelation comes in grappling with various degrees of transaction costs, in analyzing their complexities, in devising property rights and legal procedures that help to minimize social deadweight loss.

However, there is still needed – from the pen of Coase or anyone else – a coherent analysis of just what is afoot in the non-polar real world. Anecdotes do not a science make. If the polar cases, the easy cases, are defective in their purported analysis, then the subject is still in a primitive stage of development. The concepts of transaction costs – as for example the minimum quantum of time and effort needed in ordering more of an inventory, which is basic to a realistic theory of inventory holding – are often clear cut in their usual applications. But it is a confusion to try to pigeonhole the intricacies of game-theoretic interactions under the rubric of differential-degree of property rights and of irreducible and reducible transaction costs.

In general, i.e., generically, there is an infinity of existent Pareto-Optimal states of the world; and almost all of them do involve different "allocations of resources among economic enterprises [and industries]." Only under Santa Claus specifications of conditions of "perfect competition" – constant returns to scale, partitionable ownership of inputs among numerous decentralized entities, spread of knowledge, ... – will real-world scenarios hone in on one determinate subset of that infinity. (In the Cournot duopoly myth, what Stigler considers the unique Pareto-Optimal state of the world – which is the uncountable infinity of solutions to the $q_1^* + q_2^* = 1$ ideal-monopoly solution – the myriad of consumers are losing so much that there exists an infinity of quite different truly Pareto-Optimal states of the world (involving $q_1^* + q_2^* = 2$): always the winning consumers could in principle bribe the disappointed exploiters into expanding their costless productions to that non-Stigler state. Will that happen? To whom or what ("the State?") do we give the property rights so that the Utopia (ill-defined) will prevail?

The Coase–Samuelson generation were brought up witnessing the great debate between von Mises and Lerner–Lange concerning the feasibility of socialist rational pricing to produce Utopia. (That was a reprise of earlier Pareto–Barone–Wieser–Taylor debates.) Many contemporaries believed Lerner–Lange triumphed in the debate. I came to believe that Friedrich Hayek was the true victor.

Under static conditions where all is known or knowable (to whom?), whatever optimal states laissez-faire might occasion, so could some computer solution or some algorithms of play the game of competition also achieve. But in the real world all is changing, even in the time it takes me to write this sentence. Hayek has been persuasive – not in Whig ideology or in declaring that moderate reform of laissez-faire leads inevitably down the road to totalitarian socialism but – in arguing that experience suggests that only with heavy dependence on market pricing mechanisms can there be realized quasi-efficient and quasi-progressive organization of societies involving humans as Darwinian history has equeathed them. If a reader does not find the Hayek dynamic arguments persuasive, I will not here argue the matter further.

My point is that the same thing applies to legal assignment of property rights. We have paradoxes in public-utility economics. In the Tragedy of the Open Road we encounter the Braess Paradox, in which supplying a new road segment leads under laissez-faire to a slower ride for everybody. We can contrive, in this instance, a variety of alternative property rights that would make for Pareto-Optimality. (One could be: give the State a right to impose tolls; but constrain in the property-grant the right of the bureaucrats to deviate from the just-right pattern of tolls. Or contrive an equivalent Dutch Auction to pick a private monopolist with effectively the same property rights.) But in the time it takes me to write this paragraph, exogenous change and dynamic endogenous change will cause the data of the problem to change in such a way as to entail a different set of property rights. If the Social Contract makes all earlier property rights capable of being abrogated to adjust to new Pareto-Optimal needs, we are in the old quagmire of moral hazard, inverse externalities, and so forth. No doubt wise Twenty-First-Century Hayeks or Lerners will come forward to give persuasive counsel on how a Mixed Economy will want to compromise among divergent instrumentalities so as to optimize various definitions of social and individual welfares.

## 3. Summary

Allocation of property rights – and how they are to be defined – matters mightily. They are the chips in the game of dickering, threatening, and litigating. These processes are unavoidable. And it is only in my MIT seminar room that they go on all morning long in dry runs that converge to (an infinity of) Pareto-Optimal solutions; and that at high noon an omnipotent go-between finalizes at one of these calculated optima. In the real world rivalry is incessant. Only in certain Santa Claus situations – constant returns to scale, infinite divisibility, free entry, dispersed ownership of each grade of factor, shared knowledge, complete markets – only then will Smithian self-interest be compelled to achieve Pareto-Optimality.

To try to capture all that which contributes to deadweight loss under the verbal rubric of "transactions costs" weakens a useful concept without gaining understanding of incompleteness of markets, asymmetries of information, and insusceptibilities of various technologies to decentralized pricing algorithms.

The vogue of vulgar and vague Coaseism, one hypothesizes, is strongest among libertarians and other devotees of laissez-faire who believe to find in it ammunition against regulation and voters' activism. Whether this hypothesis is close to or wide off the mark is of no importance. What does matter is how much deadweight-loss obtains in real life.

## References

Coase, R.H., 1937, The nature of the firm, Economica 4, 386–405.

Coase, R.H., 1960, The problem of social cost, Journal of Law and Economics 3, 1–44.

Coase, R.H., 1991, The institutional structure of production, Nobel Lecture, December 9, 1991, Stockholm, Sweden, The Nobel Foundation.

Cooter, R.D., 1987, Coase Theorem, in: J. Eatwell, M. Milgate and P. Newman, eds., The New Palgrave: A dictionary of economics, Vol. I (Macmillan, London) 457–460.
Cheung, S.N.S., 1987, Common property rights, in: J. Eatwell, M. Milgate and P. Newman, eds., The New Palgrave: A dictionary of economics, Vol. I (Macmillan, London) 504–506.
Hayek, F., 1945, The use of knowledge in society, American Economic Review 35, 519–530.
Lange, O., 1936, On the economic theory of socialism, Part I, Review of Economic Studies 4, 53–71.
Lange, O., 1937, On the economic theory of socialism, Part II, Review of Economic Studies 4, 123–142.
Lerner, A., 1934, Economic theory and socialist economy, Review of Economic Studies 1, 51–61.
Lerner, A., 1935, A rejoinder, Review of Economic Studies 2, 152–154.
Lerner, A., 1936, A note on socialist economics, Review of Economic Studies 4, 72–76.
Mises, L. von, 1920, Economic calculation in the socialist commonwealth, in: F. Hayek, ed., Collectivist economic planning. Critical studies on the possibilities of socialism (Routledge, London) 1935.
Samuelson, P.A., 1974, Is the rent-collector worthy of his full hire?, Eastern Economic Journal 1, 7–10. Reproduced in: The Collected Scientific Papers of Paul A. Samuelson, Vol. 4 (MIT Press, Cambridge, MA, 1977) Ch. 263.
Samuelson, P.A., 1990, When deregulation makes things worse before they get better, Essays in honor of Margaret Hall, in: C. Moir and J. Dawson, eds., Competition and markets (Macmillan, London).
Samuelson, P.A., 1992, Tragedy of the open road: Avoiding paradox by use of regulated public utilities that charge corrected Knightian tolls, Journal of International and Comparative Economics 1, 3–12.
Samuelson, P.A., 1993, Tragedy of the commons: Efficiency rents to the rescue of free-road inefficiencies and paradoxes, in: H. Ohta and J.-F. Thisse, eds., Does economic space matter? (St. Martin's Press, New York).
Stigler, G.J., 1988, Memoirs of an unregulated economist (Basic Books, New York).
Weitzman, M. and J.S. Cohen, 1975, A Marxian model of enclosures, Journal of Development Economics 1, 287–336.

# [21]

# THE COST OF COASE

*ROBERT COOTER**
*University of California School of Law*

## INTRODUCTION

THE publication of "The Problem of Social Cost" in 1960 by Ronald Coase brought together two powerful intellectual currents, namely, the economic theory of externalities and the common-law tradition concerning torts and nuisance.[1] The sea is fertile but rough where two ocean currents meet, and the same can be said of the disputes provoked by Coase. Coase developed his argument through a series of concrete examples, such as the rancher and the farmer, the railroad sparks and the corn crops, etc. He steadfastly refused to articulate the general truths underlying the examples; for example, the famous "Coase Theorem" is abstracted from the paper but not stated in it. After two decades of debate the generalizations underlying the examples are still disputed.

In this paper I will not attempt the impossible task of offering the "true" or final interpretation of Coase's paper. Hermeneutics is left for others. Rather, I will state and prove those generalizations applicable to Coase's examples which follow from familiar assumptions of economic theory. It seems to me that these generalizations frequently conflict with Coase's examples in the sense that the immediate interpretation of his examples are inconsistent with the provable generalizations. The cost of Coase's paper is that readers are confused or misled about the generalizations which follow from familiar economic assumptions.

In the first section of this paper I characterize the dispute by developing one of Coase's examples. The second section formulates some general propositions about correcting externalities through the use of liability law, taxes, and transferable property rights. The third section addresses the

* I have received numerous comments on several drafts of this paper, most recently from Henry Hansmann and the participants in the public finance seminar at the University of Toronto.

[1] R. H. Coase, The Problem of Social Cost, 3 J. Law & Econ. 1 (1960).

[*Journal of Legal Studies*, vol. XI (January 1982)]

TABLE 1
BALANCE SHEET SHOWING PRIMARY DATA

| | | Trains per Day | | | |
|---|---|---|---|---|---|
| Row | | *0* | *1* | *2* | *3* |
| 1 | RR's gross profit (fares less operating costs) | 0 | 100 | 150 | 125 |
| 2 | Damage to nonmarginal fields | 0 | −60 | −120 | |
| 3 | Damage to marginal fields if cultivated | 0 | −60 | −120 | |
| 4 | Farmers' gross profit on marginal fields (no compensation) | 10 | −50 | −110 | |

problem of bargaining and the Coase Theorem. The formal development of the argument and the proofs, some of which are interesting in their own right, are relegated to the detailed Appendix.

## I. Railroad and Farmers: The Problem

A famous example from nineteenth-century England developed by Coase concerns the crop damage caused by fires ignited by sparks emitted from railroad trains. We shall use this example to illustrate the scope of the controversy provoked by Coase. Tables 1–3 characterize the example quantitatively. The numbers in these tables are mostly reproduced from Coase, but it was necessary to supplement Coase's numbers in order to broaden the example's scope. Table 1 shows profits and losses experienced by the railroad and farmers. Crop damage is distinguished according to whether it occurs in nonmarginal or marginal fields. The marginal fields are located along the margins of the railroad tracks (fig. 1), but they are also marginal in an economic sense because the profitability of cultivating them depends upon the behavior of the railroad. By contrast, the nonmarginal fields are located far enough from the tracks so that cultivating them is profitable, regardless of the railroad's behavior.

The railroad decides how many trains to run each day and the farmers

TABLE 2
JOINT PROFITS

| | Trains per Day | | |
|---|---|---|---|
| Marginal Fields | 0 | 1 | 2 |
| Cultivate 1 + 2 + 4 | 10 | −10 | −80 |
| Fallow 1 + 2 | 0 | 40 | 30 |

TABLE 3
POLICY OUTCOMES

| Policy | No. of Trains | Cultivate or Fallow | Profits before Tax or Subsidy: RR's | Farmers' | Joint |
|---|---|---|---|---|---|
| 1. Do nothing | 2 | F | 150 | −120 | 30 |
| 2. Liability | 0 | C | 0 | 10 | 10 |
| 3. Tax on damages | 0 | C | 0 | 10 | 10 |
| | 1 | F | 100 | −60 | 40 |
| 4a. Bargaining: no liability | 1 | F | 155 | −115 | 40 |
| 4b. Bargaining: liability | 1 | F | 15 | 25 | 40 |

decide whether to cultivate or leave fallow the marginal fields. The joint profits resulting from these decisions are shown in table 2. The resource allocation which is optimal in the sense of maximizing joint profits requires the railroad to operate one train per day and the farmers to leave the marginal fields fallow, yielding joint profits of 40.

In table 3 we see the outcomes resulting from different policies. If the government does nothing to reallocate costs, then the railroad will operate two trains per day and the farmers will leave the marginal fields fallow, yielding joint profits of 30. If the railroad is required to compensate the farmers for actual damage done to crops in the marginal and nonmarginal fields, then the farmers will cultivate the marginal fields and the railroad will run no trains, yielding joint profits of 10. These are the two rules of

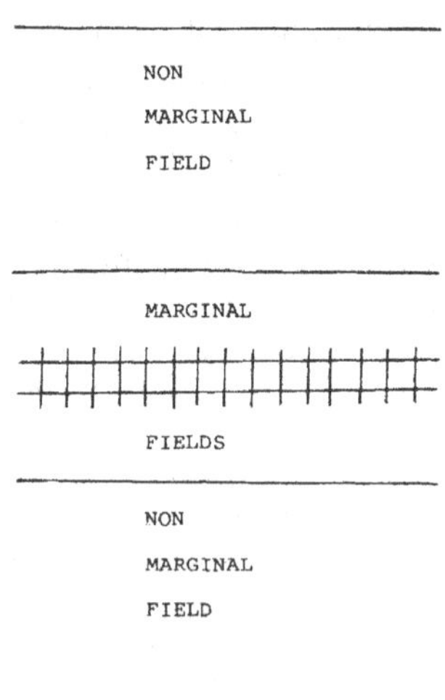


FIG. 1

law discussed by Coase in the example of the railroad and the farmers. We have expanded this example in order to consider a tax remedy. If the railroad is taxed for the actual damage done to crops, and the taxes are *not* paid to the farmers as compensation, then there are two (Nash) equilibria. Either the farmers will cultivate the marginal fields and the railroad will run no trains, or the railroad will run one train and the farmers will leave the marginal fields fallow.

The preceding paragraph assumes that the railroad and the farmers do not bargain with each other or cooperate. If the parties can bargain and cooperate, then their best course is to maximize joint profits and split the surplus from cooperation. The proposition that resource allocation is efficient, regardless of the structure of liability law, provided that bargaining is frictionless, is one version of the Coase Theorem. We illustrate this claim in rows 4a and 4b of table 3. In these two rows the activities which maximize joint profits are undertaken, regardless of the liability law, but the law of liability does influence the distribution of the cooperative surplus. The railroad is better off under "no liability" (row 4a) and the farmers are better off under "liability" (row 4b). The exact numbers are obtained by computing what each party can earn on his own without cooperation (threat values) and adding to that amount one half of the surplus from cooperation. For example, consider the rule of liability. We see from row 2 that the railroad's and the farmers' noncooperative profits are (0, 10) respectively, the cooperative surplus is $40 - (0 + 10) = 30$, and so the payoffs in row 4b are $0 + 15$ and $10 + 15$, or (15, 25).

What goes wrong with the liability and tax remedies in this example? Can we expect these remedies to fail in the usual situation? Is the Coase Theorem a mere tautology or is it a conclusion deduced from the usual economic assumptions about human behavior? These are some of the questions answered in the next two sections.

## II. Theorems on Remedies under Competitive Assumptions

In this section we formulate and explain theorems about the existence, efficiency, and stability of the liability, tax, and property rights remedies for externalities. Throughout Section II we assume that there is no bargaining, collusion, or market power on the part of the parties. This assumption is relaxed in Section III. Mathematics is relegated to the Appendix.

### *Pigouvian Tax*

How does a competitive market reach equilibrium? Economic theory usually imagines that an auctioneer adjusts prices until demand equals supply. If demand exceeds supply, then the auctioneer shouts out a higher price. Consumers and producers respond by stating their demand and supply at the new price. If demand still exceeds supply, the auctioneer raises the price again. The market equilibrates through a series of such price and quantity adjustments.[2]

In this section we imagine that a tax is levied on pollution and that this tax is adjusted in a fashion similar to the auctioneer's adjustment of market prices. We name the government auctioneer after Pigou, as distinct from the Walrasian auctioneer who controls the prices of private goods.[3] The Pigouvian auctioneer shouts out the tax-price of pollution. Polluters respond by stating how much pollution they will emit at that price, and pollutees respond by stating how much they would pay to reduce pollution. If the pollutees are willing to pay more than the tax to reduce pollution, then the auctioneer raises the tax. The pseudomarket equilibrates through a series of such price and quantity adjustments.

In order to have a concrete example, imagine that firms emit smoke and households suffer from it. When a tax-price is announced, the firms plan to pollute out to the point where the tax equals the marginal cost of smoke reduction. The households respond to the planned smoke level by adjusting their behavior so that they are less vulnerable to smoke, for example, they plan to rent homes farther from the factories. The households also reveal to the Pigouvian auctioneer how much they would be willing to pay for a marginal improvement in air quality. If the households are willing to pay more than the tax-price, then there is excess demand for clean air and the Pigouvian auctioneer raises the price of smoke. Thus our interpretation of pollution taxes is exactly parallel to the standard economic interpretation of market behavior.

We imagine that an auctioneer adjusts prices, including the tax price, upward when there is positive excess demand and downward when there is excess supply. It is easy to prove three fundamental theorems under the usual assumptions about convexity and continuity:[4]

*PI.* An equilibrium exists with the Pigouvian auctioneer setting the tax.

Furthermore, an equilibrium is efficient because the marginal benefit

[2] A sophisticated treatment of general equilibrium theorem is Kenneth Arrow & F. H. Hahn, General Competitive Analysis (1971).

[3] Walras's account of general equilibrium theory is found in Eléments d'économic politique pure (1874, 1877), translated into English by William Jaffé as Elements of Pure Economics (1954). A. C. Pigou's discussion of externalities is in his The Economics of Welfare (4th ed. 1932).

[4] A less explicit development of these theorems is in William J. Baumol, On Taxation and Control of Externalities, 62 Am. Econ. Rev. 307 (1972).

of clean air equals the marginal cost in equilibrium. Several alternative propositions about efficiency can be proved. The following formulation is especially useful:

*P2.* Equilibrium is efficient in the sense that no improvement can be made as measured by the cost benefit standard (hypothetical compensation or compensating variation.

An interesting fact proved in the Appendix is that the Pigouvian auctioneer always adjusts prices so that social value increases, as measured by the cost-benefit standard, providing income effects are small. In other words, social value increases as the economy moves along the disequilibrium path. The cost-benefit standard measures distance from the optimum, and the Pigouvian auctioneer acts to decrease this distance, from which our third proposition follows:

*P3.* If income effects are small locally, then the system is locally stable.

Propositions 1–3 imply that if the government taxes polluters for the actual cost of the pollution as recommended by Pigou, then taxes and prices will converge toward efficiency, under the usual competitive assumptions. Why does the railroad and farmers example fail to exhibit this property? An obvious reason is that in the example farmers are compensated for the market value of the crops destroyed on the marginal fields, not the loss of profits from leaving the marginal fields fallow. If the tax equaled the loss in profits on the marginal fields (10) and the nonmarginal fields (60 for one train, 120 for two trains), then the railroad would run one train and the farmer would leave the marginal fields fallow, as required for efficiency.

Some readers of Coase imagine that P1–P3 do not apply to choice of location. For example, it is said that taxing smoke from factories will cause residential housing to locate too close to the factory. But the location of residences is no different theoretically from the location of cultivated fields. What P1–P3 tell us is that the distance of cultivated fields from the railroad tracks will be efficient with Pigouvian taxes, and the same can be said about the distance of houses from stationary sources of pollution.

In passing we remark that the tax remedy is vulnerable to collusion. It is easy to see why. Suppose that there is no tax and that collusion between farmers and railroad is perfect. In that case the farmers and the railroad will maximize joint profits as required for efficiency. Now we impose a tax on sparks. The marginal cost of sparks to the joint enterprise increases by the value of the tax, so spark emissions will be reduced. But by assumption the joint enterprise was already taking efficient precautions. Thus the tax remedy is inefficient when polluter and pollutee collude, because it results in too little pollution.

### *Liability Remedy*

Assume that there is an external bad and that efficiency requires costly preventive measures on the part of both injurer and victim. Assume that obstacles to private bargains prevent the parties from voluntarily reallocating the cost between them. If the law does nothing to reallocate costs, then the injurer's prevention will be nil. If the law holds the injurer strictly liable to the victim for the full damage, then the victim's prevention will be nil. Thus no liability and strict liability are symmetrical opposites, both of which are inefficient. This is the conventional economic analysis encountered in our example of the railroad and the farmers.[5]

Now consider an example which conflicts with the conventional analysis. A factory emits smoke which dissipates with distance from the plant. The smoke damages crops but not trees. The factory can prevent the externality by reducing or eliminating smoke, and landowners can prevent the externality by growing trees. If the rule of law is no liability, then there will be too many trees and too few crops near the factory, just as predicted by the conventional model. If the rule of law is strict liability, and if compensable damages equal loss in rental value of the land caused by smoke, then there will be an efficient mix of trees and crops, as we shall show. Thus strict liability for the loss in rental value is efficient and is not the symmetrical opposite of no liability.

It is easy to explain why strict liability for loss in rental value is efficient. The income from land ownership equals rent plus compensation. Compensation equals the fall in the competitive rental value of the land due to smoke. A landowner cannot increase his compensation by renting below the market. For example, lumbering is the activity which yields the highest return on land in the shadow of the smokestack, but the compensation will be the same whether the owner uses it for lumbering or for farming. An income-maximizing landlord will put his land to the highest-valued use, whether the rule of law is strict liability for loss in rental value or no liability. Furthermore, strict liability will cause the factory to internalize the cost of smoke. Thus, strict liability for loss in rental value will produce the efficient mix of trees, crops, and smoke.

What is the difference between the conventional economic model and our example? The difference comes down to the distinction between price making and price taking. Under strict liability, the pollutee's entitlement to be free from pollution can be purchased by the polluter at a price set by the court. If compensation is based upon damage to crops, then the pollutee can influence the price which the polluter must pay for the entitlement. If compensation is based upon the fall in rental value, then the

[5] An explicit development of the conventional analysis →ı John Brown's Toward an Economic Theory of Liability, 2 J. Legal Stud. 323 (1973).

pollutee cannot influence the price which the polluter must pay for the entitlement. In other words, the pollutee is a price maker in the supply of pollution rights under strict liability for damage to crops, and the pollutee is a price taker in the supply of pollution rights under strict liability for damage to rents. The destruction of crops is affected by the decision about what fields to plant, but the rental value of the land is determined by the market. In general, the victim supplies too little precaution when a decrease in precaution increases the price paid to him for the right to pollute. The victim's precaution is efficient when the price paid to him for the right to pollute is independent of his precaution.

Strict liability for damage to crops is inefficient because the pollutee behaves like a monopolist, whereas strict liability for damage to rents is efficient because the pollutee behaves like a competitor. This is the explanation which we offered for the difference between Coase's example and our example. The same point can be made by an analogy to taxation, rather than market structure. We may think of compensation as a subsidy (negative tax) paid to the farmer by the court. If compensation is based upon the fall in market rents, which the farmer cannot influence, then the subsidy is lump sum. A lump-sum subsidy does not distort the farmer's precaution. If compensation is based upon damage to crops, which the farmer can influence, then the subsidy distorts the farmer's precaution.

Now we turn to the task of formulating the underlying generalizations. We assume that polluters are strictly liable for the actual damage done to pollutees. We also assume that the measure of damage is a fall in competitive prices, such as land rents, which no individual pollutee can influence. We refer to this rule of law as "strict competitive liability." The following propositions can be proved about a model which has a Walrasian auctioneer for market goods and courts imposing strict competitive liability for external bads:

*P1'*. An equilibrium in prices exists with a Walrasian auctioneer and strict competitive liability.

*P2'*. An equilibrium is efficient by the cost-benefit standard with a Walrasian auctioneer and strict competitive liability.

*P3'*. Assume income effects are small locally. Then the system is locally stable with a Walrasian auctioneer and strict competitive liability.

These propositions imply that the allocation of resources will converge toward efficiency if markets are competitive and if courts hold injurers strictly liable for the actual damage from external bads, provided that individual victims cannot influence their compensation.

In our example adapted from Coase, if the railroad is liable, then farmers plant the marginal fields, which is inefficient. What goes wrong? The difficulty is that the computation of damages violates the competitive assumption. Specifically, an individual farmer can influence the rate of compensation by cultivating the marginal fields or leaving them fallow. The Coase example envisions courts basing compensation upon damage to crops, which individuals control, and not on damage to rents, which the market controls. The example of the railroad and the farmers points out a problem with a liability remedy that builds monopoly power into the compensation schedule, but it does not imply a general problem with liability remedies.

What if the court wishes to compensate farmers as well as landlords, or to base compensation on damage to crops as well as rents? No difficulty arises so long as the court makes the correct distinction between temporary and permanent damage. If crop damage is unanticipated and uncompensated, then the railroad will cause profits from farming in a competitive market to be negative temporarily. This condition will persist until the amount of farming decreases enough to restore profits to their normal level. The courts may ease the pain of transition from one long-run equilibrium to another by ordering the railroad to compensate farmers for crop damage. However, this compensation must be temporary, for example, for damage done to marginal crops *last year only*. The court must not provide an incentive for continuing the inefficient practice of cultivating the marginal fields. By contrast, the damage to the rentier is permanent; for example, landlord losses equal the present value of the decline in annual rents for an infinite number of years. Strict competitive liability provides compensation for this permanent fall in rents.

Our discussion of the liability remedy focused upon strict liability. The analysis of a variety of other tort rules has been carried out elsewhere, with results similar to P1′–P3′. The point is that efficiency will be achieved under competitive conditions by mechanisms similar to those described in this section. For example, the rule of negligence is efficient if the standard of care is adjusted by the courts according to a mechanism similar to what we called the "Pigouvian auctioneer."[6]

*Property Rights Remedy*

Suppose that the government prints coupons authorizing the owner to emit one unit of smoke per coupon. No one is permitted to emit more smoke than his coupons allow. In this section we examine the competitive exchange of such pollution rights. We shall show that a competitive market will be efficient if the government adjusts the economy's endowment in coupons in a manner analogous to our Pigouvian auctioneer. In fact, the

[6] See Robert Cooter, Lewis Kornhauser, & David Lane, Liability Rules, Limited Information, and the Role of Precedent, 10 Bell J. Econ. 366 (1979).

property rights remedy is the dual of the tax remedy, with government choosing the quantity of pollution rights rather than the tax-price of pollution.

The characterization of a competitive market for pollution rights is straightforward. The government issues a certain number of pollution coupons, It does not matter whether the coupons are initially given to polluters, pollutees, or auctioned to the highest bidder, so long as the owners of the coupons are free to exchange them. We assume that there are enough participants in this market for it to be competitive. In a competitive market, the right to pollute depends upon ownership of a pollution coupon and not on the identity of the owner. We are assuming that pollution coupons do not bear the names of individuals. For example, a factory owner who wants to emit pollution that will damage John Doe can use any pollution coupon. The factory does not need a coupon conferring the "right to pollute John Doe." Our competitive assumption requires that pollution rights be impersonal and that pollutees be numerous. Consequently, an individual pollutee cannot appreciably diminish the pollution which he suffers by refusing to sell his pollution rights. All pollutees will sell their rights to polluters. If the equilibrium price is positive, then the amount of pollution will equal the number of pollution rights created by the government.

The competitive price measures the amount that polluters are willing to pay to pollute, which equals the cost of reducing pollution. The government adjusts the quantity of pollution rights in circulation by a rule just like the one the Pigouvian auctioneer used to adjust the tax rate on pollution. If the pollutee's willingness to pay for a reduction of pollution is less than the market price, then the government issues more coupons. If the willingness to pay for a reduction in pollution is more than the price, then some coupons are removed from circulation. We call this behavior "quantity determination by the Pigouvian auctioneer."

The following theorems can be proved:

*P1″*. An equilibrium exists, with the Pigouvian auctioneer setting the quantity of pollution rights and the Walrasian auctioneer setting prices.

*P2″*. Equilibrium in the exchange of pollution rights with a Pigouvian/Walrasian auctioneer is efficient in the sense that no improvement can be made as measured by the cost-benefit standard.

*P3″*. If income effects are small locally, then the system for exchanging pollution rights is locally stable with a Pigouvian/Walrasian auctioneer.

In our example of the railroad and farmers, we may imagine that government creates rights to emit sparks which it adjusts iteratively. In equilibrium the railroad will hold enough rights to operate trains at efficient intervals and farmers will cultivate at the efficient distance from the tracks. The initial allocation of pollution rights will influence the distribution of the surplus achieved by their exchange, as described in rows 4a and 4b of table 3. The efficiency of the equilibrium does not depend upon the initial allocation of rights. Efficiency is guaranteed by competitive exchange and the government's iterative adjustment of the quantity of pollution rights.[7]

Pollution rights are like coal in the ground, in the sense that in equilibrium the owners of the rights will be those who value them the most. The initial pattern of ownership does not affect efficiency. It does not matter whether the government auctions the coupons or gives them away. However, the quantity of coal in the ground is set by nature, whereas pollution rights are variable as a matter of policy. The government must create exactly the correct quantity of pollution rights to achieve efficiency. The Pigouvian auctioneer will do this by P2″.

Information is needed to adjust the quantity of pollution rights in an efficient direction. We see from our propositions that the Pigouvian auctioneer requires the identical information to adjust either the endowment in property rights or taxes. (Furthermore, the "equilibrium price" of pollution rights in a government auction with recontracting is another name for the Pigouvian tax.) These facts offer no basis for choosing between the two mechanisms for controlling pollution. The difference between them is in the disequilibrium effects. Under the tax scheme, in each disequilibrium period the firms know the tax price of pollution in advance, but government is uncertain about the quantity of pollution. Under the property rights scheme, in each disequilibrium period the government knows the quantity of pollution in advance, that is, the quantity of coupons issued, but the firms do not know the price of pollution. Policy preference between these schemes turns on whether quantity or price uncertainty is more costly to society.

Before turning to a different topic, it is worth mentioning the connection between the competitive exchange of pollution rights and the "bubble" concept with which the Environmental Protection Agency has experimented. The idea of the bubble is that air quality for a plant or district is not allowed to fall below some given level. Extant polluters are given

[7] The concept of a market for pollution rights was first analyzed mathematically by Arrow. Starrett showed that such markets may exhibit a nonconvexity. Cooter pointed out that the nonconvexity would not arise under realistic schemes for allocating the endowments in pollution rights. See K. J. Arrow, The Organization of Economic Activity: Issues Pertinent to the Choice of Market versus Nonmarket Allocation, in 1 U.S. Congress, Joint Economic Committee, The Analysis and Evaluation of Public Expenditures: The PPB System (1969), 1:47–64. David A. Starrett, Fundamental Nonconvexities in the Theory of Externalities, 4 J. Econ. Theory 180 (1972); Robert Cooter, How the Law Circumvents Starrett's Nonconvexity, 22 J. Econ. Theory 499 (1980).

the right to continue polluting at the same level for some period of time, but any new polluter must buy pollution rights from someone else. Thus the air quality within the bubble is held constant. As characterized there is no provision for adjusting the number of pollution rights in circulation toward an optimum. If the pollution rights were adjusted iteratively until the market price paid by polluters equaled the pollutee's willingness to pay for pollution reduction, then the bubble scheme would correspond to our abstract model.[8]

The Coase Theorem is sometimes interpreted to mean that competitive exchange of pollution rights will be efficient regardless of the initial allocation of rights. This version of the theorem is confirmed by P2″. However, the total endowment of pollution rights must be adjusted by government to achieve efficiency, as is done with the Pigouvian tax remedy. Most discussions of the property rights remedy envision a more limited role for government.

In Section III we consider what happens when pollution rights bear the names of individuals, so that there is an irreducible element of monopoly in their exchange. We also consider what happens when individuals can choose how many coupons to mint instead of the government making that determination.

*Caveats*

We have shown that tax, liability, and property rights remedies will solve the problem of externalities under competitive conditions. The competitive model is the natural starting point of an economic analysis because it is simple. Realism demands the relaxation of its assumptions. We shall not attempt a systematic examination of the consequences of relaxing the competitive assumptions, but we shall offer a few remarks.

A potential problem is nonconvexity in the production or consumption sets.[9] It is easy to illustrate this problem by the example of the laundry and the smoky factory. If the two plants are located far apart, then the smoke will not interfere with the laundry. As the plants are moved closer together, smoke interferes with the laundry more and more, as illustrated in figure 2. The end points of the production frontier do not change because there is no interference when all resources are devoted to producing only one good, but the interior points collapse toward the origin as the plants are located closer together. Obviously a nonconvexity will be pro-

[8] EPA's Widening Embrace of the "Bubble" Concept: The Legality and Availability of Intra-Source Tradeoffs, 9 Env'l L. Rep. 10027 (1979).

[9] See Baumol, *supra* note 4; also see Starrett & Cooter, *supra* note 7.

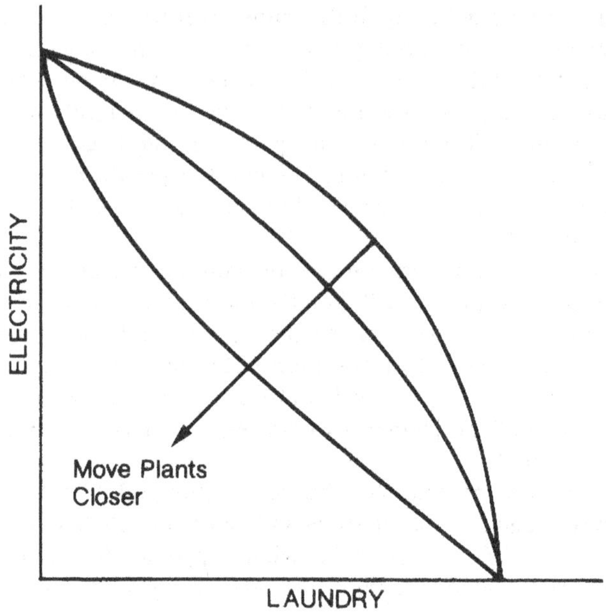


FIG. 2

duced if interference is large when the plants are close together. If the production or consumption sets display large nonconvexities, then our proofs of existence, efficiency, and stability will fail.

Another problem concerns imperfect information. For the tax or property rights remedy to work, the government must know the true damages suffered by victims. For the liability remedy to work, the courts must know the actual fall in rents caused by the pollution. Under each of these arrangements the parties have an incentive to provide distorted information to the government. It is not certain that government could obtain the needed facts.

There is also a problem concerning government motives. We have shown that the tax and property rights remedies will work if government behaves like the Pigouvian auctioneer. In fact government officials have little incentive to mimic the market. Our models suffer from the usual defect of assuming ideal government behavior without offering an account of incentives which would produce such behavior.

Finally, there are a host of second-best problems. How does insurance affect the liability remedy? What happens when compensation is partial, rather than complete? What happens to the tax remedy when some markets are monopolized? Can pollution rights be allocated without political chicanery? We must pass over these questions in order to consider the bargaining interpretation of Coase's Theorem.

## III. Bargaining and the Coase Theorem

Coase gave his name to a fundamental theorem on externalities and tort law, but he left to others the job of stating exactly what the theorem says.[10] The basic idea of the theorem is that the structure of the law which assigns property rights and liability does not matter so long as transaction costs are nil; bargaining will result in an efficient outcome no matter who bears the burden of liability. The conclusion may be drawn that the structure of law should be chosen so that transaction costs are minimized, because this will conserve resources used up by the bargaining process and also promote efficient outcomes in the bargaining itself.[11]

It has been suggested that the Coase Theorem is a tautology, like the proposition "All husbands are married."[12] But a tautology conveys no information to someone who is competent in the language, whereas the Coase Theorem is the basis for a theory of externality and the evolution of property rights. Most discussions of the Coase Theorem do not treat it as an empty tautology; rather, it is taken to suggest a definite approach to policy and legislation—use the law to lubricate private bargaining. In order to account for the Coase Theorem's power, it must be regarded as being what its name proclaims, a theorem not a tautology.

It is helpful to keep in mind the distinction between them. A tautology is true by virtue of the definition of words. A theorem is true by virtue of its deduction from the assumptions of a theory. Tautologies are based upon linguistic conventions and theorems are based upon theoretical assumptions. The power of Coase's Theorem is explained by the fact that it is treated as if it were an economic theorem, that is, a proposition deduced from standard economic assumptions. The proof has never been con-

[10] The theorem is suggested by arguments in his classic paper, The Problem of Social Cost, *supra* note 1. I am told that he stated the theorem explicitly in a seminar at the University of Chicago.

[11] For example this is a theme in Richard Posner's Economic Analysis of Law (2d ed. 1977).

[12] "In such a frictionless society, transactions would occur until no one could be made better off as a result of further transactions without making someone else worse off. This, we would suggest, is a necessary, indeed a tautological, result of the definitions of Pareto-optimality and of transaction costs which we have given." Guido Calabresi & A. Douglas Melamed, Property Right, Liability, Rules and Inalienability: One View of the Cathedral, 85 Harv. L. Rev. 1089 (1972); reprinted in Economic Foundations of Property Law (Bruce Ackerman ed. 1975); 31–48, esp. 34.

structed, but there is widespread conviction that it could be constructed if sufficient care were taken in arranging the assumptions.

We shall argue that the central version of the Coase Theorem cannot be deduced from economic assumptions. The widespread belief to the contrary is symptomatic of confusion about bargaining. This confusion results in blindness toward certain outcomes of policy. We shall try to restore accurate vision by explaining the relations among liability law, bargaining, and the economic assumptions of rational behavior.

*Bargaining Problem*

The Coase Theorem identifies a set of conditions under which the legal assignment of liability makes no difference. The phrase "makes no difference" has two interpretations: (*i*) the allocation of resources is invariant, or (*ii*) the allocation of resources is efficient. There was a confused debate about invariance versus efficiency, but now there is agreement that the invariance version is untenable.[13] It is the efficiency version which we shall consider.

There is no agreed-upon interpretation of the conditions suggested by Coase under which the rule of liability does not affect efficiency. One tradition of exegesis interprets Coase as requiring competitive markets, so that no one has any bargaining power. For example, Richard Zerbe has offered the following statement of the Coase Theorem: "In a world of perfect competition, perfect information, and zero transaction costs, the allocation of resources will be efficient and invariant with respect to legal rule of liability."[14] We have already observed that the invariance interpretation is discredited, so the phrase "and invariant" should be deleted. The idea is that a complete set of markets can be achieved by liability law, even in the presence of externalities, and that these markets are efficient when competitive.

This form of the Coase Theorem is true. It is an application of proposition P2″ where we stated that competitive exchange of property rights achieves efficiency, regardless of the initial assignment of pollution coupons. However, the government must create exactly the right number of pollution coupons in order to achieve efficiency. The government's role in adjusting the total quantity of pollution coupons was shown to be the dual of the government's role in adjusting a Pigouvian tax. This activist

[13] See comments by Bruce Ackerman, in Economic Foundations of Property Law, *supra* note 12, at 23.

[14] Richard O. Zerbe, The Problem of Social Cost: Fifteen Years Later, Theory and Measurement of Economic Externalities 29 (Steven A. Y. Lin ed. 1976).

role of government is not what the commentators had in mind when discussing the Coase Theorem. Consequently, we shall not discuss any further the interpretation of the Coase Theorem which assumes competitive exchange.

Another interpretation of the Coase Theorem does not mention a requirement of competitive markets. For example, Polinsky has offered this compact statement of Coase's Theorem: "If transaction costs are zero the structure of the law does not matter because efficiency will result in any case."[15] The meaning of transaction costs is not well-standardized in the literature. Calabresi says, "By transaction costs, I have in mind costs like those of getting large numbers of people together to bargain, and the cost of excluding freeloaders."[16] The transaction costs of bargaining refer to the cost of communicating among the parties (including the value of time used up in sending messages), making side payments (the cost of the transaction, not the value of what is exchanged), and the cost of excluding people from sharing in the benefits exchanged by the parties. In the case of contingent commodities, the cost of obtaining information on the actions of the players is also treated as a transaction cost, so the inefficiencies from moral hazard and adverse selection are swept under the blanket of transaction costs. We shall not quarrel with the expansion of transaction costs to cover such diverse phenomena. Our objection is more fundamental.

The mechanism for achieving efficiency in the absence of competitive markets is bargaining. For example, Calabresi formulated the Coase Theorem as follows: "If one assumes rationality, no transaction costs, and no legal impediments to bargaining, *all* misallocation of resources would be fully cured in the market by bargains."[17] This formulation apparently presupposes a general proposition about bargaining, namely, "Bargaining games with zero transaction costs reach efficient solutions."[18]

In order to evaluate this interpretation of Coase, we must explain the place of bargaining in game theory. A zero-sum game is a game in which total winnings minus total losses equals zero. Poker is an example. A zero-sum game is a game of pure redistribution, because nothing is created or destroyed. By contrast, a coordination game is a game in which the players have the same goal. For example, if a phone conver-

[15] A. Mitchell Polinsky, Economic Analysis as a Potentially Defective Product: A Buyer's Guide to Posner's Economic Analysis of Law, 87 Harv. L. Rev. 1165 (1974).

[16] Guido Calabresi, Transaction Costs, Resource Allocation, and Liability Rules—A Comment, 11 J. Law & Econ. 67 (1968).

[17] Calabresi, *supra* note 16, at 68.

[18] Donald H. Regan, The Problem of Social Cost Revisited, 15 J. Law & Econ. 427 (1972).

sation is cut off, then the callers face a coordination problem. The connection cannot be restored unless someone dials, but the call will not go through if both dial at once. The players win or lose as a team, and winning is productive, so coordination games are games of pure production.

A bargaining game involves distribution and production. Typically, there is something to be divided called the *stakes*. For example, one person may have a car to sell and the other may have money to spend. The stakes are the money and the car. If the players can agree upon a price for the car, then both of them will benefit. The *surplus* is the joint benefits from cooperation, for example, consumer's surplus plus seller's surplus in our example of the car. If the players cannot agree upon how to divide the stakes, then the surplus will be lost. In brief, bargaining games are games in which production is contingent upon agreement about distribution.

The bargaining version of the Coase Theorem takes an optimistic attitude toward the ability of people to solve this problem of distribution. The obstacles to cooperation are portrayed as the cost of communicating, the time spent negotiating, the cost of enforcing agreements, etc. These obstacles can all be described as transaction costs of bargaining. Obviously, we can conceive of a bargaining game in which these costs are nil.

A pessimistic approach assumes that people cannot solve the distribution problem, even if there are no costs to bargaining. According to this view, there is no reason why rationally self-interested players should agree about how to divide the stakes. The distribution problem is unsolvable by rational players. To eliminate the possibility of noncooperation, we would have to eliminate the problem of distribution, that is, to convert the bargaining game into a coordination game. But it makes no sense to speak about a bargaining game without a problem of distribution.

Our example of selling a car illustrates the collision of these two viewpoints. The costs of communicating, writing a contract, and enforcing its terms are the transaction costs of buying or selling a car. These costs sometimes constitute an obstacle to exchange. However, there is another obstacle of an entirely different kind, namely the absence of a competitive price. The parties must haggle over the price until they can agree upon how to distribute the gains from trade. There is no guarantee that the rational pursuit of self-interest will permit agreement. If we interpret zero transaction costs to mean that there is no dispute over price, then we have dissolved the bargaining game.

The polar opposite of the optimistic bargaining theorem can be stated as follows: "Bargaining games have noncooperative outcomes even when the bargaining process is costless." This line of thought suggests the polar opposite of the Coase Theorem: "Private bargaining to redistribute external costs will not achieve efficiency unless there is an institutional mechanism to dictate the terms of the contract." We have already discussed one institutional mechanism to achieve efficiency, namely a competitive market, which eliminates the power of parties to threaten each other. Another such institution is compulsory arbitration.

The conception of law which is the polar opposite to Coase is articulated in Hobbes and is probably much older. It is based upon the belief that people will exercise their worst threats against each other unless there is a third party to coerce both of them. The third party for Hobbes is the prince or leviathan—we would say dictatorial government—who has unlimited power relative to the bargainers. Without his coercive threats, life would be "nasty, brutish, and short."[19] We shall refer to the polar opposite of the Coase Theorem as the Hobbes Theorem.

The Coase Theorem identifies the problem of externalities with the cost of the bargaining process, whereas the Hobbes Theorem identifies the problem with the absence of an authoritative distribution of the stakes. We shall argue that both theorems are false. However, they are illuminating falsehoods because they offer a guide to structuring law in the interest of efficiency.

In real situations faced by policymakers, transaction costs are positive. The Coase Theorem suggests that the role of law is to assign entitlements to the party who values them the most, so that the costly process of exchanging the entitlement is unnecessary. There are many similar versions of this proposition, for example, liability for accidents should be assigned to the party who can prevent them at lowest cost, or the cost of breach of contract should be assigned to the party who is the best insurer against nonperformance. If the party who values the entitlement the most cannot be identified, then it should be assigned to the party who can initiate an exchange at the least cost.[20]

The Hobbes Theorem suggests that the role of law is to minimize the inefficiency that results when bargaining fails, by restricting the threats

[19] In a state of nature men live in "continual fear, and danger of violent death; and the life of man [is] solitary, poor, nasty, brutish, and short." Thomas Hobbes, Leviathan 100 (Collier-MacMillan ed. 1973).

[20] "Suppose we are not sure whether rubber bumpers or wearing fluorescent clothing is the 'cheapest way' of handling the car-pedestrian accident problem. In this case it may become necessary to consider the following question: Is an erroneous placing of liability on car owners or an erroneous placing of liability on pedestrians more likely to be corrected in the market? Whether car owners (or car makers) can bribe pedestrians more cheaply than pedestrians can bribe car owners or makers, becomes the relevant issue." Calabresi, *supra* note 16, at 72.

which the parties can make against each other. In the jargon of game theory, law increases the value of the noncooperative solution by eliminating elements of the payoff matrix with low value. This function is obvious in criminal law, where threats of violence against property or persons are punished. This function of law is also apparent in regulation of collective bargaining and strike activity. We claim that the same principle is at work where the threat is, say, to pollute a stream, to not perform on a contract, or to not take precautions against accidents.

For example, suppose that efficiency requires both the injurer and the victim to take precautions against accidents. According to the Hobbes Theorem, liability should be assigned to the party whose lack of precaution is most destructive. Put technically, liability should be assigned to the party for whom the excess of joint benefits over the private costs of precaution is largest. Alternatively, consider the problem of nonperformance on a contract by the promisor. According to the Hobbes Theorem, liability should be assigned to the promisee if excessive reliance by the promisee results in more net damage than insufficient precaution by the promisor against the events causing nonperformance. A detailed example from contract law will be developed in a subsequent section of this paper.

The Coase Theorem and the Hobbes Theorem have contradictory implications for the size of government. We can see this point most clearly by considering the policy implications in the ideal world of zero transaction costs. According to the Coase Theorem, there is no continuing need for government under these conditions. Like the deist god, the government retires from the scene after creating some rights over externalities, and efficiency is achieved regardless of what rights were created. According to the Hobbes Theorem, the coercive threats of government or some similar institution are needed to achieve efficiency when externalities create bargaining situations, even though bargaining is costless. Like the theist god, the government continuously monitors private bargaining to insure its success.

The Coase Theorem represents extreme optimism about private cooperation and the Hobbes Theorem represents extreme pessimism. Perhaps the Coase Theorem is more accurate than the Hobbes Theorem in the sense that gains from trade in bargaining situations are more often realized than not, or perhaps the Hobbes Theorem is more accurate from the perspective of lawyers who must pick up the pieces when cooperation fails. We shall not attempt an allocation of truth. The strategic considerations are not normally insurmountable, as suggested by Hobbes, or inconsequential, as suggested by Coase. An informed policy choice must balance the Coase Theorem against the Hobbes Theorem in light of the ability of the parties to cooperate. Our next task is to develop a theory of bargaining, based upon standard economic assumptions, which facilitates thinking about the obstacles to cooperation.

*Bargaining Model*

Our concern is with games in which everyone has an interest in avoiding the worst outcomes, but the outcome which is best from one player's viewpoint is not best from another's. The objective of a skillful bargainer is to convince others that he intends to act in such a way that it is in their best interest to do what is in his best interest. He transmits information and makes side payments in order to maneuver his opponents into a position where perceived self-interest compels them to do what is to his advantage. Inefficient outcomes occur when the players miscalculate and fail to anticipate the moves that others will make; for example, "I think that your sincere threat is a bluff." In such cases everyone is rational in the Bayesian sense of maximizing expected utility, but the best move ex ante turns out to be a bad move ex post.

Dissimulation is part of bargaining skill, and the low cost of communication is what enables players to practice it. It is implausible to claim that no one would mistake a sincere threat for a bluff if they could communicate costlessly. Perfect information requires not only the declaration of intentions, it also requires the certification of their truthfulness. Certifying an intention is an act which destroys a player's freedom.[21] Some examples are burning the bridges behind an advancing army, exchanging hostages, or signing a legal contract. The advantage of eliminating your freedom in a bargaining situation is that it makes you unable to compromise; that responsibility devolves upon your opponents. Typically, nature does not provide the means for certifying your intentions (for example, the rivers are in the wrong place), and the law denies those means by deliberate design. For example, in collective bargaining the law does not recognize contracts of the form, "Our union will strike unless management. . . ." If the law were to enable unions to certify their threats to strike, then it would enable them to destroy their ability to compromise. The laws governing collective bargaining are designed to facilitate compromise solutions, not inhibit them. Since the law is designed so that some threats cannot be certified, there is room for dissimulation, bluffs, and negotiating skill; there is also room for miscalculations and inefficiency.

In this section we develop an economic model of bargaining which captures many of the features just described. Specifically, the players are assumed to be rational in the Bayesian sense of maximizing subjectively

[21] See Thomas C. Schelling, Strategy of Conflict (1960).

expected utility, and the equilibrium is a situation in which bargaining sometimes breaks down. This model will allow us to contrast the Coase Theorem and the Hobbes Theorem.

We can describe the model in the abstract language of bargaining theory. The players face a problem of agreeing upon how to divide the stakes in the game. If they reach agreement, then they enjoy the surplus from cooperation. If they cannot agree, then the surplus is lost. Bargaining proceeds through an exchange of offers and counteroffers for dividing the stakes. A bargaining strategy is a contingency plan for making offers. A strategy calls for a particular offer contingent upon the prior offers and counteroffers. Mathematically, a strategy is a sequence of functions in which the actual value of the offer at any point in time is a function of all the preceding offers and counteroffers.

To flesh out the model, assume that the law assigns a property right to individual farmers to be free from sparks. In other words, the government provides each victim with pollution coupons bearing the victim's name, and the injurer must hold one coupon for each unit of pollution to which a victim is exposed. The railroad could not emit one unit of sparks unless each farmer along the tracks sold one coupon to the railroad. There is an irreducible element of bargaining power in these situations because pollution rights are assigned to individuals by name.

In the event of noncooperation the farmers will cultivate the marginal fields, yielding joint profits of 10, and in the event of cooperation the farmers will leave the marginal fields fallow, yielding joint profits of 40. Thus the surplus from cooperation is $40 - 10 = 30$. For simplicity assume that the farmers can be treated as a single bargaining unit. Bargaining consists of exchanging offers and counteroffers for dividing the surplus or, equivalently, for dividing pollution rights and profits (the stakes). A strategy is a plan prescribing the offer to be made at each round of negotiations, given the prior history of offers and counteroffers.

Let us consider the problem of strategy from the railroad's viewpoint. The railroad plans to make concessions and expects the farmer to make concessions. If the railroad concedes too fast, then his share of the surplus will be low. If the railroad concedes too slowly, then the parties may fail to reach an agreement. Usually there will be a time limit on bargaining (for example, the crops must be planted by a certain date). If the railroad concedes too slowly relative to the farmers, then the date will arrive for planting the crops without an agreement and cooperation will no longer be possible. Thus the optimal strategy is found by trading off a higher payoff in the event of settlement against a lower probability of settlement.

The strategy chosen by a player depends upon his subjective probability distribution over his opponent's strategy. It is necessary to specify the mechanism for forming expectations. There are various economic models for the formation of expectations, but the model which is entitled to be called the most fundamental is a model of "rational expectations."[22] This phrase means that expectations contain no systematic bias, that is, the subjective expectations correspond to the objective frequencies of the random event.

For example, consider a class of accidents for which there are many injurers and victims. The objective frequency is the actual frequency with which injurers or victims adopt a particular bargaining strategy, for example, the frequency with which railroads adopt a particular bargaining strategy when dealing with farmers. If the subjective expectations of the farmers correspond to the objective frequency of bargaining strategies among railroads, then the farmers' expectations are rational.

Rational expectations are the result of a learning process by which bias is corrected. There is a mechanism for learning in the legal setting. In our example the railroad and the farmers would probably seek legal counsel. The lawyers would be experienced with such bargaining situations. It is easy to see how bias would be eliminated from a lawyer's expectations. A lawyer expects a particular strategy on the part of his client to result in noncooperation a certain proportion of the time. If his expectations are disappointed, then he will revise them repeatedly until they are accurate. For example, if the railroad adopts the conciliatory strategy of demanding only 20 percent of the stakes, and the lawyer expects this strategy to produce cooperation in every case, but the farmers persist in rejecting the offer, then the lawyer will have different expectations the next time a similar case occurs.

The learning process which we have described will result in revision of the subjective probabilities until they correspond to objective frequencies. The process will cease when expectations are rational. Thus the equilibrium of the game is a situation in which subjective probabilities correspond to objective frequencies. The equilibrium can be called a "Bayesian Nash equilibrium."[23] It is Bayesian in the sense that each player's optimal strategy is derived from a subjective probability distribution over his opponent's move, and it is Nash in the sense that no one cares to revise his strategy given the distribution of the strategies of others.

[22] The idea that expectations about macroeconomics should be rational has been developed into an elaborate theory. The first paper in this tradition is apparently John F. Muth, Rational Expectations and the Theory of Price Movements, 29 Econometrica 315 (1961).

[23] John Harsanyi, Games with Incomplete Information Played by "Bayesian Players," 41 J. Management Sci. 320 (1968), esp. at pt. 2.

Let us summarize our bargaining model. Bargaining occurs in a context of uncertainty about how opponents will react to offers and counteroffers. The basic approach in economics to choice under uncertainty involves a two-step process: first, form your best expectations about the likelihood of each possible outcome from acting, and second, calculate your maximal move. The two-step process is called expected utility maximization with Bayesian probabilities. The fundamental problem in game theory is that one player's expectations about another's move depend upon the other player's expectations about the first player's move. How can the two-step process be applied simultaneously by everyone? The paradox is resolved by specifying expectations in the first step which are confirmed in the second step. Rational expectations have this characteristic because the subjective expectations correspond to objective frequencies. When expectations are rational, each player's strategy is optimal against the distribution of an opponent's strategies, but not necessarily optimal against a particular opponent drawn randomly from the distribution. The optimal strategy balances an increased share of the stakes associated with a harder strategy against a higher probability of noncooperation.

The error in the bargaining version of the Coase Theorem is to suppose that the obstacle to cooperation is the cost of communicating, rather than the strategic nature of the situation. Bargainers remain uncertain about what their opponents will do, not because it costs too much to broadcast one's intentions, but because strategy requires that true intentions be disguised. The error in the Hobbes Theorem is to suppose that bargainers increase their demands without regard to the reduction in probability of settlement. In equilibrium when expectations are rational, players do not adopt strategies which always lead to noncooperation, nor do they adopt strategies which always lead to cooperation.

An interesting question is whether lowering transaction costs will increase the frequency of cooperation. A natural interpretation of transaction costs in this model is the cost of transmitting offers and counteroffers. Lowering transaction costs will reduce the incentive to settle early. Noncooperation occurs when the deadline on bargaining is reached before settlement. Consequently, lowering transaction costs will delay settlement and make noncooperation more likely. Thus, lowering transaction costs results in fewer settlements in this model, which is counter to the Coase tradition.

Policymakers require a detailed account of how observable variables influence the probability of settlement. A list of relevant variables might include cost of transmitting information, payoff while awaiting resolution of the dispute, discount rate (time preference), risk aversion, and spitefulness. A model connecting these variables to the probability of cooperation would tell a policymaker whether the Coase Theorem or the Hobbes Theorem is a better guide in a particular situation. This paper is not the place to develop such a theory.[24] Instead, we shall consider in detail a recent court decision on a contract dispute.

Before leaving the discussion of the abstract bargaining model, we should mention its relationship to some familiar bargaining theories. There have been many attempts in bargaining theory to eliminate uncertainty and insure cooperation in every case. This approach postulates that a rational player will accept a payoff based upon his bargaining strength, which is gauged by his power to hurt others.[25] It is unreasonable for anyone to expect a payoff greater than his bargaining strength warrants and unnecessary to accept less, according to these theories. The scheme for distribution is, "To each according to his threat point."[26] It is an appealing picture, reminiscent of ritual combat among animals in which the victory goes without a fight to the contender who would win if the fight were to occur. Unfortunately these stipulated solutions have not gained a strong hold upon reality. Litigation drags on for months, strikes occur, nations persist in wars, hostages are killed, common resources are wasted, etc. Apparently the stipulated solutions were never meant to be predictive or descriptive.[27]

## *Austin Instrument* v. *Loral*

In order to give concrete meaning to our argument, we shall consider an example of an appellate decision which fits the Hobbes Theorem better than the Coase Theorem.

In 1971 the Court of Appeals of New York extended the concept of duress in deciding the case of *Austin Instrument, Inc.* v. *Loral Corporation.*[28] Loral had been awarded a general contract from the Navy for the

[24] Robert Cooter & Steve Marks, Bargaining in the Shadow of the Law: Model of Strategic Behavior (1981).

[25] I have in mind the Nash-Zeuthen solution and the Shapely value. For a discussion see R. Duncan Luce & Howard Raiffa, Games and Decisions (1957). A different kind of stipulated solution is presented by J. C. Harsanyi, The Tracing Procedure: A Bayesian Approach to Defining a Solution for n-Person Noncooperative Games, 4 Int'l J. Games Theory 61 (1975).

[26] The phrase is due to John Rawls.

[27] "Certainly it [Nash's solution] is not a prediction of what actually happens in bargains—it is easy to cite empirical cases where an agreement is not reached and the players end up at the [inefficient] status quo point. Nash contends that his solution is a 'fair' division which purportedly should reflect the 'reasonable expectancies' of 'rational bargainers.' " Luce & Raiffa, *supra* note 25, at 128.

[28] Austin Instrument, Inc. v. Loral Corporation, 316 N.Y.S.2d 528 (1970); Austin Instrument, Inc. v. Loral Corporation, 324 N.Y.S.2d 22 (1971).

production of radar sets, and Austin was one of its subcontractors. A year later Loral was awarded a second contract from the Navy and solicited a bid from Austin to construct some of the component parts. This second bid was solicited at a time when Austin had not completed delivery on items prescribed in its first contract with Loral. Austin threatened nonperformance on the remainder of its first contract unless Loral awarded the second contract on terms that favored Austin, including a retroactive price increase on the remaining items from the first contract. Austin was not the lowest bidder on some items covered by the second contract. Loral needed the items from the first contract to meet its delivery deadline with the Navy and escape the penalty clauses for late delivery in its general contract. Loral could have challenged Austin and sued for breach of contract in the event of nonperformance. Instead, Loral capitulated to Austin's demands but made clear in a letter to Austin that it did so under duress. Deliveries proceeded on schedule, but after receiving all of the items specified in the two contracts with Austin, Loral withheld its last payment and both parties sued.

The New York Supreme Court decided the case in favor of Austin on the grounds that Loral had access to the traditional legal remedy for breach of contract. In that court's view Loral had not established that the normal legal remedy for breach would be inadequate or ineffectual. However, the Court of Appeals reversed the lower court's ruling and found in favor of Loral. The higher court held that duress was established by the fact that the threatened party could not obtain the goods from another source in the event of default.

We can understand the higher court's finding in terms of Hobbesian bargaining theory. If Loral had responded to Austin's initial threat by a counterthreat, namely the threat to sue for breach of contract, Austin might have capitulated and the outcome would have been efficient. But if Austin did not capitulate, then the outcome would have been costly to both parties. A judge following the Hobbes Theorem would want to reduce the destructiveness of noncooperation. This end was accomplished by allowing Loral the option of postponing its challenge until after Austin completed performance, as permitted by the rule of duress. The structure of the law was chosen to eliminate the worst consequences of nonperformance.

The skeleton of the situation is portrayed in the payoff matrices in tables 4 and 5. If the lower court's ruling had stood, then the parties would play the game of default pictured in table 4. If Austin does not perform, the damage to joint profits is − 200, plus an additional −100 in legal costs if there is a suit. If Austin performs on the first contract, but is not awarded the second contract, then joint profits are highest (+300). If

TABLE 4
JOINT PROFITS IN DEFAULT GAME

| | LORAL | | |
|---|---|---|---|
| AUSTIN | Sue if Austin Defaults | Do Not Sue & Do Not Give Austin Second Contract | Do Not Sue and Give Austin Second Contract |
| Nonperformance | −300 (noncooperative) | −200 | . . . |
| Performs on 1st contract | . . . | +300 (cooperative) | . . . |
| Performs on 1st & 2nd contracts | . . . | . . . | +200 |

NOTE.—Numbers are illustrative.

Austin is awarded the second contract, then joint profits fall (+200) because Austin cannot produce the items in the second contract at lowest cost.

In the game of duress depicted in table 5, we assume that Austin has already fulfilled the first and second contracts. The remaining uncertainty is whether Loral will make the last payment on the second contract and whether Austin will sue if Loral does not perform. Loral's payment or nonpayment is purely redistributive. Austin's decision to sue would reduce joint profits (+200) by the cost of legal fees (−100), as shown.

The cooperative solution to a bargaining game maximizes the joint profits. In the game of default, the cooperative solution requires Austin to perform on the first contract and Loral not to award the second contract to Austin, yielding joint profits of +300. In the game of duress, the cooperative solution requires Austin not to sue, yielding joint profits of +200. Profits are lower in the game of duress because Austin builds parts under the second contract, for which it is not the lowest-cost supplier.

TABLE 5
JOINT PROFITS IN DURESS GAME

| | LORAL | |
|---|---|---|
| AUSTIN | Nonperformance | Performance |
| Sue | 100 (noncooperative) | . . . |
| Not sue | 200 (cooperative) | 200 (cooperative) |

NOTE.—Numbers are illustrative.

The noncooperative solution occurs when the parties act upon their worst threats. In the game of default, noncooperation occurs if Austin does not perform on the first contract and Loral sues, yielding joint profits of −300. In the game of duress, noncooperation occurs if Loral does not perform and Austin sues, yielding joint profits of +100.

We have seen that the game of default has a higher cooperative and a lower noncooperative solution than the game of duress. A court concerned with efficiency would prefer the game of default if it were optimistic about cooperation in two-party bargaining, and it would prefer the game of duress if it were pessimistic. Apparently, the Court of Appeals was pessimistic and chose the game of duress, as commended by the Hobbes Theorem.

The Coase Theorem and the Hobbes Theorem are both too flexible and vague to permit construction of a decisive example in which they are contradictory. No doubt a true believer in the Coase Theorem could find a way to explain the higher court's decision. However, the Hobbes Theorem is the more immediate, less forced explanation.

In passing we mention that other cases of duress have been decided according to the Hobbesian theory. A case in point is *Harris* v. *Watson,* which was decided in 1791, considered a leading case by Williston.[29] The master of a ship offered his seamen a five-guinea bonus to exert themselves to save their ship from danger, but he refused to pay after the danger had passed. Lord Kenyon ruled that there was no obligation to pay, because "if sailors were in all events to have their wages, and in times of danger were entitled to insist on an extra charge on such a promise as this, they would in many cases suffer a ship to sink, unless the captain would pay any extravagant demand they might think proper to make." The judge reasoned that sailors would from time to time act upon their worst threat and sink ships if masters could not void contracts created under duress. This is another example where the game of duress has a less destructive noncooperative outcome than its alternative, so the courts defined the law to give players access to the game of duress.

## *Conclusion*

"The Problem of Social Cost" brought together two divergent intellectual traditions, and its poignant examples continue to be a valuable instrument for teaching the economic analysis of law. But this classic has its costs. The examples are often misleading about the underlying

[29] Harris v. Watson, Peake 102, 170 Eng. Rep. 94 (1791); discussed in Grant Gilmore, Death of Contract C. 25 (1974); Gilmore refers to Williston, Contracts § 130 (1920).

generalizations. In this paper we showed that the tax remedy, liability remedy, and competitive market for pollution rights have desirable microeconomic properties. Specifically, an equilibrium exists and it is both stable and efficient. We showed that strict liability is efficient even when remedies are bilateral, provided that compensation is independent of the individual victim's behavior; for example, compensation equals the fall in rental value of land. We also showed that the Pigouvian tax remedy and the competitive exchange of liability rights are dual remedies, that is, the government follows the same procedure and uses the same information to adjust the tax rate or the quantity of liability rights in order to achieve an efficient equilibrium. The competitive exchange of liability rights is efficient regardless of their initial allocation, as stated in the competitive market interpretation of the Coase Theorem, but the role of the government in this remedy is no less than in the Pigouvian tax remedy.

We also considered the bargaining interpretation of the Coase Theorem, which states that externalities will be cured by private bargains, even in the absence of competitive prices, provided that there are no obstacles to the bargaining process. Inspired by Hobbes, we formulated the polar-opposite theorem: Externalities will not be cured by private bargains unless someone coerces the parties to agree about the price. The Coase Theorem and the Hobbes Theorem are illuminating falsehoods. The Coase Theorem is false because the final obstacle to private noncompetitive bargains is the absence of a rule for dividing the surplus, not the cost of bargaining. In fact, it is cheaper to engage in strategic behavior when communication is inexpensive. The Hobbes Theorem is false because bargainers moderate their demands in order to increase the likelihood of agreement. The Coase Theorem is illuminating because it suggests that liability rights should be allocated by the court in the way that they would be if cooperative agreements were always achieved. The Hobbes Theorem is illuminating because it suggests that legal rights should be structured to eliminate the most destructive noncooperative outcomes, that is, the cells in the payoff matrix with low value should be inaccessible to the players.

In order to explain our view of Coase's Bargaining Theorem, we developed a bargaining model in which strategic behavior sometimes results in noncooperative outcomes. In our model the equilibrium is rational in the sense that every individual is maximizing his expected utility, and everyone's expectations are accurate, but noncooperative outcomes still occur. Noncooperative outcomes occur because each player's strategy is best against opponents on average, but not best against every individual opponent. Reducing the transaction costs of bargaining in this model does not generally increase the probability of cooperation.

Coase created a new field out of poignant examples. After twenty years we ought to get clear about the underlying generalizations.

## APPENDIX

### AI. Firms and Households

Notation is as follows:

$p = (p_1, p_2, \ldots, p_N)$, vector of prices;

$p_s = \tau$, tax on smoke;

$y = (y_1, y_2, \ldots, y_N)$, supply vector;

$y_s = -s$, supply of clean air, or minus smoke, an element of $y$;

$x = (x_1, x_2, \ldots, x_N)$, net demand vector;

$f(y) \leqslant 0$, continuously differentiable production set;

$u(s,x)$, continuously differentiable utility function;

$I = \alpha(\pi + \tau s)$, income of a household, equal to its share of profits and taxes on smoke;

$v(s,p,I)$, indirect utility.

Optimization by households and firms:

$$E(s,p,v) \equiv \min_x p \cdot x \,|\, u(s,x) \geqslant v \Rightarrow \text{demand } E_p = x(s,p,v),$$
$$\text{where } v = v(s,p,I),$$
$$\pi(p) \equiv \max_y p \cdot y \,|\, f(y) \leqslant 0 \Rightarrow \text{supply } \pi_p = y(p).$$

Define excess demands:

$$i \neq s : Z_i(s,p,I) \equiv E_{pi} - \pi_{pi},$$
$$i = s : Z_s(s,p,I) \equiv E_s - \tau.$$

### AII. Tax Remedy

Pigouvian auctioneer's rule $R$:

$$p_i(0) > 0 \text{ all } i,$$
$$\dot{p}_i(t) = kp_iZ_i \text{ all } i, \text{ where } k > 0.$$

Define equilibrium: Set of prices $p(t)$ such that $\dot{p}(t + \Delta) = 0$ for all $\Delta \geqslant 0$.

*P1. An Equilibrium Exists for Pigouvian Rule* R

*Proof.* We shall construct a mapping with a fixed point. Express all prices as price relatives, $p_i/\Sigma_i p_i$, so that $p \in S_N$ where $S_N$ is the unit simplex with $N$ sides. Pick any positive price vector $p \in S_N$. The prices determine supply $y(p)$ and profits $\pi(p)$. Supply and profits determine smoke and income to households: $s = -y_s(p)$ and $I = \alpha[\pi(p) + \tau s]$. Prices, smoke, and income determine demands: $x = x(s,p,I)$. Supply and demand determine excess demand: $Z = y - x$. Excess demand and prices determine new prices by the rule $R$. The mapping is from the compact, convex set $S_N$ into itself. It is continuous for continuously differentiable $E$ and $\pi$.

*Definition.* The cost-benefit standard of social value of a change in smoke, prices, and income from $(s^*,p^*,I^*)$ to $(s,p,I)$ is the income equivalent given by $\overline{W} = E(s,p,v^*) - E(s,p,v)$, where $v = v(s,p,I)$, and $v^* = v(s^*,p^*,I^*)$.

*P2. Equilibrium Is Efficient in the Sense That No Improvement Can Be Made as Measured by the Cost-Benefit Standard of Social Value*

*Proof.* 1. The cost benefit measure of value is, by adding and subtracting [.], equal to

$$\begin{aligned}\overline{W} &= [E(s^*,p^*,v^*)] - E(s,p,v) + E(s,p,v^*) - [E(s^*,p^*,v^*)],\\ &= I^* - I + E(s,p,v^*) - E^*,\\ &= \pi^* + \tau^* s^* - \pi - \tau s + E(s,p,v^*) - E^*.\end{aligned}$$

2. We wish to minimize $\overline{W}$ with respect to $p$ and $s$. The starred items are constants, so we minimize $W$ where

$$W \equiv E(s,p,v^*) - \pi(p) - \tau s,$$

with first order conditions

$$\begin{aligned}&E_p - \pi_p \leqslant 0 \quad \text{strictly equal for } p_i > 0,\\ &E_s - \tau \leqslant 0 \quad \text{strictly equal for } \tau > 0.\end{aligned}$$

3. By rule $R$ an equilibrium is a condition where

$$\begin{aligned}0 &= p \cdot Z = p \cdot (E_p - \pi_p),\\ 0 &= p_s Z_s \;\; = \tau(E_s - \tau).\end{aligned}$$

*Definition.* The system is locally stable if it returns to the original equilibrium after any small disturbance.

*P3. Assume That Income Effects Are Small. Then the System Is Locally Stable*

*Proof.* By P2 we know that the equilibrium $p^*$, with resulting smoke $s^* = \pi_\tau$, maximizes $W$. Differentiate $W$ fully:

$$\begin{aligned}\frac{dW}{dt} &= (E_p - \pi_p) \cdot \dot{p} + (E_s - \tau)\dot{s} \text{ evaluated at } v = v^*,\\ &= \sum_i \overline{Z}_i k p_i Z_i \text{ by rule } R, \text{ where } \overline{Z}_i \text{ is the } \textit{compensated} \text{ demand relative to } v^*.\end{aligned}$$

By assumption, income effects are small, so near the equilibrium we have $\overline{Z} \approx Z$, implying $dW/dt > 0$ for nonequilibrium values. Hence $W$ is a Lyapunov function and the system is stable.

*Definition.* Let $x_{n+1}$ and $y_{n+1}$ measure nearness to CBD for a household and a firm, where $P_{n+1}$ is the increase in rent from moving a little nearer to CBD. Hence $y_{n+1}$ is an argument in $f(y)$, and $u(\cdot)$ includes both $x_{n+1}$ and $y_{n+1}$ as arguments.

*P4. Propositions 1–3 Also Apply to the Choice of Location*

*Proof.* This is merely a reinterpretation of variables using the preceding definition.

## AIII. Liability Remedy

Households: Each household assumes that compensation for smoke damage is based upon harm as computed by a measure which no individual household can influence. Thus smoke, prices, and compensation $C$ are taken as given by households

$$E(s,p,v) \equiv \min_x p \cdot x \mid u(s,x) \geqslant v \Rightarrow E_p = x(s,p,v),$$
$$v = v(s,p,I),$$
$$I = \propto \pi + C.$$

Compensation Rule $\bar{R}$: Compensable smoke damage equals the damage which the typical household suffers,

$$C = E(s,p,v) - E(0,p,v).$$

$C$ may be interpreted as the fall in rent that is suffered by identical households.

Firms: Maximize profit net of compensation,

$$\pi(p,v) \equiv \max_y p \cdot y - C(s) \mid f(y) \leqslant 0.$$

Auctioneer's Rule $R'$:

$$P_s = \tau = 0 \text{ (no Pigouvian tax)},$$
$$p_i(0) > 0 \text{ for } i \neq s,$$
$$\dot{p}_i(t) = kp_i x_i \text{ for } i \neq s,\ k > 0.$$

*P1'. An Equilibrium in Prices Exists under Rules* $\bar{\text{R}}$ *and* R'

*Proof.* We require only a slight modification in the mapping to use the same proof as in P1. Let $v$ be the relative utility $v = u/\Sigma u$, so that $v \epsilon S_H$. Begin with utilities $v$ and prices $p$. Together they determine a supply vector $y$ (including smoke $s$), compensation $C$, and profits $p \cdot y$. Smoke $s$, prices $p$, compensation $C$, and profits $p \cdot y$ determine demand $x$. Smoke and demand determine a new relative utility allocation $v$. Demand and supply determine new prices $p$ by $R'$. Thus the mapping is from $S_N\ x\ S_H$ into itself. The mapping is continuous for continuously differentiable $\pi$, $E$, and $v$.

*P2'. An Equilibrium Is Efficient under Rules R and R' by the Cost-Benefit Standard*

*Proof.* The first-order conditions for a cost benefit maximum are the same as in the proof to P2. It only remains to show that these conditions are satisfied in equilibrium under liability rule $\bar{R}$. In equilibrium we have

$$0 = p_i z_i = p_i(E_{pi} - \pi_{pi}) \text{ for } i \neq s,$$
$$0 \geqslant f_s - E_s \text{ by liability rule } \bar{R}.$$

*P3'. Assume That Income Effects Are Small: Then the System Is Locally Stable*

*Proof.* Same as for P3.

### AIV. Competitive Market in Pollution Rights

Allocating pollution rights:

$$\bar{s} \equiv \text{endowment in coupons authorizing pollution;}$$

$$Z_s \equiv x_s + s - \bar{s} \leq 0,$$

$$\pi \equiv p \cdot y, \text{ profits under polluter's rights;}$$

$$I = \alpha\pi - p_s s, \text{ household income under pollutee's rights.}$$

Pigouvian auctioneer's rule $R''$ for quantity adjustments:

$$p_i(0) > 0, \text{ all } i;$$

$$\dot{p}_i(t) = kp_i Z_i, \text{ all } i \neq s, \text{ where } k > 0;$$

$$\dot{s}(t) = -kp_s z_s, \text{ where } k > 0.$$

Competitive Market Assumption: Households assume that $s$ is unaffected by an individual's buying or selling pollution rights.

*P1″. An Equilibrium in Prices Exists under Auctioneer's Rule R″*

*Proof.* Same as P1.

*P2″. If Pollution Rights Are Scarce ($p_s < 0$), Then an Equilibrium Is Efficient under Rule* R″ *If and Only If* $\bar{s}$ *Is Efficient, Regardless of Whether the Rule of Law Is Polluter's Rights or Pollutee's Rights*

*Proof.* Households solve

$$\min_x p \cdot x \mid u(s,x) \geq v.$$

By assumption $x_s$ does not affect utility directly. Under the competitive assumption, $x_s$ does not influence $s$ for any individual, so $x_s$ does not influence utility indirectly. Consequently the minimization problem is solved at $x_s = 0$, which implies that $s \leq \bar{s}$ in equilibrium. If $p_s > 0$, then by Rule $R''$ in equilibrium $z_s = s - \bar{s} = 0$. Since actual pollution equals the endowment in pollution rights, it follows that efficiency is achieved *only if* $\bar{s}$ is efficient. By repeating the proof to P2 it follows that efficiency is achieved in equilibrium if $\bar{s}$ is efficient.

*P3″. Assume That Income Effects Are Small: Then the System Is Locally Stable*

*Proof.* Same as for P3.

*Comment.* From Sections AIII and AIV we see that the government cannot avoid choosing either the price $\tau$ or the quantity $\bar{s}$ of pollution. The same efficiency results can be achieved under the property rights approach as under the Pigouvian tax by adjusting the endowment $\bar{s}$.

### AV. Bilateral Monopoly in Exchange of Pollution Rights: Bargaining

*Defining the Stakes*

*Noncooperative outcome* is the equilibrium utility and profit allocation when property rights are not exchanged. *Cooperative outcome* is the equilibrium utility and profit allocation when property rights are exchanged until efficiently allocated. *Stakes* equal the change in welfare between the noncooperative and cooperative outcomes as measured by the cost-benefit standard $\overline{W}$.

*Bargaining Process*

*Bargaining* consists in a sequence of offers and counteroffers for dividing the stakes. *Strategy* is a sequence of offer functions, in which the offer at any time $t$ depends upon the previous history of bargaining. *A harder strategy* is one in which demands are at least as great under any contingency as for the softer strategy. *Assume ranking of strategies* by hardness, where "a" is hardness of household's strategy and "b" is hardness of firm's strategv.

Bargaining rule '$R$: Cooperative outcome occurs when the pair of strategies is not too hard and noncooperation occurs otherwise, or by normalizing the hardness indexes,

$$a + b \leq 1 <=> \text{cooperation},$$

$$a + b > 1 <=> \text{noncooperation}.$$

Value of game:

$m(a,b)$ = proportion of stakes won by household in event of cooperation where $0 \leq m \leq 1$.

$V(m,w,u^H)$ = household's utility given $m$, observable traits $w$, and unobservable traits $u^H$. Note that in event of cooperation

$$V = v(s^*,p^*,I^*) \text{ where } I^* = \propto\pi + m.$$

$p(b,w)$ = subjective probability that firm adopts strategy $b$ given observable traits $w$.

Value of game to household is

$$V^H = \int_0^{1-a} p(b,w)V[m(a,b),w,u^H]db + [1 - P(1 - a,w)]V(o,w,u^H).$$

Bayesian Nash equilibrium or rational expectations equilibrium: Let $r(u^H)$ and $r(u^F)$ be the probability density function on unobservable traits of households and firms, respectively. Let $p(b,w)$ and $q(a,w)$ be the subjective probabilities on opponents' moves. Let $a(u^H, w)$ and $b\ (u^F,w)$ solve max $V^H$ and max $V^F$, respectively. An equilibrium $(p^*,q^*)$ satisfies

$$p^*[b(u^F,w)] = r(u^F)$$

$$q^*[a(u^H,w)] = r(u^H).$$

Comparative statics: The comparative statics of this model of bargaining are developed in Robert Cooter and Steve Marks, "Bargaining in the Shadow of the Law: Model of Strategic Behavior."[30] It is shown that an increase in transaction costs increases the probability of cooperation, assuming that negotiations are not broken off. This result is contrary to the Coase Theorem approach.

[30] Robert Cooter and Steven Marks, "Bargaining in the Shadow of the Law: Model of Strategic Behavior," J. Legal Stud., forthcoming.

# [22]

ELSEVIER

Journal of Public Economics 76 (2000) 309–335

JOURNAL OF PUBLIC ECONOMICS

# Does voluntary participation undermine the Coase Theorem?

Avinash Dixit*, Mancur Olson[†]

*Department of Economics, Princeton University, Princeton, NJ 08544-1021, USA*

**Abstract**

The Coase Theorem states that costless enforcement of voluntary agreements yields efficient outcomes. We argue that previous treatments fail to recognize the full meaning of 'voluntary'. It requires a two-stage game: a non-cooperative participation decision, followed by Coaseian bargaining only among those who choose to participate. We illustrate this in a simple public-goods model, and find outcomes ranging from extremely inefficient to fully efficient. However, the efficient equilibrium is not robust to even very small transaction costs. Thus, we cast doubt on Coaseian claims of universal efficiency. Finally, we outline a kind of coercion that restores efficiency. © 2000 Elsevier Science S.A. All rights reserved.

*Keywords:* Public goods, Coase Theorem

*JEL classification:* H11; H41; D71

## 1. Introduction

In his article 'The Problem of Social Cost,' Ronald Coase introduced a very powerful idea of great importance. Coase's article has been arguably the single

---

*Corresponding author.

*E-mail address:* dixitak@princeton.edu (A. Dixit)

[†]Footnote by Avinash Dixit: Mancur Olson was Distinguished Professor of Economics and Director of the Center for Institutional Reform and the Informal Sector (IRIS) at the University of Maryland. He died very suddenly on February 19, 1998, in the midst of numerous projects including a revision of this paper. I have had to prepare the final version without the benefit of his insight, scholarship, energy, and enthusiasm.


PII: S0047-2727(99)00089-4

largest influence on thinking about economic policy for the last three decades. It is one of the most — if not the most — widely cited economics article in recent times.[1]

Coase argued that, given a precise allocation of property rights and the absence of any costs of information or negotiation, two parties would arrive at a bargain that would internalize any externalities between them. Though Coase took for granted a government that allocated the property rights between the parties and a court that enforced their agreed bargain, he emphasized that an efficient outcome would occur whatever the initial allocation of legal rights.[2] Coase extended his analysis beyond two-party externalities to larger groups and even to 'amorphous' externalities or public bads like air pollution (see the Coase, 1988 book, in which the Coase, 1960 article is reprinted, pp. 24–25, 170–177, 180–182). While it is admitted that transaction costs will increase when the number of people in the group impacted by the externalities or served by the public good are large, the argument is that in Coase's idealized world of zero transaction costs, efficient outcomes can be achieved no matter how large the numbers. Thus, Coase's argument applies to public goods for large numbers as well as to local externalities. In addition, using his own earlier theory of the firm, Coase argued in Section VI of his article (Coase, 1960) that economic activity will be carried out by whatever means, market or non-market, that minimizes total costs: that is, production plus transaction costs. In short, the Pigouvian argument that government is needed to use taxes and subsidies to internalize externalities was fundamentally unsatisfactory; even in the presence of externalities and public goods, the rational bargaining of the parties in the economy would bring efficiency without any governmental intervention.

### *1.1. The narrow and the broad theorem*

Coase did not claim he had offered a theorem, but George Stigler and legions of other economists have asserted that he had. Therefore, they attribute to him a deductive result that is, within its domain of application, necessarily and universally true. Though in some formulations of the theorem there are also other claims, the most basic claim of what has come to be called the Coase Theorem is that only transaction (or bargaining) costs can prevent voluntary bargaining from attaining Pareto-efficient outcomes. The theorem can be fairly stated as follows: 'If

[1]According to the Social Science Citation Index volumes since 1972, even Milton Friedman and Paul Samuelson do not have a single publication that has been cited even half as often as 'The Problem of Social Cost.' This article was also, by a huge margin, the most widely ordered article in the Bobbs–Merrill Reprint Series in Economics.

[2]The initial distribution of legal rights affects the distribution of income, and, thus, the outcomes may be different because of income effects.

transaction costs are zero, rational parties will necessarily achieve a Pareto-efficient allocation through voluntary transactions or bargaining.'

Different economists define transaction costs differently, but all agree that the resources devoted to transactions have alternative uses and, thus, an opportunity cost. Therefore, transaction costs must be taken into account in defining the Pareto frontier. When this point is used along with a comprehensive definition of transaction costs, the Coase Theorem can easily be transformed into an even grander proposition. If the familiar Coase theorem is true, it must also be true that rational parties in an economy will make all those trades in private goods, and all those bargains to internalize externalities, provide public goods, and deal with any other potential market failures, that bring positive **net** gains — that is, gains greater than the transaction costs needed to realize them. They will not make those deals that cost more to make than they are worth, and obviously Pareto efficiency requires that such deals should not be made. Thus, if the Coase Theorem is true, so is a 'super Coase Theorem,' namely that 'rational parties will necessarily achieve a Pareto-efficient allocation through voluntary transactions or bargaining, no matter how high transaction costs might be.'

When transaction costs are important, so is the transaction technology. There are obvious incentives to come up with innovations that reduce transaction costs. The above argument then extends to say that the most cost-effective methods of reducing transaction costs will get chosen. Some innovations that reduce transaction costs are organizational rather than technological: for example money, which eliminates the transaction cost of barter which requires a double coincidence of wants. Then the theorem says that such institutions will emerge through the same process of voluntary transaction.

### *1.2. The theorem applied to politics*

Some followers of Coase, for example Cheung (1970), have taken the next logical step and pointed out that government is an organization that can reduce transaction costs. Coase also recognizes the possibility that governments, though their policies in practice typically have serious defects, could sometimes in dealing with certain problems have lower transaction costs than the private sector (Coase, 1988, p. 27). Then the comprehensive Coase Theorem extends to cover politics: rational actors in the polity will bargain politically until all mutual gains have been realized. Therefore, democratic government produces socially efficient results. It is not even necessary to start by postulating the existence of such a government; if it does not exist, but its value to the society exceeds the transaction costs of setting it up and operating it, then it will emerge through Coaseian bargaining.

A number of economists, some of whom began with strong classical-liberal or conservative world views, have thus been led, with impressive scientific honesty, by their understanding of the logic of the Coase Theorem, to an astonishingly optimistic account of economic policy in democratic governments. Notable examples are Stigler (1971, 1992) and Wittman (1989, 1995).

### *1.3. Numbers matter*

As Olson (1996) has argued, these Panglossian implications of the Coase Theorem are difficult to reconcile with the historical record. History is not only full of examples of egregiously wasteful economic policies, but also of destruction and violence, such as in holocausts and wars, that are certainly not Pareto-efficient and cannot be consistent with the Coase Theorem. Olson (1965), and several others following him, for example Hardin (1982) and Sandler (1992), have argued that the Coase Theorem often leads to absurd conclusions because it does not take account of the way that an increase in the number who must participate in the internalization of an externality or the provision of a public good makes it difficult or impossible for Coaseian bargaining to achieve Pareto efficiency. The point is not merely that transaction costs increase with numbers; that would be covered by the 'super-Coase' formulation. Rather, the key to the argument is the familiar economic problem of free riding.

The argument goes as follows. As the number who would benefit from provision of a non-exclusive public good increases, other things being equal, voluntary non-cooperative rational individual behavior leads any group to fall further short of obtaining a group-optimal level of provision. In a society consisting of $N$ identical individuals, each gets only $(1/N)$th of the total benefit of the good; therefore, each contributes too little. This problem gets worse as $N$ increases. If the individuals differ in their intensity of demand for the public good, those with the strongest demands will contribute more than their mere numbers would indicate, but the total will still fall short of the social optimum.

### *1.4. What is a voluntary agreement?*

But a non-cooperative contribution equilibrium does not allow for Coaseian bargaining, and Coaseians claim that a meeting of all potential beneficiaries will achieve unanimous agreement for a fully efficient provision of the public good. We argue that in this they fail to recognize the deep basis of free riding. It is an inherent consequence of the Coaseian requirement that agreements be voluntary. Therefore, it arises in the very act of convening such a meeting.

Suppose that the benefits accruing to $M$ people would suffice to cover the cost of providing the public good, where $M$ is less than $N$, the total population. Then no individual is pivotal or critical to the outcome. Any one can reckon that if he stays away from the meeting, the remaining $(N-1)$ will find it worth their while to contribute and provide the good anyway. Then the absentee can enjoy the benefits of the good (remember it is non-excludable) without paying any of the cost (remember that agreement has to be voluntary, so someone who was absent and did not consent cannot be compelled to pay). The potential benefit of such free riding can tempt every member of the population. If there are enough such free riders, the bus will stay in the garage — the public good will not be provided even though its total social benefit may exceed its cost by a considerable margin.

Adherents of the Coase Theorem propose to get around this free rider problem by using more complex conditional agreements of the form 'Each person will be asked to pay his share if and only if all others pay their shares,' or 'If anyone is absent from the meeting, the good will not be provided at all.' If such resolutions were credible prior commitments, then an individual contemplating staying away would recognize that he is indeed pivotal — his absence would kill the project and he would not enjoy the free rider's benefit. But remember that it is the meeting that will decide the matter. At the time the individual is deciding whether to participate, the meeting has not yet taken place, and no commitment to an 'all-or-nothing' choice has been made. If an individual is to expect that the future meeting will make such a choice, it has to be ex post optimal for the meeting to do so. In other words, it has to be a part of a properly specified forward-looking or subgame-perfect equilibrium of a two-stage game, of which the first stage is the non-cooperative choice of isolated individuals as to whether to attend a meeting, and the second stage is the cooperative action of those who have turned up for the meeting.[3]

This point is basic to the voluntary nature of Coaseian bargains. Individuals should have the right to decide freely whether to participate in them. Once participants have emerged, and have struck a deal, it will be enforced by the prevailing transactions technology. But in the strict logic of the argument, there is no such thing as society until individuals come together to form it, and statements such as 'the society will devise a conditional contract to ensure efficiency' are empty until one specifies the decision process of individuals that leads to the formation of this society.

All previous Coaseian approaches to public good provision share this defect in one way or another: they assume that all potential beneficiaries of the good have already gathered together, and proceed to analyze whether and how they can arrive at efficient solutions, constrained by the transaction cost technology. The core — for example Foley (1970), Mas-Colell (1980), and Cornes and Sandler (1986, pp. 303–306, 417–419) — is an explicitly cooperative concept of this kind. Mechanism design approaches — for example Clarke (1971), Groves and Ledyard (1977), and Cornes and Sandler (1986, Chap. 7) — start by assuming that the power to make and implement the mechanism has been handed over to someone, presumably by a duly constituted meeting of all potential participants. They do not

[3]By making the meeting a first stage, with a clearly understood time and venue, we are actually biasing the situation in favor of an efficient Coaseian outcome. Without this assumption, the act of organizing a first stage is itself a problem of providing a public good, so we cannot begin to solve the main public good problem without solving this prior one!

consider individual incentives to attend this meeting; thus, they skip what we called the vital first stage of voluntary participation.

### *1.5. Foreshadowing the model*

In Section 2 we develop a formal model that captures what we have argued as the essential and basic voluntary participation choice. Here we briefly discuss the structure of the model and the intuition for its results.

To examine the Coase Theorem in its simplest and purest form, we assume that there are no transaction costs whatever and that all agreements are costlessly and reliably enforced. We also simplify further by assuming that the public good is available in only one discrete quantity, so that we do not need to consider any bargaining about partial provision or about how much to obtain. Any obstacles to efficiency which we discover in this framework can only be magnified in more general settings with transaction costs and continuously variable amounts of the good.

We believe that it is essential to respect both aspects: voluntary participation, and costless enforcement. We do this using a two-stage game. The first stage is non-cooperative, where isolated individuals decide whether to participate in the second stage. The latter is the familiar Coaseian bargaining process, and can be modelled using any of the standard approaches like the core or mechanism design. Since we do not consider transaction costs, for us these are all equivalent, and produce an outcome that is optimal for those who have chosen to participate. But that in turn profoundly affects the Stage 1 participation decision, and, therefore, the efficiency of the outcome for society as a whole.

Consider a non-excludable, discrete public good that provides a benefit $V$ to every person in some group of $N$ individuals and costs $C$ to produce. Suppose initially that all individuals are identical. Let $M$ be the smallest integer such that $MV > C$; thus, $M$ is the smallest group that would find it advantageous to produce the good entirely at its own expense. Often $M$ will be smaller than $N$. This will be the case whenever the good provides enough of a surplus over its costs so that a subset of those who benefit from provision would gain from providing it even if they bore all of the costs. It will also be true whenever a public good that already is worth enough to cover its costs is non-rival (i.e. such that additional consumers do not reduce the consumption of others) and new people move into the group or community. When the gain to the $M$ individuals exceeds the cost $C$ of the good, it is a fortiori necessary for Pareto efficiency that it be provided when $N > M$.

Suppose some $n$ individuals of size $M$ or larger provide the good. They must still solve a bargaining problem among themselves to share the cost. Since there is no information asymmetry, we assume that they do so efficiently. For the most part, in fact, we assume that the individuals are also identical as regards their bargaining abilities, that is, they share the costs equally, and each individual pays $C/n$. However, in one crucial context this assumption contributes to a more optimistic conclusion about the good being provided. At that point we will return to the assumption and comment upon it.

Consider the $N$ individuals, initially in isolation, making independent decisions about whether they will participate in the provision of a public good or even in any discussions about mechanisms or agreements that might provide the good. We can quickly get some intuitive sense of the matter by comparing the gains to an individual if he chooses to participate and those that come if he attempts to free ride on the provision of others.

First consider a single play of this two-stage game. As usual, the subgame perfect equilibrium is found by starting with Stage 2, namely the Coaseian bargaining or mechanism design among those who have chosen to participate. If $M$ or more people show up at Stage 2, it is optimal for them to proceed to provide the good and share the cost. Thus, at least in this paper, we have no quarrel with the presumption of efficiency of Coaseian bargaining once it starts. The difficulty which we emphasize arises from free riding at the previous stage where individuals are deciding whether to participate in the whole process, rationally looking ahead to what will happen at Stage 2.

Focus on one person, whom we call Herb for sake of definiteness. The only gain to Herb from being a contributor arises in the eventuality where exactly $M-1$ others decide to contribute. In this case Herb's contribution is pivotal and his gain from contributing is $V-C/M$. The gain to Herb from deciding to free ride is that he obtains the larger gain of $V$ if $M$ or more of the others decide to contribute. When $N$ exceeds $M$ by much, the likelihood that Herb will be the pivotal contributor and, thus, gain from the decision to contribute is small; Herb is much more likely, if there is provision, to be a non-indispensable contributor, and in all such cases he is wiser to have made the decision to be a free rider. The model allows us to quantify these ideas, and shows, for example, that when $M=10$ and $N=30$, the likelihood that there will be provision is much less than one in a million.

However, limiting the game to a single play of the two stages is arbitrary, especially since we have assumed zero transaction costs. Therefore, we go on to consider a repeated version of the two-stage game. We find two equilibria, each sustained by its own internally consistent expectations. In the first equilibrium, individuals at every play of Stage 1 believe that if $M$ or more people turn up at the immediately following Stage 2 they will go ahead and provide the good on their own. This further reduces the incentive for any one individual to attend the meeting at any one play: if an error is made (too few people show up) there will be opportunities to play again. Because of this reduction of individual participation, paradoxically, repetition actually makes the outcome even less efficient. In the second equilibrium, everyone at every play of Stage 1 believes that the following Stage 2 will proceed with the provision of the good if and only if all $N$ show up. Then it is optimal for everyone to show up, and it is also ex post optimal for the meeting to follow this all-or-nothing strategy if anyone tries to test it, so long as people are very patient, that is, there is little or no discounting of payoffs in successive plays.

The second equilibrium gives everyone higher payoffs; in fact it is fully optimal. Also, it obtains when there is low discounting, that is, the waiting costs of negotiation are low, which fits naturally with our assumption of no transaction costs. Therefore, this equilibrium has some claim to attention. However, we find that it is not robust to the introduction of even small costs of attending meetings. Also, if individuals differ in their bargaining abilities, and, therefore, bear different cost shares at Stage 2, then the requirement of low discounting is even stricter than with equal shares. Therefore, we do not conclude that the repeated two-stage Coaseian procedure must yield efficient outcomes. Taking the idea of voluntary participation seriously does point out major obstacles to efficiency.

We should emphasize that our criticism pertains to the internal logic of the Coase Theorem. We do not wish to claim that public goods generally go unprovided in practice. Some large inefficiencies persist — see Olson (1996) — but groups do strive to overcome free rider problems and often succeed. Our claim is that they are unlikely to succeed if they rely solely on voluntary participation choices of individuals. Successful provision of public goods, or internalization of externalities in large groups, usually requires some form of coercion. Of course there are different types and degrees of coercion, some more palatable than others. In the concluding section we point out a particularly simple and relatively acceptable form, which is often used in practice.

## 2. Formal statement of the model

We now propose an extremely simple model that respects both the voluntary participation and costless enforcement assumed in the Coase Theorem. Our model is closely related to Palfrey and Rosenthal (1984) and we discuss the specific points of similarity and difference at appropriate places below. Our model takes both aspects of Coase's setup — voluntary agreement and costless enforcement — seriously. Agreements should be voluntary so that every individual has complete freedom to decide whether to enter into them, and they should be costlessly enforceable so that once an individual has made an agreement, he or she is held to all the commitments contained in the agreement. Each part of this duo has a reciprocal or negative aspect: there must be no coercion to enter any agreement ex ante, and there must be no escape from a contract ex post.

The first or voluntary agreement feature of the Coase Theorem makes a non-cooperative game formulation natural, and the second or perfectly reliable costless enforcement calls for a cooperative game formulation. Accordingly we develop a two-stage game. In the first stage, each individual decides whether to participate (choose IN) or not (choose OUT). In the second, those who have chosen IN play a cooperative game of Coaseian bargaining with costless enforcement of contracts. We first consider a single play of this game; then we allow it to be repeated.

In our model, note that the second stage is played only among those who have chosen IN at the first stage: people cannot be compelled to participate and contribute. But note also that there are no transaction costs: once you have declared yourself IN, you have no private information and no ability to engage in opportunistic behavior, and there are no obstacles to the achievement of an optimal bargain — among those who have declared IN. We will see that the last qualifying phrase carries a punch.

The equilibrium is found by backward induction. The participation decision in the first stage is made by looking ahead to the consequences of participation or non-participation and balancing the benefits against the costs.

Remember that the public good is discrete and non-excludable. The total population is $N$; each member gets benefit $V$ from the good; the cost of the good is $C$; and $M$ is the smallest number whose benefits cover the cost, so $MV \geq C > (M-1)V$.

We will show that as $N$ increases and $M < N$, the likelihood that the good gets provided goes down very rapidly and a Pareto-efficient outcome is extremely unlikely. Therefore, the result contradicts the Coase Theorem in a very strong sense. We postpone further discussion of our assumptions until later, in the hope that they can better be understood in the light of the analysis and the results.

## 3. Single play

We begin by supposing that the two stage game is played only once, and consider its forward-looking or subgame-perfect equilibrium. For this, we begin by finding out what happens in the second stage. That is easy: if $n$ people have chosen IN at the first stage, where $n \geq M$, it is optimal for them to produce the good in the standard Coaseian manner. Thus, here we do not quarrel with the Coaseian argument that a negotiating meeting, once convened, reaches an outcome that is efficient for the participants. However, we do not allow the participants to coerce the non-participants. Since all participants are identical, we resolve their problem of bargaining about sharing the cost of the good by assuming equal shares. Then each of the $n$ participants, where $n \geq M$, gets the net benefit of $V-(C/n)$, while each of the $(N-n)$ non-participants (free riders) gets $V$. If fewer than $M$ people choose IN, the good is not produced. (Later we introduce further rounds that will allow reconsideration.)

We pause to discuss the relation between our model and Palfrey and Rosenthal (1984). They assume that the contribution $k$ required from each participant is the same no matter what their numbers, whereas we fix the total cost of the good, $C$, so that the contribution of each participant, $(C/n)$, is inversely proportional to their number $n$. They consider two cases: the 'refund case' where if less than $M$ people participate each gets zero, and a 'non-refund case' where in such an eventuality each participant still pays $k$ even though the good is not provided, so the payoffs are $-k$ each. In the non-refund case there is a 'fear' motive for an individual to choose non-participation: if too few others show up, one merely loses one's stake. This is absent from our model. In the refund case there is a 'greed' motive for non-participation: if enough others show up, then one does better by free-riding. This greed motive has less force in our model than in Palfrey–Rosenthal: if more of the others contribute, then one's own share of the cost, and, therefore, one's own saving from free riding, is smaller. Thus, in our model the rules are actually very much more favorable to generating contributions and achieving an efficient outcome than is the case in Palfrey–Rosenthal. Nonetheless, we find that the likelihood of the good being provided is generally very small. Therefore, our negative conclusion has much more force.

Now we return to our model and examine its the first stage, where individuals decide whether to participate in the meeting, looking ahead rationally to the equilibrium outcome of that stage. We begin by looking for equilibria in pure strategies. If $M \geq 2$, there is an equilibrium where everyone chooses OUT — when everyone else is choosing OUT, one person switching to IN achieves nothing. If we accept this equilibrium the Coase Theorem is already contradicted, so we proceed to look at alternatives. There are no other pure strategy equilibria that are symmetric in the sense that all players choose the same strategy. There is a whole collection of equilibria where precisely $M$ of the $N$ players choose IN and the rest choose OUT. But this most arbitrarily requires identical players to choose different strategies in a precisely coordinated manner and it also runs against the non-cooperative nature of the first stage. Therefore, we turn to mixed-strategy equilibria. Palfrey and Rosenthal (1984) do likewise.

The same pragmatic argument in favor of choosing the symmetric mixed-strategy equilibrium, namely the difficulty of the coordination that is required for choosing one among the asymmetric pure strategy equilibria when a subset of a large group is designated to do one thing and the rest another, is also invoked in the large literature on free-riding in acceptance of corporate takeover bids; see Bagnoli and Lipman (1988) and Holmström and Nalebuff (1992). In our context, the argument for symmetry is stronger because the coordination problem is harder: the potential participants are not even identified until they show up for the meeting, whereas in the takeover context at least the identities and addresses of all the shareholders are known in advance. Even more basic theoretical support for our choice of the symmetric mixed-strategy equilibrium comes from Crawford and Haller (1990). They consider games in which identical players have identical preferences among multiple equilibria, but must learn to coordinate over which equilibrium to play by repeatedly playing the game. They find convergence with probability 1 and in finite time to an action combination that yield all players equal stage game payoffs. In our context only the symmetric mixed-strategy equilibrium has this property.

Note that as soon as we have mixed strategies, the probability that the good will be provided in equilibrium is less than 1. Thus, our choice of equilibrium is tantamount to ruling out full efficiency. But the interest in our result comes from the fact that it is far stronger than a mere recognition of *some inefficiency*. We find that the probability of the good being provided is close to zero in most situations; that is, the outcome is close to the extreme of *total inefficiency*.

We now proceed with the calculations for Stage 1. Let $P$ denote the probability that any one player chooses IN. Fix on one player — Herb — and consider the consequences of each of his two choices.

First suppose Herb chooses IN. If $(M-1)$ or more of the remaining $(N-1)$ people also choose IN, the good will get produced. If a total of $n$ (where $N \geq M$) including Herb choose IN, then Herb's net benefit is $V-(C/n)$. Using the appropriate binomial probabilities of the other people's choices, Herb's expected net benefit is:

$$\sum_{n=M}^{N} \frac{(N-1)!}{(n-1)!\,((N-1)-(n-1))!} P^{n-1}(1-P)^{(N-1)-(n-1)}\left[V-\frac{C}{n}\right] \tag{1}$$

Next suppose Herb chooses OUT. If $M$ or more of the remaining $(N-1)$ people choose IN, the good will get produced and Herb will get the free rider's benefit of $V$. The expected value of this is:

$$\sum_{n=M}^{N-1} \frac{(N-1)!}{n!(N-1-n)!} P^{n}(1-P)^{N-1-n} V \tag{2}$$

For a mixed-strategy equilibrium, Herb must be indifferent between the two pure choices. Equating the two expressions for his expected payoff yields an implicit equation defining the equilibrium $P$.

To simplify the expected payoff of IN given by (1), separate out the benefit and the cost sums, and define a new index of summation $\nu = n-1$ in the first. Then the expected payoff of IN becomes:

$$\begin{aligned}&\sum_{\nu=M-1}^{N-1} \frac{(N-1)!}{\nu!(N-1-\nu)!} P^{\nu}(1-P)^{N-1-\nu} V\\ &-\sum_{n=M}^{N} \frac{(N-1)!}{(n-1)!((N-1)-(n-1))!} P^{n-1}(1-P)^{(N-1)-(n-1)}\frac{C}{n}\end{aligned} \tag{3}$$

In the first of these sums we can relabel the dummy index of summation $\nu$ and call it $n$ instead. When we equate this expression to the benefit of OUT, namely (2), most of the terms from the first sum in (3) cancel against the sum in (2). We are left with:

$$
\begin{aligned}
0 \quad = \quad & \frac{(N-1)!}{(M-1)!((N-1)-(M-1))!} P^{M-1}(1-P)^{(N-1)-(M-1)} V \\
& - \sum_{n=M}^{N} \frac{(N-1)!}{(n-1)!((N-1)-(n-1))!} P^{n-1}(1-P)^{(N-1)-(n-1)} \frac{C}{n}
\end{aligned} \tag{4}
$$

This equation carries the intuition that was explained before. The first term on the right-hand side is the extra benefit that Herb gets from choosing IN rather than OUT — when precisely $(M-1)$ of the other $(N-1)$ people choose IN, Herb is pivotal and can get the benefit $V$ only by choosing IN. The other terms (the sum) on the right-hand side of (4) constitute the cost to Herb of choosing IN — when $n = M - 1$ or more of the rest choose IN, the good gets produced and Herb must pay his share of the cost. In the mixed-strategy equilibrium, Herb must be indifferent between the two pure choices. The value of $P$ (the same for all players) adjusts in equilibrium to bring this about.

A little regrouping of factors within each term converts (4) into a much simpler form. Define:

$$
b(N, M, P) = \frac{N!}{M!(N-M)!} P^{M}(1-P)^{N-M} \tag{5}
$$

This is just the density of a binomial distribution, namely the probability of exactly $M$ 'successes' in $N$ independent Bernoulli trials when the probability of success in each trial is $P$. Then (4) can be written:

$$
\frac{b(N, M, P)}{\sum_{n=M}^{N} b(N, n, P)} = \frac{C}{MV} \tag{6}
$$

The left-hand side of (6) is the 'hazard rate' of the binomial distribution — the density at one point divided by the cumulative density to the right of this point, or the probability of exactly $M$ successes divided by that of $M$ or more successes. Expressed as a function of $P$ for given $N$ and $M$, the hazard rate decreases monotonically from 1 to 0 as $P$ increases from 0 to 1. Fig. 1 shows the hazard rate for the case where $N = 6$ and $M = 2$. For larger values of $N$ and $M$, unless $M$ is almost equal to $N$, the decline in the hazard rate is very rapid as $P$ increases starting at 0.

On the right-hand side we have a fraction that is less than 1, but not by too much. By the definition of $MV > C$ but $(M-1)V < C$, so:

$$
\frac{M-1}{M} < \frac{C}{MV} < 1 \tag{7}
$$

For small values of $M$, the range of $C/(MV)$ can be quite substantial, but for large $M$ the fraction must be very close to 1.

Equilibrium can now be determined using Fig. 1. The hazard rate of exactly $M$ IN choices is shown as the decreasing solid curve, and the cumulative probability

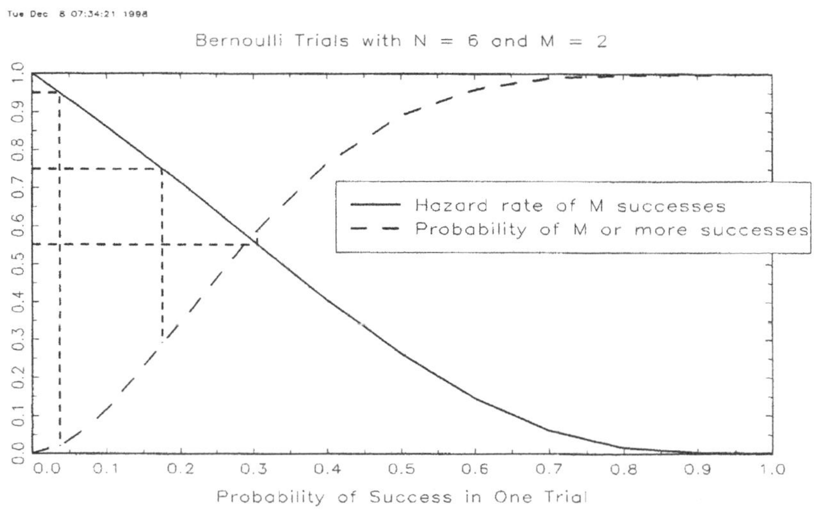


Fig. 1. Determination of equilibrium in single play.

of $M$ or more IN choices is the increasing curve in long dashes. The magnitudes of $C$ and $V$ are exogenously known, and $M$ is defined in terms of them. Then $C/(MV)$ is known, so the value of $P$ where the hazard rate equals this ratio can be read off and the cumulative probability can be found. In the figure this is shown by means of the lines in short dashes, corresponding to the values of $C/(MV)$ that are defined below.

Now we see why the equilibrium has such anti-Coaseian properties. Since $C/(MV)$ has to be close to 1, from the hazard rate graph we see that $P$ has to be small, and then from the cumulative probability graph we see that the probability that the good gets produced has to be small also.

The situation is least unfavorable to a Coaseian efficient outcome in two circumstances: (1) when the hazard rate does not decline very rapidly for $P$ close to 0; and (2) if $C/(MV)$ is close to its minimum possible value of $(M-1)/M$. The first happens when $M$ is close to $N$, that is, when almost everyone's participation is needed and everyone is quite likely to be pivotal. The second happens when an individual's pivotal contribution brings that individual a larger gain.

This is quite intuitive. The only incentive to contribute is that you might be the pivotal $M$th person. The more by which $N$ exceeds $M$, the less likely you are to be pivotal, so the less likely you are to contribute.

In addition, the larger that $M$ is, the smaller the gain that arises from being pivotal. Suppose $V=1$, $M=2$, and that the cost $C$ is the midpoint, 1.5, between the case where a single person would have just found it advantageous to provide the good ($C=1$) and where two would just barely have provided ($C=2$). The

Table 1
Individual probability, $P$, of choosing IN, and cumulative probability, $Q$, of success with $M = 10$

| | $C = 9.1$ | | $C = 9.5$ | | $C = 9.9$ | |
|---|---|---|---|---|---|---|
| $N$ | $P$ | $Q$ | $P$ | $Q$ | $P$ | $Q$ |
| 15 | 0.17 | $0.24\times10^{-4}$ | 0.10 | $0.19\times10^{-6}$ | $0.21\times10^{-1}$ | $0.60\times10^{-13}$ |
| 30 | $0.48\times10^{-1}$ | $0.76\times10^{-6}$ | $0.27\times10^{-1}$ | $0.37\times10^{-8}$ | $0.55\times10^{-2}$ | $0.66\times10^{-15}$ |
| 50 | $0.24\times10^{-1}$ | $0.31\times10^{-6}$ | $0.14\times10^{-1}$ | $0.14\times10^{-8}$ | $0.27\times10^{-2}$ | $0.23\times10^{-15}$ |
| 200 | $0.52\times10^{-2}$ | $0.14\times10^{-6}$ | $0.29\times10^{-2}$ | $0.57\times10^{-9}$ | $0.58\times10^{-3}$ | $0.86\times10^{-16}$ |

gain to the pivotal individual with $n = 2$ is $1-(1.5/2)$ or 0.25. Now suppose that $M = 1000$. Assume again that the cost is exactly at the midpoint between where $M-1$ would barely have gained from providing, and where $M$ would just have barely have provided, i.e. 999.5. The gain to an individual from providing the pivotal contribution, $(V - C/n)$, is now only $[1-(999.5/1000)]$ or 0.0005. The gain from being the pivotal $M$th contributor is 500 times higher when $M = 2$ than when $M = 1000$.

Both of these ways in which larger numbers reduce the likelihood of efficient outcomes are of great practical pertinence. As $N$ gets larger, it is likely to exceed $M$ by a larger absolute number and each individual is less likely to be pivotal. Similarly, when a public good would benefit a larger number, typically $M$ will also be larger; the dam that would protect the many that are likely to live in the flood plain of a great river is likely to cost more than a dam that would protect the few who are likely to live near a small stream. The gain to an individual from providing a pivotal contribution would then be smaller for the larger dam.

In the many important cases where $M$ is absolutely large but substantially smaller than $N$, the equilibrium $P$, and the probability of the Coaseian outcome, will be both very small. Tables 1–3 show various combinations of parameters that demonstrate this vividly.[4]

Throughout we kept $V = 1$; this is just a normalization. Table 1 shows the results for the case where $M = 10$. We allow $N$ to range from 15 to 200. We also consider three values of $C$, namely 9.1, 9.5 and 9.9. With the first of these, nine are just

Table 2
Individual probability, $P$, of choosing IN, and cumulative probability, $Q$, of success with $M = 2$

| | $C = 1.1$ | | $C = 1.5$ | | $C = 1.9$ | |
|---|---|---|---|---|---|---|
| $N$ | $P$ | $Q$ | $P$ | $Q$ | $P$ | $Q$ |
| 3 | 0.71 | 0.80 | 0.50 | 0.50 | 0.13 | $0.51\times10^{-1}$ |
| 6 | 0.31 | 0.59 | 0.18 | 0.28 | $0.37\times10^{-1}$ | $0.19\times10^{-1}$ |
| 15 | 0.11 | 0.51 | $0.59\times10^{-1}$ | 0.22 | $0.12\times10^{-1}$ | $0.13\times10^{-1}$ |
| 60 | $0.27\times10^{-1}$ | 0.48 | $0.14\times10^{-1}$ | 0.20 | $0.26\times10^{-2}$ | $0.11\times10^{-1}$ |

[4]The computations were carried out using the routines in Press et al. (1989, pp. 166–169).

Table 3
Individual probability, $P$, of choosing IN, and cumulative probability, $Q$, of success with $M = 50$

| | $C = 49.1$ | | $C = 49.5$ | | $C = 49.9$ | |
|---|---|---|---|---|---|---|
| $N$ | $P$ | $Q$ | $P$ | $Q$ | $P$ | $Q$ |
| 60 | $0.84\times10^{-1}$ | $0.60\times10^{-43}$ | $0.49\times10^{-1}$ | $0.97\times10^{-55}$ | $0.10\times10^{-1}$ | $0.11\times10^{-88}$ |
| 100 | $0.18\times10^{-1}$ | $0.27\times10^{-58}$ | $0.10\times10^{-1}$ | $0.10\times10^{-70}$ | $0.20\times10^{-2}$ | $0.26\times10^{-105}$ |
| 150 | $0.91\times10^{-2}$ | $0.74\times10^{-62}$ | $0.51\times10^{-2}$ | $0.23\times10^{-74}$ | $0.10\times10^{-2}$ | $0.48\times10^{-109}$ |
| 250 | $0.46\times10^{-2}$ | $0.56\times10^{-64}$ | $0.25\times10^{-2}$ | $0.16\times10^{-76}$ | $0.51\times10^{-3}$ | $0.28\times10^{-111}$ |

insufficient to provide the good, and with the third, 10 are just sufficient. In each case, we denote by $P$ the probability that any one individual chooses IN, and by $Q$ the cumulative probability that the good gets provided, that is, that $M$ or more individuals choose IN.

Consider first the central case with $C=9.5$. In a society of 15 people, each chooses IN with a probability of about 10%. But the total probability that these choices yield 10 or more IN votes and cause the good to be produced is only 0.00000019. We can see this more easily if we think in terms of a normal approximation to the binomial. With $N = 15$ and $P = 0.1$, the number of successes regarded as a normal variate has the mean $NP = 1.5$ and the standard deviation $\sqrt{NP(1-P)} = 1.16$. Getting 10 or more successes is an event more than 7 standard deviations beyond the mean, and, therefore, exceedingly unlikely.[5]

As $N$ increases, the probability that any one individual chooses IN decreases. We expect this, but the probability of 10 or more IN choices could still go up because there are more people making the choices. We see that this is not the case. The decrease in individual probabilities of choosing IN is the more powerful force, to the point that the probability of the good being produced very quickly falls to an even more negligible level.

The probabilities for $C = 9.1$ are a little higher, because the cost of choosing IN is lower in relation to the benefit. But the bottom line, namely the probability that the good gets produced, remains negligible. Increasing $C$ to 9.9 makes matters worse: even with $N = 15$, the probability that any one chooses IN is now only a little over 2%, and the probability that the good gets produced is virtually zero.

Table 2 shows calculations with smaller numbers. Now $M = 2$, and the values of $C$ are 1.1, 1.5 and 1.9. These are the values, for the case $N = 6$, that were used in Fig. 1. Now we examine the results for a whole range of $N$. First consider the middle column with $C = 1.5$. In a group of total size 3, each chooses IN with probability 50%, and that is also the probability that the good is produced.[6] As the

[5]Incidentally, the fact that the standard deviation is proportional to the square root of $N$ shows why the outcome for $P$ is not invariant to a proportional scaling up of both $N$ and $M$.

[6]Incidentally, for $N = 3$ and $M = 2$, the mixed-strategy equilibrium can be found in closed form, and the probability of choosing IN is exactly 50%. This is a useful check on the accuracy of our computational procedure and of the numerical calculations and FORTRAN programs we used.

group size rises to 60, the probability that any one chooses IN falls to about 1.38%. The probability that at least two people choose IN (and, thus, the good gets produced) also falls, but levels off and asymptotes to about 20%.

Next turn to the first column, where $C = 1.1$. Here $C/(MV) = 0.55$, which is about as low a value as this ratio can possibly have. Then from Fig. 1 we see that the equilibrium $P$ gets quite large; with $N = 6$ it is a little over 30%. The cumulative probability is almost 60%. This is about as favorable a case for the provision of the public good as one can find.

Conversely, in the third column, where $C$ is 1.9, all the probabilities are uniformly lower, and the asymptotic probability of the good being produced in a large group is only a little over 1%.

Table 3 shows a case with numbers more appropriate to non-trivial group decision problems. Here $M = 50$, and values of $N$ ranging from 60 to 250 are considered. The probabilities of the good being produced are uniformly close to zero.[7]

These calculations show that even when transactions costs are absent, large numbers constitute a distinct problem and can lead to grossly inefficient outcomes. Similar results obtain even when there are transaction costs; for example Mailath and Postlewaite (1990).

## 4. Repeated play

If the above game results in non-provision because fewer than $M$ people show up at the meeting (choose IN at Stage 1), then everyone stands to gain from playing the whole game again. At the minimum, under our rules, there is nothing to lose: there are no transaction costs, including costs of waiting. Therefore, we now consider the effect of such repetitions. We find that they do not rescue the Coase Theorem.[8]

A fixed finite number of repetitions clearly will not help. No one has any incentive to choose IN for any but the last play, which then degenerates into the single-play model above. However, stopping the game after a finite number of repetitions is arbitrary, and not logically consistent with our assumption of zero transaction costs. Therefore, we must consider infinite repetition.

As is well known, infinitely repeated games can have multiple equilibria, each sustained by its own internally consistent expectations. This one is no exception.

[7]We hope the $0.28 \times 10^{-111}$ in Table 3 is a record for the smallest number ever to appear in an economics paper.

[8]Related models of repeated attempts at coordination are Farrell and Saloner (1988) and Bolton and Farrell (1990).

We find two such equilibria (doubtless there are many more), with vastly different efficiency properties.

### 4.1. An inefficient equilibrium

Suppose that in any one 'play' or 'round' of the repeated game, all individuals at Stage 1 expect that the meeting at the immediately following Stage 2 will go ahead with the provision of the good if $M$ or more people are present. Call this the 'go-ahead' expectation. We will show that such expectation is indeed rational — this choice is ex post optimal for the meeting — given the individuals' responses to it. For the moment, focus on these responses. There are two effects. For each individual in each round, the incentive to choose IN is reduced because there is the prospect of further rounds if too few people show up at this round. Thus, the equilibrium $P$ in each play is lower. But for the group as a whole, there are more rounds, and the prospect that enough people will show eventually in one of the rounds is greater for any given $P$. The overall effect is the balance of the two, and it turns out that the balance tilts toward even greater inefficiency.[9]

We illustrate this by considering the special case where $N = 2$ and $M = 1$, and then build the general case. We also develop the theory with discounting, and then take the limit as the discount rate goes to zero, as required for our assumption of zero transaction costs. Write $\beta$ for the discount factor. As usual, $\beta = 1/(1 + r)$ where $r$ is the discount rate, so the no-transaction-cost limit corresponds to $r = 0$ or $\beta = 1$. Also, write $W$ for the equilibrium payoff or value of the game to each player.

Now the payoff matrix for the two players at Stage 1 is as shown in Table 4. The notation and the explanation is as follows. If both players choose IN, the good is provided and the cost shared; each gets $V - \frac{1}{2}C$. If one chooses IN and the other OUT, then given the temporarily assumed expectations about Stage 2, the good is still provided, the IN player bears the cost and gets $V - C$; the OUT player free-rides and gets $V$. If both choose OUT, the good is not provided and the game

Table 4
Payoff matrix for Stage 1 under go-ahead expectations

| | | Player B | |
|---|---|---|---|
| | | IN | OUT |
| Player A | IN | $V - \frac{1}{2}C, V - \frac{1}{2}C$ | $V - C, V$ |
| | OUT | $V, V - C$ | $\beta W, \beta W$ |

[9] It might be argued that if fewer than $M$ people turn up in the first round, they can commit themselves not to go ahead unless everyone turns up. But they cannot make a similar commitment on behalf of others who have not shown up at this round and might do so at later rounds.

is repeated starting next period; the payoff from this is $W$ to each player starting one period later, so its discounted present value today is $\beta W$.

In the mixed-strategy equilibrium each player should be indifferent between choosing IN and OUT, and the common payoff of the two is by definition the value of the game, $W$. Therefore:

$$W = P\left(V - \frac{1}{2}C\right) + (1 - P)(V - C) \tag{8}$$

and

$$W = PV + (1 - P)\beta W, \quad \text{or } W = PV/[1 - \beta + \beta P] \tag{9}$$

These two simultaneous equations in $P$ and $W$ as unknowns can be solved for the equilibrium.

Fig. 2 graphs these two equations, and shows that there is a unique solution in the range [0, 1] for $P$. The values are normalized so that $V = 1$, and for sake of illustration I have chosen $C = 0.6$ so that $V - C = 0.4$ and $V - \frac{1}{2}C = 0.7$. (There is another solution with $P > 1$ but that is economically irrelevant.) At this solution the value to each player is more than $(V - C)$ — what he would get by paying the full cost of the good himself — but is less than $(V - \frac{1}{2}C)$ — the efficient outcome where the cost is shared. Thus, the total payoff to the pair is less than $(2V - C)$: some inefficiency remains.

Given this solution for Stage 1, consider the ex post optimality of actions for the IN group at Stage 2. If both happen to have chosen IN, the group of 2 should

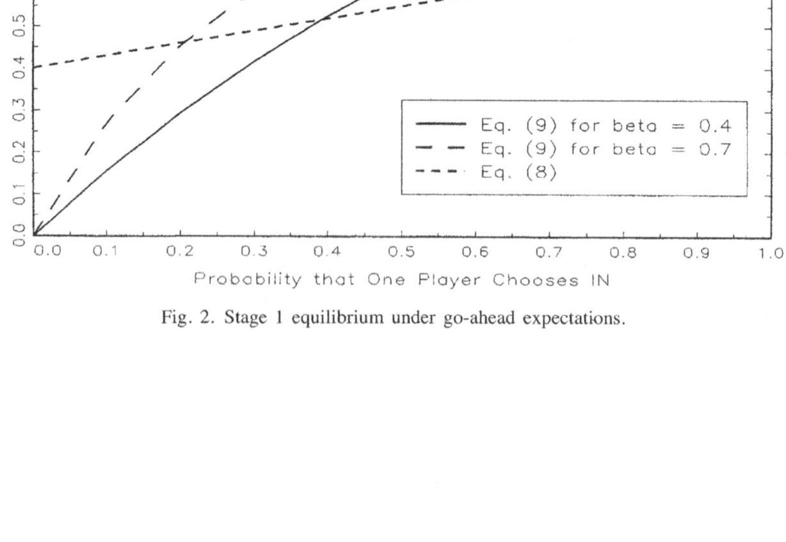


Fig. 2. Stage 1 equilibrium under go-ahead expectations.

clearly go ahead. If, say, A has chosen OUT, then B gets $V-C$ by going ahead, and $\beta W$ by deviating and sending the game to another round. (By Raiffa's Theorem it is enough to check single deviations.) This deviation is unprofitable if $V-C>\beta W$. We now check this.

Eqs. (8) and (9) can be written as:

$$V-W=C\left(1-\frac{1}{2}P\right), \quad V-W=(1-P)(V-\beta W)$$

Therefore:

$$(V-\beta W)/C=\left(1-\frac{1}{2}P\right)\Big/(1-P)>1$$

so $V-C>\beta W$ as required. Thus, we have a self-consistent equilibrium of expectations and actions.

Now we examine the properties of this equilibrium. Fig. 2 shows that the value $W$ lies between $V-C$ and $V-\frac{1}{2}C$. Thus, each player gets higher payoff than by bearing the whole cost of the good, but less than that in the efficient outcome. Thus, some inefficiency remains.

As $\beta$ increases, the curve representing (9) shifts up as shown in the figure; the equilibrium shifts to the left along the line (8) and the expected value of the game to each player falls. Thus, greater patience — lower transaction cost — paradoxically leaves both players worse off. The reason is that greater patience makes each shirk more in any one round ($P$ goes down). In the limit with total patience, $\beta \to 1$; then $P \to 0$ and $W \to V-C$, and the outcome is as if each player had to bear the full cost of the good.

The result for the general case is similar. The payoffs from choosing IN is:

$$W=\sum_{n=1}^{M-1} b(N-1,n-1,P)\beta W+\sum_{n=M}^{N} b(N-1,n-1,p)(V-C/n) \tag{10}$$

and that from choosing OUT is:

$$W=\sum_{n=1}^{M} b(N-1,n-1,P)\beta W+\sum_{n=M+1}^{N} b(N-1,n-1,P)V \tag{11}$$

As $\beta \to 1$, (11) becomes:

$$W\left[1-\sum_{n=1}^{M-1} b(N-1,n-1,P)\right]=V\sum_{n=M}^{N} b(N-1,n-1,p)$$

The two probability sums are equal, so either each of the sums is zero (which corresponds to $P \to 0$), or $W=V$. But the latter is impossible since (10) shows $W$ to be a weighted average of terms all of which are less than $V$. (This corresponds to the irrelevant solution $P>1$ of the two-player case.)

Now write (10) as:

$$W = \frac{\sum_{n=M}^{N} b(N-1, n-1, p)(V - C/n)}{1 - \beta + \beta \sum_{n=1}^{M-1} b(N-1, n-1, P)}$$

As $\beta \to 1$ and $P \to 0$, the numerator and the denominator both go to zero. But the first term in the numerator combines with the probability sum in the denominator to form the hazard rate for $M$ successes in $N$ trials, which goes to 1. Then $W \to V - C/M$. The value to each player is the same as if only the minimal coalition of $M$ people forms; there is no benefit of lower cost from larger coalitions of participants. The reason is again the increase in the incentive to shirk in any one play.

The total value to all $N$ players is:

$$NW = NV - (N/M)C < NV - C$$

so the outcome is inefficient. The measure of this inefficiency, or the shortfall in the total payoff, is $(N/M)C - C$. For large numbers, where as we saw above, $C/M$ is approximately equal to $V$, the shortfall is almost $NV - C$. That is, the inefficiency is almost 100%.

### 4.2. *An efficient equilibrium*

Now suppose the expectation about Stage 2 of any round is as follows. If all $N$ players have chosen IN, the meeting will go ahead and produce the good. If not, the meeting will adjourn without providing for the good, and the game will proceed to its next round. Call this the 'all-or-nothing' expectation. Again we will show later that this choice is rational for the meeting, given the individuals' responses in its expectation, and provided the discount factor is sufficiently close to 1. For now we examine the individual responses at Stage 1.

Given these expectations, the Stage 1 payoff matrix changes to that shown in Table 5.

If $V - \frac{1}{2}C > \beta W$, then IN is the dominant strategy for each player, and the resulting payoff is $W = V - \frac{1}{2}C$, confirming the requirement for dominance. It only remains to check that, given the resulting Stage 1 equilibrium, the all-or-nothing response is optimal at Stage 2.

If both players have chosen IN at Stage 1, going ahead is clearly optimal. But if,

Table 5
Payoff matrix for Stage 1 under all-or-nothing expectations

| | | Player B | |
|---|---|---|---|
| | | IN | OUT |
| Player A | IN | $V - \frac{1}{2}C, V - \frac{1}{2}C$ | $\beta W, \beta W$ |
| | OUT | $\beta W, \beta W$ | $\beta W, \beta W$ |

say, A tests the matter by staying OUT at Stage 1, what should B do? A deviation by going ahead and providing the good gets him $V - C$. Adherence to the strategy gets $\beta W = \beta(V - \frac{1}{2}C)$. Therefore, the deviation is unprofitable if:

$$\beta > (V - C)/\left(V - \frac{1}{2}C\right)$$

This is true for $\beta$ sufficiently close to 1. Therefore, with sufficiently patient players (sufficiently low transaction cost of bargaining), the all-or-nothing response is credible and the resulting (efficient) equilibrium is subgame-perfect.

The analysis for the general case is similar: the all-or-nothing strategy is ex post optimal if:

$$\beta > \frac{V - [C/(N-1)]}{V - (C/N)} \tag{12}$$

This is again true for $\beta$ sufficiently close to 1.

Note the difference between this and the claims of some Coaseians: they argue that someone can take the lead *before* the meeting (at Stage 1) and threaten a would-be free rider that unless everyone participated the good would not be provided. But no assertions before the meeting carry any automatic credibility about what the meeting will decide. The argument here is that *during* the meeting at Stage 2, the all-or-nothing choice will be found ex post optimal. Therefore, this is a credible expectation to entertain for someone doing the calculation of IN vs. OUT in isolation at Stage 1. In other words, we have found another self-consistent equilibrium of the repeated game.

### 4.3. Choosing between the equilibria

When a game has multiple equilibria, one must look for some other consideration that will help select one of them. There are different criteria of this kind, and we examine some of them.

#### 4.3.1. Focal point

Schelling (1960, Chap. 3) introduced the best-known consideration of this kind, namely a focal point. If the expectations of all players can converge on one of the equilibria, then everyone will play his part in it, expecting everyone else to do likewise. Schelling showed how various historical, cultural or linguistic forces can create such a convergence of expectations on one equilibrium. We have not specified any such details, but there is an argument which suggests that the efficient equilibrium has a greater claim to be a focal point.

This comes from the comparison of the payoffs themselves. Given our assumption of zero transaction costs, every player in isolation at Stage 1 has full knowledge of the data ($N$, $V$ and $C$), and can costlessly figure out both or all equilibria, each with its self-consistent expectations. Then each thinks whether everyone else will think that . . . one of these is to be favored. He knows that everyone else has done the same calculation, and so everyone knows that one of the equilibria offers higher payoffs to everyone than any other. Therefore, each should think that all will think that . . . it should be chosen.

### *4.3.2. Robustness to small transaction costs*

Many would regard the focal point argument to be compelling, and we admit its force. But we point out another consideration which cuts the other way. This is to ask that the equilibrium be robust to a small perturbation of the model. Our main focus is on the case of zero transaction costs. But if we were to change the model by introducing very small transaction costs, would it have an equilibrium close to the one for the zero-transaction-cost case?[10]

We have already constructed the model by introducing one form of transaction cost, namely the cost of waiting while the negotiation goes on through its rounds. This is implicit in the discount factor $\beta$. Although our main interest was in the limiting case as $\beta \rightarrow 1$, in the process we found that the limit proceeded continuously. This was true of the inefficient equilibrium as well as the efficient one; both are robust to the introduction of a small cost of waiting.

Now we consider another kind of cost, namely of attending a meeting. Here we find a great difference: the inefficient equilibrium above is robust, while the efficient one is not — it disappears when there is some cost of each type, waiting and attending meeting, no matter how small each may be. Again we show this in the two-person context; the general case is then obvious.

Consider the inefficient equilibrium first. Let $\epsilon$ denote the cost of attending a meeting, measured in the same units as $V$ and $C$. Then the payoff matrix of Stage 1, given the go-ahead expectations about Stage 2, is shown in Table 6. The equilibrium is again in mixed strategies, and the equations, replacing (8) and (9), are:

$$W = P\left(V - \frac{1}{2}C - \epsilon\right) + (1 - P)(V - C - \epsilon) \tag{13}$$

and

Table 6
Payoff matrix for Stage 1 under go-ahead expectations and attendance cost

| | | Player B | |
|---|---|---|---|
| | | IN | OUT |
| Player A | IN | $V - \frac{1}{2}C - \epsilon, V - \frac{1}{2}C - \epsilon$ | $V - C - \epsilon, V$ |
| | OUT | $V, V - C - \epsilon$ | $\beta W, \beta W$ |

[10] Anderlini and Felli (1997) introduce small contracting costs, and consider a different implication, namely a hold-up problem. This also leads to an anti-Coase result.

$$W = PV + (1 - P)\beta W, \quad \text{or } W = PV/[1 - \beta + \beta P] \tag{14}$$

The solution can be found as in Fig. 2. The sole difference is that the straight line representing (8) is vertically lowered by $\epsilon$ to get (13). This reduces $P$ and $V$, and the change is small when $\epsilon$ is small.

The condition for the go-ahead behavior to be ex post optimal at Stage 2 is $V - C > \beta W$, and it is easy to verify that it is satisfied. In fact it is easier to satisfy now, since the cost of attending another meeting makes it even more desirable (albeit only slightly so when the cost is small) for one person to go ahead without waiting for the other to show up in the next round.

Thus, we continue to have the inefficient equilibrium with self-sustaining expectations, and it changes continuously as a small cost of attendance is introduced.

The efficient equilibrium changes dramatically. The Stage 1 payoff matrix, given all-or-nothing expectations about Stage 2, becomes as shown in Table 7. Choosing IN is no longer the dominant strategy, and an equilibrium in mixed strategies must be found.

Using the by-now familiar notation and technique, the two equations defining the probability $P$ of playing IN and the value $W$ of the game are:

$$W = P\left(V - \frac{1}{2}C - \epsilon\right) + (1 - P)(\beta W - \epsilon) \tag{15}$$

and

$$W = P\beta W + (1 - P)\beta W = \beta W \tag{16}$$

So long as $\beta < 1$, no matter how small the difference (no matter how small the cost of waiting), Eq. (16) admits only one solution, namely $W = 0$. Then Eq. (15) gives:

$$P = \epsilon / \left(V - \frac{1}{2}C\right)$$

Thus, the probability of participation is very small, and the value of the game is very low, namely zero. The only good thing about this situation is that it cannot be an equilibrium with self-sustaining expectations. If one person tests it out by

Table 7
Payoff matrix for Stage 1 under all-or-nothing expectations and attendance cost

| | | Player B | |
|---|---|---|---|
| | | IN | OUT |
| Player A | IN | $V - \frac{1}{2}C - \epsilon, V - \frac{1}{2}C - \epsilon$ | $\beta W - \epsilon, \beta W$ |
| | OUT | $\beta W, \beta W - \epsilon$ | $\beta W, \beta W$ |

staying OUT, at Stage 2 the other would find it optimal to wait and go another round if $\beta W > V - C$, which is not true as $W = 0$ but $V > C$.

Thus, the efficient equilibrium does not survive the simultaneous existence of even extremely small costs of waiting and of attending meetings. The attendance cost brings a 'no-refund' feature to the game, analogous to the case considered by Palfrey and Rosenthal (1984), and, therefore, further increases the temptation to free-ride. But in our setting of the repeated game, this makes a much more dramatic difference.

#### *4.3.3. Unequal cost shares*

Our assumption throughout the formal analysis has been that whenever $n$ ($\geq M$) individuals find themselves IN at Stage 2 and provide the good, they share its cost equally. This was harmless in the cases where the equilibrium had very low participation probabilities and was, therefore, very inefficient. But the efficient equilibrium of the repeated game is much more vulnerable to relaxation of this assumption. Suppose $(N - 1)$ people find themselves present at Stage 2, while the remaining person is testing out their resolve to go through with the strategy of letting the game go another round and wait for everyone to show up. For this strategy to be optimal, the players must now be sufficiently patient, or their discounting of the future must be sufficiently low, to make it optimal for them to outwait even the $N$th person who is most reluctant to join, that is, the one who faces the prospect of the highest cost share among all individuals. Then condition on $\beta$ that replaces (12) is even stricter, that is, $\beta$ must be even closer to 1 than before to sustain the efficient equilibrium. This is not strictly a problem in the simplest Coaseian world with zero transaction costs, where the discount factor can be assumed to be as close to 1 as needed. But it does make the efficient equilibrium even less robust to small changes in the assumptions, and, therefore, even more suspect as a practical guide.

## 5. Conclusions

What can one conclude from this? Some people would accept the argument that when one equilibrium is Pareto-better than another, it should emerge as a focal point. They would, therefore, say that we have pointed out a new non-cooperative way of achieving Coaseian efficiency. Others would regard the non-robustness to the introduction of very small transaction costs as fatal; they would say that we have disproved the Coase Theorem. We prefer not to take a dogmatic stand on the issue, but we do say that at the very least we have raised some serious doubts about the validity of Coaseian claims that in the absence of transaction costs, starting from a total tabula rasa, a set of individuals will create procedures that lead to Pareto-efficient outcomes.

When we cast doubt on the claims of universal efficiency on the basis of the

Coase Theorem, and exhibit equilibria that are grossly inefficient, our quarrel is with the logic of that argument. We do not wish to push this so far as to claim that public goods will almost never get provided in large societies. Even if a group starts trapped in such a cycle, where few or none participate, the manifest inefficiency will prompt some efforts at remedies. Providing such remedies is itself a public good and, therefore, subject to similar difficulties, but these are often overcome in practice. To examine how, and, therefore, to draw policy prescriptions, would take us too long in what is already a long paper. Therefore, we leave that task for another occasion. But in conclusion we wish to point out one possible, and commonly used, approach.

The starting point is the observation that every groups faces several collective action problems simultaneously. Individuals do not have the option of participation (in our jargon the choice of IN and OUT) separately for each issue. The choice must be made once and for all; choosing IN reveals one's identity and subjects one to compulsory participation in all the public issues facing that group. We see this as deliberate strategy, the idea being that every individual will derive private benefit from participation in some issue, and this will be sufficient to induce him to choose IN for the whole package. For example, getting a driving license makes one liable for jury service. Such bundling, and restricting individuals to say IN or OUT to the whole bundle, is a kind of coercion. But it is a relatively gentle kind of coercion, relying on individuals' self-interest, and, therefore, not unlike the price system in its rationing role.

This is how non-governmental or special interest groups often overcome free rider problems; labor unions, the AARP, etc. offer enough excludable private benefits to induce people to become members, and then a part of their membership fee is used in lobbying for the non-excludable public (really, group) good. The role of such 'selective incentives' in solving the collective action problems of interest groups was examined by Olson (1965, p. 51) and Wilson (1974, pp. 33–34). Governments can be regarded as similar mechanisms writ large.

If this method is important for achieving voluntary participation in public good provision in practice, it also offers a new explanation of why several private excludable goods are publicly provided. Economists are often puzzled by this phenomenon, and almost unanimous in advocating privatization of these activities. But the public provision of private goods may be playing an important role: packaging them with other genuinely public goods may serve to give individuals sufficient incentives to participate in the provision of those latter goods, which might otherwise suffer because of free riding.[11] In other words, the bundling with private goods can induce selfish individuals to sign on to 'society' and to participate in its public good activities.

---

[11]Of course for this to work, competing private supply of these private goods will have to be forbidden.

## Acknowledgements

A previous version of this paper was circulated and presented in several seminars under a different title, and numerous people offered perceptive criticisms and suggestions of it. We thank them all, but feel we must make specific mention of seminars at Chicago, Munich, and Princeton, and of Austan Goolsbee, Patrick Bolton, Gene Grossman, Thomas Palfrey, Howard Rosenthal, and Jakob von Weizsäcker. The literature on the Coase Theorem is far too large to cite in full. We ask all authors to kindly accept this collective acknowledgement; in the text we cite only those works which are most directly related to our own arguments. Dixit thanks the National Science Foundation, and Olson thanks the US Agency for International Development, for financial support of this research.


## References


Anderlini, L., Felli, L., 1997. Costly Coasian Contracts, Working Paper, London School of Economics.

Bagnoli, M., Lipman, B.L., 1988. Successful takeovers without exclusion. Review of Financial Studies 1 (1), 89–110.

Bolton, P., Farrell, J., 1990. Decentralization, duplication, and delay. Journal of Political Economy 99 (4), 803–826.

Cheung, S., 1970. The structure of a contract and the theory of a non-exclusive resource. Journal of Law and Economics 13 (1), 49–70.

Clarke, E.H., 1971. Multipart pricing of public goods. Public Choice 11 (1), 19–33.

Coase, R., 1960. The problem of social cost. The Journal of Law and Economics 3 (1), 1–44.

Coase, R., 1988. The Firm, The Market and The Law, University of Chicago Press, Chicago.

Cornes, R., Sandler, T., 1986. The Theory of Externalities, Public Goods, and Club Goods, 2nd Edition, Cambridge University Press, Cambridge, UK.

Crawford, V.P., Haller, H., 1990. Learning how to cooperate: Optimal play in repeated coordination games. Econometrica 58 (3), 571–595.

Farrell, J., Saloner, G., 1988. Coordination through committees and markets. Rand Journal of Economics 19 (2), 235–252.

Foley, D.K., 1970. Lindahl's solution and the core of an economy with public goods. Econometrica 38 (1), 66–72.

Groves, T., Ledyard, J., 1977. Optimal allocation of public goods: A solution to the free rider problem. Econometrica 45 (3), 783–809.

Hardin, R., 1982. Collective Action, Resources for the Future, Johns Hopkins University Press, Baltimore, MD.

Holmström, B., Nalebuff, B., 1992. To the raider goes the surplus? A reexamination of the free-rider problem. Journal of Economics and Management Strategy 1 (1), 37–62.

Mailath, G.J., Postlewaite, A., 1990. Asymmetric information bargaining problems with many agents. Review of Economic Studies 57 (3), 351–367.

Mas-Colell, A., 1980. Efficiency and decentralization in the pure theory of public goods. Quarterly Journal of Economics 94 (4), 625–641.

Olson, M., 1965. The Logic of Collective Action, Harvard University Press, Cambridge, MA.

Olson, M., 1996. Big bills left on the sidewalk: Why some nations are rich, and others poor. Journal of Economic Perspectives 10 (2), 3–24.

Palfrey, T.R., Rosenthal, H., 1984. Participation and the provision of discrete public goods: A strategic analysis. Journal of Public Economics 24 (2), 171–193.

Press, W.H., Flannery, B.P., Teukolsky, S.A., Vetterling, W.T., 1989. Numerical Recipes: The Art of Scientific Computing (FORTRAN version), Cambridge University Press, New York.

Sandler, T., 1992. Collective Action, University of Michigan Press, Ann Arbor, MI.

Schelling, T.C., 1960. The Strategy of Conflict, Harvard University Press, Cambridge, MA.

Stigler, G.J., 1971. The theory of economic regulation. Bell Journal of Economics and Management Science 2 (1), 3–21.

Stigler, G.J., 1992. Law or economics? The Journal of Law and Economics 35 (2), 455–468.

Wilson, J.Q., 1974. Political Organizations, Basic Books, New York.

Wittman, D.A., 1989. Why democracies produce efficient results. Journal of Political Economy 97 (6), 1395–1424.

Wittman, D.A., 1995. The Myth of Democratic Failure, University of Chicago Press, Chicago.

# [23]

*The Economic Journal*, **116** (*January*), 223–245. © Royal Economic Society 2006. Published by Blackwell Publishing, 9600 Garsington Road, Oxford OX4 2DQ, UK and 350 Main Street, Malden, MA 02148, USA.

# TRANSACTION COSTS AND THE ROBUSTNESS OF THE COASE THEOREM*

*Luca Anderlini and Leonardo Felli*

This paper explores the extent to which *ex ante* transaction costs may lead to failures of the Coase Theorem. In particular we identify the basic 'hold-up problem' that arises whenever the parties to a Coasian negotiation have to pay *ex ante costs* for the negotiation to take place. We then show that a 'Coasian solution' to this problem is not available: a Coasian solution typically entails a negotiation about the payment of the costs associated with the future negotiation, which in turn is associated with a fresh set of *ex ante* costs, and hence a new hold-up problem.

The Coase theorem (Coase, 1960) has had a profound influence on the way economists and legal scholars think about *inefficiencies*. It guarantees that provided that *property rights* are allocated, fully informed rational agents involved in an inefficient situation will ensure through negotiation that there are no unexploited gains from trade and hence an efficient outcome obtains.

In its strongest formulation, the Coase theorem is interpreted as guaranteeing an efficient outcome regardless of the 'way in which property rights are assigned' (Nicholson, 1989, p. 725) and whenever the potential mutual gains 'exceed [the] necessary bargaining costs' (Nicholson, 1989, p. 726).[1]

The predictions entailed by the stronger version of the Coase theorem are startling. Whenever property rights are allocated, we should observe only outcomes that are *constrained efficient* in the sense that all potential gains from trade (net of transaction costs) are exploited. This clearly contradicts even the most casual observation of empirical facts. There are many obvious instances of situations in which Pareto improving negotiation opportunities are available, but are left unexploited by the parties involved.[2]

If we were to believe the predictions of the 'strong' Coase theorem, all these apparent inefficiencies would not be real inefficiencies at all. They should simply

* We are grateful to one of the Editors of this Journal, David de Meza, and to two anonymous referees for extremely useful feedback. An early version of this paper was circulated as a working paper entitled 'Costly Coasian Contracts' (Anderlini and Felli, 1998). Revisions and further work were completed while Leonardo Felli was visiting the Department of Economics at the University of Pennsylvania and the Department of Economics of the Stern School of Business at NYU. Their generous hospitality is gratefully acknowledged. Both authors thank the ESRC (Grant R000237825) for financial support. We are also grateful to Ian Gale and to seminar participants at the ISER 2000 in Siena for stimulating comments. This paper was submitted before Leonardo Felli was invited to become an editor of the Journal and accepted for publication by the previous editorial board.

[1] This stronger version of the Coase theorem does *not* correspond to what is claimed in Coase (1960), but it is an interpretation of it that is sufficiently common to have found its way into basic micro-economic text-books such as the one quoted above.

[2] Of course, we are not claiming that these observed inefficiencies can necessarily be traced to the sources we identify in our analysis below. In many cases a simple appeal to 'irrational expectations' suffices to explain observed failures to exploit potential gains from trade. See our discussion of some anecdotal evidence that we believe fits our model well in Section 2 below.

be viewed as the result of transaction costs that are 'high' relative to the potential gains from trade. We take the view that this is not a satisfactory explanation of these observed facts.

Our aim in this article is to take issue with this strong version of the Coase theorem and show that the impact of transaction costs can extend over and above their size relative to the potential gains from trade. This stems from the *strategic role* that transaction costs may play in a Coasian negotiation. It turns out that a key factor in determining the strategic role of transaction costs is whether they are payable *ex ante* or *ex post*; after the negotiation concerning the distribution of the unexploited gains from trade takes place. We show that in the presence of *ex ante* transaction costs a *constrained inefficient* outcome may obtain.

In Anderlini and Felli (2001*a*) (henceforth AF) we introduce *ex ante* costs in each round of an alternating offers bargaining model (Rubinstein, 1982). In each period, both the proposer and the responder must pay a cost for the negotiation to proceed. If either player declines to pay, the current round of offer and response is cancelled and play moves on to the next round.

In that article we show that it is always an equilibrium for both players *never* to pay the *ex ante* costs and hence never to agree on a division of the potential surplus, although the sum of the *ex ante* costs is strictly lower than the surplus itself. Moreover, we show that this is the *unique* equilibrium outcome in both the following cases:

(1) If the sum of the *ex ante* costs is not 'too low' (but still less than the available surplus) and/or the distribution of these costs across the players is sufficiently asymmetric, and
(2) If we impose that the equilibrium must be robust to the possibility that the players might find a way to renegotiate out of future inefficiencies.[3]

Thus, in AF we show that when the distribution of surplus across contracting parties is endogenous (it is the outcome of the bargaining – if it ever takes place), transaction costs that are payable *ex ante* can have a devastating effect on efficiency.

In this article, we take it as given that if the negotiating stage is reached an agreement will result and, for simplicity, we take as (parametrically) given the parties' shares of surplus in this agreement. We then introduce transaction costs that are payable *ex ante*: the negotiation stage is reached only if these costs are paid. We find that for some combinations of bargaining power (determining surplus shares) and *ex ante* costs adding up to less than the available surplus, no agreement will take place because the costs will not be paid.

A natural further question follows at this point. Suppose that we allow the parties to negotiate some compensating transfers *before* the *ex ante* costs are payable. In

[3] In AF we actually propose a modification of the extensive form that is meant to capture the requirement of renegotiation-proofness. This is because, there, we take the view that 'black-box' renegotiation is not an appropriate modelling ingredient in a model of the actual negotiation between players.

other words, suppose that we endow the parties with the possibility of undoing the effects of the *ex ante* transaction costs in a Coasian way ahead of time. Is it then the case that the inefficiencies we found will disappear? The answer we obtain is 'no', provided that the negotiation of the compensating transfers is itself associated with a fresh set of *ex ante* transaction costs, *regardless of how small these new costs are.*

Proceeding with a simple stripped-down model of the negotiating phase (in essence a single parameter between 0 and 1) has a two-fold advantage. First of all, it safely allows us to abstract from the problem analysed in AF, so that we know that the efficiency failures that we find here come from a different source than the one pinpointed there. Secondly, it allows us to check the robustness of our results to some basic changes in the way *ex ante* costs are payable, keeping the analysis at a very tractable level. In particular, below we show that our results are 'pervasive' in the sense that they survive when it is enough that *one* party pays, and when the *ex ante* costs are modelled as 'strategic complements'.

We begin our analysis with a brief review of the related literature (Section 1) and a discussion of the possible interpretations of the *ex ante* transaction costs (Section 2). We then proceed in Section 3 to present the simplest possible model of the basic hold-up problem associated with a surplus-enhancing negotiation. This problem is analysed in the case in which the *ex ante* costs associated with the Coasian negotiation are either complements or substitutes. In Section 4 we address the question of whether a Coasian solution to our basic hold-up problem is plausible. We do this by analysing the possibility of a negotiated transfer from one party to the other before the payment of the transaction costs that are at the origin of the hold-up problem. In Section 5 we look at how the allocation of property rights may or may not alleviate the inefficiencies stemming from *ex ante* transaction costs. Section 6 offers some concluding remarks. To ease the exposition, we have relegated all proofs to the Appendix.

## 1. Related Literature

What has become known as the Coase theorem (Coase, 1960) assumes the absence of transaction costs or other frictions in the bargaining process. Coase (1960) himself does provide an extensive discussion of the role of transaction costs.[4] Indeed, Coase (1992) describes the result as provocative and intended to show how unrealistic is the world without transaction costs.

Here and in AF, we go further by identifying the strategic role played by *ex ante* transaction costs (as opposed, for instance, to transaction costs that are payable *ex post*) which may lead to an outcome that is *constrained inefficient.*

The source of inefficiencies in this article is a version of the 'hold-up problem' (Grout, 1984; Grossman and Hart, 1986; Hart and Moore, 1988, among many others). The problem is particularly acute in our setting since it may be impossible for the negotiating parties to find a 'Coasian solution' to this hold-up problem. Closely linked to the literature on the hold-up problem is the literature on the

[4] de Meza (1988) provides an extensive survey of the literature on the Coase theorem, including an outline of its history and possible interpretations.

effects of the allocation of property rights when contracts are incomplete (Grossman and Hart, 1986; Hart and Moore, 1990; Chiu, 1998; de Meza and Lockwood, 1998; Rajan and Zingales, 1998, among many others). It turns out that the effects of the allocation of property rights on the version of the hold-up problem we analyse here depends on how the parties' outside options affect the division of surplus. We devote Section 5 below entirely to this point.

We are certainly not the first to point out that the Coase theorem no longer holds when there are frictions in the negotiation process. There is a vast literature on bargaining models where the frictions take the form of incomplete and asymmetric information. With incomplete information, efficient agreements often cannot be reached and delays in bargaining may obtain.[5] By contrast, the reduced form negotiation that we consider in our analysis is one of complete information. The source of inefficiencies in this article can therefore be traced directly to the presence of transaction costs.

Dixit and Olson (2000) are concerned with a classical Coasian public good problem in which they explicitly model the agents' *ex ante* (possibly costly) decisions of whether to participate or not in the bargaining process. In their setting they find both efficient and inefficient equilibria as opposed to the unique constrained inefficient equilibrium we derive in our setting. They also highlight the inefficiency of the symmetric (mixed-strategy) equilibria of their model.

## 2. *Ex Ante* Transaction Costs

We are concerned with Coasian negotiations in which the parties have to incur some *ex ante* transaction costs, before they reach the stage in which the actual negotiation occurs.

The interpretation of these *ex ante* transaction costs which we favour is that of time spent 'preparing' for the Coasian negotiation. Typically, a variety of tasks need to be carried out by the parties involved before the actual negotiation begins.

In those cases in which the negotiation of an agreement contingent on a state of nature is concerned, both parties need to conceive of, and agree upon, a suitable language to describe the possible realisations of the state of nature precisely. The parties also need to collect and analyse information about the 'legal environment' in which the agreement will be embedded. For instance, in different countries the same agreement will need to be drawn-up differently to make it legally enforceable.

In virtually all settings in which a negotiation is required, the parties need to spend time arranging a way to 'meet' and they need to 'earmark' some of their time schedules for the actual meeting.

In many cases, before a meaningful negotiation can start, the parties will need to collect and analyse background information that may be relevant to their understanding of the actual trading opportunities. These activities may range from

[5] See Muthoo (1999) for an up-to-date coverage as well as extensive references on this strand of literature and other issues in bargaining theory.

collecting information about (for instance the creditworthiness of) the other party, to actual 'thinking' or 'complexity' costs incurred to understand the negotiation problem. We view this type of *ex ante* transaction costs as both relevant and important for the type of effects which we identify in our analysis below. However, it should be emphasised that our model does not *directly* apply to this type of costs. This is because in our model the size of the gains from trade is fixed and known to the parties. On the other hand, the lack of information and/or understanding of the negotiation setting that we have just described, would clearly make the size of the surplus uncertain for the parties involved. We have not considered the case of uncertain surplus for reasons of space and analytical convenience. However, we conjecture that the general flavour of our results generalises to this case.

Where does one look for evidence of transactions that never took place because of *ex ante* costs? This is obviously no easy endeavour, aside perhaps from small things like not inspecting a used car because the negotiation can only take place after sinking the cost of travelling to where the car is kept.

There is a well known colourful story – an anecdotal piece of evidence – that, in our view, fits the bill well enough to be mentioned here.[6] In 1980, IBM (then the unchallenged dominant player in the computer industry) decided to enter the market for Personal Computers. IBM did not have an operating system for PCs. To acquire an operating system from an outside source they sent a delegation to visit the offices of Microsoft to negotiate. At the time, however, Microsoft did not own an operating system either, and so they referred the visitors from IBM to a small company – Intergalactic Digital Research – that had a working operating system for PCs. The surprise match between IBM and Digital Research never reached the actual negotiation stage. The founder of Digital Research (Gary Kildall) refused to meet with the IBM delegation because he had 'other plans'. His wife (Dorothy Kildall) met with the representatives of IBM but refused their request to sign a non-disclosure agreement. Eventually, the IBM representatives left without any negotiation concerning the actual deal having taken place.

The interpretation of events in line with our main point in this paper is clear. If the negotiating stage had been reached, IBM's bargaining power would have been extreme. As a result Digital Research did not pay the *ex ante* costs necessary to reach the actual negotiation stage: Gary Kildall decided that his time was better employed elsewhere and Dorothy Kildall was put off by the non-disclosure agreement, a likely signal of the length and complexity of the negotiation to come, as well as a possible direct liability. The inefficiency of the outcome reached is

[6] The story was the subject of a documentary series aired in 1996 by PBS television stations in the US. The documentary was entitled *Triumph of the Nerds: The Rise of Accidental Empires*. The transcripts can be found at http://www.pbs.org/nerds/. The documentary series was in turn based on Cringely (1992). The basic facts summarised here seem to be reasonably uncontroversial. However, it should also be pointed out that the story is so widely known that differing interpretations and versions of some of its details can be found in copious amounts on the World Wide Web. These include disputed accounts of a subsequent meeting between Gary Kildall of Digital Research and IBM. If this meeting did take place, clearly it did not generate an operative deal. Of course, the interpretation of the facts that we give is our own.

apparent: ownership of the dominant operating system for PCs turned out to be worth tens of billions of dollars in the following two decades alone.[7]

We conclude this Section with an observation. In many cases the parties to a negotiation will have the opportunity to delegate to outsiders many of the tasks that we have mentioned as sources of *ex ante* transaction costs. The most common example of this is the hiring of lawyers. Abstracting from agency problems (between the negotiating party/principal and the lawyer/agent), which are likely to increase the *ex ante* costs anyway, our analysis applies, unchanged, to the case in which the *ex ante* transaction costs that we have described are payable to an agent.

## 3. The Basic Hold-up Problem

We focus on three basic cases in which the presence of *ex ante* transaction costs generates the hold-up problem we have outlined informally above.

The three cases we pursue in detail are chosen with a two-fold objective in mind. First of all they are the simplest models that suffice to put across the main point. Second, the range of cases they cover is meant to convey the fact that the inefficiency we find is 'pervasive' in the sense that it obtains in a whole variety of extensive forms. In Anderlini and Felli (2001*b*) we show that the basic hold-up problem identified here survives when we allow transaction costs to be continuous as opposed to the binary choice considered here.

### 3.1. *Perfect Complements*

Consider two agents, called $A$ and $B$, who face a 'Coasian' opportunity to realise some gains from trade. Without loss of generality we normalise to one the size of the surplus realised if an agreement is reached. We also set the parties' payoffs in the case of disagreement to be equal to zero.

In the first two cases we look at, once the negotiating phase is reached the division of surplus between the two agents is exogenously given and cannot be changed by the agents.[8]

Let $\lambda \in [0, 1]$ be the share of the surplus that accrues to agent $A$ if the parties engage in the negotiation and $1 - \lambda$ the share of the surplus that accrues to $B$.

For the negotiation to start, each agent has to pay a given *ex ante transaction cost*. In other words, the agents reach the negotiating phase only if they both pay a

[7] The enormity of the value of the missed transaction raises an obvious question: were Digital Research simply 'dumb' as some of the characters involved seem to suggest in the transcripts of the documentary cited above? (see footnote 6). Our reply is two-fold. First, the value of the failed transaction was surely highly uncertain at the time. To measure it with its *realised* value more than 20 years later does not seem correct. Second, the realised value of the failed transaction is measured by the subsequent success of Microsoft. However, while Microsoft *did* supply IBM with an operating system for PCs soon after the events we have described, they did not *sell* it, but rather they *licensed* it to IBM. Microsoft concluded a deal with IBM using a contractual device that, as it turns out, shifted the division of surplus dramatically in its favour.

[8] See our introduction for a discussion of AF where the division of surplus is endogenously determined by the model.

certain amount before the negotiation begins.[9] These costs should be thought of as representing a combination of the activities necessary for the gains from trade to materialise which we discussed in some detail in Section 2.

Let $c_A > 0$ and $c_B > 0$ be the two agents' *ex ante* costs. Clearly, if $c_A + c_B > 1$ then the two agents will never reach the negotiation stage that yields the unit surplus. Clearly, neither would a social planner since the total cost of the negotiation exceeds the surplus which it yields. We are interested in the case in which it would be socially efficient for the two agents to negotiate an agreement. Our first assumption guarantees that this is the case.

ASSUMPTION 1: *The surplus that the negotiation yields exceeds the total ex ante costs that are payable for the negotiation to occur. In other words* $c_A + c_B < 1$.

Our two agents play a two-stage game. In period $t = 0$ they both simultaneously and independently decide whether to pay their *ex ante* cost. An agreement yielding a surplus of size one at $t = 1$ is feasible only if both agents pay their *ex ante* costs at $t = 0$.[10] The game at $t = 1$ is a simple 'black box', yielding payoffs of $\lambda$ to $A$ and $1 - \lambda$ to $B$. If one or both agents do not pay their *ex ante* costs at $t = 0$, the game at $t = 1$ is trivial: the negotiation that yields the unit surplus is not feasible; the agents have no actions to take and they both receive a payoff of zero.

Throughout the article, unless otherwise stated, by equilibrium we mean a *subgame perfect* equilibrium of the game at hand. The normal form that corresponds to the two-stage game we have just described is depicted in Figure 1. From this it is immediate to derive our first Proposition, which therefore is stated without proof.

| | pay $c_B$ | not pay $c_B$ |
|---|---|---|
| pay $c_A$ | $\lambda - c_A$, $1 - \lambda - c_B$ | $-c_A$, 0 |
| not pay $c_A$ | 0, $-c_B$ | 0, 0 |

Fig. 1. *Normal Form of the Two-stage Game with Ex Ante Costs*

PROPOSITION 1: *If either* $c_A > \lambda$ *or* $c_B > 1 - \lambda$ *the unique equilibrium of the two-stage game represented in Figure 1 has neither agent paying the ex ante cost and therefore yields the no-agreement outcome.*

We view Proposition 1 as implying that in the presence of *ex ante* transaction costs, if the *distribution* of *ex ante* costs across the parties is sufficiently 'mis-matched' with the distribution of surplus, then the *ex ante* costs will generate a version of the hold-up problem which will induce the agents not to negotiate an agreement even though it would be socially efficient to do so.

[9] Notice therefore that we are implicitly assuming that the agents have some endowments of resources out of which the *ex ante* costs can be paid.

[10] Notice that we are therefore assuming that the two agents' *ex ante* costs are *perfect complements* in the 'technology' that determines whether the surplus-generating negotiation is feasible or not. We examine the cases of perfect substitutes, and of strategic complements in Subsections 3.2 and 3.3 below respectively.

The intuition behind Proposition 1 is simple enough. If negotiating an agreement involves some costs that are payable *ex ante*, the share of the surplus accruing to each party will not depend, in equilibrium, on whether the *ex ante* costs are paid. Therefore, the parties will pay the costs only if the distribution of the surplus generated by the negotiation will allow them to recoup the cost *ex post*. If the distribution of surplus and that of *ex ante* costs are sufficiently 'mis-matched', then one of the agents will not be able to recoup the *ex ante* cost. In this case, an agreement will not be reached, even though it would generate a total surplus large enough to cover the *ex ante* costs of both agents.

As a polar benchmark, consider the alternative setup in which both parties can pay the costs $c_A$ and $c_B$ after the negotiation has occurred and an agreement is reached. In other words the transaction costs can be paid *ex post* rather than *ex ante*.[11] In this case the extensive form of the game is equivalent to a simple negotiation in which the size of the gains from trade is $1 - c_A - c_B$. The assumption we made on the black-box negotiation implies that in this case the two parties do indeed reach an agreement. Party $A$ receives the share of surplus $\lambda(1 - c_A - c_B)$ while party $B$ receives the share $(1 - \lambda)(1 - c_A - c_B)$. In other words when transaction costs can be paid *ex post* the strong version of the Coase Theorem holds and a constrained efficient outcome is guaranteed.

We conclude this subsection with two observations. First of all, the simultaneity in the payment of the *ex ante* costs is not essential to Proposition 1. The result applies to the case in which the *ex ante* costs are payable sequentially by the two agents before the actual negotiation begins.

Second, while the model has a unique equilibrium for the parameter configurations identified in Proposition 1, it has multiple equilibria whenever this proposition does not apply. It is clear that, whenever both $\lambda > c_A$ and $(1 - \lambda) > c_B$, the model has two equilibria. One in which the *ex ante* costs are paid and an agreement is reached, and another in which neither agent pays the *ex ante* costs simply because he expects the other agent not to pay his cost either. The equilibrium in which the agreement is reached strictly Pareto-dominates the no-agreement equilibrium. Clearly, the multiplicity of equilibria disappears if the costs are payable sequentially. The latter observation will become relevant again in Section 4 below.

### 3.2. *Perfect Substitutes*

We now turn to our second simple model. The next Proposition tells us that when the agents' *ex ante* costs are *perfect substitutes* our constrained inefficiency result of Subsection 3.1 still holds, although the inefficiency may take a different form.

The intuition behind the next results is straightforward. In an environment in which the *ex ante* costs may be paid by *either* agent the negotiation leads to a constrained efficient outcome if *at least one* of the two *ex ante* costs is smaller than the size of the surplus. It is then easy to envisage a situation in which the share of

[11] These *ex post* costs could, for example, be associated with registering the agreement with the relevant authorities.

the surplus accruing to each agent is strictly smaller than his *ex ante* costs although there is enough surplus to cover the smallest of these costs. In this case, in equilibrium, the parties will not reach an agreement although it would be socially efficient to do so.

When the *ex ante* costs are perfect substitutes, a new type of inefficiency can also arise in equilibrium. In particular, it is possible that the agents reach an agreement, but the equilibrium involves the highest of the two *ex ante* costs being paid.

Formally, when the *ex ante* costs are perfect substitutes Assumption 1 needs to be modified. Assumption 2 below identifies the range of *ex ante* costs that guarantee that negotiating an agreement is socially efficient in this case.

ASSUMPTION 2. *The surplus that the agreement yields exceeds the minimum ex ante cost payable for the negotiation to become feasible. In other words* $\min\{c_A, c_B\} < 1$. *Without loss of generality (up to a re-labelling of agents) let* $c_A \leq c_B$. *Hence* $c_A < 1$.

Consider now the model with *ex ante* transaction costs that are perfect substitutes and let Assumption 2 above hold. The normal form corresponding to the new two-stage game is depicted in Figure 2.

| | pay $c_B$ | not pay $c_B$ |
|---|---|---|
| pay $c_A$ | $\lambda - c_A,\ 1 - \lambda - c_B$ | $\lambda - c_A,\ 1 - \lambda$ |
| not pay $c_A$ | $\lambda,\ 1 - \lambda - c_B$ | $0,\ 0$ |

Fig. 2. *Normal Form When the Ex ante Costs are Perfect Substitutes*

As we mentioned above, the inefficiency generated by the *ex ante* costs can now take two forms, which our next proposition identifies. As before, it is stated without proof since it is immediate from the payoffs in Figure 2.

PROPOSITION 2. *If* $1 > c_A > \lambda$ *and* $c_B > 1 - \lambda$ *the only equilibrium of the two-stage game represented in Figure 2 has neither agent paying the* ex ante *cost, and therefore yields the no-agreement outcome.*

*If instead* $1 > c_A > \lambda$ *and* $c_B < 1 - \lambda$ *then the only equilibrium of the two-stage game represented in Figure 2 has agent A not paying the ex ante cost* $c_A$, *and B paying the ex ante cost* $c_B > c_A$.

### 3.3. *Strategic Complements*

Our goal in this subsection is to show that the analogue of Proposition 1 holds when the *ex ante* costs are technologically perfect substitutes but are 'strategic complements' in the game-theoretic sense.[12] We conjecture that this is true more generally but limit our formal analysis to a simple model closely related to the previous two.

[12] Intuitively, two decision variables are strategic complements if an increase in one induces an increase in the optimal choice (the 'best response' of the opposing player) of the other. See Fudenberg and Tirole (1996, ch. 12).

At $t = 0$ both agents decide simultaneously and independently whether to pay their *ex ante* costs. If both agents decide not to pay the *ex ante* costs, then negotiation is not feasible and both receive a payoff of zero. If either agent $i \in \{A, B\}$ pays the *ex ante* cost $c_i$ at $t = 0$ the negotiation of an agreement yielding one unit of surplus becomes feasible. If both pay their *ex ante* costs at $t = 0$ the distribution parameter $\lambda$ determines the agreement that is negotiated and *A*'s and *B*'s payoffs are $\lambda - c_A$ and $1 - \lambda - c_B$ respectively.

However, if only one agent, say *A*, pays the *ex ante* cost at $t = 0$, he is allowed to make a take-it-or-leave-it offer $\ell$ to *B* at $t = 1$. The value of $\ell$ is interpreted as an offer to make *A*'s and *B*'s payoffs equal $\ell$ and $1 - \ell$ respectively, minus any costs paid. This can be thought of as a crude way to say that if only one agent pays the *ex ante* cost then the bargaining power shifts dramatically in his favour.

Moreover, we assume that *A*, if he alone has paid the *ex ante* cost, can, in principle, make some offers that would push agent *B* below his individual rationality constraint. In other words we assume that the take-it-or-leave-it offer $\ell$ must be in the interval $[-\epsilon, 1 + \xi]$ with $\epsilon$ and $\xi$ some (possibly small) positive numbers.

At $t = 2$, *B* has two choices. He can either pay an *ex ante* cost $c'_B > 0$ or pay nothing.[13] If he does not pay he does not observe *A*'s offer, but is still allowed to accept or reject it blind. If *B* decides to pay his *ex ante* cost, he can then observe *A*'s offer and subsequently decide to accept or reject it.

The description of the extensive form that is played if it is *B* alone who pays the *ex ante* cost at $t = 0$ is symmetric to the case we have just described.

Notice that the strategic complementarity of the two agents' *ex ante* costs is built into the extensive form game we have described precisely via the shift in bargaining power that obtains when one agent alone pays the *ex ante* costs at $t = 0$.

Suppose now that the parameters $\lambda$, $c_A$ and $c_B$ are such that the agents would not negotiate an agreement in the model described in Subsection 3.1. Our next proposition then tells us that, in the model with strategic complementarities we have just described, they will not negotiate an agreement either.

PROPOSITION 3. *Consider the model with ex ante costs that are strategic complements described above in this subsection. Assume that either $\lambda < c_A$ or $1 - \lambda < c_B$. Then the unique equilibrium outcome of the model has neither agent paying the ex ante cost at $t = 0$, and hence the no-agreement outcome obtains.*

## 4. The Impossibility of a Coasian Solution

In Section 3 we have argued that *ex ante* transaction costs may give rise to a version of the hold-up problem which in turn generates an inefficient (no-agreement) outcome. The next natural question to ask is whether a Coasian solution to the hold-up problem is generally available in the present set up. In other words: is it

[13] Notice that while Proposition 3 below restricts the values of $c_A$ and $c_B$ to be in an appropriate range, $c'_B$ can take any positive (small) value.

possible to add another stage of negotiation to our model (say $t = -1$), prior to the stage in which the *ex ante* costs are incurred, in which the agents can negotiate a 'grand agreement', which will resolve the hold-up problem and hence restore efficiency?

The answer to the above question is trivially 'yes', if at $t = -1$ a *truly grand* agreement can be negotiated *costlessly*, that specifies everything, including the payment of the *ex ante* costs, *and* the division of the actual surplus at time $t = 1$. The answer, however, changes dramatically if the 'grand agreement' is itself costly.

We specify two crucial details of the grand agreement negotiation stage. First of all we assume, as seems plausible in the present context, that in order to be able to negotiate an agreement at $t = -1$ a fresh set of *ex ante* costs must be incurred by the parties before $t = -1$, say at $t = -2$. Second, we restrict the agents to negotiate a *compensating transfer* at $t = -1$. In other words, we take a specific view on the agreements that the agents can enter at $t = -1$. We restrict them to be transfers *contingent* on the payment of *ex ante* costs at $t = 0$. This seems to be in the spirit of our model of Section 3, in that, in principle, it allows the agents to transfer surplus effectively between them but it keeps the distribution of surplus in the last stage of the negotiating process, $t = 1$, exogenously fixed as before.

It is worth emphasising at this point that we find that the presence of any *strictly positive* 'second tier' *ex ante* costs is sufficient to keep the addition of a grand agreement negotiation stage from resolving the hold-up problem of Section 3. We view this as a strength of the results we present in this Section. In many situations it would be sensible to assume that the second tier *ex ante* costs are in fact at least as large as the 'first tier' *ex ante* costs, on the grounds that the negotiation of a grand agreement, in an intuitive sense, is a more complex object than the negotiation of the agreement itself.

Formally, we modify the first model of Section 3 as follows. There are now four time periods, $t \in \{-2, -1, 0, 1\}$. The sequence of decisions and events for the two agents (depicted schematically in Figure 3) is as follows. In period $t = -2$, the two agents decide simultaneously and independently whether to pay the second tier *ex ante* costs $(c_A^2, c_B^2)$. If either or both agents decide not to pay these *ex ante* costs, the period $t = -1$ compensating transfers to be described shortly are automatically set equal to 0, and the agents effectively move directly to time $t = 0$. If, on the other hand both agents pay the second tier *ex ante* costs, then period $t = -1$ compensating transfers can be negotiated.

For simplicity, we assume that (provided that both pay the second tier costs) at $t = -1$, both agents make simultaneous offers of contingent compensating transfers to each other. Formally, each agent $i \in \{A, B\}$ chooses a real number $\sigma_i \geq 0$, which is interpreted as a commitment to transfer the amount of wealth $\sigma_i$ to the other agent, $j \neq i$, if and only if $j$ pays the first tier *ex ante* cost $c_j^0$ in period $t = 0$. Immediately after choosing $\sigma_i$, still in period $t = -1$, $A$ and $B$ simultaneously choose whether to accept or reject the other agent's offer of compensating transfer. Those offers which are accepted at this stage are binding in period $t = 0$.

The decisions and events in periods $t = 0$ and $t = 1$ are analogous to those described in Subsection 3.1. At $t = 0$, both agents choose simultaneously and independently whether to pay the first tier *ex ante* costs $(c_A^0, c_B^0)$. If he chooses to

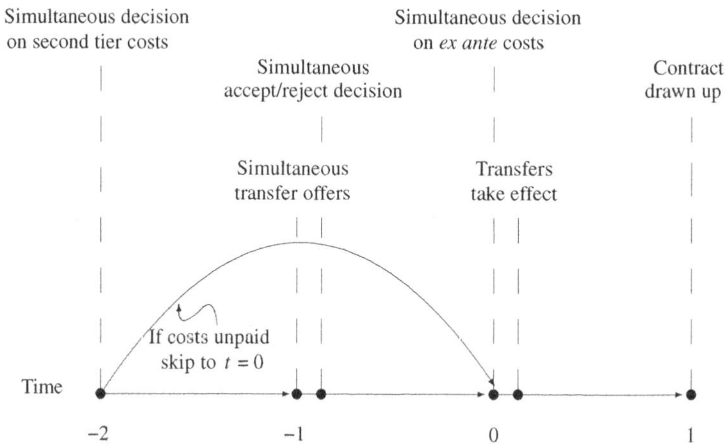


Fig. 3. *Timing in the Two Tier Model*

pay, each agent $i \in \{A, B\}$ then incurs an *ex ante* cost of $c_i^0$ at this time, and subsequently receives a compensating transfer of $\sigma_j$ from agent $j \neq i$. Only if both agents have paid the first tier *ex ante* costs does the $t = 1$ negotiation of the surplus-generating agreement becomes possible.

Provided both agents have paid their first tier *ex ante* costs their payoffs are $\lambda - \gamma_A$ and $1 - \lambda - \gamma_B$ respectively, where $\gamma_i$ denotes the total *ex ante* costs paid by agent $i \subset \{A, B\}$ during the entire game, minus any compensating transfer received from agent $j \neq i$, and plus any compensating transfers paid by $i$ to $j$. If the surplus-generating agreement is not negotiated, then the two agents payoffs are simply $-\gamma_A$ and $-\gamma_B$ respectively.

The assumption that the total (for both tiers) of *ex ante* costs must be low enough so that it is socially efficient for the parties to negotiate a grand agreement is easy to state for this version of our model.

Assumption 3. *Let* $c_i = c_i^2 + c_i^0$ *for* $i \in \{A, B\}$. *Then* $c_A + c_B < 1$.

It is apparent from the description of our model with compensating transfers above (cf. Figure 3) that this model, viewed from $t = 0$, is in fact identical to the simple model of Subsection 1, whenever both agents have chosen not to pay the second tier *ex ante* costs. We can therefore ask whether the parameters of our model with compensating transfers are such that according to Proposition 1, in the absence of compensating transfers, the no-agreement is the unique equilibrium outcome of the model. This motivates our first Definition.

Definition 1. *Assume that either* $c_A^0 > \lambda$ *or* $c_B^0 > 1 - \lambda$ *so that, provided that neither agent has paid the second tier ex ante cost, then no agreement is the only equilibrium outcome of the model (see Proposition 1 above). We then say that the model with compensating transfers 'yields the no-agreement outcome in the final stage'.*

We are now ready to state our next Proposition. It tells us that, if the parameters of the model of Subsection 3.1 yield the no-agreement outcome, then adding a new stage to the model, with a second tier of positive *ex ante* costs and compensating transfers, may not solve the hold-up problem generated by the first tier *ex ante* costs. In particular, the model with compensating transfers has multiple equilibria and at least one equilibrium that yields the no-agreement outcome.

PROPOSITION 4. *Consider the model with compensating transfers. Suppose that $c_A^0$, $c_B^0$ and $\lambda$ yield the no-agreement outcome in the final stage (cf. Definition 1), and assume that the second tier ex ante costs are strictly positive for both agents ($c_i^2 > 0$ for $i \in \{A, B\}$). Then the model has multiple equilibria. In particular, an equilibrium always exists in which neither agent pays either tier of ex ante costs, and hence yields the no-agreement outcome. Moreover, there is also an equilibrium in which both agents pay both tiers of ex ante costs and an agreement is negotiated.*

The reason why the model with compensating transfers always has one equilibrium in which none of the costs are paid is obvious. Recall that at each stage the two agents decide simultaneously and independently whether to pay their *ex ante* costs. Moreover an agreement is (or compensating transfers are) feasible only if both agents pay. It is then clear that if one agent expects the other not to pay his *ex ante* cost he should not pay either. The cost would be wasted since it has no effect on the remainder of the game. Therefore it is an equilibrium for both agents to pay none of the costs.

The intuition behind the existence of a subgame perfect equilibrium in which the parties do pay both tiers of *ex ante* costs and negotiate a grand agreement is less straightforward.[14]

Imagine that some compensating transfers have been agreed. If the transfers are such that the first tier *ex ante* costs are 'covered' for both agents (which is always possible in principle because of Assumption 3), then the terminal subgame of the model has two equilibria. One in which an agreement is negotiated, and another one in which neither agent pays the first tier *ex ante* cost and the no-agreement outcome obtains. Note that these equilibria are Pareto-ranked.

It is then possible to construct an equilibrium in which the agents switch (off-the-equilibrium-path) between equilibria of the terminal subgame, according to what transfers have been offered and agreed in the first stage of the game. The 'switching point' can always be constructed in such a way that it is in the interest of the agent whose share of the surplus exceeds his costs to compensate the other for the shortfall between his share of the surplus and both tiers of *ex ante* costs. The threat of switching to the inefficient equilibrium is viable because the no-agreement outcome is always one of the possible equilibrium outcomes of the terminal subgame.

[14] We are indebted to Stephen Matthews for pointing out the existence of this type of equilibrium in the model.

Two observations come to mind with respect to the equilibrium we just described. First, even if the agreement is successfully negotiated this is done by paying two tiers of *ex ante* costs rather than one. Therefore, even when an agreement is reached the equilibrium of the model is constrained inefficient.

Second, and in our view more importantly, the equilibria of our model, with compensating transfers in which an agreement is negotiated, rely on the agents playing (off-the-equilibrium-path) an equilibrium in the terminal subgame that is strictly Pareto-dominated by another equilibrium of the same subgame. This runs against the intuition that the parties to a negotiation will be able to re-negotiate *ex post* to an equilibrium that makes them both better off when one is available.

Imagine now that we impose the restriction that in the terminal subgame the agents must play the Pareto-efficient equilibrium when the subgame has two equilibria. Then, after the second tier *ex ante* costs have been paid, they are *sunk* in a strategic sense. This means that the agent who has a 'deficit' in the last stage of the game, by subgame perfection, will accept any offer of compensating transfer that leaves him with a positive continuation payoff. Therefore in any equilibrium that obeys this new restriction, the compensating transfers will *not* take into account the second tier *ex ante* costs. Therefore, one of the two agents will find it profitable not to pay the second tier *ex ante* cost for which he would not possibly be compensated. This, in turn, means that compensating transfers will not be observed in equilibrium, and therefore yields the no-agreement outcome. This is the focus of Proposition 5 below.

The idea that some type of renegotiation-proofness is an appealing additional restriction to impose on the set of subgame perfect equilibria is not new. Examples are to be found in contract theory (Grossman and Hart, 1986; Hart and Moore, 1988; Rubinstein and Wolinsky, 1992; Segal, 1999; Che and Hausch, 1999), in the mechanism design and implementation literature (Maskin and Moore, 1999; Segal and Whinston, 2002), and in game theory in general (Farrell and Maskin, 1989; Abreu *et al.*, 1993, Benoît and Krishna, 1993) among others.

We give an informal definition of a *renegotiation-proof* equilibrium which applies to our model of this Section.

DEFINITION 2. *A subgame perfect equilibrium of the model with compensating transfers is renegotiation-proof if and only if the equilibria played in every proper subgame are not strictly Pareto-dominated by any other equilibrium of the same subgame.*[15]

Our next result says the if we restrict attention to renegotiation-proof equilibria, then the possibility of compensating transfers does not resolve the hold-up problem identified in Section 3. It is true that the model always has an equilibrium in which transfers take effect and an agreement is negotiated. But this equilibrium is not renegotiation-proof. Thus, although it may be tempting to select (in a Coasian fashion) the equilibrium with agreement among the two mentioned in Proposition 4 simply because it Pareto-dominates the no-agreement equilibrium, this type of selection is open to an objection that is, in our view, fatal.

[15] Notice that our informal definition is made particularly simple by the fact that our model with compensating transfers only has one 'level' of proper subgames.

Surely, if we are willing to select among Pareto-ranked equilibria in favour of the dominating one, we should also be willing to apply the same logic to every subgame? After all, once entered, every subgame is just like a game. However, if we apply this selection criterion to every subgame (in a recursively consistent way, of course), the only equilibrium of the entire game that survives is the constrained inefficient one, in which the no-agreement outcome obtains.

PROPOSITION 5. *Consider the model with compensating transfers. Suppose that $c_A^0$, $c_B^0$ and $\lambda$ yield the no-agreement outcome in the final stage and that $c_A^2 > 0$ and $c_B^2 > 0$. Then every renegotiation-proof subgame perfect equilibrium of the model involves neither agent paying either tier of ex ante costs and therefore yields the no-agreement outcome.*

We view Proposition 5 as saying that the possibility of compensating transfers does not resolve the hold-up problem identified in Section 3 in the following sense. Either, we are willing to accept the multiple equilibria identified in Proposition 4, and therefore to accept the no-agreement equilibrium as being just as plausible as the one in which an agreement is negotiated. Or, we attempt to select among Pareto-ranked equilibria in favour of the efficient ones. However in this case, we should apply this logic consistently to every subgame, and hence single out those equilibria that are renegotiation-proof. In this case only the no-agreement outcome survives.

Notice that the multiplicity of equilibria in the terminal subgame of our model is crucially dependent on the fact that the *ex ante* costs are payable simultaneously by the agents. Therefore if the game is modified so that the costs are payable sequentially, all subgames have a unique equilibrium and the no-agreement outcome is certain to prevail.

In particular, consider the following modification of the extensive form depicted in Figure 3. At $t = 0$ $A$ decides whether to pay the *ex ante* cost $c_A^0$. Then $B$ observes $A$'s choice and decides whether to pay the *ex ante* cost $c_B^0$. The rest of the extensive form is identical to the one in Figure 3. The following proposition characterises the equilibria of this modification of the model with compensating transfers.[16]

PROPOSITION 6. *Consider the modified model with compensating transfers that we have just described. Suppose that $c_A^0$, $c_B^0$ and $\lambda$ yield the no-agreement outcome in the final stage and that $c_A^2 > 0$ and $c_B^2 > 0$. Then, the unique subgame perfect equilibrium of the model is for neither agent to pay either tier of ex ante costs, and hence yields the no-agreement outcome.*

## 5. Property Rights?

Since the seminal contribution of Grossman and Hart (1986), whenever a hold-up problem prevents contracting parties from achieving an efficient outcome, it is natural to ask whether an appropriate (re)allocation of property rights might

[16] The alternative game, in which $B$ decides whether to pay the *ex ante* cost before $A$, is just a relabelling of the one we have just described. Proposition 6 obviously applies to this extensive form as well.

alleviate the inefficiency. Our next task is to investigate whether a reallocation of property rights can fulfil this role in our set up.

First of all, we notice a key difference between our framework and the Grossman and Hart (1986) model. The hold-up problem in Grossman and Hart (1986) gives rise to inefficiently low levels of *relationship-specific investment*. These are investments that enhance the surplus available from the contractual relationship. In that framework, it is also natural to assume that, to some extent at least, the parties' investments improve their *outside options* available outside the contractual relationship.

The hold-up problem in our set up is generated by (*ex ante*) *transaction costs*. These are *uniquely* related to the potential transaction at hand. It is therefore natural to assume that whether they are paid or not has *no effect* on the value of the parties' outside options. This key difference is what drives our findings below. Our set up is one in which it is natural to assume that the allocation of property rights affects the parties' outside options, regardless of the payment of the *ex ante* transaction costs.

Once the above observation is granted, we find that whether the allocation of property rights matters or not depends on whether and how outside options matter in the division of surplus between the parties. In other words, whether and how outside options affect the bargaining outcome.

Purely for the sake of simplicity, we introduce the parties' outside options as $o_A$ and $o_B$ respectively and we take them to be such that $o_A + o_B = 0$.[17] An allocation of property rights in our model is then simply a choice of $o_A$ and $o_B$ summing to 0 as above. The obvious interpretation being that asset ownership increases what an agent can get outside of the contractual relationship.

We now consider once more our simple model of Subsection 3.1, in which both parties must pay their *ex ante* transaction costs for the surplus to materialise.

We begin with the outside options having the same role in the parties' bargaining as in Grossman and Hart (1986). In this case, if the negotiation takes place, each party receives his outside option, plus a share of the available surplus over and above the sum of the outside options (the gains from trade).[18]

Using the fact that $o_A + o_B = 0$, in this case the normal form corresponding to the two-stage game is as in Figure 4. We can then conclude that in this case, the reallocation of property rights cannot resolve the hold-up problem created by the *ex ante* transactions costs. As is apparent from the normal form in Figure 4, the model will have a unique equilibrium in which neither party pays his *ex ante* cost and hence the no contract outcome obtains *regardless* of $o_A$ and $o_B$, provided that

[17] It is easy to check that nothing we say here depends on the outside options summing to 0. All our arguments apply virtually unchanged if we assume that $o_A + o_B$ is equal to some constant $k$, that is less than $1 - c_A - c_B$. The analysis will change, however, if the sum of the outside options depends on the allocation of ownership rights. We briefly consider this case below at the end of the Section.

[18] There is a sizeable literature in bargaining theory on what justifies the parties outside options affecting the outcome in different ways. The Nash bargaining solution of course suggests that they should have exactly the role they have in Grossman and Hart (1986). In extensive form bargaining, their role depends on the details of the extensive form and can range from being the same as in the Nash bargaining solution to acting as a constraints that only matter if they become binding (Binmore, 1986; Binmore *et al.*, 1986; Sutton, 1986).

| | pay $c_B$ | not pay $c_B$ |
|---|---|---|
| pay $c_A$ | $\lambda + o_A - c_A,\ 1 - \lambda + o_B - c_B$ | $o_A - c_A,\ o_B$ |
| not pay $c_A$ | $o_A,\ o_B - c_B$ | $o_A,\ o_B$ |

Fig. 4. *Normal Form with Nash Bargaining Outside Options*

the distribution of *ex ante* costs and bargaining power are sufficiently 'mis-matched' exactly as we found in Proposition 1 above.

Both de Meza and Lockwood (1998) and Chiu (1998) analyse the effect of the allocation of property rights in a hold-up model in which outside options play a different role in the bargaining outcome.[19] In these models outside options act as a *constraint* on the bargaining outcome. So, an agent's payoff will be his share in the bargaining over the whole surplus, if neither outside option is binding. If either outside option is binding, then the party for whom it is binding receives a share of surplus equal to his outside option and the other party gets the rest.

To write down the normal form corresponding to the two-stage game in this case it is convenient to consider two separate cases: $o_A > 0$ and $o_B > 0$.[20] When $o_A > 0$, it is only possible that *A*'s outside option binds, while for *B* it must be not binding. Symmetrically, when $o_B > 0$, it is only possible that *B*'s outside option binds, while for *A* it must be not binding. The normal form corresponding to the two-stage game therefore is either as in Figure 5, or as in Figure 6 depending on which case applies.

In this case it is immediate from the normal forms in Figures 5 and 6 that a reallocation of property rights is in fact capable of resolving the hold-up problem we have identified. In fact it is straightforward to check that, whatever $\lambda \in (0, 1)$ and $c_A$ and $c_B$ satisfying Assumption 1, we can always choose $o_A$ ad $o_B$ so that both $\lambda - c_A > o_A$ and $1 - \lambda - c_B > o_B$ hold.[21] Given these outside options from Figures 5 and 6 it is clear that the model has an equilibrium in which both *A* and *B* pay their *ex ante* transaction costs and an agreement is reached.[22]

Clearly, the two conditions we have found can be rewritten as $\lambda > c_A + o_A$ and $1 - \lambda > c_B + o_B$. Thus, in the second case we have analysed, the allocation of property rights can be used to 're-align' the distribution of *ex ante* transaction costs with the distribution of bargaining power when they are 'mis-matched'. To this end the property rights must be allocated in favour of the agent with the highest bargaining power.

In this Section, we have so far assumed that the sum of the outside options is independent of the allocation of ownership rights. This is of course a special case.

[19] Rajan and Zingales (1998) analyse a related model in which the focus is the role of the allocation of power, defined as the control of 'access' to a physical asset.

[20] Clearly, because $o_A + o_B = 0$ these two cases are mutually exclusive. Since the case $o_A = o_B = 0$ corresponds to our previous model, the cases we consider here are also exhaustive of all configurations of interest.

[21] These conditions can be satisfied simultaneously because $o_A + o_B = 0$. In fact they can always be satisfied simultaneously provided that $c_A + c_B + o_A + o_B < 1$. This is equivalent to asserting that trade is in fact efficient, given the transaction costs and the parties' outside options. See footnote 17.

[22] As in our analysis of Subsection 3.1 above, there is always another equilibrium in which neither agent pays the *ex ante* transaction cost and no agreement is reached. As before, this equilibrium disappears if the *ex ante* transaction costs are payable sequentially.

| | pay $c_B$ | not pay $c_B$ |
|---|---|---|
| pay $c_A$ | $\max\{\lambda, o_A\} - c_A,\ 1 - \max\{\lambda, o_A\} - c_B$ | $o_A - c_A,\ o_B$ |
| not pay $c_A$ | $o_A,\ o_B - c_B$ | $o_A,\ o_B$ |

Fig. 5. *Normal Form with Outside Options as Constraints:* $o_A > 0$

| | pay $c_B$ | not pay $c_B$ |
|---|---|---|
| pay $c_A$ | $1 - \max\{1 - \lambda, o_B\} - c_A,\ \max\{1 - \lambda, o_B\} - c_B$ | $o_A - c_A,\ o_B$ |
| not pay $c_A$ | $o_A,\ o_B - c_B$ | $o_A,\ o_B$ |

Fig. 6. *Normal Form with Outside Options as Constraints:* $o_B > 0$

In general, the allocation of ownership rights affects the sum, as well as the distribution, of the outside options. If no deal is struck between the parties about say the common use of a tract of land, it may well be the case that the second best alternative is for one party and not the other to have access to the land. So, we now briefly consider the case in which the sum of $o_A$ and $o_B$ may change as we vary the allocation of property rights.

If we continue to assume that signing a contract is more efficient than not signing one so that whatever the allocation of property rights we have that $o_A + o_B < 1 - c_A - c_B$,[23] it is easy to check that nothing changes in the case of outside options as constraints summarised in Figures 5 and 6. It is still the case that some (re)allocation of property rights will in fact induce the efficient outcome (the *ex ante* costs are paid and the contract is signed) to be an equilibrium.

In the first case we considered (outside options in Nash bargaining), summarised in Figure 4 the situation is quite different. Assume that the parameters of the problem are such that either $\lambda < c_A$ or $1 - \lambda < c_B$. In this case the unique equilibrium is such that neither party pays the *ex ante* costs and hence the no contract outcome obtains. This conclusion is independent of whether the sum of the outside options is affected by the distribution of ownership rights. The efficient allocation of ownership rights is then the one that maximises the sum of the outside options. In other words, as already conjectured in Coase (1960), when transaction costs prevent the contracting parties from reaching the efficient agreement the allocation of ownership rights does matter. The property rights over the tract of land that we mentioned above should be allocated to the party that will make the most efficient (second best) use of it.

## 6. Concluding Remarks

If the parties involved in a Coasian negotiation need to sink some *ex ante* transaction costs before they can reach the negotiating phase of their interaction, the *ex ante* costs may generate a version of the hold-up problem. If the distribution of *ex ante* costs and the distribution of surplus generated by the negotiation are sufficiently 'mis-matched', one of the two parties to the negotiation will not find it

[23] See footnotes 17 and 21.

to his advantage to pay the *ex ante* cost, even though the surplus generated by the agreement would be sufficient to cover the total *ex ante* costs associated with it. Therefore, in equilibrium the agreement will not be negotiated. We have verified this claim in a variety of simple models.

Unlike many other versions of this problem, under appropriate conditions, the hold-up problem generated by *ex ante* transaction costs is unlikely to have a 'Coasian solution'. This is because the Coasian negotiation that attempts to solve the hold-up problem is likely to generate a fresh set of *ex ante* transaction costs and hence a new hold-up problem.

Lastly, we have explored the effect of the allocation of property rights on the hold-up problem we identified. Whether property rights can resolve the problem or not depends crucially on the role that outside options play in the parties' bargaining.

## Appendix

*Proof of Proposition 3.* Since either $\lambda < c_A$ or $1 - \lambda < c_B$, it is clear that there is no equilibrium in which both agents pay the *ex ante* cost at $t = 0$.

We only show that it is not possible that in any pure strategy equilibrium $A$ alone pays the *ex ante* cost at $t = 0$. Any equilibrium in which $B$ alone pays the *ex ante* cost at $t = 0$ can be ruled out in a symmetric way and we omit the details. Mixed strategy equilibria can be ruled out using standard arguments and we omit the details.

Suppose then that there is an equilibrium in which only $A$ pays the *ex ante* cost at $t = 0$. There are two cases to consider. Either $B$ pays his cost to see $A$'s offer or he does not.

Suppose next that there is an equilibrium in which $A$ only pays the *ex ante* costs at $t = 0$ and subsequently $B$ either accepts or rejects $A$'s offer without seeing it. Note that in this case $B$ cannot condition his decision to accept or reject on the value of $\ell$ since he does not pay to see it. If $B$ accepts in equilibrium, clearly $A$ will set $\ell = -\epsilon$. But this would give an equilibrium payoff of $-\epsilon$ to $B$, and therefore yields a contradiction since $B$ can always guarantee himself a payoff of zero by not paying any costs and rejecting any offer. If $B$ rejects $A$'s offer blind in equilibrium, then $A$'s equilibrium payoff is $-c_A$ since no agreement is negotiated and $A$ pays his *ex ante* cost at $t = 0$. This is again a contradiction since $A$ can guarantee himself a payoff of zero by not paying the *ex ante* cost at $t = 0$ (and rejecting any offers made by $B$ if he pays his *ex ante* cost).

Lastly, consider the possibility of an equilibrium in which $A$ alone pays the *ex ante* costs at $t = 0$ and subsequently $B$ pays his *ex ante* cost $c'_B$ to see the value of $\ell$, and then accepts or rejects $A$'s offer. Notice that now $B$ can condition his decision to accept or reject $A$'s offer on the actual value of $\ell$. Using subgame perfection, it is immediate to see that, in equilibrium, it must be the case that $B$ accepts all offers that guarantee that $1 - \ell > 0$ (his *ex ante* cost is *sunk* when the accept/reject decision is made). Therefore, in equilibrium, $A$ will offer precisely $\ell = 1$. It follows that in any equilibrium in which $A$ alone pays the *ex ante* cost at $t = 0$ and subsequently $B$ pays to see $A$'s offer, $B$'s payoff is at most $-c'_B$. But this is a contradiction since $B$, as before, can guarantee himself a payoff of zero by not paying any costs and rejecting any offer.

LEMMA A.1: *Consider the terminal subgame of the model with simple compensating transfers described in Subsection 4 which occurs after the pair of compensating transfers* $(\sigma_A, \sigma_B)$ *has been agreed, as a function of the pair* $(\sigma_A, \sigma_B)$. *If the following inequalities are satisfied*

$$\lambda - \sigma_A + \sigma_B - c_A^0 \geq 0 \tag{A.1}$$

$$1 - \lambda + \sigma_A - \sigma_B - c_B^0 \geq 0 \tag{A.2}$$

*the subgame has two equilibria. If both inequalities are strict one equilibrium strictly Pareto-dominates the other. The Pareto-superior equilibrium is such that both parties pay the ex ante costs* $(c_A^0, c_B^0)$ *and the agreement is successfully negotiated leaving the parties with continuation payoffs* $(\lambda - \sigma_A + \sigma_B - c_A^0)$ *and* $(1 - \lambda + \sigma_A - \sigma_B - c_B^0)$. *The inferior equilibrium is such that both parties do not pay the ex ante costs* $(c_A^0, c_B^0)$ *and yields the no-agreement outcome. If either or both inequalities* (A.1) *and* (A.2) *are violated the terminal subgame has a unique equilibrium in which neither agent pays the ex ante costs* $(c_A, c_B)$, *and hence yields the no-agreement outcome.*

*Proof.* The claim follows immediately from the fact that an agreement is feasible only if both $A$ and $B$ pay the *ex ante* costs $(c_A^0, c_B^0)$, and from the observation that either agent $i$ can guarantee a continuation payoff of zero by not paying his *ex ante* cost $c_i^0$.

LEMMA A.2: *Consider the model with simple compensating transfers described in Section 4. If there exists an equilibrium of the model in which both* $\sigma_A > 0$ *and* $\sigma_B > 0$, *then there exists another, payoff equivalent, equilibrium of the model in which the transfers take the values* $\tilde{\sigma}_A = \sigma_A - \sigma_B$ *and* $\tilde{\sigma}_B = 0$ *if* $\sigma_A \geq \sigma_B$, *and* $\tilde{\sigma}_A = 0$ *and* $\tilde{\sigma}_B = \sigma_B - \sigma_A$ *if* $\sigma_B \geq \sigma_A$.

*Proof.* We only examine the case in which $\sigma_A \geq \sigma_B$. The other case is a simple re-labelling of this one. To construct the new equilibrium, let the strategies of both agents be identical to the strategies in the original equilibrium, except for the way actions are conditioned on the other agents' compensating transfer offer. In the new equilibrium, each agent $i \in \{A, B\}$ responds to any offer $\tilde{\sigma}_j$ (with $j \neq i$) exactly as he would respond to the offer $\tilde{\sigma}_j + \sigma_i$ in the original equilibrium.

*Proof of Proposition 4.* Recall that both tiers of *ex ante* costs are payable simultaneously by the agents and that an agreement (compensating transfer) is feasible only if both agents have paid the first (second) tier of *ex ante* costs. Therefore it is obvious that a pair of strategies that prescribe not paying any *ex ante* costs for both agents (and some equilibrium behaviour off-the-equilibrium-path) constitutes an equilibrium. This proves our first claim.

We now move to the construction of a subgame perfect equilibrium of the model with simple compensating transfers in which the parties do negotiate an agreement.

We only deal with the case in which $1 - \lambda < c_B^0$. The case in which $\lambda < c_A^0$ is a simple re-labelling of this one and we omit the details.

Consider the subgame occurring after the transfers $(\sigma_A, \sigma_B)$ have been agreed. If $\sigma_B \geq \sigma_A$ the only equilibrium of this subgame is such that both parties do not pay the *ex ante* costs $(c_A^2, c_B^2)$. If instead $\sigma_A \geq \sigma_B$ then by Lemma A.2 we can restrict attention to transfers that satisfy $\sigma_A > 0$ and $\sigma_B = 0$.

If $\sigma_A$ is such that inequalities (A.1) and

$$1 - \lambda + \sigma_A \geq c_B^0 + c_B^2 \tag{A.3}$$

are satisfied, we assume that the agents play the Pareto-superior of the two equilibria described in Lemma A.1 in which the agreement is successfully negotiated. If instead $\sigma_A$ is such that inequality (A.3) is *not* satisfied while (A.1) and (A.2) are satisfied we assume that the agents play the Pareto-inferior of the two equilibria described in Lemma A.1 that yields the no-agreement outcome. If either or both (A.1) and (A.2) are violated then the agents play the unique subgame perfect equilibrium of the subgame.

Proceeding backwards, it is then a best reply for $B$ to accept any offer $\sigma_A > 0$ such that inequality (A.3) is satisfied. Indeed, if $B$ rejects the offer his continuation payoff is zero while by accepting the offer his continuation payoff is non-negative.

It is then optimal for $A$ to make an offer $\sigma_A$ such that

$$\sigma_A = c_B^2 + c_B^0 - (1 - \lambda). \tag{A.4}$$

This offer is associated with a positive continuation payoff for $A$. A higher offer is associated with a smaller continuation payoff while a lower offer is associated with a continuation payoff of zero, since the parties expect to play the inefficient equilibrium whenever (A.3) is violated.

Therefore, in equilibrium both parties pay the second tier *ex ante* costs $(c_A^2, c_B^2)$. Paying the cost, $B$ obtains the payoff of zero that coincides with the payoff he gets by not paying. By paying, $A$ gets a strictly positive payoff while he gets a payoff of zero by not paying. This concludes the proof.

*Proof of Proposition* 5. We only deal with the case in which $1 - \lambda < c_B^0$. The case in which $\lambda < c_A^0$ is a simple re-labelling of this one and we omit the details.

Since we are assuming that the parameters of the model yield the no-agreement outcome in the final stage, any renegotiation-proof subgame perfect equilibrium that yields an agreement as an outcome must have both agents paying both tiers of *ex ante* costs.

Assume by way of contradiction that such an equilibrium exists and denote by a superscript '*' the equilibrium values of all variables in this equilibrium.

Notice first of all that if $\sigma_B^* \geq \sigma_A^*$ we have an immediate contradiction since in this case $\gamma_B^* > c_B$ and therefore $B$'s equilibrium payoff must be negative. Since $B$ can guarantee a payoff of zero by not paying any of the *ex ante* costs this is a contradiction.

By Lemma A.2, we can then assume without loss of generality that $\sigma_A^* > 0$ and $\sigma_B^* = 0$.

Next, consider the subgame that starts after the transfers $(\sigma_A^*, \sigma_B^*)$ have been agreed. We now claim that every renegotiation-proof subgame perfect equilibrium must be such that

$$1 - \lambda + \sigma_A^* - c_B^0 = 0. \tag{A.5}$$

To see this notice that Definition 2 and Lemma A.1 imply that every renegotiation-proof subgame perfect equilibrium must prescribe that in this subgame when

$$\lambda - \sigma_A - c_A^0 > 0 \tag{A.6}$$

$$1 - \lambda + \sigma_A - c_B^0 > 0 \tag{A.7}$$

are satisfied the parties play the Pareto superior equilibrium. This equilibrium involves both agents paying the costs $(c_A^0, c_B^0)$, negotiating an agreement and obtaining the strictly positive continuation payoffs: $1 - \lambda + \sigma_A - c_B^0$ and $\lambda - \sigma_A - c_A^0$. However, any offer $\sigma_A$ that satisfies (A.7) cannot be payoff maximising for $A$. Therefore the only renegotiation-proof subgame perfect equilibrium offer has to satisfy (A.5).

It follows directly from (A.5) that $B$'s payoff in this renegotiation-proof subgame perfect equilibrium would be $-c_B^2$. But this is a contradiction since $B$ can guarantee a payoff of zero by not paying any *ex ante* costs. This is enough to prove the proposition.

*Proof of Proposition* 6. The proof can be constructed in a way that is completely analogous to the one of Proposition 5 once we observe that when inequalities (A.6) and (A.7) are satisfied the unique subgame perfect equilibrium of the terminal subgame starting at $t = 0$ is for both parties to pay the costs $(c_A^0, c_B^0)$, negotiated an agreement and obtain payoffs: $1 - \lambda + \sigma_A - c_B^0$ and $\lambda - \sigma_A - c_A^0$.

Indeed, if $A$ has paid his cost $c_A^0$ it is optimal for $B$ to pay the cost $c_B^0$ as well, given that $B$ obtains a strictly positive continuation payoff by doing so, while he gets a continuation payoff of zero by not paying. On the other hand, if $A$ does not pay his *ex ante* cost $c_A^0$ then it is optimal for $B$ not to pay his cost $c_B^0$ either. If $B$ does not pay he gets a payoff of zero while if he does pay he gets a negative payoff. Therefore the unique subgame perfect equilibrium of this subgame is for both parties to pay their costs $(c_A^0, c_B^0)$ and negotiate an agreement.

We omit the details of the remaining part of the proof.

*Georgetown University*
*London School of Economics*

*Submitted: 4 February 2003*
*Accepted: 12 December 2004*

## References

Abreu, D., Pearce, D. and Stacchetti, E. (1993). 'Renegotiation and symmetry in repeated games', *Journal of Economic Theory*, vol. 60, pp. 217–40.

Anderlini, L., and Felli, L. (1998). 'Costly Coasian contracts'. Theoretical Economics Discussion Paper TE/98/362, STICERD, London School of Economics.

Anderlini, L., and Felli, L. (2001*a*). 'Costly bargaining and renegotiation'. *Econometrica*, vol. 68, pp. 377–411.

Anderlini, L., and Felli, L. (2001*b*). 'Transaction costs and the robustness of the Coase theorem', Theoretical Economics Discussion Paper TE/01/409, STICERD, London School of Economics.

Benoît, J.-P., and Krishna, V. (1993). 'Renegotiation in finitely repeated Games', *Econometrica*, vol. 61, pp. 303–23.

Binmore, K. (1986). 'Bargaining and coalitions', in (A. Roth, ed.) *Game Theoretic Approaches to Bargaining Theory*, Cambridge: Cambridge University Press.

Binmore, K., Rubinstein, A. and Wolinsky, A. (1986). 'The Nash bargaining solution in economic modeling', *Rand Journal of Economics*, vol. 17, pp. 176–88.

Che, Y.-K., and Hausch, D. (1999). 'Cooperative investments and the value of contracting', *American Economic Review*, vol. 89, pp. 125–47.

Chiu, Y. S. (1998). 'Noncooperative bargaining, hostages, and optimal asset ownership', *American Economic Review*, vol. 88, pp. 882–901.

Coase, R. H. (1960). 'The problem of social cost', *Journal of Law and Economics*, vol. 3, pp. 1–44.

Coase, R. H. (1992). 'The institutional structure of production', *American Economic Review*, vol. 82, pp. 713–9.

Cringely, R. X. (1992). *Accidental Empires*, Boston: Addison Wesley.

de Meza, D. (1988). 'Coase Theorem', in (P. Newmann, ed.) *The New Palgrave Dictionary of Economics and the Law*, pp. 270–82, Bastingstoke: Macmillan.

de Meza, D. and Lockwood, B. (1998). 'Does asset ownership always motivate managers? Outside options and the property rights theory of the firm', *Quarterly Journal of Economics*, vol. 113, pp. 361–86.

Dixit, A., and Olson, M. (2000). 'Does voluntary participation undermine the Coase theorem?', *Journal of Public Economics*, vol. 76, pp. 309–35.

Farrell, J. and Maskin, E. (1989). 'Renegotiation in repeated games', *Games and Economic Behavior*, vol. 1, pp. 327–60.

Fudenberg, D., and Tirole, J. (1996). *Game Theory*, Cambridge, MA: M.I.T. Press.

Grossman, S. J., and Hart, O. D. (1986). 'The costs and benefits of ownership: a theory of vertical and lateral integration', *Journal of Political Economy*, vol. 94, pp. 691–719.

Grout, P. (1984). 'Investment and wages in the absence of binding contracts: a Nash bargaining solution', *Econometrica*, vol. 52, pp. 449–60.

Hart, O. D. and Moore, J. (1988). 'Incomplete contracts and renegotiation', *Econometrica*, vol. 56, pp. 755–85.

Hart, O. D. and Moore, J. (1990). 'Property rights and the nature of the firm', *Journal of Political Economy*, vol. 98, pp. 1119–58.

Maskin, E., and Moore, J. (1999). 'Implementation and renegotiation', *Review of Economic Studies*, vol. 66, pp. 39–56.

Muthoo, A. (1999). *Bargaining Theory with Applications*, Cambridge: Cambridge University Press.

Nicholson, W. (1989). *Microeconomic Theory: Basic Principles and Extensions*, 4th International Edn. Chicago: Dryden Press.

Rajan, R. and Zingales, L. (1998). 'Power in a theory of the firm', *Quarterly Journal of Economics*, vol. 113, pp. 387–432.

Rubinstein, A. (1982). 'Perfect equilibrium in a bargaining model'. *Econometrica*, vol. 50, pp. 97–110.

Rubinstein, A., and Wolinsky, A. (1992). 'Renegotiation-proof implementation and time preferences', *American Economics Review*, vol. 82, pp. 600–14.

Segal, I. (1999). 'Complexity and renegotiation: a foundation for incomplete contracts', *Review of Economic Studies*, vol. 66, pp. 57–82.

Segal, I. and Whinston, M. D. (2002). 'The Mirrlees approach to mechanism design with renegotiation (with applications to hold-up and risk sharing)', *Econometrica*, vol. 70, pp. 1–45.

Sutton, J. (1986). 'Non-cooperative bargaining theory: an introduction', *Review of Economic Studies*, vol. 53, pp. 709–24.

# [24]

JOURNAL OF ECONOMIC THEORY 6, 606–613 (1973)

# Limitations of the "Coase Theorem" on Liability Rules

KEN-ICHI INADA AND KIYOSHI KUGA*

*Institute of Social and Economic Research,*
*Osaka University, Toyonaka, Osaka, Japan*

Received January 19, 1973; revised March 26, 1973

It is well known that the presence of externalities in the ordinary competitive price mechanism forms an obstacle to a Pareto-optimal allocation of resources. An answer worked out by Coase [1] to cope with this difficulty was the introduction of artificial "markets" for externalities. For example, when an externality is such that activities of a unit causes damage to other units in society, then the "market" takes the form of negotiations between the damaging part and the suffering part.

He asserts that the introduction of "markets" enables an economy under externalities to attain a Pareto-optimal allocation of resources, and that an identical Pareto-optimal allocation will result whether a damaging part is placed liable for the damage it causes or a suffering part is placed to pay for inducing the damager to abstension of his activity. The key assumptions used to derive these conclusions are that each "market" works competitively without cost, and that in each "market" an *ex ante* consensus about an externality allowance level[1] can be taken for granted. Also remarkable is his conclusion that the final outcome is independent of these allowance levels in the case of production externalities.

This optimistic view is, however, open to the following difficulties:

(i) The Coase system presupposes an *ex ante* consensus about an externality allowance level. But as a matter of fact, such a consensus cannot be a datum. It must be determined in one way or other, possibly through exchange of demonstration and counterproof (or recognition) of damage between the parties affected, and also through tiresome negotiations that follow. To find then a point of consensus about an ex-

* The authors have benefitted from valuable comments of an anonymous referee.

[1] This may be interpreted either as an initial point of negotiation, or as a vested right of the externality level or the *status quo*. Throughout this paper, $\bar{Q}_2$ is used to designate this entity.

ternality allowance level would be a harder task than to determine an equilibrium price of externality with a given allowance level.

More formally, determining an appropriate allowance level of externality is not much different from considering a redistribution of wealth in the private ownership economy, and naturally there will be much friction in this process.

(ii) The economic environment under externality is subject to a feature which is peculiar to such a circumstance. It is, however, the case that the Coase-type solutions [1–3] have so far been worked out without due attention to this fact. Thus, apart from the problem of the *ex ante* consensus about the allowance level, there still remains a problem to examine if the Coase procedure really functions so that it may lead the economy to a Pareto optimum under externality.

These two difficulties may have equal importance. But it would be difficult to reach conclusion in the first case where value judgement may outweigh, and for which we will not go farther than pointing out the problem. In this paper we will be concerned only with the second kind of difficulty, dealing with

(I) A market approach, an analogy of a competitive market to match the demand and supply of an external variable [3], and

(II) A bargaining approach, a process for adjusting marginal external profit and loss [2].

These approaches are useful, but there are cases in which the proposed procedures fail to attain the desired goal, when they are examined in a set of assumptions proper to externality.

Davis and Whinston [3] proposed a process in which the demand for and supply of external variable are matched by the parametric role of the "externality-price." This proposal is a natural extension of the usual nonexternal competitive market mechanism to the case where externalities exist. That a Pareto optimum may be attained by this extended process is intuitively clear, if it really works as expected. But as shown below it cannot be free from an indeterminacy problem.

Let us consider two firms 1 (suffering firm) and 2 (damaging firm) whose production functions are given by

$$Q_1 = f^1(x_1\,;\,Q_2); \qquad \frac{\partial f^1}{\partial x_1} > 0, \quad \frac{\partial f^1}{\partial Q_2} \leqslant 0$$

and

$$Q_2 = f^2(x_2),$$

where

$Q_i$ : output of firm $i$,

$x_i$ : input of factor $x$ by firm $i$.

Here we are assuming that the production of $Q_1$ is affected by $Q_2$, and that the damage firm 1 suffers at a given level of its own input has a one-to-one correspondence with the level of $Q_2$. In other words, $Q_2$ is used to designate the output of firm 2 as well as the extent of externality. $\tilde{Q}_2$ below also follows this rule of representation.

Coase's liability situations in terms of Davis and Whinston's interpretation [3] may be represented by the following

*Situation A* : Firms behave so as to

$$\max_{Q_1, x_1, Q_2^D} P_1Q_1 - wx_1 - \rho(\tilde{Q}_2 - Q_2^D) \tag{1}$$

subject to $Q_1 = f^1(x_1 ; Q_2^D)$, and

$$\max_{Q_2^S, x_2} P_2Q_2^S - wx_2 + \rho(\tilde{Q}_2 - Q_2^S) \tag{2}$$

subject to $Q_2^S = f^2(x_2)$, where

$P_i$ : price of $Q_i$,

$w$ : factor price of $x$,

$\tilde{Q}_2$ : allowance level of externality.

(If $Q_2 - \tilde{Q}_2 > 0$, the damaging firm is placed liable to the extent of $\rho(Q_2 - \tilde{Q}_2)$. On the other hand, if $Q_2 - \tilde{Q}_2 < 0$, then the suffering firm is placed to pay the sum of $\rho(\tilde{Q}_2 - Q_2)$)[2],

$\rho$ : externality price,

$Q_2^D$ : firm 1's request regarding the output level of $Q_2$,

$Q_2^S$ : firm 2's decision on its own output level.

The problems (1) and (2), in which $\rho$ is a parameter and $P_1$, $P_2$ and $w$ are given constants, enable us to write $Q_2^D$ and $Q_2^S$ as functions of $\rho$, i.e., $Q_2^D(\rho)$ and $Q_2^S(\rho)$. The Davis and Whinston [3]'s procedure is a bargaining process to determine a suitable $\rho^*$ that equates $Q_2^D(\rho^*)$ and $Q_2^S(\rho^*)$ for given $P_1$, $P_2$, and $w$. A solution to Situation $A$, if such

[2] See also footnote 1.

exists, is possibly a Coase–Pareto solution, because the problems (1) and (2) lead to the following conditions:

$$\begin{aligned} P_1 \cdot \frac{\partial f^1}{\partial x_1}(x_1^*; Q_2^{D*}) &= w, \\ -P_1 \cdot \frac{\partial f^1}{\partial Q_2{}^D}(x_1^*; Q_2^{D*}) &= \rho^*, \\ (P_2 - \rho^*) \cdot \frac{\partial f^2}{\partial x_2}(x_2^*) &= w, \\ Q_2^{D*} &= Q_2^{S*}, \end{aligned} \tag{3}$$

and because these marginal conditions are also the necessary conditions for the merger profit maximization to be attained. It is also to be noted that the solution to (3) is independent of $\tilde{Q}_2$.

There is a case, however, in which Situation $A$ fails to have a solution. In order to show this, we assume

$$f^1(0; Q_2) = 0 \qquad \text{for any} \quad Q_2 \geqslant 0. \tag{$*$}$$

The meaning of $(*)$ is that no output of $Q_1$ is producible from zero factor input, and that this zero–zero correspondence is independent of the level of $Q_2$.

The following argument proceeds under this assumption. Suppose $\rho > 0$ in Situation $A$. Then the firm 1 is able to plan to make its profit as large as it wishes by requesting $Q_2{}^D$ to be infinitely large while neglecting its own activity. That is, the suffering firm under $(*)$ choose to live a parasite life rather than to earn its own living. It means that there exists no point of intersection for the two curves $Q_2{}^D(\rho)$ and $Q_2{}^S(\rho)$, as long as $\rho > 0$.[3] The last possibility is $\rho = 0$. But this is nothing but the situation without externality payment. Therefore, no solution exists to the Davis and Whinston process [3] as long as $(*)$ prevails.

[3] (1) and (2) are the counterparts of (32) and (33) of Davis and Whinston [3, pp. 314–315]. Our approach differs from theirs in that the former is based on production functions whereas the latter is based on cost functions. The aforementioned difficulty, however, is also shown even if we take the cost function approach. Let $f^1 = \sqrt{x_1}/[1 + (Q_2)^2]$. Then the cost function to produce $Q_1$ becomes $w[1 + (Q_2)^2]^2 \cdot (Q_1)^2$ and the profit maximization problem formulated along their line (i.e., (32)) take the following form

$$\max_{Q_1, Q_2{}^D} P_1 Q_1 - w[1 + (Q_2{}^D)^2]^2 \cdot (Q_1)^2 - \lambda_1 Q_1 + \lambda_2 Q_2{}^D,$$

where $\lambda_i$'s are the externality prices in their notation. Then it is not difficult to see that the above maximand is unbounded as long as $\lambda_2 > 0$, and that the condition $(*)$ gives rise to this difficulty.

An argument may be made, however, that there may exist an upper limit, say $\bar{Q}_2$, to $Q_2^D$ and $Q_2^S$, provided possibly by a law or a regulation. Unfortunately this expediency is not so effective as one may suppose. An illustration will help.

Let $f^1 = \sqrt{x_1}/[1 + (Q_2)^2]$ and $f^2 = \sqrt{x_2}$, and consider

$$\max_{Q_1, x_1, Q_2^D} P_1 Q_1 - w x_1 - \rho(\tilde{Q}_2 - Q_2^D) \tag{1'}$$

subject to $Q_1 = f^1(x_1 ; Q_2^D)$

$$\bar{Q}_2 \geqslant Q_2^D$$

and

$$\max_{Q_2^S, x_2} P_2 Q_2^S - w x_2 + \rho(\tilde{Q}_2 - Q_2^S) \tag{2'}$$

subject to $Q_2^S = f^2(x_2)$

$$\bar{Q}_2 \geqslant Q_2^S.$$

Then the solutions to (1′) and (2′) which we designate respectively by $\hat{Q}_2^D(\rho)$ and $\hat{Q}_2^S(\rho)$ take the forms

$$\left.\begin{array}{l} \hat{Q}_2^D(\rho) = \text{the smaller of} \left\{ Q_2^D \,\middle|\, \rho = \dfrac{(P_1)^2}{w} \dfrac{Q_2^D}{[1 + (Q_2^D)^2]^3} \right\}^4 \\ \qquad \text{for} \quad 0 \leqslant \rho \leqslant \dfrac{25\sqrt{5}}{216} \dfrac{(P_1)^2}{w} = \alpha \\ \hat{Q}_2^D(\rho) = \bar{Q}_2 \qquad \text{for} \quad \rho \geqslant \alpha \end{array}\right\} \text{for } \sqrt{5}/5 < \bar{Q}_2,$$

$$\left.\begin{array}{l} \hat{Q}_2^D(\rho) = \text{the smaller of} \left\{ Q_2^D \,\middle|\, \rho = \dfrac{(P_1)^2}{w} \dfrac{Q_2^D}{[1 + (Q_2^D)^2]^3} \right\} \\ \qquad \text{for} \quad 0 \leqslant \rho \leqslant \dfrac{(P_1)^2}{w} \dfrac{\bar{Q}_2}{[1 + (\bar{Q}_2)^2]^3} \\ \hat{Q}_2^D(\rho) = \bar{Q}_2 \qquad \text{for} \quad \rho \geqslant \dfrac{(P_1)^2}{w} \dfrac{\bar{Q}_2}{[1 + (\bar{Q}_2)^2]^3} \end{array}\right\} \text{for } \sqrt{5}/5 \geqslant \bar{Q}_2,$$

and

$$\hat{Q}_2^S(\rho) = \min[\bar{Q}_2, (P_2 - \rho)/2w].$$

[4] That this set consists of two points for $0 \leqslant \rho < \alpha$ and is empty for $\rho > \alpha$ can be seen from the following diagram.

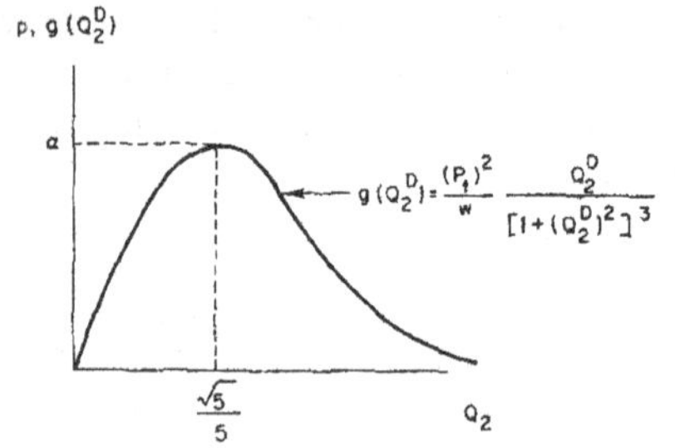

Putting these together, we obtain four different patterns according to the variation of the values of $P_i$'s, $w$, and $\bar{Q}_2$, as can be depicted by the following diagrams.

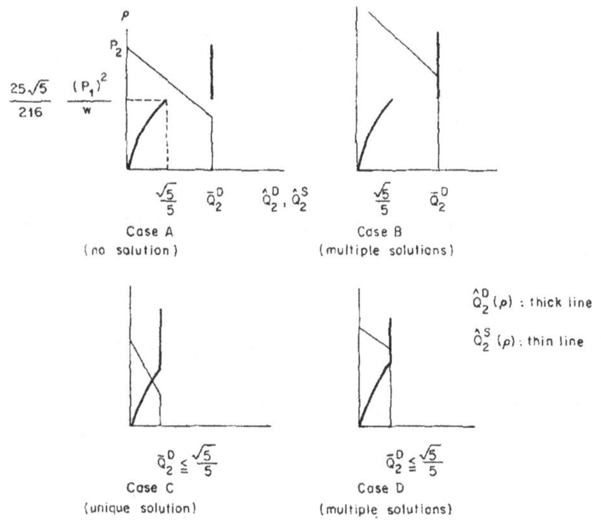

We can see from these diagrams that there still remains the possibility of the nonexistence of equilibrium point.

Another approach to externality is an adjustment process of marginal external profit and loss. Davis and Whinston [2] formulated this process in the case when externalities are characterized by dependence of one consumer's utility on the activities of other individuals. Hereafter we will formulate an analogous process for the case of production externality and show where a difficulty emerges.

The framework of the second approach is as follows: The damaging firm (firm 2) determines its own production plan under a provisional value of $\rho$, and informs the suffering firm (firm 1) of its provisional plan of $Q_2^S(\rho)$ and the associated payment $\rho(\tilde{Q}_2 - Q_2^S(\rho))$. $Q_2^S(\rho)$ is the solution to (2). The firm 1 takes these $\rho$ and $Q_2^S(\rho)$ as given and plans to

$$\max_{Q_1, x_1} P_1 Q_1 - w x_1 - \rho(\tilde{Q}_2 - Q_2^S(\rho)) \tag{4}$$

subject to $Q_1 = f^1(x_1 ; Q_2^S(\rho))$.
Then both firms enter negotiations, where the marginal external loss $-P_1 \cdot (\partial f^1/\partial Q_2^S)$ and the marginal payment rate $\rho$ are the concern of the parties. When the former exceeds the latter, the suffering firm puts claim that the payment rate is low compared to its marginal external loss, and the damaging firm responds with a rise in $\rho$. In the opposite case, the damaging firm claims that it is overpaying, and a reduction in $\rho$ results. These procedures repeat until the marginal external loss and the marginal payment rate coincide finally.

More formally the process is represented by

$$\frac{d\rho}{dt} = -\beta \left[\rho + P_1 \frac{\partial f^1}{\partial Q_2^S}(x_1(Q_2^S(\rho)); Q_2^S(\rho))\right], \tag{5}$$

where $\beta > 0$ is an adjustment coefficient and $x_1(Q_2^S(\rho))$ is a solution to (4). The process is globally stable and reaches a unique Coase–Pareto solution, if $f^1$ and $f^2$ are concave with respect to all arguments.

So far so good. But this argument does not take into account the important fact that the presence of externality does not preserve the concavity of a production function.

The reason why this is so is plain. We are assuming $\partial f^1/\partial Q_2 \leqslant 0$, so if we further assume $\partial^2 f^1/\partial Q_2^2 < 0$, then the nonnegativity of $f^1$ (i.e., the condition (*)) has to be sacrificed. Put otherwise, the properties $\partial f^1/\partial Q_2 \leqslant 0$ and $f^1 \geqslant 0$ on the whole domain contradicts to the concavity of $f^1$ with respect to $Q_2$. This striking feature peculiar to the externality has been neglected so far.

It, therefore, follows that a production function under externality with $\partial f^1/\partial Q_2 \leqslant 0$ and $f^1 \geqslant 0$ should have other property than the concavity with respect to $Q_2$. A natural case would then be that the marginal externality effect increases in its early stage but decreases gradually as $Q_2$ increases, i.e., $\partial^2 f^1/\partial Q_2^2 > 0$ for small $Q_2$ but turns negative as $Q_2$ increases. The consequence of this observation is that a possibility is to arise for (5) to have multiple stationary solutions, and that production programs corresponding to some of them are not Pareto-optimal.

We use the same example as above. Let

$$f^1 = \sqrt{x_1}/[1 + (Q_2)^2] \quad \text{and} \quad f^2 = \sqrt{x_2}\,.$$

Then the stationary solutions to (5) with these $f^i$'s must satisfy

$$\rho = -P_1 \frac{\partial f^1}{\partial Q_2{}^S} [x_1(Q_2{}^S(\rho)); Q_2{}^S(\rho)] \qquad \text{by (5),}$$

$$Q_2{}^S(\rho) = (P_2 - \rho)/2w \qquad \text{by (2),}$$

$$2w\sqrt{x_1} = P_1/[1 + (Q_2{}^S(\rho))^2] \qquad \text{by (4).}$$

Arranging these conditions, we obtain

$$0 = P_2 - 2wQ_2{}^S(\rho) - \frac{(P_1)^2}{w} \cdot \frac{Q_2{}^S(\rho)}{[1 + (Q_2{}^S(\rho))^2]^3}. \tag{6}$$

Then for the values of $P_2 = 0.33$, $w = 0.09$, and $(P_1)^2/w = 1$, the equation (6) has at least three solutions as the following table suggests.

| $\rho$ | 0.024 | 0.150 | 0.222 | 0.330 |
|---|---|---|---|---|
| $Q_2{}^S(\rho)$ | 1.7 | 1.0 | 0.6 | 0.0 |
| right side of (6) | − | + | − | + |

Thus, the alternating theorem on stable and unstable points applies. The final outcome of process (5) depends on the initial value of $\rho$. Among the stationary solutions, the smallest $\rho$ corresponds to a true Pareto-optimum, the middle of them does to a saddle point of the joint profit curve, and the largest $\rho$ does to a locally joint-profit maximizing point.[5] The latter two solutions are not Pareto-optimal.

## REFERENCES

1. R. H. COASE, The problem of social cost, *The Journal of Law and Economics*, III (1960), 1–44.
2. O. A. DAVIS AND A. B. WHINSTON, Some notes on equating private and social cost, *Southern Economic Journal*, XXXII (1965), 113–126.
3. D. A. DAVIS AND A. B. WHINSTON, On externalities, information and the government-assisted invisible hand, *Economica* XXXIII (1966), 303–318.

[5] The approximate values of these stationary solutions are $\rho$ = 0.0.3165, 019275, and 0.25665 to which correspond such values of sum of profits as 0.31752, 0.09927, and 0.30340, respectively.

# [25]

# THE COASE THEOREM AND THE EMPTY CORE*

*VAROUJ A. AIVAZIAN and JEFFREY L. CALLEN*
*McMaster University*

THE Coase theorem, which states that in the absence of transaction costs resource allocation is neutral with respect to liability rules, is usually demonstrated in a two-participant scenario of either two firms or two consumers.[1] This is so in Coase's original verbal discussion, as well as in the more recent literature that treats the Coase argument within the confines of the neoclassical paradigm.[2] As we will show, this is an unfortunate state of affairs, because with more than two participants the Coase theorem cannot always be demonstrated.

The reader's initial response to our claim is undoubtedly skeptical; he may believe that we have underestimated the power and robustness of the zero transaction cost assumption. We wish to emphasize, however, that our result is not predicated on the existence of transaction costs, be they information costs, bargaining costs, or (damage) valuation costs. Our assumptions include those made explicitly or implicitly by Coase.[3] Furthermore, our contentions are not based on novel notions but rather on some well-known results from the theory of the core, a theory which plays an important role in mathematical economics and game theory.[4] The fact that our type of critique of the Coase theorem has not appeared in the literature until now is primarily a function of the slow diffusion of mathematical economics to the remainder of the profession rather than a function of our incisive analysis.

We will show, utilizing a three-participant example, that the Coase

* We wish to acknowledge the very helpful comments of Professor Andrew Schotter on an earlier version of this paper. The usual disclaimers apply.

[1] R. H. Coase, The Problem of Social Cost, 3 J. Law & Econ. 1 (1960).

[2] See, for example, James R. Marchand & Keith P. Russell, Externalities, Liability, Separability, and Resource Allocation, 63 Am. Econ. Rev. 611 (1973); Ken-Ichi Inada & Kiyoshi Kuga, Limitations of the "Coase Theorem" on Liability Rules, 6 J. Econ. Theory 606 (1973); and Peter H. Greenwood & Charles A. Ingene, Uncertain Externalities, Liability Rules, and Resource Allocation, 68 Am. Econ. Rev. 300 (1978).

[3] Coase assumed away wealth effects and bargaining threats.

[4] One of the most comprehensive analyses of the theory of the core and its applications to economics is provided by Lester Telser, Competition, Collusion, and Game Theory (1972).

theorem cannot be proved if the core of the game is empty under one of the liability rules. This is in contradistinction to the two-participant case, for which the core is always nonempty so that the Coase theorem can always be demonstrated. Besides questioning the general validity of the Coase theorem, we will illustrate that it cannot be studied meaningfully (or rigorously) by employing the familiar neoclassical paradigm. The Coase theorem is a statement about nonmarket allocations and the predilection of the extant literature to impose competitive market structure parameters or specific adjustment paths on the bargaining process is limiting at best and, probably, self-defeating.[5] The only tool we are aware of that is capable of providing the appropriate insights into nonmarket allocations is game theory.

In what follows, Section I describes an example for which the Coase theorem cannot be demonstrated. Although the example is somewhat stylized and simplified, it captures the crux of the argument. Section II provides the intuition for the breakdown of the Coase theorem in the context of the example. Section III demonstrates the argument in a more rigorous fashion, while Section IV discusses the implications of our results.

## I. Description of the Example[6]

Consider two factories labeled $A$ and $B$ polluting a neighborhood laundry, firm $C$. The laundry does not emit pollutants. Let the function $V$ denote profits per day. In the absence of negotiations, profits per day for the three firms are thus assumed: $V(A)$ = \$3,000; $V(B)$ = \$8,000; and $V(C)$ = \$24,000.

Since there are no transaction costs, firms will negotiate or, equivalently, merge to mitigate the impact of the pollution. In the spirit of game theory such mergers will be called coalitions and $V$ the characteristic function. Define $V(A,B,C)$ to be the joint profits of the (grand) coalition of all three firms. Similarly, $V(A,B)$ will denote the joint profits of the coalition of firms $A$ and $B$ and so on. We will assume the following joint profits for all potential coalitions: $V(A,B)$ = \$15,000; $V(A,C)$ = \$31,000; $V(B,C)$ = \$36,000; and $V(A,B,C)$ = \$40,000.

These values should be interpreted to mean that if, for example, $A$ and $C$ negotiate or merge, sufficient pollution can be eliminated so that both firms earn \$31,000. This is in contradistinction to the \$27,000 they would have earned in the absence of negotiations. To simplify matters we will

[5] See the references cited in note 2 *supra*.

[6] The numerics (but not the context) of this example are from Jan Mossin, Merger Agreements: Some Game-Theoretic Considerations, 41 J. Bus. 460 (1968).

assume that the merger or negotiation between $A$ and $C$, if consummated, will close the polluter $A$ down.[7] Thus, all the potential benefits from mergers between the laundry and either factory comes from the closing down of the polluter. If $A$ and $C$ do merge without $B$, then $B$ is assumed to keep polluting and earning \$8,000 per day.

Should all three firms negotiate or merge, the resulting grand coalition will earn joint profits of \$40,000 per day rather than the \$35,000 they earned by acting independently of each other. Again we assume that, should the grand coalition form, both $A$ and $B$ stop producing.

Although $A$'s and $B$'s pollution activities do not affect each other's outputs, they are also assumed to have the incentive to merge since $V(A,B) > V(A) + V(B)$. In the context of our example, one can assume that this incentive is due to economies of scale in production.[8] To keep the example tractable, it is assumed that the $A,B$ coalition does not affect the level of pollutants so that the laundry continues to earn $V(C)$.[9]

We have assumed in our example that profits accruing to each of the potential coalitions is greater than what these firms would have earned by acting independently. In the merger literature this phenomenon is known as synergy. In the game-theory literature the characteristic function $V$ is said to be superadditive. Superadditivity implies that $V(A) + V(B) + V(C) \leq V(A,B) + V(C) \leq V(A,B,C)$. Similar relationships would of course hold for the other potential coalitions. Far from being a restrictive assumption, superadditivity is obviously a necessary condition for the bargaining process to be initiated and for the Coase theorem to be valid.

## II. Breakdown of the Coase Theorem

We now show that the Coase theorem breaks down for this example. Let us first analyse the simple case in which $A$ and $B$ are liable for the pollution damages to $C$. It is immediately obvious that the grand coalition solution must obtain and neither $A$ nor $B$ are allowed to produce. Thus, if $X_A$, $X_B$, and $X_C$ denote the profit allocations to firms $A$, $B$, and $C$, respectively, the solution in the case where $A$ and $B$ are liable is $X_A = X_B = 0$

[7] Otherwise, we would have to specify each firm's production function or, equivalently, a tableau of outputs for each level of pollution. This assumption does not affect the qualitative nature of our results.

[8] On first blush, one is tempted to argue that, if $A$ and $B$ have the incentive to merge because of economies of scale, they will merge and we are back in a two-firm world. However, this is only one potential merger and there are others. It is because there is more than one merger possibility that the Coase theorem fails to hold in our example.

[9] Again, we could complicate the example by providing a tableau of $C$'s earnings for each level of pollution from the merged firm. This would provide more realism with no more insight.

and $X_C$ = \$40,000. This is the correct solution because the maximum bribe that $A$ and $B$ can offer is \$15,000, but their combined liabilities total \$16,000. Therefore, $C$ obtains the maximum benefits of \$40,000 while $A$ and $B$ shut down.[10]

The alternative case in which $A$ and $B$ are not liable for the pollution damages to the laundry is far more complex. Since $A$ and $B$ are not liable, $C$ has the incentive to bribe either $A$ or $B$, or perhaps both, to reduce their pollution activities. Suppose $C$ bribes $B$ but not $A$, so that the distribution of profits is \$3,000 to $A$ and \$36,000 to $B$ and $C$. Since firm $C$ could earn \$24,000 in spite of the pollution, the maximum bribe $C$ will offer $B$ is \$12,000 and, of course, the minimum bribe $B$ is willing to accept is $V(B)$ or \$8,000.

Let us suppose initially that $C$ captures all the potential gains and $B$ is willing to accept the minimum bribe. This distribution of profits ($X_A$ = \$3,000; $X_B$ = \$8,000; and $X_C$ = \$28,000) is inherently unstable. In a transaction-costless world, firm $A$ has the incentive to offer $B$ an additional \$500 to join in a coalition involving only $A$ and $B$ in which $X_A$ = \$6,500 and $X_B$ = \$8,500. Since $A$ and $B$ are better off in this latter case than before, they can block the original distribution of profits involving the coalition of $B$ and $C$ by forming their own coalition. Of course the story does not end here since $C$ could come back and offer $B$ \$9,000 to join the original $B,C$ coalition. Therefore, $B$ can play $A$ against $C$ until, ultimately, it would appear, $B$ captures all the potential benefits by forming a coalition with either $A$ or $C$.

Suppose, in fact, that $B$ forms a coalition with $C$, as initially hypothesized, but now $B$ is offered the maximum bribe so that $C$ earns only \$24,000. This distribution is again unstable since $A$ will now bribe $C$ (say by an additional \$500), blocking the latest coalition. Thus, $C$ can play $A$ against $B$ and, again, try to appropriate the maximum benefit.

Even if a two-firm coalition could be found to be stable, these coalitions are unstable relative to the grand coalition. In our example, every two-member coalition yields total profits of \$39,000 which is less than the benefits from the grand coalition of \$40,000. Thus, given a specific distribution of profits in a two-firm coalition, one can always find an alternative

[10] The discussion throughout the paper implicitly assumes that the characteristic function itself does not depend on the particular liability rule. This assumption can readily be relaxed by assuming that, where $A$ and $B$ are liable for the damages, the characteristic function takes on these values: $V(A) = 0$; $V(B) = 0$; $V(C) = 24{,}000$; $V(A,B) = 0$; $V(A,C) = 31{,}000$; $V(B,C) = 36{,}000$; $V(A,B,C) = 40{,}000$. This means that, if $A$ and $B$ are liable for the damages and if the lost profits to $C$ due to pollution are greater than the realized profits accruing to $A$ and $B$ due to production, then the best $A$ and/or $B$ can do is not to produce. If they do produce, they would be liable to pay $C$ more than they earned by producing. In this example again, the core exists and the unique imputation is $X_A = X_B = 0$ and $X_C$ = \$40,000.

distribution in the grand coalition which makes each firm better off. Therefore, one might be tempted to argue that the grand coalition must result. But in our example even the grand coalition is unstable. To see why this is so consider the grand coalition distribution of profits: $X_A =$ \$4,750; $X_B =$ \$9,750; and $X_C =$ \$25,500. Although each firm earns more than it would in the absence of negotiations, there are many two-member coalitions which could, and presumably would, block this particular distribution. For example, the coalition of $B$ and $C$ where $X_B =$ \$10,000 and $X_C =$ \$26,000 is preferred by $B$ and $C$ to the grand coalition solution given above.

Our discussion thus far has tried to highlight a number of the coalition possibilities and why these coalitions are infeasible. Specifically, a coalition is infeasible if any firm earns less than it would by independent action. In addition, no coalition can succeed if the resulting distribution of profits can be blocked by an alternative coalition. As we prove rigorously below, these two latter conditions cause all the potential coalitions in our example to be unstable. Ironically, in a world of zero transaction costs, the inherent instability of all coalitions could result in endless recontracting among the firms.

## III. The Empty Core

In a three-participant scenario, coalitional stability requires that the resulting allocation of profits satisfy the following conditions:

$$X_A \geqslant V(A),\ X_B \geqslant V(B),\ X_C \geqslant V(C) \tag{1}$$

$$X_A + X_B \geqslant V(A,B),\ X_A + X_C \geqslant V(A,C),\ X_B + X_C \geqslant V(B,C) \tag{2}$$

$$X_A + X_B + X_C = V(A,B,C). \tag{3}$$

The set of allocations which satisfies these conditions is called the core.

In our example, the core is empty. To see this, note that if all the two-coalition inequalities in (2) are added together then

$$(X_A + X_B + X_C) \geqslant \frac{1}{2}[V(A,B) + V(A,C) + V(B,C)] \tag{4}$$

so that substituting (3) into (4) yields

$$V(A,B,C) \geqslant \frac{1}{2}[V(A,B) + V(A,C) + V(B,C)]. \tag{5}$$

This last condition is violated by our example since the right-hand side of the inequality turns out to be equal to \$41,000 and the left-hand side to \$40,000.

This situation could never occur in the two-participant case, where the core is always nonempty. With two participants, say $A$ and $B$, the core is defined by the constraints

$$X_A \geqslant V(A), X_B \geqslant V(B) \tag{6}$$

$$X_A + X_B = V(A,B). \tag{7}$$

But these constraints must be satisfied by at least one allocation since $V(A,B) \geqslant V(A) + V(B)$.

## IV. Discussion and Conclusion

We have provided an example in which liability rules have an asymmetrical impact on resource allocation. It was seen that when firms $A$ and $B$ are liable for damages they will stop producing and firm $C$ earns \$40,000 per day. On the other hand, when firms $A$ and $B$ are not liable, negotiations cannot be consummated because the core is empty. In a world of zero transaction costs, negotiations could be endless. Even if some merger is negotiated, it will be the grand coalition only by happenstance.

It could be argued that, if the core is empty and no solution is forthcoming, the participants may agree to accept a set of allocation rules that will yield the desired outcome. The Shapley and Von Neumann-Morgenstern allocations are just two of many game-theory solutions which do not depend on the existence of the core.[11] Moreover, since these solutions are Pareto optimal (by assumption), the grand coalition obtains and the allocative outcome is independent of the liability rule. Thus, it may be argued the Coase theorem is valid once more.

The problem with this approach is that it makes a tautology out of the Coase theorem. If the core does not exist, the participants may accept an alternative solution concept; then again they may simply stop negotiating. It is an empirical question as to what happens when the core is empty. We do not know. Of course, one can impose a Pareto-optimal solution on the participants such as the Shapley allocation. To do so, however, would be tantamount to assuming what Coase was trying to prove, namely, that a Pareto-optimal solution will be forthcoming independent of the liability rule *and* independent of the bargaining structure. We have demonstrated that for one bargaining structure at least, the Coase theorem cannot be proved.

The Coase theorem fundamentally derives its importance from a world with positive transaction costs. It makes it clear that the existence and rationalization of specific contractual arrangements rests on an examination of the transaction costs associated with potential (market or nonmar-

[11] For a brief description of the Shapley and Von Neumann-Morgenstern solutions see Michael D. Intriligator, Mathematical Optimization and Economic Theory (1971).

ket) exchanges which would arise in the absence of such contracts. The nonexistence of the core furnishes yet a further rationale for the existence of particular contractual arrangements in that these contracts may be useful in eliminating potential bargaining situations that defy solution. Contractual arrangements will evolve to force a solution on the bargaining process.

Empirically, however, it is difficult to differentiate between contractual arrangements that arise because of the nonexistence of the core from those that arise from transaction costs when there is a core. The nonexistence of the core will also manifest itself in transaction costs either because of the opportunity cost of (negotiation) time or because of the erosion of the potential exchange opportunity as it is postponed. One should not make the mistake of assuming, however, that once "time is money" this will force a Pareto-optimal solution. No one knows what actually happens when the core is empty. Do the participants agree to a Pareto-optimal solution or will they merely stop negotiating? This is an empirical question.

Finally, we would like to emphasize that the simplicity of our example belies its potential generality. Examples of negotiations where the core does not exist are easy to concoct and may be quite common in practice. External diseconomies, increasing returns to scale, and nonconvex preference functions are all factors which may lead to an empty core.[12]

[12] See Lloyd S. Shapley & Martin Shubik, On the Core of an Economic System with Externalities, 59 Am. Econ. Rev. 678 (1969); and Telser, *supra* note 4, at 81.

# [26]

# *COASE v. PIGOU* REEXAMINED

*A. W. BRIAN SIMPSON**

ABSTRACT

Coase's thesis in "The Problem of Social Cost" is reexamined, with particular reference to criticisms of Pigou as an enthusiast for state intervention and to Coase's understanding of the history of English tort law; the litigation in *Sturges v. Bridgman* illustrates the analysis. Pigou is defended, and his function as a straw man in a rhetorical form of argument described. An analysis of Coase's thesis—that Pigou perpetrated a fundamental error in analysis—when related to the realities of land use disputes between neighbors suggests that the logic of the Coasean theory as to the correct analysis in terms of efficiency is incapable of generating any general rule as to what should be the legal response to the problem of social cost. Unless certain problems can be solved, it cannot provide guidance for the law.

RONALD H. Coase's celebrated article, "The Problem of Social Cost,"[1] has generated a massive literature, much the product of fascination with the Coase theorem. Anyone setting out to add to this literature must do so with some diffidence. There seem, however, to be some difficulties which are internal to the original article and which have not been addressed by other writers. They center on Coase's criticisms of the late Arthur C. Pigou. I should make it clear that I approach the article from the point of view of a historian and lawyer, not that of an economist.

At the outset, Coase explained that "[t]his paper is concerned with those actions of business firms which have harmful effects on others. The standard example is that of a factory, the smoke from which has harmful effects on those occupying neighboring properties."[2] In the common law this problem was primarily handled by indictments for public nuisance,

* Charles F. and Edith J. Clyne Professor of Law at the University of Michigan. I am indebted to Valerie Brondyke, Bronwyn Croxson, Merritt Fox, John Griffith, Richard Helmholz, Jim Krier, Neil Duxbury, Richard Posner, and Barbe Vaccaro for assistance and comments.

[1] First published R. H. Coase, The Problem of Social Cost 3 J. Law & Econ. 1–44 (1960) and reprinted in R. H. Coase, The Firm, the Market and the Law 95 (Chicago, 1988). This includes additional relevant material: ch. 1 on The Firm, the Market and the Law, at 1–31, and ch. 6 on Notes on the Problem of Social Cost, at 157–85. All references are to this reprint unless otherwise indicated.

[2] *Id.* at 95.

[*Journal of Legal Studies*, vol. XXV (January 1996)]

which Coase does not discuss, by tort actions for private nuisance for damages, and by suits for injunctions.[3] Where there was some tangible harmful escape, other forms of tort action, such as the action for cattle trespass, might be used. Coase illustrated the problem through a number of nuisance cases, several having been determined in the nineteenth century.[4] One, *Sturges v. Bridgman* (1879),[5] figures prominently both in "The Problem of Social Cost" and in his earlier article, "The Federal Communications Commission."[6] I shall follow him by providing an account of it and later use it to illustrate certain difficulties in his analysis.

## I. *Sturges v. Bridgman*

*Sturges v. Bridgman* involved a successful suit by a doctor to restrain a confectioner, operating his business in adjacent premises, from using machinery causing noise and vibration. It is possible to say a little more about this case than is in the law reports.[7] The plaintiff, Dr. Octavius Sturges, was a medical man of distinction.[8] Born in London in 1833, he was educated at Addiscombe, the military seminary of the East India Company. He entered the service of the Company as a second lieutenant with the Bombay Artillery in 1853. In 1883, with the assistance of his niece, Mary Sturges, he published an autobiographical novel on his expe-

[3] These are not found before the nineteenth century; see John P. S. McLaren, Nuisance Law and the Industrial Revolution—Some Lessons from Social History, 3 Oxford J. Legal Stud. 155, 186 ff. (1983). Until 1854 an attempt to obtain an injunction involved litigation both at common law and in Chancery, and until the fusion on the courts in 1876 this practice might still be followed, as in Tipping v. St. Helen's Smelting Company (1865), on which see note 14 below.

[4] See in particular section 5 of his article, *supra* note 1, at 104–14.

[5] Sturges v. Bridgman, 1877 § 233, 11 Ch. D. 852.

[6] R. H. Coase, The Federal Communications Commission, 2 J. Law & Econ. 1–40, 27 (1959).

[7] Before the Master of the Rolls, Sir George Jessel, on May 31, 1878, in the Court of Appeal (Lord Justices Thesiger, James, and Baggallay) on June 13, 14, and 16 and on July 1. My account is based on the report in 11 Ch. D. 852; on the law report entitled Law Report, High Court of Justice, June 3 Chancery Division (before the Master of the Rolls), Sturges and Bridgman, in the Times, June 4, 1878; and on papers in the Public Record Office: J54/80 S.223 (pleadings); C32/322 (cause book); J15/1385, 1386, and 1387 (orders made in the course of the litigation); and J4/660 (S650–S654) and J4/663 (1440–42) (affidavits filed). The case is not noted in the Bakers Record and General Advertiser or in the Lancet or British Medical Journal, but is noted under the headline Quiet Consulting Room, in the Medical Times and Gazette for July 20, 1878.

[8] What follows is based on 3 Frederic Boase, Modern English Biography (1965); obituaries in the Times (November 6, 7, and 9, 1894) and in the Lancet and the British Medical Journal; the British Library Catalogue; and copies of the annual London and Provincial Medical Directory.

riences, *In the Company's Service: A Reminiscence.*[9] The hero is Norman Farquhar, one of four fellow Addiscombe cadets; one or all of them embody his own experiences. Farquhar is killed in the Mutiny of 1857, which presumably Sturges experienced. The book reflects some disgust at the ferocity with which it was put down. Sturges resigned his commission and entered St. George's Hospital as a medical student. He studied in Cambridge at Emmanuel College, and then returned to London, becoming medical registrar at St. George's Hospital in 1863. In 1868 he became associated with the Westminster Hospital, becoming physician in 1875; from 1878 he was also assistant physician to the Great Ormond Street Hospital for Children. He held both these appointments for the rest of his life. He lectured in the Westminster Medical School, and published extensively; his specialisms were pneumonia and chorea. Directories show that until 1865 he lived at 35 Connaught Square, when he purchased the lease of 85 Wimpole Street.

His opponent was also a person of distinction. Frederick Horatio[10] Bridgman was, by appointment, confectioner to Her Majesty the Queen and to His Royal Highness the Prince of Wales. In an affidavit he recounted how, in 1830, he had succeeded his late father John in the business of a cook and confectioner at 30 Wigmore Street; indeed, "my said Father and I have or one of us, during the last sixty years and upwards, uninterruptedly and in succession to each other carried on the Business."[11] So the business had been in the same premises, unaltered for 50 or probably 60 years, since about the time of Waterloo. Frederick would have started working with his father in 1828 or so, being born in about 1814.

Mid-nineteenth-century Wigmore Street was predominantly commercial. The principal trade was clothing—there were dressmakers, milliners, lace cleaners, and the like. Other businesses included a bell hanger, wax chandlers, and buttermen and, for the medical men of Wimpole Street, a dealer in medical rubber. There were no doctors in Wigmore Street. In elegant Wimpole Street, which intersects it at right angles, doctors were much in evidence. The street was primarily residential, with professionals conducting business from their homes, as did Dr. Sturges. The medical profession had been colonizing Wimpole Street for some time. Whereas in 1871 there had been only 19 physicians, of the 95 properties listed in *Kelly's Post Office Directory*[12] for 1878, 38 were occupied

[9] Octavius Sturges with Mary Sturges, In the Company's Service: A Reminiscence (1883).

[10] No doubt after Admiral Nelson.

[11] Affidavit by F. H. Bridgman. See note 7 *supra*.

[12] Kelly's Post Office Directory (79th ed. 1878).

by physicians or surgeons, and there were some dentists too. There was also Mrs. Wilson's Institute for Nurses: "For upwards of ten years the most eminent of the medical profession, and the public, have been supplied at a moments notice with my nurses, who reside at 90 Wimpole Street."[13] By 1888 another essential ancillary trade, that of undertaker, had moved in at number 3b; at the time of the litigation, medical failures had to seek this service elsewhere. In 1878 and even later, other trades remained—a diamond merchant, a confectioner, and a stocking maker, for example, and many private residences, such as that of William Patchett, Q.C. There had recently even been a future Lord Justice of Appeal in residence, Sir William Milbourne James.

So the litigation did not raise a zoning problem—do we want predominantly residential or business use in the area? Dr. Sturges was in an appropriate location, and so was Mr. Bridgman. The problem arose because effects crossed the boundary between a commercial and a residential area. Courts typically have to face the problem of social cost, if they face it all, only when either a stationary or a moving boundary is involved. The most notable of all Victorian nuisance cases, *Tipping v. St. Helen's Smelting Company* (1865),[14] which I do not discuss here, arose because a gentleman's residence and estate was close to an expanding industrial area and suffered pollution from a copper smelting plant.

Next door to Dr. Sturges—he was to be there for many more years—was Thomas Aldington Wallworth, a professor of singing. But in his affidavit Dr. Sturges does not give Wallworth's activities as the reason for his decision, in 1873, 8 years after he moved in, to build a consulting room in the very small "yard or garden" at the back of his house. There was no other suitable room; the other ground floor room was his dining room, and after 1873 the waiting room for his patients. Before 1873 his work was probably confined to hospital practice and writing; his first book, *An Introduction to the Study of Clinical Medicine,* appeared in 1873. So a boundary was being moved in the autumn of 1873 by his decision to see patients in the new consulting room. But this use was not continuous. Between 1873 and late 1875, or early 1876, he saw patients from 10 A.M. to 1 P.M. He also used the room at these hours for preparing his lectures before he left for his hospital work. The noise from Mr. Bridgman's kitchen soon began to cause him "great discomfort and annoyance."[15]

[13] Advertisement in London and Provincial Medical Directory 1878.

[14] Tipping v. The St. Helen's Smelting Company, 4 B. & S. 608, 616, 122 E.R. 588, 591. XI H.L.C. 642, 11 E.R. 1483, 1 Ch. App. Cas. 66. See my Leading Cases in the Common Law (Oxford, 1995), ch. 7.

[15] Affidavit by O. Sturges. See note 7 *supra*.

The wall which separated the two properties, and formed the wall of Mr. Bridgman's kitchen, was a party wall, one and a half bricks thick. The new consulting room was built against this party wall, adding to it a thickness of half a brick.[16] In the kitchen were two 16-inch marble mortars near its northeastern corner, close to the southwest corner of the consulting room, both set in brickwork built against the party wall. One had been there for 50 or even 60 years, the other for 26 years. They were used for crushing loaf sugar, almonds, and indeed meat and were worked by lignum vitae pestles, operated by one man. These pestles, when in operation, "are each passed through a socket in a bearer secured to a plank bolted onto or as I believe right through the said wall . . . [that is the party wall, but not the half-brick thick wall of the consulting room]." The affidavit of J. T. Christopher, an architect and surveyor employed by Dr. Sturges, went on: "A more effectual means of communicating or conveying sound and vibration could hardly be devised." Although experts hired by Mr. Bridgman disputed the passage of vibration, employing the unsophisticated balancing egg test, there was no conflict over the noise, described by Dr. Sturges as "of a thumping character . . . Every blow is distinctly heard and felt." The noise "interfered materially with the comfort of my house as a residence and its use for my professional purposes." In particular it prevented "my carrying on any work requiring continuous thought" and interfered with the use of the stethoscope; it also annoyed his patients. Similar accounts were given in affidavits by colleagues: Dr. J. W. Haward, a surgeon at St. George's; Dr. W. H. Allchin, a physician who lived at 94 Wimpole Street; and Dr. H. Donkin, a Harley Street physician. They emphasized that the noise would seriously interfere with the use of the room for normal domestic purposes. Thus, Dr. Haward said that "the noise was of a kind which would have materially interfered with one's domestic comfort if one was using the room for ordinary purposes." This was to head off the argument that it was only the peculiar nature of the use to which Dr. Sturges put the room which created the problem.[17]

This was the situation which gave rise, eventually, to the litigation. One point needs perhaps to be made at the outset. My account of the source of the dispute is based on the way lawyers packaged it in the light of their knowledge of the law and of what factors it made relevant; their work survives in the British Public Record Office, principally in affidavits. These do not directly address the problem of *social* cost (or social

[16] A standard brick is 9 × 4½ inches. The party wall was (with mortar) approximately 14 inches thick, and the consulting room increased the thickness to approximately 19 inches.

[17] Affidavits. See note 7 *supra*.

gain) at all. Clearly all sorts of people might be indirectly affected by the outcome of the dispute—Her Majesty the Queen, the Prince of Wales, Mr. Bridgman's employees, Dr. Sturges's patients—but the lawyers conceived of the dispute as only involving two individuals, unable to agree over the boundaries of their property rights. That the matter should be conceived in this way was, and is, part of the conventional ideology of the common law, and of the function of courts within the system. Anyone who suggests that such a dispute should be conceived in some different way needs to address the consequences which would follow in the way the case would have to be presented for decision.

## II. Basic Ideas in "The Problem of Social Cost"

Let me now return to Coase's article and attempt to bring out certain basic ideas in it. There seem to me to be five.

The first idea, which runs through all Coase's writings, is deep skepticism as to the desirability of government intervention. Various expressions are used, but the thought is the same.[18] In "The Problem of Social Cost" this skepticism is very mildly expressed; he argues that action against a smoke-emitting factory will lead to results which "are not necessarily, or even *usually,* desirable."[19] In *The Firm, the Market and the Law* Coase hardens his position, arguing that whether government intervention is desirable or not is a "factual question" and that economic theory does not support any presumption in its favor. He goes on: "The ubiquitous nature of 'externalities' suggests to me that there is a *prima facie* case against intervention, and the studies of the effects of regulation which have been made in recent years in the United States, ranging from agriculture to zoning, which indicate that regulation has commonly made matters worse, lend support to this view."[20] There is a change of emphasis here from the original article, which was more anxious to demonstrate the significance of transaction costs, rather than that of externalities. Indeed, although the effect on third parties, and on society generally, of decisions in cases of conflict is mentioned, the expression "externality"

[18] These expressions include "direct governmental regulation," "governmental administrative regulation," "governmental regulation," "governmental action," "corrective governmental action," "State action," and "governmental intervention"; see Coase, The Problem of Social Cost, as reprinted *supra* note 1, at 117, 199, 131, 133, 135. In ch. 1 of Coase, The Firm, the Market and the Law, *supra* note 1, at 22, we have "public intervention" as well. I do not think the varied expressions used alter the basic thought. Richard A. Posner, Overcoming Law 413 (Cambridge, Mass., 1995), describes hostility to public intervention except when this will maximize wealth as a "leitmotif" of Coase's work.

[19] Coase, The Problem of Social Cost, as reprinted *supra* note 1, at 96. My italics.

[20] Coase, *supra* note 1, at 26.

is not used. Coase has explained that his failure to use the term, and his preference for the expression "harmful effects," was deliberate.[21]

The second idea is the corollary of the first; since government intervention is suspect, the alternatives to government intervention are viewed sympathetically. The drift of the argument favors leaving matters to the market. This possibility is dramatized by the thesis which has come to be called the Coase theorem: that in the absence of transaction costs the allocation of resources reached by negotiation and bargain, assuming economic rationality,[22] would be unaffected by the rule as to legal liability. This is stated in the discussion of *Sturges v. Bridgman:* "With costless market transactions, the decision of the courts concerning liability for damage would be without effect on the allocation of resources."[23] This of course is a purely theoretical view as to what would happen in a world which does not exist.[24] But Coase relates his thinking to real life by arguing, surely correctly, that in a case such as *Sturges v. Bridgman* the parties might have reached an economically satisfactory position by a bargain, or at least a position which seemed satisfactory to them, a point which is clear enough without the Coase theorem and quite independent of it.[25] Presumably, the reason why they did not is, pace Coase, either the impediment of transaction costs or the fact that one or other or both did not behave with economic rationality or because of differing expectations as to the probable outcome of litigation. Of course, litigation will involve considerable additional costs, as it did in this case.

Elsewhere, Coase gives an account of the alternatives to government intervention, which he lists: "inaction, the abandonment of earlier governmental action, or the facilitating of market transactions."[26] What "inaction" means is unclear, but I shall return to the point later. Obviously, market transactions might be facilitated by measures taken to reduce transaction costs—free legal services for the handling of negotiations, free research materials, free telephones, or whatever. This all sounds like government intervention. The implication of Coase's argument is that given facilitation, leaving the outcome to the market is the best solution.

[21] Coase, *id.* at 27.

[22] There may be other assumptions which I do not here discuss if the allocation is to be efficient—for example, some sort of embargo on violence. It may also be necessary, given the marginal utility of income, to make some assumption about relative wealth.

[23] Coase, *supra* note 1, at 106.

[24] For an account of what happened in the real nineteenth-century world in which the use of the law was extremely expensive, see McLaren, *supra* note 3; and Simpson, *supra* note 14, ch. 7.

[25] Coase, *supra* note 1, at 105–6.

[26] *Id.* at 24.

The third idea is not easy to reproduce accurately; it is most simply put by saying that the problem of social cost is, at least to an economist, a reciprocal problem. The idea, at one level, may be illustrated from *Sturges v. Bridgman*. Alterations in behavior by either Dr. Sturges (giving up the practice of medicine, selling his house to a deaf person, writing his lectures elsewhere, etc.) or by Mr. Bridgman (retirement, moving his mortars, using them at a different time of the day, etc.) will cause the problem to go away. It only arises because of the relationship between two people and their behavior. Coase however puts this in two other ways. One is negative: it rejects the idea of the arrow of causation. It is wrong to suppose that Mr. Bridgman's activities were harming Dr. Sturges, with the implication that it is Mr. Bridgman who must be restrained. The other is positive: since a decision either way will impose economic costs on the loser, the real question is—who is to be allowed to harm whom? In one passage Coase says: "If we are to discuss the problem in terms of causation, both parties cause the damage."[27] I am not convinced that it is necessary to Coase's economic argument to do this violence to the everyday conception of causation or to reject the evaluative distinction which everyday thought makes between harms and costs, but, be that as it may, his view certainly sets him apart from lawyers, who everywhere make use of causal notions and do not treat harms and costs as equivalent. A worrying implication of Coase's reciprocity is that from an economists's point of view, deciding a case such as *Sturges v. Bridgman* ought to involve evaluating a wide and perhaps unlimited range of alternative courses of action which would solve the problem. There is a tendency to discuss the reciprocal character of the problem of social cost in terms of just two activities—running railways or growing crops, making cakes or seeing patients. This can mislead; once the reciprocal nature of the problem is conceded, there is just no end to the possibilities—they include Dr. Sturges's and Mr. Bridgman's mutual suicide. The reciprocal nature of human interaction can raise emotive issues, as when women object to the idea that the way to stop sexual assaults on the streets at night is for them to stay at home. Even if they are the cheapest cost avoiders, ought this to be conclusive?

The fourth idea is much less easy to state with any precision, perhaps because it involves a number of intimately related ideas. It concerns the role of law. In the real world, as opposed to some ideal world in which there were no transaction costs, there is of course, in Coase's view, a role for law. One reason is that in his view rights have to be defined or allocated before you can have bargains. Coase argues that because

[27] *Id.* at 112.

transactions are not costless: "[T]he initial delimitation of legal rights does have an effect on the efficiency with which the economic system operates."[28] So if the initial allocation is inefficient then it may not be possible, given high transaction costs, for the parties to reallocate them efficiently. Those of more left-wing sympathies often make this point in saying that in a world in which, wherever you start, property rights are very unequally allocated, assets will not necessarily end up in the hands of those who can make the best use of them. So Coase concludes: "Even when it is possible to change the legal delimitation of rights through market transactions, it is obviously desirable to reduce the need for such transactions and thus reduce the employment of resources in carrying them out."[29] So the law should tend to allocate rights in the way in which they would be allocated by the market in a world in which the costs of market transactions, and presumably other imperfections, were not an impediment. This is a somewhat startling thesis unless it is assumed that the law should somehow at the same time not upset the existing unequal allocation of property rights, and Coase does not address the point. Although skeptical Coase concedes that there may be some situations—smoke nuisance affecting a large number of other people, where transaction costs are likely to be large—in which government intervention is appropriate: "[T]here is no reason why, on occasion, such governmental administrative regulation should not lead to an improvement in economic efficiency."[30] It all depends on the circumstances.

What seems to me to be curious is that Coase, who on questions of allocation and delimitation of rights has in mind private law, nowhere treats judicial decisions in private law by the courts of the state as a form of governmental intervention or action. Private law, evolving through judicial decisions, is, for reasons never made explicit, privileged against the criticisms he directs against government intervention. When he instances "inaction" as one possible reaction to the problem of social cost what he must really mean is leaving the matter to the common law. Since courts cannot simply wash their hands of disputes, this never means doing nothing. In the case of a smoke nuisance, it might mean imposing strict liability, liability for negligence, or no liability at all; whatever is decided entails taking sides. It may be possible to divine why Coase is sympathetic to leaving matters to the common law from his doubts about governmental decisions, which arise because they are "subject to politi-

[28] *Id.* at 115. Coase does not discuss the fact that making use of the allocation of legal rights by litigation is not costless.

[29] *Id.* at 119.

[30] *Id.* at 118.

cal pressures and operating without any competitive check."[31] So judicial decisions, though not obviously subject to competitive checks, are better because they are apolitical. This view is of course controversial. Another possible reason is that whereas the parties can contract out of a common-law ruling, they normally cannot do this where there is regulatory control, such as zoning, at least if they wish their contract to be legally effective. Coase is critical of others for discussing the problem of social cost without specifying the institutional context, as by discussing, for example, laissez-faire without telling the reader what monetary, legal, or political system is assumed to be in force.[32] However, he does not himself specify what other assumptions he is making about the state of the law. For example, in *Sturges v. Bridgman,* given a state of nature, Dr. Sturges might well have solved the problem by using his acquired military skills and bayoneting Mr. Bridgman, or Mr. Bridgman might have crowned the good doctor with one of his lignum vitae pestles.[33] Doing nothing about the problem of social cost might or might not mean that the state did not intervene in such circumstances. But this criticism goes I think more to the understanding of the Coase theorem, which is not the subject of this article.

The fifth idea may perhaps be viewed as intimately connected with his view as to the role of law. It is that the right way to decide cases involving the problem of social cost (he has in mind private nuisance cases in which an injunction is sought) is to ask "whether the gain from preventing the harm is greater than the loss which would be suffered elsewhere as a result of stopping the action which produced the harm."[34] Although the point is variously expressed, Coase's argument seems to be that in such a case as *Sturges v. Bridgman* what is needed is a cost benefit analysis—residential and medical uses of property to be weighed against cakes.[35] But, given the reciprocal nature of the problem, why just medicine and cakes? Should we not take into account a very wide and perhaps limitless range of alternative courses of action? I find Coase is not very explicit

[31] *Id.*

[32] *Id.* at 154.

[33] See note 22 *supra.*

[34] Coase, *supra* note 1, at 132.

[35] See *id.* at 106: "[T]he solution of the problem depends essentially on whether the continued use of the machinery adds more to the confectioner's income than it subtracts from the doctor's." At 107 the point is put a little differently: "And it would be desirable to preserve the areas [Wimpole Street] for residential or professional use [by giving nonindustrial users the right to stop the noise, vibration, smoke, etc., by injunction] only if the value of the additional residential facilities obtained was greater than the value of the cakes . . . lost." I have omitted references to another hypothetical case.

here, and he does not explain how, in terms of legal procedure, if that is what he has in mind, such an inquiry would proceed. I shall return to the question later.

## III. The Pigovian Tendency

I now turn to the structure of the article, or rather to one striking aspect of it. This takes the form of a criticism of the work of Pigou. Coase attacks views on social policy which he attributes in particular to Pigou's *The Economics of Welfare* (1920),[36] a textbook developed out of Pigou's earlier *Wealth and Welfare* (1912).

Pigou, who was born in 1877 and died on March 7, 1959, succeeded Alfred Marshall as Professor of Political Economy in Cambridge in 1908 and held the chair until 1943.[37] Pigou was an example of a type of Oxbridge don once ubiquitous but now almost extinct—a lifelong bachelor, petrified of women, who enjoyed the company of young men but, so far as is known, abstained from any sort of close entanglement, let alone physical relationship, with them.[38] He was an undergraduate at King's, where he was a pupil of Oscar Browning, and apart from noncombatant service in the First World War, he spent his whole adult life in the college until his death in 1959. My colleague Beverley Pooley can recall him pottering about, disheveled, in old age, moving backward around the court in bedroom slippers. In recent times he has achieved a curious and undeserved notoriety; J. Costello in his *Mask of Treachery* presented him as having sinister Russian contacts and also awarded him a knighthood, which I fear he never received or could have received, since he had been a conscientious objector in the war.[39] A mountain climber of considerable ability, who even climbed with George Mallory, later to die on Everest, he suffered in 1927 a severe breakdown in health, developing fibrillation

[36] A. C. Pigou, Wealth and Welfare (1912); A. C. Pigou, The Economics of Welfare (4th ed. 1932). Coase gives references to the fourth edition of The Economics of Welfare published in 1932, and I shall follow his practice. The other editions were the second (1924) and third (1929). The fourth edition was reprinted several times (in 1938, 1946, 1948, 1950, and in 1952 with eight appendices). There may have been other reprints.

[37] Ronald Coase in his Economics and Economists (Chicago, 1991), ch. 10, gives an account of Pigou's appointment.

[38] Biographical account based on correspondence with the late Sir Austin (E. A. G.) Robinson in 1992 and Lord Noel Annan in 1994; an unsigned obituary attributed to Robinson in the *Times* for March 9, 1959; an article by Robinson in The Dictionary of National Biography 814–17 (1951–60); an article by J. de V. Graaff in 3 The New Palgrave: A Dictionary of Economics 876 (John Eatwell, Murray Milgate, & Peter Newman eds., 1994) and an article by Robert Skidelsky on John Maynard Keynes in 2 *id.* at 282, 286–87, 367, 702; and other accounts as cited below.

[39] John Costello, The Mask of Treachery 149, 176, 181 (New York, 1988).

of the heart. Thereafter, he was a shadow of his former self; he became eccentric and reclusive, and his misogyny became grotesque. Even in his country cottage in the Lake District, where he tended to unwind, and was even civil to the wives of his friends, he was hostile to talking about economics. As the late Sir Austin Robinson recorded: "[E]conomics was taboo. I have never had a serious economic discussion with Pigou."[40] He thus differed from the type of Oxbridge don—examples are the philosophers Ludwig Wittgenstein and J. L. Austin—whose ideas were disseminated orally through seminars and discussion with colleagues.

As an economist he was an uncritical follower of the views of his predecessor Marshall. Indeed, as Sir Austin told me, he tended to be intolerant of anyone who presumed to criticize the views of the master.[41] He published extensively and lectured somewhat repetitively in a style which was then quite normal.

As an economist "he set out to investigate the full conditions for maximum satisfaction, the conditions in which private and social net product (as he called them) might diverge, and the measures which could be taken to bring them into equality, and maximize satisfaction."[42] Pigou did not investigate every good thing in society, but only those which could readily be related to monetary value. Since the measures which he thought might, in principle, be employed to correct divergence would principally be legal measures, typically the collection of taxes or payment of bounties, Pigou had an economic theory as to how law might promote welfare, though he never laid any emphasis on the point, and perhaps never realized this.

Coase treats Pigou as his principal target and presents the Pigovian theory—what he calls his "basic position" or "central tendency"—thus: "[W]hen defects were found in the working of the economic system, the way to put things right was through some form of governmental action."[43] In his *Essays on Economics and Economists* (1994), Coase presents Pigou as influencing a school of economists: "Some fifteen or twenty years

[40] Don Patinkin & J. Clark Leith, Keynes, Cambridge, and *The General Theory:* The Process of Criticism and Discussion Connected with the Development of *The General Theory* 30 (London, 1978).

[41] Letters from Sir Austin Robinson to author, May 26, 1992, and June 6, 1992.

[42] In Pigou, Wealth and Welfare, *supra* note 36, ch. 7, at 148–71, Pigou gives examples of divergences. Some arise out of the form of contracts, for example in leases which provide no incentive for the tenant to maintain the fertility of the land or improve it. Examples are given of uncompensated services such as the light thrown onto a street by lamps at the entrance of private houses (see *supra,* at 158–69), and these are followed by cases where the social net product falls short of the private net product, as where motor cars wear out roads (*supra,* at 162 ff.).

[43] Coase, *supra* note 1, at 20.

ago economists, under the influence of Pigou and others, thought of the government as waiting beneficently to put things right whenever the hidden hand pointed in the wrong direction."[44] Coase has also indicated that Pigou was not really very clever. Thus, in the first chapter of *The Firm, the Market and the Law* of 1988 he records how he proposes to present to the Regenstein Library of the University of Chicago Pigou's copy of E. W. Bemis's *Municipal Monopolies;* the markings and annotations "will indicate Pigou's manner of working."[45] The context in which this is said suggests that these markings and annotations are not the product of a superior intellect, nor evidence of a sound manner of working. I have not inspected the book, and for all I know this may very well be true. In the account Coase gives of Pigou's appointment to the Cambridge chair, in which Marshall was influential, Coase remarks: "It seems clear to me that Pigou did not fulfil the high hopes which Marshall had of him. In many respects his influence on the development of economics has been bad. He seems to have lacked any feeling for the working of economic institutions."[46]

Somewhat surprisingly, Coase in *The Firm, the Market and the Law* more or less concedes that Pigou nowhere expresses the view attributed to him, or if he does, hedges it with "numerous qualifications." On the page where he makes this concession he refers to the Pigovian *tradition,* meaning thereby to refer to a view which was in some loose sense associated with Pigou, or fathered on him in oral tradition, rather than anything he actually wrote or said.[47] As I have explained Pigou's ideas were not likely to have been transmitted orally, given his dislike of discussing economics, so the source of any Pigovian tradition is likely to have been his written works, or glosses put on them by others. I shall later return to this curiosity.

## IV. Pigou and Sparks from Locomotives

Coase uses a particular Pigovian illustration, involving the law relating to uncompensated fire damage caused by sparks escaping from steam railway locomotives, as an example of Pigou's failings. I shall discuss the law in more detail later; here it is enough to know that the victim of such

[44] *Id.* at 30; compare at 56. Pigou's most radical political view, not original to him, was that because of the differing marginal utility of income, wealth transfers from rich to poor would enhance utility. Coase does not discuss this view.

[45] *Id.* at 22 n.33. The work is cited by Pigou, for example, in The Economics of Welfare, *supra* note 36, at 296.

[46] *Id.* at 166 n.32.

[47] *Id.* at 20.

damage might be unable to recover compensation for it without proving negligence. This might be difficult—for example, it might be difficult to identify which locomotive was the source. In "The Problem of Social Cost,"[48] Coase discusses the sparks illustration in considerable detail. He makes three claims, based on Pigou's use of it in *The Economics of Welfare*.[49]

The first is that Pigou thought that there should be "state action" to force the railways to make compensation. This statement of Pigou's supposed view is expressed in a different form by others, for example by R. D. Cooter in an article on the Coase theorem in *The New Palgrave: A Dictionary of Economics:* "Pigou used economics to defend the common law principle that a party who caused a nuisance should be enjoined or required to pay damages. According to Pigou, the common law rules tend to promote economic efficiency by internalizing social costs."[50] But this, besides being wrong, is quite at odds with Coase's presentation.

The second claim is that the legal situation to which Pigou referred, which in Pigou's view, so Coase claims, amounted to an imperfection in the working of the economic system, was in reality itself the *consequence* of state action. So Pigou in favoring state action had dramatically got hold of the wrong end of the stick.[51] He returns to the same point in *The Firm, the Market and the Law:* "For example, as I pointed out in 'The Problem of Social Cost,' the situation in which sparks from a railway locomotive could start fires which burnt woods on land adjoining the railway without the railway having to pay compensation to the owners of the woods (the legal position in England at the time Pigou was writing and one of which he had perhaps heard) had come about not because of a lack of governmental action but in consequence of it."[52] Underlying these first two claims is Coase's general skepticism about state action.

The third claim I shall for the moment leave on one side.[53]

## V. Sparks, Pigou, and State Action

As for the first claim, Pigou nowhere said that the state should do anything at all about uncompensated damage caused by sparks from rail-

[48] *Id.* at 135–42.

[49] Pigou, The Economics of Welfare, *supra* note 36, at 134. It is not used in Wealth and Welfare in the relevant passage in pt. 2, ch. 7, in particular at 162–64, but at 159 he mentions the use of devices which reduce smoke emissions as conferring an unpaid-for service on third parties.

[50] Article on "The Coase Theorem," in 1 The New Palgrave: A Dictionary of Economics, *supra* note 38, at 459.

[51] Coase, *supra* note 1, at 135–38.

[52] *Id.* at 23; see also 131.

[53] See Section IX below.

way locomotives. Much less does Pigou "defend the common law principle," as Cooter claims in the passage I have quoted.

Pigou's example has a context. He used it merely to show how social and private net products—in simple language, economic advantage or disadvantage to society generally on the one hand and to the individual actor on the other—might diverge: "It might happen, for example, as will be explained more fully in a later chapter, that costs are thrown upon people not directly concerned, through, say, uncompensated damage done to surrounding woods by sparks from railway engines."[54] Pigou was drawing attention to what economists now call "externalities."

He never used this example in discussing the merits of government intervention. It appears in the edition of *The Economics of Welfare* of 1920[55] and in all later editions, unaltered in substance. The terminology of the 1920 edition was slightly different from that used in the fourth edition quoted by Coase. In the first edition Pigou contrasted "social net product" ("the aggregate contribution made to the national dividend") with "trade net product" ("the contribution . . . that is capable of being sold and the proceeds added to the earnings of those responsible for the industry under review".)[56] Pigou was trying to make the point that in calculating private (or earlier "trade") and social net products, "All such effects must be included—some of them will be positive, others negative elements."[57] In assessing the social net product of running a railway, you have to include in the balance sheet all the effects of the operation, good or bad, on everyone who is affected, however indirectly; how this daunting undertaking was to be conducted Pigou did not explain, and as we shall see he later recognized the difficulty.[58] That is the only use to which he puts the illustration.

Coase says that Pigou's use of the example "is presumably intended to show how it is possible 'for State action to improve on "natural" tendencies.' "[59] The passage quoted from Pigou comes from Pigou's book, but not from the section in which he deals with sparks. Coase's claim seems mistaken.

Later in the first edition, in speaking of the reasons why there could be divergence, Pigou explains, without mentioning the sparks example, that "technical considerations" might prevent "compensation being en-

[54] Pigou, *supra* note 36, at 134.

[55] Pigou, The Economics of Welfare 115 (1st ed. 1920).

[56] Pigou, *supra* note 36 (4th ed.), at 149. The terminology used in the later editions of The Economics of Welfare is that used in his Wealth and Welfare.

[57] *Id.* at 134.

[58] See text around notes 62 and 85 *infra*.

[59] Coase, *supra* note 1, at 137.

forced on behalf of the injured parties" where A, in providing a service to B, renders some disservice to C.[60] He makes the same point over benefits conferred on third persons, but not paid for by them. In the fourth edition he refers to "the technical difficulty of enforcing compensation for incidental disservices."[61] It is obscure to me what Pigou meant by "technical difficulty." Conceivably, he was talking about the state of tort law, but whether he was or not, the passage makes it clear that he accepted the fact that not all damage would be compensable.

Pigou also gave no hints as to how, as a matter of principle, practicalities apart, you identify all the effects of an activity, such as running a railway, in order to take them into account. He seems to assume some sort of commonsense notion of causation. Later in his *Socialism versus Capitalism,* published in 1937, he came to the conclusion that quantifying the effects would be very difficult, though he does not there discuss how one sets bounds to the enterprise.[62] The problem is not discussed by Coase. Plainly, you cannot engage in cost benefit analysis without some scheme for allocating consequences or effects to the activity under consideration.

Why did Çoase think that Pigou favored state intervention over engine sparks? Coase reaches his conclusion by relying on a much later passage in Pigou's *The Economics of Welfare,* chapter 20 of part 2. In this chapter Pigou explicitly discusses intervention by public authorities. The conclusion Pigou reaches is accurately stated in his own summary of paragraphs 4 and 5 of this chapter: "The mere failure of private industry, when left free from public interference, to maximize the national dividend does not of itself warrant intervention; for this *might* make things worse. Certain modern developments have, however, rendered government agencies better fitted for intervention than they were in former times."[63] Here Pigou is not discussing changes in private tort law. He is discussing regulatory "control over concerns left in private hands" or their "direct public management." He argues that the principal disadvantages—he lists four in particular—which had in the past adversely affected intervention by public authorities can be obviated, and he speaks favorably of "the recently developed device of Commissions or ad hoc Boards, that is to say, bodies of men appointed for the express purpose of industrial operation or control."[64] He instances the Railway Department of New South

[60] Pigou, *supra* note 49, at 159.

[61] Pigou, *supra* note 36, at 185.

[62] Arthur C. Pigou, Socialism versus Capitalism, ch. 3, 31–46 (1937).

[63] Pigou, The Economics of Welfare, *supra* note 36, at xix.

[64] *Id.* at 334.

Wales and the Port of London Authority as examples of commissions for "operation" (we would today say "management") and the Interstate Railway Commission in the United States as one for "control" (we would today say "regulation").[65] In his later *Socialism versus Capitalism* of 1937, Pigou expresses the same preference; he was not disposed to favor management by government departments, as in the case of the Post Office.[66] In a passage in *The Firm, the Market and the Law* Coase claims that in his discussion, "starting with a statement about the imperfections of government, Pigou discovers the perfect form of governmental organization and is therefore able to avoid enquiring into the circumstances in which the defects of public intervention would mean that such intervention would tend to make matters worse."[67] I can see no basis for this in what Pigou wrote; he never suggested that the newer institutions were perfect. He did say that the newer agencies did not suffer from some of the defects of the older, having in mind principally municipal authorities. His cautious approach is thus presented in *The Economics of Welfare:* "It is not sufficient to contrast the imperfect adjustments of unfettered private enterprise with the best adjustment that economists in their studies can imagine."[68]

Indeed, there is no particular reason why Pigou should have wanted private tort law to be changed. Assuming, for the sake of argument, that Pigou was reasonably well informed on the law, he was referring to the fact that most railways in Britain were not "strictly" liable, that is, liable without proof of negligence or fault. They were not immune from liability. This was the position both before and after the passage of the Railway Fires Acts of 1905 and 1923, though this legislation introduced some exceptions.[69] Pigou could well have accepted this state of the law as

[65] Coase points out that Pigou means the Interstate Commerce Commission, established in 1887.

[66] Pigou, *supra* note 62, at 138. See also his Alfred Marshall and Current Thought (1953), written in the light of the actions of the postwar British Labour government.

[67] Coase, *supra* note 1, at 21–22.

[68] Pigou, The Economics of Welfare, *supra* note 36, at 296–99.

[69] The Railway (Fires) Act of 1905 imposed strict liability for some fire damage (basically, damage to agricultural land or crops) caused by railways up to a limit of £100, subject to certain procedural requirements. The Railway (Fires) Amendment Act of 1923 put the limit up to £200. Damage outside the scope of these acts could only be claimed by showing negligence. The Act of 1905 was first introduced in 1901 as the Compensation for Damage to Crops Bill (see Parl. Deb. 90, cols. 737–63). For its passage see Parl. Deb. 142 (4th ser.), cols. 348–74 (1901); Parl. Deb. 148 (4th ser.), cols. 1478–92 (1905). One ground for opposition was that when part of a tract of land was acquired for a railway, the price paid by way of compensation commonly included a figure for severance. This could be viewed as providing compensation for future damage; in some instance apparently the conveyance transferring the land included a provision to this effect.

reasonable. In the history of tort law there have always been some who think liability should be based on fault and others who favor some version of strict liability based on causation alone. One practical aspect of the latter is that it considerably reduces the cost of litigation to the plaintiff for proof of negligence may involve, for example, expensive expert witnesses.

Pigou's writings do not, however, suggest that he had any interest in tort law; liability for damage through sparks only momentarily attracted his attention. About tort law generally Pigou is silent; I imagine he neither knew nor cared about it. This would be typical of economists of his generation, and of virtually all the nineteenth-century political economists, though some did have an interest in accidents.[70] They showed scant interest in the private law structure of the world they discussed. I have not investigated the matter, but it would not be surprising if Coase himself was the first economist to devote any attention to tort law. The only legal arrangements which Pigou actually mentions for encouraging activities leading to desirable third-party effects, or discouraging those which led to undesirable ones, are administrative control by regulatory bodies, bounties, and taxes.[71] Neither Pigou nor Coase considers the possible development of the law of unjust enrichment to cope with situations when there are beneficial effects on third parties; at the time they were writing, this branch of the law was in England very little developed.

My belief that Pigou never considered changes in tort liability is strengthened by another of his publications. One of his *Essays in Applied Economics* discusses, as a question of ethics informed by economics, how individuals should spend their money.[72] He argues that "in our selection of objects on which to spend, it is our duty to take account of certain indirect consequences which our action produces upon other people. Some sorts of spending cause labor and equipment to be employed in ways that inflict injury on members of the general public, for which they receive no compensation. . . . *Per contra* other sorts of spending indi-

[70] John Ramsey McCulloch favored imposing liability on factory and mine owners; see his Principles of Political Economy with Some Inquiries Respecting their Application and a Sketch of the Rise and Progress of that Science 307 (Edinburgh, 1849). Edwin Chadwick, a follower of the political economists, thought the same; see S. E. Finer, The Life and Times of Sir Edwin Chadwick 61, 93, 148–50 (London, 1980). Neither had in mind tort law as the instrument. See Simpson, *supra* note 14, at 129–32.

[71] See Pigou, Wealth and Welfare, *supra* note 36, at 164; Pigou, The Economics of Welfare, *supra* note 36, at 192–96; and A. C. Pigou, A Study in Public Finance (3d rev. ed. 1947), pt. 2, ch. 8, at 94–100, on Taxes and Bounties to Correct Maladjustment. Coase, *supra* note 1, at 151 refers to this discussion, his reference being to the third edition of 1947, which I have not seen.

[72] A. C. Pigou, The Private Use of Money, in Essays in Applied Economics 1 ff. (rev. ed. 1924).

rectly confer a benefit on members of the general public, for which they pay no price."[73] Here was an opportunity to say that ethics requires the actor to pay compensation to those injured, or required that those benefited should pay for what they gain. Pigou does not take this opportunity.

There seems to be no warrant for Coase's claim that the use by Pigou of the example of uncompensated damage caused by sparks from railway engines "is presumably intended to show how it is possible 'for State action to improve on natural tendencies.' "[74] Had he said that he would of course have been right, as Coase concedes—the critical word is *possible*.

Indeed, Pigou would have been completely off his head if he had argued in favor of intervention, either by regulation or administrative control, or by bounties and taxes, in every situation where a divergence existed between social and private net product. His examples show that he was perfectly well aware of the ubiquity of externalities. Pigou seems to have viewed them as part of the natural order of things.

From Pigou's writings his real views on government intervention can readily be discovered. They are similar to those of Henry Sidgwick, whose lectures he attended. Sidgwick made the point that utility to the individual and utility to society might diverge. He concluded that there was, in consequence, a case for state intervention, but added a caution lest it be thought a compelling case: "It does not of course follow that wherever *laisser faire* falls short government interference is expedient: since the inevitable drawbacks and disadvantages of the latter may, in any particular case, be worse than the shortcomings of private industry."[75] Pigou's own view is most fully explained in a work which Coase does not cite, *Economics in Practice: Six Lectures on Current Issues*.[76] Here he argues that "it sometimes happens that only a portion of the benefit or damage due to a person's private action is reflected in the reward that person receives; and, consequently, that he tends to carry that action less far or further than the general interest of society requires."[77] He gives examples of harmful and beneficial effects.[78] He ar-

[73] *Id.* at 9.

[74] Coase, *supra* note 1, at 137.

[75] H. Sidgwick, The Principles of Political Economy, bk. 3, ch. 2, 419 (London, 1883). See the Dictionary of National Biography article, *supra* note 38.

[76] A. C. Pigou, Economics in Practice: Six Lectures on Current Issues (London, 1935). Four of these lectures were delivered at the University of London in 1934, but the relevant one, lecture 5 on State Action and Laisser-Faire, was not.

[77] *Id.* at 118 ff.

[78] In the first edition the examples are a little different. Thus, the rabbit damage is caused by game-preserving activities. With regard to smoke prevention devices, he argues that in many instances they might actually be profitable to the users, but that the public interest requires their use even though they may not "pay" the installer. See *id.* at 160–61.

gues that in such cases "there is a *prima facie* case for State intervention, in the first case by restriction, in the second by stimulation." As these terms indicate he has in mind here bounties and taxes. The same remedies for what he calls "maladjustments" are mentioned in his *A Study in Public Finance*, which Coase does cite.[79] He speaks here of "a discommodity for which those on whom it is inflicted are unable to exact compensation." He gives examples and then sets out possible disadvantages of the use of taxes or bounties.[80]

He seems blissfully unaware of the relevance of tort law, though another passage in his lectures indicates that he assumes a background of what he calls, vaguely, "the ordinary forms of law": "When private self-interest, acting freely, subject only to the ordinary forms of law, does not lead to the best results from a general social point of view, there is, as I have indicated, a *prima facie* case for State action."[81] Pigou then goes on to set out numerous problems about state action and again argues that governmental institutions, such as Public Service Boards and Commissions, are better than they used to be. The conclusion is: "The issue about which popular writers argue—the principle of laissez-faire *versus* the principle of State action—is not an issue at all. There is no principle involved on either side. Each particular case must be considered on its merits in all the detail of its concrete circumstance."[82]

The simple point Pigou made, which seems to me to be wholly unaffected by Coase's criticisms, is that if individuals act out of self-interest, narrowly defined,[83] they will tend not to take into account third-party effects for which they do not have to pay if harmful, or for which they will not be paid if beneficial. Consequently, it may be economically though not ethically rational for them to act in ways which do not enhance general welfare, or fail to act in ways which would. Taxes and bounties may be used to provide incentives to deal with this problem, but intervention may do more harm than good. It is hardly an exaggeration to say that Pigou demonstrated that self-interest operating through the market is unlikely to lead to an optimal use of resources but that he had no developed idea as to what, if anything, should be done about this. Curiously enough, Pigou does not anywhere argue, as I suppose he might have done, that in the absence of corrective measures the lack of respon-

[79] See Pigou, note 71 *supra*. In this work the examples given of losses inflicted on third parties do not include damage from sparks or rabbits.

[80] *Id.* at 99–100.

[81] *Id.* at 124.

[82] *Id.* at 127–28.

[83] If altruistic conduct, or conduct motivated by a desire to appear noble or the like, is defined as self-interested, then the analysis is different.

sibility for the creation of public harms accompanied by the lack of reward for the creation of public goods will tend to produce a world in which there are more of the former than of the latter.

By 1937, when he published his *Socialism versus Capitalism*, he had come to have grave doubts even about the use of bounties and taxes in either a capitalist or a communist system. The problem, as he saw it, was that although economists had suggested the use of these devices, no government has ever tried to use them,[84] and the economists "have never attempted the quantitative study that would be necessary before the suggestion could be applied in practice."[85] His idea was that such study would be needed to settle the level of taxation. Ignorance of the facts militated against the use of these possible remedies.[86] Curiously enough, his view here is similar to that presented by Coase in his "Note to the Problem of Social Cost," but much less developed.[87]

Pigou's view was thus much the same as that of Coase, though he was marginally less skeptical about the merits of state action. A curiosity of Pigou's view is that taxes for damage do not compensate those harmed, since it is not suggested that the tax revenue should go to them. Perhaps the explanation is that compensation is usually justified on the ground of its being just or fair to the individual, whereas Pigou supposed himself to be interested in providing incentives to discourage activities which were harmful to society generally; his taxes serve the same purpose as deterrent punishment in the criminal law, which does not directly benefit the immediate victim. Bounties, however, do benefit directly the person who provides the service.[88]

[84] In fact they had—the imposition of tolls to reward those who ran lighthouses is a form of taxation. See David E. Van Zandt, The Lessons of the Lighthouse: "Government" or "Private" Provision of Goods, 22 J. Legal Stud. 47, 61 ff. (1993).

[85] See Pigou, *supra* note 62, ch. 2, at 42–44.

[86] William J. Baumol in On Taxation and the Control of Externalities, 62 Am. Econ. Rev. 307 (1972) has set out a practical scheme for getting around this difficulty, using the example of a smoke-producing factory and adjacent laundries. After fixing a desired level of pollution/cleanliness, you impose a tax and adjust it in the light of experience until the desired level is achieved. He further argues that compensation must not be paid to the laundries. One reason is that this might encourage too many laundries (or whatever) to move into the area—"an excessive influx of neighbours." The influx might be excessive if the aggregate harm resulting was greater than it had been without compensation, when trades sensitive to smoke would keep away. Baumol does not in a short treatment attend to the complexity of his scheme, under which those who moved in, once pollution was reduced, might not be laundries but orchid growers, nudists, or whatever. He also relies on a theoretical argument: public harms are to be analogized to public goods, when one person's use does not reduce the supply of the good to others. So the fact that one adjacent laundry is harmed does not reduce the amount of harm available to another laundry. It is not easy to see why this is an argument against providing compensation.

[87] Coase, *supra* note 1, at 184.

[88] *Id.* at 151.

The subject of interference by government had long excited the political economists, and they tended to say much the same as each other, relying not on formal proofs or empirical studies, but on appeals to common sense and assertions of the supposedly obvious. Thus, J. R. McCulloch back in 1849 ended his chapter on the subject with a typical fanfare, couched in appropriately loaded language: "It cannot, however, be too strongly impressed upon those in authority, that non-interference should be the leading principle of their policy, and interference the exception only; that in all ordinary cases individuals should be left to shape their own conduct according to their own judgement and discretion; and that no interference should ever be made on any speculative or doubtful grounds, but only when its necessity is apparent, or when it can be clearly made out that it will be productive of *public* advantage."[89] The practice was to assert in rhetorical tones, as this example illustrates, the validity of propositions so broad as to be quite incapable of falsification or demonstration. That this technique could be effective cannot be doubted; the most notable victims of the early political economists were the Irish peasants who died in the Great Famine, for Charles Trevelyan, the civil servant responsible, was passionately committed to the view that government intervention in the Irish food market would only make things worse, failing to attend to the fact that so far as the peasantry were concerned there was, as an institution, no food market.[90]

## VI. Pigou as Straw Man

Since Pigou did not express or apparently hold the view attributed to him, the question arises as to what he is doing in the article at all. One possibility is that he functions as a surrogate for what Coase calls the Pigovian tradition. It may well be that in the exposition of Pigou's supposed views by others, but not by him, ideas were expressed by economists, and passed on to their pupils, which conform to Coase's account and formed a coherent oral tradition.[91] Yet if Coase is not really criticizing an economic doctrine purveyed by Pigou, but merely some sort of pervasive sentiment in favor of regulation by the state, it remains hard to see why Pigou is treated as a target.

[89] McCulloch, *supra* note 70, at 308.

[90] By "market" I mean a set of institutional arrangements which facilitate exchange. See C. Woodham-Smith, The Great Hunger (1977), generally and especially at 54–55; Christine Kinealy, This Great Calamity: The Irish Famine, 1845–1852 (1994), esp. ch. 9.

[91] Coase, *supra* note 1, at 149–53. For an example see 1 Hugh Dalton, Call Back Yesterday: Memoirs 1887–1931, at 58 (London, 1953), cited in E. Durbin, New Jerusalems: The Labour Party and the Economics of Democratic Socialism 5 (London, 1985). Durbin's book suggests that control over pollution was not a topic which excited left-wing economists.

The explanation is perhaps this. Coase is anxious to convince his readers that his own skepticism as to the merits of government intervention in the economy is so justified as to raise a presumption against it. Yet it is hard to see how this could be demonstrated. It does not seem to be self-evidently true; as for empirical proof the claim is of such an all-embracing generality that there is no way in which it could be either supported, or attacked, by deploying some body of scientific knowledge called economics. No doubt in particular cases it is possible to come up with evidence of a persuasive or fairly compelling character, but the global claim is neither supportable nor falsifiable. It has no truth value. Those who put forward such global claims report their own political preferences and are reduced to attempting to convince others by rhetoric. For the claim hardly falls short of the assertion that, prima facie, government is a bad thing; it seems difficult to think of any form of government intervention which does not affect the working of the economy. This may or may not be true, but there is just no way of being sure or even mildly confident. Hence Coase, in the tradition of the political economists, adopts a rhetorical device, which is first of all to attribute a commitment to the merits of government intervention to Pigou and then to present Pigou as a deeply confused thinker. The form of the argument then is this: if you believe X, then you are in bad company, for you believe something particularly associated with the thinking of Y, a deeply confused economist. The very fact that Y believed X becomes itself a reason for skepticism.

The function of Coase's second claim relates to this rhetorical device: it is to show how confused a thinker Pigou was.

This second claim is, as I have explained, that in his use of the sparks example Pigou got hold of the wrong end of the stick. The immunity of railways from liability for fire damage, insofar as such immunity exists or used to exist, was itself a *consequence* of governmental action.[92] In *The Firm, the Market and the Law* Coase repeats his point in a passage I have already quoted.[93] In another passage Coase puts his belief that the partial immunity under discussion was the consequence of government action in an even stronger form: "In the real world Pigou's example could only exist as a result of *a deliberate choice of the legislature*."[94] By "governmental action" Coase apparently had in mind some kind of ministerial or cabinet decision expressed in legislation, or at least a decision by Parliament embodied in legislation. In another passage Coase, after

[92] Coase, *supra* note 1, at 138.

[93] See text around note 52 above.

[94] Coase, *supra* note 1, at 138 (my italics).

quoting from an American case,[95] dramatizes his argument. Most economists seem to be unaware that

> [w]hen they are prevented from sleeping at night by the roar of jet planes overhead (publicly authorized and perhaps publicly operated), are unable to think (or rest) in the day because of the noise and vibration from passing trains (publicly authorized and perhaps publicly operated), find it difficult to breathe because of the odour from the local sewage farm (publicly authorized and perhaps publicly operated), and are unable to escape because their driveways are blocked by a road obstruction (without any doubt, publicly devised), their nerves frayed and mental balance disturbed, they proceed to declaim about the disadvantages of private enterprise and the need for governmental regulation.[96]

As R. A. Posner puts it, "Coase appears to be blaming all pollution on government."[97] Of course, horrors of the character of those mentioned by Coase have existed throughout history, long before the rise of the modern regulatory state.[98]

But did Pigou really misunderstand the matter in so serious a way? To answer this question requires some account of the history of this branch of the law.

Railways were never immune from liability; the immunity in question was partial, an immunity from strict liability only. Coase based his view on a passage in *Halsbury's Laws of England,*[99] and although there is a doctrinal sense in which this is correct, it misled Coase. To explain why requires a somewhat tedious analysis of a complex body of nineteenth-century case law.

In the past fires were a major scourge of cities; reported cases are curiously rare, and the problem was handled largely by regulatory controls and techniques other than tort actions.[100] Liability for the escape of fire existed in medieval common law and originally seems to have been centered on house fires, deliberately kindled.[101] In *Turberville v. Stampe* (1697),[102] this liability was extended to cover agricultural fires deliberately kindled. Whether in pre-nineteenth-century law liability for the escape of

[95] Smith v. New England Aircraft Co. (1930), 270 Mass. 511, 170 N.E. 385, at 390.

[96] Coase, *supra* note 1, at 131.

[97] Posner, *supra* note 18, at 410 n.18.

[98] For an account of pollution in Victorian England, see McLaren, *supra* note 3.

[99] Railways and Canals, vol. 31 in Halsbury's Laws of England (Viscount Simonds ed. 1952–64), at 474–75.

[100] Frank Sharman, Fires and Fire Laws up to the Middle of the Eighteenth Century, 22 Cambrian L. Rev. 42 (1991).

[101] The Year Book case is Beaulieu v. Finglam (1401), Y.B. 2 Hen.IV, folio 18, plea 5.

[102] Turberville v. Stampe (1697), 1 Ld.Raym. 264, 91 E.R. 1072.

fire was strict, or based on negligence, or some sort of hotchpotch between them, is obscure. It may be an unreal question, since standards of liability were then matters of jury discretion, rather than questions of law to be settled by the judiciary.

During the eighteenth century a series of fire prevention statutes was passed; they include provisions dealing with fires which began "accidentally."[103] In 1774 a comprehensive *Fires Prevention (Metropolis) Act* was passed;[104] section 86 appears to assume that at common law there might be liability, possibly strict, for fires which escaped from premises but had not been deliberately kindled, but the provision is obscure. The underlying assumption seems to have been that fires which caused damage to neighbors would normally either have been deliberately kindled, and allowed by negligence to spread, or have begun through negligence, but that there might be situations where a fire was accidental in the sense that it had not spread through negligence.[105] The Act of 1774 does not clearly indicate what the standard of liability was then supposed to be, perhaps for the reason I have explained. However, Blackstone in his *Commentaries* (1765–69) thought that the effect of the Act was to exonerate a householder from liability either for his own negligence or that of his servant.[106] However, a servant responsible was made liable to a penalty, with imprisonment in default of payment. Since serious fires would commonly leave a potential defendant without means, tort actions may have had little value.

The first reported nineteenth-century case which explicitly addressed the standard of liability as a matter of law was *Vaughan v. Menlove* (1837).[107] The fire arose from the spontaneous combustion of a hayrick and was spread by the wind to adjacent property. All the lawyers involved assumed that liability must be based on proof of negligence. The case is, indeed, notable as laying down, for the first time, the objective test of negligence in tort law. It contains no suggestion that strict liability applied. *Filliter v. Phippard* (1847) held that the exemption for accidental

[103] 6 Anne c.31 (1707) was a temporary act. It provided that in the case of a fire which began accidentally, the defendant could, if sued, plead the general issue and give this in evidence. The implication is that the jury might treat it as a defense. This act was made perpetual by 10 Anne c.14 (1711) s.1. There were further Acts in 1760 (33 Geo.II c.73) and 1772 (12 Geo.III c.73).

[104] 14 Geo.III c.78.

[105] I base this on a comparison of sections 134 and 136 of the Fires Prevention (Metropolis) Act of 1774.

[106] 1 William Blackstone, Commentaries on the Laws of England 419 (facsimile 1st ed. of 1765–69, Chicago, 1979).

[107] Vaughan v. Menlove (1837), 3 Bing. N.C. 468, 132 E.R. 490, 7 Car. & P. 525, 173 E.R. 232, 4 Scott 244, 3 Hodges 51.

fires provided by the Act of 1772 did not apply to fires begun or spread by negligence, but does not clearly indicate what the common-law rule was then thought to be. It suggests that there was only liability for negligence.[108]

In *Viscount Canterbury v. Attorney General* (1843),[109] Lord Lyndhurst thought that common-law liability was for negligence and was unaffected by the Act of 1774; he referred, in addition to *Vaughan v. Menlove,* to an unreported decision at nisi prius by Baron Alderson, where liability was so based. He decided the case before him on another ground and commented on the curious lack of case law on the matter.

However, during the nineteenth century the idea that liability for accidental damage ought to depend on proof of negligence was in competition with the idea that those who caused damage, or those from whose activities damage resulted, ought to be strictly liable. Strict liability received support some years later in *Rylands v. Fletcher* (1868),[110] a case which did not, however, involve the escape of fire, but of water. Shortly after the decision of the Court of Exchequer Chamber in that case, and in the same year, *Jones v. Festiniog Railway,*[111] which did involve fire, came before the courts. The defendant company had been empowered by an Act of 1832[112] to make and maintain a railway. But the private act gave no express power to operate locomotive steam engines. Probably the original scheme was to use horse-drawn trains. By the mid–nineteenth century the company was using steam locomotives to draw passenger trains. Sparks from an engine burnt the plaintiff's hayrick. Mr. Justice Blackburn, formulator of the "rule in *Rylands v. Fletcher,*" who had delivered the opinion of the Court of Exchequer Chamber in that case, took the view that his rule applied to the escape of fire as well.[113]

Between 1837 and 1860, the latter being the date of *Vaughan v. Taff Vale Railway,*[114] which, as we shall see, was the critical decision on the partial immunity of railways from liability for fire damage, it is by no means easy to say what the common-law principle governing escape of

[108] Filliter v. Phippard (1847), 11 Q.B. 346, 116 E.R. 506.

[109] Viscount Canterbury v. Attorney-General (1843), 1 Phillips 306, 41 E.R. 648.

[110] L.R. 1 H.L. 330.

[111] Jones v. The Festiniog Railroad Company (1868), L.R. 3 Q.B. 733.

[112] 2 Wm.IV c.cxlviii.

[113] The Queen's Bench decided this case on June 26, 1868. Rylands v. Fletcher was decided by the Court of Exchequer Chamber on May 14, 1866, and by the House of Lords on July 17, 1868. By the time the report of *Jones* was published, it was possible to insert a reference to the House of Lords decision.

[114] Vaughan v. The Taff Vale Railway Company (1860), 3 H. & N. 743, 157 E.R. 667, 5 H. & N. 679, 157 E.R. 1351. The case is mentioned by Coase, *supra* note 1, at 137.

fire from steam powered locomotives onto adjacent land was. The point was, as lawyers say, arguable.[115] But all the reported actions against railways for the escape of fire were for negligence.

In 1860, however, *Vaughan v. Taff Vale Railway* ruled, for the first time, that an action against a statutorily authorized railway for the escape of fire had to be based on negligence. But it was not until 1868 that *Jones v. Festiniog Railway* ruled that the common law, in the absence of statutory authorization, imposed strict liability. Hence from 1868 onward such railways as the Taff Vale Railway were thought to enjoy an exemption from what had now become the normal rule. Before 1868 it was by no means clear that this was an exemption. So the partial immunity which Coase discusses was only established, as such, in 1868.

## VII. The Doctrinal Background to *Vaughan v. Taff Vale Railway*

The background to the decision in *Vaughan v. Taff Vale Railway* was as follows.

Railways could be operated without statutory authority, but most sizable ones were authorized by Local and Personal Acts of Parliament—"special" Acts.[116] One reason for these Acts was that the undertakers required power to override private property rights for survey or during construction, and to acquire land compulsorily, on payment of compensation. An enormous range of privately operated utilities were so authorized—canals, turnpike roads, markets, bridges, reservoirs, docks, and of course railways. They were the principal legal underpinning of both the agricultural and the industrial revolutions.[117] Originally each Act would be individually tailored to the particular promotion, but Parliament came to insist on the inclusion of certain standard clauses. The next step was general legislation—"Clauses" Acts—whose provisions were automatically incorporated into individual special Acts. Thus, from 1845 onward all Railway Acts were governed both by the Land Clauses and Railway Clauses (Consolidation) Acts of that year, as well as by the provisions in the special Act.[118]

[115] Further uncertainty arose because a case involving fire damage could be categorized as a nuisance case, and although in a nuisance action it no doubt helped to show that the defendant's operations were negligently conducted, it was not thought essential to do so.

[116] See generally R. W. Kostal, Law and English Railway Capitalism, 1825–1875 (Oxford, 1994), pt. 1. Kostal does not, however, deal with the law relating to property damage caused by railways.

[117] See A. W. B. Simpson, Legal Liability for Bursting Reservoirs: The Historical Context of Rylands v. Fletcher, 13 J. Legal Stud. (1984), at 209, 252–54, and generally.

[118] Rex v. Pease (1832), 8 and 9 Vict. c.18 and c.20. Other examples are the Waterworks Clauses Act of 1847 and Town Police Clauses Act of the same year.

Neither special Acts, nor Clauses Acts, clearly spelled out how the operations of authorized undertakings fitted into the scheme of common-law liability. Only by degrees did there emerge a clear body of principle. The judicial task was not made easier by the fact that during this period the common law itself was not some settled body of doctrine—it too was in a state of flux; the legal culture embodied ideas which pulled in different directions.

The starting point was a criminal case, ***Rex v. Pease*** (1832).[119] It concerned the Stockton and Darlington Railway, the first to be open to public use, constructed and operated under two special Acts.[120] The permitted line ran close to a highway, and trouble arose when steam locomotives were used. The undertakers were indicted at the York Lent Assizes for public nuisance. The indictment alleged that the operation of the railway close to the highway made its use dangerous because "the said engines, furnaces and stoves, and the fires burning therein as aforesaid, exhibit terrific and alarming appearances, and make divers loud explosions, shocks and noises." In defense of the company, J. F. Pollock[121] argued: "The enterprise in this case is private: but it is one in which the public are largely interested. Like Waterloo Bridge, or the London Docks, it has a mixed object; profit for the adventurers, and public benefit." The trial judge, Sir James Parke,[122] influenced by this analysis, based his decision on section 8 of the special Act: "[I]t shall and may be lawful for the said company . . . to make and erect such and so many locomotive or moveable engines as the said company shall from time to time think proper and expedient, and to use and employ the same in and upon the said railway and tramroads."[123] This he thought incompatible with holding that operating the railway was in itself indictable—a nuisance per se. However, neither this nor any other section said anything specific about criminal or civil liability, and he went on to consider whether the act gave the company an absolute power to run the railway without incurring criminal liability: "or only with some implied condition or qualification, that they should employ all practicable means to protect the public against any injury from them." Such means might include building screens, or laying the railway further from the road; if the power was

[119] The King against Edward Pease and others (1832), 4 B. & Ad. 30, 110 E.R. 366. Edward Pease, who came from a Darlington Quaker family, was the entrepreneur principally responsible for the building of the Stockton and Darlington Railway.

[120] 1 & 2 Geo.IV c.xliv and 4 Geo. IV c.xxxiii.

[121] Pollock lived from 1783 to 1870; he was later Chief Baron Pollock.

[122] He was later to become Lord Wensleydale.

[123] 4 Geo. IV c.33.

merely conditional, the running of the railway might or might not be a public nuisance, depending on the circumstances. He might well have taken this view, and many years later, in *Metropolitan Asylum District v. Hill* (1881),[124] the House of Lords applied a doctrine which came close to it. The reasoning in that case could have led to a conviction in *Rex v. Pease,* so long as it would have been possible to site or manage the railway so as not to cause a nuisance. But in the event, the judge held that there was no such qualification. There was nothing unreasonable, he thought, in supposing that the legislature knew that the railway would inconvenience the public, but would compensate for this in the public benefit conferred. The idea that if an activity which would normally constitute a public nuisance could be shown to confer a public benefit, it might not for this reason rank as an indictable nuisance, may have derived from *Rex v. Russell* (1827).[125] The question to be considered was, "Did the public benefit countervail the prejudice to individuals?" This was to become a common argument for immunity in tort law.

The application of this notion to civil liability is first met in an argument presented by Serjeant Bompas in *Aldridge v. Great Western Railway Co.* (1841).[126] However, the court expressed no opinion; the question did not arise, since the action was based on negligence. In another action against a railway, *Piggot v. Eastern Counties Railway Co.* (1846),[127] it was assumed that the common law imposed liability only for negligence and that an authorized railway would be so liable. *Rex v. Pease* was not mentioned, and as the issue was there conceived, no immunity or exception to a general common-law rule was involved.

The application of *Rex v. Pease* to civil liability is first considered judicially in *Vaughan v. Taff Vale Railway* (1857–60).[128]

This case had a curious history. It was tried before Baron Bramwell at the Glamorgan Spring Assizes in 1857. A fire damaged a wood on the Aberdare branch of the railway; it had caught fire on several previous occasions. The action was based on allegations of negligence; at this time it would be supposed in the profession that proof of negligence was necessary, following *Vaughan v. Menlove* (1837). One count alleged negligence in the operation

[124] Metropolitan Asylum District v. Hill (1881), 6 App. Cas. 193.

[125] The King against Russell and others (1827), 6 B. & C. 566, 108 E.R. 560. This was questioned in R. v. Ward (1836), 4 Ad. & E. 385 at 400, 111 E.R. 832 at 837, and in 1873 held to be overruled in Jollife v. Wallasley Local Board (1873), L.R. 9 C.P. 62.

[126] Aldridge v. The Great Western Railway Company (1841), 3 Man. & Gr. 515, 133 E.R. 1246, 4 Scott N.R. 156.

[127] Piggot v. The Eastern Counties Railway Company (1846), 3 C.B. 229, 136 E.R. 92.

[128] November 20, 1858, before the Court en banc 3 H. & N. 743, 157 E.R. 667; before the Exchequer Chamber May 12, 1860, 5 H.& N. 679, 157 E.R. 1351.

of the railway, the other in the management of the bank of the railway. The trial judge, Baron Bramwell, strongly believed in the idea that industry should, as we would now say, internalize its costs. J. P. S. McLaren has pointed out in his classic article how Bramwell believed as strongly in the conception of individual responsibility. In consequence, his decisions were erratic, according to which idea prevailed in a particular case.[129] In *Vaughan v. Taff Vale Railway*, internalization won. He told the jury that "if, to serve his own purposes, a man does a dangerous thing, whether he takes precautions or not, and mischief ensues, he must bear the consequences: that running engines which cast forth sparks, is a thing intrinsically dangerous, and that if a railway engine is used, which in spite of the utmost care and skill . . . is dangerous, the owner must pay for any damage occasioned thereby." This sounds like strict liability, but Baron Bramwell's point was that there must have been negligence or the fire would never have happened. He suggested precautions which might have been taken—the railway banks might have been made of gravel and not covered with inflammable grass. Bramwell's view that the facts spoke for themselves was to be dignified as "res ipsa loquitur" in *Byrne v. Boadle* (1863).[130] The jury obediently found the defendants liable, apparently on the first count. The claim based on the supposedly negligent management of the bank was not taken any further.

The case then went before the full Court of Exchequer. No doubt because it seemed difficult to uphold the direction of Baron Bramwell, if negligence was the basis of liability, counsel now argued that running railway engines was like keeping a dangerous animal, such as a tiger, for which liability was strict. At the time such liability was sometimes explained by saying that keeping a dangerous animal was in itself an unlawful act. Chief Baron Pollock responded to this, distinguishing keeping tigers from running this railway, which the defendants were empowered to run by statute. He referred to *Rex v. Pease*, in which he had as we have seen been counsel for the winning side. It is from this intervention that the civil immunity of authorized railways and other utilities from liability, in the absence of negligence, derives. But as we have seen it was not until some years later, after *Jones v. Festiniog Railway* (1868),[131] that their legal position can be *contrasted* with a normal common-law regime of strict liability. In the event, the court treated the case as a negligence action, and, in an opinion delivered by Baron Bramwell himself, held that his direction was unobjectionable.

[129] McLaren, *supra* note 3.

[130] Byrne v. Boadle (1863), 2 H. & C. 722. Bramwell was one of the judges but delivered no separate opinion.

[131] Jones v. Festiniog Railway Company (1868), L.R. 3 Q.B. 733.

The case then went to the Court of Exchequer Chamber.[132] It ruled that Baron Bramwell had misdirected the jury. Chief Justice Cockburn picked up Pollock's reference to *Rex v. Pease,* saying that if the action of running the railway was authorized, then there was only liability for negligence. The doctrine derived from *Pease* would only of course make a difference if the normal common-law standard of liability, which would apply to fires caused by locomotives operated without express statutory authority, was strict, and the case contains no ruling that this was so. However the reliance on *Pease* made it unnecessary for the court to go into the matter.[133]

Although the Taff Vale Railway Company won the case, it paid the damages, perhaps to head off an appeal to the House of Lords and the risk of a decision unfavorable to the railway interest. Mr. Justice Willes was involved: "[T]he parties afterwards came before me in Chambers and I made an order by consent, staying the proceedings on payment of the damages and costs. The Company in that case had allowed the embankments of the railway to be in such a state as to be peculiarly liable to ignite from anything that might fall from an engine."[134] So the outcome of the case turned on an aspect of the claim never pressed in the actual trial.

The next two cases to raise the matter were *Jones v. Festiniog Railway,*[135] decided by the Queens Bench, consisting of Blackburn and Lush JJ., on June 26, 1868, and *Brand v. Hammersmith and City Railway Co.,*[136] which was before the courts between November 1865 and July 13, 1869, when it was finally determined by the House of Lords.

As we have seen in *Jones v. Festiniog Railway,* Blackburn applied the principle of *Fletcher v. Rylands*[137] to the defendant company. It was conceded that under *Rex v. Pease,* as applied in *Vaughan v. Taff Vale*

[132] Chief Justice Cockburn and Justices Williams, Crompton, Willes, Byles, and Blackburn comprised the court.

[133] Bramwell himself did not rely in any way on *Pease* in supposing that the common-law liability of railways for causing fires depended on proof of negligence. And Bramwell later took the view that both *Pease* and *Vaughan* had been wrongly decided; see Brand v. Hammersmith and City Railway Co. when before the Exchequer Chamber (1867), 2 Q.B. 223, at 230–31.

[134] Sir Thomas Freemantle Bt. and Bliss v. London and North Western Railway Co., 10 C.B. N.S. 89, 142 E.R. 383, and at nisi prius 2 F. & F. 341, 175 E.R. 1088.

[135] Jones v. Festiniog Railway (1868), L.R. 3 Q.B. 733. The action had been heard in the County Court of Carnaervonshire at Portmadoc, and came before the Queen's Bench on a case stated.

[136] Brand v. Hammersmith and City Railway Co. (Nov. 27, 1865), L.R.1 Q.B. 130 (1867), L.R. 2 Q.B. 223 (July 3, 6, 1868, April 22, July 13, 1869), 4 H.L. 171.

[137] Litigated between September 1862 and July 17, 1868. The decision of the Court of Exchequer Chamber was delivered by Blackburn on May 14, 1866. The citation was to the decision of the Court of Exchequer Chamber; see L.R. 1 Ex. 265, 279.

*Railway*, the company would only have been liable for negligence if their operation of steam locomotives had been authorized, but they had not been. Hence, the company was liable even though it had taken all reasonable precautions. And by 1878 Blackburn, now a Lord of Appeal in Ordinary, was able to say in *Geddes v. Proprietors of Bann Reservoir:*[138] "For I take it, without citing cases, that it is now thoroughly well established that no action will lie for doing that which the legislature has authorized, if it be done without negligence."

The reason for Blackburn's confidence was the fact that the House of Lords had, on July 13, 1869, decided the highly controversial case of the *Brand v. Hammersmith and City Railway Co.*[139] in which two out of the three House of Lords judges, Lords Chelmsford and Cairns, expressly approved the *Pease* and *Vaughan* doctrine. Thereafter it was regarded as settled and beyond argument, though it was to be much refined. Decisions of the Lords were at this time binding both on all inferior courts and on the House itself. In 1880, in *Powell v. Fall,*[140] in conformity with the doctrine, the operator of a steam locomotive on the highway, who was not viewed as being statutorily authorized, was held to be strictly liable for a fire caused by escape of sparks.

The line of cases from *Rex v. Pease* through *Vaughan v. Taff Vale Railway* to *Geddes v. Proprietors of Bann Reservoir* settled the partial immunity of railways and other utilities from common-law liability to pay damages for the fires they caused. There was no government decision to this effect, in the sense in which Coase uses this concept. Instead, the doctrine was evolved by the judges, just like the common law itself.

One cannot conclude that Pigou got the history of the matter right; there is absolutely no evidence that he ever addressed the matter. But he did not get hold of the wrong end of the stick; rather, he never got hold of the stick at all. His supposed error serves to dramatize the confusion embodied, so it is argued, in the Pigovian tradition.

## VIII. Dr. Sturges Has Recourse to Litigation

I shall continue to postpone consideration of Coase's third claim and return to *Sturges v. Bridgman*. One of Coase's points is that problems arising from conflicting land use can be settled by a bargain between the parties. The sort of bargain he has in mind involves a one-way payment,

[138] Geddes v. Proprietors of Bann Reservoir (1878), 3 App. Cas. 430, at 455–56.

[139] L.R. 1 Q.B. 130, 2 Q.B. 223, 4 H.L. 171.

[140] Powell v. Fall (1880), 5 Q.B.D. 597 (Court of Appeal, Lord Justices Bramwell, Baggallay and Thesiger). Bramwell said that the hearing had hardened his view that *Pease* and *Vaughan* were wrongly decided.

based on a rational calculation of respective alternatives and costs: "The solution of the problem depends essentially on whether the continued use of the machinery adds more to the confectioner's income than it subtracts from the doctor's."[141] He adds, "Note that what is taken into account is the change in income after allowing for alteration in methods of production, location, character of product, etc." In this passage he seems to be thinking of a bargain after the case was decided, but his reasoning would apply to one preceding litigation as well.

Dr. Sturges did try negotiation, first complaining personally, and then, in the spring of 1876, through his solicitor. The precise form of the negotiations is unrecorded, but from what Mr. Bridgman said in reply we may guess that there was some suggestion that he might arrange to use the mortars at times when the consulting room was not in use. Apparently, the problem was most serious during the London season, that is, from May to the end of July, when the upper classes repaired to London to engage in conspicuous consumption; the defendant's business consequently increased. Dr. Sturges at least believed that the problem had progressively worsened. There are hints in the affidavits of deteriorating personal relations; thus, Dr. Sturges's surveyor was refused access to Mr. Bridgman's property on the second occasion on which he tried to inspect it.

In his affidavit Mr. Bridgman took the line that it was the doctor's problem, not his. He pointed out that Dr. Sturges had "instead of building a separate and distinct wall . . . utilized the North Wall of my said kitchen." He went on to state the length of time the mortars had been in use, and the fact that there had previously been only one complaint, in about 1848. An invalid lady then living in number 85 had asked him not to use the mortars before 8 A.M.; he had explained that in his business this was impossible, and she never complained again. Nor had there been any complaints for 18 months after the consulting room was built. He had done what he could to confine the use of the mortars to times which did not trouble Dr. Sturges; since July 1876 all sugar had been pounded between 8 A.M. and 9.30 A.M., and, in response to the doctor's request, pounding between 11 A.M. and 1 P.M. had been avoided so far as possible. He could do no more if he was to run his business. So it was that nothing was achieved in the negotiations, and the dispute came to litigation, presumably at very considerable cost, much greater in all probability than those eventually incurred by Mr. Bridgman in conforming to the court's order. In the event, Mr. Bridgman would have had to pay these costs.

Negotiation will normally precede litigation in nuisance cases of this

[141] Coase, *supra* note 1, at 106.

character. The story which emerges from the affidavits is a very everyday account of a dispute between neighbors of this kind, with an attempt to work things out amicably. Although we do not know the details, it would be astonishing if Dr. Sturges considered for one moment the possibility of paying Mr. Bridgman money to change his ways, much less that Mr. Bridgman would have considered offering Dr. Sturges money to change his, for example, by reducing the number of patients he saw, or seeing them in his dining room, or whatever. Much less is there any hint that either Dr. Sturges or Mr. Bridgman considered moving elsewhere or changing their employment. It would also be quite astonishing if the doctor and the confectioner approached the matter by supposing that "[t]he solution of the problem depends essentially on whether the continued use of the machinery adds more to the confectioner's income than it subtracts from the doctor's"[142] or that they engaged in some elaborate cost benefit analysis of the infinite range of options open to them. The calculations required would include an assessment—by both Dr. Sturges and Mr. Bridgman of course—of the potential loss of income which Dr. Sturges "would suffer from having to move to a more costly or less convenient location, from having to curtail his activities at this location or (and this was suggested as a possibility) from having to build a separate wall which would deaden the noise and vibration." In fact nobody suggested building a separate wall. The function of the reference to the wall in the affidavit was merely argumentative: Mr. Bridgman was making the point that the trouble was not his fault, but arose because Dr. Sturges's builder did not do a good job.

The elaborate calculations envisaged may perhaps take place in situations in which two forms of land use are, in practical terms, suspected of being quite incompatible. There may be situations in which relocation turns out to be the only viable solution; given the costs of litigation, and the English rule as to responsibility for them, there must, in the nineteenth century, have been many cases in which the victim of pollution relocated, but they do not feature in law reports.[143] Coasean cost benefit analysis bears little relationship to how neighbors usually behave in real life in situations where the situation is not so intolerable as to present the stark choice between litigation or relocation. If they are trying to solve a dispute, they have to accept the broad outlines of the situation: the confectioner's kitchen is going to remain in operation, the consulting room will continue to be used for consulting. To reach an amicable ar-

[142] *Id.*

[143] For nineteenth-century examples of situations in which litigation in private or public nuisance induced a polluting enterprise to relocate, see Simpson, *supra* note 14, ch. 7.

rangement they must accept each other's rights, and concentrate on finding some simple or cheap method whereby the exercise of these rights may be mutually accommodated. No doubt Mr. Bridgman thought he had a perfect right to go on using his mortars as he and his father had done in the past, and you do not offer to pay people money for a right you already possess. He was prepared to behave reasonably and thought he had done so; anyway the trouble was all Dr. Sturges's fault. And no doubt Dr. Sturges, perhaps after taking legal advice from his solicitor, thought that he had a right to peace and quiet in his home, so that he could see his patients and write his lectures, and again you do not offer to pay people money for what is yours already. It was all Mr. Bridgman's fault; all he had to do was to employ an engineer to come up with a new way of arranging his machinery, or perhaps alter his working schedule. In short, I doubt if either of the two men questioned for one moment the right of the other to continue to pursue their business on their property. An offer of money by Dr. Sturges to help over any costs involved in moving or insulating the mortars might well have been socially acceptable, but anything more than that on either side would surely have bordered on the offensive.

The reason why a market transaction in the sense of a purchase and sale of rights is usually not possible in such situations is that the parties are not willing to place their rights in the market. Once this is understood it becomes offensive not to respect this unwillingness. Life would indeed be quite intolerable if individuals did not in general respect social limits to the market—when invited to a dinner party it is unacceptable for a guest to make offers for the silverware or the wine or the pictures which adorn the dining room, or to attempt to sell life insurance to fellow guests.

Hence, solving a conflict of this character does not entail attempting to reach an economically efficient solution to the general question of how the two tracts of land should be used. Nor does it mean agreeing to a market transaction whose paradigm is a sale. It means agreeing on some form of mutual accommodation which brings the dispute to an end, and this will usually be marginal in character. The process resembles the manner in which large numbers of people contrive, by a process of cooperative adjustment, to use a sidewalk without colliding with each other. The aim of the negotiations is not to maximize the value of production; it is more modestly to avoid the costs, in particular legal costs, which will be imposed on both parties if a dispute is not resolved. If what is perceived as expenditure is needed to settle the dispute, then the smaller the expenditure, the better the chances of a solution being agreed. The possibility of reaching some form of marginal accommodation entails accepting the idea that the problem is a reciprocal one, but only in a weak sense which severely limits the range of optional adjustments which the parties are prepared to consider.

Coase argues that an essential prerequisite to the sort of market transaction which he has in mind is that the rights of the parties must be settled or be well defined. Thus, he says: "It is necessary to know whether the damaging business is liable or not for damage caused, since without the establishment of this initial delimitation of rights there can be no market transactions to transfer and recombine them."[144] This may be true of buying and selling, but it is certainly not true over negotiated settlements of problems of land use conflict between neighbors. Even if both Dr. Sturges and Mr. Bridgman agreed to differ on whether or not Bridgman had a right to make the noise, they could perfectly well reach an agreement which resolved any dispute about it. The significance of allocation of rights in a case such as this is surely that it allocates power in negotiations, not that it permits them. If Dr. Sturges is legally in a position to stop Mr. Bridgman from using the mortars, he does not have to bargain with him at all, and he can reject offers from Mr. Bridgman which, if he was rational homo economicus, he would accept. This is sometimes called the problem of hold out, but this characterization is a mistake. In a system of private property law it is not a problem at all. It is, instead, central to the institution, as Sir William Blackstone long ago explained: "There is nothing which so generally strikes the imagination, and engages the affections of mankind, as the right of property; or that sole and despotic dominion which one man claims and exercises over the external things of the world, in total exclusion of the right of any other individual in the universe."[145] Despotic dominion is what the right of private property is all about, and it includes the right to behave in ways which make no contribution whatsoever to the national wealth.

In the event, the negotiations failed, and the case came to court. The judge was Sir George Jessel, Master of the Rolls, and the evidence made it pretty clear, and indeed there was really no dispute, that Mr. Bridgman's activities were seriously interfering with Dr. Sturges's enjoyment of his property. There was no suggestion that Dr. Sturges's activities were causing any problem for Mr. Bridgman. So from a legal point of view, the first question to settle was whether Mr. Bridgman was, as he claimed, entitled to continue his noisy activities, through having, over the years, acquired a right to do so under the fictitious doctrine of lost

[144] Coase, *supra* note 1, at 104. Compare at 158: "the delimitation of rights is an essential prelude to market transactions . . . the ultimate result (which maximizes the value of production) is independent of the legal decision."

[145] Blackstone, *supra* note 106, vol. 2, at 2.

grant. It was more or less conceded that unless Bridgman could show that he had acquired a right to make the noise, he had invaded the rights of Sturges. The judge ruled that no such right had been acquired. It is possible in English law to acquire such a right by long use and acquiescence on the other side, but the judge took the view that until the consulting room came into use the noise was not causing any trouble, and was thus not actionable, nor was Dr. Sturges or his predecessor in a position to stop it. Hence, it would have been wrong to infer that the doctor and previous occupiers of 85 Wimpole Street had in any way acquiesced in the noise.

So Mr. Bridgman had not acquired a right to make the noise, and Dr. Sturges was given his injunction. Plainly, the issue in the case, as seen by Sir George Jessel, had nothing whatever to do with the Coasean question—"whether the continued use of the machinery adds more to the confectioner's income than it subtracts from the doctors."[146] In his scheme of things that was not a matter for a court to decide. The injunction did not go into specifics as to what should be done; it maximized the liberty of the defendant property owner by merely requiring Mr. Bridgman not to use his pestles and mortars "in such a manner or at such times as to be a nuisance to the plaintiff." There was no suggestion that his business must be closed down or relocated. Indeed, Sir George Jessel gave time to Mr. Bridgman "to make the necessary alterations to his premises; and no doubt he would find some skillful mechanic in London who would tell him how to work these machines without making any noise at all." So the injunction was not enforceable until August 1, 1878. This was to reduce the cost of making the accommodation required and minimize the risk of further costly procedures. So here economics indeed played a role, but at the margins.

The case was then taken on appeal, and the main issue ventilated was the same—had Mr. Bridgman acquired a right to make the noise? The judges thought that he had not. An analogy was offered with a hypothetical case: a noisy blacksmith's forge situated in what had long been a barren moor, near which a residence has recently been built:

> As regards the blacksmith's forge, this is really an *idem per idem* case with the present. It would be on the one hand in a very high degree unreasonable and undesirable that there should be a right of action for acts which are not in the present condition of the adjoining land, and possibly never will be any annoyance or inconvenience to either its owner or occupier; and it would be on the other hand in an equal degree unjust, and from a public point of view, inexpedient,

146 See note 35 *supra*.

that the use and value of adjoining land should, for all times and under all circumstances, be restricted or diminished by reason of the continuance of acts incapable of physical interruption, and which the law gives no power to prevent. The smith in the case supposed might protect himself by taking a sufficient curtilage to ensure what he does from being at any time an annoyance to his neighbor, but the neighbor himself would be powerless in the matter.

This opinion of Lord Justice Thesiger claims that any other principle would "produce a prejudicial effect upon the development of land for residential purposes."[147]

The judicial opinions in the case, like the affidavits on which they are based, make not the least attempt to investigate the economic or social value of the activities of either the doctor or the confectioner; legally speaking, such specific questions were quite irrelevant, as they must in general be in a capitalist system which respects the right of private property. It is not the business of the courts to substitute their despotic dominion for that of the litigants. As occupiers of property the parties must be treated equally, respecting their rights to do what they like on their property, however inefficient, so long of course as this does not violate some legal prohibition. The whole point of the law of nuisance is to protect that equality, and in consequence the law intervenes when either party engages in activities which significantly abridge the freedom of their neighbor. Valuable though the distinction is, confusion can be caused here by contrasting entitlements protected by property rules from entitlements protected by liability rules, or property *rights* with liability *rules*.[148] The statement of a property right is the statement of an entitlement which the law protects; in a sense it represents the statement of an ideal. The mechanisms whereby property rights are protected are complex, involving both the criminal and the civil law; legal remedies and procedures represent as it were the outworks of rights. A landowner's property rights are protected by criminal law, property rules, liability rules, not to mention such institutions as that of testamentary succession, contract law, etcetera. The enthusiasm or intensity of protection varies, so that in the case of personal property, much of which is socially fungible, orders for specific restitution are commonly not available. To view this as a legal recognition that people can take other peoples' personal property so long as they pay for it seems to me to be mistaken; in the world we live in, partially structured by law, that is not the understanding. Hence, to do

[147] Sturges v. Bridgman, 11 Ch. D. 865–66.

[148] See William M. Landes & Richard A. Posner, The Economic Structure of Tort Law 29 (Cambridge, 1987), based on Guido Calabresi and A. D. Melamed, Property Rules, Liability Rules and Inalienability: One View of the Cathedral, 85 Harv. L. Rev. 1089 (1972).

so will usually, though not always, constitute a criminal offense. With rights in land, specific recovery in cases of dispossession is available partly because it is more practicable, and partly because land is not treated as fungible. For interference involving entry but no dispossession there are in some instances criminal sanctions, and the civil action of trespass. But the protection provided by trespass would in some contexts be inadequate unless less tangible interference was remedied, and the law of private nuisance offers a remedy. In nineteenth-century English law substantial interference was actionable, giving rise to a right to damages and, by mid-century, an injunction. After some controversy it came to be settled that this basic principle was not to be displaced by the public interest in economic development.[149] The common law rejected the idea of permitting what has come to be called the economically efficient level of pollution. I suppose, though this is nowhere said, that the common law thereby adopted a position of strong defense of the autonomy of property owners and left the hidden hand to worry about economic development. However, the judges, and no doubt juries, in determining what is to rank as an actionable nuisance, have always accepted the idea that some level of mutual tolerance and adjustment between landowners is necessary if life is to go on, given the fact that effects of land use are bound to cross boundaries, and a rough and ready economic calculus has no doubt been significant at the margins. To this weak extent the reciprocal nature of problems of conflicting land use has been accepted by the oracles of the law, and no doubt also by juries. In modern American law such decisions as that in the well-known and controversial case of *Boomer v. Atlantic Cement Co.*[150] have retreated from the protection of property rights by refusing injunctions in situations in which, although there is substantial interference, the cost of abating a nuisance is thought to be very much greater than the damage caused; given certain arrangements about the recovery of damages, this may allow a polluting landowner to acquire the right to pollute without the consent of the victim on payment of a price fixed by the court, a bizarre state of affairs in a capitalist society. But even today, and certainly not in the nineteenth century, courts do not enter into general open-ended investigations of the efficient use of adjacent tracts of land and allocate rights accordingly. To do that would be the end of the right of private property. The Boomer

[149] See Simpson, *supra* note 11, ch. 7, discussing Tipping v. St. Helen's Smelting Co. (1865), 4 B. & S. 608, 616, 122 E.R. 588, 591, 11 H.L.C. 642, 11 E.R. 1483, 1 Ch. App. Cas. 66.

[150] Boomer v. Atlantic Cement Company (1970), 26 N.Y. 2d. 219, 257 N.E. 2d. 870, 309 N.Y.S. 2d. 312. For discussion, see Landes & Posner, *supra* note 148, at 44 ff.

case certainly seriously weakens the protection of that right. In nineteenth-century law economic considerations operated only at the margins, and then impressionistically, as when Jessel in *Sturges v. Bridgman* guessed that Mr. Bridgman would find some fairly cheap way of dealing with the problem caused by his mortars.

The judge seems to have been right, for Mr. Bridgman, somehow or other, dealt with the problem. The business did not move as a result of the litigation, and in due course Bridgman's son, whose name was James, joined him, appearing for example in *Kelly's Directory* for 1888 and 1889. But in 1891 James is in business at 792 Old Kent Road, and the Bridgmans do not figure in the *Directory* for 1890, so we may assume that Frederick died or retired in that year. Figures produced for the litigation, designed to rebut the argument that the nuisance was increasing, indicated that in 1878 the gross income of Bridgman's business had been falling for some years—in 1852–53 it had been £9,416, but in 1876–77 it was £5,340, and it presumably eventually became unprofitable. At about the turn of the century, 28–34 Wigmore Street was redeveloped and became Norfolk Mansions, the building which now stands on the site.

As for Dr. Sturges he practiced from 85 Wimpole Street until his death. In spite of the success of his action, he became rather deaf, and he did not hear the approach of a rubber-tired hansom cab which knocked him down in Cavendish Square on October 16, 1894. He died of internal injuries at his home on November 3. The premises at 85 Wimpole Street, however, remain just as they were at the time of the litigation and are now occupied by Adlers, a firm of Surveyors, Estate Agents, and Property and Development Consultants, who use Dr. Sturges's consulting room for their meetings. If you visit there you will see the original roof light, installed no doubt to enable the doctor the more easily to examine his patients and indicating to this day the original function of the room.

## IX. Pigou's Fundamental Error

It is now time to return to Coase's third claim, again based on the sparks example. It is that the Pigovian conclusion—that the railway be required to compensate—was based on a fundamentally flawed analysis. The Pigovian view, so Coase argued, was that a divergence between social and private net products justified state action to correct the divergence; hence, what needed to be compared was social and private net product. According to Coase what needs to be compared is the social net product without government action and the social net product with government action. Is the world a better place after intervention than it was before? And Coase's instinct is to expect that commonly it will be worse. Whether this expectation is correct or not, Coase certainly shows that it can be worse. He gives a hypothetical example, giving figures as to crop loss and so on, which show that if the railway was liable to compensate it would not be run. But if it was run, then the value of total production would be increased by $20. He goes on: "Of course, by altering the figures, it could be shown that there are other cases in which it would be desirable that the railway should be liable for the damage it causes. It is enough for my purpose to show that, from an economic point of view, a situation in which there is 'uncompensated damage done to surrounding woods by sparks from railway engines' is not necessarily undesirable. Whether it is desirable or not depends on the particular circumstances."[151] This illustration is intended to show that the Pigovian analysis is fundamentally flawed.

The next paragraph explains why. Now one basic reason why Pigovian analysis might be wrong, and which would be compatible with much of what Coase says, is this. Whenever the government intervenes in the world, the world can and does alter in response to that intervention. The world with the intervention is not just the same world as it was before, with the intervention added. It is a world changed in other respects. It may respond in ways which may bring about a worse state of affairs than the one we started with. Thus, suppose the city of Pigovia has a considerable rat population, and news of the approach of bubonic plague induces the government to introduce a bounty system to encourage rat control, fifty cents for each rat tail delivered to the local rat bounty office. Enterprising children find it profitable to breed rats in disused buildings in order to collect the bounty; their security arrangements are lax, and many rats escape. Soon the bounty-issuing officers find it profitable to resell tails back to those presenting them for forty cents or less; tails may under this system be presented numerous times. Entrepreneurs import tails from abroad. In order to counter these and other abuses, the City has to expend considerable sums enhancing customs control and policing the bounty offices. Rumors of a change in the bounty rate induce entrepreneurs to establish a rat tail futures market; this outrages local citizens who believe in animal rights, who start a powerful Save the Rat movement. Riots break out, and the premises of those selling rat traps and rat poison are burned down. The City diverts funds from public health to riot control. Soon there are more rats in Pigovia than there ever were before. . . . Awareness that this sort of thing may happen does not of

[151] Coase, *supra* note 1, at 140–41. It is of course undesirable for the owner of the wood, whose interests are to be sacrificed to some conception of the common good. Note how Coase himself here employs the notion of causation to set up the example.

course point to any particular view as to the merits of government intervention in general; all we can do is our best in a world in which information is often lacking and prediction difficult.

Secondary responses might be the crux of the matter. But in the bulk of the paragraph which follows the illustration, Coase does not identify Pigou's fundamental error in this way at all.[152] What he says is quite different. He writes:

> The question at issue is not whether it is desirable to run an additional train or a faster train or to install smoke preventing devices; *the question at issue is whether it is desirable to have a system in which the railway has to compensate those who suffer damages from the fires which it causes or one in which the railway does not have to compensate them.* When an economist is comparing alternative social arrangements, the proper procedure is to compare the total social product yielded by these different arrangements. The comparison of private and social products is neither here nor there.

Coase gives the example of a motorist who, because he would otherwise be fined, stops at a red traffic light although there is no risk of an accident if he did not stop. If he passed the light, the social product would be increased since he would reach his destination earlier; he stops because private product would be decreased by the fine. The invitation is to agree that this would be no reason for altering the general rule whereby motorists who cross red light are fined. We need to compare a system in which motorists have to stop with one in which they do not, and Coase seems to think it obvious what the answer would be; he does not consider a range of possible other systems.[153] So the Pigovian error is not to compare the social product of systems.

At the end of the paragraph, however, he makes a point which is much closer to my first suggestion: "The Pigovian analysis shows us that it is possible to conceive of better worlds than the one in which we live. But the problem is to devise practical arrangements which will correct defects in one part of the system *without causing more serious harm in other parts.*"[154] Elsewhere, when criticizing the use of the notion of causation, which notion he himself here uses, he hints at a quite different point: the Pigovian error is failing to see that the farmer (in the sparks example)

[152] *Id.* at 141–42 (my italics).

[153] For example, permitting the motorist to turn right on red or whatever.

[154] Coase, *supra* note 1, at 142 (my italics). This, for better or for worse, is one of the classic conservative arguments for resisting change, familiar to anyone who has sat through a few faculty meetings.

might be the cheapest cost avoider.[155] This is a familiar interpretation of his essay.

So it does not seem to me to be entirely clear what the Pigovian error is. Perhaps a fair interpretation would be to say that Pigou did not realize that what must be compared, in the case of fire damage from engines, was the world with and the world without a system of enforced compensation and that in constructing the two worlds for comparison we must take into account all possible courses of action, and not just changes in behavior by one party identified by the conception of active causation. This would be a sort of amalgam of the points which Coase makes. One could perhaps add another point, which is that in the calculus any public good produced by the railway ought to be included—perhaps its activities give enormous pleasure to railway buffs.

It also does not seem to me to be absolutely clear whether Coase, in "The Problem of Social Cost," is suggesting that courts ought, in deciding cases such as *Sturges v. Bridgman,* to engage in economic analysis along the lines he recommends. Some passages seem consistent with the view that he does think this. Thus, he criticizes the judges who decided the case for being unaware of the correct economic analysis of the problem presented by the litigation; the only point of being aware of it would be for it to influence their decision.[156] He argues that because transaction costs may impede the reaching of an economically efficient solution by bargain it is desirable to reduce the need for bargains; this implies that courts ought to pay heed to considerations of efficiency by coming to a conclusion as to what bargain the landowners would have reached in an ideal world people by homines economici.[157] He also suggests in what seem to be tones of approval that to a limited extent the judges did consider the economic consequences of their decision in *Sturges v. Bridgman.*[158] From a passage which I have already quoted, which is in the opinion of Lord Justice Thesiger, Coase drew the conclusion that the judges thought they were "settling how the land involved in the case was to be used"[159] But other passages appear to concede that courts and economists are engaged in different enterprises and that courts may be

[155] *Id.* at 96–97.

[156] *Id.* at 107.

[157] *Id.* at 119.

[158] *Id.* at 107, 122.

[159] *Id.* at 107. The passage continues by saying that this belief would only be true "in the case in which the costs of carrying out the necessary market transaction exceeded the gain which might be achieved by any arrangement of rights." I do not think Coase's interpretation of the opinion of Thesiger is correct, but that does not affect the argument here.

properly influenced by noneconomic considerations.[160] I do not think it is possible to obtain from "The Problem of Social Cost" any clear picture of the degree to which Coase thinks that courts should allow economic considerations to condition their decisions; it was not a subject which he directly addressed. Others may have read into Coase's article views which are not really to be found there. And certainly Coase does not address the procedural complexities.

I suppose it is conceivable that a court might, in a case like *Sturges v. Bridgman,* allocate the rights of the parties in such a way as to maximize their view of economic efficiency. One thing this would mean would be that the court would decide whether peace and quiet for Dr. Sturges would contribute more to the gross national product than pounded loaf sugar for Mr. Bridgman. Under the strong sense of reciprocity, a more or less infinite range of alternative courses of action is open to the doctor and the confectioner, and the resulting cost benefit analysis, unless some sort of limit was imposed on its scope, would occupy the court for a lifetime. In any event, the data required did not then exist, and would not exist today in a comparable case. The imagination boggles at the complexities. The idea seems wholly fanciful. This is certainly not the way the judges approached the matter, nor is it the way the parties asked them to approach it. The affidavits presented by the parties address four questions—the severity of the noise, the length of time the mortars have been in use, whose fault it is that the problem exists, and the practicality and cost of some adjustment in behavior which might make the problem go away. They are simply not concerned with questions of social net product, nor do they address alternative possibilities.

Suppose for one moment that the court, in allocating the rights of the parties, did attend to general considerations of economic efficiency along the lines suggested by Coase's argument, and suppose, for the sake of argument, that a cost benefit analysis was practicable. There is an even more radical difficulty. The comparison I have suggested, if limited to the circumstances of the dispute between doctor and confectioner, would not be a comparison of *systems*. To put the point in a slightly different way, a cost benefit analysis of the facts of a particular dispute will generate no general rule even as to what should be done about disputes between doctors and confectioners, or denizens of Wigmore and Wimpole Street. It inexorably follows from Coase's analysis that imposing liability may in some cases makes things better, in others worse. But law has to operate through generalization refined only to a limited extent by excep-

[160] *Id.* at 114. See in particular the passage at the top of the page.

tions. This conclusion has no doubt occurred to him, and in the passage I have already quoted, which seems to me to be of critical importance, he seems to try to escape his own logic and propose a way in which economic analysis can generate a general rule. Hence the sudden appearance of systems. Let me quote it again: "[T]he question at issue is whether it is desirable to have a *system* in which the railway has to compensate those who suffer damage from the fires which it causes or one in which the railway does not have to compensate them."[161] So, in terms of law, railways either have to compensate, or not.

How one can compare two *systems* in terms of their contribution to wealth creation is nowhere explained, and the idea seems again to be wholly fanciful, the complexity being quite limitless.

Nor is this the only problem. In addition there is a critical question of initial definition: what systems do you compare? A system for railways limited to sparks from engines, another for straying cattle? Or atmospheric pollution? Or cats? Or more generally, a system covering all damage to neighbors? There is the further problem of allocating effects to a particular activity. Cost benefit analysis is no doubt a valuable activity, but cost benefit analysis in the air is the stuff of dreams or nightmares, not of practical government and law.

In view of the problems I have indicated, it is not easy to see how Coasean economics can provide guidance for lawyers, whose business is with general rules, as to what ought to be done about the problem of social cost. Everything will turn on the particular facts of different situations; on this at least Pigou was right, and the consequence is that no general economic solution is possible.

My conclusion is that the arguments presented by Coase in his criticism of Pigou, and the use to which Pigou is said to have put the sparks example, are unconvincing, and that the idea of employing economic analysis and the Coasean conception of reciprocity, with all its implications, to resolve problems which are currently handled by courts as raising questions of social, political, or moral rights is beset with some very serious difficulties. It is at least arguable, though I myself can see no strict way in which this could be demonstrated, that courts make their most useful contribution to economic efficiency in a capitalist system when they studiously avoid attempting to second-guess the operations of the hidden hand and confine their activities to the vigorous protection of rights.

[161] *Id.* at 141–42 (my italics).

# Part VII
# Experimental Tests of the Coase Theorem

# [27]

# THE COASE THEOREM: SOME EXPERIMENTAL TESTS*

*ELIZABETH HOFFMAN* *and* *MATTHEW L. SPITZER*
*Purdue University* *University of Southern California*

## I. Introduction

In *The Problem of Social Cost,*[1] Ronald Coase investigated the economic effects of liability rules for externalities when the affected parties can bargain with each other. More specifically, Coase posited that a change in a liability rule will leave the agents' production and consumption decisions both unchanged and economically efficient within the following (implicit) framework: (*a*) two agents to each externality (and bargain), (*b*) perfect knowledge of one another's (convex) production and profit or utility functions, (*c*) competitive markets, (*d*) zero transactions costs; (*e*) costless court system,[2] (*f*) profit-maximizing producers and expected utility-maximizing consumers, (*g*) no wealth effects, (*h*) agents will strike mutually advantageous bargains in the absence of transactions costs. This result—commonly called the "Coase Theorem"—has generated a great deal of economic and legal discussion, much of it aimed at exploring the effects of weakening one or another of the model's assumptions.[3] Some of the most common theoretical discussions focus on the

* We wish to thank Frank Easterbrook, Daniel Fischel, Charles R. Plott, Daniel Polsby, Alvin Roth, and members of the Northwestern University School of Law Workshop, the Stanford University Law and Economics Workshop, and the University of Illinois at Champaign-Urbana Regulation Workshop for their helpful comments. All errors are, of course, our own. Research support was provided by Northwestern University's College of Arts and Sciences and School of Law.

[1] R. H. Coase, The Problem of Social Cost, 3 J. Law & Econ. 1 (1960).

[2] This assumption includes the existence of enough basic contract and tort law and enforcement that the parties can deal with one another. On the philosophy of such an assumption, see David W. Carroll, Two Games That Illustrate Some Problems Concerning Economic Analysis of Legal Problems, 53 S. Cal. L. Rev. 1371 (1980).

[3] Literature on the Coase Theorem has explored, among other things, the following topics. (*A*) The long-run wealth effects of a change in liability rules: see, for example, Harold Demsetz, Wealth Distribution and the Ownership of Rights, 1 J. Legal Stud. 223 (1972); H. E. Frech, III, Pricing of Pollution: The Coase Theorem in the Long Run, 4 Bell J. Econ. & Manag. Sci. 316 (1973); H. E. Frech, III, Extended Coase Theorem and Long-Run Equilib-

[*Journal of Law & Economics,* vol. XXV (April 1982)]

effects of transaction costs, especially those costs generated either by imperfect knowledge of one another's production and profit functions[4] or by the need to include many agents in a bargain.[5] Many observers have theoretically assumed (or deduced) that imperfect information or multiple agents in a bargain will tend to preclude contracting by the affected parties.[6] A great deal of legal and economic work rests directly on these two theoretical assumptions.[7]

---

rium: The Nonequivalence of Liability Rules and Property Rights, 17 Econ. Inquiry 254 (1979); T. T. Maloney, The Coase Theorem and Long-Run Industry Equilibrium, 17 Q. Rev. Econ. & Bus. 113 (1977); G. Warren Nutter, The Coase Theorem on Social Cost: A Footnote, 11 J. Law & Econ. 503 (1968); Donald H. Regan, The Problem of Social Cost Revisited, 15 J. Law & Econ. 427 (1972); William Schulze & Ralph C. d'Arge, The Coase Proposition, Information Constraints, and Long-Run Equilibrium, 64 Am. Econ. Rev. 763 (1974). (*B*) The property rule/liability rule distinction: see, for example, Guido Calabresi & A. Douglas Melamed, Property Rules, Liability Rules and Inalienability: One View of the Cathedral, 85 Harv. L. Rev. 1089 (1972); Harold Demsetz, When Does the Rule of Liability Matter? 1 J. Legal Stud. 13 (1972); Harold Demsetz, The Exchange and Enforcement of Property Rights, 7 J. Law & Econ. 11 (1964); Roger Feldman, Liability Rules and the Transfer of Economic Rents, 3 J. Legal Stud. 499 (1974): Frech, "Extended Coase Theorem and Long-Run Equilibrium," *supra* note 3*A*; Ken-Ichi Inada & Kiyoshi Kuga, Limitations of the "Coase Theorem" on Liability Rules, 6 J. Econ. Theory 606 (1973). (*C*) A definition of transaction costs and their effect on the efficient assignment of legal rules: see, e.g., Guido Calabresi, Transaction Costs, Resource Allocation, and Liability—a Comment, 11 J. Law & Econ. 67 (1968); Thomas D. Crocker, Externalities, Property Rights, and Transaction Costs: An Empirical Study, 14 J. Law & Econ. 451 (1971); George Daly, The Coase Theorem: Assumptions, Applications, and Ambiguities, 12 Econ. Inquiry 203 (1974); A. Mitchell Polinsky, Economic Analysis as a Potentially Defective Product: A Buyers Guide to Posner's Economic Analysis of Law, 87 Harv. L. Rev. 1655, 1671–74 (1974); Richard A. Posner, Economic Analysis of Law, 34 (2d ed. 1977). (*D*) The consequences of imperfect information and the need for a well defined theory of "rational" behavior: see, for example, Otto A. Davis & Andrew B. Whinston, Externalities, Welfare and the Theory of Games, 70 J. Pol. Econ. 241 (1962); Regan, *supra* note 3A; Schulze & d'Arge, *supra* note 3*A*; George J. Stigler, The Theory of Price, 113 (3d ed. 1966); Cento G. Veljanovski, The Coase Theorem—the Says Law of Welfare Economics, 53 Econ. Record 535 (1977). (*E*) The inclusion of large numbers of agents in the contracting situation: see, for example, William J. Baumol, On Taxation and the Control of Externalities, 62 Am. Econ. Rev. 307 (1972); Calabresi & Melamed, *supra* note 3*B*; Daly, *supra* note 3*C*; Posner, *supra* note 3*C*; Stanislaw Wellisz, On External Economies and the Government Assisted Invisible Hand, 31 Economica 345 (n.s. 1964).

[4] See *supra* note 3, those publications dealing with the consequences of imperfect information and the need for a well-defined theory of "rational" economic behavior.

[5] See *supra* note 3, those publications dealing with the inclusion of large numbers of agents in the contracting situation.

[6] See, for example, Davis & Whinston, *supra* note 3*D*; Regan, *supra* note 3*A*; Schulze & d'Arge, *supra* note 3*A*; Stigler, *supra* note 3*D*; Veljanovski, *supra* note 3*D*; Baumol, *supra* note 3*E*; Calabresi & Melamed, *supra* note 3*B*.

[7] See, for example, Stanley M. Besen, William G. Manning, & Bridger M. Mitchell, Copyright Liability for Cable Television: Compulsory Licensing and the Coase Theorem, 21 J. Law & Econ. 67 (1978); Guido Calabresi, The Decision for Accidents: An Approach to

In 1972, Donald Regan pointed out that assumption *h* is quite unlike assumptions about agents' behavior in most economic models.[8] For example, a proof of the existence of the competitive equilibrium might presume that an individual maximizes utility subject to a budget constraint in the face of fixed prices by purchasing commodities in a market. In contrast, *h* posits that two specific individuals who find themselves in a position to strike a mutually advantageous bargain *will do so*. This assumption is, in essence, a statement that parties in non–zero-sum games

Nonfault Allocation and Costs, 78 Harv. L. Rev. 730 (1965); Reuben A. Kessel, Transfused Blood Serum Hepatitis and the Coase Theorem, 17 J. Law & Econ. 265 (1974); Frederic L. Kirgis, Effective Pollution Control in Industrialized Countries: International Economic Disincentives, Policy Responses, and the GATT, 70 Mich. L. Rev. 859 (1972).

[8] Regan, *supra* note 3*A*. Assumption *h* is clearly needed to prove the theorem; none of the other assumptions guarantees that two agents who are in a position to strike a mutually advantageous deal will do so. The assumption of profit-maximizing producers (or expected utility-maximizing consumers) guarantees only *individual* rationality. Most economic models take such assumptions about individual rationality and impose some sort of mechanism or institution, such as a market, which combines the individually rational choices into a group outcome. The Coase Theorem proffers only the existence of basic contract law, which will be perfectly and costlessly enforced by the court system. The Coase Theorem also needs an assumption which provides for combining individually rational behavior into a group outcome. Instead of providing some specific mechanism, such as allowing one of the two parties to propose a deal and let the other accept if and only if accepting the deal would increase the acceptor's individual utility (or profits), assumption *h* makes the most general proposition that eventually some sort of deal will be struck. Hence, assumption *h* is the analog, in the Coase Theorem, of the assumption in a market model that consumers *will actually purchase* the goods and services, subject to a budget constraint, which maximize their utilities. Furthermore, assumption *h* is not captured by the assumption of zero transaction costs. It may be that even though the parties can negotiate and transact costlessly, one or both of the parties may behave strategically so as to capture more profits for himself. As Regan, *supra* note 3*A*, p. 430, notes, the essence of making credible threats is to carry them out, sometimes. But once a threat is carried out the Coase Theorem has failed. Even if such threats are not carried out, each party may continually threaten to refuse to agree to a deal unless that party receives quite favorable treatment. Parties can refuse to agree to the deal indefinitely. The only way to handle this dilemma for the Coase Theorem is to assume that the parties *will* strike a deal. Consider, in this vein, the argument found in William M. Landes & Richard A. Posner, Salvors, Finders, Good Samaritans, and Other Rescuers: An Economic Study of Law and Altruism, 7 J. Legal Stud. 83, 91 (1978): "Even where there is both mental capacity and adequate time for negotiating, the process of voluntary exchange may not work efficiently. Suppose the sinking ship is far out at sea—though in no immediate danger of sinking—and a potential rescuer comes upon it by chance or by responding to its distress signal. There is time for negotiation but little likelihood of another ship's chancing on the scene. The potential rescuer therefore has a monopoly position which he can use to try to extract the victim's promise, prior to initiation of any rescue efforts, to pay him all or most of the value of the ship and cargo. At the same time, because the rescuer has no alternative customer for his rescue services at the place where he has found the ship in distress, the "rescuee" has a monopoly position, making the situation one of bilateral monopoly. Transaction costs under bilateral monopoly are high because there is a range of possible prices which invites haggling. The haggling may be protracted, costly, and sometimes unsuccessful in producing agreement on terms." Assumption *h* also rules out both

will choose a Pareto optimal allocation.[9] As such, assumption *h* represents a departure from the conventional wisdom, which is that outcomes of non-zero-sum games are quite uncertain. Hence, Coase's Theorem is much more a proposition than a typical economic theorem. Once the analyst fully accepts this point, the Coase Theorem's appeal depends on the reasonableness of assumption *h* in a typical Coase Theorem setting. In other words, one must know whether two people who are in a situation satisfying assumptions *a* through *g* will tend to act in accordance with assumption *h*.

In addition, as is noted above, a great deal of important legal and economic work stands on the supposition that either including many parties to a bargaining situation (assumption *a*) or including imperfect information (assumption *b*) tends to preclude the formation of mutually advantageous contracts.[10] For example, Calabresi and Melamed use these suppositions to analyze the differences between property rules and liability rules.[11] To test these suppositions, one must know of the effects of relaxing assumption *a* (multiple parties) in the presence of assumptions *b* through *h*, of relaxing assumption *b* (imperfect information) in the pres-

---

personal or social pressures which militate against contracting. If one of the parties to an externality were to believe that contracting is inherently evil, or that the behavior involved in the externality is terrible, the individual might refuse to ever sign a contract which pertained to the externality, and the Coase Theorem might fail. Social pressures could affect willingness to contract in an asymmetric fashion. For example, in Coase's original example of a rancher and a farmer, there were no social pressures on the two parties to resist economic forces. However, if cows were considered sacred to the extent that one who signed a contract to limit the number of cows kept on a ranch would be shunned by his friends, but no such attitude would exist toward a contract which increased the number of cows to be kept, then the following results might be obtained. First, if the farmer had a property right to exclude cows, so that the rancher had to obtain the farmer's permission to have a herd, then the farmer and rancher would strike a deal allowing the rancher to keep some cows. Second, if the rancher had a property right to have as many cows as he wished, so that the rancher and farmer could joint-profit maximize only by striking a deal to limit the number of cows the rancher would keep, then no deal would be struck. Such a pair of results would violate the Coase Theorem, and assumption *h* rules out all such problems. Of course, to the extent that the reader remains unconvinced that assumption *h* does not flow naturally from the other assumptions, he will not be particularly interested in (or surprised by) the strong appeal of the Pareto optimal outcome in the two-person, full-information experiments. Such a reader, however, should still be quite interested in the three-person and partial information variations on the Coase scenario which we test.

[9] A Pareto optimal allocation has the property that it is not possible to make one person better off without making another person worse off. In a non-zero-sum game a Pareto optimal allocation maximizes the joint profits from the game.

[10] See Crocker, *supra* note 3*C*; Mark Kelman, Consumption Theory, Production Theory and Ideology in the Coase Theorem, 52 S. Cal. L. Rev 669 (1979); Matthew Spitzer & Elizabeth Hoffman, A Reply to Kelman's Consumption Theory, Production Theory, and Ideology in the Coase Theorem, 53 S. Cal. L. Rev. 1187 (1980).

[11] Calabresi & Melamed, *supra* note 3*B*.

ence of assumptions *a* and *c* through *h*, and of relaxing assumptions *a* and *b* (multiple parties and imperfect information) in the presence of assumptions *c* through *h*.

## II. Review of the Literature

There is a large and growing experimental literature on two- and three-person bargaining games. Many of the experiments illuminate one or more of the axioms discussed above, but almost no work has specifically tested the Coase bargaining problem in the specific ways discussed above.[12] However, we can make some important generalizations, which have significant implications for the design of an experiment. The main issue is whether parties to a bargain will choose a Pareto optimal allocation. Although subjects playing non–zero-sum games have not universally chosen Pareto optimal outcomes, in general they have tended to choose Pareto optimal outcomes more often when the experimental conditions have looked more like the Coase axioms. In particular, Pareto optimal choices seem to be more frequent under the following conditions: (1) When subjects play for significant amounts of real money,[13] (2) when all parties can engage in free face-to-face communications,[14] (3) when parties can make

[12] Jerome Chertkoff & James K. Esser, A Review of Experiments in Explicit Bargaining, 12 J. Experimental Soc. Psych. 464 (1976); Melvin J. Guyer & Barbara Perkel, Experimental Games: A Bibliography (1945–1971), 293 U. Mich. Mental Health Research Inst. Com. (1972); J. Keith Murningham, Models of Coalition Behavior: Game Theoretic, Social Psychological and Political Perspectives, 85 Psych. Bull. 1130 (1978). The only paper specifically on the Coase Theorem of which we are aware is Yves Coffi Prudencio, The Voluntary Approach to Externality Problems: An Experimental Test (Discussion Paper, 81-4, U. Ariz., Dep't Econ., 1981). The design of the experiments reported in that paper are quite different from the design of the experiments reported here.

[13] Victor Daniels, Communication, Incentive, and Structural Variables in Interpersonal Exchange and Negotiation, 3 J. Experimental Soc. Psych. 47 (1976); Philip S. Gallo, Jr., & Charles G. McClintock, Cooperative and Competitive Behavior in Mixed-Motive Games, 9 J. Conflict Resolution 68 (1965); H. H. Kelly *et al.*, A Comparative Experimental Study of Negotiation Behavior, 16 J. Personality & Soc. Psych. 411 (1970); Charles G. McClintock & Steven P. McNeel, Reward Level and Game Playing Behavior, 10 J. Conflict Resolution 98 (1966); Charles G. McClintock & Steven P. McNeel, Prior Dyadic Experience and Monetary Reward as Determinants of Cooperative and Competitive Game Behavior, 5 J. Personality & Soc. Psych. 282 (1967); Steven M. Medlin, Effects of Grand Coalition Payoffs on Coalition Formation in Three-person Games, 21 Behavioral Sci. 48 (1976).

[14] Chertkoff & Esser, *supra* note 12; Daniel Druckman, The Influence of the Situation in Inter-party Conflict 15 J. Conflict Resolution 523 (1971); Rudy V. Nydegger and Guillermo Owen, Two-person Bargaining: An Experimental Test of the Nash Axioms, 1 Int'l J. Game Theory 239 (1975); Alvin Roth & Michael Malouf, Game-theoretic Models and the Role of Information in Bargaining, 588 (Working Paper, U. Ill. at Urbana-Champaign, C. Com. and Bus. Ad. Faculty 1979); Richard G. Swennsson, Cooperation in the Prisoner's Dilemma Game I: The Effects of Asymmetric Payoff Information and Explicit Communication, 12 Behavioral Sci. 314 (1967); Harvey Wickman, Effects of Isolation and Communication on Cooperation in a Two-person Game, 16 J. Personality & Soc. Psych. 114 (1970).

enforceable contracts with one another,[15] (4) when there is an equal-split allocation among the Pareto optimal allocations,[16] (5) when all parties have full information about one another's payoffs,[17] and (6) when prizes are paid in public.[18] The first five conditions are all clearly contained in the Coase axioms. The last condition seems to be a natural extrapolation from Coase's perfect information and zero transaction costs assumptions.

A second issue, which Coase himself does not raise but which has troubled some commentators,[19] is how parties to a bargain typically divide the profits from a joint decision. The experimental literature differs on this issue. On the one hand, many articles conclude that subjects divide profits either equally or in proportion to the effort each party expends.[20] On the

[15] Peter Murdoch, Development of Contractual Norms in a Dyad, 6 J. Personality & Soc. Psych. 206 (1967); Harold H. Kelley, Linda Linden Beckman, & Claude S. Fisher, Negotiating the Division of a Reward under Incomplete Information, 3 J. Experimental Soc. Psych. 361 (1967); Robert Radlow & M. F. Weidner, Unenforced Commitments in Cooperative and Non-cooperative None-constant Sum Games, 10 J. Conflict Resolution 497 (1966); John Thibaut, The Development of Contractual Norms in Bargaining: Replications and Variation, 12 J. Conflict Resolution 102 (1968); John Thibaut & Claude Faucheaux, The Development of Contractual Norms in Bargaining Situations under Two Types of Stress, 1 J. Experimental Soc. Psych. 89 (1965); John Thibaut & Charles L. Gruder, Formulation of Contractual Agreements between Parties of Unequal Power, 11 J. Personality and Soc. Psych. 59 (1969).

[16] Lawrence E. Fouraker & Sidney Siegel, Bargaining Behavior (1963); H. Andrew Michener, Irving J. Ginsberg, & Kenneth Yuen, Effects of Core Properties in Four-person Games with Side Payments, 24 Behavioral Sci. 263 (1979); Sidney Siegel & Lawrence E. Fouraker, Bargaining and Group Decision Making: Experiments in Bilateral Monopoly (1960).

[17] William P. Smith, Reward Structure and Information in the Development of Cooperation, 4 J. Experimental Soc. Psych. 199 (1968).

[18] Druckman, *supra* note 14.

[19] See Demsetz, *supra* note 3*B*; Bruce A. Ackerman, Economic Foundations of Property Law (Questions 2–5) (1975).

[20] See, for example, Irving M. Lane & Lawrence A. Messe, Equity and the Distribution of Rewards, 20 J. Personality & Soc. Psych. 1 (1971); Gerald S. Leventhal, James W. Michaels, & Clifford Sanford, Inequity and Interpersonal Conflict: Reward Allocation and Secrecy about Reward as Methods of Preventing Conflict, 23 J. Personality & Soc. Psych. 88 (1972); Bernhardt Lieberman, Not an Artifact, 15 J. Conflict Resolution 113 (1971); Lawrence A. Messe, Robin R. Vallacher, & James L. Phillips, Equity and the Formation of Revolutionary and Conservative Coalitions in Triads, 31 J. Personality & Soc. Psych. 1141 (1975); William R. Morgan & Jack Sawyer, Bargaining Expectations and the Preference for Equality over Equity, 6 J. Personality & Soc. Psych. 139 (1967); Rudy V. Nydegger & Guillermo Owen, The Norm of Equity in a Three-person Majority Game, 22 Behavioral Sci. 32 (1977); Nydegger & Owen, *supra* note 14; Anatol Rapoport, Oded Frenkel, & Josef Perner, Experiments with Cooperative 2 × 2 Games, 1 Theory & Decision 67 (1967); Anatol Rapoport, Melvin J. Guyer, & David G. Gordon, The 2 × 2 Game (1976); Anatol Rapoport & Carol Orwant, Experimental Games: A Review, 7 Behavioral Sci. 1 (1962); Harry T. Reis & Joan Grunzen, On Mediating Equity, Equality and Self-Interest: The Role of Self-Preservation in Social Exchange, 12 J. Experimental Soc. Psych. 478 (1976); Roth & Malouf, *supra* note 14; E. Gary Shapiro, Effect of Expectations of Future Interaction on Reward

other hand, an almost equally large literature concludes that subjects try to maximize their own profits and refuse to settle for less than they could command by operating alone.[21]

The difference in results seems to be generated at least in part by different instructions and different information about payoffs given to the subjects. Subjects who divide the profits equally either tend to know all monetary payoffs[22] or tend to be told that their "task" is to divide up a sum of money. Conversely, subjects who bargain to unequal payoffs generally either tend to be ignorant of one another's payoffs[23] or tend to be instructed by the experimenter to try to make as much money as possible.[24] Where the instructions are less pointed about subject motivation, the results seem more mixed.[25] In general, the following experimental conditions seem to be associated with more equal splitting of profits: (1) repeated, face-to face negotiations;[26] (2) the ability to choose a Pareto optimal allocation which is also an equal split;[27] (3) public payoffs;[28] and (4) full information about one another's profits.[29]

---

Allocations in Dyads: Equity or Equality, 31 J. Personality & Soc. Psych. 873 (1975); Elaine Walster, Ellen Berscheid, & G. William Walster, New Directions in Equity Research, 25 J. Personality & Soc. Psych. 151 (1973).

[21] See, for example, Jerome M. Chertkoff, Coalition Formation as a Function of Differences in Resources, 15 J. Conflict Resolution 371 (1971); Sandra G. Funk, Amnon Rapoport, & James P. Kahan, Quota versus Positional Power in Four-person Apex Games, 16 J. Experimental Soc. Psych. 77 (1980); Kelley, Beckman, & Fischer, *supra* note 15; Michener, Ginsberg, & Yuen, *supra* note 16; H. Andrew Michener, Kenneth Yuen, & Irving J. Ginsberg, A Competitive Test of the $M_1$ (im) Bargaining Set, Kernel, and Equal Share Models, 22 Behavioral Sci. 341 (1977); Charles E. Miller, Coalition Formation in Characteristic Function Games: Competitive Tests of Three Theories, 16 J. Experimental Soc. Psych. 61 (1980); J. Keith Murningham, Strength and Weakness in Four Coalition Theories, 23 Behavioral Sci. 195 (1978); Amnon Rapoport & James P. Kahan, When Three Is Not Always Two against One: Coalitions in Experimental Three-person Cooperative Games, 12 J. Experimental Soc. Psych. 253 (1976); Thibaut and Gruder, *supra* note 15.

[22] See Roth & Malouf, *supra* note 14, and Rudy V. Nydegger, Independent Utility Scaling and the Nash Bargaining Model, 22 Behavioral Sci. 283 (1977), for discussions of the effect of knowledge of payoffs on payoff splits. Melvin J. Guyer & Anatol Rapoport, Information Effects in Two Mixed-Motive Games, 15 Behavioral Sci. 467 (1969), also find this result.

[23] See note 22 *supra*.

[24] Particularly Kelley, Beckman, & Fisher *supra* note 15; Michener, Ginsberg, & Yuen *supra* note 16; Michener, Yuen, & Ginsberg, *supra* note 21; and Murningham, *supra* note 21.

[25] See, for example, Funk, Rapoport, & Kahan, *supra* note 21; Morgan & Sawyer, *supra* note 20; and Lane & Messe, *supra* note 20.

[26] Josi Greenberg, Group vs. Individual Equity Judgments—Is There a Polarization Effect? 15 J. Experimental Psych. 504 (1979); Rapoport, Guyer, & Gordon, *supra* note 20; E. Gary Shapiro, *supra* note 20.

[27] Note 16 *supra*.

[28] Leventhal, Michaels, & Clifford Sanford *supra* note 20; Reis & Gruzen, *supra* note 20.

[29] Note 22 *supra*.

While the experimental literature summarized above has improved our understanding of how individuals bargain under a variety of different conditions, the general bargaining problem described by Coase has received little attention prior to the work reported here. There have been very few experiments which have both required subjects to bargain over a variety of different discrete choices and allowed them to make side payments to one another at the same time.[30] In Coase's view, the person owning the liability right gets compensated. For example, in bilateral monopoly experiments subjects bargain over discrete choices as individuals might bargain over levels of pollution, but side payments are generally forbidden.[31] On the other hand, most of the games which implicitly allow side payments involve only two or three alternatives from which to choose and are described in coalitional rather than discrete alternative form.[32] Typically, in such a game, subjects are given the following infor-

[30] Two such experiments are reported in Michener, Ginsberg, & Yuen *supra* note 16; Michener, Yuen, & Ginsberg, *supra* note 21.

[31] Edward H. Chamberlin, An Experimental Imperfect Market, 56 J. Pol. Econ. 95 (1948); Daniel Druckman & Thomas V. Bonoma, Determinants of Bargaining Behavior in a Bilateral Monopoly Situation II: Opponent's Concession Rate and Similarity, 21 Behavioral Sci. 252 (1976); Dan S. Felsenthal, Bargaining Behavior When Profits Are Unequal and Losses Are Equal, 22 Behavioral Sci. 334 (1977); Fouraker & Siegel, *supra* note 16; Melvin J. Guyer, An Analysis of Duopoly Bargaining, 11 General Systems 215 (1966); Donald L. Harnett & Larry L. Cummings, Bilateral Monopoly Bargaining: An International Study, in 3 Contributions to Experimental Economics 100 (Heinz Sauermann ed. 1971); Harold L. Johnson & Arthur M. Cohen, Experiments in Behavioral Economics: Siegel and Fouraker Revisited, 12 Behavioral Sci. 353 (1967); S. S. Komorita & Arline R. Brenner, Bargaining and Concession Making under Bilateral Monopoly, 9 J. Personality & Soc. Psych. 15 (1968); Heinz Sauermann & Reinhard Selton, An Experiment in Oligopoly, 5 Society for General Systems Research (1960).

[32] Murningham, *supra* note 12, reviews much of this literature; other examples include Theodore Caplow, A Theory of Coalitions in the Triad, 21 Am. Soc. Rev. 489 (1956) and Two Against One (1968); Chertkoff, *supra* note 21; Jerome Chertkoff & James K. Esser, A Test of Three Theories of Coalition Formation When Agreements Can Be Short-Term or Long-Term, 35 J. Personality & Soc. Psych. 237 (1977); Steven G. Cole, An Examination of the Power-Inversion Effect in Three-person Mixed-Motive Games, 11 J. Personality & Soc. Psych. 50 (1969); Funk, Rapoport, & Kahn, *supra* note 21; William A. Gamson, Experimental Studies of Coalition Formation, in 1 Advances in Experimental Social Psychology (Leonard Berkowitz ed. 1964); The Study of Coalition Behavior (Sven Groennings, E. W. Kelley, and Michael Leiserson eds. 1970); Abraham D. Horowitz & Amnon Rapoport, Test of the Kernel, and Two Bargaining Set Models in Four and Five-person Games in Game Theory as a Theory of Conflict Resolution (Anatol Rapoport ed. 1974); James P. Kahn & Amnon Rapoport, Test of the Bargaining Set and Kernel Models in Three-person Games in *id*; Harold H. Kelley & A. John Arrowood, Coalitions in the Triad: Critique and Experiment, 23 Sociometry 231 (1960); Medlin, *supra* note 13; H. Andrew Michener, John A. Fleishman, & Jerry J. Vaske, A Test of the Bargaining Theory of Coalition Formation in Four-person Groups, 34 J. Personality & Soc. Psych. 1114 (1976); Michener, Ginsberg, & Yuen, *supra* note 16; Michener, Yuen, & Ginsberg, *supra* note 21; H. Andrew Michener & Richard A. Zeller, The Effects of Coalition Strength on the Formation of Contractual Norms, 35 Sociometry 290 (1972); Miller, *supra* note 21; Murningham, *supra* note 21; J.

mation. Alone you make \$$x$. If you form a coalition with a second person, the two of you can split \$$2x$ + \$$y$ and the odd person gets \$$x$. If all three players form a coalition, they split \$$3x$ + \$$y$ + \$$z$.

A set of experiments conducted by Michener, Yuen, and Ginsberg comes very close to a Coase bargaining situation.[33] Three subjects per experiment bargained over outcomes (instead of coalition divisions), and they could make side payments. Subjects were told to maximize their own payoffs. More than half, but by no means all, of the choices were Pareto optimal, and the mean payoff splits were far from equal. The authors concluded that the payoff splits generally fit the Shapley value,[34] which predicts that the payoffs will be in proportion to one's power in the game. However, the experimental situation above differs crucially from a Coase bargaining situation in that no one player could unilaterally choose the allocation as can the owner of a property right.

Experiments which have granted some unilateral power to one of the parties in a bargaining game have generally involved somewhat different decision tasks from that described by the Coase Theorem. For example, in one study, two players were given individual values and a joint value they could divide. One player was given the right to divide the joint reward if the other player did not depart from a joint cooperative strategy, and the subjects could write enforceable contracts specifying what each player would do. If the subjects wrote no contract, they were given their indi-

---

Keith Murningham & Alvin E. Roth, The Effects of Communication and Information Availability in an Experimental Study of a Three-person Game, 23 Manag. Sci. 1336 (1977) and Large Group Bargaining in a Characteristic Function Game, 22 J. Conflict Resolution 299 (1978); Rapoport & Kahan, *supra* note 21; William H. Riker, Bargaining in a Three-person Game, 61 Am. Pol. Sci. Rev. 642 (1967); Loyda M. Shears, Patterns of Coalition Formation in Two Games Played by Male Tetrads, 12 Behavioral Sci. 130 (1967); W. Edgar Vinacke & Abe Arkoff, An Experimental Study of Coalitions in the Triad, 22 Am. Rev. 406 (1957); Karl E. Weick & Donald D. Penner, Triads: A Laboratory Analogue, Organization Behavior & Human Performance 191 (1966); Richard H. Willis, Coalitions in the Tetrad, 25 Sociometry 358 (1962).

[33] Note 21 *supra*.

[34] Lloyd S. Shapley, A Value for N-Person Games, in Contributions to the Theory of Games (H. W. Kuhn & A. W. Tucker eds. 1953). The Shapley value of each player in a game is that player's expected payoff, computed as follows:

$$EP_i = \sum_{S \subseteq N} \{[(s - 1)!\,(n - s)!\,]/n!\}\,[v(S) - v(S - i)],$$

where $N$ = number of coalitions player $i$ could join, $S$ = a particular coalition, $s$ = number of players in $S$, $n$ = number of players in the game, $V(S)$ = payoff coalition $S$ can command, and $V(S - i)$ = payoff coalition $S$ could command if $i$ did not join. The interpretation of the Shapley value focuses on the power player $i$ can command as the pivotal player in a number of coalitions. The more coalitions $i$ can join and the more $i$ contributes to the payoffs commanded by those coalitions, the more intrinsic power $i$ has and the more total payoff $i$ can expect from playing the game.

vidual values.[35] In another experiment the subjects could divide the rewards, and both could write a contract specifying the division.[36] The authors of these two studies concluded that the ability to write enforceable contracts fosters the attainment of Pareto optimal outcomes.

Another important question raised by Coase's critics is whether a proposition describing two-person bargaining can be extended to larger groups. Experiments with three- and four-person games suggest that Pareto optimal outcomes can be achieved,[37] but experiments with larger groups have generally concluded that free-rider problems take over unless special allocation mechanisms are imposed.[38] However, these larger group experiments have not allowed open communication, side payments, and enforceable contracts.

This paper reports the results of a set of controlled experiments designed specifically to test the Coase proposition in two- and three-person bargains. The results strongly favor the Coase proposition and also strongly suggest that parties engaging in repeated negotiations with one another may split profits equally even though in single-shot negotiations they are more likely to choose individually rational divisions. Of the 114 experimental decisions, 89.5 percent were Pareto optimal. Sixty-two of those dictated that payoffs be divided nearly equally.

## III. Experimental Design

### A. *Two-person Experiments*

#### 1. Perfect Information: Instructions

As the subjects arrived at a designated room they were randomly assigned the letters A or B. Each pair was placed in a separate room, with a monitor being the only other person present. The monitor provided the following set of instructions to the subjects, who first read the instructions silently and then listened to the monitor read them aloud.

[35] Murdoch, *supra* note 15.

[36] Thibaut & Gruder, *supra* note 15.

[37] For example, Michener, Ginsberg, & Yuen, *supra* note 16; Michener, Yuen, & Ginsberg, *supra* note 21; Miller, *supra* note 21; Rapoport & Kahan, *supra* note 21; Medlin, *supra* note 13; Rapoport et al., Three Person Non-Zero-Sum Negotiable Games, 7 Behavioral Sci. 38 (1962).

[38] John R. Chamberlin, The Logic of Collective Action; Some Experimental Results, 23 Behavioral Sci. 441 (1978) and Provision of Public Goods as a Function of Group Size, 68 Am. Pol. Sci. Rev. 707 (1974); R. Mark Isaac & Charles R. Plott, The Opportunity for Conspiracy in Restraint of Trade: An Experimental Study (Working Paper No. 255, Cal. Inst. Tech. Soc. Sci. 1979); Charles R. Plott, Externalities and Corrective Policies in Ex-

## INSTRUCTIONS

*General*

You are about to participate in an experiment in decision making. The purpose of the experiment is to gain insight into certain features of complex economic processes. If you follow the instructions carefully you might earn a considerable amount of money. You will be paid in cash at the end of the experiment.

*Specific Instructions to Participants*

You will be asked to make several choices. Each choice will involve choosing a number. The cash value to you of the number is given in the set of payoff sheets attached to your instructions (see pp. ———). For example, if \$5 were next to number 2 on your payoff sheet and if number 2 were chosen, then you would be paid \$5. In the example shown below, for instance, you might be person B. Your payoff sheets[39] list not only the value of each number to you, but also the value of each number to the other participant.

Two of you will participate together on each decision. One of you will be designated the "controller." The controller may, if he or she wishes, choose the number by himself or herself and inform the monitor, who will stop the experiment and pay both participants. The other participant may attempt to influence the controller to reach a mutually acceptable joint decision; the other participant may offer to pay part or all of his or her earnings to the controller.

*Example*

Assume that A is the controller and that participants A and B have the following payoffs associated with numbers 0, 1, and 2:

| Number | A's Payoff (\$) | B's Payoff (\$) |
|---|---|---|
| 0 | 4 | 1 |
| 1 | 5 | 2 |
| 2 | 3 | 5 |

perimental Markets (1977) 180 (Working Paper No. 180, Cal. Inst. Tech. Soc. Sci. 1977); Vernon L. Smith, Incentive Compatible Experimental Processes for the Provision of Public Goods in 1 Research in Experimental Economics (Vernon L. Smith ed. 1979). One exception to the conclusion that free-rider problems are insurmountable is a six-person Prisoner's Dilemma experiment in which subjects could discuss and decide on a strategy halfway through the iterated game; V. Edwin Bixenstine, Clifford A. Levitt, & Kellogg V. Wilson, Collaboration among Six Persons in A Prisoner's Dilemma Game, 10 J. Conflict Resolution 488 (1966). While they could not legally enforce their strategy, they could subtly punish defectors. The results were that groups that knew all the payoffs and could discuss a strategy cooperated almost 100 percent of the time after their discussions. Groups which did not discuss cooperated much less and did not change significantly at any time.

[39] Sample payoff functions are reproduced in Table 1 below.

If A and B were to agree to set the number at 0, and further agree that B should get $1 from A's payoff, then the monitor would terminate the experiment, pay A $3 (representing the $4 payoff less the $1 transfer to B) and pay B $2 (representing the $1 payoff plus the $1 transfer from A).

If a joint agreement is reached, *both* parties must sign the attached agreement form, stating both what the chosen number will be and how much money will be transferred from one participant's earnings to the other's. *No physical threats are allowed.* If a joint agreement is made and the form is signed, the monitor will terminate the experiment and pay each participant according to the terms set forth in the agreement.

Are there any questions? We ask you to answer the questions on the attached sheet to make sure you understand the instructions.

QUESTIONS

(Refer to your payoffs on p.———.)

1. Number——— makes me the most money. Number——— makes me the least money.
2. If the other participant is the controller and he picks number 4, I make———.
3. If I agree to pay $2 to the other participant and we agree on number 1, I make ———.

AGREEMENT FORM

A and B agree to set the number at ———.
A and B agree that, from the award $——— should be paid ——————— to ———————.

Signed ———————
A

———————
B

In essence, these instructions told subjects that they had to choose one of a given set of numbers and that they would be paid different amounts of money, *in cash*, depending on which number was chosen. In this formulation, the numbers are analogous to the productive decisions in the Coase Theorem. For example, subjects A and B might correspond to the adjacent rancher and farmer in Coase's original model. Similarly, the chosen numbers might correspond to the size of the rancher's herd, and the money that was paid to the subjects might represent the rancher's and farmer's profits. The subjects were also told that one of them had the power to choose the number unilaterally. This power is analogous to a property right in the Coase situation.[40] For example, the controller's abil-

[40] Although Coase contrasted a liability rule in favor of farmers with a property rule in favor of ranchers, we have chosen to contrast opposite property rules because they are so much easier to model.

ity to choose the number might correspond to the farmer's right to obtain an injunction preventing the rancher from allowing his cows to wander onto the farmer's land. Finally, the instructions allowed subjects to transfer, by contract, payoffs from one party to another. This feature of the experiment directly mimics the contract mechanism which is central to the Coase Theorem.

Each of the instructions included some information telling the participant how much cash he would be paid (depending on which number was chosen).[41] Table 1 shows representative payoffs for two-party bargaining situations.[42] Notice that each schedule has a clear joint-profit maximizing number, which pays at least $1.00 more than the next highest number. After reading the instructions and examining their payoffs, subjects were tested on their understanding of the rules and the consequences of decisions they might make.[43] After both subjects had answered all of the questions correctly, and after the monitor had answered all of the subjects' remaining uncertainties about the rules of the game, the experimenter flipped a coin, and the winner of the toss was designated the controller. The subjects were then instructed to proceed with the experiment (by choosing a number).

## 2. Experimental Institutions

In all of the two-person experiments the bargaining was face-to-face and public and involved more money than most students can earn for an hour's work in their next best alternative employment. Side payments were allowed; contracts were in writing and strictly enforced. All payments were made in public. Subjects were given no motivational instructions; subjects were not told what their objectives should be in choosing a number or in forming contracts.

The instructions above for the first set of experiments modeled an environment as close as possible to one satisfying all the sufficient conditions for the Coase Theorem to hold: two parties who are fully informed about one another's payoffs and who have no transactions costs. Because we suspected that parties to a bargain might divide the profits differently if their relationship were to continue than if they were to make only one decision, there were two versions of this first set of experiments.

[41] See Vernon L. Smith, Experimental Economics: Induced Value Theory, 66 Am. Econ. Rev. 274 (1976), for a theoretical justification for inducing preference orderings with monetary payoffs.

[42] A variety of different payoff functions with the same structure was randomly used. The object of randomizing the payoff functions was to minimize possible experimenter effects.

[43] Tests are included with the instructions.

TABLE 1
SAMPLE PAYOFFS SCHEDULES ($)

A. TWO-PERSON EXPERIMENTS

| Decision 1 | | | Decision 2 | | |
|---|---|---|---|---|---|
| Number | A | B | Number | A | B |
| 0 | 0.00 | 12.00 | 0 | 0.00 | 11.00 |
| 1 | 4.00 | 10.00 | 10 | 1.00 | 10.00 |
| 2 | 6.00 | 6.00 | 20 | 2.00 | 8.00 |
| 3 | 8.00 | 4.00 | 30 | 4.00 | 6.00 |
| 4 | 9.00 | 2.00 | 40 | 5.50 | 5.50 |
| 5 | 10.00 | 1.00 | 50 | 9.00 | 4.00 |
| 6 | 11.00 | 0.00 | 60 | 10.50 | 1.00 |
| | | | 70 | 9.00 | 0.00 |

B. THREE-PERSON EXPERIMENTS

| Decision 1 | | | | Decision 2 | | | |
|---|---|---|---|---|---|---|---|
| Number | A | B | C | Number | A | B | C |
| 1 | 1.00 | 7.00 | 7.00 | 1 | 0.00 | 8.50 | 8.50 |
| 2 | 5.00 | 5.50 | 5.50 | 2 | 3.00 | 7.00 | 7.00 |
| 3 | 10.00 | 4.00 | 4.00 | 3 | 5.50 | 5.50 | 5.50 |
| 4 | 12.00 | 0.00 | 0.00 | 4 | 11.00 | 4.00 | 4.00 |
| | | | | 5 | 13.00 | 0.00 | 0.00 |

*a*) *Sequential.* Six pairs of subjects made two decisions each, in sequence. The coin was flipped to decide who was the controller before deliberation began on each decision. The subjects thus knew they would make two decisions together, but during the first decision, they did not know who would be controller for the second. The object was to simulate a legal environment in which the assignment of rights was uncertain but the parties knew they would have to maintain a continuing relationship. This models, for example, a nuisance case in which the parties will interact over a period of time but in which the legal assignment of liability is not clear.

*b*) *Nonsequential.* Two groups of four subjects who did not know one another made six single, pairwise decisions each. The object was to model a legal environment in which one bargain would be struck between two parties who would never have to communicate again.

### 3. Two-person, Limited Information

The next set of experiments modeled an environment less favorable to Coase than the first. Subjects were only told their own payoffs. They were allowed to reveal their payoffs to the other subject in a bargain, but they did not have to do so. The instructions for this pair of experimental institutions were identical to the instructions for the pair above, with one crucial exception. Where the instructions above stated, "Your payoff sheets list not only the value of each number to you, but also the value of each number to the other participant," the instructions for the limited information bargains stated, "Your payoff sheets list only the value of each number to you. The other participant is free to tell you anything he or she wishes to about the value of each number to him or her." Otherwise, these experiments were exactly the same as the first. These experiments were also divided into (*a*) *sequential*—four pairs made two decisions each, and (*b*) *nonsequential*—two groups of four each made six single pairwise decisions.

### *B. Three-person Experiments*

#### 1. Full-Information Instructions

As the subjects arrived at a designated room they were randomly assigned the letters A, B, or C. Each triad was placed in a separate room, with the monitor being the only other person present. The monitor provided the following set of instructions to the subjects, who first read the instructions silently and then listened to the monitor read them aloud.

INSTRUCTIONS

*General*

You are about to participate in an experiment in decision making. The purpose of the experiment is to gain insight into certain features of complex economic processes. If you follow the instructions carefully, you might earn a considerable amount of money. You will be paid in cash at the end of the experiment.

*Specific Instructions to Participants*

You will be asked to make several choices. Each choice will involve choosing a number. The cash value to you of the number is given in the set of payoff sheets[44] attached to your instructions (see pp. ———). For example, if $10 were next to number 2 on your payoff sheet and if number 2 were chosen, then you would be paid $10. In the example shown below, for instance, you might be person B. Your payoff sheets list not only the value of each number to you, but also the value of each number to each of the other participants.

You three people will participate together. Either one of you will be chosen as the "controller" or two of you will be chosen as "joint controllers."

[44] Sample payoff functions are reproduced in Table 1.

*a*) If *one* of you is chosen, then the controller may, if he or she wishes, choose the number by himself or herself and inform the monitor, who will stop the experiment and pay all three participants. The other two participants may attempt to influence the controller to reach a mutually acceptable group decision; either or both of the other participants may offer to pay part or all of his or her earnings to the controller.

*b*) If *two* of you are chosen as joint controllers, then either joint controller may, if he or she wishes, *attempt* to choose the number. (This is done by filling out one of the attached forms and handing it to the monitor.) The joint controller who chooses the *lower* number will determine the number. If, for example, one joint controller chooses number 2 and the other joint controller chooses number 1, then the monitor will set the number at 1 and pay the participants accordingly. The remaining participant (the one who is *not* a joint controller) may attempt to influence either or both of the remaining parties to reach an acceptable group decision; any party may offer to pay all or part of his or her earnings to one or both of the remaining parties.

In order to reach a group agreement, the following procedures must be followed:

*a*) If *one* person has been designated the controller, then either one or both of the other participants can join the controller in a group decision by filling out and signing one of the attached agreement forms. All of the parties to an agreement must sign, and if any portion of any participant's earnings is to be paid to someone else, then the participant agreeing to pay must sign the agreement form before the agreement will be enforced by the monitor. Otherwise, the controller can choose the number alone.

*b*) If *two* participants have been chosen joint controllers, then *both* joint controllers must join in a group decision before it will become effective. Otherwise, the number will be chosen in accord with the procedure described in the preceding paragraph (that is, the joint controller choosing the lower number sets the number). The remaining participant may also be a party to a group agreement. Again, all of the parties to a group agreement must sign, and if any portion of any participant's earnings is to be paid to someone else, then the participant agreeing to pay must sign the agreement form before the agreement will be enforced by the monitor. *No physical threats are allowed.* If either party makes a physical threat, the threatened party will be paid his or her maximum payoff, and the threatening party will get nothing. When a group agreement is reached and the forms are signed, the monitor will end the experiment and pay the participants.

*Examples*

1. Assume that A is the only controller.

| Number | A's Payoff ($) | B's Payoff ($) | C's Payoff ($) |
|---|---|---|---|
| 1 | 40 | 30 | 30 |
| 2 | 50 | 10 | 10 |

If B and C agree on number 1, but A chooses number 2, then number 2 has been chosen and the monitor will pay accordingly.

If A and B sign an agreement form choosing number 1 and directing the monitor to pay all of C's payoff to B, the monitor will disregard the agreement, unless C also signs it.

If A, B, and C sign an agreement form choosing number 1 and directing that $10 of A's payoff be paid to C, the monitor will terminate the experimental period, pay A $30 (representing the $40 payoff less the $10 transfer to C), pay B $30, and pay C $40 (representing a $30 payoff plus the $10 transfer from A).

2. Assume that B and C are joint controllers.

| Number | A's Payoff ($) | B's Payoff ($) | C's Payoff ($) |
|---|---|---|---|
| 1 | 40 | 30 | 30 |
| 2 | 50 | 10 | 10 |

If A and B sign an agreement form, choosing number 2, and C chooses number 1, then number 1 has been chosen and the monitor will pay accordingly.

If B and C sign an agreement form choosing number 1 and directing that A's payoff should be split equally among them, the monitor will disregard the agreement unless A signs it.

If A, B, and C sign an agreement form choosing number 1 and directing that $10 of A's payoff be transferred to C and $5 of B's payoff be transferred to C, then the monitor will terminate the experiment, pay A $30 (representing a $40 payoff less the $10 transfer to C), pay B $25 (representing a $30 payoff less the $5 transfer to C) and pay C $45 (representing a $30 payoff plus the $10 transfer from A and the $5 transfer from B).

Are there any questions? We would like you to answer the questions on the attached page. These should help you understand the instructions.

QUESTIONS

(Refer to the decision on p. ———)

1. Level ——— makes me the most money. Level ——— makes me the least money.
2. If C is the only controller and if C chooses number 4, I make ———.
3. If B and C are joint controllers and if B chooses 2 and C chooses 1, I make ———.
4. If A is the controller and he reaches an agreement with B and C which chooses number 2 and directs B to pay A $2 and C to pay A $3, I make ———.
5. If B and C are joint controllers and they reach an agreement with A in which the number is set at 1 and A agrees to pay B and C each $0.50, I make ———.
6. If I am the only controller, I may set the number by myself, true or false? ———.

GROUP AGREEMENT FORM

(Three-person Experiments)

Number Chosen ———

$——— from ———'s payoff to be paid to ————.

$——— from ———'s payoff to be paid to —————.
$——— from ———'s payoff to be paid to —————.

Signed: ——————
A

——————
B

——————
C

These instructions are meant to model a pollution externality; A might correspond to a factory which wished to dump the by-products of its production process into a stream, and B and C might be downstream riparian owners who dislike increased levels of pollution. The choice of a number would correspond to the choice of a level of pollution. If A were the controller, his power to choose the number unilaterally would represent the factory's right to pollute as much as it wished, without having to pay anyone anything. If B and C were joint controllers, their shared power might represent each riparian owner's independent right to obtain an injunction preventing the factory from dumping any pollutants. Under such circumstances, B and C's right to attempt to set the number independently would correspond to each riparian owner independently telling the factory the maximum level of pollution the riparian owner will tolerate. The factory obviously may not pollute to any greater extent than the lowest level allowed from among the independent riparian owners. In just this way, if B and C attempt to set the number independently, the lower of their choices controls. For this very reason, all riparian owners would have to join in an agreement not to seek an injunction before the factory could rely on the agreement. Similarly, in the experiment, both B and C must join in a group agreement in order for A to be able to rely on it.

Each of the instructions included information telling each participant how much cash he and each of the other participants would be paid (depending on which number was chosen). Table 1 shows representative payoffs for three-party bargaining situations. Once again, notice that each schedule has a clear joint-profit maximizing number, which pays at least $1.00 more than the next highest number.

After reading the instructions and examining their payoffs, subjects were tested on their understanding of the rules and the consequences of the decisions they might make. After all three subjects had answered all of the questions correctly, and after the monitor had answered all of the subjects' remaining uncertainties about the rules of the game, the experimenter flipped a coin, and the winner of the toss (either A alone or B and

C together) was designated the controller. The subjects were then instructed to proceed with the experiment (by choosing a number).

### 2. Experimental Institutions

The three-person, full-information experimental institutions were almost identical to the two-person, limited-information sequential institutions. Again, all bargaining was face-to-face and involved more money then most students can earn for an hour's work in their next best alternative employment. Side payments were allowed, and contracts were in writing and strictly enforced.[45] All cash payments were made in public. Subjects were given no motivational instructions. Seventeen groups of three subjects made two decisions each, sequentially.

### 3. Three-person, Limited Information

This final set of experiments completes a square design of two and three subjects crossed with limited and full information making sequential decisions. The instructions are exactly the same as the three-person instructions given above, except for the crucial insert about knowledge of one another's payoffs. Where the instructions above stated, "Your payoff sheets list not only the value of each number to you, but also the value of each number to each of the other participants," the instructions for the limited information bargains state, "Your payoff sheets list only the value of each number to you. The other participants are free to reveal to you anything they wish about their payoffs." Eighteen groups of three subjects made two decisions each, sequentially.

## IV. Experimental Results

Table 2 summarizes the results of all 114 experimental decisions. Overall, 89.5 percent of the decisions are Pareto optimal. In fact, the only deviation from nearly 100 percent joint-profit maximization is with three persons to a bargain, joint controllers, and limited information. These results clearly demonstrate that the Coase Theorem is supported under the following conditions: (1) two parties to a bargain, with and without full information; (2) three parties to a bargain and a single controller, with and without full information; and (3) three parties to a bargain, joint controllers, and full information.

Controllers' behavior regarding splitting the profits fell neatly into two groups. With only fifteen exceptions controllers either agreed to split the

[45] Contract forms are included with the instructions.

TABLE 2
EXPERIMENTAL RESULTS

| EXPERIMENT | $N$ | $N_1$: JOINT PROFIT MAXIMUM | PAYOFF DIVISION | | | | |
|---|---|---|---|---|---|---|---|
| | | | $N_2$: Equal Splits | $N_3$: Within $1 Different from Equal Split | $N_4$: Controller Received Exactly the Individual Maximum | $N_5$: Controller Received More than the Individual Maximum | Other |
| Two person: | | | | | | | |
| Full information: | | | | | | | |
| Sequential | 12 | 12 | 12 | 0 | 0 | 0 | 0 |
| Nonsequential | 12 | 11 | 5 | 0 | 4 | 3 | 0 |
| Limited information: | | | | | | | |
| Sequential | 8 | 8 | 6 | 0 | 2 | 0 | 0 |
| Nonsequential | 12 | 11 | 3 | 3 | 3 | 1 | 2 |
| Three person, sequential: | | | | | | | |
| Limited information: | | | | | | | |
| Single controller | 21 | 19 | 3 | 4 | 2 | 5 | 7 |
| Joint controller | 15 | 9 | 2 | 3 | 5 | 4 | 1 |
| Full information: | | | | | | | |
| Single controller | 13 | 12 | 3 | 2 | 1 | 2 | 5 |
| Joint controller | 16 | 15 | 9 | 2 | 1 | 3 | 1 |
| Coin flip barred by subjects on second decision | 5 | 5 | 4 | 1 | 0 | 0 | 0 |
| Total | 114 | 102 | 47 | 15 | 18 | 18 | 16 |

payoffs nearly evenly or demanded at least their individual maxima. The second strategy is individually rational for each play of the game and is generally predicted by game-theoretic solutions to the bargaining problem. The first strategy is more in keeping with the results of the social psychological experiments which did not instruct subjects to be individually rational.[46] If we define sharing as an allocation within $1.00 of an equal split, sixty-seven controllers shared and thirty-six bargained to a core allocation.[47]

Sharing occurred most frequently in two-person sequential decisions, and the presence or absence of full information seems to have made no difference. Eighteen of twenty controllers in two-person sequential decisons shared, compared with only eleven of twenty-four in two-person, nonsequential decisions. This suggests that controllers are more likely to share when the parties to a two-person agreement have a continuing relationship than when they do not. Joint controllers also frequently shared in three-person, sequential, full-information decisions. In addition, a number of three-person, sequential, full-information subject groups insisted on signing a sharing agreement covering both decisions. They would sign two agreement forms during discussion of the first decision.

It is possible that we would have observed fewer equal splits if we had not used college students as subjects. College students may not be as rationally self-interested as those who are older. This possible lack of self-interest might also derive from a feeling of "kinship" with fellow students.

Indeed, to the extent that the sharing behavior indicates that either the subjects were failing to profit maximize or were maximizing interdependent utility functions which might violate one of the axioms of the Coase Theorem, our results cannot be taken to verify the theorem. Since the initial conditions were not all satisfied, assumption *h* might not have received a good test. However, if our assumption regarding individual motivations were incorrect, then these results may take on even more significance, for they seem to indicate that the Coase Theorem's prediction about production still has great power; the Pareto optimum was chosen almost 90 percent of the time. These experiments would seem to say

[46] Note 20 *supra*.

[47] A core allocation is individually rational, Pareto optimal, and rational for every possible winning coalition of players. Some might argue that our results do not support Coase's hypothesis because so many subjects split equally instead of bargaining to a core allocation. It seems to us, however, that Coase's efficiency prediction has been the crucial part of his hypothesis in shaping legal and economic policy. It is on that basis that we claim our results support the Coase Theorem. We recognize that Coase *expected* the income distribution would favor the controller. That expectation is, of course, not confirmed in general by our results.

that in two- and three-person situations a scholar might be able to assert with some confidence that groups will behave *as if* all of the Coase Theorem's assumptions were satisfied. Nevertheless, the pattern of sharing vis-à-vis individual maximizing behavior may not be inconsistent with rational behavior in the fact of uncertainty. Sharing buys "good will" in a continuing relationship, especially one in which the other person might be controller the next time. While the expected value of demanding at least the individual maximum may be higher, the expected utility may be lower.[48]

Moreover, the pattern in the three-person, sequential, full-information experiments is consistent with a downward-sloping demand curve for risk avoidance. Once the coin has been flipped for the first decision and the outcome is known, adopting a sharing strategy for *both* decisions requires that single controllers on the first decision give up more than joint controllers relative to the *minimum* expected payoffs they can command. On the first decision a single controller commands at least $12.00, while a

[48] Richard Posner has recently suggested an economic rationale for the prevalence of sharing behavior in primitive (preliterate) societies. Posner hypothesizes that in a culture that produces food that cannot be stored from one period to another, voluntary "gifts" of surplus food production to needy individuals will form the basis of a primitive form of insurance against hunger and starvation. Those who produce surplus in one period may be needy the next. As long as the fortunate give to the needy in each period, everyone's chance of starving is greatly reduced. Posner explores the ramifications of these insights in A Theory of Primitive Society with Special Reference to Primitive Law, 23 J. Law & Econ. 1 (1980). Unfortunately, however, our results cannot be explained through Posner's analysis. Each subject's production was perfectly storable from one experiment to the next. Hence, the controller on the first of two sequential decisions could *self-insure* against the possibility of losing control on the second decision by refusing to share his surplus. Furthermore, Posner's thesis cannot explain any of the sharing behavior that we observed in nonsequential decisions or in the *second* of two sequential decisions, since there is no longer any insurance to be bought. Of course, the sharing behavior might be the "natural" outcome of this bargaining game if the subjects were to view *all* of the money to be paid to them as "profits" rather than just regard the additional money which can be earned by cooperating as profits. The Nash bargaining solution is to split evenly all profits where neither party has greater power within the game. This solution would suggest that the controller would take his individual maximum plus one-half of the surplus from cooperation. If, for some reason, the controller failed to fully appreciate his complete control over the amount he could command by himself (although each subject answered questions indicating that he *did* have such an appreciation), then the observed equal splits would correspond, in some sense, to the Nash bargaining solution. To test this possibility, we wish to run additional two- and three-person experiments, identical in all respects to the previous experiments, with one important change. When the coin is flipped and the controller is chosen, we will take an amount of cash equal to the maximum the controller can command by himself and give it to the controller immediately. The controller will be told that the cash is his and that it is up to him whether the experiment proceeds. If the experiment proceeds, the procedures will be unchanged. However, to effect an equal split, the controller will have to give up some of the cash in hand to the other party or parties. We suspect that such a change in procedure will reduce the number of equal splits.

TABLE 3
THREE-PERSON, SEQUENTIAL, FULL-INFORMATION RESULTS

| | Number | Number Which Shared |
|---|---|---|
| First decision: | | |
| Single controller | 8 | 4 |
| Joint controllers | 9 | 7 |
| Second decision: | | |
| Binding contract: | 5 | 5 |
| Single controller on first decision | 2 | 2 |
| Joint controllers on first decision | 3 | 3 |
| Single controller: | 5 | 1 |
| Single controller shared on first decision | 1 | 1 |
| Joint controllers shared on first decision | 1 | 0 |
| Joint controller: | 7 | 4 |
| Single controller shared on first decision | 1 | 1 |
| Joint controllers shared on first decision | 3 | 3 |

joint controller commands a minimum of only $7.00. The second decision (before the coin flip) has an expected value of at least $6.50 to the single controller and an expected value of at least $4.25 to each joint controller. A sharing strategy yields $12.33 to each participant. Hence, the decision to share requires a single controller on the first decision to trade away an expected return of at least $6.50 on the second decision in exchange for $0.33 with certainty. Joint controllers, however, may gain $5.33 with certainty by trading away their expected value of at least $4.25. Therefore, we would expect joint controllers to share more often than single controllers.

As Table 3 shows, in three-person, sequential, full-information experiments joint controllers were more likely to share than single controllers on both decisions. Moreover, all second-decision sharing was linked to a binding or implicit contract among the participants. Thus, either the participants had actually signed such a contract, or they had shared on the first decision, creating an implicit contract to share all proceeds.

## V. CONCLUSION AND SUGGESTIONS FOR FURTHER RESEARCH

The experimental results presented in this paper provide strong support for Coase's proposition that agents will bargain to a joint-profit-maximizing outcome when it exists in two- and three-party bargaining situations under full information and when one party has the right to make the decision unilaterally under limited information. It is too early to tell whether the experimental departures from Pareto optimality jointly controlled, three-person, partial-information games are significant. Four of the six departures occurred in the first of two decisions and were followed by a Pareto optimal decision. Thus, it may be that the game is more difficult to learn with joint controllers. In that case we might simply be observing an experience effect which was not evident in the easier games. This hypothesis requires further testing.

However, if these indications of failure to achieve Pareto optimal results in jointly controlled, three-person, partial-information games are confirmed by future testing, we may be able to derive substantial policy implications for the law. The choice of remedies for the area of nuisance law[49] provides a good example. Assume that a particular new land use, for example, a cement factory, interferes with other land uses, for example, homeowning, so as possibly to constitute a "nuisance" under the law.[50] Regardless of whether the court finds the new factory to be a nuisance, the court must confront the thorny issue of whether to grant the winning side the right to an injunction or to limit that side to a damages remedy.[51] These are the two *injunctive* remedies, which were modeled in our experiment, from which the court must choose: (1) Factory's right—the factory may pollute at any level it chooses. (2) Homeowners' right—any homeowner is entitled to an order of the court directing the factory to emit no pollutants. The court may also choose from these two *damages* remedies: (1*a*) Factory's right—the homeowners may obtain an order of the court directing the factory to emit no pollutants if and only if the homeowners pay the factory all damages it suffers from reducing its level of pollution. (2*a*) Homeowner's right—the factory may pollute at any level it chooses, but it must pay homeowners for any damage caused by the pollution.

There are problems[52] associated with both damages and injunctive rem-

[49] See Maurice T. Van Hecke, Robert N. Leavell, & Grant S. Nelson, Cases and Materials on Equitable Remedies and Restitution, 425–59 (1973), for general background on this subject.

[50] For example, Boomer v. Atlantic Cement Co., 26 N.Y.2d 219, 257 N.E.2d 870, 309 N.Y.S.2d 312 (1970).

[51] We realize that there are other possibilities, but restricting the discussion to these two alternatives simplifies the textual discussion. For a good discussion of a hybrid remedy, see Robert C. Ellickson, Alternatives to Zoning: Covenants, Nuisance Rules, and Fines as Land Use Controls, 40 U. Chi. L. Rev. 681, 738 (1973).

[52] We assume that the law is, or should be, concerned at least in part with economic efficiency. This topic has been much discussed in the literature of law and economics. See Symposium on Efficiency as a Legal Concern, 8 Hofstra L. Rev. 485–771 (1980), and A Response to the Efficiency Symposium, 8 Hofstra L. Rev. 811–973 (1980). We recognize that the proper jurisprudential role of economics is controversial, but resolution of this controversy lies well beyond the scope of this paper.

edies.[53] Injunctive relief may be inefficient because bargaining may fail to achieve Pareto optimality. Damages remedies are plagued by the difficulty of accurately appraising damages and the increased administrative costs associated with such a valuation. Where there is only one cement factory and one homeowner, the risk associated with injunctive entitlements—the failure of contracting—has been thought to be low. Our experiments provide some confirmation of this intuition. The almost complete dominance of Pareto optimal outcomes in our two-person experiment suggests that, if there is only one homeowner, a court may choose from between rules 1 and 2 (depending on whether the factory is or is not a nuisance) with confidence that the parties will bargain to an efficient outcome. Hence, injunctive entitlements have appeal in two-party situations.

However, when there are "many" homeowners, it has commonly been feared that strategic behaviors (often termed "free-rider problems") and problems of coordination may preclude the parties' rearrangement of judicial decisions into Pareto optimal patterns. Our results provide some crucial insights. First, although such fears may be realistic in some circumstances, one cannot know whether to be worried about injunctive remedies merely by counting all of the parties to a lawsuit and asking if there are "many" parties. The dominance of Pareto optimal outcomes in single controller, three-person games suggests that, if there are two homeowners, a court may choose rule 1 with good confidence that the parties will bargain efficiently. However, with exactly the same parties, our results to date imply that a court may not choose rule 2 with the same high level of confidence about optimal bargaining.[54] Furthermore, a court may have to begin worrying about such concerns when there are only two homeowners.[55] All together, these insights suggest that, in contexts like

[53] These problems are discussed in much greater detail in Calabresi & Melamed, *supra* note 3*B*.

[54] Moreover, if our hypothesis that inexperience is responsible for some departures from Pareto optimality is confirmed, then the courts should behave differently when they suspect parties will make only one bargain than when the courts suspect they will bargain repeatedly. If agents are to bargain repeatedly, they may converge quickly to the efficient outcome under either rule 1 or rule 2, but if one single bargain is to stand for many years the court may have to worry about rule 2.

[55] Discussions in the law and economics literature tend to avoid addressing the question of how many is "many"; instead the literature discusses only situations in which there are hundreds of homeowners, thereby sidestepping the problem. For example, in discussing the sources of high transactions costs, Judge Richard Posner (then Professor Posner) stated in his treatise: "The costs of transacting are highest where elements of bilateral monopoly coincide with a large number of parties to the transaction—a quite possible conjunction. For example, if homeowners have a right to be free from pollution, the factory that wishes to acquire the right to pollute must acquire it from every homeowner. If only one out of a thousand refuses to come to terms, the rights that the factory has purchased from the other 999 are worth nothing (why?) Because the holdout can extract an exorbitant price, as in our

our example, a judge must begin worrying about problems with rule 2 when he does not yet have to worry about rule 1.[56] We can derive similar (tentative) policy conclusions about the law of easements and equitable servitudes on land with such an analysis. Of course, further experimental work with joint controllers and larger bargaining parties is needed before we can say that the Coase Proposition is confirmed experimentally as a more general behavioral prediction.[57]

---

right-of-way example in the previous section, each homeowner has an incentive to delay coming to terms with the factory; the process of negotiation may therefore be endlessly protracted." Richard Posner, *supra* note 3*C*, at 45. Posner also discusses the possibility of bargaining breakdown in two-party discussions. *Id.* Also see the discussion in Calabresi & Melamed, *supra* note 3*B* (100,000 citizens).

[56] Obviously, further experimental research is needed to ascertain the point at which, if a court finds no nuisance, "many" homeowners prevent efficient contracting. We are currently engaged in such tests.

[57] The results also provide some support for predictions about how agents in such bargaining situations will divide the profits. Controllers in two-person sequential bargains and, more generally, those with a previous experience sharing profits or a monetary incentive to share are more likely to share. Others are somewhat more likely to demand their individual maxima. We feel that it is premature, at this stage, to draw normative conclusions from the sharing behavior between subjects in these experiments. However, before one may draw such normative implications for the Coase Theorem one would need a theory of how subjects (or people in general) ought to behave with respect to exploiting economic rights. Such a theory might stem from a notion of just deserts. For example, one might feel that full exploitation of an economic right was justified only where the owner of the right had acquired it through labor. Under such a theory the subjects in our experiment, who acquired the right to be controller through a flip of the coin rather than through labor, should share the profits. Alternatively, one might feel that one may morally exploit a property right if and only if the other party with whom one is dealing is wealthier, of a higher caste, etc. Under this theory, we would have to know the relative status of controllers and noncontrollers in our experiments before being able to make any normative pronouncements on the sharing behavior. The development of a general, normative theory lies well beyond the scope of this paper. Even if we had a well-developed normative theory of exploitation of economic rights, our data are far too sketchy to allow any meaningful application. We intend to return to these questions upon completing the full set of Coase Theorem experiments.

# [28]

# EXPERIMENTAL EVALUATION OF THE COASE THEOREM*

*GLENN W. HARRISON* *and* *MICHAEL MCKEE*
*University of Western Ontario* *University of Windsor*

## I. Introduction

THE Coase Theorem is a theoretical proposition describing the outcomes of mutually advantageous bargains in the face of the generation of an externality. The traditional Coasian framework is summarized in the set of assumptions adopted by Hoffman and Spitzer in their behavioral evaluation of the Theorem: "(*a*) two agents to each externality (and bargain), (*b*) perfect knowledge of one another's (convex) production and profit or utility functions, (*c*) competitive markets, (*d*) zero transactions costs, (*e*) costless court system, (*f*) *profit-maximizing* producers and expected *utility-maximizing* consumers, (*g*) no wealth effects, (*h*) agents will strike mutually advantageous bargains in the absence of transactions costs."[1]

The Coase Theorem is generally stated in terms of the neutrality of the resulting level of the externality to the initial assignment of property rights between the two parties. That is, irrespective of which party has the unilateral property right (UPR) to impose the externality on the other party, we should find the Pareto-optimal level of externality generation. The compelling feature of this Coasian result is that it is brought about by the self-interest of each party and does not rely on their altruism with respect to one another or the visible hand of the state.

In an important study, Hoffman and Spitzer provide an experimental evaluation of the behavioral relevance of the Coase Theorem.[2] They claim

* We are grateful to the Centre for Economic Analysis of Property Rights for financial support, and to Jack Hirshleifer, Sumner LaCroix, John Palmer, E. E. Rutsröm, and Ron Wintrobe for helpful comments.

[1] Elizabeth Hoffman & Matthew L. Spitzer, The Coase Theorem: Some Experimental Tests, 25 J. Law & Econ. 73 (1982). Footnote omitted, emphasis added.

[2] For related experimental studies see Yves C. Prudencio, The Voluntary Approach to Externality Problems: An Experimental Test, 9 J. Envtl. Econ. & Mgmt. 213 (1982); Elizabeth Hoffman & Matthew L. Spitzer, Experimental Tests of the Coase Theorem with

[*Journal of Law & Economics*, vol. XXVIII (October 1985)]

that their results provide strong support for the Coase Theorem. Indeed their results have been employed in at least one standard textbook exposition.[3] Following Regan,[4] Hoffman and Spitzer focus on the behavioral implications of assumption *h* above. This assumption implies *two* distinct behavioral outcomes: (i) that the two parties will agree on a Pareto-optimal level for the externality; and (ii) that any such agreement will be attained by means of a mutually advantageous bargain between the two parties. Hoffman and Spitzer present experimental results that overwhelmingly support the first outcome but reject the second outcome. Pooling over all their experiments, 89.5 percent of all bargains resulted in a Pareto optimal solution. However, in 60.8 percent of those solutions the two parties essentially[5] agreed to split the total payoff equally, even though this represented a disadvantageous bargain for one of the parties (the "controller," or holder of the UPR) relative to the payoff attainable without any bargaining.

Hoffman and Spitzer explicitly recognize the problem with their results:

> A core allocation is individually rational, Pareto optimal, and rational for every possible winning coalition of players. Some might argue that our results do not support Coase's hypothesis because so many subjects split equally instead of bargaining to a core allocation. It seems to us, however, that Coase's efficiency prediction has been the crucial part of his hypothesis in shaping legal and economic policy. It is on that basis that we claim our results support the Coase Theorem. We recognize that Coase *expected* the income distribution would favor the controller. That expectation is, of course, not confirmed in general by our results.[6]

Ignoring the exegetical issue of what Coase "really meant,"[7] we can argue that the policy significance of the Coase Theorem derives primarily from the view that the delimitation of UPR serves to facilitate the inter-

---

Large Bargaining Groups, 15 J. Legal Stud. (1986), forthcoming; and Elizabeth Hoffman & Matthew L. Spitzer, Entitlements, Rights and Fairness: An Experimental Examination of Subjects' Concepts of Distributive Justice, 14 J. Legal Stud. 259 (1985).

[3] Jack Hirshleifer, Price Theory and Applications 490 (3d ed. 1984).

[4] Donald H. Regan, The Problem of Social Cost Revisited, 15 J. Law & Econ. 427 (1972).

[5] The word "essentially" allows for divisions of the total payoff that are within $1.00 of an equal split.

[6] Hoffman & Spitzer, *supra* note 1, at 93 n.47.

[7] For an exchange on the question of the relevance of the core concept for the Coase Theorem see Varouj A. Aivazian & Jeffrey L. Callen, The Coase Theorem and the Empty Core, 24 J. Law & Econ. 175 (1981); and R. H. Coase, The Coase Theorem and the Empty Core: A Comment, 24 J. Law & Econ. 183 (1981). In the original paper Coase actually refers to "mutually satisfactory bargains": see R. H. Coase, The Problem of Social Cost, 3 J. Law & Econ. 1, 4 (1960), for example.

nalization of externalities through individually rational bargaining. Hirshleifer notes that from a "policy point of view, Coase's Theorem strongly suggests that the *unambiguous assignment of exchangeable property rights,* whatever the specific nature of the assignment may be, might be an important step in promoting the achievement of efficiency."[8] Similarly, Cooter observes that the Coase Theorem "is taken to suggest a definite approach to policy legislation—use the law to lubricate private bargaining."[9] The critical behavioral presumption, then, is that the affected parties act in a self-interested fashion in the bargaining context defined by the initial property rights assignment. This presumption is not supported by the results of Hoffman and Spitzer's experiments.

An alternative line of defense of their results is offered by Hoffman and Spitzer, based on the interpretation of their results as reflecting the altruism of their subjects:

> Indeed, to the extent that the sharing behavior indicates that either the subjects were failing to profit maximize or were maximizing interdependent utility functions which might violate one of the axioms of the Coase Theorem, our results cannot be taken to verify the theorem. Since the initial conditions were not all satisfied, assumption *h* might not have received a good test. However, if our assumption regarding individual motivations were incorrect, then these results may take on even more significance, for they seem to indicate that the Coase Theorem's prediction about production still has great power; the Pareto optimum was chosen almost 90 percent of the time. These experiments would seem to say that in two- and three-person situations a scholar might be able to assert with some confidence that groups will behave *as if* all of the Coase Theorem's assumptions were satisfied.[10]

In short, the Coase Theorem is behaviorally "right for the wrong reasons." Moreover, if we can rely on economic agents to be altruistic with respect to the generation of externalities, why do we need UPR (or Pigouvian taxes, for that matter) to internalize the problem? In this light, the Coase Theorem is rendered behaviorally vacuous for policy purposes.

In the next section we develop an experimental design that allows a careful evaluation of the Coase Theorem in the simplest possible context: two parties, full information concerning each other's payoffs, and nonsequential bargaining (that is, no subject has any continuing experimental relationship with any other subject).[11] Our experimental results are pre-

[8] Hirshleifer, *supra* note 3, at 491.

[9] Robert Cooter, The Cost of Coase, 11 J. Legal Stud. 1, 14 (1982).

[10] Hoffman & Spitzer, *supra* note 1, at 93–94.

[11] Note that this is just one of the many experimental designs considered by Hoffman and Spitzer (HS). It is, however, the one that HS present as most directly relevant for the evaluation of the Coase Theorem (that is, the other designs involve relaxing one or more of the assumptions of the theorem).

TABLE 1
ALTERNATIVE PAYOFF SCHEDULES

| Schedule | Number | Payoff to A | Payoff to B | Joint Payoff |
|---|---|---|---|---|
| I | 1 | .00 | 4.00 | 4.00 |
| | 2 | .50 | 3.50 | 4.00 |
| | 3 | 2.00 | 3.00 | 5.00 |
| | 4 | 2.50 | 1.00 | 3.50 |
| | 5 | 3.00 | .50 | 3.50 |
| | 6 | 4.00 | .00 | 4.00 |
| II | 1 | .00 | 4.00 | 4.00 |
| | 2 | .50 | 3.50 | 4.00 |
| | 3 | 2.50 | 3.50 | 6.00 |
| | 4 | 2.50 | 1.00 | 3.50 |
| | 5 | 3.00 | .50 | 3.50 |
| | 6 | 4.00 | .00 | 4.00 |
| III | 1 | .00 | 4.75 | 4.75 |
| | 2 | .50 | 4.50 | 5.00 |
| | 3 | 1.75 | 4.25 | 6.00 |
| | 4 | 2.50 | 2.50 | 5.00 |
| | 5 | 4.50 | .50 | 5.00 |
| | 6 | 4.75 | .00 | 4.75 |

NOTE.—The joint payoff values were not provided to subjects.

sented in Section III. We find that the comparable Hoffman-Spitzer results that are inconsistent with individual rationality are attributable to a lack of understanding by certain subjects of the meaning of UPR. We are also able to demonstrate that the Coase Theorem is *not* behaviorally vacuous for policy purposes, by illustrating the necessity of an initial assignment of property rights for mutually advantageous bargaining to produce an efficient outcome.

## II. EXPERIMENTAL DESIGN AND HYPOTHESES

As far as possible our design and instructions followed Hoffman & Spitzer. All subjects were recruited from the economics undergraduate program at the University of Western Ontario. None had received any formal exposure to the Coase Theorem or game theory. The subjects were told in effect that they would be bargaining in three successive sessions, each time with a different opponent. The complete experimental instructions, reproduced in Appendix A, carefully avoid (as far as possible) the use of any "loaded" word such as "bargaining" or "opponent." Each participant was to be paid according to a publicly posted payoff schedule. This schedule showed the monetary value to each subject of six numbers (see Table 1). The exact monetary amount paid depended on whether the subject was designated "person A" or "person B" (decided by a coin flip) *and* on the number eventually chosen (by way of agreement or disagreement). Subjects were told that they would be paid by check at the end of a series of experiments.[12] Physical threats were not allowed: all bargaining negotiations were monitored to reinforce this requirement.

Subjects were told that there could be either an "agreement outcome" or a "disagreement outcome" in each session. The former was simply an agreement between the two parties as to which number to choose *and* how much of the total payoff would go to each participant. In response to a public question from one subject in the initial experiments, it was explained to all subjects that the agreement form could be used solely to agree upon a number without any sidepayments being made. In subsequent experiments this point was made orally during the initial public reading of the instructions. In one series of experiments, designated "No Property Rights," we prohibited explicit contractual sidepayments; Appendix B presents the modified instructions used in these experiments.

Subjects were informed that one of three alternative disagreement outcomes would apply—random, zero, and controller—and that they would be told at the beginning of each session which one applied to them. The instructions defining each of these outcomes are reproduced in Appendix A. In the *random* outcome, a number is drawn at random and applied to both participants. Each number is equally likely to be drawn at random. In the *zero* outcome both participants receive zero payoff for the session. The *controller* outcome follows when one player is designated the "controller" at the outset of each session, based on a coin flip. The controller may choose the number by himself or herself and inform the monitor, who will stop the experiment and pay both participants. The other participant may attempt to influence the controller to reach a mutually acceptable joint decision; the other participant may offer to pay part or all of his or her earnings to the controller.

Subjects were given a demonstration of our "random number generator" (a die) and a simple example of a *hypothetical* controller outcome. They were then asked to answer privately a brief series of *hypothetical* questions designed, among other things, to see if they understood what a controller's "property rights" were (specifically, that the controller can unilaterally choose any number, with or without the "opponent's" agreement). All subjects answered each question correctly. Each bargaining

[12] Subjects also knew that none of the subsequent experiments would involve bilateral bargaining with any of their opponents in the current experiments. Payment of earning with a lag probably served to reinforce the importance of the explicit agreement form in our experiments (as the only effective or credible way to transfer any of the joint payoffs from a decision).

session could last for ten minutes, with several warnings provided about the time remaining.[13] Very few of the observed outcomes were decided "at the wire," and this time limit did not appear to be a binding constraint on negotiating behavior. Table 1 lists the payoff schedules adopted in each experiment, and Table 2 presents our experimental design.

The first series of experiments involves a "replication" of Hoffman and Spitzer's design with our subject pool and our (relatively trivial) modifications to their instructions.[14] These experiments adopt unilateral property rights (UPR) in each of the three sessions, with the social surplus equal to $1.00 or $2.00. In addition to providing a behavioral benchmark for subsequent treatments, these experiments allow us to examine two hypotheses concerning Hoffman and Spitzer's results:

H1. The altruistic divisions of the joint payoff are due to learning behavior (that is, they occur primarily in sessions 1 or 2, and not in session 3).

H2. The altruistic divisions of the joint payoff are an artifact of a small social surplus (that is, increasing the surplus from $1.00 to $2.00 will reduce the number of observed altruistic divisions).

The first hypothesis is suggested by a comparison of the sequential and nonsequential two-person, full-information results of Hoffman and Spitzer. In the former experiments, which were conducted in just one session, 100 percent of the divisions were exactly altruistic; in the latter experiments, which were conducted (like ours) in three successive sessions, "only" 45.5 percent of the Pareto-optimal decisions were altruistically divided. Given the importance of learning behavior and sequential replication in other areas of experimental behavior, it is important to check if

[13] HS apparently allowed an indeterminate amount of time for bargaining. Don Coursey, Bilateral Bargaining, Pareto Optimality, and the Empirical Frequency of Impasse, 3 J. Econ. Behav. & Organization 243 (1982) provides a systematic study of the effect of time constraints on the observed frequency of impasse in bilateral bargaining experiments. We regard the introduction of a time constraint as a potentially important modification of the HS design for two reasons: (i) it avoids the problem of extraneous pressures on the time allowed for bargaining (for example, one subject may have a pressing appointment at a certain time), which may lead to different subjective costs of continuing to bargain (or, in Coasian jargon, "transactions costs"); and (ii) it allows us to ensure that our financial incentives are salient for any particular subject pool (that is, we can ensure that the potential payoffs are commensurate with the opportunity cost of the time involved in the experiment).

[14] Examples of these modifications are the time limit constraint and the payment of subjects with a lag. Although we have a strong prior expectation that these are behaviorially innocuous modifications for present purposes, it is important to confirm this before studying less trivial modifications. If this prior is not accepted, then our experiments do not constitute a literal replication of HS, but they do stand as an independent series of experiments. Moreover we may then examine the effect of the important modifications in an orthogonal fashion, irrespective of the extent to which we "replicate" HS.

TABLE 2
EXPERIMENTAL DESIGN

| Institution | Experiment | Session | Disagreement Outcome | Training Session | Social Surplus ($) | Payoff Schedule (See Table 1) |
|---|---|---|---|---|---|---|
| Unilateral property rights | UPR(1) | 1 | Controller | . . . | 1 | I |
| | | 2 | Controller | UPR(1) | 1 | I |
| | | 3 | Controller | UPR(1) | 1 | I |
| | UPR(2) | 1 | Controller | . . . | 2 | II |
| | | 2 | Controller | UPR(2) | 2 | II |
| | | 3 | Controller | UPR(2) | 2 | II |
| No property rights | NPR(Z) | 1 | Zero | . . . | 1 | III |
| | | 2 | Zero | NPR(Z) | 1 | III |
| | | 3 | Zero | NPR(Z) | 1 | III |
| | NPR(R) | 1 | Random | . . . | 1 | III |
| | | 2 | Random | NPR(R) | 1 | III |
| | | 3 | Random | NPR(R) | 1 | III |
| Joint property rights | JPR(Z) | 1 | Zero | . . . | 1 | I |
| | | 2 | Zero | JPR(Z) | 1 | I |
| | JPR(R) | 1 | Random | . . . | 1 | I |
| | | 2 | Random | JPR(R) | 1 | I |
| Unilateral property rights | UPR(Z) | 3 | Controller | JPR(Z) | 1 | I |
| | UPR(R) | 3 | Controller | JPR(R) | 1 | I |

this simple explanation accounts for the observed altruism (Hoffman and Spitzer do not report the results for their nonsequential experiments by session). The second hypothesis addresses the issue of the opportunity cost, in terms of forgone monetary payoff, of altruism in these experiments.[15] Alternatively, hypothesis H2 is also suggested by vague notions of the opportunity cost of "understanding the property rights of a controller" (presuming such comprehension requires some mental exertion that is valued by the subject).

The second series of experiments establishes a no property rights (NPR) bargaining environment with alternative disagreement outcomes. Here the subjects could agree on a particular number, but could not *contractually* transfer any of the resulting joint payoff from one party to the other. The payoff schedule used in these experiments (schedule III in Table 1) yields a Pareto-optimal outcome (3) that maximized the joint payoff and a *different* Pareto-optimal outcome (4) that divided the joint payoff (which was $1.00 less than the maximum joint payoff) equally between the two parties. We have the following hypothesis in these experiments:

H3. In the absence of transferable property rights the parties will not choose the joint payoff maximum.

Clearly, if this hypothesis is rejected, we do not have an "externality problem" to solve (by Coasian or other means). The importance of establishing that there is indeed a behavioral problem to solve, before examining the ability of certain institutions to solve it behaviorally, is long established in the experimental literature.[16]

[15] HS randomized over payoff schedules, noting that "each schedule has a clear joint-profit maximizing number, which pays at least $1.00 more than the next highest number." Hoffman & Spitzer, *supra* note 1, at 85. In a personal communication, Elizabeth Hoffman notes that for the two-person full-information HS experiments the social surplus was always $2.00 or more. HS do not report the results obtained for different levels of the social surplus.

[16] See, for example, Vernon L. Smith, Incentive Compatible Experimental Processes for the Provision of Public Goods, 1 Research in Experimental Econ. 59 (1979), sec. 4, on the "free-rider problem" for public goods; on the "monopoly problem," see Vernon L. Smith, An Empirical Study of Decentralized Institutions of Monopoly Restraint, in Essays in Contemporary Fields of Economics (G. Horwich & J. Quirk eds. 1981); Don Coursey, R. Mark Isaac & Vernon L. Smith, Natural Monopoly and Contested Markets: Some Experimental Results, 27 J. Law & Econ. 91 (1984); and Glenn W. Harrison & Michael McKee, Monopoly Behavior, Decentralized Regulation, and Contestable Markets: An Experimental Evaluation, 16 Rand J. Econ. 51 (1985); on the "externality problem," see Charles R. Plott, Externalities and Corrective Policies in Experimental Markets, 93 Econ. J. 106 (1983); and on the "predatory pricing problem," see Glenn W. Harrison, Predatory Pricing in Experiments (May 1985) (unpublished manuscript, Univ. Arizona, Dep't Econ.); and R. Mark Isaac & Vernon L. Smith, In Search of Predatory Pricing, 93 J. Pol. Econ. 320 (1985).

The third series of experiments establishes joint property rights (JPR), in the sense that no party has the right *unilaterally* to choose any number that can guarantee a positive payoff, but that the two parties have the right to choose any number *jointly* and divide the total payoff as they wish. The alternative to coming to a joint agreement is that neither party can be certain of receiving a positive payoff (the random disagreement outcome) *or* they are certain to receive nothing (the zero disagreement outcome). The following hypotheses are proposed:

H4. The establishment of joint property rights increases the number of joint maximum payoff outcomes.

H5. The total payoff received under joint property rights will be equally split between the two parties.

Hypothesis H4, if accepted, may be taken as consistent with a weak behavioral form of the Coase Theorem: that it is only necessary *for efficiency* that JPR be established. Hypothesis H5 is consistent with the Nash solution for bargaining games of this form.[17]

The final series of experiments establishes unilateral property rights (UPR) for one party. An essential feature of our design is that these UPR experiments follow "training sessions" consisting of JPR experiments (with zero or random disagreement outcomes). This sequential feature reinforces the delimitation of *unilateral* property rights that is at the heart of the Coasian individual rationality question. We therefore hypothesize:

H6. The establishment of unilateral property rights increases the number of joint maximum payoff outcomes.

H7. The establishment of unilateral property rights increases the number of individually rational bargains by the property right holder.

It is interesting to note the rather close approximation of this final design to the stylized facts describing the manner in which naturally occurring legal decisions are made. One can view the trial process—wherein property rights are assigned—as a final stage of a bargaining *series* in which the initial periods involve incompletely specified property rights.[18] The behavioral implication of our design is that the pre-property-rights negotiation will impress the value of the property right on the person ultimately designated as controller. Hypothesis H7 expresses the impact of the "pretrial" bargaining process on the posttrial allocation of re-

[17] John F. Nash, The Bargaining Problem, 18 Econometrica 155 (1950); and John F. Nash, Two Person Cooperative Games, 21 Econometrica 128 (1953).

[18] See Robert Cooter & Stephen Marks, with Robert Mnookin, Bargaining in the Shadow of the Law: A Testable Model of Strategic Behavior, 11 J. Legal Stud. 225 (1982).

sources. If not rejected, H7 may be considered as consistent with a strong behavioral form of the Coase Theorem.

## III. Experimental Results

Table 3 presents the detailed results of our experiments, along with those reported by Hoffman and Spitzer for their nonsequential two-person full-information design. In Table 4 we present the results of several $\chi^2$ tests to determine if the behavioral outcomes discussed below differ significantly between experiments.[19] Note that the test adopted is two sided, and that the direction of any difference in outcome is not predicted. The "critical level" shown in Table 4 is the *smallest* significance level at which the null hypothesis could be rejected (that is, a critical level of .490 indicates that one would have to have at least 49 percent confidence in the alternative hypothesis in order to reject the null). We report on rejection of the null hypothesis in Table 4 at a stringent 2 percent critical level.

Hypothesis H1 is rejected on the basis of the UPR(1) results for each session: there is no apparent learning behavior across the three sessions. This result is confirmed in Table 4 by a $\chi^2$ test on the UPR(1) results reported in Table 3, indicating that the probability of altruistic outcomes is not significantly different in session 3.

Comparing Hoffman and Spitzer's pooled results with the UPR(1) series of our experiments we find that 45.5 percent (five of eleven) of their Pareto-optimal decisions were accompanied by equal-split (altruistic) outcomes, while 60.0 percent (nine of fifteen) of our bargains yielded this result. We cannot reject the hypothesis that these results are identical (the appropriate $\chi^2$ statistic is .540 with a critical level of .4627). Our results therefore replicate those of Hoffman and Spitzer, indicating that the *minor* changes we made to their procedures are indeed behaviorally unimportant. This confirms our use of the UPR(1) experiments as a base from which to evaluate the remaining experimental institutions.

Hypothesis H2 is supported by a comparison of the UPR(1) and UPR(2) results: increasing the social surplus significantly reduced the number of altruistic divisions from 60.0 percent (nine out of fifteen) to a mere 11.1 percent (one out of nine). Although the strength of this treatment is remarkable, it indicates that the individual irrationality of Hoffman and Spitzer's results may be due in part to the adoption of payoff schedules involving a "small" social surplus.[20]

[19] W. J. Conover, Practical Nonparametric Statistics 144–51 (2d ed. 1980) provides a formal explanation of the $\chi^2$ test used.

[20] Note that we varied the size of the social surplus in an absolute sense (from $1.00 to

TABLE 3
EXPERIMENTAL RESULTS

| | | | | PAYOFF DIVISION | | | | | |
|---|---|---|---|---|---|---|---|---|---|
| EXPERIMENT | SESSION | NUMBER OF DECISIONS (N) | NUMBER OF JOINT PROFIT MAXIMUM DECISIONS ($N_1$) | Equal Splits ($N_2$) | Within \$1.00 of Equal Splits ($N_3$) | Controller Receives Exactly the Individual Maximum ($N_4$) | Controller Receives More than Individual Maximum ($N_5$) | Other ($N_6$) | Disagreement Outcome ($N_7$) |
| HS | All | 12 | 11 | 5 | 0 | 4 | 3 | 0 | n.a. |
| UPR(1) | 1 | 5 | 5 | 3 | 1 | 0 | 1 | 0 | 0 |
| | 2 | 5 | 5 | 2 | 0 | 1 | 2 | 0 | 0 |
| | 3 | 5 | 5 | 3 | 0 | 2 | 0 | 0 | 0 |
| | All | 15 | 15 | 8 | 1 | 3 | 3 | 0 | 0 |
| UPR(2) | 1 | 3 | 3 | 1 | 0 | 0 | 2 | 0 | 0 |
| | 2 | 3 | 3 | 0 | 0 | 1 | 2 | 0 | 0 |
| | 3 | 3 | 3 | 0 | 0 | 0 | 3 | 0 | 0 |
| | All | 9 | 9 | 1 | 0 | 1 | 7 | 0 | 0 |
| NPR(Z) | 1 | 2 | 0 | 2 | 0 | n.a. | n.a. | 0 | 0 |
| | 2 | 2 | 0 | 2 | 0 | n.a. | n.a. | 0 | 0 |
| | 3 | 2 | 0 | 2 | 0 | n.a. | n.a. | 0 | 0 |
| | All | 6 | 0 | 6 | 0 | n.a. | n.a. | 0 | 0 |
| NPR(R) | 1 | 2 | 0 | 1 | 0 | n.a. | n.a. | 0 | 1 |
| | 2 | 2 | 0 | 0 | 0 | n.a. | n.a. | 0 | 2 |
| | 3 | 2 | 0 | 0 | 0 | n.a. | n.a. | 0 | 2 |
| | All | 6 | 0 | 1 | 0 | n.a. | n.a. | 0 | 5 |
| NPR (Z and R) | All | 12 | 0 | 7 | 0 | n.a. | n.a. | 0 | 5 |
| JPR(Z) | 1 | 7 | 7 | 6 | 1 | n.a. | n.a. | 0 | 0 |
| | 2 | 7 | 7 | 7 | 0 | n.a. | n.a. | 0 | 0 |
| | All | 14 | 14 | 13 | 1 | n.a. | n.a. | 0 | 0 |
| JPR(R) | 1 | 10 | 10 | 9 | 1 | n.a. | n.a. | 0 | 0 |
| | 2 | 10 | 9 | 8 | 0 | n.a. | n.a. | 0 | 2 |
| | All | 20 | 19 | 17 | 1 | n.a. | n.a. | 0 | 2 |
| JPR (Z and R) | All | 34 | 33 | 30 | 2 | n.a. | n.a. | 0 | 2 |
| UPR(Z) | 3 | 7 | 6 | 2 | 0 | 2 | 3 | 0 | 0 |
| UPR(R) | 3 | 10 | 9 | 0 | 1 | 5 | 3 | 1* | 0 |
| UPR (Z and R) | 3 | 17 | 15 | 2 | 1 | 7 | 6 | 1 | 0 |

NOTE.—Refer to Table 2 for a description of the experimental design; n.a. means outcome not applicable.
* Controller chose his individual maximum and transferred \$1.00 to the other player. This outcome was implemented by the agreement form, with both subjects signing.

TABLE 4
STATISTICAL TESTS

| Hypothesis | Population 1 | | Population 2 | | Class 1 | | |
|---|---|---|---|---|---|---|---|
| | Experiment | Sessions | Experiment | Sessions | Definition | Population 1 Value | Population 2 Value |
| H1 | UPR(1) | 1 | UPR(1) | 3 | $N_2 + N_3$ | 4 | 3 |
| | UPR(1) | 2 | UPR(1) | 3 | $N_2 + N_3$ | 2 | 3 |
| | UPR(1) | 1 & 2 | UPR(1) | 3 | $N_2 + N_3$ | 6 | 3 |
| H2 | UPR(1) | All | UPR(2) | All | $N_2 + N_3$ | 9 | 1 |
| H3 | NPR | All | UPR and JPR | All | $N_1$ | 0 | 72 |
| H4 | NPR | All | JPR | All | $N_1$ | 0 | 33 |
| H6 | UPR(Z and R) | All | NPR | All | $N_1$ | 15 | 0 |
| | UPR(Z and R) | All | JPR | All | $N_1$ | 15 | 33 |
| | UPR(Z and R) | All | NPR and JPR | All | $N_1$ | 15 | 33 |
| H7 | UPR(Z and R) | All | UPR(1) | All | $N_4 + N_5$ | 13 | 6 |

Hypothesis H3 is overwhelmingly supported: none of the twelve decisions in the NPR experiments involved choosing the joint profit maximum. In the NPR(Z) series all of the agreements involved the equal-split outcome, whereas in the NPR(R) series 83.3 percent (five out of six) of the negotiations ended with the disagreement outcome.[21] We therefore conclude that there is indeed a behavioral "externality problem" to solve.

Hypothesis H4, implying a weak behavioral form of the Coase Theorem, is convincingly supported. Fully 97.1 percent (thirty-three out of thirty-four) of the decisions with JPR were agreements to choose the joint-profit-maximizing number. This contrasts significantly with the results just discussed for the NPR experiments (with none of the decisions being the joint-profit maximum). Hypothesis H5 is also strongly supported: 97.0 percent (thirty-two out of thirty-three) of the Pareto-optimal payoffs in the JPR experiments were divided virtually equally between the two parties. This result is, of course, perfectly consistent with Nash *and* Coasian solutions, given that UPR are not assigned to one party.

Hypothesis H6 is firmly supported, with 88.2 percent (fifteen out of seventeen) of the decisions in the experiments that establish UPR in session 3 being Pareto optimal. This again contrasts sharply with the

$2.00) *and* relative to the disagreement outcome payoff to the controller. An interesting area for subsequent research would be to determine which of these two interpretations of "increased social surplus" is the more important. Neither interpretation has any behavioral significance from the perspective of formal game theory, which predicts individually rational bargains in either case.

[21] Note that the *expected* monetary payoff to player B from the random disagreement outcome in the NPR(R) experiments exceeded the equal-split payoff by $0.25. This expected payoff was $1.75 less than the payoff this party received at the joint maximum payoff decision.

TABLE 4 (*Continued*)

| Definition | CLASS 2 | | NULL HYPOTHESIS | ALTERNATIVE HYPOTHESIS | $\chi^2$ TEST STATISTIC | CRITICAL LEVEL | REJECT NULL HYPOTHESIS? |
|---|---|---|---|---|---|---|---|
| | Population 1 Value | Population 2 Value | | | | | |
| $N - N_2 - N_3$ | 1 | 2 | $P_1 = P_2$ | $P_1 \neq P_2$ | .476 | .490 | No |
| $N - N_2 - N_3$ | 3 | 2 | $P_1 = P_2$ | $P_1 \neq P_2$ | .400 | .527 | No |
| $N - N_2 - N_3$ | 4 | 2 | $P_1 = P_2$ | $P_1 \neq P_2$ | .0 | 1.0 | No |
| $N - N_2 - N_3$ | 6 | 8 | $P_1 = P_2$ | $P_1 \neq P_2$ | 5.531 | .0187 | Yes |
| $N - N_1$ | 12 | 3 | $P_1 = P_2$ | $P_1 \neq P_2$ | 66.816 | .0 | Yes |
| $N - N_1$ | 12 | 1 | $P_1 = P_2$ | $P_1 \neq P_2$ | 41.213 | .0 | Yes |
| $N - N_1$ | 2 | 12 | $P_1 = P_2$ | $P_1 \neq P_2$ | 21.933 | .0 | Yes |
| $N - N_1$ | 2 | 1 | $P_1 = P_2$ | $P_1 \neq P_2$ | 1.594 | .207 | No |
| $N - N_1$ | 2 | 13 | $P_1 = P_2$ | $P_1 \neq P_2$ | 1.862 | .172 | No |
| $N - N_4 - N_5$ | 4 | 9 | $P_1 = P_2$ | $P_1 \neq P_2$ | 4.394 | .0361 | Yes |

NOTE.—See W. J. Conover, Practical Nonparametric Statistics 144–51 (2d ed. 1980) for an explanation of all statistical terminology, Table 2 for a description of each experiment, and Table 3 for the definition and values for each class. The null hypothesis states that the probability of the class 1 outcome in population 1 is equal to the probability of the class 1 outcome in population 2.

previously discussed result for the NPR experiments. However, it is not possible to discern any significant difference in the *efficiency* properties of the JPR and UPR experiments (this result follows from the strong acceptance of hypothesis H4).

Finally, we find that we cannot reject hypothesis H7 on the basis of the results reported in Table 3. Under UPR, with "trained" subjects that had bargained initially under the JPR property rights specification, 76.5 percent (thirteen out of seventeen) of the decisions involved individually rational outcomes while the initial UPRT(1) experiments (our replication of Hoffman and Spitzer) generated only 40.0 percent (six out of sixteen) individually rational outcomes for the controller.[22] Table 4 indicates that this difference in behavior is statistically significant. This is dramatic support for the strong behavioral form of the Coase Theorem.

## IV. CONCLUSION

The experimental results reported here strongly support the Coase Theorem. This is in contrast to Hoffman and Spitzer's results, which

[22] Our UPR results are not significantly different from the results in Hoffman & Spitzer, *supra* note 2, in which 87.5 percent (twenty-one out of twenty-four) of all decisions in their comparable "game-trigger" experiments were individually rational. These experiments utilized a prebargaining "trigger game" (such as tic-tac-toe) in which the winner "earned the right" to be the controller in the bargaining game. Issues of moral authority aside, this trigger clearly served to reinforce the significance of being a controller. Our experimental design does the same thing in a less artificial way. Moreover, our results demonstrate that the "moral authority" of such a game trigger is not necessary (although it may be sufficient) to encourage individually rational outcomes.

violate the individual rationality requirement of the Coase Theorem (as well as game theory). It would be interesting to undertake the boundary experiments[23] identified by Hoffman and Spitzer (limited information concerning opponent payoffs and/or larger bargaining groups) with our experimental design, given that the Coase Theorem has now been established for the bargaining environment in which it was originally presented (full-information, two-person bargaining).

## APPENDIX A

### Experimental Instructions

#### *General*

You are about to participate in an experiment in decision making. The purpose of the experiment is to gain insight into certain features of complex economic processes. If you follow the instructions carefully you might earn a considerable amount of money. You will be paid by a check at the end of the experimental series.

#### *Specific Instructions*

You will be asked to make several choices over three sessions. Each choice will involve choosing a number. The cash value to you of the number is given in the payoff schedule written on the blackboard. For example, if $5 were next to number 2 on the payoff sheet (for the column pertaining to you), then you would be paid $5 if number 2 were chosen. In the example shown below, for instance, you might be person B. The payoff schedule lists the value of each number to you as well as the value of each number to the other participant.

Two of you will participate together on each decision. Although we will have three sessions, you will make only one decision with any particular person. That is, you will not participate with the same person in more than one session (and, hence, one decision). Each session will last ten minutes.

#### *Agreement Outcomes*

You may arrive at an agreement with the other participant as to which number to choose and how to allocate the resulting monetary payoff. If a joint agreement is reached, *both* parties must sign the attached agreement form, stating both what the chosen number will be *and* how much money will be transferred from one participant's earnings to the other's. *No physical threats are allowed.* If a joint agreement is made and the form is signed, the monitor will terminate the experiment and pay each participant according to the terms set forth in the agreement.

[23] See Vernon L. Smith & Arlington W. Williams, The Boundaries of Competitive Price Theory: Convergence, Expectations and Transactions Costs (June 1982) (unpublished manuscript, Indiana Univ., Dep't Econ.) for an example of boundary experiments; and Vernon L. Smith, Microeconomic Systems as an Experimental Science, 72 Am. Econ. Rev. 923, 942 (1982) for a general discussion of their methodological role.

*Disagreement Outcomes*

If you cannot come to an agreement before the end of each session, one of three alternative disagreement outcomes will be imposed on both of you. You will be informed by the monitor at the beginning of each session which of the three alternatives applies. The possible disagreement outcomes are:

1. Random: one of the numbers will be drawn at random, and will apply to both participants. Each number is equally likely to be drawn at random.
2. Zero: both participants receive zero payoff in that session.
3. Controller: one of you will be designated the "controller" at the outset of each session. This will be decided by a coin flip. The controller may, if he or she wishes, choose the number by himself or herself and inform the monitor, who will stop the experiment and pay both participants. The other participant may attempt to influence the controller to reach a mutually acceptable joint decision; the other participant may offer to pay part or all of his or her earnings to the controller.

*Example*

The following example illustrates a decision in which one participant is a controller.

Assume that A is the controller and that participants A and B have the following payoffs associated with numbers 0, 1, and 2:

| Number | A's Payoff ($) | B's Payoff ($) |
|---|---|---|
| 0 | 4 | 1 |
| 1 | 5 | 2 |
| 2 | 3 | 5 |

If A and B were to agree to set the number at 0, and further agree that B should get $1 from A's payoff, then the monitor would terminate the experiment, pay A $3 (representing the $4 payoff less the $1 transfer to B) and pay B $2 (representing the $1 payoff plus the $1 transfer from A).

An illustrative agreement form is shown below.

AGREEMENT FORM (Example)

A and B agree to set the number at ____.
A and B agree that $_____ from the monetary payoff should be paid from _____ to _____.

Signed: A: __________________
B: __________________

Do you have any questions? Please answer the following questions to make sure that you understand the instructions.

QUESTIONS

(Refer to the payoffs marked EXAMPLE on the blackboard)

1. Number ___ makes me the most money.
   Number ___ makes me the least money.
2. If the other participant is the controller and he picks number 4, I make $_____.
3. If I agree to pay $2 to the other participant and we agree on number 1, I make $_____.

## APPENDIX B

### OUR EXPERIMENTAL INSTRUCTIONS

#### *General*

You are about to participate in an experiment in decision making. The purpose of the experiment is to gain insight into certain features of complex economic processes. If you follow the instructions carefully you might earn a considerable amount of money. You will be paid by a check at the end of the experimental series.

#### *Specific Instructions*

You will be asked to make several choices over three sessions. Each choice will involve choosing a number. The cash value to you of the number is given in the payoff schedule written on the blackboard. For example, if $5 were next to number 2 on the payoff sheet (for the column pertaining to you), then you would be paid $5 if number 2 were chosen. In the example shown below, for instance, you might be person B. The payoff schedule lists the value of each number to you as well as the value of each number to the other participant.

Two of you will participate together on each decision. Although we will have three sessions, you will only make one decision with any particular person. That is, you will not participate with the same person in more than one session (and, hence, one decision). Each session will last ten minutes.

#### *Agreement Outcomes*

You may arrive at an agreement with the other participant as to which number to choose. If a joint agreement is reached, *both* parties must sign the attached agreement form, stating the chosen number. *No physical threats are allowed.* If a joint agreement is made and the form is signed, the monitor will terminate the experiment and pay each participant according to the terms set forth in the agreement.

#### *Disagreement Outcomes*

If you cannot come to an agreement before the end of each session, one of two alternative disagreement outcomes will be imposed on both of you. You will be informed by the monitor at the beginning of each session which of the alternatives applies. The possible disagreement outcomes are:

1. Random: one of the numbers will be drawn at random, and will apply to both participants. Each number is equally likely to be drawn at random.
2. Zero: both participants receive zero payoff in that session.

## Bibliography

Aivazian, Varouj A., and Callen, Jeffrey L. "The Coase Theorem and the Empty Core." *Journal of Law & Economics* 24 (1981): 175–81.

Coase, R. H. "The Problem of Social Cost." *Journal of Law & Economics* 3 (1960): 1–44.

Coase, R. H. "The Coase Theorem and the Empty Core: A Comment." *Journal of Law & Economics* 24 (1981): 183–87.

Conover, W. J. *Practical Nonparametric Statistics*. 2d ed. New York: John Wiley & Sons, 1980.

Cooter, Robert. "The Cost of Coase." *Journal of Legal Studies* 11 (1982): 1–31.

Cooter, Robert, and Marks, Stephen, with Mnookin, Robert. "Bargaining in the Shadow of the Law: A Testable Model of Strategic Behavior." *Journal of Legal Studies* 11 (1982): 225–51.

Coursey, Don. "Bilateral Bargaining, Pareto Optimality, and the Empirical Frequency of Impasse." *Journal of Economic Behavior and Organization* 3 (1982): 243–59.

Coursey, Don; Isaac, R. Mark; and Smith, Vernon L. "Natural Monopoly and Contested Markets: Some Experimental Results." *Journal of Law & Economics* 27 (1984): 91–113.

Harrison, Glenn W. "Predatory Pricing in Experiments." Manuscript. Tucson: University of Arizona, May 1985.

Harrison, Glenn W., and McKee, Michael. "Monopoly Behavior, Decentralized Regulation, and Contestable Markets: An Experimental Evaluation." *Rand Journal of Economics* 16 (1985): 51–69.

Hirshleifer, Jack. *Price Theory and Applications*. 3d ed. Englewood Cliffs, N.J.: Prentice-Hall, Inc., 1984.

Hoffman, Elizabeth, and Spitzer, Matthew L. "The Coase Theorem: Some Experimental Tests." *Journal of Law & Economics* 25 (1982): 73–98.

Hoffman, Elizabeth, and Spitzer, Matthew L. "Entitlements, Rights and Fairness: An Experimental Examination of Subjects' Concepts of Distributive Justice." *Journal of Legal Studies* 14 (1985): 259–97.

Hoffman, Elizabeth, and Spitzer, Matthew L. "Experimental Tests of the Coase Theorem with Large Bargaining Groups." *Journal of Legal Studies*, 15 (1986), in press.

Isaac, R. Mark, and Smith, Vernon L. "In Search of Predatory Pricing." *Journal of Political Economy* 93 (1985): 320–45.

Nash, John F. "The Bargaining Problem." *Econometrica* 18 (1950): 155–62.

Nash, John F. "Two Person Cooperative Games." *Econometrica* 21 (1953): 128–40.

Plott, Charles R. "Externalities and Corrective Policies in Experimental Markets." *Economics Journal* 93 (1983): 106–27.

Prudencio, Yves C. "The Voluntary Approach to Externality Problems: An Experimental Test." *Journal of Environmental Economics and Management* 9 (1982): 213–28.

Regan, Donald H. "The Problem of Social Cost Revisited." *Journal of Law and Economics* 15 (1972): 427–37.

Smith, Vernon L. "Incentive Compatible Experimental Processes for the Provision of Public Goods." *Research in Experimental Economics* 1 (1979): 59–168.

Smith, Vernon L. "An Empirical Study of Decentralized Institutions of Monopoly Restraint." In *Essays in Contemporary Fields of Economics,* edited by G. Horwich and J. Quirk. West Lafayette, Ind.: Purdue University Press, 1981.

Smith, Vernon L. "Microeconomic Systems as an Experimental Science." *American Economic Review* 72 (1982): 923–55.

Smith, Vernon L., and Williams, Arlington W. "The Boundaries of Competitive Price Theory: Convergence, Expectations and Transactions Costs." Manuscript. Bloomington: Indiana University, Department of Economics, June 1982.

# [29]

# EXPERIMENTAL TESTS OF THE COASE THEOREM WITH LARGE BARGAINING GROUPS

*ELIZABETH HOFFMAN and MATTHEW L. SPITZER**

## I. INTRODUCTION

IN his path-breaking paper "The Problem of Social Cost"[1] Ronald Coase posited that a change in a liability rule will leave agents' production and consumption decisions both unchanged and economically efficient within the following (implicit) framework: (1) two agents to each bargain, (2) perfect knowledge of one another's (convex) production and profit or utility functions, (3) competitive markets, (4) zero transactions costs, (5) costless court system, (6) profit-maximizing producers and expected-utility maximizing consumers, (7) no wealth effects, and (8) agents will strike mutually advantageous bargains in the absence of transactions costs. While the theorem is "true" given these assumptions, criticism has focused on its applicability in a wider environment in which the assumptions are generally not met.

In a recent paper,[2] we reported the results of experimental tests of the Coase Theorem in situations in which there were either two or three parties to a bargain. Some experiments were conducted on a "full-information" basis, where the subjects were provided with both their own and the other subject's payoff schedules. Other experiments were conducted on a "limited-information" basis, in which subjects were only shown their own payoff schedules.[3] The results for all the two-person

* Associate Professor of Economics, Purdue University, and Professor of Law, University of Southern California, respectively. Helpful comments were provided by Richard Craswell, Glenn Harrison, Peter Ordeshook, Alan Schwartz, Barbara White, and the participants in workshops at UCLA and Washington University. Research assistance was provided by Gary Adler, Faye Anderson, Lee Ann Duffy, Felipe Prestamo, and Ellen Roth. The authors reluctantly accept responsibility for any errors. The financial support of National Science Foundation grant no. SES-8200266 is gratefully acknowledged.

[1] R. H. Coase, The Problem of Social Cost, 3 J. Law & Econ. 1 (1960).

[2] Elizabeth Hoffman & Matthew L. Spitzer, The Coase Theorem: Some Experimental Tests, 25 J. Law & Econ. 73 (1982).

[3] For full details of the experimental procedure, see *id.*

[*Journal of Legal Studies*, vol. XV (January 1986)]
 0047-2530/86/1501-0007$01.50

experiments and the three-person experiments with full information provided strong support for the Coase Theorem. Subjects chose the joint-profit-maximizing outcome over 92 percent of the time in each of the three experimental treatments. However, the results of the three-person experiments with limited information gave less support.

These results are important because they establish that agents will strike mutually advantageous bargains within the simple framework first proposed by Coase. Moreover, they suggest that simply relaxing the assumption of two parties to a bargain will not immediately lead to bargaining breakdown. On the other hand, the erosion of efficiency with three agents and incomplete information suggests that the Coase proposition's policy applications might not be as wide as its supporters claim.

In this paper we extend our previous work in order to examine the operation of the Coase Theorem when there are many parties to a bargain. As a theoretical matter, there is reason to believe that the parties will likely fail to exhaust the gains from voluntary trade as the number of parties increases, because the problem with holdouts becomes more acute. The easiest way to see the point is to assume that the population contains two types of persons, greedy and reasonable. Greedy people try to extract far more than "their share" of the surplus from any bargain and sometimes cause bargaining breakdown if the others do not give in. In the extreme situation, the presence of a single greedy person will block the formation of advantageous trades. As the number of persons needed to complete trades increases, the likelihood that one or more greedy persons will block the transaction should increase.[4] This theoretical argument

[4] A simple mathematical model demonstrates the point. Assume there are $g$ greedy individuals and $n - g$ reasonable ones, and that a greedy person will act greedily regardless of the bargaining context. If $n$ and $g$ are large enough, we can regard the selection of bargainers from the population as draws, *with replacement*, from a population. The probability of getting a greedy person on any draw is $g/n$, while the probability of getting a reasonable one is $(n - g)/n$.

A bargain will occur in a group, where the consent of at least $x$ people are needed, if and only if there are zero greedy people in the group. The probability that this will happen is

$$P = \left(\frac{n - g}{n}\right)^x.$$

To find $dP/dx$, set

$$\ln P = x \ln\left(\frac{n - g}{n}\right)$$

$$\frac{1}{P}\frac{dP}{dx} = \ln\left(\frac{n - g}{n}\right).$$

thus tends to point to a Hobbesian, not a Coasian, view of the world.[5]

The literature contains, however, very little empirical work on this general proposition. This paper is an effort to fill that gap. It reports the results of experiments designed to test the Coase Theorem for large groups. Using an experimental design similar to that in our previous work, we conducted experiments with both four and ten parties to a bargain under full and limited information, and with twenty parties to a bargain under limited information. The results provide continued overwhelming support for Coase's proposition. Overall, 93 percent of the decisions were efficient and there was no deterioration as the bargaining groups got larger. If anything, efficiency improved with larger groups. On the other hand, there was some deterioration in moving from full to limited information. Virtually 100 percent of the full-information bargains were efficient, but efficiency was closer to 90 percent with limited information.

These results provide significant implications for property, tort, and contract law. In the traditional language of political economy, the Coase Theorem is the cornerstone of a laissez-faire legal and economic policy governing contract and property law. One implication of our results is that policymakers should recognize the power of voluntary agreements to overcome externality problems, even in the absence of government intervention. More specifically, these results produce a presumption in favor of the Coase Theorem for disputes involving substantial numbers of parties. By a "presumption in favor of the Coase Theorem" we mean that a judge or legislator who is considering choosing a rule to govern a dispute in tort, contract, or property that involves as many as thirty-eight parties should assume that the parties can and will exhaust the gains from trade by voluntary agreement. One who would show that bargaining breakdown is likely must bear the burden of proof.

---

Therefore,

$$\frac{dP}{dx} = P \ln\left(\frac{n-g}{n}\right) = \left(\frac{n-g}{n}\right)^x \ln\left(\frac{n-g}{n}\right) < 0,$$

because $0 < (n - g)/n < 1$. Thus, this model predicts that the probability of reaching an agreement declines as the size of the bargaining group increases. On more realistic assumptions, the presence of one or more greedy parties need not block all voluntary transactions. It is possible that some transactions may go forward, with the greedy persons taking the lion's share of the surplus. Nonetheless, the likelihood of failure in these situations will likely increase with the number of parties, because several greedy persons may appear in any random draw.

[5] Robert Cooter, The Cost of Coase, 11 J. Legal Stud. 1 (1982).

## II. Experimental Design

### A. *General*

In all the experiments[6] the subjects bargained "face-to-face" in public[7] for more money than most students can earn for an hour's work in their next best alternative employment. Side payments were allowed, and contracts were in writing and strictly enforced. All payments were made in public. Subjects were given no motivational instructions, in that they were not told what their objectives should be in choosing a number or in forming contracts.

We placed each bargaining group in a separate room (with the monitor being the only other person present) and randomly assigned payoff charts to the subjects. The monitor provided the subjects with the instructions that are given in the appendix. The subjects first read the instructions silently and then listened as the monitor read them aloud.

These instructions told subjects that they would be divided into two groups and that they had to choose one of a given set of numbers. They would be paid different amounts of money, in cash, depending on which number was chosen. In the full-information experiments each subject was given payoff information for all other subjects. In the limited-information experiments each subject was only given his own payoffs. Each set of payoff schedules had a unique and clearly identifiable joint-profit-maximizing number. If the subjects chose that number and reallocated the payoffs through side payments, each participant could make at least one dollar more than at the next best alternative.

In this formulation the numbers that the subjects choose are analogous to pollution levels in an externality problem. For example, one group of subjects preferred higher numbers and might represent upstream factories that pollute a river. The other group preferred lower numbers and might represent downstream users who need clean water.

The subjects were told that one of the two groups would be chosen "joint controllers." Joint controllers could choose a number in the following manner. If all joint controllers agreed on a number, then that agreed-on number was chosen. However, if any joint controller disagreed with the others, he might choose the number by himself. For example, if ten subjects, placed in the position of pollutees, were joint controllers and had to choose a number (pollution level), then any one of the joint controllers could insist on a lower number (level of pollution) than the other joint controllers wished. Even if the other nine joint controllers were willing to

[6] Instructions for all experiments are available in an appendix on request from the authors.

[7] The monitors observed the bargaining.

choose a higher number (to tolerate a higher level of pollution), the subjects outside the controlling group would not be helped unless the tenth joint controller also agreed to choose the higher number (to tolerate the pollution). If the tenth joint controller chose a lower number, the lower number controlled as the group's choice. If the subjects in the position of polluters were joint controllers, the number was chosen in exactly the same fashion, except that individual subjects could force the group to choose higher numbers. The "joint controllers" arrangement models a right to pollute (for polluters) or a right to an injunction forbidding pollution and guaranteeing clean water (for pollutees).

The subjects were also allowed to transfer, by contract, payoffs from any party to any other party.[8] This feature of the experiment directly mimics the contract mechanism that is central to the Coase Theorem.

After reading the instructions and examining their payoffs, subjects were tested on their understanding of the rules and the consequences of any decisions they might make.[9] After all the subjects in a particular experiment had answered all the questions correctly, and after the monitor had answered all the subjects' remaining uncertainties about the rules of the game, the monitor used one of the mechanisms described below for choosing joint controllers. The subjects were then instructed to proceed with the experiment (by choosing a number).

### *B. Four-Person, Coin-Flip Experiments*

We began this experimental project as an extension of the experimental design we had used for the two- and three-person experiments in our previous work.[10] We used four parties to a bargain, either two against two (2 × 2) or one against three (1 × 3), and the right to be joint controllers was decided by a coin flip. Each grouping was run under both full and limited information, and each group made three decisions together, sequentially. Table 1 summarizes the number of experimental sessions of three decisions each we conducted under each of the four treatments.

### *C. Game-Trigger Experiments*

The subjects in the experiments described above almost always chose the joint-profit maximum, thereby strongly supporting Coase. But they seldom chose payoff divisions that gave the controller or controllers at least their individual maxima—the amount controllers could make with-

[8] Payoff sheets are included with the instructions.

[9] Tests are included with the instructions.

[10] Hoffman & Spitzer, *supra* note 2.

TABLE 1
FOUR-PERSON, COIN-FLIP EXPERIMENTAL TREATMENTS

| | JOINT CONTROLLERS | |
|---|---|---|
| | 2 × 2 | 1 × 3 |
| Full information | 3 | 25 |
| Limited information | 15 | 18 |

out cooperating with anyone else. More than half the time the subjects split the payoffs equally, as though controllers were not self-regarding, a point we have analyzed elsewhere.[11]

In order to elicit more self-regarding payoff divisions, we developed a new experimental design and set of instructions. We hypothesized that subjects who won the coin flip did not feel they had the morally justifiable right to exercise the entitlement of the controller's position, which led them to bargain as if they were in a symmetric game and chose an equal split of the payoffs—the Nash solution. We then induced feelings of moral justification in the controller by making that individual "earn" the entitlement by winning a simple game. We also told the controller he or she had actually earned that right by winning the game.[12]

1. *Two-Person* (1 × 1) *Experiments*. We first tested this new experimental design in the basic two-person setting. We ran two-person experiments with both full and limited information, each with both sequential decisions and nonsequential decisions. In the sequential decisions two subjects made two decisions together. In the nonsequential decisions each pair of subjects only made one decision together. Table 2 summarizes how many pairs of subjects participated in each treatment.[13]

2. *Three-Person* (1 × 2) *Nonsequential*. We next tested this new experimental design with three-person (2 × 1) experiments. We were particularly interested in replicating these experiments because the limited-

[11] *Id.*

[12] In another paper, Elizabeth Hoffman & Matthew L. Spitzer, Entitlements, Rights, and Fairness: An Experimental Examination of Subjects' Concepts of Distributive Justice, 14 J. Legal Stud. 259 (1985), we report the results of two-person, full-information experiments. We found that changes in the nature of the instructions had no effect on the likelihood of the parties to reach the joint efficient outcome: with both sets of instructions, nearly 100 percent of the choices were optimal. But changes in instructions did influence the division of the gains. Winning a game and having the monitor reinforce the winner's moral authority resulted in the controller's obtaining his or her individual maximum more than half the time. When the controller was chosen by coin flip without reinforcement, only about a quarter of the payoff divisions were individually rational. Glenn W. Harrison & Michael McKee, Experimental Evaluation of the Coase Theorem, 28 J. Law & Econ. 653 (1985), essentially replicate our results using a different mechanism for inducing self-regarding behavior.

[13] Results of these experiments are reported in Hoffman & Spitzer, *supra* note 12.

TABLE 2
PARTICIPANTS IN TWO-PERSON, GAME-TRIGGER EXPERIMENTS

| | INFORMATION | |
|---|---|---|
| | Full | Limited |
| Sequential | 11 | 10 |
| Nonsequential | 24 | 18 |

information environment was likely to be quite unfavorable to the Coase Theorem, given our previous results. To put additional stress on the Coase Theorem, we also ran these experiments in the nonsequential mode. In other words, each group of three people (who did not know one another) made only one decision together. Thus there was no incentive for controllers just to behave altruistically and split the payoffs equally in hopes of receiving similar treatment in subsequent decisions. Twenty-four experimental decisions were made under full information and twenty-four were made under limited information.

3. *Four-Person, Nonsequential.* The next three sets of experiments simply extended the three-person experiments to four parties to each bargain. We ran 1 × 3 joint controllers with both full and limited information and 2 × 2 joint controllers with only limited information. We only ran limited information for the 2 × 2 joint controllers because the full-information, symmetric experiments had been almost 100 percent efficient. Since 1 × 2 joint controllers had presented some problems, we ran the 1 × 3 with full as well as limited information. Twelve full-information and twelve limited-information decisions were made with 1 × 3 joint controllers; twelve limited-information decisions were made with 2 × 2 joint controllers.

4. *Ten-Person, Sequential.* We then conducted experiments with ten subjects to see if the Coase Theorem remained robust in large groups. Here we returned to the sequential experimental design. First we ran experiments with five subjects on each of two teams (5 × 5 experiments). The teams were organized similarly to the 2 × 2 teams in the four-person experiments. Six groups of ten subjects made two decisions each under full information, and five groups made two decisions each under limited information. Then we ran 1 × 9 joint controllers with both full and limited information. Five groups of ten subjects made two decisions each under full information, and five groups made two decisions each under limited information.

5. *Twenty-Person, Sequential.* Having completed the ten-person experiments, it was clear that the Coase Theorem was quite robust, even in moderately large groups. We then doubled the group size once again and

focused only on the treatment showing any deviation from complete efficiency: one controller against many controllers under limited information. On the basis of the four- and ten-person experiments, we concluded that if the Coase Theorem was robust under that experimental treatment, we could be reasonably certain it would be robust with equal-size bargaining groups or full information. We planned to conduct the experiments in the other treatment cells only if this cell failed to support the Coase Theorem. Four groups of twenty subjects made two decisions each using $1 \times 19$, limited-information experimental instructions.

### *D. Subjects*

Subjects were undergraduate economics and management majors and management graduate students at Purdue University; upper-level undergraduate economics majors at Northwestern University; and law students, undergraduate arts and sciences students, and university staff at the University of Southern California. They were recruited in classes and by telephone and told only that they would participate in an economics decision. They were promised $4.00 per hour plus their earnings. Extra subjects were recruited in case of no-shows and paid at least $2.00 just for showing up. All subjects were inexperienced in this particular kind of experiment, and friends were not allowed to participate together. After each experiment we explained the nature of the experiment and the scientific importance of not telling their friends about it. Later subjects appeared to be as naive about the experiment as earlier subjects had been, and there did not seem to be a time trend in the results.

## III. Experimental Results

Table 3 summarizes the results of all 445 experimental decisions. For all sizes of bargaining groups, the results strongly support the Coase Theorem. If anything, larger bargaining groups were more likely to choose the joint-profit maximum than small groups were. Overall, 93 percent of the experimental decisions chose the profit-maximizing outcome; 98 percent of the ten- and twenty-subject decisions chose it. Efficiency is somewhat lower (91 percent) with limited than with full information (94 percent), but—critically—it is at least 90 percent for all but a few experimental treatments. Surprisingly, the only deviations from nearly 100 percent efficiency are among the four-person coin-flip experiments, which had the highest proportions of equal-split payoff divisions. In fact, these results strongly suggest that, in general, efficiency is compatible with self-regarding payoff divisions. The game-trigger experiments were more efficient (94 percent) than the coin-flip experiments (91 percent). The game-trigger experiments also yielded far more (81 percent) self-regarding divisions than the coin-flip experiments (only 33 percent).

It is possible to hazard an explanation for the seemingly anomalous situation in which the large groups cooperated more effectively than small ones. Subjects in large experiments created ad hoc institutions to help the transacting process. In the twenty-person experiments, for example, the nineteen people always shared information about payoffs with one another. They tended to caucus and select two or three of their number to deal directly with the single opponent. After some discussions the representatives would report back to the rest of their group, and then return to speak with the single opponent. In essence, the group of nineteen devised an informal institution that allowed them to overcome the problems of large numbers. By organizing themselves they were able to exhaust the gains from trade in fairly short order. The longest of these experiments took no more than two hours.

## IV. Implications of the Results for Analysis of Nonlaboratory Environments

In this section we explore the applicability of our results to nonlaboratory settings and then consider some implications of our findings for the choice of common-law remedies, such as damages or injunctions.

### A. *Applicability of Results*

To what extent do our experimental results supporting the Coase Theorem extend to nonlaboratory environments, assuming they could be replicated? To answer this question we will explore two different types of reasons for not using these results. First, subjects might not behave in the laboratory as they do in naturally occurring environments. Second, the experimental treatments used might not capture essential aspects of nonlaboratory environments.

1. *Laboratory Effects.* One important set of issues concerns the transferability of our results from the laboratory to the world at large. In a fundamental sense this problem is asymmetrical. If our experimental results had indicated substantial departures from efficiency, we would be able to say that the Coase Theorem was not supported and was, perhaps, wrong. If a theory cannot work in a laboratory that has been designed to focus on the assumptions underlying the theory, it is unlikely the theory will work in a naturally occurring environment, except by chance. If the Coase Theorem had failed in the laboratory setting, then we would have no cause to believe it would be valid in the field.

TABLE 3
RESULTS

| Experiment | $N$ | $N_1$ | $N_2$ | $N_3$ | $N_4$ |
|---|---|---|---|---|---|
| I. Coin flip | | | | | |
| A. Two-person | | | | | |
| 1. Sequential* | | | | | |
| a. Full information | 12 | 12 | 12 | 0 | 0 |
| b. Limited information | 8 | 8 | 6 | 2 | 0 |
| 2. Nonsequential | | | | | |
| a. Full information | 12 | 11 | 5 | 7 | 0 |
| b. Limited information | 12 | 11 | 6 | 4 | 2 |
| B. Four-person sequential | | | | | |
| 1. 3 × 1 Controllers | | | | | |
| a. Full information | 75 | 75 | 49 | 15 | 11 |
| Single controller | 41 | 41 | 25 | 6 | 10 |
| Joint controller | 31 | 31 | 21 | 9 | 1 |
| No flip | 3 | 3 | 3 | 0 | 0 |
| b. Limited information | 54 | 42 | 28 | 20 | 6 |
| Single controller | 23 | 18 | 8 | 10 | 5 |
| Joint controller | 28 | 21 | 17 | 10 | 1 |
| No flip | 3 | 3 | 3 | 0 | 0 |
| 2. 2 × 2 Controllers | | | | | |
| a. Full information | 9 | 6 | 1 | 6 | 2 |
| b. Limited information | 45 | 42 | 16 | 20 | 9 |
| Coin flip totals | 227 | 207 | 123 | 74 | 30 |
| Percentages | | 91 | 54 | 33 | 13 |
| II. Game trigger | | | | | |
| A. Two-person | | | | | |
| 1. Sequential | | | | | |
| a. Full information | 22 | 21 | 7 | 15 | 0 |
| b. Limited information | 20 | 18 | 7 | 11 | 2 |
| 2. Nonsequential | | | | | |
| a. Full information | 24 | 20 | 2 | 21 | 1 |
| b. Limited information | 18 | 18 | 0 | 10 | 8 |
| B. Three-person nonsequential | | | | | |
| 1. Full information | 24 | 23 | 1 | 23 | 0 |
| Single controller | 8 | 8 | 0 | 8 | 0 |
| Joint controller | 15 | 14 | 0 | 15 | 0 |
| No game | 1 | 1 | 1 | 0 | 0 |
| 2. Limited information | 24 | 23 | 3 | 18 | 3 |
| Single controller | 5 | 5 | 1 | 3 | 1 |
| Joint controller | 19 | 18 | 2 | 15 | 2 |
| C. Four-person nonsequential | | | | | |
| 1. 3 × 1 Controllers | | | | | |
| a. Full information | 12 | 12 | 1 | 11 | 0 |
| Single controller | 6 | 6 | 1 | 5 | 0 |
| Joint controller | 6 | 6 | 0 | 6 | 0 |
| b. Limited information | 12 | 10 | 1 | 10 | 1 |
| Single controller | 2 | 2 | 0 | 1 | 1 |
| Joint controller | 10 | 8 | 1 | 9 | 0 |
| 2. 2 × 2 Controllers | | | | | |
| a. Limited information | 12 | 12 | 0 | 12 | 0 |

TABLE 3 (*Continued*)

| Experiment | $N$ | $N_1$ | $N_2$ | $N_3$ | $N_4$ |
|---|---|---|---|---|---|
| D. Ten-person sequential | | | | | |
| 1. 5 × 5 Controllers | | | | | |
| a. Full information | 12 | 11 | 0 | 12 | 0 |
| b. Limited information | 12 | 12 | 0 | 11 | 1 |
| 2. 9 × 1 Controllers | | | | | |
| a. Full information | 8 | 8 | 0 | 7 | 1 |
| b. Limited information | 10 | 10 | 1 | 8 | 1 |
| E. Twenty-person, sequential, limited information | 8 | 8 | 0 | 7 | 1 |
| Game-trigger totals | 218 | 206 | 23 | 176 | 19 |
| Percentages | | 94 | 11 | 81 | 8 |
| Grand totals | 445 | 413 | 146 | 250 | 49 |
| Percentages | | 93 | 33 | 56 | 11 |
| Full information | 210 | 199 | 78 | 117 | 15 |
| Percentages | | 95 | 37 | 56 | 7 |
| Limited information | 235 | 214 | 68 | 133 | 34 |
| Percentages | | 91 | 29 | 57 | 14 |

NOTE.—$N$ = total number of decisions; $N_1$ = number of joint profit maximums; $N_2$ = number of equal splits ± $1.00; $N_3$ = number of individually rational divisions; $N_4$ = other payoff divisions.

* From Elizabeth Hoffman & Matthew L. Spitzer, Entitlements, Rights, and Fairness: An Experimental Examination of Subjects' Concepts of Distributive Justice, 14 J. Legal Stud. 259 (1985).

The more difficult inferences run in the opposite direction, as several reasons might be suggested why our results would not be as robust in the field as they are in the laboratory. In particular, in a laboratory setting, subjects might regard money differently, or they might take different attitudes toward bargaining generally. These differences might be produced either by observer effects or by some substantial difference between our subject pool (mainly young, well-educated adults) and the population at large.

In order to explore this hypothesis it is useful to ask at the outset whether any evidence of laboratory effects appears in the data. The non-self-regarding nature of many of the controller's decisions might be taken as evidence of these effects, given the common assumption that people generally act in a self-regarding manner in naturally occurring environments. Two considerations suggest that this possibility should not present problems for the applicability of our results. First, the degree of self-regarding behavior increased markedly when we switched the experimental treatment from coin flip to game trigger, suggesting that the laboratory setting (as distinct from a naturally occurring setting) was not producing that behavior. Second, the results of the experiments with self-regarding controllers supported the Coase Theorem just as strongly as did the experiments with non-self-regarding controllers. Thus, even if people are, on average, less self-regarding in the laboratory than in naturally occurring environments, it seems to pose no threat to our test of the Coase

Theorem. The theorem is quite robust with regard to differences in subjects' willingness to be self-regarding in a laboratory environment.

Despite the theorem's robustness in the laboratory, however, observer effects and differences between the subject pool and the population at large could render our results inapplicable in naturally occurring environments. Subjects might bargain to efficient outcomes merely because of a desire to appear to be "nice" because they were being watched by the experimenter. But if simply being observed could drive people to bargain to efficient outcomes, our results would apply to many nonlaboratory settings. Little "real-world" bargaining takes place in absolute secrecy. The results, and often the bargaining process itself, of virtually all important business deals are scrutinized by management, boards of directors, stockholders, or governmental organizations.

The subject pool in our experiments is also quite similar to the group of people who make the kind of business deals and get involved in the kind of lawsuits the Coase Theorem models. These subjects, who tended to be juniors, seniors, and graduate students between twenty and twenty-five years of age, will be the business leaders and propertied individuals of the next generation. We do not think that our subjects were too young and inexperienced in bargaining to provide a model for bargaining behavior. Most of the subjects were management students and law students, and both groups get instruction and practice in bargaining. They all seemed to take the experiments very seriously, and the results suggest that they did. Only if our subjects were to become less able to contract to efficient outcomes as they grew older and more experienced would one question their usefulness for a test of the Coase Theorem. But why expect people to be less likely to contract to the efficient outcomes as they grow older and more experienced? Forcing a bargaining breakdown is self-defeating behavior. An experienced negotiator learns over time to get as much as possible from a bargain, not to assure the bargain's failure.

2. *Experimental Treatment Effects.* A policy analyst might hesitate to trust our conclusions, however, on the ground that our experiments failed to incorporate enough of the naturally occurring phenomena. In particular, we have not modeled three crucial sources of bargaining breakdown.

First, certain important bargaining and coordination costs were absent in our experiments. We only went up to twenty parties to a bargain and we brought them together face-to-face for the purpose of bargaining with one another. We did not forbid them to make joint-maximizing deals including side payments. We have no reason to believe they disliked the task of bargaining with one another. And we included institutions, such as standard form contracts and an hourly wage for bargainers, that undoubtedly reduced the costs of bargaining and facilitated the achievement of efficient outcomes.

Naturally occurring bargains may not occur or be efficient if large groups cannot get organized to sit down together or if government regulations forbid them to do so. If they were to sit down together, they might not reach an efficient outcome if they could not enforce their agreements or if the bargaining took a great deal of time and the bargainers were not being paid. In addition, if the parties hate each other so much that they either will not talk or they prefer to hurt one another instead of maximizing jointly, no efficient bargaining is likely to take place. For such reasons, our results may not be applicable in a pollution dispute involving hundreds of unorganized homeowners (very large numbers), a price-fixing deal between large corporations (legally unenforceable agreement), or a divorce settlement (animosity between parties).

Second, informational deficiencies or asymmetries might also produce inefficient outcomes. Our experiment did not model situations in which parties did not know their own profit functions or could not learn how their own activities interfered with others' profits. In such situations individuals might try to joint maximize, given their information, but still be unable to do so. In some sense, however, one could argue that such behavior does not violate the spirit of the Coase Theorem. We simply need to reformulate the theorem with informational constraints, just as standard economic welfare theory[14] and bargaining theory[15] are being reformulated subject to those constraints. The theorem's predictions would undoubtedly be different, however, and we would want to test the new predictions with a limited-information set.

Third, we modeled no significant wealth effects in our experiments. Large changes in a consumer's wealth can cause substantial variations in the amount the consumer would be willing to pay for a "good," such as freedom from pollution. Usually, the wealthier he is the more he will pay for a good. In our experiments, when one side or the other gained the controller's position, its wealth was increased. However, our experiment did not change the subjects' payoffs according to which side became the controller. By keeping the payoffs constant, we kept wealth effects out of the experiment. If we had changed payoffs, thereby modeling large wealth effects on consumer demand, the payoff changes alone should have led to different outcomes. In this way, large wealth effects on consumer demand preclude application of the invariance result of the Coase Theorem.[16]

[14] See, for example, Milton Harris & Robert M. Townshend, Resource Allocation under Asymmetric Information, 49 Econometrica 33 (1981).

[15] Roger Myerson, Two-Person Bargaining Problems with Incomplete Information, 52 Econometrica 461 (1984).

[16] Another closely related possibility is that people attach value to the ownership rights, per se, and would pay more to avoid losing their rights than they would pay to acquire those

Despite all these precautionary statements, however, we still believe that our results produce a presumption in favor of a Coase Theorem–type mechanism in a substantial class of conflicts. Such a class would include at least situations where bargaining and enforcement costs are low, where there are few informational problems, and where no more than twenty people are involved. Would this class of conflicts extend to disputes with more than twenty people? We think so. First, note that the Coase Theorem worked perfectly with 1 × 19 joint controllers. Second, note that it also worked perfectly in the ten-person, 5 × 5 experiments. If these results are not idiosyncratic, then we should expect the Coase Theorem to work in a 19 × 19 setting. Hence, our range of confidence should probably extend to disputes involving as many as thirty-eight parties. This is quite a substantial number, and it allows us to extend the presumption in favor of the Coase Theorem to a substantial class of disputes, such as landowner disputes involving rights to light and air,[17] small nuisances, such as dog kennels,[18] neighborhood aesthetics, such as ugly houses and funeral parlors,[19] and contractual claims involving a number of people.

What do we mean by a "presumption in favor of the Coase Theorem"? We suggest that in choosing a legal rule to govern disputes such as those listed above, a judge or a legislator should start his analysis by presuming that the parties can and will, in general, exhaust the gains from trade through private bargaining. Someone who claims the opposite, that bargaining breakdown will generally occur in some particular setting, must bear the burden of proof. He must point to some phenomenon, such as very high transactions costs, and show how the phenomenon is likely to

same rights. Then they would not necessarily behave in accordance with the Coase Theorem. For a discussion of the implications of this asymmetry with regard to rights, see Mark Kelman, Consumption Theory, Production Theory, and Ideology in the Coase Theorem, 52 S. Cal. L. Rev. 669 (1979). It is attacked on methodological grounds in Matthew L. Spitzer & Elizabeth Hoffman, A Reply to Consumption Theory, Production Theory, and Ideology in the Coase Theorem, 53 S. Cal. L. Rev. 1187 (1980). The empirical work on this issue is mixed. Jack L. Knetch & J. A. Sinden, Willingness to Pay and Compensation Demanded: Experimental Evidence of an Unexpected Disparity in Measures of Value, 99 Q. J. Econ. 507 (1984), strongly suggest that this may be a concern in consumer contexts. On the other hand, Don L. Coursey, John J. Hovis, & William D. Schulze, A Comparison of Alternative Valuation Mechanisms for Non-market Exchange (1983) (unpublished manuscript, Univ. Wyoming), find that if they use an incentive-compatible method to elicit willingness to accept responses, the difference between willingness to pay and willingness to sell goes away.

[17] See, for example, Fontainebleau Hotel Corp. v. Forty-five Twenty-five, Inc., 18 Fla. Supp. 74, 114 So.2d 357 (Fla. App. 1959).

[18] See, for example, Ensign v. Walls, 323 Mich. 49, 34 N.W.2d 549 (1948).

[19] See, for example, Matthewson v. Primeau, 64 Wash.2d 929, 395 P.2d 183 (1964); and C. Gregory, H. Kalven, Jr., & R. Epstein, Cases and Materials on Torts 524 (1977).

prevent contracting between the parties. Only if the person who predicts bargaining breakdown makes his case should the judge or legislator act with the presumption of bargaining breakdown.

This placement of the burden of proof, and the resultant framing of work on disputes, represents a substantial step forward. Previously, discussions had avoided dealing with disputes with twenty or thirty parties either by always assuming 1,000 or more parties in a large dispute[20] or by simply referring to "many" without specifying how many.[21] Assuming our results can be replicated, we have provided a first step in using the Coase Theorem in the analysis of a substantial class of disputes. Henceforth, "many" may still be read to include 1,000 parties, but it probably will not include thirty-eight.[22]

### *B. Examples of the Use of Our Results for Legal Policy*

Our results may provide implications for the law of remedies in property, tort, and contract, where they support a preference for injunctive remedies as opposed to damages.[23]

1. *Nuisances Involving Relatively Few Parties.* The law of nuisance[24] is replete with cases in which relatively few parties may and need bargain among themselves over the reassignment of property rights. In disputes between a kennel owner and nearby homeowners, for example, the parties can easily locate each other, so that the possible outcomes reduce to a familiar set of four. There are two injunctive remedies: (1) kennel's

[20] See, for example, Richard A. Posner, Economic Analysis of Law 45 (2d ed. 1977) (1,000 parties); and Guido Calabresi & A. Douglas Melamed, Property Rules, Liability Rules and Inalienability: One View of the Cathedral, 85 Harv. L. Rev. 1089 (1972) (100,000 citizens).

[21] See, for example, Stanley M. Besen, Willard G. Manning, Jr., & Bridger M. Mitchell, Copyright Liability for Cable Television: Compulsory Licensing and the Coase Theorem, 21 J. Law & Econ. 67, 82 (1978); Stephen G. Breyer & Richard B. Stewart, Administrative Law and Regulatory Policy 284, n.81 (1979).

[22] At this point the moderate departures from optimality in the three- and four-person, joint-controller, limited-information, coin-flip experiments are best viewed as statistical outliers, especially in view of the overwhelmingly high percentage of efficient outcomes in the three-, four-, ten-, and twenty-person, joint-controller experiments. Hence, our tentative conclusions in Hoffman & Spitzer, *supra* note 2, at 96–98, that joint controllers pose a problem for the Coase Theorem, should be discarded.

[23] We assume the law is, or should be, concerned at least in part with economic efficiency, but we also recognize that the proper jurisprudential role of economics is controversial. See text at notes 36–39 *infra*. Resolution of this controversy lies well beyond the scope of this paper.

[24] See Maurice T. Van Hecke, Robert N. Leavell, & Grant S. Nelson, Cases and Materials on Equitable Remedies and Restitution 425–60 (1973), for general background on this subject.

right—the kennel may emit noise and odors, and (2) homeowner's right—any homeowner is entitled to an order of the court enjoining the kennel to emit no noise or odors.

The court may also choose from two damages remedies: (*a*) kennel's right—the homeowners may obtain an order of the court directing the kennel to emit no noise and odors if and only if the homeowners pay the kennel all damages it suffers from reducing its level of pollution, or (*b*) homeowner's right—the kennel may pollute at any level it chooses, but it must pay homeowners for any damage caused by the noise and odors.[25]

The great risk of either injunctive remedy is commonly thought to arise from the risk that, where the court assigns the right to the party who values it least, voluntary negotiations will not be able to correct the original allocative error. Alternatively, damage remedies impose considerable administrative costs on the courts and may not be entirely accurate. Our results suggest that the choice should be between rule 1 and rule 2 because risk of breakdown in voluntary negotiations is ordinarily low, perhaps even if there are as many as thirty-eight parties to the dispute. Where the kennel is not enjoined as a nuisance, then the homeowners can by agreement pay the kennel operator money to reduce the pollution. Where the kennel operation is so enjoined, the optimal level of pollution can be achieved, this time with payments from the kennel operator to the homeowners.

The strength of these results may depend in part on the nature of the participants to the dispute. If the homeowners are relatively homogeneous in their income and preference, the dispute may be more easily resolved than it would be if they differed among themselves in these respects. In addition, our results do not tell us anything about disputes involving, for example, a factory and hundreds or thousands of landowners who may not even know of each others' existence. In such a situation, contracting to a Pareto optimum may still be unlikely, and the court may prefer to choose a damages entitlement. If the factory is a nuisance, the court may choose rule *b*, which allows the factory to pollute at any level as long as it pays landowners all judicially determined amounts of damage. Such a rule would prevent the landowners from holding out, and would encourage the factory to take into account the cost of its pollution. It might, however, suffer from possible inaccuracies in the court's valuation of damages from pollutants.

[25] There are other possibilities, but restricting discussion to these two alternatives simplifies the textual discussion. For a good discussion of a hybrid remedy, see Robert C. Ellickson, Alternatives to Zoning: Covenants, Nuisance Rules, and Fines as Land Use Controls, 40 U. Chi. L. Rev. 681, 738 (1973).

If the factory is not a nuisance, choosing a damage rule becomes more problematic. Rule *a* would allow the factory to pollute until the landowners paid it an amount equal to the added costs it would incur from reducing its pollution. Unfortunately, such a rule might be plagued by substantial holdout problems. Unless some incentive-compatible taxation scheme were devised to get money from the landowners, such a rule would probably fail to produce worthwhile reductions in pollution. Hence, a court that was interested in efficiency might prefer to find the factory a nuisance and choose rule *b*.

2. *Enforcement of Old Servitudes.* Other legal rules may be analyzed in an entirely analogous fashion. Consider the enforcement of old servitudes that burden some parcels of land.[26] Neighboring landowners frequently execute agreements, called equitable servitudes, to restrict in advance the right of any landowner to use his land in ways injurious to other landowners. For example, a group of landowners might all promise to use their land only for single family dwellings. If any landowner were to attempt to use his property in a manner inconsistent with his promise, any of the other landowners could go to court and get an injunction forbidding the inconsistent use.[27] In this manner the landowners become "joint controllers" with respect to inconsistent uses; all landowners must consent to any one owner's inconsistent use of land before the inconsistent use will be permitted.

Many years after the creation of equitable servitudes, the nature of the neighborhood may change so much that the original servitudes have lost their utility. For example, the neighborhood adjacent to the single family homes that are restricted to that use may now include a large feedlot operation that emits a great deal of noise and odor. If one of the single family homeowners were to open a dog kennel, the extra noise and odor might matter little, if at all, to the neighbors.

If one of the neighbors sues to stop the dog kennel, a court must choose between injunctive and damages remedies. The two injunctive remedies, analogous to those discussed within nuisance, are (1) kennel's right ("doctrine of changed conditions")[28]—the kennel may exist, and the court will

[26] See Jesse Dukeminier & James E. Krier, Property 959–1092 (1981) on the general subject of servitudes on land.

[27] Just who counts as a promiser turns out to be a tricky issue. *Id* at 1004–17. If a number of technicalities are complied with, the promises will also bind successive owners of the land. *Id.* at 1030–59.

[28] The doctrine of changed conditions generally works to void the servitude if the servitude seems to have no purpose other than allowing the beneficiary of the servitude to hold out and possibly cause bargaining breakdown. Courts are often chary of applying the doctrine of changed conditions, however. See Rick v. West, 34 Misc. 2d 1002, 228 N.Y.S.2d 195 (1962); Western Land Co. v. Truskolaski, 88 Nev. 200, 495 P.2d 624 (1972).

refuse to enforce the servitude, and (2) homeowner's right—the homeowner is entitled to an order of the court enjoining the kennel's existence. There are also two damages remedies: (*a*) kennel's right—the homeowner may obtain an injunction against the kennel's existence if and only if the homeowner pays the would-be kennel owner all damages he suffers from the injunction, and (*b*) homeowner's right—the kennel owner must pay the homeowner all damages the homeowner suffers from the kennel's existence.

Again, where risk of bargaining breakdown is very small, the court should choose between rules 1 and 2. Subject to the caveats noted in the nuisance example, our experimental data again suggest that the risk of contractual breakdown is small where there are up to thirty-eight parties to the servitude arrangement. Where the numbers are larger, the increased risk of bargaining breakdown points to the increased desirability of damage remedies.[29]

3. *Treatment of Secured Creditors in Bankruptcy.* Our analysis may be extended beyond the traditional common-law areas of tort, contract, and property. In particular, it might prove to be of special importance in determining the property treatment of secured creditors in bankruptcy. Generally a secured creditor has the right to invoke the power of the court to seize the pledged assets, to sell them, and to use the proceeds of the sale to satisfy the debt and necessary expenses, refunding any excess proceeds to the debtor. In contrast, general creditors must respect the priority of secured claims when they seek the aid of the court for the collection of their claims, and they cannot seize or sell pledged property in ways that destroy or prejudice the interests of secured creditors.[30] One important question is whether the priorities of secured creditors should be altered in bankruptcy so that the secured creditor must release some

[29] The choice of remedies for enforcing servitudes on land is, in itself, a complex and convoluted topic. The orthodox learning is that equitable servitudes are enforced only by injunction. To obtain damages, one must demonstrate that a "real covenant" exists. As a practical matter, there is very little difference between an equitable servitude and a real covenant, and courts have begun to enforce both types of servitude by both damages and injunctive relief. See Uriel Reichman, Toward a Unified Concept of Servitudes, 55 S. Cal. L. Rev. 1179 (1982).

[30] See Uniform Commercial Code §§ 9-301, 9-311 (1977). The unsecured creditor may, in theory, levy against secured assets, which will then be sold subject to the original security interest. Of course, unless the asset is worth significantly more than the debt secured by the asset, no rational third party will pay anything for the asset. As a practical matter, courts seem to treat secured versus unsecured creditor conflicts in a highly variegated fashion. Jack B. Justice, Secured Parties and Judgment Creditors—the Courts and Section 9-311 of the Uniform Commercial Code, 30 Bus. Lawyer 433 (1975).

alternative payment, such as a right to a stream of payment over several years, which may or may not be secured by the original pledged assets.[31]

Why might the law do such a thing? Thomas Jackson has argued as follows. A court may choose two different entitlements to protect a creditor's security interest: (1) secured creditor's property rights—the secured creditor can invoke the power of the court to sell the pledged asset and use the proceeds to satisfy the debt, or (2) secured creditor's damages right—the trustee in bankruptcy can stop the secured creditor from exercising his right to sell the asset, but must award the creditor a right to a set of payments worth the amount of the debt.[32] Selling the asset will often be economically inefficient, either because the asset may have a higher value within the debtor's business than outside, or because selling the asset may destroy the existence of the debtor's business, which destroys goodwill.

If the court chooses rule 1 and enforces the creditor's right to sell the assets, the creditor will have to agree not to sell the asset so as to avoid the economic loss. The debtor and its other creditors must persuade the secured creditor, probably by paying it some of the savings from not selling the asset, a loss that otherwise falls on the other creditors. In this situation the secured creditor may behave strategically and demand a large share of the savings from not selling the asset and thereby produce a large chance of bargaining breakdown and the attendant economic inefficiency. To avoid this result the court can choose rule 2, and give the secured creditor a damages right.

Our results suggest that the fear of bargaining breakdown, at least where there are relatively few creditors, may be overemphasized in such an analysis. If the risk of bargaining breakdown is small, then perhaps the law should enforce security interests in bankruptcy with a property entitlement[33] and allow the creditors to work things out, selling the asset in exactly those situations where it is efficient to do so. Once again, the law could utilize a presumption in favor of the Coase Theorem, leaving it to the other creditors to show that bargaining is difficult in any particular case in their attempt to persuade the court to use rule 2.

[31] Thomas H. Jackson, Bankruptcy, Non-bankruptcy Entitlements, and the Creditor's Bargain, 91 Yale L. J. 857, 872–77 (1982).

[32] *Id.* at 868–71.

[33] Of course, even a small risk of bargaining breakdown may be unacceptable if there is a very large loss when such a breakdown occurs. If one were certain that assets were *always much more valuable* in the debtor's going concern than on the open market, then rule 2 might be appropriate. However, Jackson does not seem to believe that this is the case, for he spends several pages attacking the failure to grant secured creditors full damages because sometimes it is efficient to sell the asset on the open market, rather than retain it in the debtor's going concern. *Id.* at 874–77.

Of course, our experiments have little to say about bankruptcies involving hundreds of creditors. In such proceedings, the risk of bargaining breakdown may be very high, and the law should choose rule 2, and, if the law cannot choose different rules for cases involving few parties and many parties, then perhaps it should choose rule 2 for all cases. But the law need not choose 2 for all cases because of an excessive fear of bargaining breakdown in cases involving few parties.

4. *Litigation and Settlement.* There are some recent data on dispute resolution that suggest that our experimental support for the Coase Theorem is correct. When litigants sue each other there are strong incentives to settle the case before it gets to trial. Trial is very expensive for all sides involved in a dispute. If all parties to a lawsuit agree on the probabilities of one side or another prevailing, and the parties are motivated by money, then a group agreement to settle the litigation can make all parties better off by saving litigation expenses for everyone. Through side payments in the settlement agreement this saving can be distributed in any manner among the litigants. Of course, litigants may have an incentive to hold out, behave strategically, and threaten to cause bargaining breakdown. The empirical question arises, How often, and under what circumstances, will litigants settle before trial?

Marc Galanter reports that approximately 90 percent of all lawsuits are settled before trial.[34] Further, he gives a breakdown of those that do not settle. They are almost all suits whose description clearly places them outside the theoretical bounds of the Coase Theorem. Such nonsettling suits:

1. cannot be settled, such as divorce cases, because a judicial decree is needed before the suit can end;
2. are very cheap to process, thereby providing little saving from settling;
3. involve a special value from a judicial decree, either because one of the parties wants the court to take moral responsibility for the action, wants to signal to a principal that there has been no shirking, or wants to establish a reputation with adversaries in future suits;
4. involve a special value from a judicial decree, because one of the parties wants to effect a change in the rule of law for future cases;
5. involve a "fundamental value" that the parties cannot monetize with ease; or

[34] Marc Galanter, Reading the Landscape of Disputes: What We Know and Don't Know (and Think We Don't Know) about Our Allegedly Contentious and Litigious Society, 31 UCLA L. Rev. 4, 28–30 (1983).

6. involve high transactions costs of settlement relative to the gains of doing so.

In sum, then, Galanter's results on litigation and settlement tend to reinforce our experimental results.

5. *Land Assembly.* There is, however, other real-world evidence that suggests that the problem of bargaining failure may well be more difficult. Steven N. S. Cheung recounts the failure of Hong Kong landlords and tenants to agree to vacate old uneconomic buildings, tear down the structures, and build new and larger apartment buildings.[35] Because post–World War II rent control statutes in Hong Kong gave tenants property rights—in essence making tenants joint controllers—landlords had to negotiate with dozens of tenant families to secure unanimous agreement among tenant families to move out. Cheung reports that conversations with people who remember the 1947–55 period suggest that holdouts always produced bargaining breakdown. Cheung could find no record of a successfully negotiated deal.

Cheung's work is intriguing, but for several reasons it cannot show that our experiments are inapplicable to the natural world. First, it is unclear how many parties were involved in these landlord and tenant negotiations. Cheung's own figures suggest that many of the negotiations could involve more than fifty parties. Second, Cheung's data are all anecdotal, and give no clue as to the "true" subjective values involved. Therefore, we cannot be sure that deals that were not consummated would have been value-increasing. Anecdotes from those involved in trying to assemble sites for large scale developments in the United States indicate that the fiercest holdouts are old people who have strong emotional ties to their dwelling places.[36] In such cases the old people cannot be made better off by a deal. Third, direct payments to tenants in exchange for their promise to leave were technically illegal (although Cheung indicates this may not have been a practical problem). On balance, Cheung's data should prompt us to question with care, but not totally to reject, our experimental data.

6. *Economic Efficiency as a Legal Norm.* Our results also change the tenor of the current jurisprudential debate about economic efficiency as a norm in the law. As used in the literature, which has grown around Richard Posner's various defenses of his "wealth maximization" norm, economic efficiency has been equated with the Hicks-Kaldor compensa-

[35] Steven N. S. Cheung, Rent Control and Housing Reconstruction: The Postwar Experience of Prewar Premises in Hong Kong, 22 J. Law & Econ. 27, 31–32 (1979).

[36] Joanne Lipman, The Holdouts, Wall St. J., May 22, 1984, at 1, col. 1.

tion criterion.[37] One of the central difficulties with the Hicks-Kaldor version of economic efficiency is that the criterion directs some to be made worse off, while some are made better off, merely because everyone could (but will not be) made better off. Where a judge must choose one of two allocations of a property right, and where bargaining is too expensive, the rights will remain where they are judicially placed. The criterion of economic efficiency leads the judge to imagine a world in which bargaining, coordination, and enforcement costs are zero, to predict which of the claimants would purchase the right at auction, and then to actually award the right to that claimant.[38] Richard Posner defends such an approach by arguing that economic efficiency can be equated with Pareto superiority in the long run. This position has been attacked on many different grounds.[39]

Regardless of the ultimate success of the arguments for and against Posner's version of the economic efficiency criterion, however, our experimental results should affect the tenor of the arguments. One who is arguing for the use of the efficiency norm may now claim that the norm describes what parties to a bargain will decide to do for themselves. The judge, then, is simply facilitating an inevitable process and is justifiably concerned about promoting economic efficiency. By simply choosing the efficient outcome, the judge merely saves society the legal costs that would be incurred during a long bargaining process.

Those who argue against economic efficiency as a norm may also find support in our results. After all, if the parties can be trusted to contract an efficient solution by themselves, a judge may ignore efficiency concerns and concentrate instead on effecting a "fair" distribution of income or on setting a precedent for an appealing theory of rights. Only in circumstances in which the Coase Theorem cannot be applied with confidence should economic efficiency have any claim on judicial attention.

In general, therefore, the form of the debate alters when one is fairly certain that the Coase Theorem is applicable. Our experimental results show that the Coase Theorem shifts the tone of the debate in a substantial number of cases.

[37] See, for example, Richard A. Posner, Utilitarianism, Economics, and Legal Theory, 8 J. Legal Stud. 103 (1979). We neither defend nor attack this criterion as a norm in this paper. Instead, we show how the Coase Theorem, and our results, might affect the nature of the debate.

[38] Richard A. Posner, The Ethical and Political Basis of the Efficiency Norm in Common Law Adjudication, in Symposium on Efficiency as a Legal Concern, 8 Hofstra L. Rev. 485, 485–771 (1980).

[39] See, for example, all of the other articles in Symposium on Efficiency as a Legal Concern, 8 Hofstra L. Rev (1980); and also A Response to the Efficiency Symposium, *id.* at 811, 811–973.

## V. Conclusions

Our experimental results provide very strong support for the Coase Theorem as a tool for analyzing decisions of groups of twenty persons or fewer, when bargaining, coordination, and enforcement costs are low and there are few information problems. We suggest they can be extended to similar groups of thirty-eight persons. Although a policy analyst should be quite careful about applying these results to a nonlaboratory setting, where he may do so with some confidence he can produce substantial implications for the law of remedies in tort, contract, and property.

# [30]

*The Economic Journal*, **97** (*June* 1987) 388–402
*Printed in Great Britain*

# COASIAN SOLUTIONS TO THE EXTERNALITY PROBLEM IN EXPERIMENTAL MARKETS*

*Glenn W. Harrison, Elizabeth Hoffman, E. E. Rutström and Matthew L. Spitzer*

This paper evaluates Coasian solutions to the externality problem in a series of experimental markets. In an important and innovative study Plott (1983) establishes that there is indeed a *behavioural* externality problem to solve, in the sense that competitive markets with externalities do converge to a private equilibrium that ignores social costs. Plott (1983) then considers a series of alternative corrective policies designed to remedy this problem. The policies considered are 'Pigouvian taxes', 'standards', and 'marketable licences'. In each case the regulator is assumed to have sufficient information to apply the optimal policy. This informational restriction is readily justified by the exploratory nature of the enquiry.[1] We extend the study of possible remedies to include decentralised Coasian bargains, where the only role for the government (or the legal system) is to define transferable property rights.

Experimental studies by Harrison and McKee (1985) and Hoffman and Spitzer (1982; 1986) have demonstrated that the Coase Theorem (1960) is behaviourally 'alive and well' in relatively sterile and abstract bargaining environments. In these experiments subjects were given payoff tables which told them that if the group decision were a particular number they, individually, would receive those payoffs. In addition, one subject (or group of subjects) was allocated the right to make the decision without consulting the other subject (or subjects). This subject was designated the controller. Those not allocated that right could offer to transfer some of their earnings in order to persuade the controller to enter into a joint agreement.

Following Regan (1972), we take the Coasian approach as implying two distinct behavioural outcomes: (i) that the parties will agree on a Pareto optimal level for the externality-generating activity, and (ii) that any such agreement will be attained by means of a mutually advantageous bargain between the parties. Harrison and McKee (1985) and Hoffman and Spitzer (1985; 1986) present experimental evidence for small and large bargaining groups that overwhelmingly support both outcomes. Hoffman and Spitzer (1982) support the first but not the second outcome.

Regarding the second outcome, both Harrison and McKee (1985) and

* The financial support of the National Science Foundation and the Social Sciences and Humanities Research Council of Canada is gratefully acknowledged. Helpful comments were provided by two referees and seminar participants at the Econometric Society Meetings (New York, 1985), the Public Choice Society Meetings (Baltimore, 1986), the University of Arizona and the University of Tasmania.

[1] There have been several interesting proposals for informationally decentralised versions of some of the schemes considered by Plott (1983): see Kwerel (1976), Montgomery (1972) and Roberts and Spence (1976) for further discussion. One obvious extension of our study would be to compare such schemes against the informationally decentralised Coasian approach we evaluate.

Hoffman and Spitzer (1985; 1986) found that some mechanism for inducing self-regarding behaviour in subjects appeared to be necessary. Hoffman and Spitzer (1985; 1986) used a game-trigger, in which the winner of a simple game (like 'tic-tac-toe') *earned* the right to be controller. Harrison and McKee (1985) had the bargainers' experience an environment in which property rights were not defined.

The experiments reported in this paper extend those previous experiments to a much richer informational environment. First we operationalise the Harrison and McKee (1985) mechanism by allowing subjects to participate in a market with an externality for five trading periods before allowing them to strike Coasian bargains. However, in contrast to Harrison and McKee (1985), the no-property-rights (or disagreement) outcome was not known with certainty as the result of a previous bargaining session or experimental design. It was the outcome of a market process which was converging to equilibrium, and the distribution of the trading surplus could vary from one trading period to another.

The trading environment also made the bargaining environment far more informationally complex than the previous experimental environments had been. In order to determine the Pareto optimal outcome, subjects had to compute the net social surplus at each quantity from cost and redemption information which was initially private to each subject and which differed substantially across subjects.

We divided the experiment into two phases to provide subjects with both an externality and a Coasian market. The first phase simply replicated the externality experiments of Plott (1983). In the second phase any subset of subjects was allowed to sign an agreement that permitted the subjects to restrict purchases and sales, and to effect any monetary sidepayments desired. In six experiments we found that subjects were able, after several periods of learning, both to identify the social optimum quantity and to agree to enforce a voluntary restriction on that quantity. Moreover, the bargaining outcome was generally mutually advantageous. These findings may suggest a role for Coasian bargaining in the regulation of externalities.

In two experiments we imposed a time-limit on bargaining activity in each period, in order to conduct a greater number of periods in the Coasian phase and thereby to induce more self-regarding distributions of the social surplus. Our results suggest that this modification does encourage subjects in one experiment to move away from simple rules, such as equal division, for dividing the surplus. Indeed some of the observed bargaining behaviour may be interpreted as roughly consistent with strategic game-theoretic notions of bargaining 'power'. Moreover, in attempting to articulate their rationale for a non-equal share, some agents were able to encourage slower witted cohorts to agree to a more efficient overall outcome.

The structure of the paper is as follows. In Section I we present the experimental design. In Section II we develop some basic theoretical predictions and in Section III we evaluate those predictions. Section IV indicates the implications of our results for naturally occurring environments and further research. Space constraints force us to omit discussion of many details of our design and results; interested readers are referred to Harrison *et al.* (1986) for these details.

## I. EXPERIMENTAL PROCEDURES AND DESIGN

Six experiments were conducted, and will be denoted E1–E6. Each experiment consisted of five periods with an unrestricted externality in what we refer to as Phase 1, followed by a variable number of periods in Phase 2 which allow for Coasian bargaining to possibly restrain the externality. The trading institution adopted is the double-oral auction. Subject valuations were stationary across all periods, and are listed in Table 1 and displayed in Fig. 1.

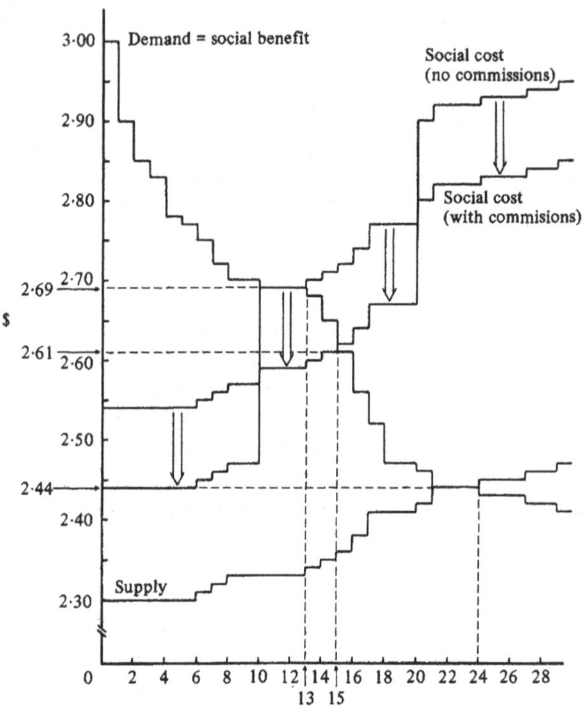


Fig. 1. Supply, demand and social cost.

In addition to these private valuations, each subject was given an initial Capital Payment of $0·70 in each period and a schedule listing the monetary damages 'due to the operating environment'. These damages represent the externality in our market. For every unit traded in the market, irrespective of which specific agents make the trade, every subject incurs a known monetary damage. This damage is set at $0·02 for each of the first ten units traded, at $0·03 for each of the next ten units, and finally at $0·04 for all subsequent units.

These damages imply a Social Cost of market activity in excess of Private Cost, as illustrated in Fig. 1.[2]

Our parameter values essentially follow those adopted by Plott (1983). The major differences are the allocation of valuations to individual subjects and the distribution of Capital Payments. Inspection of Fig. 3 of Plott (1983, p. 110) indicates that his sellers 1, 2 and 3 are allocated all of the infra-marginal units at the Private Equilibrium (seller 4 has two marginal units). Similarly, his buyers 7, 8 and 9 are allocated all but one of the infra-marginal units at the Private Equilibrium. It is therefore understandable why Plott (1983, table 1, p. 109) skewed the Capital Payments in favour of the six other marginal and extra-marginal traders. We were much more equitable in our allocation of private valuations, and hence were similarly egalitarian with respect to Capital Payments. We made this change in order to avoid a bargaining 'clique'

Table 1

*Private Redemption Values and Costs*

| | | Unit | | | | | | | | | |
|---|---|---|---|---|---|---|---|---|---|---|---|
| Agent | Type | 1 | 2 | 3 | 4 | 5 | 6 | 7 | 8 | 9 | 10 |
| 1 | Seller | $2·30 | 2·33 | 2·41 | 2·44 | 2·45 | 2·49 | 2·49 | 2·74 | 5·00 | 5·00 |
| 2 | Seller | 2·30 | 2·33 | 2·36 | 2·42 | 2·46 | 2·48 | 2·51 | 2·63 | 2·95 | 5·00 |
| 3 | Seller | 2·30 | 2·33 | 2·34 | 2·41 | 2·45 | 2·48 | 2·52 | 2·60 | 2·75 | 5·00 |
| 4 | Seller | 2·30 | 2·33 | 2·33 | 2·41 | 2·46 | 2·48 | 2·54 | 2·58 | 2·85 | 5·00 |
| 5 | Seller | 2·30 | 2·32 | 2·35 | 2·44 | 2·45 | 2·48 | 2·55 | 2·63 | 3·05 | 5·00 |
| 6 | Seller | 2·30 | 2·31 | 2·38 | 2·44 | 2·47 | 2·48 | 2·56 | 2·70 | 5·00 | 5·00 |
| 7 | Buyer | $3·00 | 2·69 | 2·52 | 2·44 | 2·43 | 2·40 | 2·34 | 2·25 | 0·0 | 0·0 |
| 8 | Buyer | 2·90 | 2·69 | 2·61 | 2·44 | 2·42 | 2·39 | 2·33 | 2·30 | 2·28 | 0·0 |
| 9 | Buyer | 2·85 | 2·70 | 2·68 | 2·47 | 2·43 | 2·40 | 2·36 | 2·30 | 0·0 | 0·0 |
| 10 | Buyer | 2·83 | 2·70 | 2·69 | 2·47 | 2·42 | 2·40 | 2·32 | 0·0 | 0·0 | 0·0 |
| 11 | Buyer | 2·78 | 2·72 | 2·65 | 2·46 | 2·43 | 2·40 | 2·39 | 0·0 | 0·0 | 0·0 |
| 12 | Buyer | 2·77 | 2·75 | 2·56 | 2·44 | 2·41 | 2·40 | 2·37 | 2·25 | 0·0 | 0·0 |

emerging consisting of the relatively small number of infra-marginal traders. We therefore give the Coasian approach a more severe test by requiring all agents to become involved in bargaining (if fully efficient outcomes are to obtain). On the other hand, we may have made Coasian bargaining easier in that we defuse a potential breakdown in bargaining due to 'distributional disputes' emerging *within* each group of buyers or sellers.

Each subject received and was made familiar with a series of instructions describing the two 'Phases' of each experiment. Phase 1 consisted of five periods of an unregulated market subject to an externality – our procedures here followed Plott (1983) closely. Subjects were not permitted to collude or otherwise cooperate in any overt fashion. The instructions explaining Phase 2 of the experiment were as follows:

> In the second phase of the experiment we will run another market as in the first phase. However, in the second phase you may reveal to any

[2] Social Cost is simply the Supply Curve (Private Cost) plus $0·24 for units 1–10, plus $0·36 for units 11–20, and plus $0·48 for all subsequent units.

of the other participants anything you wish about your costs or redemption values. In addition, you are free to enter into a group agreement with one or more of the other subjects. A group agreement may specify the maximum number of units an individual seller is allowed to sell or the maximum number of units an individual buyer is allowed to buy. The agreement may also specify that one or more subjects will transfer portions of their earnings to other subjects. Those transfers may be specified in absolute or percentage terms.

There is a group agreement form on pages 8 and 9 and all parties to a group agreement must sign the form before it will become effective. *No agreement* may limit the sales or purchases of any participant *who does not sign* or transfer money from a person *who does not sign* to someone else.

Participants will have the opportunity to enter into a group agreement before each trading period. Once such an agreement is signed, it will become totally binding on the parties. Buyers and sellers who agree to limit purchases or sales will receive chits for the units they are allowed to buy or sell. Buyers or sellers who are not limited may have as many chits as they have units to buy or sell on their payoff sheets. Each time a transaction is made, the participants entering into the transaction must turn in chits. If a participant who is limited tries to complete a transaction without having a chit, the monitor will reduce that participant's earnings to zero for that trading period. (To ensure that you do not mistakenly place a bid or offer on a unit you may not buy or sell, we recommend that you cross out the units you may not transact that trading period.)

*No Physical Threats Are Allowed.* If any participant threatens another participant, the threatening party will lose all units for purchase or sale during that trading period and the threatened party will receive compensation equal to his average earnings for all other trading periods.

Once a group agreement is made and the form is signed, the market will proceed as in phase 1, except that buyers and sellers must submit chits in order to make transactions.

When all of the trading periods are completed, the monitor will pay each participant individually in cash as he or she leaves.

The record sheets adopted were standard and follow those reproduced by Plott (1983). Due to space constraints, the complete instructions are not reproduced here; they are available in Harrison *et al.* (1986).

In experiments E5 and E6 an oral announcement was made to the effect that a maximum of ten minutes would be allowed for 'discussions' in each period in Phase 2. This feature of our experiments follows Harrison and McKee (1985); Hoffman and Spitzer (1982; 1986) allowed an indeterminate amount of time for bargaining, as we did in experiments E1–E4. Harrison and McKee (1985; footnote 13) regarded this as a potentially significant modification of the earlier design for two reasons:

(i) it avoids the problem of extraneous pressures on the time allowed for bargaining (for example, one subject may have a pressing appointment at a certain time), which may lead to different subjective costs of continuing to bargain (or, in Coasian jargon, 'transactions costs'); and (ii) it allows us to ensure that our financial incentives are salient for any particular subject pool (that is, we can ensure that the potential payoffs are commensurate with the opportunity cost of the time involved in the experiment).

Coursey (1982) provides a systematic study of the effect of time constraints on the observed frequency of impasse in bilateral bargaining experiments. In experiments E3 and E4, subjects were told at the outset that we would try to conduct five periods in each Phase. In experiments E5 and E6 we indicated at the outset that we expected to be able to conduct ten periods in Phase 2.

All subjects were economics undergraduates with no formal knowledge in game theory or the Coase Theorem. Some care was taken to ensure that subjects from the same classes or years did not participate in the same experiment. Experiments E1 and E2 were conducted at Purdue University and the remainder at the University of Western Ontario (the Canadian exchange rate at the time of the experiments was approximately US\$1 = C\$1·33). All subjects were inexperienced in this particular design. This accords with the inexperienced subjects used by Plott (1983) in his experiments 1–6.

## II. THEORETICAL PREDICTIONS

In Phase 1 of our experiments we apply the law of supply and demand to predict that individual agents will only consider their private costs and benefits when deciding whether or not to trade (and thereby generate an externality on all). By inspection of Fig. 1, we therefore predict a price of \$2·44 and a quantity of 24 at the Private Equilibrium outcome. Note that each subject receives a trading commission of \$0·05 per trade in order to overcome presumed subjective costs of transacting. Therefore we predict that trading volume will be 24 instead of only 21 (the last three units do not generate any trading surplus before commissions).

Plott (1983) defines the Socially Optimal outcome by the intersection of the Social Cost schedule *excluding* trading commissions with the Social Benefit (or Demand) schedule. Again, trading commissions merely play the role of encouraging marginal units to be traded. Thus he predicts a Social Optimum when price is \$2·69 and quantity is 13 units. For the corrective policies and 'no policies' experiments conducted by Plott (1983), this definition is completely satisfactory.

When we consider Coasian bargaining solutions, however, one cannot identify the Social Optimum quite so precisely. Table 2 presents the relevant calculations of the maximum social surplus attainable for different quantity levels. The 'maximum' trading surplus shown in Table 2 is found by simply pairing-off the lowest (private) cost sellers and the highest (private) value buyers. The price they trade at is of no relevance here. Next in Table 2 we show the total amount of trading commissions earned. We shall see that it makes some difference if these commission earnings are included in the social surplus

14-2

calculations or not. The total damages shown in Table 2 reflect, of course, the externality of higher volume in the market.

We next compute the net social surplus, alternatively not including commissions or including them. In the first case we note that social surplus is indeed maximised at \$2·52 when volume is 13 units, *but that the same surplus is attained for 10, 11 or 12 units as well.* Thus the Social Optimum is indeterminate in this quantity range. When we include commissions in our computation of net social surplus, however, we obtain a unique optimal quantity level of 15 units. In Fig. 1 we have drawn in Social Costs *with* commissions (it is uniformly \$0·10 below

Table 2

*Maximum Social Surplus* (dollars)

| Quantity | Maximum trading surplus | Trading commissions | Total damages | Net social surplus: No commissions | Net social surplus: With commissions |
|---|---|---|---|---|---|
| 1 | 0·70 | 0·10 | 0·24 | 0·46 | 0·56 |
| 2 | 1·30 | 0·20 | 0·48 | 0·82 | 1·02 |
| 3 | 1·86 | 0·30 | 0·72 | 1·14 | 1·44 |
| 4 | 2·39 | 0·40 | 0·96 | 1·43 | 1·83 |
| 5 | 2·87 | 0·50 | 1·20 | 1·67 | 2·17 |
| 6 | 3·34 | 0·60 | 1·44 | 1·90 | 2·50 |
| 7 | 3·78 | 0·70 | 1·68 | 2·10 | 2·80 |
| 8 | 4·18 | 0·80 | 1·92 | 2·26 | 3·06 |
| 9 | 4·55 | 0·90 | 2·16 | 2·39 | 3·29 |
| 10 | 4·92 | 1·00 | 2·40 | 2·52 | 3·52 |
| 11 | 5·28 | 1·10 | 2·76 | 2·52 | 3·62 |
| 12 | 5·64 | 1·20 | 3·12 | 2·52 | 3·72 |
| 13 | 6·00 | 1·30 | 3·48 | 2·52 | 3·82 |
| 14 | 6·34 | 1·40 | 3·84 | 2·50 | 3·90 |
| 15 | 6·64 | 1·50 | 4·20 | 2·44 | 3·94 |
| 16 | 6·89 | 1·60 | 4·56 | 2·33 | 3·93 |
| 17 | 7·07 | 1·70 | 4·92 | 2·15 | 3·85 |
| 18 | 7·18 | 1·80 | 5·28 | 1·90 | 3·70 |
| 19 | 7·24 | 1·90 | 5·64 | 1·60 | 3·50 |
| 20 | 7·30 | 2·00 | 6·00 | 1·30 | 3·30 |
| 21 | 7·34 | 2·10 | 6·48 | 0·86 | 2·96 |
| 22 | 7·34 | 2·20 | 6·96 | 0·38 | 2·58 |
| 23 | 7·34 | 2·30 | 7·44 | 0·10 | 2·40 |
| 24 | 7·34 | 2·40 | 7·92 | −0·58 | 1·82 |

the Social Cost schedule excluding commissions). The point of its intersection with the Social Benefit schedule is at a volume of 15 units.

One issue of importance for our theoretical predictions, then, is whether or not commissions should be viewed as implicitly compensating individual traders for the 'onerous' task of submitting bids and offers or not. If one accepts this interpretation, as the bulk of the experimental literature does, then the issue turns on the trading logistics used to generate trading surplus in our experiments. In Phase 1 these logistics necessarily involved the nerve-racking, real-time, hustle-and-bustle of ordinary double-oral auction markets. Accordingly we have no hesitation in viewing commissions as appropriately offsetting the individual's costs of particpating in that market; see Smith and Williams (1983) for some evidence on the value of those costs. On the other hand, the logistics of generating *trading* surplus in many of the periods of Phase 2 were downright genteel and sedate. Everything of importance had been decided during the bargaining stage, and the 'trading' stage was merely akin to the 'reading of the (long-probated) will'. In such cases, which are fortunately quite easy to identify *ex post*, we have no hesitation in viewing commissions as available for distribution with the rest of the social surplus. Certainly this was the way some of the subjects viewed matters.

Finally we note that, providing that more than 6 units are sold, any reduction from 22 units (or 24 units if commissions are included) in Phase 1 will *increase* efficiency, whether or not it is due to Coasian bargaining. Such a reduction may, for example, be due to sellers organising as a collusive (uniform-price) monopoly when buyers behave non-cooperatively. In this scenario the profit maximising quantity is only 14 units, whether or not the seller cartel internalises the externality. The benefit of an experimental methodology is that we can readily identify such scenarios during Phase 2, allowing us to see precisely what type of behaviour is generating such outcomes. We illustrate this point in the next Section with a discussion of experiment E4.

## III. EXPERIMENTAL RESULTS

### III. 1. *Trading Behaviour*

Table 3 presents a summary of the observed trading behaviour in all six experiments. By and large we are able to replicate the two five-period experiments reported in Plott (1983) that have no corrective policies imposed. Our Phase 1 results in each experiment *rapidly converge to the Private Equilibrium* price of $2·44 and the corresponding quantity of 24. Any discrepancies observed from these precise predictions are minor and generally statistically insignificant. Moreover, they are obviously much closer to the predicted equilibrium than to the Social Optimum outcome (however defined).

The reported Phase 2 'trading' behaviour in Table 3 can be somewhat misleading, in the sense that it represents in most cases (e.g. periods 7, 8 and 9 of E2) an arbitrary series of trades simply designed to generate the social surplus. However, one general and important result to note from the Phase 2 trading behaviour is that the *trading volume decreases in all experiments to within one unit of either definition of the Social Optimum* (i.e. 13 units ignoring commissions or 15 units including them).

### III. 2. *Bargaining Behaviour*

Space constraints preclude an extended discussion of the bargaining behaviour in our experiments (see Harrison *et al.* (1986) for such a discussion). However, experiment E4 is particularly instructive. In period 6 of this experiment neither buyers nor sellers signed an explicit agreement form. Instead, each 'side' viewed Phase 2 as providing an opportunity for cartel formation. The discussions

Table 3
*Observed Trading Behaviour*

| Period | Mean | Standard deviation | Volume | Mean | Standard deviation | Volume | Mean | Standard deviation | Volume |
|---|---|---|---|---|---|---|---|---|---|
| | | Experiment E1 | | | Experiment E2 | | | Experiment E3 | |
| 1 | $2·466 | $0·090 | 22 | $2·541 | $0·079 | 22 | $2·460 | $0·049 | 23 |
| 2 | 2·464 | 0·062 | 27 | 2·493 | 0·028 | 21 | 2·424 | 0·029 | 22 |
| 3 | 2·449 | 0·055 | 24 | 2·483 | 0·031 | 23 | 2·426 | 0·036 | 22 |
| 4 | 2·436 | 0·034 | 26 | 2·466 | 0·028 | 24 | 2·437 | 0·021 | 24 |
| 5 | 2·429 | 0·022 | 22 | 2·463 | 0·020 | 23 | 2·423 | 0·015 | 24 |
| 6 | 2·570 | 0·000 | 6 | — | — | 0 | 2·324 | 0·023 | 17 |
| 7 | — | — | 0 | 2·321 | 0·019 | 16 | 2·321 | 0·019 | 16 |
| 8 | 2·573 | 0·010 | 12 | 2·321 | 0·019 | 16 | 2·318 | 0·017 | 15 |
| 9 | 2·603 | 0·013 | 4 | 2·321 | 0·019 | 16 | 2·318 | 0·017 | 15 |
| 10 | 2·575 | 0·025 | 12 | — | — | — | 2·318 | 0·017 | 15 |
| 11 | 2·603 | 0·015 | 12 | — | — | — | — | — | — |
| 12 | 2·613 | 0·004 | 12 | — | — | — | — | — | — |
| 13 | — | — | — | — | — | — | — | — | — |
| 14 | — | — | — | — | — | — | — | — | — |
| 15 | — | — | — | — | — | — | — | — | — |
| | | Experiment E4 | | | Experiment E5 | | | Experiment E6 | |
| 1 | $2·412 | $0·041 | 18 | $2·371 | $0·023 | 16 | $2·414 | $0·041 | 21 |
| 2 | 2·433 | 0·015 | 23 | 2·395 | 0·041 | 23 | 2·427 | 0·035 | 18 |
| 3 | 2·440 | 0·018 | 20 | 2·414 | 0·056 | 20 | 2·437 | 0·023 | 23 |
| 4 | 2·435 | 0·012 | 20 | 2·425 | 0·048 | 21 | 2·439 | 0·043 | 22 |
| 5 | 2·441 | 0·004 | 19 | 2·427 | 0·045 | 24 | 2·436 | 0·019 | 23 |
| 6 | — | — | 0 | — | — | 0 | 2·440 | 0·0 | 6 |
| 7 | 2·560 | 0·0 | 4 | 2·430 | 0·006 | 5 | 2·413 | 0·005 | 3 |
| 8 | 2·313 | 0·014 | 12 | 2·450 | 0·050 | 12 | — | — | 0 |
| 9 | 2·316 | 0·015 | 14 | 2·318 | 0·017 | 15 | 2·321 | 0·019 | 16 |
| 10 | 2·318 | 0·017 | 15 | 2·318 | 0·017 | 15 | — | — | 0 |
| 11 | — | — | — | 2·318 | 0·017 | 15 | 2·321 | 0·019 | 16 |
| 12 | — | — | — | 2·318 | 0·017 | 15 | 2·321 | 0·019 | 16 |
| 13 | — | — | — | 2·318 | 0·017 | 15 | 2·321 | 0·019 | 16 |
| 14 | — | — | — | 2·318 | 0·017 | 15 | 2·321 | 0·019 | 16 |
| 15 | — | — | — | 2·318 | 0·017 | 15 | 2·321 | 0·019 | 16 |

preceding 'trading' were relatively brief (only about 8 minutes), and focused on what price to aim for and which agent was to be the spokesman. Trading opened with a bid of $2·60, counter offers at $1·30, 1·50 and 2·30, a reply bid of $2·58 and a final counter offer of $2·32. Neither side appeared willing to reduce the bid-ask spread. Given the total absence of any further haggling, it appears as though each side had defined uniform group limit prices for their negotiators to work with.

In period 7 there was again virtually no mention of the possibility of coordinated action by both sides, let alone any concern by either side for the externality they were generating. The focus, yet again, was on bilateral cartel strength and strategy. In this case each side appeared to be less rigid in their instructions to negotiators, with these two establishing a price of $2·56 in relatively short order. However, after a mere four transactions at these prices the remaining buyers and sellers began to posture for bargaining leverage again, with a widening bid-ask spread. It appeared as though the relatively sober negotiators were powerless to return to the 'trading floor' to settle on a price given that two buyers and two sellers had not yet sold their first units. Such an action by the negotiators may have been misinterpreted by others as chiseling on the tacit agreement to bargain as a coalition.

Finally in period 8 the two (frustrated) negotiators in the two previous periods managed to convince their respective partners to cooperate in Coasian fashion in order to extract the available surplus and then for each side to worry about how to divide their 50% share of that surplus. Distributional considerations did not play much of a role in bargaining discussions until the final period, by which time there was considerable peer pressure on the individual agitators not to rock the boat 'for peanuts' in what was known to be the terminal period.

### III. 3. *Efficiency Comparisons*

Table 4 presents a summary statement of the efficiency values for all periods in our experiments. An asterisk beside a value indicates that we employ the efficiency measure that includes commissions (in those periods for which the 'trading' activity was obviously pre-arranged).[3] For comparison purposes we also present the efficiency values reported by Plott (1983, p. 118) for each of his eight experiments.

The first comparison to be drawn from Table 4 is the most obvious: market efficiency in Phase 2 of our experiments is overwhelmingly higher than in Phase 1. The role of Coasian bargaining is clearly demonstrated in our experiments.

The next comparison is certainly more surprising: Coasian bargaining tends to enhance efficiency, by one statistical measure, even when compared to Plott's 'policy' experiments. This conclusion is *not* suggested by the simple pooled values for efficiency. Those pooled values indicate that the implicit use of 'centralised' full information when designing the policies evaluated in Plott's experiments leads to greater efficiency than our informationally decentralised Phase 2 experiments. This performance ranking would not be surprising, given the noted differences in the informational requirements of the various institutions.

However, a non-parametric Mann–Whitney test[4] of the differences in efficiency reverses the conclusion based solely on pooled efficiency values. This test supports the hypothesis that our Phase 2 outcomes are more efficient than the tax policy, the policy standard, and the licence policy with 95, 100 and 77% confidence, respectively. The reason for this discrepancy between the pooled

[3] More precisely, the Efficiency measure with no asterisk is calculated as Trading Surplus, less Total Damages, all divided by \$2·52 (recall Table 2). The Efficiency measure with an asterisk is calculated as Trading Surplus plus Total Commissions less Total Damages, all divided by \$3·94. These efficiency measures are standard to the experimental economics literature. When calculating pooled values for efficiency we always adopt the measure including commissions for those periods in which it is clearly the better measure (e.g. periods 9 and 11–15 in experiment E6).

[4] See Conover (1980, pp. 216 ff.) for a complete discussion. We employ one-sided hypothesis tests.

Table 4

*Efficiency Comparisons*

| | Present study | | | | | | | Plott (1983) experiments | | | | | | | |
|---|---|---|---|---|---|---|---|---|---|---|---|---|---|---|---|
| | | | | | | | | No policy | | Tax policy | | Policy standard | | Licence policy | |
| Period | E1 | E2 | E3 | E4 | E5 | E6 | E1–E6 | 1 | 2 | 1 | 2 | 1 | 2 | 1 | 2 |
| 1 | −25 | 19 | 27 | 54 | 67 | 16 | 26 | 36·1 | 15·9 | 68·3 | 65·5 | 51·5 | 54·4 | 88·6 | 90·7 |
| 2 | −68 | 25 | 46 | 14 | 2 | 58 | 13 | −111·9 | −25·8 | 83·3 | 93·6 | 22·2 | 17·7 | 95·9 | 93·9 |
| 3 | −57 | −6 | 13 | 34 | 44 | 5 | 6 | −40·9 | −42·8 | 89·7 | 81·4 | 32·1 | 59·1 | 96·5 | 88·4 |
| 4 | −28 | −33 | −5 | 31 | 37 | 13 | 3 | −85·3 | −34·1 | 92·1 | 92·1 | 22·6 | 45·6 | 98·3 | 99·5 |
| 5 | −38 | 3 | −4 | 24 | −23 | 4 | −6 | −25·4 | −38·5 | 96·4 | 95·2 | 56·3 | 36·1 | 96·0 | 97·2 |
| Phase 1 | −43 | 2 | 15 | 31 | 25 | 19 | 8 | −45·5 | −25·1 | — | — | — | — | — | — |
| 6 | 63 | 0 | 98* | 0 | 0 | 75 | 39 | — | — | 96·8 | 98·0 | −0·4 | 53·6 | 99·6 | 98·8 |
| 7 | 0 | 100* | 100* | 55 | 73 | 34 | 60 | — | — | — | 98·0 | 39·7 | 72·6 | † | 97·6 |
| 8 | 95 | 100* | 100* | 94* | 94* | 0 | 81 | — | — | — | — | −9·5 | — | 99·4 | † |
| 9 | 52 | 100* | 100* | 97* | 100* | 100* | 92 | — | — | — | — | 4·7 | — | 99·5 | 98·4 |
| 10 | 94* | — | 100* | 99* | 100* | 0 | 79 | — | — | — | — | — | — | 99·0 | † |
| 11 | 99 | — | — | — | 100* | 100* | 100 | — | — | — | — | — | — | — | 96·3 |
| 12 | 96 | — | — | — | 100* | 100* | 99 | — | — | — | — | — | — | — | 99·6 |
| 13 | 72 | — | — | — | 100* | 100* | 91 | — | — | — | — | — | — | — | — |
| 14 | — | — | — | — | 100* | 100* | 100 | — | — | — | — | — | — | — | — |
| 15 | — | — | — | — | 100* | 100* | 100 | — | — | — | — | — | — | — | — |
| Phase 2 | 71 | 75 | 100 | 69 | 77 | 71 | 78 | — | — | 87·8 | 89·4 | 24·4 | 48·4 | 97·0 | 96·0 |

* Indicates the efficiency including commissions; a † indicates that a recording error during the experiment does not allow a measure to be calculated (see Plott (1983, p. 118)).

values and the Mann–Whitney test is simply the *extreme* efficiency values in our Phase 2 experiments. The impact of zero efficiency values is more important when pooling (or averaging) values than when conducting a Mann–Whitney test (i.e., a zero value in the latter test is no more 'serious' than a value epsilon below the comparison value, whereas it is more serious when taking averages).

One major drawback of our Coasian process as compared to Plott's policy instruments is the variation in the efficiency results of the former. The tax policy and licence policy results are far more stable, with efficiency steadily increasing towards 100%. One might argue that stability of outcomes is more important than the high average efficiency accompanied by occasional extreme variations observed in the Coasian experiments.

Finally, it should be noted that the efficiency outcomes in our Phase 2 experiments and the tax and licence policy experiments are virtually identical *for the last three periods*. This comparison allows for subjects to learn about the incentives provided by each institution by stationary replication over time. It is standard in the experimental literature to focus on such comparisons of the 'terminal' behaviour of institutions. On this basis, all three institutions deserve equal consideration for policy purposes.

## IV. IMPLICATIONS FOR NATURALLY OCCURRING ENVIRONMENTS

Before we can analyse the implications of our experiment for nonlaboratory settings, we must ask what types of nonlaboratory environments were, or were not, modelled well by our experiment. There are two types of arguments *against* applying our results to a nonlaboratory setting. Subjects might behave differently in the laboratory than elsewhere. We do not find such arguments convincing.[5] On the other hand, the experiments may have failed to capture

[5] What are the most likely laboratory effects in our experiments? The subjects might have regarded money differently, or they might have had different attitudes towards bargaining. These differences might have been produced either by important differences between our subject pool and the target population, or by observer effects. Is there any evidence of laboratory effects in the data? Nothing in the prices at which units traded hands suggest any laboratory effects. Informal observation of the subjects also failed to suggest anything. No one tried to 'buy high, sell low' and subjects traded hard in Phase 1 and bargained very hard in Phase 2. Despite this informal reassurance, observer effects and differences between our subject pool and target populations could prevent applying our results to natural settings. Observer effects would be present if subjects were to bargain to efficient outcomes because they were being watched and wished to be thought of as 'nice' or 'worthy'. Observer effects should not preclude applying our results to natural environments. Is it plausible to think of subjects trading to the private cost curve in Phase 1, and to the social cost curve in Phase 2 out of a desire to appear nice? We do not think so. But it is possible that subjects may have behaved in such a fashion (at least in Phase 2) because some of them thought that this was what the experimenter wished, and they were trying to comply. However, if so, we would expect similar observer effects in natural environments. Few (legal) markets of any size are organised in secret, and any bargaining in an attempt to limit harmful externalities would likely be observed by people hoping for a successful contract. Differences, if any, between our subject pool and target populations also provide no reason to refrain from using our results. Our subjects tended to be undergraduate students, about twenty years old, who will soon be adult citizens potentially involved in the lawsuits that the Coase Theorem models. Did their relative youth make a difference? Probably not. They seemed to be adept at bargaining, took the experiment very seriously, and routinely bargained to the efficient outcome. If we were to expect subjects to become *less* likely to bargain to efficient outcomes as they grow older, we would have grounds to suspect our results. But why expect this? In the long run, people are more likely to learn that bargaining-breakdown is costly for everyone, and thus learn to be proficient at making deals.

the essential features of particular natural settings.[6] Some of these arguments are worthy of further scrutiny. A policymaker should refrain from applying our results to any natural setting if the essential features of that setting were not incorporated into our design. There are four important sources of bargaining breakdown that were not incorporated into our experiments.

First, we excluded most sources of transaction costs by bringing the parties together, including only six parties on each side of the market, and paying the subjects for their time. This eliminated most sources of such friction in the natural world.[7] Second, all of the externalities in our market fell on the market participants themselves. Where the effects fall on those who are strangers to the market, all of the problems of friction alluded to above will be exacerbated.

Third, we excluded most informational deficiencies that might cause bargaining breakdown by giving each subject enough information so that the entire group *could* pool the information and deduce the social cost function. Subjects also had enough information, *if pooled*, to compute the profits each participant would make under each proposed solution to the experiment in Phase 2. Moreover, we provided a *costless verification technology* for subjects to use to assess the credibility of other subjects' information about private costs or valuations. Even under these conditions of certainty, disputes over division stymied formation of mutually advantageous contracts in some periods. Without the information or the ability to communicate it, subjects might have been unable to determine the social cost function. And even if they had deduced the function, suspicions about strategic behaviour by other subjects might have led them to refuse to contract in the absence of a verification technology (costless or not). Of course, to be confident about these possibilities for bargaining breakdown, we would have to promulgate a model involving uncertainty and test it. Natural environments are likely to include such uncertainties (e.g., see Wiggins and Libecap (1985) on contractual failure in the case of US oil field unitisation), so we again counsel caution in directly applying our results.

Fourth, and in some ways most important, we provided our subjects with standard form contracts that were perfectly enforced. In contrast, contracts in natural environments would be subject to antitrust laws. A contract between market participants whose object was to restrict output, and possibly reallocate profits realised at the resulting higher prices, would likely be regarded as illegal and would subject the contracting parties to possible monetary damages and prison terms. Moreover, this result would rest on a 'solidly established' (albeit intellectually fragile) foundation, for allowing market participants to combine to restrict output raises the *per se* spectre of anticompetitive combinations. Before we could recommend allowing participants in naturally occurring markets to

[6] Many of the arguments governing the extent to which the results of such laboratory experiments may be applied to natural environments have been considered extensively by Plott (1982) and Smith (1982) in general and by Hoffman and Spitzer (1982) in the context of Coasian bargaining. We therefore provide only a brief review at this juncture.

[7] Examples include situations in which the parties do not know each other, there are hundreds or thousands of parties to the dispute, and situations in which the bargaining process is very costly. The case of many small manufacturers selling small items that cause environmental blight (for example, styrofoam cups) to millions of consumers would contain, to some degree, all of these sources of friction. Our results should not be applied uncritically to problems of this kind.

execute contracts such as those modelled in our experiment, by creating an exception to the antitrust laws, we would have to be satisfied that an exemption could be fashioned which would do more good than harm. But such a conclusion can only follow from an extended institutional analysis, which is beyond the scope of this work.[8]

## V. CONCLUDING REMARKS

We have replicated the experimental demonstration by Plott (1983) that a behavioural externality problem exists in double-oral auction markets. We have also demonstrated that a Coasian approach to the externality problem generates solutions, after an initial learning period, that are efficient and informationally decentralised. The efficiency of the observed Coasian solutions, like the efficiency of the optimal informationally centralised approaches, is very high. Although these results are encouraging, further work must be done before we can confidently urge applying one or another of these systems to natural environments. The first obvious direction for further research is to compare the behavioural efficiency of the bargaining approach considered here with informationally decentralised versions of the Pigouvian and marketable licence approaches that have been proposed. Next, experiments should be undertaken including negotiating costs, uncertainty about calculating social cost, and externalities falling on strangers to the market. When such experiments are complete, we may be in a position to begin proposing policies for natural environments.

*University of Western Ontario*

*Purdue University and University of Wyoming*

*Stockholm School of Economics*

*University of Southern California*

*Date of receipt of final typescript: September 1986*

## References

Coase, Ronald H. (1960). 'The problem of social cost.' *Journal of Law and Economics*, vol. 3, pp. 1–44.

Conover, William J. (1980). *Practical Nonparametric Statistics*, 2nd ed. New York: Wiley.

Coursey, Don L. (1982). 'Bilateral bargaining, Pareto optimality, and the empirical frequency of impasse.' *Journal of Economic Behavior and Organization*, vol. 3, pp. 243–59.

Harrison, Glenn W., Hoffman, Elizabeth, Ruström, E. E. and Spitzer, Matthew L. (1986). 'Coasian solutions to the externality problem in experimental markets.' *Research Paper No.* 43. (February). Department of Economics, University of Melbourne.

—— and McKee, Michael (1985). 'Experimental evaluation of the Coase theorem.' *Journal of Law and Economics*, vol. 28, pp. 653–70.

Hoffman, Elizabeth and Spitzer, Matthew, L. (1982). 'The Coase theorem: some experimental tests.' *Journal of Law and Economics*, vol. 25, pp. 73–98.

[8] For example, an exemption which allowed market participants to execute an output-limiting agreement whenever there was a significant externality generated by the market might work acceptably well for a market in which there are six sellers and six buyers. However, in a market with six sellers and six thousand buyers we would expect only the sellers to organise. The resultant market outcome might be worse than one without any agreement, although it might be even better under some circumstances (recall the discussion of seller-cartel-behaviour at the end of Section II).

Hoffman, Elizabeth (1985). 'Entitlements, rights and fairness: an experimental examination of subjects' concepts of distributive justice.' *Journal of Legal Studies*, vol. 14, pp. 259–97.
—— (1986). 'Experimental tests of the Coase theorem with large bargaining groups.' *Journal of Legal Studies*, vol. 15, pp. 149–71.
Kwerel, Evan (1976). 'To tell the truth: imperfect information and optimal pollution control.' *Review of Economic Studies*, vol. 52, pp. 595–601.
Montgomery, W. David (1972). 'Markets in licences and efficient pollution control programs.' *Journal of Economic Theory*, vol. 5, pp. 395–418.
Plott, Charles, R. (1982). 'Industrial organization theory and experimental economics.' *Journal of Economic Literature*, vol. 20, pp. 1485–27.
—— (1983). 'Externalities and corrective policies in experimental markets.' ECONOMIC JOURNAL, vol. 93, pp. 106–27.
Regan, Donald H. (1972). 'The problem of social cost revisited.' *Journal of Law and Economics*, vol. 15, pp. 427–37.
Roberts, Marc J. and Spence, Michael (1976). 'Effluent charges and licences under uncertainty.' *Journal of Public Economics*, vol. 5, pp. 193–208.
Smith, Vernon L. (1982). 'Microeconomic systems as an experimental science.' *American Economic Review*, vol. 72, (December) p. 923–55.
—— and Williams, Arlington W. (1983). 'An experimental comparison of alternative rules for competitive market exchange.' In (eds. R. Engelbrecht-Wiggans, M. Shubik and R. Stark). *Auctions, Bidding and Contracting: Uses and Theory*. New York: New York Publishing Press.
Wiggins, Steven, N. and Libecap, Gary D. (1985). 'Oil field unitization: contractual failure in the presence of imperfect information.' *American Economic Review*, vol. 75, pp. 368–85.

# [31]

# Experimental Tests of the Endowment Effect and the Coase Theorem

Daniel Kahneman

*University of California, Berkeley*

Jack L. Knetsch

*Simon Fraser University*

Richard H. Thaler

*Cornell University*

Contrary to theoretical expectations, measures of willingness to accept greatly exceed measures of willingness to pay. This paper reports several experiments that demonstrate that this "endowment effect" persists even in market settings with opportunities to learn. Consumption objects (e.g., coffee mugs) are randomly given to half the subjects in an experiment. Markets for the mugs are then conducted. The Coase theorem predicts that about half the mugs will trade, but observed volume is always significantly less. When markets for "induced-value" tokens are conducted, the predicted volume is observed, suggesting that transactions costs cannot explain the undertrading for consumption goods.

## I. Introduction

The standard assumptions of economic theory imply that when income effects are small, differences between an individual's maximum

Financial support was provided by Fisheries and Oceans Canada, the Ontario Ministry of the Environment, and the behavioral economics program of the Alfred P. Sloan Foundation. We wish to thank Vernon Smith for encouraging us to conduct these experiments and for providing extensive comments on earlier drafts. Of course, the usual disclaimer applies.

[*Journal of Political Economy*, 1990, vol. 98, no. 6]

willingness to pay (WTP) for a good and minimum compensation demanded for the same entitlement (willingness to accept [WTA]) should be negligible (Willig 1976). Thus indifference curves are drawn without reference to current endowments; any difference between equivalent and compensating variation assessments of welfare changes is in practice ignored;[1] and there is wide acceptance of the Coase theorem assertion that, subject to income effects, the allocation of resources will be independent of the assignment of property rights when costless trades are possible.

The assumption that entitlements do not affect value contrasts sharply with empirical observations of significantly higher selling than buying prices. For example, Thaler (1980) found that the minimal compensation demanded for accepting a .001 risk of sudden death was higher by one or two orders of magnitude than the amount people were willing to pay to eliminate an identical existing risk. Other examples of similar reported findings are summarized in table 1. The disparities observed in these examples are clearly too large to be explained plausibly by income effects.

Several factors probably contribute to the discrepancies between the evaluations of buyers and sellers that are documented in table 1. The perceived illegitimacy of the transaction may, for example, contribute to the extraordinarily high demand for personal compensation for agreeing to the loss of a public good (e.g., Rowe, d'Arge, and Brookshire 1980). Standard bargaining habits may also contribute to a discrepancy between the stated reservation prices of buyers and sellers. Sellers are often rewarded for overstating their true value, and buyers for understating theirs (Knez, Smith, and Williams 1985). By force of habit they may misrepresent their true valuations even when such misrepresentation confers no advantage, as in answering hypothetical questions or one-shot or single transactions. In such situations the buying-selling discrepancy is simply a strategic mistake, which experienced traders will learn to avoid (Coursey, Hovis, and Schulze 1987; Brookshire and Coursey 1987).

The hypothesis of interest here is that many discrepancies between WTA and WTP, far from being a mistake, reflect a genuine effect of reference positions on preferences. Thaler (1980) labeled the increased value of a good to an individual when the good becomes part of the individual's endowment the "endowment effect." This effect is a manifestation of "loss aversion," the generalization that losses are weighted substantially more than objectively commensurate gains in

[1] For example, the conventional prescription for assessing environmental and other losses is that, "practically speaking, it does not appear to make much difference which definition is accepted" (Freeman 1979, p. 3).

TABLE 1

SUMMARY OF PAST TESTS OF EVALUATION DISPARITY

| STUDY AND ENTITLEMENT | MEANS | | | MEDIANS | | |
|---|---|---|---|---|---|---|
| | WTP | WTA | Ratio | WTP | WTA | Ratio |
| Hypothetical surveys: | | | | | | |
| Hammack and Brown (1974): marshes | $247 | $1,044 | 4.2 | | | |
| Sinclair (1978): fishing | | | | 35 | 100 | 2.9 |
| Banford et al. (1979): | | | | | | |
| Fishing pier | 43 | 120 | 2.8 | 47 | 129 | 2.7 |
| Postal service | 22 | 93 | 4.2 | 22 | 106 | 4.8 |
| Bishop and Heberlein (1979): goose hunting permits | 21 | 101 | 4.8 | | | |
| Rowe et al. (1980): visibility | 1.33 | 3.49 | 2.6 | | | |
| Brookshire et al. (1980): elk hunting* | 54 | 143 | 2.6 | | | |
| Heberlein and Bishop (1985): deer hunting | 31 | 513 | 16.5 | | | |
| Real exchange experiments: | | | | | | |
| Knetsch and Sinden (1984): lottery tickets | 1.28 | 5.18 | 4.0 | | | |
| Heberlein and Bishop (1985): deer hunting | 25 | 172 | 6.9 | | | |
| Coursey et al. (1987): taste of sucrose octa-acetate† | 3.45 | 4.71 | 1.4 | 1.33 | 3.49 | 2.6 |
| Brookshire and Coursey (1987): park trees†‡ | 10.12 | 56.60 | 5.6 | 6.30 | 12.96 | 2.1 |

* Middle-level change of several used in study.
† Final values after multiple iterations.
‡ Average of two levels of tree plantings.

the evaluation of prospects and trades (Kahneman and Tversky 1979; Tversky and Kahneman, in press). An implication of this asymmetry is that if a good is evaluated as a loss when it is given up and as a gain when it is acquired, loss aversion will, on average, induce a higher dollar value for owners than for potential buyers, reducing the set of mutually acceptable trades.

There are some cases in which no endowment effect would be expected, such as when goods are purchased for resale rather than for utilization. A particularly clear case of a good held exclusively for resale is the notional token typically traded in experimental markets commonly used to test the efficiency of market institutions (Plott 1982; Smith 1982). Such experiments employ the induced-value technique in which the objects of trade are tokens to which private redemption values that vary among individual participants have been assigned by the experimenter (Smith 1976). Subjects can obtain the prescribed value assigned for the tokens when redeeming them at the end of the trading period; the tokens are otherwise worthless.

No endowment effect would be expected for such tokens, which are valued only because they can be redeemed for cash. Thus both buyers and sellers should value tokens at the induced value they have been assigned. Markets for induced-value tokens can therefore be used as a control condition to determine whether differences between the values of buyers and sellers in other markets could be attributable to transaction costs, misunderstandings, or habitual strategies of bargaining. Any discrepancy between the buying and selling values can be isolated in an experiment by comparing the outcomes of markets for real goods with those of otherwise identical markets for induced-value tokens. If no differences in values are observed for the induced-value tokens, then economic theory predicts that no differences between buying and selling values will be observed for consumption goods evaluated and traded under the same conditions.

The results from a series of experiments involving real exchanges of tokens and of various consumption goods are reported in this paper. In each case, a random allocation design was used to test for the presence of an endowment effect. Half of the subjects were endowed with a good and became potential sellers in each market; the other half of the subjects were potential buyers. Conventional economic analysis yields the simple prediction that one-half of the goods should be traded in voluntary exchanges. If value is unaffected by ownership, then the distribution of values in the two groups should be the same except for sampling variation. The supply and demand curves should therefore be mirror images of each other, intersecting at their common median. The null hypothesis is, therefore, that half of the goods provided should change hands. Label this predicted volume $V^*$. If there is an endowment effect, the value of the good will be higher for sellers than for buyers, and observed volume $V$ will be less than $V^*$. The ratio $V/V^*$ provides a unit-free measure of the undertrading that is produced by the effect of ownership on value. To test the hypothesis that market experience eliminates undertrading, the markets were repeated several times.

A test for the possibility that observed undertrading was due to transaction costs was provided by a comparison of the results from a series of induced-value markets with those from the subsequent goods markets carried out with identical trading rules. Notice that this comparison can also be used to eliminate numerous other possible explanations of the observed undertrading. For example, if the instructions to the subjects are confusing or misleading, the effects should show up in both the induced-value markets and the experimental markets for real goods. Section II describes studies of trading volume in induced-value markets and in consumption goods markets. Section III provides a further test for strategic behavior and demonstrates that the disparity findings are not likely caused by this. Section IV investigates the extent to which the undertrading of goods is produced by reluctance to buy and reluctance to sell. Section V examines undertrading in bilateral negotiations and provides a test of the Coase theorem. Section VI describes an experiment that rules out income effects and a trophy effect as explanations of the observed valuation disparity. Implications of the observed effects are discussed in Section VII.

## II. Repeated Market Experiments

In experiment 1, 44 students in an advanced undergraduate law and economics class at Cornell University received a packet of general instructions plus 11 forms, one for each of the markets that were conducted in the experiment. (The instructions for all experiments are available from the authors.) The first three markets were conducted for induced-value tokens. Sellers received the following instructions (with differences for buyers in brackets):

> In this market the objects being traded are tokens. You are an owner, so you now own a token [You are a buyer, so you have an opportunity to buy a token] which has a value to you of $\$x$. It has this value to you because the experimenter will give you this much money for it. The value of the token is different for different individuals. A price for the tokens will be determined later. For each of the prices listed below, please indicate whether you prefer to: (1) Sell your token at

> this price and receive the market price. [Buy a token at this price and cash it in for the sum of money indicated above.] (2) Keep your token and cash it in for the sum of money indicated above. [Not buy a token at this price.] For each price indicate your decision by marking an X in the appropriate column.

Part of the response form for sellers follows:

> At a price of $8.75 I will sell _____ I will not sell _____
>
> At a price of $8.25 I will sell _____ I will not sell _____

The same rectangular distribution of values—ranging from $0.25 to $8.75 in steps of $0.50—was prepared for both buyers and sellers. Because not all the forms were actually distributed, however, the induced supply and demand curves were not always precisely symmetrical. Subjects alternated between the buyer and seller role in the three successive markets and were assigned a different individual redemption value in each trial.

Experimenters collected the forms from all participants after each market period and immediately calculated and announced the market-clearing price,[2] the number of trades, and the presence or absence of excess demand or supply at the market-clearing price.[3] Three buyers and three sellers were selected at random after each of the induced markets and were paid off according to the preferences stated on their forms and the market-clearing price for that period.

Immediately after the three induced-value markets, subjects on alternating seats were given Cornell coffee mugs, which sell for $6.00 each at the bookstore. The experimenter asked all participants to examine a mug, either their own or their neighbor's. The experimenter then informed the subjects that four markets for mugs would be conducted using the same procedures as the prior induced markets with two exceptions: (1) One of the four market trials would subsequently be selected at random, and only the trades made on this

[2] The instructions stated that "*it is in your best interest to answer these questions truthfully.* For any question, treat the price as fixed. (In economics jargon, you should act as 'price takers'.)" All the subjects were junior and senior economics majors, so they were familiar with the terms used. If subjects asked how the market prices were determined, they were told, truthfully, that the market price was the point at which the elicited supply and demand curves intersected. The uniformity of the results across many different experiments suggests that this information had no discernible effect on behavior. Furthermore, the responses of the subjects in the induced-value portion of the experiments indicate that nearly all understood and accepted their role as price takers. See also experiment 5, in which a random price procedure was used.

[3] When this occurred, a random draw determined which buyers and sellers were accommodated.

trial would be executed. (2) In the binding market trial, *all* trades would be implemented, unlike the subset implemented in the induced-value markets.[4] The initial assignment of buyer and seller roles was maintained for all four trading periods. The clearing price and the number of trades were announced after each period. The market that "counted" was indicated after the fourth period, and transactions were executed immediately. All sellers who had indicated that they would give up their mugs for a sum at the market-clearing price exchanged their mugs for cash, and successful buyers paid this same price and received their mugs. This design was used to permit learning to take place over successive trials and yet make each trial potentially binding. The same procedure was then followed for four more successive markets using boxed ballpoint pens with a visible bookstore price tag of $3.98, which were distributed to the subjects who had been buyers in the mug markets.

For each goods market, subjects completed a form similar to that used for the induced-value tokens, with the following instructions:

> You now own the object in your possession. [You do not own the object that you see in the possession of some of your neighbors.] You have the option of selling it [buying one] if a price, which will be determined later, is acceptable to you. For each of the possible prices below indicate whether you wish to: (1) Sell your object and receive this price [Pay this price and receive an object to take home with you] or (2) Keep your object and take it home with you. [Not buy an object at this price.] For each price indicate your decision by marking an X in the appropriate column.

The buyers and sellers in the consumption goods markets faced the same incentives that they had experienced in the induced-value markets. Buyers maximized their potential gain by agreeing to buy at all prices below the value they ascribed to the good, and sellers maximized their welfare by agreeing to sell at all prices above the good's worth to them. As in the induced-value markets, it was in the best interest of the participants to act as price takers.

As shown in table 2, the markets for induced-value tokens and consumption goods yielded sharply different results. In the induced-value markets, as expected, the median buying and selling prices were identical. The ratio of actual to predicted volume ($V/V^*$) was 1.0,

[4] The experimental design was intended to give the markets for consumption goods every possible chance to be efficient. While in the induced-value markets not everyone was paid, in the consumption goods markets everyone was paid. Also, the consumption goods markets were conducted after the induced-value markets and were repeated four times each, to allow the subjects the maximum opportunity for learning.

TABLE 2

RESULTS OF EXPERIMENT 1

INDUCED-VALUE MARKETS

| Trial | Actual Trades | Expected Trades | Price | Expected Price |
|---|---|---|---|---|
| 1 | 12 | 11 | 3.75 | 3.75 |
| 2 | 11 | 11 | 4.75 | 4.75 |
| 3 | 10 | 11 | 4.25 | 4.25 |

CONSUMPTION GOODS MARKETS

| Trial | Trades | Price | Median Buyer Reservation Price | Median Seller Reservation Price |
|---|---|---|---|---|
| | | Mugs (Expected Trades = 11) | | |
| 4 | 4 | 4.25 | 2.75 | 5.25 |
| 5 | 1 | 4.75 | 2.25 | 5.25 |
| 6 | 2 | 4.50 | 2.25 | 5.25 |
| 7 | 2 | 4.25 | 2.25 | 5.25 |
| | | Pens (Expected Trades = 11) | | |
| 8 | 4 | 1.25 | .75 | 2.50 |
| 9 | 5 | 1.25 | .75 | 1.75 |
| 10 | 4 | 1.25 | .75 | 2.25 |
| 11 | 5 | 1.25 | .75 | 1.75 |

aggregating over the three periods. In contrast, the median selling prices in the mug and pen markets were more than twice the median buying prices, and the $V/V^*$ ratio was only .20 for mugs and .41 for pens. Observed volume did not increase over successive periods in either the mug or the pen markets, providing no indication that subjects learned to adopt equal buying and selling prices.

The results of the first and last markets for coffee mugs are also displayed in figure 1. There are five features to notice in this figure: (1) Both buyers and sellers display a wide range of values, indicating that in the absence of an endowment effect there would be enough rents to produce gains from trade. Indeed, the range of values is similar to that used in the induced-value markets, which had near-perfect market efficiency. (2) The distribution of selling prices has a single mode, unlike some recent results in which an evaluation discrepancy could be explained by a bimodal distribution of compensation demanded (Boyce et al. 1990). (3) The payment of a small commission for trading, such as $0.25 per trade, would not significantly alter the results. (4) The mugs were desirable. Every subject assigned a positive value to the mug, and the lowest value assigned by a seller

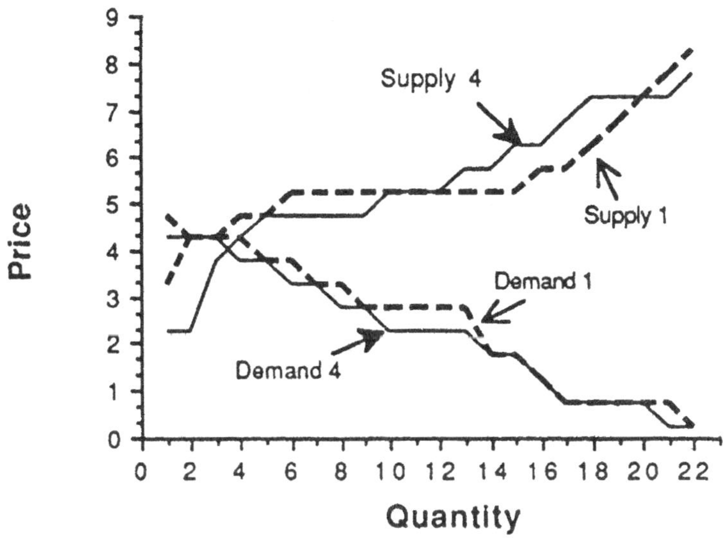


FIG. 1.—Supply and demand curves, markets 1 and 4

was \$2.25. (5) Neither demand nor supply changed much between the first and last markets.

Experiment 2 was conducted in an undergraduate microeconomics class at Cornell ($N = 38$). The procedure was identical to that of experiment 1, except that the second consumption good was a pair of folding binoculars in a cardboard frame, available at the bookstore for \$4.00. The results are reported in table 3.

In experiments 3 and 4, conducted in Simon Fraser University undergraduate economics classes, the subjects were asked to provide minimum selling prices or maximum buying prices rather than to answer the series of yes or no questions used in experiments 1 and 2. The induced-value markets were conducted with no monetary payoffs and were followed by four markets for pens in experiment 3 and five markets for mugs in experiment 4. In experiment 3, subjects were told that the first three markets for pens would be used for practice, so only the fourth and final market would be binding. In experiment 4, one of the five markets was selected at random to count, as in experiments 1 and 2. Other procedures were unchanged. The results are shown in table 4.

Experiments 2–4 all yielded results similar to those obtained in experiment 1. Summing over the induced-value markets in all four experiments produced a $V/V^*$ index of .91. This excellent performance was achieved even though the participants did not have the

TABLE 3

RESULTS OF EXPERIMENT 2

INDUCED-VALUE MARKETS

| Trial | Actual Trades | Expected Trades | Price | Expected Price |
|---|---|---|---|---|
| 1 | 10 | 10 | 3.75 | 4.25 |
| 2 | 9 | 10 | 4.75 | 4.25 |
| 3 | 7 | 8 | 4.25 | 4.75 |

CONSUMPTION GOODS MARKETS

| Trial | Trades | Price | Median Buyer Reservation Price | Median Seller Reservation Price |
|---|---|---|---|---|
| | Mugs (Expected Trades = 9.5) | | | |
| 4 | 3 | 3.75 | 1.75 | 4.75 |
| 5 | 3 | 3.25 | 2.25 | 4.75 |
| 6 | 2 | 3.25 | 2.25 | 4.75 |
| 7 | 2 | 3.25 | 2.25 | 4.25 |
| | Binoculars (Expected Trades = 9.5) | | | |
| 8 | 4 | 1.25 | .75 | 1.25 |
| 9 | 4 | .75 | .75 | 1.25 |
| 10 | 3 | .75 | .75 | 1.75 |
| 11 | 3 | .75 | .75 | 1.75 |

benefit of experience with the trading rules, there were limited monetary incentives in experiments 1 and 2, and there were no monetary incentives in experiments 3 and 4. In the markets for consumption goods, in which all participants faced monetary incentives and experience with the market rules gained from the induced-value markets, $V/V^*$ averaged .31, and median selling prices were more than double the corresponding buying prices. Trading procedures were precisely identical in markets for goods and for induced-value tokens. The high volume of trade in money tokens therefore eliminates transaction costs (or any other feature that was present in both types of markets) as an explanation of the observed undertrading of consumption goods.

It should be noted that subjects in the position of buyers were not given money to use for purchases, but rather had to make transactions using their own money. (Subjects were told to bring money to class and that credit and change would be available if necessary. Some subjects borrowed from friends to make payments.) The aim was to study transactions in a realistic setting. While the present design makes potential sellers slightly wealthier, at least in the first market, the magnitude of the possible income effect is trivial. In one of the

TABLE 4

RESULTS OF EXPERIMENTS 3 AND 4

| Trial | *N* | Object | Actual Trades | Expected Trades | Ratio of Seller Median Value to Buyer Median Value |
|---|---|---|---|---|---|
| | | | Experiment 3 | | |
| 1 | 26 | Induced | 5 | 6.5 | |
| 2 | 26 | Pen | 2 | 6.5 | 6.0 |
| 3 | 26 | Pen | 2 | 6.5 | 6.0 |
| 4 | 26 | Pen | 2 | 6.5 | 5.0 |
| 5 | 26 | Pen | 1 | 6.5 | 5.0 |
| | | | Experiment 4 | | |
| 1 | 74 | Induced | 15 | 18.5 | |
| 2 | 74 | Induced | 16 | 18.5 | |
| 3 | 74 | Mug | 6 | 18.5 | 3.8 |
| 4 | 74 | Mug | 4 | 18.5 | 2.8 |
| 5 | 72 | Mug | 4 | 18 | 2.2 |
| 6 | 73 | Mug | 8 | 18 | 1.8 |
| 7 | 74 | Mug | 8 | 18.5 | 1.8 |

markets the equilibrium price was only $0.75, and the prices in other markets were never above a few dollars. Also, as shown in experiments 7 and 8 below, equal undertrading was found in designs that eliminated the possibility of an income effect or cash constraint.

As shown in tables 2–4, subjects showed almost no undertrading even in their first trial in an induced-value market. Evidently neither bargaining habits nor any transaction costs impede trading in money tokens. On the other hand, there is no indication that participants in the markets for goods learned to make valuations independent of their entitlements. The discrepant evaluations of buyers and sellers remained stable over four, and in one case five, successive markets for the same good and did not change systematically over repeated markets for successive goods.

A difference in procedure probably explains the apparent conflict between these results and the conclusion reached in some other studies, that the WTA-WTP discrepancy is greatly reduced by market experience. The studies that reported a disciplinary effect of market experience assessed this effect by comparing the responses of buyers and sellers in preliminary hypothetical questions or nonbinding market trials to their behavior in a subsequent binding trial with real monetary payoffs (Knez et al. 1985; Brookshire and Coursey 1987; Coursey et al. 1987). In the present experiments, the markets for consumption goods were real and potentially binding from the first trial, and the WTA-WTP discrepancy was found to be stable over a series of such binding trials.

It should be stressed that previous research did not actually demonstrate that the discrepancy between buyers and sellers is eliminated in markets. Although the discrepancy between the final selling and buying prices in the sucrose octa-acetate experiment of Coursey et al. (1987) was not statistically significant, the ratio of median prices of sellers and buyers was still 2.6.[5] If the buyers and sellers had been allowed to trade according to their final bids, a total of nine advantageous exchanges would have occurred between the two groups, compared to the theoretical expectation of 16 trades (for details, see Knetsch and Sinden [1987]). This $V/V^*$ ratio of .56 is quite similar to the ratios observed in experiments 1–4. In the study by Brookshire and Coursey (1987), the ratio of mean prices was indeed reduced by experience, from a high of 77 for initial hypothetical survey responses to 6.1 in the first potentially binding auction conducted in a laboratory. However, the ratio remained at 5.6 in the final auction.

## III. Testing for Misrepresentation

As previously stated, subjects faced identical incentives in the induced-value and consumption goods phases of experiments 1–4. Therefore, it seems safe to attribute the difference in observed trading to the endowment effect. However, some readers of early drafts of this paper have suggested that because of the way market prices were determined, subjects might have felt that they had an incentive to misstate their true values in order to influence the price, and perhaps this incentive was perceived to be greater in the consumption goods markets. To eliminate this possible interpretation of the previous results, experiment 5 was carried out in a manner similar to the first four experiments, except that subjects were told that the price would be selected at random. As is well known, this is an incentive-compatible procedure for eliciting values (see Becker, DeGroot, and Marschak 1964).

Each participant received the following instructions (with appropriate alternative wording in the buyers' forms):

> After you have finished, one of the prices listed below will be selected at random and any exchanges will take place at that price. If you have indicated you will sell at this price you will receive this amount of money and will give up the mug; if you have indicated that you will keep the mug at this price

[5] The ratio of the mean selling and buying prices is 1.4 if all subjects are included. However, if one buyer and one seller with extreme valuations are excluded, the ratio is 1.9. These numbers were reported in an earlier version of Coursey et al. (1987).

> then no exchange will be made and you can take the mug home with you.
>
> . . . Your decision can have no effect on the price actually used because the price will be selected at random.

The experiment was conducted in a series of six tutorial groups of a business statistics class at Simon Fraser University. The use of small groups helped assure complete understanding of the instructions, and the exercises were conducted over the course of a single day to minimize opportunities for communication between participants. Each group was divided equally: half of the subjects were designated as sellers by random selection, and the other half became buyers. A total of 59 people took part.

Two induced-value markets for hypothetical payoffs and a subsequent third real exchange market for money and mugs were conducted with identical trading rules used in all three. All participants maintained the same role as either buyers or sellers for the three markets. As in experiments 1 and 2, the prices that individuals chose to buy or to sell were selected from possible prices ranging from $0.00 to $9.50 listed by increments of $0.50.

The results of this experiment were nearly identical to the earlier ones in which the actual exchanges were based on the market-clearing price. Even though possibly less motivating hypothetical values were used in the two induced-value markets, nearly all participants pursued a profit-maximizing selection of prices to buy or sell the assets. Fourteen exchanges at a price of $4.75 were expected in the first induced-value market on the basis of the randomly distributed values written on the forms. Thirteen trades at this price were indicated by the prices actually selected by the participants. The results of the second hypothetical induced-value market were equally convincing, with 16 of the 17 expected exchanges made at the expected price of $5.75. The procedures and incentives were apparently well understood by the participants.

Mugs, comparable to those used in other experiments, were distributed to the potential sellers after the induced-value markets were completed. A mug was also shown to all the potential buyers. The following form with instructions, nearly identical to the ones used in the induced-value markets, was then distributed (with the alternative wording for buyers in brackets):

> You now [do not] have, and own a mug which you can keep and take home. You also have the option of selling it and receiving [buying one to take home by paying] money for it.
>
> For each of the possible prices listed below, please indicate

whether you wish to: (1) Receive [pay] that amount of money and sell your [buy a] mug, or (2) Not sell your [buy a] mug at this price.

After you have finished, one of the prices listed below will be selected at random and any exchanges will take place at that price. If you have indicated you will sell [buy] at this price you will receive this amount of money [a mug] and will give up the mug [pay this amount of money]; if you have indicated that you will keep the [not buy a] mug at this price then no exchange will be made and you can take the mug home with you [do not pay anything].

Notice the following two things: (1) Your decision can have no effect on the price actually used because the price will be selected at random. (2) It is in your interest to indicate your true preferences at each of the possible prices listed below.

For each price indicate your decision by marking an X in the appropriate column.

| | I Will Sell [Buy] | I Will Keep [Not Buy] the Mug |
|---|---|---|
| If the price is $0 | _____ | _____ |
| If the price is $0.50 | _____ | _____ |
| ⋮ | | |
| If the price is $9.50 | _____ | _____ |

After the instructions were read and reviewed by the experimenter and questions were answered, participants completed the forms indicating either their lowest selling price or their highest buying price. A random price, from among the list from $0.00 to $9.50, was then drawn, and exchanges based on this price were completed.

The results again showed a large and significant endowment effect. Given the 29 potential buyers, 30 potential sellers, and the random distribution of the mugs, 14.5 exchanges would be expected if entitlements did not influence valuations. Instead, only six were indicated on the basis of the values actually selected by the potential buyers and sellers ($V/V^* = .41$). The median selling price of $5.75 was over twice the median buying price of $2.25, and the means were $5.78 and $2.21, respectively.

## IV. Reluctance to Buy versus Reluctance to Sell

Exchanges of money and a good (or between two goods) offer the possibilities of four comparisons: a choice of gaining either the good or money, a choice of losing one or the other, buying (giving up money for the good), and selling (giving up the good for money) (Tversky and Kahneman, in press). The endowment effect results from a difference between the relative preferences for the good and money. The comparison of buying and selling to simple choices between gains permits an analysis of the discrepancy between WTA and WTP into two components: reluctance to sell (exchanging the good for money) and reluctance to buy (exchanging money for the good).

Experiments 6 and 7 were carried out to assess the weight of reluctance to buy and reluctance to sell in undertrading of a good similar to the goods used in the earlier experiments. The subjects in experiment 6 were 77 Simon Fraser students, randomly assigned to three groups. Members of one group, designated sellers, were given a coffee mug and were asked to indicate whether or not they would sell the mug at a series of prices ranging from $0.00 to $9.25. A group of buyers indicated whether they were willing to buy a mug at each of these prices. Finally, choosers were asked to choose, for each of the possible prices, between a mug and cash.

The results again reveal substantial undertrading: While 12.5 trades were expected between buyers and sellers, only three trades took place ($V/V^* = .24$). The median valuations were $7.12 for sellers, $3.12 for choosers, and $2.87 for buyers. The close similarity of results for buyers and choosers indicates that there was relatively little reluctance to pay for the mug.

Experiment 7 was carried out with 117 students at the University of British Columbia. It used an identical design except that price tags were left on the mugs. The results were consistent with those in experiment 6. Nineteen trades were expected on the basis of valuation equivalence, but only one was concluded on the basis of actual valuations ($V/V^* = .05$). The median valuations were $7.00 for sellers, $3.50 for choosers, and $2.00 for buyers.

It is worth noting that these results eliminate any form of income effect as an explanation of the discrepant valuations since the positions of sellers and choosers were strictly identical. The allocation of a particular mug to each seller evidently induced a sense of endowment that the choosers did not share: the median value of the mug to the sellers was more than double the value indicated by the choosers even though their choices were objectively the same. The results imply that the observed undertrading of consumption goods may be largely due to a reluctance to part with entitlements.

## V. Bilateral Bargaining and the Coase Theorem

According to the Coase theorem, the allocation of resources to individuals who can bargain and transact at no cost should be independent of initial property rights. However, if the marginal rate of substitution between one good and another is affected by endowment, then the individual who is assigned the property right to a good will be more likely to retain it. A bilateral bargaining experiment (experiment 8) was carried out to test this implication of the endowment effect.

The subjects were 35 pairs of students in seven small tutorials at Simon Fraser University. The students were enrolled in either a beginning economics course or an English class. Each student was randomly paired with another student in the same tutorial group, with care taken to assure that students entering the tutorial together were not assigned as a pair. A game of Nim, a simple game easily explained, was played by each pair of participants. The winners of the game were each given a 400-gram Swiss chocolate bar and told it was theirs to keep.

An induced-value bargaining session was then conducted. The member of each pair who did not win the Nim game, and therefore did not receive the chocolate bar, was given a ticket and an instruction sheet that indicated that the ticket was worth $3.00 because it could be redeemed for that sum. The ticket owners were also told that they could sell the ticket to their partner if mutually agreeable terms could be reached. The partners (the chocolate bar owners) received instructions indicating that they could receive $5.00 for the ticket if they could successfully buy it from the owner. Thus there was a $2.00 surplus available to any pair completing a trade.

The pairs were then given an unlimited amount of time to bargain. Subjects were told that both credit and change were available from the experimenter. Results of the bargaining sessions were recorded on their instruction sheets.

Of the 35 pairs of participants, 29 agreed to an exchange ($V/V^* =$ .83). The average price paid for the 29 tickets was $4.09, with 12 of the exchange prices being exactly $4.00. Payments of the redemption values of the tickets were made as soon as the exchanges were completed. These payments were made in single dollar bills to facilitate trading in the subsequent bargaining session. After the ticket exchanges were completed, owners of the chocolate bars were told that they could sell them to their partners if a mutually agreeable price could be determined. The procedures used for the tickets were once again applied to these bargaining sessions.

An important effect of the preliminary induced-value ticket bargains was to provide the ticket owners with some cash. The average gain to the ticket owners (including the six who did not sell their tickets) was $3.90. The average gain to their partners (the chocolate bar owners) was only $0.76. Thus the potential chocolate bar buyers were endowed with an average of $3.14 more than the owners, creating a small income effect toward the buyers. Also, to the extent that a windfall gain such as this is spent more casually by subjects than other money (for evidence on such a "house money effect," see Thaler and Johnson [1990]), trading of chocolate bars should be facilitated.

Results of the chocolate bar bargains once again suggest reluctance to trade. Rather than the 17.5 trades expected from the random allocations, only seven were observed ($V/V^* = .4$). The average price paid in those exchanges that did occur was $2.69 (the actual prices were $6.00, $3.10, $3.00, $2.75, $2.00, $1.00, and $1.00). If the six pairs of subjects who did not successfully complete bargains in the first stage are omitted from the sample on the grounds that they did not understand the task or procedures, then six trades are observed where 14.5 would be expected ($V/V^* = .414$). Similarly, if two more pairs are dropped because the prices at which they exchanged tickets were outside the range $3.00–$5.00, then the number of trades falls to four, and $V/V^*$ falls to .296. (No significant differences between the students in the English and economics classes were observed.)[6]

To be sure that the chocolate bars were valued by the subjects and that these valuations would vary enough to yield mutually beneficial trades, the same chocolate bars were distributed to half the members of another class at Simon Fraser. Those who received chocolate bars were asked the minimum price they would accept to sell their bar, while those without the bars were asked the maximum price they would pay to acquire a bar. The valuations of the bars varied from $0.50 to $8.00. The average value ascribed by sellers was $3.98, while the buyers' average valuation was $1.25. (The median values were $3.50 and $1.25.)

## VI. The Endowment Effect in Choices between Goods

The previous experiments documented undertrading in exchanges of money and consumption goods. A separate experiment (Knetsch 1989) establishes the same effect in exchanges between two goods. Participants in three classes were offered a choice between the same two goods. All students in one class were given a coffee mug at the

[6] We conducted two similar bargaining experiments that yielded comparable results. Twenty-six pairs of subjects negotiated the sale of mugs and then envelopes containing an uncertain amount of money. Buyers had not been given any cash endowment. These sessions yielded six and five trades, respectively, where 13 would be expected. Also, some induced-value bilateral negotiation sessions were conducted in which only $0.50 of surplus was available (the seller's valuation was $1.50 and the buyer's was $2.00). Nevertheless, 21 of a possible 26 trades were completed.

beginning of the session as compensation for completing a short questionnaire. At the completion of the task, the experimenters showed the students a bar of Swiss chocolate that they could immediately receive in exchange for the mug. The students in another class were offered an opportunity to make the opposite exchange after first being given the chocolate bar. The students in a third class were simply offered a choice, at the beginning of the session, between a chocolate bar and a mug. The proportion of students selecting the mug was 89 percent in the class originally endowed with mugs ($N = 76$), 56 percent in the class offered a choice ($N = 55$), and only 10 percent in the class originally endowed with chocolate bars ($N = 87$). For most participants a mug was more valuable than the chocolate when the mug had to be given up but less valuable when the chocolate had to be given up. This experiment confirms that undertrading can occur even when income effects are ruled out. It also demonstrates an endowment effect for a good that was distributed to everyone in the class and therefore did not have the appeal of a prize or trophy.

## VII. Discussion

The evidence presented in this paper supports what may be called an instant endowment effect: the value that an individual assigns to such objects as mugs, pens, binoculars, and chocolate bars appears to increase substantially as soon as that individual is given the object.[7] The apparently instantaneous nature of the reference point shift and consequent value change induced by giving a person possession of a good goes beyond previous discussions of the endowment effect, which focused on goods that have been in the individual's possession for some time. While long-term endowment effects could be explained by sentimental attachment or by an improved technology of consumption in the Stigler-Becker (1977) sense, the differences in preference or taste demonstrated by more than 700 participants in the experiments reported in this paper cannot be explained in this fashion.

The endowment effect is one explanation for the systematic differences between buying and selling prices that have been observed so often in past work. One of the objectives of this study was to examine an alternative explanation for this buying-selling discrepancy, namely that it reflects a general bargaining strategy (Knez and Smith 1987) that would be eliminated by experience in the market (Brookshire

[7] The impression gained from informal pilot experiments is that the act of giving the participant physical possession of the good results in a more consistent endowment effect. Assigning subjects a chance to receive a good, or a property right to a good to be received at a later time, seemed to produce weaker effects.

and Coursey 1987; Coursey et al. 1987). Our results do not support this alternative view. The trading institution used in experiments 1–7 encouraged participants to be price takers (especially in experiment 5), and the rules provided no incentive to conceal true preferences. Furthermore, the results of the induced-value markets indicate that the subjects understood the demand-revealing nature of the questions they were asked and acted accordingly. Substantial undertrading was nevertheless observed in markets for consumption goods. As for learning and market discipline, there was no indication that buying and selling prices converged over repeated market trials, though full feedback was provided at the end of each trial. The undertrading observed in these experiments appears to reflect a true difference in preferences between the potential buyers and sellers. The robustness of this result reduces the risk that the outcome is produced by an experimental artifact. In short, the present findings indicate that the endowment effect can persist in genuine market settings.

The contrast between the induced-value markets and the consumption goods markets lends support to Heiner's (1985) conjecture that the results of induced-value experiments may not generalize to all market settings. The defining characteristic of the induced-value markets is that the values of the tokens are unequivocally defined by the amount the experimenter will pay for them. Loss aversion is irrelevant with such objects because transactions are evaluated simply on the basis of net gain or loss. (If someone is offered $6.00 for a $5.00 bill, there is no sense of loss associated with the trade.) Some markets may share this feature of induced-value markets, especially when the conditions of pure arbitrage are approached. However, the computation of net gain and loss is not possible in other situations, for example, in markets in which risky prospects are traded for cash or in markets in which people sell goods that they also value for their use. In these conditions, the cancellation of the loss of the object against the dollars received is not possible because the good and money are not strictly commensurate. The valuation ambiguity produced by this lack of commensurability is necessary, although not sufficient, for both loss aversion and a buying-selling discrepancy.

The results of the experimental demonstrations of the endowment effect have direct implications for economic theory and economic predictions. Contrary to the assumptions of standard economic theory that preferences are independent of entitlements,[8] the evidence

[8] Although ownership can affect taste in the manner suggested by Stigler and Becker (1977), in the absence of income effects, it is traditional to assume that the indifference curves in an Edgeworth box diagram do not depend on the location of the endowment point.

presented here indicates that people's preferences depend on their reference positions. Consequently, preference orderings are not defined independently of endowments: good A may be preferred to B when A is part of an original endowment, but the reverse may be true when initial reference positions are changed. Indifference curves will have a kink at the endowment or reference point (see Tversky and Kahneman, in press), and an indifference curve tracing acceptable trades in one direction may even cross another indifference curve that plots the acceptable exchanges in the opposite direction (Knetsch 1989).

The existence of endowment effects reduces the gains from trade. In comparison with a world in which preferences are independent of endowment, the existence of loss aversion produces an inertia in the economy because potential traders are more reluctant to trade than is conventionally assumed. This is not to say that Pareto-optimal trades will not take place. Rather, there are simply fewer mutually advantageous exchanges possible, and so the volume of trade is lower than it otherwise would be.

To assess the practical significance of the endowment effect, it is important to consider first some necessary conditions for the effect to be observed. Experiments 6 and 7 suggest that the endowment effect is primarily a problem for sellers; we observed little reluctance to buy but much reluctance to sell. Furthermore, not all sellers are afflicted by an endowment effect. The effect did not appear in the markets for money tokens, and there is no reason in general to expect reluctance to resell goods that are held especially for that purpose. An owner will not be reluctant to sell an item at a given price if a perfect substitute is readily available at a lower price. This reasoning suggests that endowment effects will almost certainly occur when owners are faced with an opportunity to sell an item purchased for use that is not easily replaceable. Examples might include tickets to a sold-out event, hunting licenses in limited supply (Bishop and Heberlein 1979), works of art, or a pleasant view.

While the conditions necessary for an endowment effect to be observed may appear to limit its applicability in economic settings, in fact these conditions are very often satisfied, and especially so in the bargaining contexts to which the Coase theorem is applied. For example, tickets to Wimbledon are allocated by means of a lottery. A standard Coasean analysis would imply that in the presence of an efficient ticket brokerage market, winners of the lottery would be no more likely to attend the matches than other tennis fans who had won a similar cash prize in an unrelated lottery. In contrast, the experimental results presented in this paper predict that many winners of Wimbledon tickets will attend the event, turning down opportunities to sell their tickets that exceed their reservation price for buying them.

Endowment effects can also be observed for firms and other organizations. Endowment effects are predicted for property rights acquired by historic accident or fortuitous circumstances, such as government licenses, landing rights, or transferable pollution permits. Owing to endowment effects, firms will be reluctant to divest themselves of divisions, plants, and product lines even though they would never consider buying the same assets; indeed, stock prices often rise when firms do give them up. Again, the prediction is not an absence of trade, just a reduction in the volume of trade.

Isolating the influence of endowment effects from those of transaction costs as causes of low trading volumes is, of course, difficult in actual market settings. Demonstrations of endowment effects are most persuasive where transaction costs are very small. By design, this was the case in the experimental markets, where the efficiency of the induced-value markets demonstrated the minimal effect of transaction costs, or other impediments, on exchange decisions, leaving the great reluctance to trade mugs and other goods to be attributable to endowment effects.

Endowment effects are not limited to cases involving physical goods or to legal entitlements. The reference position of individuals and firms often includes terms of previous transactions or expectations of continuation of present, often informal, arrangements. There is clear evidence of dramatically asymmetric reactions to improvements and deteriorations of these terms and a willingness to make sacrifices to avoid unfair treatment (Kahneman, Knetsch, and Thaler 1986). The reluctance to sell at a loss, owing to a perceived entitlement to a formerly prevailing price, can explain two observations of apparent undertrading. The first pertains to housing markets. It is often observed that when housing prices fall, volume also falls. When house prices are falling, houses remain on the market longer than when prices are rising. Similarly, the volume for stocks that have declined in price is lower than the volume for stocks that have increased in value (Shefrin and Statman 1985; Ferris, Haugen, and Makhija 1988), although tax considerations would lead to the opposite prediction.

Another manifestation of loss aversion in the context of multiattribute negotiations is what might be termed "concession aversion": a reluctance to accept a loss on any dimension of an agreement. A straightforward and common instance of this is the downward stickiness of wages. A somewhat more subtle implication of concession aversion is that it can produce inefficient contract terms owing to historic precedents. Old firms may have more inefficient arrangements than new ones because new companies can negotiate without the reference positions created by prior agreements. Some airlines, for example, are required to carry three pilots on some planes while others—newer ones—operate with two.

Loss aversion implies a marked asymmetry in the treatment of losses and forgone gains, which plays an essential role in judgments of fairness (Kahneman et al. 1986). Accordingly, disputes in which concessions are viewed as losses are often much less tractable than disputes in which concessions involve forgone gains. Court decisions recognize the asymmetry of losses and forgone gains by favoring possessors of goods over other claimants, by limiting recovery of lost profits relative to compensation for actual expenditures, and by failing to enforce gratuitous promises that are coded as forgone gains to the injured party (Cohen and Knetsch 1989).

To conclude, the evidence reported here offers no support for the contention that observations of loss aversion and the consequential evaluation disparities are artifacts; nor should they be interpreted as mistakes likely to be eliminated by experience, training, or "market discipline." Instead, the findings support an alternative view of endowment effects and loss aversion as fundamental characteristics of preferences.

## References


Banford, Nancy D.; Knetsch, Jack L.; and Mauser, Gary A. "Feasibility Judgements and Alternative Measures of Benefits and Costs." *J. Bus. Admin.* 11, nos. 1, 2 (1979): 25–35.

Becker, Gordon M.; DeGroot, Morris H.; and Marschak, Jacob. "Measuring Utility by a Single-Response Sequential Method." *Behavioral Sci.* 9 (July 1964): 226–32.

Bishop, Richard C., and Heberlein, Thomas A. "Measuring Values of Extramarket Goods: Are Indirect Measures Biased?" *American J. Agricultural Econ.* 61 (December 1979): 926–30.

Boyce, Rebecca R.; Brown, Thomas C.; McClelland, Gary D.; Peterson, George L.; and Schulze, William D. "An Experimental Examination of Intrinsic Environmental Values." Working paper. Boulder: Univ. Colorado, 1990.

Brookshire, David S., and Coursey, Don L. "Measuring the Value of a Public Good: An Empirical Comparison of Elicitation Procedures." *A.E.R.* 77 (September 1987): 554–66.

Brookshire, David S.; Randall, Alan; and Stoll, John R. "Valuing Increments and Decrements in Natural Resource Service Flows." *American J. Agricultural Econ.* 62 (August 1980): 478–88.

Cohen, David, and Knetsch, Jack L. "Judicial Choice and Disparities between Measures of Economic Values." Working paper. Burnaby, B.C.: Simon Fraser Univ., 1989.

Coursey, Don L.; Hovis, John L.; and Schulze, William D. "The Disparity between Willingness to Accept and Willingness to Pay Measures of Value." *Q.J.E.* 102 (August 1987): 679–90.

Ferris, Stephen P.; Haugen, Robert A.; and Makhija, Anil K. "Predicting Contemporary Volume with Historic Volume at Differential Price Levels: Evidence Supporting the Disposition Effect." *J. Finance* 43 (July 1988): 677–97.

Freeman, A. Myrick. *The Benefits of Environmental Improvement.* Washington: Resources for the Future, 1979.

Hammack, Judd, and Brown, Gardner Mallard, Jr. *Waterfowl and Wetlands: Toward Bio-economic Analysis.* Baltimore: Johns Hopkins Press (for Resources for the Future), 1974.

Heberlein, Thomas A., and Bishop, Richard C. "Assessing the Validity of Contingent Valuation: Three Field Experiments." Paper presented at the International Conference on Man's Role in Changing the Global Environment, Italy, 1985.

Heiner, Ronald A. "Experimental Economics: Comment." *A.E.R.* 75 (March 1985): 260–63.

Kahneman, Daniel; Knetsch, Jack L.; and Thaler, Richard. "Fairness as a Constraint on Profit Seeking: Entitlements in the Market." *A.E.R.* 76 (September 1986): 728–41.

Kahneman, Daniel, and Tversky, Amos. "Prospect Theory: An Analysis of Decision under Risk." *Econometrica* 47 (March 1979): 263–91.

Knetsch, Jack L. "The Endowment Effect and Evidence of Nonreversible Indifference Curves." *A.E.R.* 79 (December 1989): 1277–84.

Knetsch, Jack L., and Sinden, J. A. "Willingness to Pay and Compensation Demanded: Experimental Evidence of an Unexpected Disparity in Measures of Value." *Q.J.E.* 99 (August 1984): 507–21.

———. "The Persistence of Evaluation Disparities." *Q.J.E.* 102 (August 1987): 691–95.

Knez, Marc, and Smith, Vernon L. "Hypothetical Valuations and Preference Reversals in the Context of Asset Trading." In *Laboratory Experiments in Economics: Six Points of View,* edited by Alvin E. Roth. Cambridge: Cambridge Univ. Press, 1987.

Knez, Peter; Smith, Vernon L.; and Williams, Arlington W. "Individual Rationality, Market Rationality, and Value Estimation." *A.E.R. Papers and Proc.* 75 (May 1985): 397–402.

Plott, Charles R. "Industrial Organization Theory and Experimental Economics." *J. Econ. Literature* 20 (December 1982): 1485–1527.

Rowe, Robert D.; d'Arge, Ralph C.; and Brookshire, David S. "An Experiment on the Economic Value of Visibility." *J. Environmental Econ. and Management* 7 (March 1980): 1–19.

Shefrin, Hersh, and Statman, Meir. "The Disposition to Sell Winners Too Early and Ride Losers Too Long: Theory and Evidence." *J. Finance* 40 (July 1985): 777–90.

Sinclair, William F. *The Economic and Social Impact of Kemano II Hydroelectric Project on British Columbia's Fisheries Resources.* Vancouver: Dept. Fisheries and Oceans, 1978.

Smith, Vernon L. "Experimental Economics: Induced Value Theory." *A.E.R. Papers and Proc.* 66 (May 1976): 274–79.

———. "Macroeconomic Systems as an Experimental Science." *A.E.R.* 72 (December 1982): 923–55.

Stigler, George J., and Becker, Gary S. "De Gustibus Non Est Disputandum." *A.E.R.* 67 (March 1977): 76–90.

Thaler, Richard. "Toward a Positive Theory of Consumer Choice." *J. Econ. Behavior and Organization* 1 (March 1980): 39–60.

Thaler, Richard, and Johnson, Eric J. "Gambling with the House Money and Trying to Break Even: The Effects of Prior Outcomes on Risky Choice." *Management Sci.* 36 (June 1990).

Tversky, Amos, and Kahneman, Daniel. "Reference Theory of Choice and Exchange." *Q.J.E.* (in press).

Willig, Robert D. "Consumer's Surplus without Apology." *A.E.R.* 66 (September 1976): 589–97.

# Experimental Tests of Core Theory and the Coase Theorem: Inefficiency and Cycling

Varouj A. Aivazian *University of Toronto*
Jeffrey L. Callen *University of Toronto*
Susan McCracken *McMaster University*

## Abstract

We examine experimentally the bargaining process and the final allocation of payoffs in games that differ in terms of whether the core exists and in the initial allocation of property rights among the players. This paper highlights the interaction among property rights, transaction costs, and the empty core. Our experimental results indicate that the existence of the core is an important determinant of bargaining generally and the Coase theorem in particular. They confirm our conjecture that when the core is empty and property rights are ill defined, Coasean efficiency breaks down. Among other results, our experiments show that the number of inefficient (non-Pareto-optimal) agreements and bargaining rounds with cycling are significantly greater when the core is empty than when the core exists, especially when property rights are ill defined. Our results suggest an economic role for specific property right arrangements to resolve the empty core.

## 1. Introduction

The Coase theorem asserts that, given well-defined property rights and absent transaction costs, Pareto-efficient allocations will emerge via bargaining among players to internalize any externality among them, regardless of the initial assignment of property rights.[1] Coase (1960) highlights the central importance of transaction costs and property rights for resource allocation, focusing on efficient property right structures when transaction costs are significant. This is in contrast to many subsequent interpretations of the paper that focus their analyses on a

We wish to thank the Social Sciences and Humanities Research Council of Canada for partial support. We also wish to acknowledge an anonymous referee, John P. Gould (editor), Ron King, and seminar participants at McMaster University for helpful comments. We thank Tat-kei Lai for research assistance.

[1] We believe it is important to clarify the assumptions and to analyze the robustness of the Coase theorem because it continues to be a central paradigm for economists and public choice and legal scholars. As Dixit and Olson (2000, pp. 309–10) write, "Coase's article has been arguably the single largest influence on thinking about economic policy for the last three decades."

[*Journal of Law and Economics*, vol. 52 (November 2009)]

world of zero transaction costs and on the efficiency of the final allocations and their invariance to initial property right assignments.

In terms of core theory, the Coase theorem can be interpreted as asserting that, regardless of the initial allocation of property rights among the players, and irrespective of whether or not the core of a superadditive characteristic function exists, the grand coalition will always emerge (for a review of core theory, see Telser 1994). However, Aivazian and Callen (1981) show that with more than two players, in a setting in which there are gains from cooperating and forming coalitions to internalize the externality, the Coasean efficiency result may fail. Specifically, using a three-participant example, they demonstrate that it is possible for the core to be empty under one set of property rights, although the core is nonempty under an alternative set of property rights. Aivazian and Callen (2003) further demonstrate that the breakdown of Coasean efficiency because of the empty core becomes more likely if transaction costs are imposed on the negotiations.[2]

The purpose of this paper is to test experimentally important implications of the theory of the core and to shed light on the robustness of the Coase theorem. The experiments involve alternative bargaining scenarios in which there are pecuniary gains to the players from cooperating and forming coalitions. The observed bargaining process and the final allocation of payoffs among the players in these experiments serve as tests of the implications of the Coase theorem and of core theory generally.[3]

Our experiments address not only the robustness of the Coasean efficiency result but also the issue of bargaining in the empty core generally.[4] Economic theory is ambiguous about bargaining in the empty core. On the one hand, theory predicts that bargaining when the core of the game is empty leads to cycling and either inefficient solutions or solutions that involve long periods of

[2] Aivazian and Callen (2003) make the reasonable assumption that the costs of forming a coalition are convex in the number of players in the potential coalition. It is wrong to conclude that once transaction costs are introduced, the problem of the empty core disappears and a Pareto-optimal solution obtains. Rather, in such circumstances, negotiations may break down more quickly, and which specific coalition structure (the grand coalition or a proper subcoalition) obtains cannot be specified a priori. Even if transaction costs were to force the equilibrium, nothing ensures that the equilibrium is Pareto optimal.

[3] Existing experimental results on the Coase theorem do not account for bargaining situations in which the core is empty (Hoffman and Spitzer 1982, 1986; Harrison and McKee 1985; Harrison et al. 1987). Indeed, in all previous experimental tests of the Coase theorem, the underlying game is assumed to have a core. In view of the Harrison and McKee (1985) result that the Coase theorem holds experimentally when the core exists, it is important to see experimentally what happens when the core of the bargaining game is empty, especially since the empty core highlights the importance of coalitional rationality.

[4] It is worth noting that technological nonconvexities can induce inefficiency and instability even when the core exists. On double-auction experiments, see Van Boening and Wilcox (1996) and the literature cited therein.

bargaining and many bargaining rounds.[5] As a consequence, the nonexistence of the core may engender not only transaction costs associated with direct bargaining and the opportunity costs of (negotiation) time but also costs associated with a decrease in the value of the exchange opportunity as it is delayed by prolonged bargaining and the prospect of settling on a non-Pareto-optimal coalition. On the other hand, there exists a large game theory literature arguing that when the core is empty, bargaining participants will utilize alternative strategies or solution concepts that result in Pareto-optimal outcomes or that when the core is empty, constraints on coalitional actions may emerge to induce efficiency.[6]

The paper is organized as follows: Section 2 develops the hypotheses to be tested. Section 3 describes the experimental setup, and Section 4 reports the results. Section 5 briefly concludes.

## 2. Development of Hypotheses

The Coase theorem is silent about the bargaining process, including the length of bargaining time, the number of bargaining proposals needed to reach agreement, and the possibility of cycling instead of converging to a Pareto-optimal outcome. The presumption is that when transaction costs are zero, none of these factors are significant or have a bearing on the achievement of Pareto-optimal outcomes. Yet when the core is empty, cycling and bargaining time may come into play as emphasized by Shubik (1983, p. 150) and Aivazian and Callen (1981, 2003). Indeed, Bernholz (1997, p. 422) argues that the empty core is isomorphic to cyclical preferences.

Core theory suggests that, when the core is empty, bargaining is bound to be more protracted because of cycling, and Pareto-optimal agreements are less likely to obtain than when the core exists. The time it takes to reach a resolution and the number of bargaining proposals proxy for the erosion of exchange opportunities. We hypothesize that the cost of exchange opportunities lost to bargaining

[5] Shubik (1983, p. 150) writes, "A game that has a core has less potential for social conflict than one without a core, since every cooperative or collusive effective demand can be granted. A coreless game, on the other hand, must leave at least one coalition unsatisfied, that is, short of its potential. At least one group of players can always do better by dropping out and going it alone. If they try it, though, another group will be able to make a better offer to some of the dropouts in a new alignment, and the bargaining may continue at great length." Of course, it is possible that participants will recognize that the core is empty, which causes them to settle on a suboptimal (proper subcoalition) outcome quickly, recognizing that allocations in the grand coalition (composed of all bargaining group members) cannot satisfy all of the individual and coalitional rationality constraints. However, it is more likely that participants will recognize that the core is empty only after trying to bargain to a grand coalition and failing to reach consensus as cycling ensues. Telser (1994) provides examples of trading situations with empty cores.

[6] For example, Shubik (1983, p. 151) writes, "In a coreless game then, some constraints on coalitional activity must be operative in the society or else they will be engendered during the play of the game." Similarly, Telser (1994) discusses the role of various mechanisms or constraints on the bargaining process to resolve an empty core and yield efficient outcomes, and Bernholz (1997) posits a similar role for binding contracts.

is greater when the core is empty than when the core exists. We expect that reaching a bargaining solution requires more cycles, longer time, and more bargaining proposals when the core is empty, especially if the initial allocation of property rights is also ill defined.

Although both transaction costs and the empty core may attenuate the achievement of an efficient outcome, and although it may be hard to distinguish between these two effects in practice, the transaction technology is fixed in our experimental design. Any differences that occur should be due to the empty core and not the transaction costs structure. Our experiments in effect control for transaction costs.[7]

These considerations lead to the following hypotheses expressed in the alternative:

**Hypothesis 1A.** The number of inefficient agreements (including no agreement) reached is greater when the core is empty than when the core is nonempty.

**Hypothesis 2A.** The amount of cycling is greater when the core is empty than when the core is nonempty.

**Hypothesis 3A.** Bargaining time is greater when the core is empty than when the core is nonempty.

**Hypothesis 4A.** The number of bargaining proposals is greater when the core is empty than when the core is nonempty.

The results of Hoffman and Spitzer (1982, 1986) suggest that when the core is nonempty, so bargaining is more likely to reach an efficient resolution, participants are likely to split payoffs equally on the basis of fairness considerations. We conjecture that when the core is empty, efficient solutions, including even splits, are less likely. This yields the following hypothesis:

**Hypothesis 5A.** The number of even-split solutions is lower when the core is empty than when the core is nonempty.

The Coase theorem asserts that efficiency obtains independent of initial property rights. However, it is precisely when property rights are ill defined that bargaining ensues and an empty core is more likely to arise. To test whether

[7] An alternative solution concept to the core is the bargaining set (Aumann and Maschler 1964). While the core represents allocations to which there are no objections, the bargaining set is based on the notions of objections and counterobjections. For example, the bargaining set $M_1^{(i)}$ is the set of all individually rational allocations that are coalitionally stable in the sense that every objection by an individual has a counterobjection. As Aivazian, Callen, and Lipnowski (1987) show, from the perspective of the Coase theorem, the bargaining set $M_1^{(i)}$ definition of coalitional stability is problematic. Every coalition structure, including no coalition at all, is potentially stable. This means that the attainment of the grand coalition is not assured. Thus, perhaps a different interpretation of our results is that instead of cycling, players reach stable subcoalitional agreements outside the (Pareto-optimal) grand coalition. Such an interpretation would be consistent with the bargaining set notion of stability, but it is important to note that these Pareto-suboptimal outcomes are inconsistent with the Coase theorem.

initial property rights matter, we investigate scenarios with and without a controller. The controller has the initial property rights, including the right to unilaterally appropriate for herself all bargaining gains. In contradistinction, no player has specific property rights in the no-controller situation. These considerations lead to the following parallel hypotheses about the controller:

**Hypothesis 1B.** The number of inefficient agreements reached (including no agreement) is greater when there is no controller than when there is a controller, especially when the core is empty.

**Hypothesis 2B.** The amount of cycling is greater when there is no controller than when there is a controller, especially when the core is empty.

**Hypothesis 3B.** Bargaining time is greater when there is no controller than when there is a controller, especially when the core is empty.

**Hypothesis 4B.** The number of bargaining proposals is greater when there is no controller than when there is a controller, especially when the core is empty.

**Hypothesis 5B.** The number of even-split solutions is less when there is no controller than when there is a controller, especially when the core is empty.

## 3. Research Design and Method

### *3.1. Participants and Administration*

Three hundred six senior business and economics students from a large Canadian university participated in the experiment.[8] Students were recruited via classroom announcements, flyers, and e-mail newsletters. They were guaranteed a flat sum of $10 for participating as well as a chance to make additional income based on their performance in the experiment.[9] Students signed up and agreed to appear at a specific time to participate.

The sessions were run via networked computers in a research trading laboratory. One of the researchers was present at all times. A maximum of 12 students could participate at one time, and sessions ran consecutively throughout the day. As students arrived for their assigned sessions, they were randomly assigned to one of the four treatment groups. Each group was composed of three players, and the participants did not know the identity of the other two people in their group. The experiment took about 1 hour to complete.

### *3.2. Experimental Design and Materials*

A 2 × 2 factorial design experiment was used to test the hypotheses. The two independent variables, manipulated between subjects, were the existence of a

[8] Two groups were dropped from the analysis (one group did not understand the materials, and for one group there was a computer malfunction), which left 300 students, or 100 groups.

[9] Ethics approval required the participants to be informed that they could earn up to $25 more than the show-up fee. This information functioned as an incentive for participation but, on the basis of the results, did not appear to influence the negotiation behavior.

core and the existence of a controller, yielding four cases: (1) an empty core and a controller ($N = 26$), (2) a nonempty core and a controller ($N = 26$), (3) an empty core and no controller ($N = 25$), and a nonempty core and no controller ($N = 23$).[10]

### 3.2.1. The Core

The only difference between the non-empty-core condition and the empty-core condition was the maximum payoff amount if all three members of a group were party to an agreement. When the core existed, the maximum amount the three players could split was 600 lire.[11] Alternatively, when the core was empty, the maximum amount the three players could split was 500 lire. All other instructions were the same.

### 3.2.2. The Controller

In the experimental conditions with a controller, one member of each three-person group was assigned the role of controller at the beginning of each trial on the basis of a random draw. The controller had the right to decide unilaterally how to split the payoff amount. For example, the controller could decide to take all of the money for herself. In the no-controller conditions, each member of the group had equal rights.[12] The remaining materials were identical irrespective of the controller condition.

### 3.2.3. Procedures

The experiment required that the participants first read the instructions individually. The instructions informed the participants of their experimental label or name—a single letter A through L—and that they would be asked to attempt to obtain an agreement with two other parties in each of five trials. In each trial, the groups were asked to split specific amounts of money among themselves. The materials were very careful to avoid any mention of negotiation, bargaining, or opponent. Instead, participants were asked to come to an agreement regarding

[10] Each group participated in five negotiation trials, and the rules and members of the group remained the same in each trial. The trials differed only with respect to the player who was randomly assigned to be the controller. Panel data techniques are used in the regression analyses to control for the number of trials.

[11] An exchange rate of 100 lire = Can$1 was employed for payment to participants.

[12] We operationalized the controller slightly differently from previous experimental studies (Hoffman and Spitzer 1982, 1986; Harrison and McKee 1985) but in a manner more consistent with the analysis of Aivazian and Callen (1981, 2003). In prior experimental papers, the controller unilaterally selects from a discrete set of options that includes a specific allocation to the controller and the other party. Once an option is chosen, the other party can bargain in order to influence the controller and reach a mutually acceptable joint decision. In our study, the controller had the absolute right to choose (1) the maximum payoff, (2) which players she would like to include in the agreement, and (3) the allocation of the payoff among the players, including the option of keeping it all for herself. Here too the other participants could try to influence the controller to reach a mutually acceptable joint decision. The essential difference is that in our case, given the maximum payoff chosen by the controller, the allocation among the parties was continuous rather than discrete.

Table 1
Maximum Amounts to Split (in Lire)

| Players | Empty Core | Nonempty Core |
|---|---|---|
| 3 | 500 | 600 |
| 2 | 400 | 400 |
| 1 | 0 | 0 |

how to split the money.[13] The pool of money to be split depended on the number of parties in the agreement and whether or not the core exists (see Table 1).

The instructions also informed the participants assigned to controller conditions that the controller would be randomly selected at the beginning of each of the five negotiation trials. No mention of the controller was made in the materials for the no-controller conditions. Once all participants read the instructions, the researcher reviewed the instructions and answered any questions.[14] We believe, on the basis of the questions asked by participants, observations of the sessions, verification checks between the online bargaining and the hard copies handed in by the participants, and our analysis of the online bargaining, that the participants understood the materials and the experimental procedures.

At the start of each of the five negotiation trials, the researcher announced the identity of the randomly selected controller in the experimental conditions with a controller. The researcher then started the trial, and the participants communicated via the computer to determine how to split the money. All communication was done via an e-mail-type program in which the participants typed in messages and sent them to their counterparts. The messages appeared immediately in the recipients' mailboxes and were stored there, with the most recent ones appearing at the top of the screen. Participants were not required to respond to any message or offer, while side agreements were possible. Information was symmetric, as all messages could be observed by all members of the three-person group. However, members could choose to address a message to only one group member.

For each trial, the participants were given 10 minutes to reach an agreement, which was ample time based on pretesting results and observations of the sessions. If an agreement was reached, the players logged out of that particular negotiation trial and completed the hard-copy questions for the trial. If an agreement was not reached within the 10-minute allotment, the computer program shut off, and all communications between the participants stopped. The

[13] The materials are based on those used in the earlier experimental literature (Hoffman and Spitzer 1982; Harrison and McKee 1985).

[14] Initial pretests involved paper-and-pencil tasks and face-to-face bargaining. However, the face-to-face bargaining resulted in participants almost always evenly splitting the payoffs. The even-split solutions appeared to be a function of the fact that many of the subjects were classmates and knew each other and is consistent with the well-known fairness bias in bargaining games (Hoffman et al. 1994). To mitigate this bias, an anonymous electronic format was developed instead. The materials were pretested several times for understandability as well as to ensure that the software was functioning appropriately.

participants then completed the questions for that particular trial. When no agreement was reached, the parties in that group earned no income for that trial.

Once all five negotiation trials were completed, the participants answered questions about the experiment as well as demographic questions. The participants were then paid the show-up fee of $10 and any income earned during the experimental sessions.

## 4. Experimental Results

### *4.1. Univariate Statistics*

Table 2 summarizes the data and variable definitions.[15] The data were individually coded by two graduate students unaware of the purpose of the study. The two coders agreed over 90 percent of the time on the rate of cycling, the number of bargaining proposals made, time spent negotiating, and negotiation outcomes. The remaining coding differences were resolved by one of the researchers. This researcher also performed test checks of the coding and found no discrepancies.

Table 2 indicates that, on average, 14 percent of the bargaining trials ended in an inefficient solution, that is, other than a grand coalition. The same percentage of trials exhibited cycling behavior. A trial took about 5 minutes on average and resulted in approximately three proposals. About 59 percent of the rounds ended in an even split among the three subjects. Even splits were defined as 200 lire each for the nonempty core participants and 166–170 lire each for the empty-core participants.

Table 3 shows univariate statistics comparing the nonempty core and the empty core. The *t*-statistics and the Wilcoxon test yield similar results. Consistent with the theory of the core and in contradiction to the Coase theorem, the empty-core case is characterized by significantly (at conventional levels) more inefficient outcomes, more trials with cycling, more time spent bargaining, and more proposals than the case of a nonempty core.[16] The empty-core case is also characterized by splits that are significantly less even. This latter result holds even though the experimental stakes were relatively low and, hence, so are the costs of being fair.[17]

Table 4 shows univariate statistics comparing the controller and no-controller cases. Again, the *t*-statistics and the Wilcoxon test yield similar results. Consistent

[15] Note that the cycling definition excludes three-player coalitions who have decided to collude and who are bargaining only about the appropriate allocation.

[16] It bears emphasizing that the statistical significance of the extra time and proposals induced by the empty core does not tell us about their economic significance, that is, the magnitude of the extra economic costs.

[17] Therefore, our results are consistent with the idea that fairness is more prevalent for high stakes than low stakes because of the relative cost of fairness, as found by Telser (1995) in the ultimatum game. However, other studies provide evidence that the size of the stake has little effect on fairness in the ultimatum game. See Hessel, Sloof, and Van De Kuilen (2004).

Table 2
Summary Data

| | Mean | Median | SD | Min | Max |
|---|---|---|---|---|---|
| INEFF | .14 | .00 | .35 | .00 | 1.00 |
| CYCLE | .14 | .00 | .36 | .00 | 1.00 |
| TIME | 5.04 | 4.65 | 2.57 | .63 | 10.0 |
| PROPOSAL | 2.82 | 2.00 | 2.77 | .00 | 20.0 |
| EVEN | .59 | 1.00 | .49 | .00 | 1.00 |

**Note.** INEFF = number of inefficient (non-Pareto-optimal) agreements in a bargaining round (trial); CYCLE equals one if the bargaining round exhibits cycling and zero otherwise, where cycling occurs if (1) two players propose to collude and a third player interjects with an alternative two- or three-player coalition proposal, or (2) two players propose to collude and one of these players breaks away and proposes to collude with the third player, or (3) three players propose to collude and two of these propose to break away and form a two-party coalition; TIME = time expended to reach an agreement in a bargaining round (in minutes); PROPOSAL = number of proposals made in a bargaining round, where a proposal is defined as any suggestion put forward by one of the players as to how to split the payoff; EVEN = number of even splits in a bargaining round.

with the Coase theorem, there is no statistical difference between the number of inefficient cases with a controller and without a controller, nor is there a significant difference in cycling behavior.[18] Nevertheless, cases with a controller are characterized by significantly more time spent bargaining and more proposals than the no-controller cases. Not surprisingly, there are significantly fewer even splits when there is a controller (who can unilaterally appropriate the payoffs for herself) relative to the no-controller scenario.

Table 5 shows summary data for each of the four core/controller possibilities. The no-controller/empty-core case is the most interesting since it is the most inimical to the Coase theorem, involving both ill-defined initial property rights and an empty core. Indeed, in comparison with the other three cases, this case shows the greatest number of inefficiencies and trials in which cycling occurs. As indicated by the superscript letters, these latter differences are also significant at the 5 percent level (on the basis of a *t*-test). However, other cases have significantly longer bargaining times and a greater number of proposals.

Table 5 also allows comparisons between the empty core with a controller and without a controller for the various outcomes, and such comparisons are quite important. Since the empty-core Pareto-optimal solution (500 lire) yields less overall profit than the non-empty-core Pareto-optimal solution (600 lire), it could be argued that incentives alone, and not the emptiness of the core, drive the observed inefficiencies.[19] By holding the empty core constant, our comparison removes the incentive issue. Indeed, untabulated results show that having an empty core without a controller yields significantly more inefficiencies (.26 versus

[18] These efficiency results for the nonempty core and controller/no-controller scenarios are in line with the findings of Hoffman and Spitzer (1982, 1986), who had inefficiency rates of 10.5 percent and 7 percent, respectively.

[19] We do not find this argument compelling since we believe that it is precisely the issue of incentives that distinguishes core existence from the empty core for all but rather uninteresting cases.

Table 3
Impact of Core Existence on Performance Outcomes

| | Empty Core | Nonempty Core | $t$-Statistic | Wilcoxon Test |
|---|---|---|---|---|
| INEFF | .21 (.00) | .07 (.00) | 4.86 [.00] | 4.71 [.00] |
| CYCLE | .20 (.00) | .10 (.00) | 3.11 [.00] | 3.09 [.00] |
| TIME | 5.36 (5.19) | 4.70 (4.20) | 2.88 [.00] | 2.72 [.01] |
| PROPOSAL | 3.52 (3.00) | 2.10 (1.00) | 5.98 [.00] | 6.87 [.00] |
| EVEN | .42 (.00) | .77 (1.00) | −8.36 [.00] | −7.81 [.00] |

Note. Values are means (medians) and univariate statistics. Two-tailed $p$-values are in square brackets.

Table 4
Impact of the Controller on Performance Outcomes

| | Controller | No Controller | $t$-Statistic | Wilcoxon Test |
|---|---|---|---|---|
| INEFF | .13 (.00) | .15 (.00) | −.87 [.38] | −.88 [.38] |
| CYCLE | .13 (.00) | .16 (.00) | −.94 [.35] | −.94 [.35] |
| TIME | 5.41 (5.33) | 4.63 (4.11) | 3.43 [.00] | 3.37 [.00] |
| PROPOSAL | 3.24 (2.00) | 2.37 (1.00) | 3.61 [.00] | 3.37 [.00] |
| EVEN | .50 (1.00) | .69 (1.00) | −4.25 [.00] | −4.17 [.00] |

Note. Values are means (medians) and univariate statistics. Two-tailed $p$-values are in square brackets.

.16; $p = .05$) and more trials with cycling (.26 versus .14; $p = .00$) than having an empty core with a controller.

### *4.2. Panel Data Regression Analyses*

Table 6 shows fixed-effects panel regressions for each of a number of dependent variables on a core existence dummy variable and a controller dummy variable. The panel data techniques control for learning by the experimental subjects over multiple trials.

Consistent with hypothesis 1A and core theory, results for INEFF show that there are significantly more inefficient bargaining resolutions when the core is empty than when the core exists, which contradicts Coasean efficiency. In contrast, initial property rights do not appear to matter, which is consistent with Coase and inconsistent with hypothesis 1B.

The results for CYCLE indicate that there is significantly more cycling when the core is empty than when the core exists. Contrary to hypothesis 2B, the results suggest that cycling is unrelated to initial property rights.

The results for TIME show that it takes longer to reach an agreement when the core is empty than when the core exists, consistent with cycling. Since a longer time to reach an agreement implies a greater erosion of exchange opportunities, this result appears to contradict the Coase theorem. Furthermore, the existence of a controller also increases the time it takes to reach an agreement, contrary to the claim that the Coase theorem holds independent of initial property rights.

The results for PROPOSAL show that more bargaining proposals are required

Table 5
**Impact of Core Existence and the Controller on Performance Outcomes**

| | Nonempty Core | | Empty Core | |
|---|---|---|---|---|
| | Controller | No Controller | Controller | No Controller |
| INEFF | .09[a,b] (.00) | .03[b] (.00) | .16[a] (.00) | .26[c] (.00) |
| CYCLE | .13[a] (.00) | .07[a] (.00) | .14[a] (.00) | .26[c] (.00) |
| TIME | 5.07[a] (4.93) | 4.29[b] (3.95) | 5.76[c] (5.83) | 4.95[a] (4.45) |
| PROPOSAL | 2.54[a] (2.00) | 1.60[b] (1.00) | 3.95[c] (3.00) | 3.08[a] (3.00) |
| EVEN | .68[a] (1.00) | .86[c] (1.00) | .32[d] (.00) | .53[b] (1.00) |

Note. Values are means (medians) and univariate statistics. Cells with the same superscript letters are not significantly different from one another at the 5% two-tailed significance level.

to reach an agreement when the core is empty than when the core exists, consistent with cycling. Again, more proposals are offered when there is a controller than when there is no controller. Unlike expenditure of time, these results do not overtly contradict the Coase theorem since more proposals do not automatically translate into a waste of resources. Nevertheless, they indicate that bargaining when the core is empty differs from bargaining when the core exists.

The results for EVEN show that when the core is empty, there are fewer even splits than when the core exists, consistent with hypothesis 5A, and, not surprisingly, there are fewer even splits when there is a controller who can unilaterally appropriate the payoffs, consistent with hypothesis 5B.[20]

Table 7 is similar to Table 6 but includes an interaction term that takes on the value of one when the core is empty and there is no controller and zero otherwise. As mentioned above, the case of an empty core and ill-defined property rights (no controller) is precisely where Coasean efficiency is expected to fail. Indeed, Table 7 shows that the number of inefficiencies is significantly greater when the core is empty and there is no controller than in all other possible combinations. Similarly, the number of trials in which cycling occurs is significantly greater when the core is empty and there is no controller than in all other possible combinations. In comparison, the interaction term is insignificant for all other outcomes.

### *4.3. Sensitivity Analyses*

We performed sensitivity analyses by replicating Tables 6 and 7 using random-effects rather than fixed-effects panel data techniques. The results are almost

[20] We replicated Table 6 after controlling for the proportion of women in the group, the average age of the group, and the average number of economics and business courses taken by the group. The signs, statistical significances, and values of the estimated coefficients on CORE and CONTR are very similar to those of Table 6. We also find that the greater the proportion of women in the group, the fewer the number of inefficient solutions, and the less time and the fewer proposals needed to reach an agreement. On average, women appear to be better at bargaining than men. The greater the average age of the group, the greater the number of inefficient solutions, the greater the extent of cycling, and the more time spent bargaining. The average number of economics and business courses taken by the group has no significant effect in any of the regressions.

Table 6

**Fixed-Effects Panel Data Regressions of Five Performance Measures on the Existence of the Core and Controller**

| | Estimation Method | CORE | CONTR | Fit Statistic | Log Likelihood |
|---|---|---|---|---|---|
| INEFF | Logit | 1.34** [4.46] (.00) | −.21 [−.79] (.43) | 24.04** (.00) | −190.46 |
| CYCLE | Logit | .84** [3.05] (.00) | −.26 [−.99] (.33) | 10.70** (.00) | −177.13 |
| TIME | Ordinary least squares | .68** [3.07] (.00) | .80** [3.60] (.00) | 11.00** (.00) | −3,198.51[a] |
| PROPOSAL | Negative binomial | .53** [9.50] (.00) | .32** [5.98] (.00) | 123.61** (.00) | −1,066.89 |
| EVEN | Logit | −1.61** [−7.80] (.00) | −.94** [−4.59] (.00) | 71.24** (.00) | −295.06 |

**Note.** CORE equals one if empty and zero if not empty; CONTR equals one if there is a controller and zero if there is no controller. The panels (suppressed) are the trial numbers (1, . . . , 5). The fit statistic is an *F*-value for TIME and $\chi^2$-values for all other dependent variables. The *t*-statistics are in square brackets, and two-tailed *p*-values are in parentheses.

[a] $R^2 = .04$.

** $P < .01$.

Table 7

**Fixed-Effects Panel Data Regressions of Five Performance Measures on the Existence of the Core, Controller and an Interaction Term**

| | Estimation Method | CORE | CONTR | CORE × (1 − CONTR) | Fit Statistic | Log Likelihood |
|---|---|---|---|---|---|---|
| INEFF | Logit | .64[+] [1.65] (.10) | 1.04[+] [1.75] (.08) | 1.65** [2.47] (.01) | 30.81** (.00) | −174.75 |
| CYCLE | Logit | .14 [.38] (.71) | .65 [1.41] (.16) | 1.42** [2.49] (.01) | 17.15** (.00) | −173.90 |
| TIME | Ordinary least squares | .70* [2.26] (.02) | .78** [2.46] (.01) | −.03 [−.08] (.94) | 7.29** (.00) | −3,198.51[a] |
| PROPOSAL | Negative binomial | .37** [4.04] (.00) | .35** [3.16] (.00) | .17 [1.17] (.24) | 50.98** (.00) | −997.33 |
| EVEN | Logit | −1.53** [−5.71] (.00) | −1.05** [−3.19] (.00) | −.19 [−.45] (.65) | 85.48** (.00) | −278.62 |

**Note.** CORE equals one if empty and zero if not empty; CONTR equals one if there is a controller and zero if there is no controller. The interaction term equals one when the core is empty and there is no controller and zero otherwise. The panels (suppressed) are the trial numbers (1, . . . , 5). The fit statistic is an *F*-value for TIME and $\chi^2$-values for all other dependent variables. The *t*-statistics are in square brackets, and two-tailed *p*-values are in parentheses.

[a] $R^2 = .04$.

[+] $p < .10$.

* $p < .05$.

** $p < .01$.

identical to those of Tables 6 and 7. We also employ a panel data Poisson regression for PROPOSAL and obtain results similar to the negative binomial. We further use panel data probit regressions in place of the logit regressions for INEFF, CYCLE, and EVEN and again obtain similar results. We also employ panel data ordinary least squares regressions for all dependent variables and obtain qualitatively similar results.

In additional sensitivity analyses, we redefine cycling as the number of cycles (rather than if cycling occurs in the trial). This new definition of cycling yielded very similar results.[21] For all regressions, the conventional standard errors were reestimated to obtain jackknife standard errors and bootstrap standard errors. The bootstrap standard errors are based on 50 data points per run. Overall, the jackknife and bootstrap standard errors were the same or smaller than the conventional standard errors.

## 5. Conclusion

Our experimental results highlight the interaction among property rights, transaction costs, and the empty core. They show that efficiency may not obtain under some property rights structures when the core is empty. Specifically, they indicate that the number of inefficient (non-Pareto-optimal) solutions and the number of bargaining rounds (trials) with cycling are significantly greater when the core is empty than when the core exists, irrespective of the initial allocation of property rights. Furthermore, we find that when the core is empty, both inefficiencies and cycling during the bargaining process are significantly more likely to occur, especially when property rights are ill defined. We also find that bargaining time and the number of bargaining proposals are significantly greater when the core is empty than when the core exists. However, we fail to find that time to resolution and the number of bargaining proposals are greater when initial property rights are ill defined even when the core is empty. We further find that the number of even splits of the payoffs among the players is affected significantly by both the existence of the core and the initial allocation of property rights.

Our results have potential implications for economic policy. They imply that voluntary bargaining mechanisms cannot always be relied on to internalize externalities and to generate mutually advantageous outcomes. As a consequence, there may be an economic role for constraints on the bargaining process—for example, specific property rights arrangements or contractual provisions—to resolve the empty core.

[21] Negative binomial regressions were estimated instead of logistic regressions since cycling is a count variable under the new definition.

## References

Aivazian, Varouj A., and Jeffrey L. Callen. 1981. The Coase Theorem and the Empty Core. *Journal of Law and Economics* 24:175–81.

———. 2003. The Core, Transaction Costs, and the Coase Theorem. *Constitutional Political Economy* 14:287–99.

Aivazian, Varouj A., Jeffrey L. Callen, and Irwin Lipnowski. 1987. The Coase Theorem and Coalitional Stability. *Economica* 54:517–20.

Aumann, Robert J., and Michael Maschler. 1964. The Bargaining Set for Cooperative Games. Pp. 443–76 in *Advances in Game Theory*, edited by Melvin Dresher, Lloyd S. Shapley, and Albert W. Tucker. Princeton, N.J.: Princeton University Press.

Bernholz, Peter. 1997. Property Rights, Contracts, Cyclical Social Preferences and the Coase Theorem: A Synthesis. *European Journal of Political Economy* 13:419–42.

Coase, R. H. 1960. The Problem of Social Cost. *Journal of Law and Economics* 3:1–44.

Dixit, Avinash, and Mancur Olson. 2000. Does Voluntary Participation Undermine the Coase Theorem? *Journal of Public Economics* 76:309–35.

Harrison, Glenn W., Elizabeth Hoffman, Elisabet Rutstrom, and Mathew L. Spitzer. 1987. Coasian Solutions to the Externality Problem in Experimental Markets. *Economic Journal* 97:388–402.

Harrison, Glenn W., and Michael McKee. 1985. Experimental Evaluation of the Coase Theorem. *Journal of Law and Economics* 28:653–70.

Hessel, Oosterbeek., Randolph Sloof, and Gijs Van De Kuilen. 2004. Cultural Differences in Ultimatum Game Experiments: Evidence from a Meta-Analysis. *Experimental Economics* 7:171–88.

Hoffman, Elizabeth, Kevin McCabe, Keith Shachat, and Vernon Smith. 1994. Preferences, Property Rights and Anonymity in Bargaining Games. *Games and Economic Behavior* 7:346–80.

Hoffman, Elizabeth, and Mathew L. Spitzer. 1982. The Coase Theorem: Some Experimental Tests. *Journal of Law and Economics* 25:73–98.

———. 1986. Experimental Tests of the Coase Theorem with Large Bargaining Groups. *Journal of Legal Studies* 15:149–71.

Shubik, Martin. 1983. *Game Theory in Social Sciences: Concepts and Solutions*. Cambridge, Mass.: MIT Press.

Telser, Lester. 1994. The Usefulness of Core Theory in Economics. *Journal of Economic Perspectives* 8:151–64.

———. 1995. The Ultimatum Game and the Law of Demand. *Economic Journal* 105: 1519–23.

Van Boening, Mark V., and Nathaniel T. Wilcox. 1996. Avoidable Cost: Ride a Double Auction Roller Coaster. *American Economic Review* 86:461–77.